The Seneca Restoration, 1715–1754

Published in cooperation with the Society for Historical Archaeology

UNIVERSITY PRESS OF FLORIDA

Florida A&M University, Tallahassee
Florida Atlantic University, Boca Raton
Florida Gulf Coast University, Ft. Myers
Florida International University, Miami
Florida State University, Tallahassee
New College of Florida, Sarasota
University of Central Florida, Orlando
University of Florida, Gainesville
University of North Florida, Jacksonville
University of South Florida, Tampa
University of West Florida, Pensacola

The Seneca Restoration, 1715–1754

An Iroquois Local Political Economy

Kurt A. Jordan

University Press of Florida
Gainesville/Tallahassee/Tampa/Boca Raton
Pensacola/Orlando/Miami/Jacksonville/Ft. Myers/Sarasota

Copyright 2008 by The Society for Historical Archaeology
Printed in the United States of America on recycled acid-free paper
All rights reserved
Published in cooperation with the Society for Historical Archaeology

First cloth printing, 2008
First paperback printing, 2011

This book was published with the generous support of the Hull Memorial Publication Fund of Cornell University.

Library of Congress Cataloging-in-Publication Data
Jordan, Kurt A.
The Seneca restoration, 1715/1754 : an Iroquois local political economy / Kurt A. Jordan.
p. cm.
"Published in cooperation with the Society for Historical Archaeology"--T.p. verso.
Includes bibliographical references and index.
ISBN 978-0-8130-3251-1 (cloth)
ISBN 978-0-8130-3685-4 (pbk.)
1. Townley-Read Site (N.Y.) 2. Seneca Indians--New York (State)--Townley-Read Site--Antiquities. 3. Land settlement patterns--New York (State)--Townley-Read Site. 4. Excavations (Archaeology)--New York (State)--Townley-Read Site. 5. Geneva (N.Y.)--Antiquities. I. Society for Historical Archaeology. II. Title.
E99.S3J67 2008
974.7'8602--dc22
2008014476

The University Press of Florida is the scholarly publishing agency for the State University System of Florida, comprising Florida A&M University, Florida Atlantic University, Florida Gulf Coast University, Florida International University, Florida State University, New College of Florida, University of Central Florida, University of Florida, University of North Florida, University of South Florida, and University of West Florida.

University Press of Florida
15 Northwest 15th Street
Gainesville, FL 32611-2079
www.upf.com

Contents

List of Figures   vii

List of Tables   ix

Acknowledgments   xi

1. Introduction: Colonialism and Decline in Eighteenth-Century Iroquois Studies   1
2. Local Political Economy   26
3. Toward a History of the Seneca Homeland, 1677–1754   49
4. New Ganechstage in the Library, Museum, and Archive   93
5. Archaeology at the Townley-Read Site, 1996–2000   121
6. Seneca Settlement Pattern and Community Structure, 1677–1779   163
7. The Logic of Dispersed Settlement   198
8. Iroquois Housing, 1677–1754: Terminology and Definitions   225
9. Iroquois Housing, 1677–1754: Archaeological and Documentary Evidence   247
10. Archaeology and Townley-Read's Economy: Faunal Remains, Red Stone, and Alcohol Bottles   278
11. Turning Points in Iroquois History: A Re-Evaluation   317
12. Conclusion: Archaeology and the Seneca Restoration   339

Notes   357

Bibliography   365

Index   401

Figures

1.1. The Iroquois Region in 1725   5
2.1. The Locality and Region of the Townley-Read Site   43
3.1. Beaver Pelts Exported from North America to Paris and London, 1720–1760   76
4.1. Seneca Sites between Canandaigua and Seneca Lakes, Occupied circa 1688–1779   94
4.2. Aerial Photograph of the Townley-Read Site Facing North   96
4.3. Detail from Lewis Evans's "A General Map of the Middle British Colonies," 1755   109
4.4. Detail from "N.W. Parts of New York, No. 156," circa 1758–1764   110
4.5. George S. Conover's Sketch Map of Seneca Sites in the Geneva, New York, Area   113
5.1. Topographic Map of the Townley-Read Site, Showing Areas Investigated   122
5.2. Surface Density of Animal Bone and Tooth Fragments in Areas D and H, showing DRCs   129
5.3. Definite and Possible Eighteenth-Century Cultural Features Excavated in DRC 1, Area D   132
5.4. The Author Inspects Sub-plowzone Traces of Structure 1 in DRC 1   133
5.5. Structure 1 Post Molds and Features in DRC 1, Area D   134
5.6. Profile of Feature 5, DRC 1, Area D   139
5.7. Excavations Conducted in DRC 3, Area H, Townley-Read Site   149
5.8. Students at Work in the Buried Plowed Midden Area, DRC 3   151
6.1. Seneca Settlements, circa 1540–1687   164
6.2. Seneca Settlements, 1687   169
6.3. Seneca Settlements, 1700   173
6.4. Topography of the Snyder-McClure Site, Occupied 1688 to circa 1710–1715   174
6.5. Seneca Settlements, circa 1720   177

6.6. Topography of the New Ganechstage Site Complex, Occupied circa 1715–1754 179

6.7. Seneca Settlements, 1750 185

6.8. Seneca Settlements, 1779 188

7.1. Model of an Eighteenth–Century Seneca House Lot in a Dispersed Community 206

8.1. Plan View of a Traditional Iroquois Longhouse 228

8.2. Origin and Development of the Midland Log Cabin 231

9.1. Plan View of Short Longhouse Structure at Ganondagan State Historic Site 249

9.2. Tracing of a French Map of the Onondaga Village Burned by the Frontenac Expedition in 1696 251

9.3. Plan View of Excavations at the Caughnawaga Site 252

9.4. Detail from "A Mapp of Coll. Romer . . . ," 1700 256

9.5. Plan View of Excavations at the Conestoga Site 259

9.6. Interpretation of Size and Internal Features of Structure 1, Townley-Read Site 266

9.7. Plan View of Short Longhouse Structure at the Onondaga Atwell Site, circa 1525–1575 268

10.1. Faunal Remains Recovered during Feature 5 Excavation, Townley-Read Site 285

10.2. Red Stone Artifacts Recovered during Townley-Read Fieldwork 306

10.3. Eighteenth-Century Bottle Glass Fragments Recovered during Townley-Read Fieldwork 313

Tables

3.1. Seneca Population Estimates, 1677–1774   55

5.1. Summary of Fieldwork Conducted at Townley-Read, 1996–2000   124

5.2. Faunal Remains Found in Strata I and II of Feature 5   141

5.3. Glass Beads Recovered at the Townley-Read Site   159

6.1. Occupation Spans for Selected Seneca Sites, 1670–1779   166

6.2. Seneca Settlement Typology   167

6.3. Seneca Settlements Destroyed by the American Sullivan Expedition, 1779   189

8.1. Post Mold Diameter Figures for Selected Iroquoian Sites   240

8.2. Iron Nail Density at Selected Iroquois Sites   242

10.1. Mammalian Specimens from the Townley-Read Site Identifiable as to Genus or Species   279

10.2. Species Frequencies of Mammalian NISP for Mohawk Subsistence Patterns and the Seneca Townley-Read Site   281

10.3. Body Part Distribution of Mammalian Remains in the East Fields at Townley-Read   283

10.4. Percentage of White-Tailed Deer Specimens within Each Locus at Townley-Read   284

10.5. Distribution of Seneca Red Stone Artifacts in the RMSC Collections, 1688–1754   307

10.6. Olive and Light Blue-Green Bottle Glass at Seneca Sites, 1688–1754   312

11.1. Iroquois Village Size and Demography in 1677   321

Acknowledgments

This volume relies in main part on archaeological data collected at the Townley-Read site near Geneva, New York. The Townley-Read/New Ganechstage Project, codirected by Dr. Nan Rothschild of Columbia University and myself, conducted archaeological investigations at the site from 1996 to 2000. The book would not have been possible without the dedicated labor of the 1998 and 1999 Columbia University Summer Field Schools, the fall 1999 dig crew (primarily from Cornell University), and the spring 2000 Hobart and William Smith Colleges Field Course in Iroquois Archaeology. Special thanks to crew chiefs Heather Atherton, Kelly Britt, Liz Dysert, Dave MacDonald, and Olivia Ng, and to our advisor Pete Jemison, who helped initiate a valuable dialogue between the project and the Seneca Nation.

Field and museum research was made possible by a number of institutions and individuals. Exploration of collections and field records at the Rochester Museum and Science Center (RMSC) was funded by a 1995 Arthur C. Parker Graduate Student Fellowship provided by the Rock Foundation. Archaeological field classes at the Townley-Read site were sponsored by Columbia University and Hobart and William Smith Colleges. Additional fieldwork at the site was funded by a 1999 National Science Foundation Grant (BCS-9908795) and a 1999 John S. Watson Grant by the Early American Industries Association. Subsequent research has been undertaken using research funds provided by the Cornell University Anthropology Department and American Indian Program, and Cornell's Hirsch Fund for Archaeological Research. I would like to thank current and former RMSC staff members Connie Bodner, Gian Cervone, Charles Hayes, Don Manchester, George McIntosh, Kathryn Murano, Brian Nagel, Annette Nohe, Betty Prisch, Lorraine Saunders, and Martha Sempowski. I am grateful to Charlotte Hegyi and Linda Clark Benedict at the Hobart and William Smith Colleges Archives, and to Wilma Townsend and Edward J. Varno at the Ontario County Historical Society for locating and allowing me to reproduce manuscript materials by George S. Conover. Above all, I thank the Minns family for allowing me access to their farm.

Research and writing was funded by a Richard Carley Hunt Fellowship from the Wenner-Gren Foundation for Anthropological Research. Firm editorial guidance was supplied by Rebecca Allen, Kirsteen Anderson, Vince Ercolano, Julie Jordan, Jon Parmenter, and Beth Ryan; Naomi Linzer supplied the index. I also am grateful to Bill Engelbrecht, Bob Kuhn, Martha Sempowski, and two anonymous reviewers provided by the Society for Historical Archaeology for their comments. Susan Albury, Kirsteen Anderson, Eli Bortz, John Byram, Jody Larson, Nevil Parker, and Heather Romans at the University Press of Florida, and Rebecca Allen and Ronald Michael of the Society for Historical Archaeology helped guide the work toward publication. The Hull Memorial Publication Fund of Cornell University provided financial assistance for production of the volume.

Mike Carmody, Jessica Herlich, Kevin McGowan, Jack Rossen, Nerissa Russell, Scott Stull, Stephen Cox Thomas, Adam Watson, and Michael West undertook specialist analyses of the Townley-Read materials. Nina Versaggi and the staff of the Public Archaeology Facility (PAF) at Binghamton University supplied invaluable help with the flotation samples. Papers and original research by students Julie French, Vera Giannaris, Jessica Herlich, Mara Horowitz, Amber Kling, Chris Mooney, Scott Mooney, Sam Oppenheim, and Lynn Richardson proved quite useful to this project. Tom Cuddy and Christine Flaherty guided me through the ins and outs of mapmaking software and helped with many of the graphics presented herein.

Rani Alexander, Sherene Baugher, Frank Bonamie, Charles Cobb, Gordon DeAngelo, Bob DeOrio, Adam Dewbury, Bill Engelbrecht, Neal Ferris, Eugene Frost, Mike Galban, Fred Gleach, George Hamell, John Henderson, Dan Hill, Rick Hill, Chris Hohman, Paul Huey, Pete Jemison, Danna Kinsey, Rodney Lightfoote, David Maracle, Chris Matthews, Ian Merwin, Alyssa Mt. Pleasant, Kirsten Olson, Beth Ryan, Michael Sanders, Martha Sempowski, Dean Snow, Bill Starna, Kathleen Sterling, Robert Venables, Nina Versaggi, Tom Volman, Gary Warrick, and Rachel Weil made comments and suggestions that greatly improved the course of my thinking and this volume. Input from my colleagues at the Cornell University American Indian Program—Eric Cheyfitz, Jane Mt. Pleasant, Jon Parmenter, and Audra Simpson—has been invaluable. My use (and abuse) of the information received from all of these people is, of course, strictly my own doing.

I thank Jim Folts, George Hamell, Nancy Herter, Bob Kuhn, Wayne Lenig, and Jon Parmenter for providing me with copies of or leads to primary source materials describing eighteenth-century Iroquois communities, housing, and lifeways. Valuable information on Iroquoian sites outside the Seneca region was provided by Monte Bennett, Bob DeOrio, Bob Gorall, Wayne Lenig, Jeff Maymon, Dean Snow, and Greg Sohrweide. Linda

Clark Benedict, Adam Dewbury, Jim Folts, Sara Gronim, Bill Hecht, Paul Huey, Paul Johnson, Bob Kibbee, Kathryn Murano, Martha Sempowski, Greg Sohrweide, Dean Snow, and Thomas Wien helped with the images.

Portions of this work have been previously published in *Northeast Anthropology* and *The Bulletin: Journal of the New York State Archaeological Association* (K. Jordan 2003, 2004). I am grateful to the editors of these publications for allowing me to reuse this material. Ideas used in the book also were presented at conferences sponsored by the Society for American Archaeology, Society for Historical Archaeology, New York State Archaeological Association, Rochester Museum and Science Center, Cayuga Museum (Auburn, New York), and the Annual Conference on Iroquois Research.

I could not have completed this book without my nuclear family—Jeannie Vallely, Ben, and Claire, some of whom have been living with this project for their entire lives! Members of my extended family and in-laws—Eric Jordan, Julie Jordan, Jennifer Jordan Kelley, Briana Kelley, Pete Vallely, Jeanne Vallely, Julie Vallely, and Peggy Vallely—helped out in the field. Special thanks to my sister Julie who read through and commented on the entire manuscript several times.

Finally, I would like to thank those people who have given me exceptional support and mentoring over the years, without whom I'm sure I would not have become interested in or persisted in anthropology. In chronological order, they are Paul Toomey (deceased) and Steve Sangren at Cornell University; Bob Sonderman, Deborah Hull-Walski, and Marian Creveling at the National Park Service; Mark Leone at the University of Maryland–College Park; Nan Rothschild, Terry D'Altroy, Chris Matthews, Rani Alexander, Abe Rosman, and Glenn Stone at Columbia University; Gerald Sider at the City University of New York Graduate Center; David Hurst Thomas of the American Museum of Natural History; Kathleen Allen of the University of Pittsburgh; Martha Sempowski and Lorraine Saunders at the Rochester Museum and Science Center; and Nina Versaggi at the Public Archaeology Facility at Binghamton University.

1

Introduction

Colonialism and Decline in Eighteenth-Century Iroquois Studies

This volume addresses a significant problem in the historical anthropology of Six Nations Iroquois (or Haudenosaunee) peoples, namely the scholarly interpretation of eighteenth-century Iroquois society. In this book I argue that anthropologists' and historians' interpretations of this period have relied excessively on models and rhetoric that foreground crisis and decline, and that these interpretations have been based more on mistaken assumptions than on sustained engagement with documentary and archaeological sources. Detailed examination of locally specific evidence—involving the collection of new archaeological data and a fresh look at documentary sources and museum collections—provides an account of eighteenth-century Iroquois society far different from depictions found in the existing literature. In particular, this work uses data from the 1715–1754 Seneca Townley-Read site near present-day Geneva, New York, to assert that Iroquois construction of dispersed communities during this time was an opportunistic innovation with a myriad of economic and ecological benefits; that the house forms used by Iroquois peoples in 1715–1754 exhibited much less European "influence" than scholars usually assert; and that the fur trade economy of western Iroquois nations remained viable at least through the mid-eighteenth century.

That there is a deficit in scholarly treatment of the Iroquois may come as a surprise to some, since Six Nations peoples have received continuous attention from anthropologists and historians since budding ethnologist Lewis Henry Morgan chose them as the subject of his research in the 1840s. Morgan's *League of the Ho-de-no-sau-nee, or Iroquois* (1962 [1851]) was one of the earliest systematic modern attempts to describe another culture. While Morgan's subsequent work (for example, 1965 [1881], 1985 [1877],

1997 [1871]) addressed a much wider geographic and temporal range of cultures and was explicitly comparative in nature, it explored themes and problems first encountered during his Iroquois research and drew heavily on Six Nations examples, reinforcing the central place of the Iroquois in American anthropology. Since Morgan, past and present Six Nations peoples and their Northern Iroquoian neighbors have served as subjects for many classic pieces of anthropological scholarship (for example, Bradley 1987; Fenton 1940, 1998; Heidenreich 1971; Parker 1910; Shimony 1994 [1961]; Speck 1995 [1940]; Tooker 1991 [1964]; Trigger 1985, 1987 [1976]; Tuck 1971; Wallace 1969).

However, the various domains of Iroquois history have not received equal attention from anthropologists, archaeologists, and historians. The years from 1687 to 1779, which Fenton (1940) terms the "Era of Colonial Wars," are a case in point. Writing on the era has been copious (for example, Aquila 1983; Brandão 1997; Fenton 1940, 1998; Graymont 1972; Haan 1976; Havard 2001; Jennings 1984, 1988; Norton 1974; Parmenter 1999, 2007a; Richter 1992; Tiro 1999; Wallace 1969), but almost all of it concentrates on diplomatic and military concerns. Daily life, economy, and ecology at particular Iroquois villages have not been subjects of systematic and sustained investigation.

This lack of attention has not impeded the production of scholarly opinion about developments at the community and household levels. Researchers, mainly in brief sketches contained within military and diplomatic histories, have claimed that a number of dramatic transformations in Iroquois settlement pattern, community structure, and household organization took place during 1687–1779, including (1) a change from nucleated to dispersed community forms; (2) abandonment of multifamily bark longhouses in favor of nuclear-family log cabins; (3) cessation of palisade construction; (4) an increase in settlement duration; (5) a decrease in cemetery size; and (6) the disintegration of traditional social organization (Abler and Tooker 1978; Aquila 1983; Fenton 1940, 1951, 1998; Grumet 1995; Hamell 1980, 1992a; Jones 2006; Morgan 1962 [1851], 1965 [1881]; Richter 1992; Snow 1989, 1994, 1995, 1997; Taylor 1995; Trubowitz 1983; Wallace 1969, 1978; Wray 1973, 1983). There is little scholarly consensus over the timing, causes, or even occurrence of these reputed changes, and there has been little attempt to examine the exact sequence in which changes took place in particular regions of Iroquoia (K. Jordan 2002: 12–32). This book attempts to rectify some of the gaps in scholarly attention by exploring these issues using Seneca Iroquois evidence.

Space and Time

Senecas, who call themselves Onodowaga (meaning "People of the Great Hill") are a Northern Iroquoian group whose traditional homeland is in what is now western New York State (for general histories of the Seneca people, see Abler and Tooker 1978; Bilharz 1998; Porter 2002; Wallace 1969). The term *Northern Iroquoian* is applied to a number of American Indian nations that spoke related languages and shared similar subsistence systems, forms of social and political organization, and cosmologies (for overviews of Northern Iroquoian culture patterns see Engelbrecht 2003; Fenton 1978, 1998; Morgan 1962 [1851]; Snow 1994; Tooker 1991 [1964]; Trigger 1990; Wallace 1969). During the Late Precolumbian era (circa 1350–1500),[1] these nations practiced extensive farming of maize, beans, and squash supplemented by hunting, fishing, and gathering. They lived in compact, palisaded villages containing up to several thousand people dwelling in multiple-family longhouses. Villages were moved every fifteen to twenty-five years, likely due to local resource depletion. Northern Iroquoian groups practiced matrilineal, matrilocal social organization and shared clan membership across national boundaries. By 1600, Northern Iroquoian peoples were living adjacent to the Great Lakes from western Ontario to the Hudson River, and south into Pennsylvania. They included the Iroquois Confederacy of Five Nations—the Seneca, Cayuga, Onondaga, Oneida, and Mohawk nations (the Tuscaroras joined the Confederacy as the sixth nation in 1722)—who lived in what is now New York State, as well as the Hurons and Petuns of western Ontario, Neutrals and Wenros on either side of Niagara Falls, Eries on the south shore of Lake Erie, and Susquehannocks on the middle Susquehanna River.

By 1700 European influences had been felt in Five Nations territory for at least 175 years, and direct engagement between Iroquois peoples and Europeans had taken place for more than 90 years. The first encounters between indigenous peoples and Europeans in the Northeast likely occurred between coastal groups and European fishermen exploiting the rich North Atlantic fishing grounds during 1500–1525; coastal Native groups subsequently traded European materials inland for pelts (Noble 2004; Trigger and Swagerty 1996; Turgeon 1998). The period of indirect European influence from 1500 to 1609 was a time of frequent migration and sweeping cultural transformation in the interior as Iroquoian groups became thoroughly enmeshed in the European beaver trade (Bradley 1987; B. Kent 1993; Snow 1994; Trigger 1990). Five Nations people first encountered Europeans directly when an expedition led by Samuel de Champlain ventured south from the St. Lawrence River valley and attacked a group of Mohawks in 1609. Recent research fairly conclusively proves that European-borne diseases did not have major effects on Iroquoian populations until 1634; many groups lost half of their populations in the years shortly after 1634 (Snow 1992; Warrick 2003). From the mid-1630s to the 1670s, the Five Nations fought a series of wars with Indian groups on their borders, likely due to both communities' encouragement for warfare (to generate captives for adoption or torture in order to assuage grief over deceased relatives) and the need to access territories with ample supplies of beaver pelts (Richter 1992). While the Iroquois prevailed in many of their early conflicts, they began to suffer greater battlefield losses and endure enemy incursions into their homeland with regularity after 1687, particularly when they faced combined western Indian and French forces. Many scholars (for example, Fenton 1940; Jennings 1984) place the Five (and after 1722, Six) Nations in a radically different political-economic position in relation to the European powers after the 1687 destruction of Seneca villages by the French-led Denonville expedition. Figure 1.1 presents a map of the Iroquois and their neighbors in the year 1725.

This volume explores the archaeological and documentary evidence for eighteenth-century settlement, household, and economic change among the Seneca Iroquois. The Seneca Nation was selected for this study for both pragmatic and historical reasons. Pragmatically, Seneca archaeology has been the focus of a longstanding research effort by avocational and professional researchers associated with the Rochester Museum and Science Center (RMSC). Charles Wray and Harry Schoff (1953) compiled a relatively complete sequence of Seneca village sites occupied after 1565 and provided a preliminary temporal framework for them. RMSC staff have completed the first three stages of a mammoth project to document and analyze materials from these sites, testing and refining the temporal framework and generating fine-grained data about Seneca daily life and social interactions as they proceed (Wray et al. 1987, 1991; Sempowski and Saunders 2001). Study of eighteenth-century Seneca archaeology taps into this research framework and benefits from the large collections of artifacts and field notes amassed at RMSC.

Historically, individual Iroquois nations were affected by divergent geographical factors, interacted with differing Native groups along their borders, and had comparatively lesser or greater engagement with Europeans. Social, economic, and ecological conditions in Iroquoia also varied

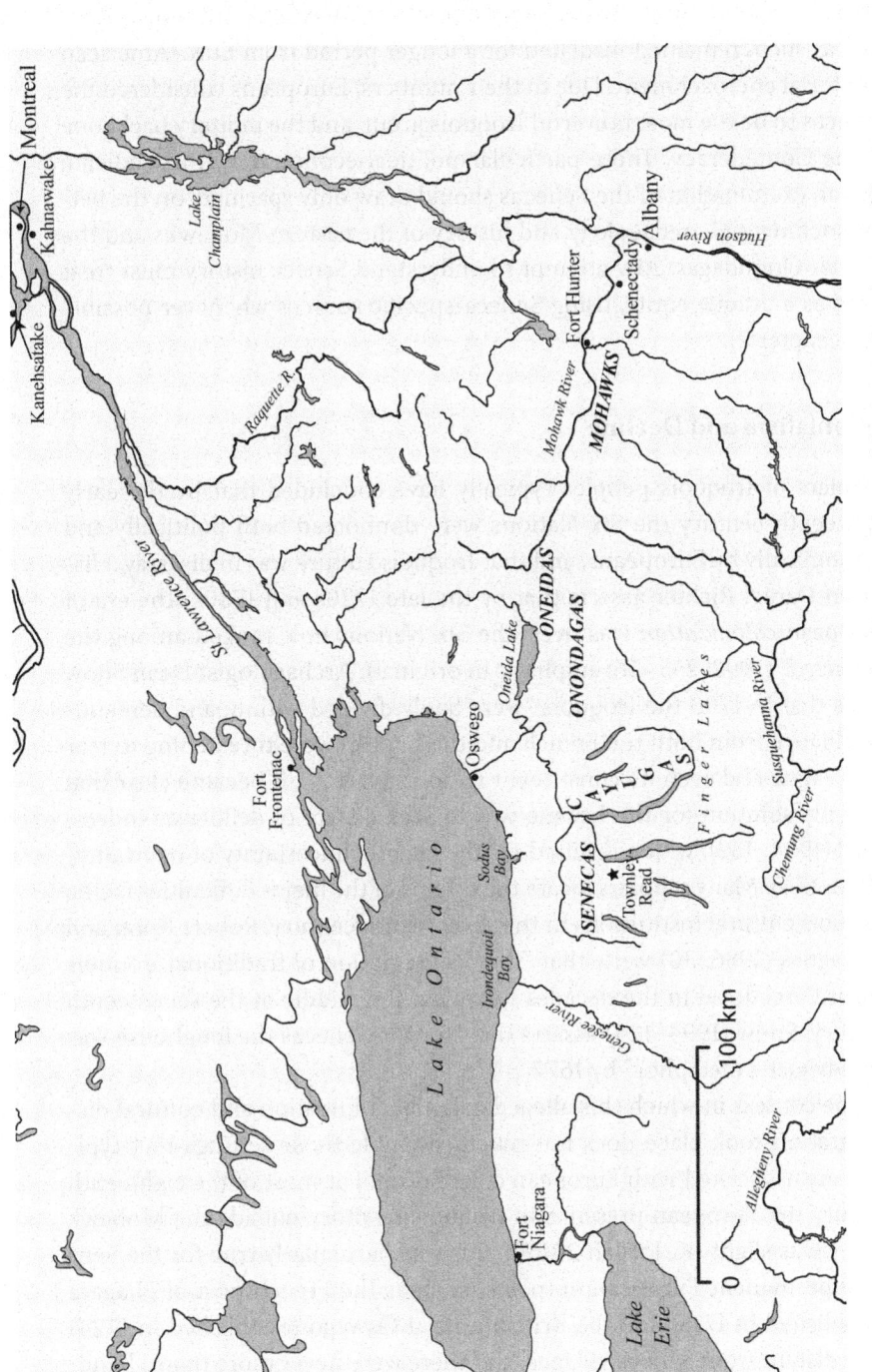

Figure 1.1. The Iroquois region in 1725, showing locations of the Townley-Read site; territories of the Iroquois nations; and European settlements, trading posts, and forts. (Base map adapted from Premier USA Map Collection, Map Resources, Lambertville, N.J., 2002 edition.)

considerably over time. The Senecas were the westernmost Iroquois nation and, as such, remained insulated for a longer period from Euro-American territorial encroachment. Due to their numbers, Europeans considered the Senecas to be the most powerful Iroquois group and the military backbone of the Confederacy. These particular political-economic factors indicate that an examination of the Senecas should draw only sparingly on the better-documented archaeology and history of the eastern Mohawks and the smaller Onondagas. Any attempt to understand Seneca history must treat them as a unique entity, using Seneca-specific sources whenever possible (see chapter 2).

Colonialism and Decline

Scholars of Iroquois peoples typically have concluded that by the early eighteenth century the Six Nations were dominated both politically and economically by Europeans, and that Iroquois culture was in disarray. Historian Daniel Richter asserts that by the late 1720s and 1730s "the era of European *colonization* was over; the Six Nations now ranked among the *colonized*" (1992: 255–56; emphasis in original). Archaeologist Dean Snow notes that in 1700 the Iroquois "were badly divided within, and demands for alliance from both the French and the English were threatening to tear the League and even its constituent nations apart . . . it became clear that the only solution for the League was to seek a state of deliberate indecision" (1994: 132), which resulted in "the chaotic uncertainty of neutrality" (1994: 134). Many scholars locate the origins of the major difficulties facing Iroquois cultural institutions in the seventeenth century. Robert Kuhn and colleagues (1986: 30) write that "the disintegration of traditional Iroquois culture" occurred in the decades following the middle of the seventeenth century. Snow (1994: 124) asserts that "for the Senecas the longhouse was already just a metaphor" by 1677.

The context in which this alleged colonial domination and cultural disintegration took place does not much resemble those settings that typically are associated with European colonialism. For most of the eighteenth century the European presence in Iroquois territory outside the Mohawk Valley was slight (K. Jordan 2009). This was particularly true for the Senecas: permanent European outposts, such as the French post at Niagara (established in 1718) and the British post at Oswego (established in 1724) were distant from Seneca villages, and there were never more than a handful of traders, diplomats, soldiers, smiths, and missionaries in Seneca territory at any given time.² While major European territorial encroachment did take place in the Mohawk Valley starting in 1711 (K. Jordan 2009) and in Oneida territory in the 1760s (Tiro 1999), the Seneca, Cayuga, and Onondaga homelands remained relatively free from European land pressure until well after the American Revolution, when the Six Nations ceded territory through controversial treaties with the new American government and its component states. The conventional model of "colonized" Iroquois people therefore requires that European colonialism took place without day-to-day surveillance of and immediate control over Iroquois actions.

Anthropologists and historians typically emphasize three factors that undermined the autonomy of the Six Nations: demography, military power, and the fur trade. Iroquois populations experienced dramatic losses due to European-borne epidemics and warfare, and also incorporated many non-Iroquois peoples into their ranks as captives or refugees (Lynch 1985). Scholars claim that population decline and increased proportions of outsiders corroded matrilineal social institutions (Ramenofsky 1987; Snow 1989, 1994, 1995, 1996, 1997). Analysts also have posited that Iroquois military losses—particularly during what Aquila (1983) terms the "Twenty Years' War" of 1680–1701—were extensive enough to have undermined their ability to act unilaterally in warfare (Fenton 1998: 330; Jennings 1984: 187, 191). Iroquois efforts to preserve their neutrality between the French and English after 1701 often are seen as a reflection of Iroquois weakness (for example, Snow's "chaotic uncertainty of neutrality" [1994: 134]). The beaver trade was a fundamentally unsustainable enterprise, as local beaver populations frequently were depleted by Native hunters (Kuhn and Funk 2000), and declining local beaver populations may have led Iroquois groups to war on their neighbors in order to open up distant territories for hunting (Trigger 1978a). As the seventeenth century progressed Iroquois men had to engage in increasingly lengthy, dangerous travel to engage in warfare and obtain pelts. Other interpretations emphasize that the fur trade led to Iroquois "dependence" on European trade goods and alcohol, and opened up Iroquois territory to European trading posts/forts (Haan 1976; Richter 1992).

Scholarly constructions in each of these three domains—demographic, military, and economic—share a similar emphasis on gradual decline. The prevalent view asserts that Iroquois populations were consistently troubled by demographic issues, military losses, and the unsustainability of the fur trade throughout the seventeenth century. While particular events—the epidemics of 1634, the Denonville expedition of 1687, the construction of European forts at Niagara and Oswego in 1718–1724—initiated episodic crises, the standard long-term picture is one of steady attenuation. In this view, the cumulative undermining of Iroquois autonomy was complete by the early 1700s, and Iroquois peoples had become colonized. However, relations between the Iroquois and Great Britain and the United States truly began to resemble the standard depiction of European colonialism only after the Revolutionary War when demilitarized Iroquois populations were confined to shrinking reservations, movement was crimped, and massive changes in subsistence practices took place (Doxtator 1996; Hauptman 1999; Taylor 2006; Wallace 1969). If the Iroquois were weak and divided, why didn't this sort of colonial encroachment take place at an earlier date, as it did, for example, in Pennsylvania? The territorial integrity of most of the Iroquois homeland through the American Revolution suggests that the standard scholarly view of the eighteenth century as the culmination of a long period of decline requires a second look.

Those writing Native American history must be vigilant about their use of tropes of decline. This involves more than the (very real) danger of writing history from the perspective of its outcome and thus falsely interpreting the dynamics of previous eras. Historically, the narrative structures scholars used to interpret American Indian cultures and histories often were framed by the erroneous preconception that Native American peoples were soon to disappear, either to die out or to be incorporated into the melting pot of mainstream society. This had as its corollary the assumption that Indian cultural institutions would naturally give way to the superior ways of Euro-Americans. These preconceptions of inevitable dissipation were codified when systematic scholarly inquiry into the past and present of Native American populations began in the nineteenth century (see Bieder 1986; Hinsley 1981; Thomas 2000). Methods and theories such as "salvage ethnography," "memory culture," trait lists, acculturation, and modernization theory were devised for measuring Native populations' inevitable conversion to Euro-American ways as "traditional" practices (often defined with utmost narrowness) withered away (see Darnell 1998; P. Deloria 1998; Lightfoot 2005: 222–33; Rubertone 2000; Simpson 2004). These theories provided not only powerful justifications for ethnocentrism and colonialism but also narrative structures for conceiving of American Indian lives, histories, and cultures. While the more egregious theories (such as unilinear evolution and polygenism) currently are regarded as curiosities from the history of anthropology, the narrative structures they generated have proved more tenacious. Much research and writing, even in the twenty-first century, has been unable to escape fully from the shadow of these persistent ways of thinking and writing.

The preconceptions encapsulated in narratives of decline are empirically inaccurate: in many instances Indian populations increased, cultural practices persisted, and opportunistic innovation took place. In most conceptions of scholarship, decline models for Indian histories and cultures and ways of writing about them should have been jettisoned years ago. Instead, they continue to be used, perpetuating misperceptions of Indians by scholars, the general public, and the legal system. The effects of these misperceptions are far from trivial—Indian people frequently are forced to demonstrate long-term historical continuity in their practice of "timeless, traditional" lifeways in order to receive individual or tribal recognition, exercise religious freedom, and regain stolen objects of cultural patrimony and the bones of ancestors (V. Deloria 1991; Fine-Dare 2002; Jaimes 1992; Mihesuah 2000; Sider 2003b; Sturm 2002).

The study of Six Nations peoples inadvertently has remained a bastion for narratives of decline, as is shown by the high profile of tropes of decline in the titles of books dealing with the Iroquois, from Anthony Wallace's *The Death and Rebirth of the Seneca* (1969) to the recent synthesis of the archaeology of northeastern peoples during 1400–1700 titled *Societies in Eclipse* (Brose, Cowan, and Mainfort 2001).[3] Two factors that may predispose researchers in Iroquois studies toward narratives of decline are (1) the reliance on "indigenisms" in analyses of Iroquois material culture; and (2) the cramped notion of "tradition" adopted by prominent researchers. These recurrent scholarly practices deserve greater critical attention.

"Indigenisms" and Iroquois Material Culture

The Postcolumbian American Indian archaeological sites in the Northeast first excavated (or looted) in the nineteenth and early twentieth centuries were Native American cemeteries and those forts, battlefields, and missions where Euro-Americans featured prominently (Huey 1997a). These sites generated enthusiasm among professionals, collectors, and the general public alike as the locations of "historic" events or sources of high-quality art objects and artifacts. Indian trash middens were occasionally mined by professional and amateur archaeologists, since they typically contained dense concentrations of artifacts that could be used to form "trait list" summaries of particular Indian cultures. Domestic areas such as village precincts were usually surface-collected or metal-detected but otherwise ignored, perhaps due to the lesser density of artifacts or the assumption that wood-based architecture would be poorly preserved. Some studies in the 1950s and 1960s (for example, Guthe 1958; Hayes 1967) concentrated on house forms, frequently targeting single house plans at a sequence of sites to assess long-term housing trends. These "type site" and "type house" excavations created an overly normative picture of many aspects of Postcolumbian American Indian societies. In most areas, the 1960s New Archaeological goal of exploring variability has not come close to being realized.

The shortcomings of archaeological research on Postcolumbian Native American sites in the Northeast are extensive. Little systematic collection of regional-level data, site-level catchment information, or data from numerous contemporaneous sites (both large and small) has been performed. Additionally, excavations of multiple houses and domestic areas from the same site, or from domestic loci such as extramural activity areas and middens, have rarely taken place. The lack of data has hampered what researchers have been able to say about the Iroquois past. Bradley (1987), for example, set out to examine Onondaga material culture, settlement patterns, and subsistence practices, but the lack of systematically collected domestic-context data essentially mandated that he concentrate on material culture.

Excavations undertaken by professional and avocational archaeologists *did* produce large collections of artifacts that fill the shelves of museums, historical societies, and private collectors. These collections provide the path of least resistance for analysis of Postcolumbian dynamics, a route that is particularly susceptible to quantification. Starting in the mid-twentieth century, acculturation models and quantification dominated Postcolumbian Indian archaeology, in large part due to the work of George Quimby and Alexander Spoehr (Quimby 1966; Quimby and Spoehr 1951). Quimby and Spoehr's primary method was to determine the proportions of Native, European, and hybrid artifacts within a given assemblage.

In the Great Lakes region, the proportion of Native and hybrid goods tended to decrease and the amount of fully European goods to increase over time. Crucially, Quimby and Spoehr took this adoption of European material culture as evidence for the loss of Native culture; the only types of material that they thought proved the continued vitality of Native cultures were those forms that continued to be made across the Columbian divide. Such cultural survivals can be termed "indigenisms," and archaeologists' continuing reliance on them explicitly parallels the history of the search for "Africanisms" in the archaeology of the African diaspora (see Ferguson

1992; Singleton 1998). Many scholars of the African diaspora have concluded that efforts to uncover cultural survivals are valuable, but that obsessive concern for them is a form of theoretical tunnel vision. More strongly, Howson (1990: 81) argues that the ethnic marker and cultural survival concepts provide "an inaccurate, passive model for a dynamic process," and that the search for such markers and survivals "rests on an inadequate definition of culture ... which emphasizes complexes of traits rather than peoples' ongoing interpretation, evaluation, and creative response, the strategies and symbolic revaluing that form the basis of cultural process."

Quimby and Spoehr's emphasis on "indigenisms" was adopted in the Seneca area by Wray and Schoff (1953). Wray and Schoff analyzed artifact assemblages from Postcolumbian Seneca sites in terms of their proportions of European and Native goods, adopting a particularly narrow definition of indigenisms by ignoring Quimby and Spoehr's "hybrid" category. Wray and Schoff (1953: 56) noted that "Native material accounted for 75% of the cultural goods owned by the Seneca" at the Dutch Hollow, Factory Hollow, Fugle, and Vita-Taft sites, currently dated to approximately 1605–1625 (Sempowski and Saunders 2001: 722). By the next set of Seneca villages at Warren, Lima, and Bosley Mills, "Native material now represented only a little better than half of Seneca material culture" (1953: 56). Wray and Schoff clearly interpreted this trend as evidence for cultural loss; at the 1670–1687 sites of Rochester Junction, Boughton Hill, Kirkwood, and Beal, they state that "Seneca native culture had shrunk to a new low, representing less than 25% of their material goods" (1953: 59).

However, conclusions drawn from artifact-origin proportions alone may not hold up if the assemblages are examined from other vantage points. Silliman (2005: 68) notes that the "defining element for material culture rests at least as much in its use and negotiated meaning as in its origins." Daniel Rogers' landmark work *Objects of Change* (1990) outlines a more subtle approach to the analysis of artifact assemblages by developing a five-part typology of "artifact processes" to assess Native adoption and rejection of European goods (1990: 105–9). Of Rogers' five processes (maintenance, addition, replacement, rejection, and transformation), only transformation represents a fundamental and absolute change in Native values. Considerable quantities of European goods could be incorporated into cultural systems that maintained their indigeneity.

Bradley's (1987) and Hamell's (1992b) studies of Postcolumbian Iroquois material culture provide excellent applications of this type of logic. The European goods acquired by Iroquois peoples in the sixteenth and early seventeenth centuries predominantly were deployed as items of spiritual significance rather than for utilitarian purposes (Bradley 1987; Hamell 1992b). Items such as glass beads and rolled sheet-brass pendants had preexisting analogues (in terms of color and composition) within Native cultures. Furthermore, Five Nations peoples reworked many European artifacts (such as iron tools and copper alloy kettles) to duplicate indigenous forms. Bradley concludes that Iroquois groups "sought out and absorbed . . . European materials, not European objects" (1987: 170). Preexisting meanings and Iroquois modifications turned goods that originated in Europe into indigenisms.

However, this pattern appears to fray by the middle of the seventeenth century. Bradley (1987) demonstrates increasing Onondaga use of European goods in unmodified form over time. Unaltered European iron items such as scissors, keys, mouth harps, files, awls, nails, spikes, and chains frequently are found at Onondaga sites occupied after 1625 (1987: 145). At 1600–1620 sites, only 5 percent of copper scrap entered the archaeological record without being utilized, but by 1650 this had risen to 45 percent (1987: 132). For Bradley, this trend represented the transformation of copper from a spiritually powerful substance to a prosaic one (1987: 131). Preformed European copper alloy items of personal adornment such as bells, thimbles, buttons, and religious-motif medals and rings also gained acceptance (1987: 135), and indigenous technologies such as ceramic vessel and stone tool manufacture were employed much less frequently. Significantly, Bradley's response to these developments was to stop writing: with the exception of a brief appendix (1987: 205–7), temporal coverage in *Evolution of the Onondaga Iroquois* essentially ends in 1655. This trend is closely mirrored by other archaeological works where consideration of sites occupied after 1680 or 1700 dwindles (for example, Anselmi 2004; Jones 2006; Mandzy 1992; Wray and Schoff 1953). As the proportion of indigenisms in the material record declines after 1650, it becomes more difficult for scholars to assert continued traditionalism. Essentially, the artifactual record seems to deny the traditionalism of the inhabitants of later sites. Emphasis on indigenisms seems to lead inexorably to the conclusion that Iroquois culture was in decline.

It is certainly true that Iroquois peoples used substantial amounts of material culture produced in Europe, and that usage patterns changed dramatically throughout the course of the seventeenth century. However, scholars need to couple their analysis of material culture with examination of the organization of communities, house lots, and houses, and the specific material practices associated with subsistence. For example, were there changes in systems of plant and animal use? In ways of organizing space and gaining access to land? Material culture studies alone cannot assess the degree of continuity and change, nor do artifacts provide the only indications of innovation. This volume goes beyond the study of material culture to emphasize the *contexts of social life*, demonstrating that the two types of information may exhibit strikingly different patterns.

Cramped Notions of Tradition

A parallel to archaeologists' reliance on indigenisms in material culture lies in the adoption of a cramped notion of authentic tradition by many prominent researchers in Iroquois studies. While other examples could have been chosen (see K. Jordan 2002: 12–33), I restrict my analysis here to three leading figures in the history of Iroquois studies: Lewis Henry Morgan, William Fenton, and Anthony Wallace. I emphasize the portions of their work treating Iroquois settlement patterns and house forms, because these concerns are central to both the present volume and Morgan's, Fenton's, and Wallace's views of Iroquois culture. Each anthropologist honed in on the fact that the Haudenosaunee, the "people of the longhouse" (Morgan 1962 [1851]: 51), stopped building longhouses, and the scholars' views of Iroquois culture predisposed them to interpret this change in terms of decline and loss.

Lewis Henry Morgan's standpoint on what was (and was not) properly Iroquois has greatly influenced many subsequent researchers. Morgan's method can be characterized as "salvage ethnography" because he sought to capture the remnants of "traditional" Iroquois culture. Hinsley (1981: 23) claims that most American salvage ethnography was characterized by a "unique blend of scientific interest, wistfulness, and guilt," and Morgan's work is no exception. Morgan stated that the Iroquois "will soon be lost as a people, in that night of impenetrable darkness in which so many Indian races have been enshrouded. Already their country has been appropriated, their forests cleared, and their trails obliterated. The residue of this proud and gifted race, who still linger around their native seats, are destined to fade away, until they become eradicated as an Indian stock" (1962 [1851]: 145–46).

His melancholy views on the decline of Iroquois tradition are exemplified by a quotation from *Houses and House-Life of the American Aborigines*:

> The Iroquois long-houses disappeared before the commencement of the present century. Very little is now remembered by the Indians themselves of their form and mechanism, or of the plan of life within them. Some knowledge of these houses remains among that class of Indians who are curious about their ancient customs. It has passed into the traditionary form, and is limited to a few particulars. A complete understanding of the mode of life in these long-houses will not, probably, ever be recovered. (1965 [1881]: 128–29)

Although Morgan's emphasis on cultural loss was consistent with nineteenth-century political-economic realities where Native Americans were confined to shrinking reservations and subjected to government policies intent on converting them into "mainstream" American or Canadian citizens, it also had the effect of forcing the evidence he collected into a narrative of cultural demise. In particular, the innovative responses of Indian peoples to Euro-American colonialism occupied a difficult place in Morgan's thought. His view of the hybrid, "nontraditional" cultural products that emerged out of colonial engagements is tinged with melancholy and negativism. Here Morgan describes "modern" eighteenth-century Iroquois communities:

> The modern village was a cluster of houses, planted like the trees of the forest, at irregular intervals, and over a large area. No attempt was made at a street, or at an arrangement of their houses in a row; two houses seldom fronting the same line. They were merely grouped together sufficiently near for a neighborhood. . . . When the villages were scattered over a large area, the houses were single, and usually designed for one family; but when compact, as in ancient times, they were very long, and subdivided, so as to accommodate a number of families. . . . After they had learned the use of the ax, they began to substitute houses of hewn logs, but they constructed them after the ancient model. (1962 [1851]: 315–19)

Morgan portrays the Iroquois builders of "modern" communities as remarkably passive. Elsewhere in *League of the Ho-de-no-sau-nee*, Morgan questions the ability of Indians to innovate, declaring there was "neither progress nor invention, nor increase of political wisdom" over time (1962 [1851]: 142). Although he ranks the Six Nations "in some respects . . . in advance of their red neighbors," Morgan also questions whether Iroquois efforts ever could have been "sufficiently potent" to propel Indian people into civilization (142–43). Interestingly, Morgan's description of a hybrid house form—log houses constructed "after the ancient model" with European trade axes—confounds both his easy bifurcation between "ancient" and "modern" and his denial of Indian ability to innovate.

William Fenton, often termed the "Dean of Iroquois Studies," occupies another crucial node in the history of Iroquois studies. Fenton's work (for example, 1940, 1951, 1967, 1998) helped place Iroquois studies on a firmer footing through systematic analysis of historical documents, but the conception of culture that framed Fenton's inquiries and his particular use of "upstreaming" methodology reinforced both the melancholy and the problematic distinction between the authentic "traditional" and degenerate "modern" seen in Morgan. Fenton's melancholy and emphasis on decline are exhibited in the following quotation:

> Iroquois settlements were formerly much concentrated. Before 1687, the League Iroquois were 12 or 13 villages, ranging between 300 and 600 persons per town. . . . Two Seneca towns comprised upward of 100 houses, of which a good proportion were extended bark houses sheltering composite families. During the next century settlements dispersed and were smaller, the bark house giving way to log houses of smaller dimensions. By 1800 the bark longhouse was a thing of the past. With it went old patterns of coresidence. (Fenton 1951: 41)

Fenton's emphasis on decline was not merely rhetorical, it was also methodological. In the "upstreaming" method, scholars use ethnographic evidence (collected from the nineteenth century into the present) to explain practices in the distant past. The ethnographic data are compared to the documentary and archaeological records; when instances of similarity between the data sets indicate the persistence of cultural practices over time, the greater detail found in ethnographic evidence can be used to inform interpretations of past conduct. This form of direct historical analogy is a mainstay of ethnohistorical and archaeological interpretation; it works well when continuous links between the past and present can be demonstrated and rigorous analysis indicates that the cultural contexts surrounding enduring practices remained similar. However, Fenton used upstreaming to formulate a research program that focused his inquiries and those of his colleagues (for example, Shimony 1994 [1961]; Tooker 1970) only on "traditions" that remained consistent for decades or even centuries, in the process excluding large swaths of Iroquois experience from scholarly research (Simpson 2004).

In his opus *The Great Law and the Longhouse*, Fenton restated his view that "patterns that have persisted for the observation of ethnologists and are not demonstrably European but can be identified in the early sources represent the Iroquois cultural heritage" (1998: 19). This constricted definition of authenticity limits "the Iroquois cultural heritage" to those aspects of Iroquois life amenable to upstreaming, in the process excluding all cultural practices invented since the "early sources," those that disappeared over time, and any hybrid practices that contained "demonstrable" European influence, regardless of the degree to which they manifested indigenous roots or operated within contexts controlled by Native logics.[4]

Given the upheavals of colonialism, the inevitability of change over time, and the influence of innovation, much of Iroquois experience from the seventeenth century to the present necessarily does not meet Fenton's definition of "traditional culture" and authenticity. That "the Iroquois cultural heritage" has "declined" is an inescapable conclusion given Fenton's definition. Many contemporary Native scholars have expressed their dissatisfaction with this research program, arguing that this narrow, past-oriented approach is inattentive to or even dismissive of contemporary Iroquois realities and concerns (Alfred 1999: 147; Doxtator 1996: 35; Simpson 2004; see also Landsman 1997).

Anthony F. C. Wallace's *The Death and Rebirth of the Seneca* (1969) is a key agent in the reproduction of tropes of decline in Iroquois studies. The book is one of the highest-profile sources on eighteenth-century Seneca society; despite its focus on the spiritual leader Handsome Lake, almost half of its content is devoted to a reconstruction of pre-reservation Seneca culture and history (1969: 21–183). Sections of *The Death and Rebirth of the Seneca* exhibit the same shortcomings as Morgan and Fenton in terms of melancholy, disregard for aspects of culture that do not fit the "traditional" model, and implied passivity. For example, a remarkable passage that appears quite early in the book discusses eighteenth-century Seneca community structure, house forms, and household organization as follows:

> A Seneca village in the eighteenth century was a few dozen houses scattered in a meadow. No plan of streets or central square defined a neat settlement pattern. The older men remembered days when towns were built between the forks of streams, protected by moats and palisades, and the dwellings within regularly spaced. But these fortified towns were no longer made, partly because of their earlier vulnerability to artillery and partly because times had become more peaceful anyway after the close of the fifty-odd years of war between 1649

and 1701. Now a village was simply an area within which individual families and kin groups built or abandoned their cabins at will; such focus as the area had for its several hundred inhabitants was provided by the council house (itself merely an enlarged dwelling), where the religious and political affairs of the community were transacted. Year by year the size of a village changed, depending on wars and rumors of war, the shifts of the fur trade, private feuds and family quarrels, the reputation of chiefs, the condition of the soil for corn culture, and the nearness of water and firewood. The same village might, over a hundred years' time, meander over a settlement area ten or fifteen miles square, increasing and decreasing in size, sometimes splitting up into several little settlements and sometimes coalescing into one, and even acquiring (and dropping) new names in addition to the generic name, which usually endured. . . . The inhabitants of a longhouse were usually kinfolk. A multifamily longhouse was, theoretically, the residence of a maternal lineage. . . . But often—especially in the middle of the eighteenth century—individual families chose to live by themselves in smaller cabins, only eighteen by twenty feet or so in size, with just one fire. As time went on, the old longhouses disintegrated and were abandoned, and by the middle of the century the Iroquois were making their houses of logs. (1969: 22–23)

Wallace replicates Morgan's wistful tone, mourning the passing of traditional culture by invoking old men's memories and the doleful image of abandoned and disintegrating longhouses. Many of the words Wallace employs to describe settlement changes have negative connotations or imply passivity: eighteenth-century communities were "scattered," had no plan, were not neat, meandered, and weren't substantial enough to have a single name for themselves; council houses were "merely" enlarged dwellings that provided "such focus as the area had"; community dispersal was a response to times that "had become more peaceable anyway"; smaller "cabins" were "only eighteen by twenty feet" in size with "just" one fire.

Although a mournful and passive decline from a vibrant and virile traditional culture is what many readers take from *The Death and Rebirth of the Seneca*, the book provides a very different view of Seneca culture when discussing the reservation period (1969: ch. 7). Here Wallace lays out detailed information on the community plan, house forms (including some bark-sided houses), and daily activities at Cornplanter's Town on the Allegheny in the 1790s, based on the first-person accounts of Quaker missionaries.

Although the chapter describing reservation conditions is titled "Slums in the Wilderness"—a phrase that tends to stick in one's mind—the overall picture Wallace paints is of a culture, traditional in many ways, struggling to survive within the newly imposed limits of reservation life. Wallace's detailed case study provides a far more nuanced take on the viability of Seneca culture than does the preceding quotation. *The Death and Rebirth of the Seneca* therefore reinforces the perception of gradual decline, but also contains information that undermines decline interpretations.

Depictions of eighteenth-century Iroquois society thus are exceptionally likely to reproduce tropes of decline as a consequence of the cramped notions of tradition, passive and mournful phrasings, and problematic treatments of innovation and hybridization employed by major scholars working in Iroquois studies. The interweaving over time of cramped definitions of culture with tropes of decline appears to have suggested an interpretation of Iroquois life in the eighteenth century that both purports to explain what went on during the era and discourages further inquiry. In bold strokes, this interpretation provides a story of acculturation inextricably bound to a tale of decline. It begins with a strong, vibrant traditional culture, and puts it on a long, slow slide ending in a slum. It declares that the only way for the Iroquois to remain Indians was to stay the same, clearly an impossibility given the upheavals of their engagement with Europeans. Any change away from indigenisms is taken as evidence for decline, precluding the possibility that Six Nations peoples ever could have engaged in positive innovation. This master narrative dissuades new scholarship by purporting to tell us everything that needs to be known about Iroquois culture during the period, and perhaps also by convincing us that what happened was so depressing that it would be better not to peer into the era at all. Uncritical reliance on this narrative of decline has both perpetuated errors of fact and damaged relations among contemporary Native Americans, scholars, and the general public.

The Archaeology of Eighteenth-Century Iroquois Communities

The domestic-context archaeology of Six Nations sites dating to the eighteenth century has been poorly explored (K. Jordan 2002: 33–56), which is perhaps in part a consequence of the ubiquity of the master narrative scholars have used to interpret the eighteenth century. In most cases, excavations have (1) concentrated on mortuary rather than domestic contexts (for example, Bennett 1982; Hayes 1965; Schoff 1949, n.d.; Wray 1983, n.d.); (2) taken place on multi-component sites where eighteenth-century material was not the primary target (for example, Prezzano 1992; Ritchie 1936); (3) focused on areas within sites that proved not to contain substantial intact eighteenth-century deposits (for example, Baugher and Quinn 1996; Hagerty 1985: 275–83; Hamell n.d.; Hartgen Archaeological Associates 2002; Henry 2001: 238); or (4) relied on surface collections alone (for example, T. Tanner 1995). Several of the most successful investigations of eighteenth-century sites—such as those at the home of the Mohawk Brant family at Indian Castle (Guldenzopf 1986; Snow 1995: 485–93), the Mohawk Enders House site (Fisher 2003), and the multinational Egli site on the Susquehanna River (Hesse 1975)—concentrated on single house lots. Extensively excavated sites such as Primes Hill (Oneida; Bennett 1988), Conestoga (multinational/Seneca; B. Kent 1993), and Comfort (multinational; Elliott 1977, 1996), have not been fully reported.

Notably, prior to the excavations at Townley-Read described herein, no domestic deposits from Iroquois sites founded during the first quarter of the century had been systematically examined (although the Mohawk Fort Hunter complex of sites was first occupied around 1711, excavated remains from the Enders House there postdate 1750 [Fisher 1993, 2003; Rick 1991]). Historical documents indicate that locally dispersed settlements became common across the Iroquois heartland after approximately 1710. Although urban development and gravel mining have obliterated many of the traces of Iroquois villages from this period in the Mohawk, Onondaga, and Oneida regions (Snow 1995; Tuck 1971; Gregory Sohrweide, personal communication, 2000; Monte Bennett, personal communication, 2001), sites of this period are preserved in agricultural fields in other parts of Iroquoia, such as the Cayuga Pattington site and the Seneca Townley-Read and Huntoon sites (Grumet 1995; K. Jordan 2004).

The reasons for the lack of sustained interest in the domestic precincts of these sites is unclear. In some senses, dispersed sites are hard to find, in that excavations at this type of site are less certain to hit substantial archaeological deposits than in more nucleated settlements. Additionally, earlier excavations did not have a solid model for the structure of such dispersed sites. The model of a dispersed Seneca house lot presented in chapter 7 of this volume appears to be applicable to other Iroquois sites (see Henry 2001: 238; Prezzano 1992; Greg Sohrweide, personal communication, 2000), which may facilitate future investigations of early eighteenth-century communities.

Furthermore, several archaeologists have disparaged the possibility of doing a thorough domestic-context archaeology of eighteenth-century Iroquois sites, expressing a different sort of decline trope. Generally their statements doubt the *preservation* or the *recognizability* of eighteenth century sites. For example, Barry Kent (1993: 63) questions whether houses constructed with horizontal logs would leave any archaeological traces, since they probably would not have been built with footer trenches or frequent subsurface posts. There are alternative ways to demonstrate the past presence of horizontal log dwellings, however. Patterned storage pits or concentrations of plowzone refuse—particularly architectural artifacts such as nails—can provide evidence for horizontal-log habitations in areas without post molds, even in completely plowed sites. Lantz (1980) was able to determine the size and door locations of a reservation-period horizontal-log cabin at the circa 1790–1869 Seneca Vanatta site on the Allegheny River. He did so based on plowzone artifact concentrations and the positions of four post molds, two of which were interpreted as support posts for a porch and two as leveling blocks for the southern end of the cabin. Additionally, the issue of whether horizontal-log structures were built by the eighteenth-century Iroquois (and if so, how frequently) is a more open question than Kent acknowledges (see chapters 8 and 9).

Doubts about site recognizability are expressed more frequently. In a discussion of survey data from the Genesee Valley, Neal Trubowitz (1983: 147) claims that "site density figures for 18th century Seneca sites are expected to be misleading; except for one burial site, no sites other than the large villages are recorded, though contemporary documents indicate that some families lived in isolated cabins. In part, this should come from a lack of recognition of the smaller native sites of this period due to their acculturation to European technology." In a discussion of 1720–1779 Onondaga sites, Bradley (1987: 207) states, "During this period the adoption of European materials becomes so widespread that native refuse begins to look very much like that from colonial frontier settlements—a scatter of broken ceramics, bottle glass, clay pipes, and scraped [sic] hardware." A similar view is expounded at greater length by Robert Grumet in his overview of eighteenth-century archaeology in the trans-Appalachian region:

> Many . . . ideological, economic, and political developments [among Native populations] are well reported in British and French archives. But archaeologists looking for the physical evidence of these changes have encountered great difficulty in documenting patterns of native settlement, production, and consumption. . . . [M]ost of the region's people had stopped making temporally and culturally diagnostic ar-

tifacts from stone or clay by 1700. Deposits found in Indian sites dating after 1700, moreover, nearly always closely resemble those left by settlers. Movements from densely packed longhouse towns to widely scattered homesteads consisting of smaller structures resembling European dwellings also make it difficult to distinguish Indian sites from non-Indian settlements. (1995: 347)

Although finding and recognizing eighteenth-century Iroquois sites may be somewhat more difficult than doing work on earlier sites, these authors overstate the case. At all eighteenth-century Iroquois sites—even the elite and superficially Europeanized house lot of Mohawk Joseph Brant (Guldenzopf 1986)—characteristic Indian goods such as shell beads, brass ornaments reshaped from kettle scrap, Native-made stone or clay pipes, or red stone ornaments have demonstrated that the site was used by Iroquois people. The relative proportions of other items ostensibly used by both Native Americans and Europeans also can be telling; for example, Indian sites are likely to have a much higher percentage of glass beads. Iroquoian and Euro-American faunal assemblages are likely to be quite different in their overall composition, and even more striking differences in processing—such as marrow extraction and bone grease production (Watson 2000)—may also be evident on Iroquois sites. Analysis of reservation-period Iroquois sites dating well into the nineteenth century indicates continued distinctiveness (Hayes 1965; Kenyon and Ferris 1984; Lantz 1980). Ideas about the difficulty of doing eighteenth-century archaeology—and particularly the view that eighteenth-century Iroquois and European sites are indistinguishable—are myths that will be put to rest once archaeologists produce more field data and publications on the era.

A Seneca Restoration?

The lack of data on eighteenth-century Iroquois daily life and the ubiquity of tropes of decline in the existing literature suggest that the prevailing model of political-economic domination by Europeans and accompanying cultural disarray should be re-evaluated. In the Seneca case, the irrefutable facts that European outposts were few in number and distant from Seneca villages, that the French and British military presence was slight, and that missionary efforts (whether Jesuit or Protestant) gained little foothold after 1709 of themselves suggest that the alleged colonialism may have been less severe than the standard model asserts.

This contention is not entirely unsupported by primary-source documentary evidence. A minority of recent historical scholarship has questioned interpretations of Iroquois decline and powerlessness (Aquila 1983; Parmenter 1999, 2001b, 2002, 2007a; Tiro 2000). Richard Aquila (1983) has proposed that the Iroquois established a set of new policies in the early eighteenth century that allowed them to rebuild communities after the military defeats and village burnings of the Twenty Years' War. These policies included neutrality between the English and French empires; alliance with Indians from the upper Great Lakes and Canada; cooperation with the government of Pennsylvania; and warfare against southern Indian groups. Aquila claims that these "restoration" policies resulted in economic gain, military recovery, increased political prestige and influence, maintained sovereignty, and social benefits for the Iroquois. For Aquila, these largely successful policies allowed Iroquois nations to stabilize and maintain a prominent political-economic presence until the focus of the European fur trade shifted west to the Ohio Valley in the 1740s (see chapter 11).

Jon Parmenter (1999, 2001b, 2002, 2007a) forcefully argues that post-1701 Iroquois neutrality between France and Great Britain was an active and highly effective policy by emphasizing the role of mobility in maintaining Iroquois power. Rather than viewing Iroquois groups who migrated to the St. Lawrence Valley, Pennsylvania, and Ohio as net losses to the Confederacy, Parmenter documents extensive connections and circular mobility between homeland and satellite Iroquois communities and shows how these interconnections (such as the "illegal" fur trade between St. Lawrence mission communities and Mohawks in Albany) worked to the benefit of both communities. Parmenter (1999) also questions the widely held supposition that Iroquois populations declined during the course of the eighteenth century by reintroducing the populations of these satellite communities into discussions of Six Nations demography.

Karim Tiro (2000) uses evidence from the American Revolution to demonstrate that Iroquois warriors participating in European-led military expeditions often managed conflicts toward their own ends, particularly by alerting Iroquois fighting on the opposite side about combat plans so as to minimize casualties. Tiro shows that with only a few exceptions (such as the 1777 battle at Oriskany) conflict between Iroquois groups during the Revolution was "civil," rather than being a fratricidal "civil war." Parmenter (2007a) examines a broader period in time, finding that an "ethic of mutual nonaggression" (40) similar to that identified by Tiro extends back to 1684. In particular, Parmenter spells out the close ties maintained between homeland Iroquois and members of satellite communities nominally fighting on opposite sides in imperial conflicts.

Although Aquila and Parmenter provide well-considered frameworks for the interpretation of events and processes in Iroquoia during the first half of the eighteenth century, their accounts have two main shortcomings. First, these historians do not systematically treat differences in the experiences of individual Iroquois nations. There is, for example, only one index entry in Aquila for Fort Hunter, a reference to a 1733 land dispute (1983: 116); Aquila does not devote serious attention to the fort's construction and its facilitation of European encroachment in the Mohawk Valley (see K. Jordan 2009). While Parmenter and Aquila present a wealth of information on the different diplomatic courses taken by individual Iroquois nations, there is little discussion of the local material conditions upon which these different courses of action were based. Second, Aquila and Parmenter largely do not address the causes or consequences of eighteenth-century transformations in community structure, house forms, and household size. Aquila's few statements about Iroquois daily life in fact replicate tropes of acculturation and decline (1983: 32, 108, 115–16, 155). That Aquila incorporates such conclusions about the changes in Iroquois settlement and residence without challenging them places his overall depiction of Iroquois restoration in jeopardy. My own study remedies these deficiencies by looking at local processes in detail, concluding that local innovations went hand-in-hand with the regional-level designs of Confederacy policy.

As the title of this book indicates, my conclusions are in harmony with the restoration interpretations of eighteenth-century Iroquois life offered by Aquila, Parmenter, and Tiro. I make the case that assertions about the gradual disintegration of Iroquois culture and political economy are based less on systematic analysis of evidence than on uncritical reproduction of narrative structures and assumptions about cultural authenticity found in earlier sources. I conclude that the residents of the 1715–1754 Townley-Read site indeed experienced a "Seneca restoration."[5] Archaeological evidence obtained in 1996–2000 excavations I codirected at Townley-Read provides a localized means to re-evaluate eighteenth-century Iroquois settlement structure, house forms, and economic organization. I use this evidence to conclude that many factors previously taken as evidence for acculturation or social disintegration in fact were innovations *beneficial* to Iroquois people. The Townley-Read data and fresh examination of primary documentary sources and museum collections suggest that settlement dispersal and smaller creolized house forms were opportunistic responses to local peace that reduced daily labor demands, and that Senecas in the early part of the eighteenth century enjoyed a hard-earned period of relative prosperity. The book also demonstrates archaeology's value in providing a perspective on Native American daily life that is missing from documentary sources and proves the explanatory power of an approach rooted in specific local political-economic conditions.

Some simplifying assumptions have been made in this study. First, I have not attempted to problematize Seneca identity. Questions about ethnogenesis during both the Pre- and Postcolumbian periods (for example, Galloway 1995; Merrell 1989; see Hauptman 1980; Kuhn and Sempowski 2001; Lynch 1985; Niemczycki 1984; and Rothschild 2003 for information relevant to the Seneca case) and the formation of "Indianness" on the colonial frontier (for example, Sider 2003a, 2003b) are of vital importance; I have chosen not to take up these issues so as to keep a sharper focus on assessing the details of subsistence, settlement, and interaction in a particular political-economic context. Similarly, as part of my overriding emphasis on material concerns, I have not assessed the effects of Christian conversion on the Senecas. It is difficult to determine the degree to which missionary (primarily Jesuit) teachings penetrated Seneca lifeways, identity, and social ethics (Hefner 1993), and any form of Christianity espoused by individual Senecas was likely to have been deeply syncretized with Native beliefs. The evidence indicates that Christianization was marginal to the major patterns in Seneca labor allocation that are the primary focus of this study. This book should not be seen as an attempt to deny the importance of these issues, but rather as an effort to provide a better conception of eighteenth-century material conditions within which processes of identity formation and religious conversion occurred.

The remainder of the volume lays out evidence from the Seneca region in detail, focusing on the Townley-Read site. The chapters that follow combine excavation, museum, and documentary data at a number of scales. I start with discussion of the theoretical and methodological approach of the volume, which I term "local political economy" (chapter 2). This is followed by an overview of 1677–1754 Seneca history (chapter 3), an analysis of documentary references to Seneca sites occupied from 1709 to 1754 and prior archaeological work done at Townley-Read (chapter 4), and a summary of the 1996–2000 fieldwork at the site (chapter 5). Subsequent chapters explore themes brought up by the field and museum work: a longer-term view of Seneca settlement pattern and community structure (chapter 6); consideration of the logic of dispersed settlement (chapter 7); a scheme for the classification of eighteenth-century Iroquois house forms (chapter 8); presentation of evidence on Iroquois housing during 1677–1754 (chapter 9); and a review of data regarding subsistence and economy at Townley-Read (chapter 10). Chapter 11 evaluates five alleged turning points in Iroquois history, and the final chapter summarizes a new model of Seneca history and culture during the first half of the eighteenth century and briefly considers models of intercultural engagement used in the archaeology of the Postcolumbian European expansion.

2

Local Political Economy

During the initial centuries of Native American–European engagement, political-economic conditions in Indian country shifted dramatically from decade to decade, and frequently over even shorter periods. Postcolumbian Iroquois history, for example, supplies numerous examples of abrupt disjunctions in military rivalries, the availability of firearms, suppliers and types of trade goods, and geographical sources of furs (Aquila 1983; Bradley 1987; Brandão and Starna 1996; Haan 1976; Kuhn and Funk 2000; Sempowski and Saunders 2001). These and other political-economic discontinuities had profound effects on the local decisions about labor allocation and use of space that are reflected in the site-level archaeological record. I propose that the archaeology of Postcolumbian American Indians (see Rubertone 2000) must resist disciplinary tendencies in archaeology and history that channel research to either the macro- or microscale, and instead must concentrate research on an intermediate spatial and temporal scale that can facilitate assessment of the disjunctions that took place in specific periods.

Archaeologists tend to generalize temporally due to their emphasis on long time frames. Early stages of archaeological work in a region often try to establish long-term chronological frameworks (for example, Snow 1995; Tuck 1971; Wray and Schoff 1953); at the site level, archaeologists typically write about all of the components they excavate, which can result in scales of analysis encompassing several hundred to a few thousand years. Event-based archaeology, such as that of battlefields and shipwrecks (for example, Bruseth and Turner 2005; R. Fox 1993), offers a microscale perspective. In contrast, historians of the Iroquois tend to write about quite large spatial units. Despite Fenton's (1951) emphasis on the "locality" as the proper frame of reference for scholars (see also Abler 1992: 183; Piker 2003: 318–20), the most influential volumes in pre-reservation Iroquois historiography have been directed at the entire Confederacy rather than individual nations or communities (for example, Aquila 1983; Fenton 1998; Graymont 1972; Haan 1976; Jennings 1984; Parmenter 1999; Richter 1992). Historians also are not immune from focus on long temporal scales (for example, Fenton

1998; Richter 1992), or the microscale, as evident by biographies of prominent Native Americans (for example, Abler 1989; Kelsay 1984).

While work at all of these scales is valuable, there is a problematic gap in current approaches. Consideration of broad time frames typically results in narratives that emphasize long-term trends at the expense of the short-term considerations vital to the everyday lived experience of people in the past. Treatments of broad spatial units frequently do not adequately address issues of regional and local political and economic differentiation. Microscale studies do not allow for the interpretation of aggregate political and economic behavior that is so important to reconstructions of the era of European-Native engagement. I advocate a contrasting focus on local political economy, or the political-economic organization of particular localities during relatively brief swaths of time.

This discussion of "local political economy" is not meant to provide a new method of analysis. Recent works that I would classify as local political-economic studies include Silliman's (2004) study of indigenous laborers at Rancho Petaluma in northern California from 1834 to 1857 and Lightfoot's (2005) examination of Russia's 1812–1841 outpost in California at Colony Ross.[1] However, not all studies of localities during brief periods of time are works of local political economy. For example, Spector's (1993) classic study of the early nineteenth century Wahpeton Dakota summer planting village at the Little Rapids site neglects local political-economic concerns by failing to specify the particular operating conditions of the fur trade during the occupation of the site, to acknowledge the effects of men's increased procurement of muskrat pelts on the seasonal round of women's labor and their security, and to examine the effects of trade in alcohol, for which there is significant archaeological evidence (1993: appendixes 2–3). The remainder of this chapter offers a set of guideposts to analytical scales and methods of investigation that can help archaeologists of Postcolumbian Native American sites reconstruct the political economies of specific localities.

Conceiving of Local Political Economy

Political economy has been characterized as "an analysis of social relations based on unequal access to wealth and power" (Roseberry 1989: 44). While most political-economic concepts initially were designed for use in the analysis of capitalist states, they have proved valuable in the exploration of non-state societies as well (Cobb 1993). Anthropological political economy is situated in the tensions between the local and the global, and between culture and history (Marquardt 1992; McGuire 2002; Roseberry 1988, 1989; Roseberry and O'Brien 1991; Sider 2003a; Sider and Smith 1997; Wolf 1982, 2001). These tensions color both the lived experience of social actors in the past and scholars' representations of the past in their writing. Political-economic approaches typically emphasize that social relations should be viewed as a *process*, and that analysis should focus on the mobilization and deployment of labor. Contradictions, ambiguities, and struggle are taken to be inherent parts of social life and also vital keys for the investigation of past and present cultures.

Use of the term *local* here does not mean that political economy is restricted to the local area nor that the most important aspects of political economy occur locally. Local political economy instead serves to "situate anthropological cases in the intersection of local and global histories" (McGuire 2002: 80) at a level of resolution much more fine-grained than that of the mode of production (a concept used most productively in the sense advocated by Wolf 1982). Conception of local political economy should be temporally specific, a necessity given the massive fluctuations of the contact era. It should also be spatially specific, to allow for the possibility of differentiation between regions and also within and between communities in the same region. Local differentiation can be cultural, as Fenton (1951) famously outlined, but it is political and economic at the same time (Doxtator 1996; K. Jordan 2009). The locality frequently proves to be an "effective scale" for analysis, one "at which pattern may be comprehended or meaning attributed" (Marquardt 1992: 107).

A key to local political economy is to resist assuming that patterns found in one locality held more generally, even in the next village over. Clues to the level of heterogeneity found in eighteenth-century Iroquois localities are evident in both archaeological and documentary data. For example, detailed research indicates that contemporaneous eighteenth-century Seneca villages were physically structured in quite different ways (K. Jordan 2004). Assertions that some eighteenth-century Seneca villages were more "pro-French" and others more "pro-English" (Abler and Tooker 1978: 507) must be taken seriously and the material implications of these claims explored. Furthermore, forms of Iroquois articulation with European powers varied quite starkly at the regional level during the eighteenth century, as comparison of Seneca and Mohawk political economies attests (K. Jordan 2009). More extensive consideration of inter-community differences will expand on these indications of heterogeneity.

Analytical focus on the locality jibes particularly well with archaeology, which is typically site-based. It is especially appropriate for the archaeology of Iroquois village sites due to the frequent planned relocations of Iroquoian communities. Iroquoian sites predominantly were occupied for only ten to fifty years (Warrick 2000: 419; see also Engelbrecht 2003: 101–7), and many contain only a single archaeological component. Just as Northern Iroquoian sites provide a snapshot of local demography (for example, Snow 1992, 1996; Warrick 2003), they also provide a snapshot of local political economy.

Although the initial emphasis in this method is on particular localities, this is not the only scale at which analysis should take place (Marquardt 1992). Processes taking place at broader and narrower scales provide constraints and opportunities that both structure and are structured by processes operating at other scales. The local political-economy approach involves looking at particular historical circumstances from a number of analytical vantages, including (1) supra-local relations of alliance and conflict; (2) regional settlement pattern and community organization; (3) specific articulations of exchange; and (4) the local organization of gendered labor across space, throughout the seasons, and among households. Inquiry using increasingly tight analytical scales facilitates insight into the tensions and contradictions of everyday life, and the role of differentiation within and between local communities in particular (Sider and Smith 1997: 7). Tensions and contradictions were numerous during the era of Indian-European engagement. Some examples in the Iroquois setting include tensions between placing a village based on defensive considerations versus securing easy access to fields and water sources; between allocating labor for subsistence versus for the fur trade; between ties to matrilineal kin groups versus to nuclear families; and the tensions (or even contradictions) associated with reproducing a largely nonhierarchical society, many of whose members came from hostile groups who were recruited through captive adoption.

At present, the overall database from Postcolumbian Iroquois sites is woefully incomplete, although most periods have received more thorough treatment than the eighteenth century. Significant temporal gaps exist, data from some regions are almost exclusively from mortuary contexts, and crucially, faunal and botanical remains have been neither collected nor analyzed sufficiently to provide adequate sequential information (faunal remains from the Mohawk Valley are an important exception; see Guldenzopf 1986: 246–64; Junker-Andersen 1986; Kuhn and Funk 2000; Socci 1995).

This is a situation that is both regrettable and filled with opportunity, and archaeologists continue to assemble small parts of this puzzle. Ultimately, archaeologically based reconstruction of a broad spatial and temporal range of Iroquois local political economies has the potential to remake our understanding of historical trends in cultural entanglement and political-economic differentiation at the regional, village, and household levels. Many of the aspects of Iroquois daily life accessible through archaeology were not recorded in documentary sources, making archaeology an important supplement—or challenge—to interpretations based on standard historical sources (see B. Little 1994; Stahl 2000).

Sources for the Reconstruction of Local Political Economy

Methodologically, the building blocks of a local political-economic approach are concentrated collection and analysis of archaeological evidence (particularly from domestic contexts) through excavation and collections work, and targeted readings of thoroughly contextualized documentary evidence.

Archaeological Sources

The archaeological methods used to investigate local political economy are little different from standard approaches in the field (Hester, Shafer, and Feder 1997), with some affiliation with the horizontal excavation strategies used in household archaeology. As elsewhere, archaeological evidence must be evaluated in terms of preservation biases, natural and cultural transformations of the archaeological record, context of recovery (including the strict analytical separation of domestic and mortuary assemblages), method of recovery, and adequacy of sample (for example, Hester, Shafer, and Feder 1997; Rogers 1990; Rothschild 2003; Schiffer 1987). It is particularly important to address these concerns when dealing with assemblages from older excavations or with collections made by avocational archaeologists, which likely did not employ the standards common in the field today, particularly with regard to botanical and faunal data.

Analytically, it is important to interpret archaeological specimens as signifiers of labor processes undertaken in the past (see Bernbeck 1995; Silliman 2004). Artifacts, faunal remains, and botanical materials offer significant clues as to where and when people were acting and what choices they made from the suite of possible alternatives. One archaeological specimen alone can signal the labor involved in its production, distribution, use, maintenance, and discard. Targeting labor (rather than more abstract categories such as culture change or adaptation) facilitates additional insights. For example, the labor-based size distinction between glass beads of "embroidery" (less than 6 mm in diameter) and "necklace" (6 mm or more in diameter) sizes (Silliman 2004: 146) contributed to the tentative identification of the relatively homogenous assemblage of small beads found in the Buried Plowed Midden at Townley-Read as the by-product of on-site embroidery work (see chapter 5). This link to labor patterns would have been impossible in typical classification systems (for example, Kidd and Kidd 1983). When coupled with ethnographic or experimental information, by-products and end products can provide important signals as to other steps completed along the way—for example, grease rendering involves not only the breaking up of mammal bones but also the collection of firewood and hauling of water; nonlocal materials imply long-distance movement, trade, or both.

For this study, new excavations of eighteenth-century domestic-context archaeological deposits were undertaken at the Townley-Read site during 1996 and 1998–2000. I examined artifacts and field notes from Seneca sites occupied between 1688 and 1754 held at the Rochester Museum and Science Center in Rochester, New York, and consulted nineteenth- and twentieth-century publications, manuscripts, and field notes by local historians, antiquarians, and archaeologists describing Seneca archaeological sites and artifacts. This included material by William Beauchamp (1900), Irving W. Coates (1892a–e, 1893), George S. Conover (1882, 1885, 1889, n.d.), Harrison C. Follett (n.d.), Albert Hoffman (n.d.), Arthur C. Parker (1920), Harry Schoff (1949, n.d.), and Charles Wray (1973, 1983, n.d.). Older observations of and collections from the Townley-Read site are outlined in chapter 4; results of the new excavations are discussed in chapter 5.

Evaluating and Contextualizing Primary Textual Sources

A local political-economic approach requires not only fine-grained collection and analysis of archaeological evidence, but also different use of historical documents. Alexander (2004: 23) aptly notes that "as the unit of analysis becomes smaller, either in time or space, available historical data often diminish"—making document-based studies of localities particularly difficult. Nonetheless, sticking to the local can have great rewards. Archaeologists need to go beyond conventional approaches that mine documents for information on general cultural patterns, supra-regional context, broad material trends, and dates of site founding and abandonment. In addition to these broad readings, it is imperative that archaeologists read more deeply, using a range of primary sources beyond those typically digested and quoted in secondary histories. Archaeologists must attempt to obtain site-specific information on resource use, labor allocation, material culture, supra-local political and economic relations, and particular personalities involved. Documentary information dating to ten years after a site was abandoned or from an adjacent region actually may impede reconstruction of local political economy. While documents susceptible to this type of reading are more prevalent in some eras than others, scholars can recover novel information by mining primary sources (including unpublished manuscript collections) in all time periods for specific information on local political economies.

Effective use of primary textual sources requires that they be subject to evaluation and critique prior to their use as evidence. Patricia Galloway (1991, 1995) cautions students of the Postcolumbian Indian past to evaluate vigorously the biases of textual sources and adopt formal standards as to what constitutes evidence. Attention must be paid to how the author of a document may have used the text to gain personal advantage or to minimize damage to self or career, thus bringing some aspects of a work (such as casualty figures in military reports or conversion rates in missionary accounts) into question (1991: 460). Scholars also must account for "the complex of Western ideological prejudices" (1995: 13) that color interpretations of other cultures and genders. A taller order for scholars who lack Galloway's background in comparative literature is her dictate that analysts must have a "thorough knowledge of the intertextual field likely to be available to the author" of a document (1991: 465), so as to identify the use of models and citations from the literature of the period that may obscure or envelop the transmission of empirical details. Explicit standards as to what constitutes acceptable evidence also need to be formulated (Galloway 1995: 16). Galloway suggests that "the material and overt behavioral aspects of an observation are . . . important because they are much less susceptible to ethnocentrism than the interpretive aspect" (1995: 291). Analysts also should look for information "which Europeans would have had no particular reason to falsify or distort" (305), and use all available documents about a particular incident in aggregate, as opposed to relying on what appears to be the single best source (87, 98–107).

Beyond these types of source evaluation, a local political-economic approach requires that the behavior described in documentary sources be situated first in space and second within temporally specific regional political-economic conditions. The degree to which recent treatments of Iroquois history are removed from considerations of place is remarkable (see Doxtator 1996), and this removal in some ways can be said to be accelerating rather than abating. Antiquarians and local historians in the Northeast (for example, Beauchamp 1916; Deardorff 1946) characteristically spent enormous amounts of time and energy trying to determine the exact locations of particular Indian villages and the routes taken by European explorers, soldiers, and missionaries. Perhaps in reaction to the intellectual narrowness of these endeavors, more recent historians and anthropologists have avoided this type of work and even have neglected previous scholarly work on Iroquois places. For example, the names and approximate locations of Seneca villages occupied during 1715–1754 were well known to nineteenth-century local historians such as George S. Conover (1882, 1885, 1889, 1893, n.d.). This information was incorporated into the *Handbook of American Indians North of Mexico* (Hodge 1907–1910, 1: 198–99, 2: 121–22), but was not transferred into later works on Iroquois village locations and place-names (for example, Jennings et al. 1985; H. Tanner 1987). Historical studies published since this information vanished from the scholarly record have hovered somewhere above the terrain of Seneca country, with decontextualized place-names occasionally being cited by historians but not in a way that allows the reader to understand the locations of and interrelations among Seneca communities. Determining specifically which communities and sites documentary sources refer to in itself adds considerable detail to the reconstruction of local political economy (see chapter 4).

Behaviors recorded in documentary sources also need to be situated within local political economies. One consequence of the emphasis on enduring traditions and upstreaming within scholarship on American Indians has been that evidence from disparate locations and periods frequently is collapsed into a single synthetic account. This tendency is exemplified by the "culture patterns" genre frequently used in writing on American Indians (for example, Trigger 1978b; see Fenton 1978, 1998: 19–33; Wallace 1969: 21–107 for Iroquois examples). Accounts of culture patterns provide useful overviews of the enduring practices of particular groups, but also present a number of obstacles to the study of local political economy.

First, culture patterns tend to be presented as immutable dictates—what Wolf (2001: 392) terms "dependably shaped bricks in a social-structural edifice"—when they are in actuality processes recurrently re-created (and transformed) by individual social actors in the moment. Cultural continuity cannot be assumed; its emergence out of transient behaviors linked to particular political-economic circumstances must be viewed as equally worthy of investigation as cultural change, and the reasons for both explored. Second, sources on Iroquoian culture patterns in particular have not been written with enough specificity to facilitate the detailed reconstruction of Iroquois allocation of gendered labor throughout the landscape and across the seasons; this topic will be addressed in the next section.

Third and most fundamentally, culture patterns accounts often fail to evaluate the political-economic context of the documentary sources they use. Two examples illustrate why this type of source criticism should become a fundamental part of the use of analogies in the study of Indian history. In *The Death and Rebirth of the Seneca*, Anthony Wallace (1969: 27) uses a description of Seneca public decorum and the conduct of local government by the Quaker Halliday Jackson as a source for describing similar behaviors among the Senecas of the mid-eighteenth century. Jackson's account is based on his 1798–1814 visits to the Allegheny Valley among Senecas who were both reservationized and pacified.[2] Wallace's application of this information to earlier Senecas he himself describes as "unvanquished" (21) must be questioned; local political-economic conditions were very different in each instance, and public decorum and the conduct of local governance no doubt were as well.

In a second example, scholars routinely use the Moravian Bishop Johann Cammerhoff's accounts of drunkenness and alcohol-induced violence among the Senecas in 1750 as typical instances of Iroquois alcohol use (for example, Fenton 1998: 452; Richter 1992: 266; Wallace 1969: 26–27). What these accounts fail to mention is that the incidents witnessed by Cammerhoff and his traveling companion, David Zeisberger, took place during a peak year in the eighteenth-century fur trade. Exchange had fallen to low levels during King George's War (1744–1748) due to British blockades of French shipping and safety concerns that essentially shut down the main British trading post at Oswego for the duration of the war (Norton 1974; Wien 1990). The years following 1748 however witnessed a boom in the Indian fur trade with both the French and British (Barnes 1914: 132–33; Wien 1990). The "alcohol brawls" seen by the Moravians therefore took place during a distinct period of Seneca abundance and affluence. Discounting local political-economic conditions in this instance severely distorts the historical record, unintentionally (and without warrant) reinforcing the stereotype of the "drunken Indian" in the process.

Types of Primary Textual Sources

Different primary sources emphasize the observation of Seneca material culture and behavior (and thus contribute to the reconstruction of local political economy) to varying degrees. Sources describing Seneca territory during the 1677–1779 period can be divided into four main categories: (1) diplomatic sources; (2) missionary sources; (3) military sources; and (4) travelers' accounts and captivity narratives. Generally, these sources are much less voluminous and detailed than one might expect given the firmly Postcolumbian dating of the period.

Diplomatic sources are the most numerous—they were produced in some cases on a daily basis in connection with negotiating and maintaining colonial alliances with Indian groups—and at the same time are frequently the least detailed. The root of this seeming paradox is that these documents were penned by people quite familiar with many details of Iroquois life, and this taken-for-granted information was not recorded. Furthermore, the writers of these documents frequently were posted in European settlements such as Albany or Montreal; the "field operatives" who actually visited the Iroquois villages most often reported verbally and their reports were summarized by the stay-at-homes, resulting in the loss of everyday detail.

An additional and often overlooked reason for the relative poverty of detail in diplomatic sources from the colony of New York lies not in their origin but in their subsequent abbreviation. The main diplomatic source for New York is the Minutes of the Albany Commissioners for Indian Affairs (hereafter MACIA). Originally covering the period from 1678 to 1755, the surviving 1722–1748 and 1753–1755 manuscript minutes are now housed in the National Archives of Canada and William L. Clements Library at the University of Michigan, respectively.[3] While the MACIA are available on microfilm, they have not frequently been accessed by scholars, who have preferred to use various published excerpts from and digests of the commissioners' minutes (see Parmenter 2007b for discussion of the history and use of the MACIA). The MACIA are abbreviated, summarized, and excerpted in Peter Wraxall's 1754 abridgement of the 1678–1751 records (McIlwain 1915); the Robert Livingston Indian Records of 1666–1723 (Leder 1956); Cadwallader Colden's *History of the Five Indian Nations* (1958 [1747]), which covers up to 1697, and a continuation covering 1707–1720 (1935 [1720]); the fifteen-volume *Documents Relative to the Colonial History of New York* (O'Callaghan 1969 [1853–1887], hereafter NYCD); and the four-volume *Documentary History of New York* (O'Callaghan 1849–1851, hereafter DHNY). Many of the writers who produced abbreviated versions of the MACIA—particularly Colden and Wraxall—did so for political purposes, and often were intent on casting aspersions on the conduct of the Albany Commissioners (Laird 1995: 121–24, 227–28; Parmenter 2007b). Significantly, the later abbreviations frequently deleted the names of towns and individual Indian leaders, which are crucial to the reconstruction of local political economy. Thus abbreviated sources must be used with caution and compared when possible to the original MACIA.

This study relied exclusively on English-language sources, and remains incomplete for that reason. The main diplomatic sources from New France that I have drawn upon are published in translation in the NYCD.

Missionary sources can be classified according to the denomination that sponsored missionary travel into Seneca territory. French Jesuits, who described their stays with the Iroquois in the invaluable *Jesuit Relations* (Thwaites 1959 [1896–1901]; hereafter JR), were the most influential. Jesuit missions were maintained in Seneca territory from 1668 to 1684, from 1702 to 1709, and possibly as late as 1713, when the Treaty of Utrecht formally forced their withdrawal (Hawley 1884; McKelvey 1951; Schoff 1949; A. Stewart 1970). However, the JR contain no documents describing the Seneca missions postdating formal reports published between 1668 and 1675 (JR 52, 54–59).

Jesuit documents from Iroquois missions on the St. Lawrence River are useful for comparative purposes. Published documents from these missions include 1734–1741 letters from Kahnawake by Father Luc François Nau (JR 68: 225–35, 261–85; 69: 35–49, 55–59) and from Lorette by Father Nicholas de Gonnor in 1742 (JR 69: 59–63). Father Joseph-François Lafitau's 1712–1717 residency at Kahnawake resulted in the 1724 publication *Customs of the American Indians Compared with the Customs of Primitive Times* (Fenton and Moore 1974, 1977), which contrasted Iroquois customs to those of the ancient Greeks, Romans, and Hebrews. Lafitau also wrote a memorandum in 1718 protesting the sale of alcohol to the Indians (JR 67: 39–47).

Protestant missionaries made little headway in Seneca territory during the study period. The Moravian Cammerhoff, reflecting on his brief 1750 visit to Seneca territory to assess the possibility of establishing a mission there, concluded that the Senecas were "much rougher and more savage" than the Cayugas and Onondagas (Beauchamp 1916: 77), and as a consequence the Moravians focused their attention elsewhere. Cammerhoff's journal is more properly a traveler's account and is discussed in that section. Society for the Propagation of the Gospel missionary Samuel Kirkland lived at Kanadesaga—the successor village to Townley-Read—near what is now Geneva, New York, in 1764–1765 (Pilkington 1980: 3–49); his account of this mission provides an interesting description of Seneca councils, transportation, and survival during a period of famine. Kirkland's Seneca mission was unsuccessful and he relocated to the Oneida area in 1766. Later Protestant missionaries to the Senecas concentrated on Seneca and multinational communities on the Allegheny River; the Moravian David Zeisberger's 1767–1768 journals (Hulbert and Schwarze 1912; see also Deardorff 1946; Olmstead 1997) contain accounts of unsuccessful efforts to expand his mission to the Genesee Valley.

Military sources describing Seneca territory are derived from the cornerstones of what Fenton (1940) termed the "Era of Colonial Wars"—the French-led Denonville expedition of 1687 and the American Sullivan-Clinton expeditions of 1779. Both invasions resulted in the destruction of most of the Seneca villages in existence at the time. Soldiers' accounts provide more detail on village sizes and locations, house forms, land use, fields, pathways, and the overall terrain in Seneca territory than the diplomatic or missionary sources do. Documents from the Denonville expedition are published or cited at length in DHNY 1: 237–43; Hamell (1980); JR 63: 269–81; Marshall (1848); NYCD 9: 358–69; Olds (1930); and Squier (1851: 90–95). Journals written by Sullivan-Clinton members are published in Conover (1887) and Division of Archives and History (1929).

Travelers' accounts and captivity narratives are unquestionably the most detailed and valuable sources on daily life in Iroquois villages. Since these texts attempted to provide colorful accounts for outsiders, their writers spent much more time describing Iroquois everyday life and beliefs than other types of sources. I have located three travelers' accounts and two captivity narratives that discuss the Seneca region during the period of interest. The first is Wentworth Greenhalgh's 1677 survey of all the villages of the Five Nations (Snow, Gehring, and Starna 1996: 188–92 supply the full correct text). Greenhalgh is one of the few sources that provides both house counts and population figures, and most authorities believe he describes the same Seneca villages destroyed by Denonville in 1687. The Moravian Cammerhoff's 1750 journal (Beauchamp 1916: 24–112) contains a wealth of detail on Seneca settlements, subsistence, travel, and use of alcohol. The journal supplies specific information on Seneca villages near present-day Geneva while Townley-Read was occupied, and Cammerhoff and his companions may have visited Townley-Read itself (see chapter 4).

Swedish naturalist Peter Kalm's various accounts of the French and Iroquois settlements at Niagara in 1750 (Benson 1937; Kalm 1966 [1751]) provide a third description of Seneca territory. Kalm reached Niagara by traveling via "flatbottomed boat" (Benson 1937: 695) from Oswego, so he may not have viewed the interior Seneca villages; unfortunately, the portions of Kalm's journal describing his journey from Oswego to Niagara have been lost (*Dictionary of Canadian Biography*, edited by Brown et al., hereafter DCB 4: 407). The alleged 1765 journal of Ezra Buell (published in Buell 1903) is likely to be a later fabrication by Augustus Buell (see Hamilton 1953, 1956, 1976; K. Jordan 2004: 43–44).

Luke Swetland's captivity narrative (Merrifield 1915) details his 1778–1779 capture by and residence with Senecas living at Kendaia on the east side of Seneca Lake; his account contains some interesting information on social organization and subsistence. Mary Jemison's well-known oral history (Seaver 1990 [1824]) details her long life with the Senecas in Ohio and the Genesee Valley from her capture in 1755 up to her interview with James Seaver in 1823. Travelers' accounts and captivity narratives originating outside the Seneca region that are useful for comparative purposes include John Bartram's description of Onondaga in 1743 (Bartram 1966 [1751]), James Smith's account of his 1755–1759 captivity in the Ohio region with a group of Kahnawake Mohawks (Drake 1855: 178–264), Richard Smith's description of the Mohawk, Susquehanna, and Delaware valleys in 1769 (Halsey 1906), and the account of an anonymous "American gentleman" who visited the Tuscarora reservation in 1799 ("Fort Niagara" 1997 [1799]).

Orsamus H. Marshall (1848) recorded a number of Seneca oral traditions about the 1687 Denonville expedition from residents of the Tonawanda and Cattaraugus reservations. This effort proved to be enormously fruitful, and the accounts have been crucial to the interpretive displays at Ganondagan State Historic Site. However, Iroquois oral histories and oral traditions about eighteenth-century events either were not collected or have not been shared readily with outsiders. Historic maps and drawings dating to the period in question are relatively sparse and inaccurate; they are discussed more thoroughly in chapter 4.

The Structure of Local Political Economy: Labor, Space, and Time

Examination of the mobilization and allocation of labor and the tensions these processes embody is a hallmark of local political-economic analysis.

In the woods and fields of the aboriginal Northeast, labor processes are subject to the brute forces of ecology: maize, beans, and squash need to be planted and harvested at certain times; deer browse at the woods' edge at dawn and dusk and yard in winter; bark needs to be harvested in the spring and then dried and flattened before it can be used in a house; wild strawberries are ripe for only a few weeks. These natural factors *constrain* where and when actions can take place, and do so in a recurrent and predictable manner. Mobility—which affects the ability to access these resources—also is limited by human endurance, the amount of daylight, and the state of transportation technology. These ecological and cultural factors need to be taken into account as basic structuring elements in models of local political economy.

Analysis must not cease with a depiction of cultural ecology. Constraints in time and space mean that social actors must decide what is to be done and what is to be left undone (a point beautifully illustrated by Flannery 1968); these decisions are social and political in nature. Additionally, "ecological anthropology, explaining social organization in terms of environmental factors, slights the basic point that social organization delineates—and defines—the environment from which appropriation can take place" (Sider 2003a: 82). Social factors and power relations thus are necessary parts of the picture, a point underscored when activities such as warring and trading are integrated into the spatial and temporal cycle.

The Iroquois, a people reliant on extensive agriculture, hunting, gathering, and fishing, were presented with an intricate variety of linked, overlapping, and conflicting tasks, some of which were tightly correlated with ecological factors and others which were not. This situation can be described in terms of a seasonal or even monthly round in a manner that may be more familiar to readers from studies of hunter-gatherers (for example, Binford 1980; Flannery 1968) but increasingly has been applied to agriculturalists (for example, Alexander 2004; Stone 1991, 1993, 1996; Stone, Netting, and Stone 1990). These studies indicate that it is possible to reconstruct the round of seasonal tasks through time and across the landscape with a level of specificity greater than is seen in most depictions of Northern Iroquoian culture patterns (for example, Fenton 1978, 1998).

The copious primary-source and ethnographic documentation available in the Iroquois case also lends itself to tentative reconstruction of a gendered round of activities. The present analysis relies on normative models of the Seneca gendered division of labor, using a task-differentiation approach (Spector 1991, 1993) and ethnographic analogies from Northern

Iroquoian peoples of other times and places (particularly seventeenth-century Huronia and nineteenth-century reservations). This approach is not without its problems; overly normative constructions of gender, gendered labor, and the household remain an endemic problem in archaeological studies (Hendon 1996; Joyce 2004). Although these difficulties may be hard to overcome (due to the vagaries of preservation, the cumulative nature of the archaeological record, and the shortcomings of documentary sources), the effort should still be made.

The following sections provide background on basic structuring factors that lie behind the gendered Iroquois use of seasonal resources and the landscape. These patterns are at a level of generality and abstraction greater than that required for reconstruction of a local political economy, and are subject to the same sorts of drawbacks I have previously identified for other culture patterns accounts. They are intended here to provide a baseline from which time-bound local modifications and departures readily can be identified.

Gendered Iroquois Social Actors in the Landscape

Archaeological focus on particular Iroquois village sites should not obscure the fact that such sites served as a focus for activities that took place at wider scales. Iroquois villages were year-round settlements, but they also served as bases for logistical procurement expeditions (in the sense of Binford 1980) that left the village for varying durations and traveled over both short and great distances. General accounts of Northern Iroquoian practices (for example, Engelbrecht 2003; Fenton 1978, 1998; Trigger 1990) suggest that such expeditions were mounted to trade; raid and wage war; participate in diplomatic and religious events; tend crops; and procure resources such as nuts, berries, medicines, maple sap, fish, venison and deerskins, beaver pelts, passenger pigeons, waterfowl, and raw materials for the construction of tools, houses, and palisades. While Iroquois messengers reportedly were able to cover incredible distances—Lewis Henry Morgan (1962 [1851]: 441) noted that a trained runner could travel 160 km per day and cited an instance of a runner covering 128 km before noon on a single day—the focus here is on more everyday trips. These typically would have incorporated one or more stops while tasks were undertaken, and often would have departed from the major trails used by runners.

Travel to obtain resources took place at scales that can be labeled local, regional, and extra-regional. Researchers generally have not attempted to quantify Iroquois use of the landscape beyond the immediate site catchment (for example, Fenton's contention that Iroquois hunting parties "walked several days into the forest" [1978: 298]), but provisional definitions of these terms may permit more concrete conceptualizations of the labor involved. Some of the most detailed descriptions of Iroquois travel and use of the landscape were provided by Morgan (1962 [1851]; see also Tooker 1994), who was not particularly concerned with identifying the specific Iroquois groups and time periods to which his descriptions applied. However, Morgan's work and other more detailed sources (for example, Fenton and Deardorff 1943; Recht 1995) allow for some general conclusions about the gendered Iroquois use of the landscape.

Local trips are defined here as those that did not need overnight stays but required some daylight hours for tasks to be completed at the destination. Twenty kilometers seems a reasonable one-way upper limit for local foot travel. Regional trips required overnight stays but an intermediate amount of transit time, and are defined here as those expeditions that covered a one-way distance of 80 km or less (that is, approximately two full days of one-way foot travel). This figure is supported by documentary sources. For example, Fenton and Deardorff (1943: 291) describe 1781 Seneca expeditions where groups made either two-day journeys or trips of 80 km (50 miles) to congregate at passenger pigeon nesting grounds in the Genesee Valley. In 1781, Senecas faced few restrictions on their mobility due to Euro-American encroachment. Additionally, the anonymous captivity narrative describing Oneida life in the 1660s likely penned by René Cuillerier contains accounts of Oneida women traveling 48–72 km (10–15 leagues) from their home villages during wartime (Brandão 2003: 71, 103).

Travel by water would have allowed greater distances to be covered, but its effects would not have been entirely uniform. For example, river travel involved one quick (downriver) leg and one slow (upriver) segment, rivers were easier to travel during the high-water spring and early summer seasons, and routes were complicated by portages (E. Little 1987). The effects of water-borne travel (which would have been primarily by canoe) on definitions of Iroquoian localities and regions will require additional analysis. Fenton's (1978: 303) description of the Iroquois canoe as "a clumsy craft unsuited to long voyages, dangerous for crossing lakes, and suicide in white water" is an exaggeration. Definitions of the local and the regional also were likely to have changed when pathways suitable for horse-borne travel were developed; this does not appear to have taken place in the area of the Townley-Read site by the time it was abandoned.

Figure 2.1 illustrates the 20 km radius local area and 80 km radius regional area around the Townley-Read site. The local area encompasses other 1715–1740 communities at Huntoon and Kendaia (K. Jordan 2004), as well as many resource-procurement areas (see chapter 4). The regional territory extending 80 km from the Townley-Read site encompasses most of the Finger Lakes and numerous locations on the south shore of Lake Ontario (including Irondequoit Bay near present-day Rochester) and reaches the present-day New York–Pennsylvania border to the south. The large western Seneca village at Genesee Castle, likely established between 1740 and 1745 (K. Jordan 2004), is well within the Townley-Read region. The British trading post at Oswego, established in 1724, falls on the very outer edge of Townley-Read's region as defined here.

Extra-regional trips were those with one-way distances greater than 80 km. Morgan (1962 [1851]: 346) describes Seneca hunting territory as extending to the Chemung Valley to the south, the Niagara Peninsula to the northwest, and through the Allegheny Valley to the Ohio country to the southwest. Although it is unclear to what exact time period this description refers, each of these regions probably was accessed by Senecas while the Townley-Read site was occupied; the outer reaches of each would be defined as extra-regional according to the definitions outlined here. Visits to the French trading post at Niagara (established in 1718) also required extra-regional travel.

Adults of both genders made trips of varying distances. Typically scholars associate Iroquois women with the local scale, and it is likely that many Iroquoian women spent much of their time within walking distance from their home villages. However, detailed consideration of documentary sources blurs the canonical division between the so-called women's space in the village clearing and the alleged men's space in the forest. First, Iroquois use of land and resources produced an intensively managed landscape that expanded over time as more fields were cleared and new village locations were occupied, while abandoned villages and inactive fields continued to be manipulated and used (Engelbrecht 2003: 99–106). Numerous accounts place Iroquois women in more remote portions of this intensively managed local area for farming and gathering, and also—crucially—at the regional and extra-regional scales to gather, hunt, trade, and even participate in military expeditions (Brandão 2003: 71, 103; Drake 1855: 178–264; Fenton and Deardorff 1943; Gehring and Starna 1988: 6, 36 note 48; JR 51: 129, 54: 117; Parmenter 2007a: 66; Pilkington 1980: 31–37; Seaver 1990 [1824]; Waterman 2008). Men's activities took place at every scale, with journeys to hunt, trade, negotiate, or wage war bringing them the farthest

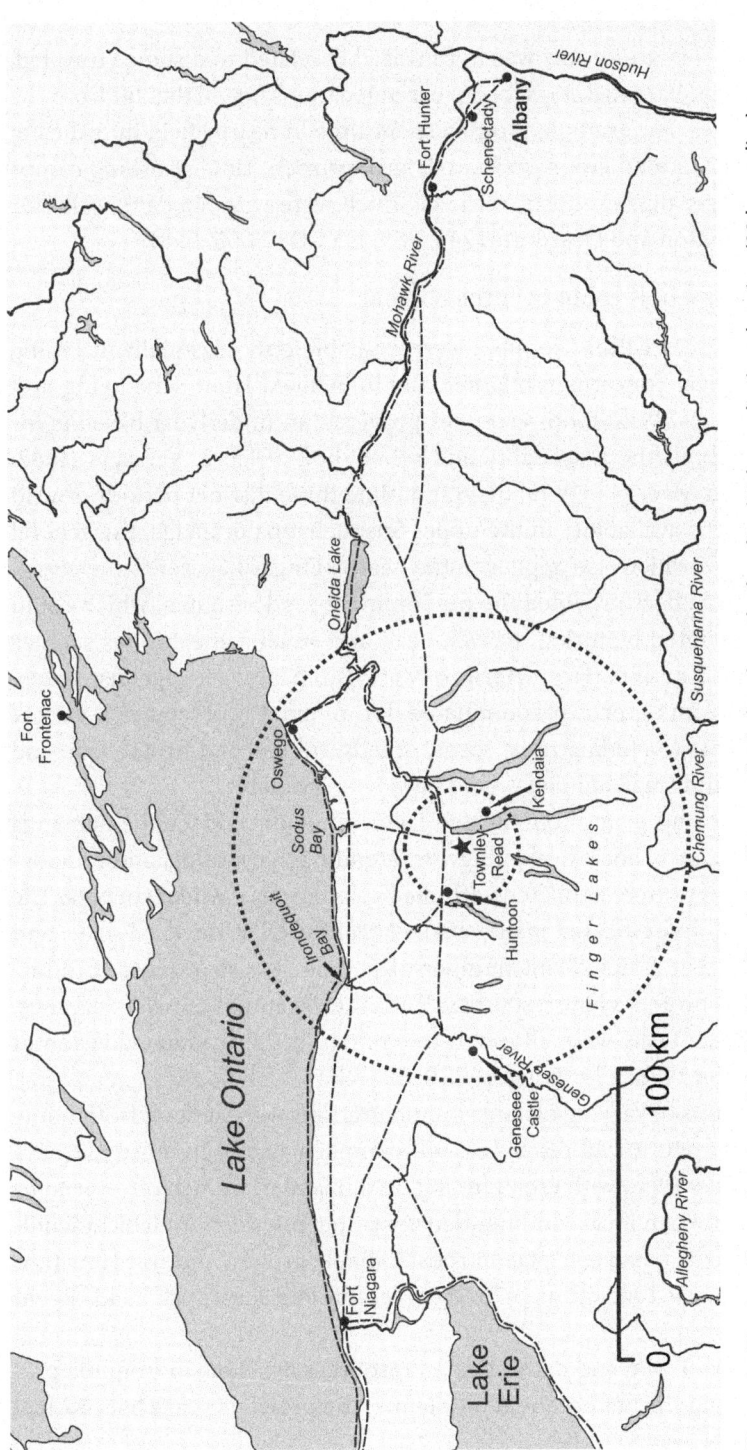

Figure 2.1. The locality and region of the Townley-Read site. Concentric circles show the locality (20 km radius) and region (80 km radius) surrounding the site, as defined in the text. Dashed lines show major west-east trade routes (both land and water) used to reach Albany, Schenectady, and Oswego. Trade-route information adapted from Morgan (1962 [1851]) and "N.W. Parts of New York" map (1750–1768). (Base map adapted from Premier USA Map Collection, Map Resources, Lambertville, N.J., 2002 edition.)

from home. Length of stay was not invariably related to distance traveled. Occasionally, extended stays took place at locations not all that far from the home villages. For example, women spent time in nearby field huts during the summer to tend crops, and family groups spent time at fishing camps and passenger pigeon roosts, some of which were within a day's walk (for example, Fenton and Deardorff 1943: 289; NYCD 4: 655, 658).

Gendered Iroquois Labor over the Seasons

Many resources within Iroquoia were available only seasonally, meaning that ecological concerns fundamentally influenced labor scheduling and travel patterns. Wild food resources provided an underlying baseline for decisions about the seasonality and scheduling of labor. Versaggi (1987: 103–10) and Madrigal (1999: 61–62) outline three distinct periods of wild food resource availability in the upper Susquehanna drainage, the general patterning of which also applies to the nearby Finger Lakes. From December to March, deer provided the predominant food resource, which could be supplemented by turkey, beaver, bear, and small game species such as squirrels and rabbits. From April to May, fish, passenger pigeons, waterfowl, tubers, and greens predominated. From June to November, a variety of wild plants (including nuts, seeds, greens, tubers, and fruits), fish, and both large and small animals would have been available.

Domesticated plants complicated labor scheduling, since the demands of field clearance, hoeing, planting, crop tending, harvesting, and processing for storage often conflicted with the exploitation of wild resources. The demands of domesticated plants were concentrated at the local scale, and demanded that a significant number of people stay at or close to home to tend and protect plant resources. With the exception of field clearance, most of these tasks were allocated to women in the Iroquois division of labor (Fenton 1978: 299; Trigger 1990: 30–33).

Expeditions of varying distances and durations were sent off from home villages to procure wild resources. Women participated in those journeys that did not conflict with crop tending. In particular, women often accompanied men when localized high-density resources were available, including deer yards, passenger pigeon roosts, maple groves, and fish runs (Engelbrecht 2003: 10; Fenton 1978: 298; Fenton and Deardorff 1943; Recht 1995).

The array of wild and domesticated resources available in Iroquoia presented one significant potential problem: if the previous year's harvest had been a poor one, by late winter or early spring, stored food might be running out and few wild resources were available as a substitute. New wild plant foods would not be ready for consumption, and many animals (such as deer) had very low fat reserves, making them much less attractive nutritionally (Speth and Spielmann 1983). During years of scarcity Iroquois peoples were "sometimes driven to borrow grain from other villages" (Fenton 1978: 301) or to consume their seed corn (Fenton and Deardorff 1943: 309). In extreme situations, maize was carried from village to village, even into the summer; Cammerhoff (in Beauchamp 1916: 85) mentions that during the summer of 1750, maize was carried overland from Onondaga to Cayuga, a distance of some 50 km. In the event of widespread failure of crops or stored resources, Iroquois famine foods included dogs, freshwater mussels, small birds, eels, muskrats, elm and basswood bark, mammal bones boiled multiple times, and rotten meat (Beauchamp 1916: 99; Junker-Andersen 1986: 101, 121; Merrifield 1915: 32; Parker 1910: 94, 104; Pilkington 1980: 29–30). This period of seasonal stress ended once wild resources began to proliferate in the late spring, most notably due to northward passenger pigeon migrations and spring fish runs (Engelbrecht 2003: 18; Fenton and Deardorff 1943).

Space, Time, and the Fur Trade

The fur trade, and the trade in beaver pelts in particular, occupies a central place in any consideration of Postcolumbian Iroquois political economy. The Iroquois dramatically (and continually) reconfigured their organization and scheduling of labor in order to procure and process furs and skins that were traded to Europeans for a variety of tools, weapons, fabrics, and nonutilitarian items (Laird 1995; Richter 1992; Wray 1973). Like other American Indian groups who reorganized themselves as commercial hunters (Jennings 1975: ch. 6; Sider 2003b: part 4), the Iroquois required a consistent supply of pelts and skins, which they acquired by a number of different means.

Six Nations groups articulated with the fur trade in six main ways (Aquila 1983, 1984; Richter 1992: 57; Trigger 1978a, 1987 [1976]: 621):

1. through direct procurement of furs and skins from local and regional sources;
2. through direct procurement of furs and skins from extra-regional territories, often involving conflict and "expelling or asserting... author-

ity over" (Trigger 1987 [1976]: 621) the group(s) laying claim to that territory;
3. through piracy, involving the taking of furs, skins, or trade goods;
4. by acting as economic middlemen—carrying trade goods to groups that still had a ready supply of peltry in their territory;
5. by acting as geographic middlemen—obtaining material benefits (including furs and skins) from groups traveling to trading posts where the main volume of exchange would take place. Advantage was secured based on the middleman group's control of trade routes; and
6. by acting as service providers (such as porters, guides, or food suppliers) to other groups more directly engaged in the trade.

The mix of articulations with the fur trade employed by the Senecas and other Iroquois nations varied over time according to Iroquois military strength, the nature of relations with neighboring groups, and regional population levels of fur-bearing animals. There is good archaeological evidence that Mohawk use of beaver supplies from their home region declined precipitously in the middle of the seventeenth century (Kuhn and Funk 2000), possibly due to overhunting. This pattern likely affected the remainder of the then–Five Nations as well.

Although some authors (for example, Rothschild 2003) have implied that declining homeland beaver populations signaled the demise of the Iroquois fur trade, continued high volumes of European trade goods at later Iroquois sites (see, for example, Ceci 1989; Sempowski 1986; Wray 1985; Wray and Schoff 1953), documentary sources (for example, NYCD 5: 911; McIlwain 1915: 164) and most scholarly opinion (for example, Norton 1974; Richter 1992) suggest that after the mid-seventeenth century the Iroquois successfully directed their efforts at acquiring beaver pelts to extra-regional sources to the north and west. A 1669 report describes four to five hundred Senecas, including women and children, departing for beaver hunting "in the direction of the Huron country" (JR 54: 117). Direct evidence for extra-regional Mohawk hunting is provided by the finds of a limited number of northern species, including wolverine and red-necked grebe, at the mid-seventeenth-century Jackson-Everson site (Kuhn and Funk 2000: 53).

Extra-regional hunting involved significant logistical problems, since most Iroquois trade still took place at European communities to the east, including Albany and Montreal, expeditions which in themselves required extra-regional trips for most Iroquois groups. Heavy furs had to be transported over very long distances, carried in canoes or on people's backs. Archaeologically, extra-regional hunting presents a potential evidential problem in that it may have had very little impact on the archaeological deposits of homeland villages. Hunters far from home would be unlikely to carry the heavy bones of pelt-bearing animals over long distances, meaning that significant amounts of durable bone material might not be present at homeland villages even if hunters had brought pelts and skins there for final processing. Therefore it is possible that a crucial economic activity might be almost invisible archaeologically.

The initial Iroquois strategy for obtaining nonlocal pelts appears to have involved warfare. Scholars have long debated the motivations for Iroquois warfare, with opinions divided as to whether economic, cultural, or a combination of factors were responsible (Abler 2000; Brandão 1997; Hunt 1940; Keener 1998; Richter 1992; Snow 1994; Starna and Brandão 2004; Trigger 1987 [1976]: 618–33). The Five Nations' consistent ability to field large numbers of warriors (Keener 1998) and the value Iroquoian cultures placed on revenge for, and in some cases demographic replacement of, persons lost to violence and disease (Richter's [1983, 1992] "mourning war complex") combined to make the Iroquois a potent military force. Following major population losses from European-borne epidemic diseases starting in 1634 (Snow 1992, 1996; Warrick 2003), the Five Nations attacked and scattered other Iroquoian groups on their borders from the mid-1630s to the 1670s, including the Hurons, Petuns, Neutrals, Wenros, Eries, and Susquehannocks. Seneca warriors appear to have been frequent participants in these conflicts, particularly against the Hurons, Eries, and Susquehannocks (Brandão 1997: table D-1; B. Kent 1993; Richter 1992; Tooker 1984; Trigger 1987 [1976]). Regardless of the motivations for conflict, one major consequence of Iroquois warfare was that it made nonlocal hunting possible. By around 1650, wars had opened up a large swath of territory to the north and west of Iroquoia for Five Nations hunting and settlement. The combined need for revenge raids and for peltry sustained additional warfare and kept Iroquois hunters and warriors in distant locations through 1700.

By 1700, Senecas also had begun to cultivate west-east trade in the lower Great Lakes, where they acted as "geographic middlemen" (see chapters 3 and 10). The west-east trade had a different dynamic than the better-studied north-south trade between Iroquois mission communities and Albany merchants (Laird 1995; Norton 1974; Parmenter 2001b), principally because it involved greater transportation distances and transit over territories of several Native groups. Additionally, there is some indication that the focus of the west-east fur trade shifted during the early eighteenth century to incorporate significant exchange of deerskins as well as beaver pelts (Cutcliffe 1981: table 1; Standen 1998). If true, this has important implications for the local political economies of the Senecas and other Iroquois nations.

3

Toward a History of the Seneca Homeland, 1677–1754

The Seneca Nation occupied a unique position at the "western door" of the Iroquois Confederacy, closer to rival western Indian groups and in some senses more isolated from European influences than other Iroquois nations. Discussions of eighteenth-century Iroquois history predominantly have focused on the Confederacy as a whole (for example, Aquila 1983; Fenton 1998; Haan 1976; Parmenter 1999; Richter 1992; Snow 1994). Scholarly focus on this spatial scale obscures the unique political-economic factors that affected the Senecas, making it necessary to revisit primary documentary sources to collect specific details on the local political economy of the Seneca homeland.[1] My review of primary and secondary textual sources reveals many instances of scholarly disagreement about the events and processes of the early to mid-eighteenth century. The inconclusiveness of this chapter serves to illustrate that archaeology has a great deal to offer as a source of new, independent data on a contested era.

The years 1677–1754 provide a swath of time sufficient to observe long-term trends in Seneca history surrounding the period during which the Townley-Read site was occupied. This chapter deals with the regional and supra-regional political-economic context that would have affected Townley-Read's residents; it supplies a *partial* and *thematic* history of the Seneca homeland rather than a fully rounded picture of the Seneca, much less the Iroquois, situation. Aquila (1983), Brandão and Starna (1996), Fenton (1998), Haan (1976), Jennings (1984, 1988), Norton (1974), Parmenter (1999, 2001a, 2001b, 2007a), Richter (1992), and Richter and Merrell (1987) treat events taking place at a distance from the Seneca region during 1677–1754, including rivalries among members of the Confederacy, specifics of treaty diplomacy, events that took place at the east and center of Iroquois territory, relations with Indians and the colonial government in Pennsylvania, interactions with Iroquois mission communities along the St. Lawrence, and raids undertaken against Indian groups in Virginia and the Carolinas.

Specific museum, documentary, and archival sources that make possible or definite reference to Townley-Read itself are discussed in chapter 4.

The 1677–1754 era is bracketed by the diplomatic visit of New York official Wentworth Greenhalgh to Seneca territory in 1677 and the beginning of the Seven Years' War in 1754. I have divided the period and the chapter into four segments based on my interpretation of political-economic conditions within the Seneca homeland: (1) the Twenty Years' War, 1677–1701; (2) a period of uncertainty, 1701–1713; (3) the "middleman" period, 1713–1724; and (4) the Oswego era, 1724–1754. A separate, final section considers the overarching issue of migration and the possible shift in French and British focus to the Ohio region.

The Twenty Years' War, 1677–1701

New York official Wentworth Greenhalgh visited Seneca territory in the summer of 1677 as part of his mission to court the alliance of the Five Nations (Snow, Gehring, and Starna 1996: 188–92). Greenhalgh recorded (likely imprecisely) that there were four nucleated Seneca villages, containing 324 houses and 1000 warriors. He observed an abundance of maize at these villages and witnessed several prisoners from the southwest being tortured to death (possibly Shawnees per Brandão [1997: table D-1]). Greenhalgh also noted that the Senecas "were very desirous to see us ride our horses, which we did; they made feasts & dancing, & invited us, that when all the maides were together, both wee & our Indyans [guides] might choose such as liked us to ly with" (Snow, Gehring, and Starna 1996: 191).

The Senecas Greenhalgh encountered were in the midst of major political-economic changes. The Five Nations had just successfully concluded a longstanding war against the Susquehannocks of Pennsylvania and were in the process of solidifying their alliance with the colony of New York, envisioned as a bright silver "covenant chain" of friendship. The Iroquois also were in the early stages of a renewed phase of warfare to the west (Brandão 1997: table D-1; JR 60: 167, 185).

In 1680, Iroquois forces began a series of major assaults in Illinois country. Aquila (1983) uses the first of these to mark the onset of what he terms the "Twenty Years' War." Subsequently, Iroquois war parties ranged as far west as the Mississippi River, threatening western Indian groups—including the Illinois, Ottawas, Foxes, Miamis, Ojibwas, and refugee Hurons known as Wyandots—and their French allies. Documentary sources do not record the full extent of post-1680 warfare, and they often fail to specify which of the Five Nations were involved in particular conflicts. Seneca participation was likely extensive and far greater than the incidents described here.

A force of 500 to 600 Iroquois warriors that captured 700 to 1200 Illinois in 1680 included Senecas (Brandão 1997: table D-1). Senecas were given extra incentive for war when the Seneca diplomat Annahac was killed by an Illinois in an Ottawa village at Michilimackinac in the autumn of 1681 (Keener 1998: 149–50, 190–91; NYCD 9: 171, 176–77). Since Hurons were present at the scene of the murder but did not retaliate against the killer, they also drew the Senecas' ire. Seneca actions affected not only western Indian groups but also the French, who were targeted due to their provisioning of Iroquois enemies with firearms and ammunition (Brandão 1997: 118–19). French official Henry de Tonty was wounded in the 1680 attack, and Senecas and other Iroquois "plundered" French traders on several occasions starting as early as 1681 (Keener 1998: 151, 188; NYCD 3: 442, 444–45; Richter 1992: 149). Two hundred Seneca and Cayuga warriors unsuccessfully besieged the French Fort Saint-Louis in Illinois territory in March 1684, and took goods that probably included guns from a French trading expedition they encountered (Brandão 1997: 57, table D-1). A French expedition led by Governor Joseph-Antoine Le Febvre de la Barre attempted to strike back at the Senecas in 1684, but stalled northeast of present-day Oswego when disease struck the French troops (Parmenter 2007a: 44–45). A series of Seneca actions in Virginia and Maryland in 1682, 1683, and 1687 (Brandão 1997: table D-1) indicates that the Senecas at least intermittently were capable of military efforts in two widely separated parts of the continent.

The Senecas eventually paid for antagonizing the French and the western "Far Indians." Conflict between the Iroquois and western nations immediately became entangled with the French-English rivalry. The European powers initially did not confront each other, but instead fought by Native proxy. The French and English did not aid their allies equally: western groups were supplied with French arms, food, trade goods, and military advisors, but the Iroquois received little support from the English despite their Covenant Chain alliance. Iroquois logistical capacities also were taxed by fielding expeditions at such a great distance from their homeland. As the military and numerical superiority of the French and their Indian allies grew, the war turned against the Five Nations.

For Senecas, the change in fortune was marked by catastrophe. On July 12, 1687, a French-led invasion force commanded by the Marquis de Denonville and numbering more than two thousand men marched south from

Irondequoit Bay into Seneca territory (Abler 1992; Coates 1893; Hamell 1980; Marshall 1848; Mohawk 1986). After a Seneca ambush of French-led forces crossing a marshy stream near what is now Victor, New York, failed, Senecas abandoned all four of their villages in anticipation of French attack. Some towns (for example, Ganondagan) were burned by the Senecas so as not to give Denonville's party the satisfaction of destroying them; others (for example, the western satellite village where Denonville found the arms of the King of England mounted "at the gate of this village" [NYCD 9: 367]) were burned by the French. As with the American expeditions that invaded Seneca territory in 1779, the French and their Native allies ended up conducting "warfare against vegetables" (Graymont 1972: 213), systematically destroying the stored food and unharvested fields left behind by the Senecas. Denonville's forces returned to Irondequoit on July 24, 1687, and then set off to build more permanent fortifications at Niagara.

Senecas and other Iroquois retaliated by laying siege to the French forts at Niagara and Fort Frontenac (now Kingston, Ontario) in late 1687. Most of the trapped French garrisons died of scurvy, and the forts were abandoned in 1688 and 1689, respectively (Abler 1992; N. Adams 1986; P. Scott 1998). Some twelve to fifteen hundred Iroquois warriors attacked the French settlement of Lachine near Montreal in August 1689, killing more than sixty-four French soldiers and civilians, capturing at least eighty people, and burning fifty-six houses (Brandão 1997: table D-1; Steele 1994: 140). Not all post-Denonville military encounters went the Senecas' way: Hurons routed a party of forty to sixty-four Senecas hunting in Michigan's Upper Peninsula in December 1687 (Brandão 1997: table D-1).

Despite military revenge, the toll inflicted on the Senecas in 1687 was considerable (compare Abler 1992; Aquila 1983: 44). In the aftermath of the Denonville expedition, Senecas wintered with the Cayugas in what must have been a season of hardship, as both nations attempted to survive on one group's stored food. In 1688 the Senecas resettled in new villages farther east at the White Springs and Snyder-McClure sites (K. Jordan 2004; Wray 1983), leaving behind a regional ecology that they had transformed through almost 150 years of intensive occupation (see figure 6.1). The mosaic of old fields and village sites, edge areas, and nut-tree groves they left likely was much more productive for human habitation than was the relatively untransformed locale of the new villages. Furthermore, Senecas constructed White Springs and Snyder-McClure without the usual several years of advance work evaluating soils, clearing fields, and stockpiling building materials that normally preceded an Iroquoian village move (Trigger 1990: 32).

In 1689, almost immediately after the new villages were established, Senecas were enveloped in King William's War between the French and the English. During this war the Five Nations were fairly closely allied with the English colonies, but even in this direct imperial conflict the English provided few resources and left the Iroquois to face the brunt of French and western Indian attacks alone. Successful attacks on Five Nations war parties and villages by the French and their allies occurred with regularity starting in 1691 (Aquila 1983: 44–45; Havard 2001: 64; Keener 1998: 146). The Senecas continued to be the most exposed to attacks from the west (Havard 2001: 64, 67), and undated Ojibwa oral traditions which Schmalz (1991: 21–30) associates with events in the 1690s suggest that major Seneca losses took place in what is now southern Ontario. French-led expeditions burned Mohawk towns in 1693 and the Onondaga and Oneida villages in 1696, meaning that in the homeland only Cayuga communities remained undamaged during the Twenty Years' War. The few large-scale English-Iroquois attacks on New France (such as those in 1690 and 1691) foundered, doomed by poor planning and inadequate logistical support.

The frequency of Iroquois diplomatic missions (both to the governors of New France and to western Indian nations) requesting peace demonstrates that the war was going badly for the Five Nations after 1693 (Richter 1992: 176). The Senecas, apparently uninterested in peace with New France in 1690, participated in unsuccessful negotiations with the French in Montreal in 1694 (Havard 2001: 56). While some peace efforts were fruitful—the Five Nations, Wyandots, and Ottawas maintained a truce during 1695–1696 (81–82)—French attacks on the Iroquois took place until the Treaty of Ryswick ended hostilities between the European powers, and the French encouraged western Indians to continue raiding even after the September 1697 treaty was signed.

Documents indicate that Seneca hunters and warriors continued to venture extra-regionally during 1689–1700, but frequently suffered defeat. French soldiers killed fifteen to twenty Senecas, likely between Montreal and Quebec, in October 1689; only ten of fifty Seneca hunters escaped a French and Indian attack near Gananoque in March 1692 (Brandão 1997: table D-1). Senecas participated in a four hundred–warrior expedition that skirmished with mission Iroquois near Kahnawake in the fall of 1692 (Parmenter 2007a: 48). In the spring of 1695, Senecas and other Iroquois captured ten western Indians (termed "Wagenhaws," probably Ottawas) near Fort Frontenac, but many Senecas were killed in an attack on Fort St. Joseph in Miami territory in southwestern Michigan (Brandão 1997: table D-1).

In 1696, a raid by Ottawas and Potawatomis killed fifty to seventy Senecas and captured over thirty more (Havard 2001: 89). More than one hundred Senecas reportedly were killed or captured by French-allied Indians in the spring of 1697, and fifty-eight Senecas were captured or killed in the Miami area in the spring of 1700 (Brandão 1997: table D-1; NYCD 9: 672). Western Indians identified as "Dowaganhaes" (again, probably Ottawas) killed five people in the immediate vicinity of a Seneca village in 1699 (NYCD 4: 597), and similar attacks took place in the Seneca homeland during 1700 (Brandão 1997: table D.1; Havard 2001: 104; NYCD 4: 768, 800). Richter (1992: 195) takes the Senecas' inability to protect local populations as an indication of their declining military power.

The Iroquois sponsored independent negotiations in 1700–1701 with numerous western Indian nations, New France, and New York, which ended open conflict and ushered in a new era in Iroquois politics. Senecas played leading roles in these negotiations (Havard 2001). The 1700–1701 treaties have been characterized as being everything from dictated by the military strength of the Iroquois (Wallace 1957) to moves of Iroquois desperation (Jennings 1984: 210). Brandão and Starna's (1996) interpretation stresses that *every* party involved in the treaties negotiated from a position of weakness. The Iroquois had been militarily depleted, and New York and New France had few resources to devote to frontier warfare. The treaty minutes also suggest that beaver had begun to become scarce in the western Indians' own hunting territories (229). The success of Iroquois efforts to establish their neutrality between the French and English and at least temporarily lull hostilities with the Far Indians in this situation of mutual weakness meant that the 1700–1701 treaties can rightly be considered a "triumph of Iroquois diplomacy" (Brandão and Starna 1996; compare Havard 2001).

The demographic consequences of this extended period of warfare on the Senecas cannot be determined precisely. Estimating American Indian populations is notoriously difficult; Brandão (1997: 153) notes that with documentary estimates one "can never be certain if shifts in population figures represent real trends or . . . the eyesight and judgment of the chroniclers." It is also likely that at least some of these figures were *intentional* misrepresentations for political purposes. Additionally, documents frequently estimate warrior rather than overall Iroquois populations, and determining what proportion of a group was made up of warriors is an inexact science (Brandão 1997: 153). While archaeological methods of calculating village populations based on site area appear to be more accurate, they require careful delineation of village sizes, something that has been done only

Table 3.1. Seneca Population Estimates, 1677–1774

Year	Number of Seneca Warriors	Overall Seneca Population
1677	1000	—
1680	—	4000
1682	1500[a]	—
1685	1200	—
1689	1300[a, b]	—
1690	—	4000
1696	1000	—
1698	600[c]	—
1700	—	2400
1710	1000	4000
1720	1000+	2800
1721	700	—
1730	—	1400
1736	350[c]	—
1740	—	2000
1750	—	2000
1760	—	4200
1763	1050	—
1768	1000	—
1770	1000	4000
1774	1000	—

Sources: Michelson (1977); Tooker (1978a); Snow (1994)
Notes: a. Brandão (1997) asserts this figure is too high.
b. Tooker (1978a) asserts this figure is too high.
c. Tooker (1978a) asserts this figure is too low.

rarely at post-1677 Seneca sites. The ratio between site area and population also varies both historically and according to how villages were physically structured (K. Jordan 2004: 48; Snow 1995: 44, 206, 216; Snow and Starna 1989).

Richter (1992: 188) claims that at least 25 percent of the Confederacy's population was lost between 1689 and 1700; Brandão (1997: 126) asserts that approximately half the Iroquois warrior population died during 1687–1698. Additionally, a "bloody flux" possibly affected Senecas in 1682 (Brandão 1997: 149–50), and smallpox may have reached Seneca territory in 1690 (Brandão 1997: 150) and definitely passed through Seneca villages in 1696 (NYCD 4: 195). Table 3.1 presents 1677–1774 Seneca population estimates. Warrior counts are derived from Michelson (1977: table I) and Tooker (1978a: table 1). Brandão (1997: table C.5) and Tooker (1978a: table 1) assess the reliability of most of these figures. Snow (1994: table 7.1) provides overall Seneca population estimates, which appear to have been formed by multiplying Tooker's (1978a) warrior population figures by four and arranging the results in ten-year intervals. By themselves these documentary figures provide little indication of overall Seneca population decline during 1677–1774. Most of the primary sources that supply these numbers do not indicate whether they included Seneca migrant communities or counted only the homeland population; Parmenter (1999: 5, 9, table 1) suggests that demographic estimates that ignore migrant and mission communities may obscure significant eighteenth-century Iroquois population growth.

Brandão (1997) and Tooker (1978a) question exactly those numbers that indicate precipitous changes in the Seneca population. That the Seneca warrior population increased between 1685 and 1689—a period which included the Denonville invasion and the forced village relocation of 1688—seems particularly unlikely, as does the increase in the total Seneca population from 2400 in 1700 to 4000 in 1710 posited by Snow. The purported sharp drop from more than 1000 warriors in 1720 to 700 warriors in 1721 occurred in the absence of any historically known epidemic or major incidents of warfare. The regularity with which seventeenth- and eighteenth-century census takers noted one thousand Seneca warriors suggests that this might better be interpreted as a rule-of-thumb estimate than an actual population figure. Brandão's (1997: 126) claim that the Five Nations lost 51 percent of their warriors during 1687–1698 is based on casualty figures derived from documentary sources. Since this estimate is derived from the accumulation of numerous small-scale observations, it is likely to provide a more accurate summation of the demographic troubles of the era than do the fluctuations in episodic estimates of the total Seneca warrior population.

There can be little doubt that the military setbacks of 1687–1700 negatively affected the economies of the Senecas and the other Iroquois nations. The main source of needed European goods remained the fur trade, supplemented by gifts given by Europeans to cement political alliances. Because beaver populations were small in the regional hunting territories of both the Iroquois *and* (if Brandão and Starna are correct) western Indians, areas north of Lake Ontario and west along the Ohio drainage depopulated during the wars of the 1630s–1650s became increasingly important sources for furs. The Seneca military setbacks of 1687–1700 probably resulted in decreased access to these productive extra-regional hunting territories; for example, western Indians drove Senecas and other Iroquois out of many settlements north of Lake Ontario by 1699 (Schmalz 1991; Snow 1994: 119). In addition to difficulties gaining direct access to peltry, the Senecas also suffered from the loss of stored food (likely including seed varieties saved for the next year's planting) and the forced relocation that resulted from the Denonville invasion. The 1687–1701 period therefore can be considered to have been troubled economically as well as militarily.

A Period of Uncertainty, 1701–1713

Aquila's (1983) survey of Iroquois diplomacy during the 1701–1754 period isolates four main elements in what he terms the Iroquois "restoration policy": (1) neutrality toward the English and French; (2) rapprochement with the powerful Far Indians of the upper Great Lakes country and Canada; (3) cooperation with the Pennsylvania government to gain hegemony over the tribes of Pennsylvania and their lands; and (4) a policy of war toward southern Indian nations, primarily located in Virginia and the Carolinas. Scholars have expressed a range of opinions on the degree of premeditation and unity that surrounded this "policy." Fenton (1998: 364) describes Confederacy actions in the first half of the eighteenth century as "ad hoc" (see also Abler 2000: 484–85; Snow 1994: 132–34). Aquila (1983: 15–16) himself emphasizes the loose political structure of the Iroquois Confederacy and its lack of coercive authority, concluding that the "program was a unified policy only in the loosest sense of the term" and questioning whether it could be considered a premeditated plan. In contrast, Parmenter (1999: 17) asserts that the Confederacy systematically developed a "consensus on neutrality" that gave the Iroquois significant "cohesion, power, and influence." Regardless of whether one views Aquila's four elements as historical trends or coherent policy, they provide important guidelines for understanding the political-economic dynamics of the 1701–1754 period, and each element was crucial to homeland Senecas.

During the first portion of the eighteenth century, restoration strategies emerged in fits and starts and were undermined as often as they were successful. Peaceful relations with New France, New York, and western Indian groups frequently were strained and occasionally broken. Although some of the political-economic gains of the 1713–1724 era (which I term the "middleman period") were presaged during 1701–1713, the earlier period was characterized by uncertainty. The main source of insecurity was the 1702–1713 French-English conflict called Queen Anne's War. Although the war never expanded into northeastern North America, it cast a long shadow over Iroquois actions by frequently threatening to do so.

The immediate challenges for the Five Nations following the Twenty Years' War were to obtain an adequate supply of pelts and maintain peace while their communities were reconstituted. The 1700–1701 agreements formally instituted joint access to western Great Lakes hunting territories by the Iroquois and western groups, including Ottawas, Potawatomis, Wyandots, Foxes, Miamis, and Ojibwas. The treaties also permitted western Indians to settle north of Lake Ontario, and the Five Nations surrendered their claim to a monopoly on western hunting territories, which had been based on their victories in these areas during the mid-seventeenth century. These treaty clauses provided official recognition for what had become de facto reality (Richter 1992: 211–15).

The Iroquois also attempted to maintain some control over these western territories. Since separate treaties were made with New York and New France, the Iroquois were able to negotiate terms to their advantage in each location and were not immediately required to resolve contradictions between the agreements. The 1701 treaty with New York contained an Iroquois "deed" granting control over western hunting grounds to the English in exchange for a nebulous guarantee of English "protection" (Brandão and Starna 1996). The Iroquois were most concerned with the Saugeen Peninsula in western Ontario, Michigan's Lower Peninsula, and the south-shore areas of Lake Erie and Lake Ontario (west of the Genesee River). The Five Nations had no clear title to these extra-regional territories, which at the time were "crawling with their victorious Indian enemies" (Richter 1992: 212). In terms of Seneca local political economy, the deed provides a clue to identifying areas that likely contained sizable populations of fur-bearing animals in 1701.

Given the competition from western Indians, Iroquois ability to continue as direct producers in the fur trade has been debated. Richter (1992: 215) claims that the western Indian presence curtailed Iroquois access to productive hunting territories. In sharp contrast, Norton (1974: 37) asserts that even after 1701 "hunters continued to be the major source of the peltry that enabled the Iroquois families to purchase European goods," a position seconded by Trelease (1962). Senecas were the closest of the Five Nations to the hunting grounds specified in the 1701 deed, so it may have been somewhat easier for Senecas than for other Iroquois nations to undertake nonlocal hunting.

Regardless of Iroquois ability to obtain pelts directly, western Indians were major suppliers for the European trade, and English and French officials both tried to gain their favor during 1701–1713. New York's trading center was in Albany; trade there benefited the English, the western Indians (who took advantage of reputedly cheaper prices for goods,[2] and did not have to travel all the way to Montreal), and the Iroquois (who could act as geographic middlemen). The Five Nations actively encouraged western Indian groups to trade with the English and permitted passage to Albany as early as 1700 (Haan 1976: 109–11, ch. 4; 1980).[3] The French viewed any trade between their western Indian allies and the English as a violation of the alliance, and they did everything in their power to make the way to Albany as difficult as possible. In part, the French tried to draw Iroquois into their orbit and make them hostile to New York; Senecas (likely with French encouragement) barred the passage of Indians from Detroit looking to trade with the English in 1702 (Havard 2001: 269). When this strategy provided poor results, the French encouraged western Indian groups to attack the Iroquois and otherwise disrupt the Albany trade (Haan 1980: 322–23). Since many independent groups of western Indians were involved, French influence prevailed on some and English on others. Trade and violence happened in rapid succession, or even simultaneously, in different parts of the Great Lakes.

Haan (1976: 157) notes that Miamis and Ottawas attacked Iroquois, and particularly Senecas, on the western border "almost yearly" during 1703–1708, motivated by revenge and French encouragement. In 1704 Miamis killed Senecas in the Great Lakes hunting grounds, Ottawas took nearly forty captives in raids upon the Seneca homeland and Iroquois settlements north of Lake Ontario, and Senecas were forced to abandon a village they had established near Fort Frontenac (Havard 2001: 174; Richter 1992: 218–19). In May 1705 Senecas told New York officials that "4 Nations of the farr Indians" were attacking them (McIlwain 1915: 44); in August Senecas met with Philippe de Rigaud de Vaudreuil, the governor of New France, to request his help in pacifying the attackers (NYCD 9: 766–69). The same month, two groups of Indians from near Detroit arrived in Seneca territory on their way to trade in Albany but were dissuaded from going farther by the French agent Louis-Thomas Chabert de Joncaire (McIlwain 1915: 44–45). New York quickly sent out an agent of its own to counter French influence (McIlwain 1915: 44–45). Another Seneca mission asked Vaudreuil to discourage anti-Iroquois actions by the Ottawas in 1706 (Jennings et al. 1985: 167).

Despite French efforts, increasing numbers of western Indians found trade with the English to be sufficiently attractive to forsake their French allies and make the long trek to Albany. Immediately after 1701 few western Indians made the trip, since they needed both the permission of their recent enemies, the Iroquois, to get to Albany, and to be in a strong enough position themselves to risk the wrath of the French. Nonetheless, appearances of Far Indians in Iroquois territory and Albany occurred more frequently as the period went on (for example, Colden 1935 [1720]: 364; Haan 1980: 322; McIlwain 1915: 52). In 1705 French officials noted a sharp decrease in the amount of trade taking place at Montreal, and only sixty Indians came to Montreal to trade in 1708 (Haan 1976: 159, 164). In 1710 a group of Ottawas negotiated for peaceful trade first with the Senecas, then with all Five Nations at Onondaga, and finally with New York officials in Albany in meetings kept secret from the French (Colden 1935 [1720]: 383–84; Haan 1976: 172–74; McIlwain 1915: 70–75). The Albany trade proved so worrisome to the French that they ordered the murder of the métis Alexander Montour, who guided western groups through Iroquois territory, in 1709 (McIlwain 1915: 64–65; Haan 1976: 164–66).

The Senecas occupied the literal middle of the controversy over the western trade. Any western group trying to get to Albany needed to go through Seneca territory. Western Indians using an inland route had to pass directly through or immediately adjacent to Seneca villages; those using a lakeside route had to stop in Seneca territory on the south shore of Lake Ontario (see figure 2.1). Either alternative meant that it was wise for any western group heading to Albany to negotiate safe passage with the Senecas, which in Native terms required formal rituals of friendship and the exchange of gifts. Many of the gifts that ended up in Seneca hands were likely pelts the westerners brought with them. The Senecas' location therefore brought them a new economic role as geographic middlemen (the impact of which is discussed more fully in the next section). Senecas appear to have been enthusiastic about attracting western Indians to Albany; for example, they told a group of Ottawas in 1710 that "The Doors stand open for you, the Beds are made for you from the Sennecas Country to the Habitation of Corlaer [Iroquois term for the governor of New York], the Path is secure & there is no Ill in our Country" (McIlwain 1915: 71).

To counter the lure of Albany, the French attempted to curry favor among the Senecas by dispatching Jesuits, agents, and smiths to Seneca territory. Jesuit missionaries provided a potentially divisive but time-tested strategy for obtaining Native allegiance; for most or all of the 1702–1709 period, Jesuits—including the aged Julien Garnier, François Vaillant de Gueslis, and Jacques d'Heu—resided with the Senecas (NYCD 9: 737, 750, 762, 775; McIlwain 1915: 43, 46, 52). French agents, particularly Louis-Thomas Chabert de Joncaire (DCB 2: 125–27; D. Kent 1974: 69–102; Severance 1906), added to their efforts. Joncaire had been captured and adopted by the Senecas in 1689 or 1690; he made use of his knowledge of the Seneca people, language, and territory during a long career as a French agent, remaining an effective voice for French concerns among the Senecas until his death in 1739. The government of New France also stationed smiths in Seneca territory to make and repair tools and weapons. Smiths were of great value on the frontier and a government lucky enough to find a smith willing to undertake dangerous service in a distant Iroquois village was likely to reap great diplomatic rewards (see K. Jordan 2001). The Senecas were said to have had a French smith "for some years in their villages" in 1709 (NYCD 9: 830).

English influence during the 1701–1713 period was less direct and more reactive. Strikingly few delegations from New York went to Seneca territory. They included groups sent to respond to Joncaire's attempts to dissuade western Indians from going to Albany in 1705; to persuade the Senecas not to let Joncaire construct a trading house in their territory in 1707; and to quell rumors about an impending French and western Indian attack on the Senecas in 1709 and again in 1710 (Leder 1956: 211–12; McIlwain 1915: 45, 51, 69; NYCD 5: 217–18). New York officials also neglected to provide customary gifts and "crassly disregarded the protocols of Indian diplomacy" (Richter 1992: 216) with the Five Nations during the first decade of the eighteenth century. English economic superiority made them confident that the Iroquois and other nations would come to them, while the French used direct contacts and the provision of services to influence the Senecas.

A series of diplomatic crises between 1708 and 1711 demonstrated the unpredictability of the Queen Anne's War years. In the summer of 1708, rumors of an impending war between New France and the New England colonies circulated in Iroquois territory (Colden 1935 [1720]: 367–69). Due to French influence, the Senecas were reported in March 1709 to be "in a great confusion amongst themselves & that most of them have a design to leave their Country but know not as of yet where they shall go to settle" (McIlwain 1915: 63–64). After the April 1709 murder of Alexander Montour, the Senecas appear to have drifted more into the British orbit. When in May Joncaire encouraged Senecas to attack Far Indians sojourning in their territory en route to Albany, the Senecas refused (McIlwain 1915: 68). The Jesuits d'Heu and Garnier and the French smith subsequently left Seneca territory "for safety's sake" (A. Stewart 1970: 116; see also DCB 2: 237; NYCD 9: 830).[4] During the summer of 1709 the British assembled a force for the invasion of Canada, mustering warriors from every Iroquois nation except the Senecas, who kept their fighting men at home—possibly due to rumors of a French and Ottawa army on their borders (Colden 1935 [1720]: 374–77; Leder 1956: 210–11). Invasion plans eventually were aborted after the British fleet that was to support the attack was diverted to Portugal (Aquila 1983: 87). Overall, Iroquois participation in the 1709 expedition has been characterized as less than enthusiastic (Parmenter 2007a: 53–54).

The early months of 1710 witnessed a partial lull in British-French hostilities. Western Indians negotiated with the Senecas for passage to Albany, and Iroquois warriors went to war against the so-called Flatheads to the south, usually an indication that they felt their homeland was secure (Aquila 1983: 207–8). Documents mention a French smith (McIlwain 1915: 79) and a British delegation (NYCD 5: 217–18) in Seneca territory. The Iroquois complained of the low price paid for beaver pelts in Albany (McIlwain 1915: 76–78).

By late 1710 or early 1711 British-French and Iroquois–western Indian hostilities had resumed. Seneca and Onondaga representatives complained of Ottawa attacks to Vaudreuil in 1710 (Havard 2001: 174). In January 1711, Five Nations representatives informed the Albany Commissioners of Indian Affairs that they intended to go to war against the "Waganhaes" (probably Ottawas) in response to 1710 attacks on Iroquois hunters that may have been instigated by the French (Aquila 1983: 89, 208; Haan 1980: 323; McIlwain 1915: 80). In 1711 another British-Iroquois force was assembled for the invasion of Canada; in sharp contrast to their nonparticipation in 1709, the Senecas sent 182 warriors to accompany the expedition (McIlwain 1915: 91). This invasion also was aborted after "fog, stormy seas, and poor leadership" sank ten of the ships that were to accompany the land force (Aquila 1983: 91). New York officials previously had convinced the Iroquois nations to post the British queen's coat of arms outside their villages; after the second failed invasion and French-spread rumors that the coats of arms represented British claims to their land, the Iroquois sent them back to Albany in anger (McIlwain 1915: 85, 92).

In 1712, a series of raids and sieges took place in the western Great Lakes in which French and Ottawas battled Foxes and Mascoutens (Edmunds and Peyser 1993: 64–76). The Seneca response to the Fox conflicts demonstrates the complicated calculus that neutrality between the French and British required. After the Foxes were defeated by the French, about one hundred of them resettled in Seneca territory, a move that clearly had anti-French overtones. However, when New York officials attempted to muster more than one thousand Iroquois warriors to avenge the Foxes that summer, the Senecas refused to participate and the expedition was cancelled (Parmenter 2007a: 56; Richter 1992: 234). In the fall of 1712 a band of Foxes based in Seneca territory attacked Frenchmen and their Indian allies as they traveled near the Niagara portage; in subsequent years the Fox-French conflict shifted back to the west (Edmunds and Peyser 1993: 76–78).

The April 1713 signing of the Treaty of Utrecht terminated Queen Anne's War. I have used this date to mark the end of the period of uncertainty. Uncertainty certainly continued, but after the resolution of the imperial conflict it took on a different character, centering on the west-east trade and the establishment of European-run trading posts in Iroquois territory rather than the possibility of open French-British warfare. Haan (1976: 193–97, 200) cites 1715 as a turning point in Iroquois history due to formal Iroquois pronouncements of neutrality to New France in 1714 and New York in 1715, and also to an important set of Ottawa-Iroquois negotiations in 1715. Trade figures cited by White (1991: 120) indicate however that the New York fur trade increased dramatically in 1713. Increased trade volume likely had a more immediate impact on Seneca local political economies than the neutrality pronouncements.

Actual conflicts with western Indians and the chronic threat of imperial war made the 1701–1713 period a fairly difficult one for Senecas. Conflict limited access to crucial extra-regional hunting territories to the north and west that still contained ample supplies of fur-bearing mammals. Attacks on Seneca localities by Ottawas and other western groups made even everyday tasks such as walking to agricultural fields or fetching water and firewood intermittently hazardous, and undoubtedly the psychological threat of attacks burdened daily life far beyond the scope of attacks that actually took place. Since the Seneca towns at the White Springs and Snyder-McClure sites were first occupied in 1688, they were probably reaching the end of their life spans by around 1710. Resources adjacent to these villages were likely to have been depleted or in decline, making for longer walks to fields and firewood sources, and waste would have built up in and around the settlements. These negative factors were somewhat offset by the new source of goods (likely including pelts) provided by western Indians in exchange for passage across Seneca territory, which was at its height from 1705 to 1709. Finally, I was unable to find any mention of epidemics or famines in Seneca territory during this period, making for a rare break in what were by this point chronic episodes of massive mortality.

The "Middleman" Period, 1713–1724

The political economy of the Great Lakes region changed dramatically after the 1713 Treaty of Utrecht as the trickle of western Indians going to Albany became a flood. The 1713–1724 period witnessed the peak movement of former Iroquois enemies across Five Nations territory to trade at Albany. The value of beaver exports from New York doubled in 1713 and doubled again in 1714 (White 1991: 120). While thirty trading canoes piloted by Far Indians (built large enough to hold twelve men; NYCD 5: 727) arrived at Schenectady during 1716 to 1720, 323 canoes arrived from 1720–1724 (NYCD 5: 739; White 1991: 121). It is likely that Senecas benefited considerably from the passage of western Indians through their territory during 1713–1724, hence its designation as the middleman period.

The use of the term *middleman* in association with the Iroquois role in the fur trade has been the subject of controversy for almost a century (Aquila 1983, 1984; Brandão 1997; Haan 1976; Hunt 1940; McIlwain 1915; Trelease 1962). Brandão (1997: 10–12) has been the most vocal of recent critics, claiming that McIlwain's (1915: introduction) use of the term projects a capitalist profit motivation upon seventeenth- and eighteenth-century Iroquois, assumes without documentary evidence that the Iroquois were carrying European goods to western Indians, and does not situate "middleman" participation within an Iroquoian cultural context.

However, Brandão fails to make the crucial distinction between *economic* and *geographic* middleman roles specified by Aquila (1983, 1984). Brandão's critique of the economic middleman role does appear to hold for the eighteenth century as well as the seventeenth: while there is some documentary evidence for Iroquois transport and peddling of goods (Aquila 1984: 52 note 4; Haan 1976: 154–55; Norton 1974: 29–30, 35; Waterman 2008), this practice appears to have been relatively rare. Instead, the major Iroquois emphasis was on negotiating with other Indian groups and persuading them to trade *directly* with certain European partners (especially the British) and to take certain routes to get to them. Encouragement of western passage to the British was a consistent element in Iroquois neutralist diplomacy from 1700 onward (Aquila 1983, 1984; Haan 1976, 1980).

The routes championed by the Five Nations were through their own territory, something that makes complete sense within the logic of Iroquoian culture. Richter (1992: 223–24) notes that by encouraging the west-east trade, the Iroquois "profited both politically and materially; each western band needed first to make peace formally with them, each trading party needed Iroquois guides, and each group needed to make appropriate ceremonial gifts as it tarried along the way in the towns of Iroquoia." The geographic middleman role thus resulted in an increased number of alliances and a greater volume of gifts circulating in Iroquoia. Both of these ends are fully consistent with traditional Iroquois forms of power: successful negotiations increased the prestige of the negotiators and provided them with sources of outside information; gifts (or the European goods for which they were exchanged) could be distributed to followers as tangible proof of the abilities of the negotiator. By some accounts, the Iroquois also obtained the reciprocal right to hunt and travel peaceably in the west as part of middleman negotiations (Aquila 1984: 55). The scale and benefits of this role were therefore far greater than the "incidental trade for provisions" with western Indians posited by those who downplay Iroquois middleman motivations (Trelease 1962: 46; Norton 1974), and it was far more than purely anti-French in its aims (as asserted by Brandão 1997: 343).

As in 1701–1713, the Senecas were located on every possible route to Albany that could have been used by western Indians (figure 2.1). There is reasonable documentation for two routes: (1) a water route to Albany by way of the south shore of Lake Ontario, the Oswego River, Oneida Lake, and the Mohawk River; and (2) a land route through Seneca territory that started at Irondequoit Bay. The Oswego route was faster and more direct, being entirely by water except for a three-mile portage near the east end of Oneida Lake (Richter 1992: 249). The portion of this route from Niagara to Sodus Bay was in Seneca territory (see map in Morgan 1962 [1851]). This stretch is more than 180 km long, a distance that would have required several overnight stops. Primary sources indicate that most of the Far Indians traveled along this route and arrived in Albany or Schenectady by water (for example, NYCD 5: 701).

Morgan's map and an anonymous historic map ("N.W. Parts of New York" 1750–1768) also show footpaths leading from Irondequoit and Sodus bays, which may have been used by western Indians. These routes went inland to the foot of Seneca Lake, from which travelers could use the Seneca River to get to Oneida Lake and there pick up the Oswego route. Missionary Samuel Kirkland and his adoptive Seneca family used the eastern portion of this route to get from Kanadesaga to Albany in 1765 (Pilkington 1980). Inland water routes starting at Irondequoit or Sodus bays also may have existed. Footpaths from Niagara and other points provided alternate but less rapid means of transit; Seneca villages were said to be "in the road from Najager [Niagara]" in 1734 (MACIA vol. 1820: 52).

In terms of the military climate, the 1713–1724 period can be characterized as one of relative local peace, with the words *relative* and *local* both requiring emphasis. Unlike the 1701–1713 period when western Indian raiders entered Seneca territory, during 1713–1724 warfare occasionally threatened the Seneca homeland but rarely took place there. In one of the few instances of homeland violence, Onondagas attacked a group of western Indians making their way across Iroquoia in June 1715 (McIlwain 1915: 103; Aquila 1983: 137). The majority of actual conflict was distant from Iroquoia, particularly in Virginia and the Carolinas, where the Five Nations continued to conduct mourning war raids on southern Indian groups throughout the period (Aquila 1983: 209–17). The change in the military climate was aided by the Anglo-French peace of 1716, in which the two European powers united in their opposition to Holy Roman Emperor Philip V; as a consequence the governor of New France was ordered to find peaceful ways to oppose the New York colony that would not alienate Britain (Haan 1976: 204–5).

Other potential conflicts did not come to fruition. The Mohawk leader Theyanoguin (also known as Hendrick) informed the New York government of secret Iroquois consideration of "making Warr on her Majestys subjects" in 1713 (Jennings et al. 1985: 170), but it is unclear whether this report was an accurate reflection of Iroquois sentiments or Theyanoguin's exaggeration. In 1715, the French attempted to get Senecas to join them in their war against the Foxes (McIlwain 1915: 103), but the Senecas instead continued their policy of "benevolent neutrality" toward the Foxes and facilitated meetings between Foxes and New York (Edmunds and Peyser 1993: 78). Rumors circulated in 1716 of a possible French and Ottawa attack on the Iroquois (Haan 1976: 208; McIlwain 1915: 115), and in 1717 a Seneca expedition departed for battle against the Illinois, only to turn back after smallpox struck (NYCD 9: 877). In 1723, the Iroquois Confederacy declared war on the Abenakis in New England (McIlwain 1915: 148–149), but did not follow through with military action.

The success of the Five Nations and New York in luring western Indians to Albany was countered by French efforts to woo the Senecas and other Iroquois groups using their standard assortment of diplomatic maneuvers, gifts, and smiths, and also by new efforts to establish an outpost in Seneca territory to capture some of the western trade. French smiths were reported to be in Seneca territory in 1715, 1716, 1717, and 1720 (McIlwain 1915: 103–4, 113, 117; NYCD 5: 550) and a French priest was there in 1716 (McIlwain 1915: 113). French traders were noted in the vicinity of Irondequoit Bay and the Niagara "carrying place" in 1714, 1715, and 1716 (McIlwain 1915: 99, 105, 106). Joncaire was ubiquitous during this period, helping to establish French outposts at Niagara and Irondequoit. He acquired nine hundred bushels of maize for the garrison at Fort Michilimackinac from the Senecas in 1715 (D. Kent 1974: 87), an indication of substantial Seneca agricultural surplus. In January 1717, Joncaire introduced his "little son" (probably Philippe-Thomas, born circa 1707) to the Senecas and asked that the boy be received favorably among them after his own death (McIlwain 1915: 117). French efforts appear to have encouraged the loyalty of at least part of the Seneca population. In 1716, twelve "considerable men of the Sennekas" were interested enough in solidifying relations with the French to petition Governor Vaudreuil to build a fort in Seneca territory (Colden 1935 [1720]: 424).

The development of each European trading post in Seneca territory followed a similar pattern. As a first step, traders would occupy a crucial transportation node during the parts of the year when Far Indians were on their way to Albany and Iroquois hunters were returning home from the north and west. The next step was to build a more formal "trading house" at that location, which usually provoked angry recriminations and threats by the opposing European power. The third step was the construction of permanent fortifications and the assignment of a military garrison to the post. During 1713–1724 the French and British competed for Irondequoit and Niagara, and trading privileges at both locations passed back and forth between the two powers.

Irondequoit Bay was within the regional territories of both the eastern and western Seneca communities (as defined in chapter 2), and the Senecas were quite careful about who could frequent Irondequoit and for how long. In 1714 New York interpreter Lawrence Claessen was sent to Seneca territory to find out about "a Settlement wch it was reported the French had made somewhere above their [Seneca] Country at a Pass where the farr Indians must come thro in order to come down to Albany" (McIlwain 1915: 99); this "Settlement" was likely to have been at Irondequoit. There were definite reports of a French presence at "Tiurundequat . . . about 32 miles [51 km] from the Sennekas Castles" by February 1716 (Colden 1935 [1720]: 424). In April of that year six Albany traders applied to the Albany Commissioners for a license "to go & try to open a Trade at Irondequat"; upon their arrival there they found five French traders and a smith (McIlwain 1915: 112–13). The next day a group of western Indians arrived and spoke with the New York delegation, prompting the New Yorkers to seek

Seneca permission to construct a permanent trading house (McIlwain 1915: 113–14). Despite these British efforts, a French post had been built at Irondequoit by the summer of 1717 (McIlwain 1915: 120). Subsequently, French focus shifted to Niagara, where they had maintained a long-standing interest.

Although the Niagara portage was more than 80 km from each of the major Seneca communities, it was a vital transportation corridor that Senecas monitored carefully. Two short-lived French forts had been built in 1678 and 1687 at the mouth of the Niagara River on Lake Ontario (now Youngstown, New York; P. Scott 1998: 46), and Joncaire and his allies in the administration of New France lobbied unsuccessfully to have a French trading post built there during 1706–1709 and again starting in 1716 (D. Kent 1974: 78–85, 89–90). Senecas and British traders also frequented the region during 1715–1720. In 1717 New York Governor Robert Hunter issued a license to Robert Livingston Jr., Johannes Cuyler, and Hendrick Hansen to open up trade to the west of the Senecas (Norton 1974: 159). An anonymous 1718 French report noted that a Seneca village of ten "cabins" had been constructed near the northern end of the 14 km portage (NYCD 9: 885). Its residents worked as porters for the French, carrying cargo along the portage around the rapids and falls in exchange for pelts, leggings, shirts, powder, and ball; some Senecas were reported to pilfer from the cargoes they transported. Maize, beans, peas, watermelons, and pumpkins were grown in the Seneca carriers' village (NYCD 9: 885), so it is likely that full family units had relocated to Niagara. In 1720 officials from New France reported that New York traders had been operating a trading house in the Niagara area "since several years ago" where they bartered merchandise and whiskey for furs (NYCD 9: 897–98).

By 1719–1720 the French had solidified their presence at Niagara by establishing a relatively permanent post just below Niagara Falls at the Artpark site (D. Kent 1974: 91–93; McIlwain 1915: 124; NYCD 5: 528; S. Scott and Scott 1998). During a July 1719 visit to Niagara, the Onondaga leader Teganissorens found both a French "fort" and Far Indians on their way to Albany (McIlwain 1915: 124; NYCD 5: 528). Haan (1976: 210) finds it noteworthy that an Onondaga, rather than the Senecas themselves, first informed New Yorkers of the French "fort" in Seneca territory. Teganissorens' report prompted New York to send Myndert Schuyler, Robert Livingston Jr., and Lawrence Claessen on a fact-finding mission to Seneca territory in 1720. The gravity of the situation is indicated by the fact that the sitting (Schuyler) and preceding (Livingston) mayors of Albany were sent on the mission (Bielinski 2002, n.d.). At Niagara Claessen and three Seneca sachems found a 12.2 m × 9.1 m trading house, inhabited by three Frenchmen who claimed to have obtained permission to build from "the young fighting men of the Senecas." The sachems denied any knowledge of this permission, and the Frenchmen rejected Claessen's demand that they tear down the building (NYCD 5: 550; McIlwain 1915: 127–28). During the same trip, Claessen also found a French smith traveling at Irondequoit (NYCD 5: 550). Joncaire and thirty men were reported to be fortifying the post at Niagara in 1721 despite Seneca opposition (McIlwain 1915: 135–36, 139). This fairly substantial French detachment deterred further British efforts at Niagara, although diplomatic initiatives to remove the post based on its violation of the Treaty of Utrecht continued (Haan 1976: 214–17). The area remained a French stronghold until its surrender to the British in 1759 during the Seven Years' War (D. Kent 1974).

New York responded to the developments at Niagara by establishing a trading post at Irondequoit, which had fallen out of French favor. In September 1721 New York Governor William Burnet sponsored Peter Schuyler Jr., the smith Myndert Wemp, and seven others for one year to establish a post at Irondequoit (DHNY 1: 289; NYCD 5: 641–42, 666, 718). In September 1722 two men were commissioned to reoccupy the area for another year (Leder 1956: 232–35). By 1724 Burnet was able to claim that he had kept smiths and traders among the Senecas "for some time" and that they had a house "near their [the Senecas'] Castle where they may live quite conveniently" (NYCD 5: 716). Despite the British presence at Irondequoit, the Senecas apparently gave Joncaire permission to construct his own post there in 1723 (McIlwain 1915: 144), although it is unclear whether he did so. European control over Irondequoit remained contested until the 1740s.

After the advent of the French outposts, New York adopted a more hands-on approach to its relations with the Senecas, offering some of the same services that the French had in the past. New York Governor Hunter ordered a smith and his journeymen to Seneca territory for a year in 1718 (McIlwain 1915: 122). A three-man expedition of 1720–1721 was explicitly instructed to oppose the designs of the French among the Senecas, but Governor Burnet later withdrew the men's salaries upon finding out they had spent their time solely in trade (McIlwain 1915: 132). By 1721 Burnet had reconsidered, granting licenses to ten private traders as long as they "did not begin selling goods before they reached the Senecas" (Norton 1974: 161). Smiths accompanied New York expeditions in 1720–1721 and 1721–1722, and probably also in 1722–1723 (McIlwain 1915: 132, 138–39; NYCD 5: 641–42, 718). One of the purposes of New York's Seneca missions was to make contact with western Indian groups and give them a good impression of the Albany trade (NYCD 5: 685).

The effects of the intermittent presence of French and British officials, traders, and smiths and the permanent French post at Niagara were likely to have been mixed, but mainly to the benefit of the Senecas (compare Haan 1976: 217). Europeans initially would have needed to provide gifts to obtain Seneca permission to build the posts, and subsequently continue the gifts to maintain good relations with their hosts. Some Senecas obtained work as carriers at Niagara. French outposts provided an alterNative source of European goods to Albany, and traveling to trading centers at Niagara or Irondequoit—regardless of whether they were French or British—required a much shorter journey than the trip to Albany.

Albany nonetheless remained the major outlet for western furs despite French efforts to capture the trade. Development of the fur market in New France was hampered by inconsistent demand (official preferences shifted from one grade of beaver pelt to another following major over-accumulation of pelts in the 1690s), and the imposition of arbitrary limits on the total number of beaver pelts that could be exported to France (Haan 1976: 203–4; Laird 1995: 12–17). French desperation was demonstrated by their attempts after 1717 to intercept canoes of western Indians on Lake Ontario and force them to turn back before they reached the shelter of the Oswego River (Haan 1976: 206). The continued predominance of Albany as a trading center meant that most western Indians still needed to make fairly lengthy stays in Seneca territory, and even those Indians who avoided Albany and traded at Niagara or Irondequoit needed to negotiate with Senecas.

The presence of the new trading centers was not entirely beneficial for the Senecas. Construction of the French posts encouraged a major outburst of factional conflict among the Senecas in 1719–1721, much of which probably was instigated by Joncaire. He approached various segments of the Seneca population until he found that the "young fighting men of the Senecas" were willing to give him permission to set up at Niagara (NYCD 5: 550). In 1719 he arranged to have the Seneca headman Kayenkwarahte (or "Blewbek"), "who had been always firmly attached to the Interest" of the New York government (Colden 1935 [1720]: 380), removed from his leadership position (432). Kayenkwarahte was reinstated in 1720 (NYCD 5: 545). In 1720 Joncaire worked feverishly to overcome the effects of the presents distributed to the Senecas by Schuyler, Livingston, and Claessen, eventually convincing at least some Senecas of the value of the new post at Niagara (D. Kent 1974: 97; NYCD 9: 898). Joncaire also spread rumors that the British were planning an attack on the Five Nations, and threatened bloodshed if the French post at Niagara was destroyed (Haan 1976: 213; NYCD 5: 563).

In 1720 pro-French sachems from the western Seneca village of "Onnahee" gave a wampum belt to Governor Vaudreuil and asked him to find a place where they could relocate; Vaudreuil provided land near Montreal and a smith to help with the construction of the new village there (NYCD 5: 550, 570–72). By September 1720, the inhabitants of one of the Seneca castles (probably "Onnahee") allowed the French to "hoist their colors" in the village, and two principal headmen and their families moved to Canada (McIlwain 1915: 129–31). More than thirty Frenchmen journeyed to Niagara in the spring of 1721; delegates from this mission successfully convinced the Senecas to oppose British plans to destroy the post (D. Kent 1974: 99–101; NYCD 5: 589–90, 9: 961). This spate of factionalism and migration may have helped convince New York to station year-round diplomatic envoys and smiths in Seneca territory.

The interpretation of the political-economic climate during this period depends on how one gauges the effects of the new posts on the fur trade. Many historians agree that the Seneca geographic middleman position provided significant benefits during 1713–1724. As in 1701–1713, documentary sources do not reveal whether the Senecas were able to obtain a significant number of beaver pelts through direct hunting. The Senecas likely constructed new dispersed villages during the middleman period (K. Jordan 2004), so after a strenuous period of house construction and field clearance, agricultural resources and firewood would have been nearby and soils fresh. As I have noted, a smallpox outbreak caused a 1717 Seneca military expedition to return home (McIlwain 1915: 120; NYCD 9: 877); there were no recorded instances of famine.

The Oswego Era, 1724–1754

The year 1724 marked a radical shift in British policy. The New York government abandoned their six-year flirtation with Irondequoit Bay in favor of a new interest in Oswego, on the shore of Lake Ontario at the mouth of the Oswego River (figure 2.1). Whereas Irondequoit was distant and difficult to access, Oswego was relatively close to Albany and directly on the fastest trade route from the west. Oswego was convenient for both western Indians, who would have less distance to travel, and New Yorkers, since it would cut out the Iroquois middlemen between Oswego and Albany and redirect to Oswego traders the goods western Indians would have used to negotiate that passage. In short, it was a classic "trader's leapfrog" (Jennings 1984: 68) that moved New Yorkers closer to a direct relationship with their suppliers. New York's renewed emphasis on the west-east fur trade also came at a time when north-south trade between Canadian mission Iroquois and Albany had been banned because it indirectly supplied British trade goods to New France (Aquila 1984: 58–59; Laird 1995: 75–80; Norton 1974: 135–48). For the Senecas, Oswego was significantly easier to access than the French stronghold at Niagara, being located on the margins of the Seneca region and connected to the Seneca towns by direct water routes (figure 2.1).

The New York government began literally to clear the path from Albany to Oswego in 1724, hiring workmen to drag trees out of waterways, build a road along the main portage from Wood Creek to the Mohawk River, and construct a bridge (Norton 1974: 164–65). That September New York Governor Burnet announced to a delegation from the now–Six Nations that he intended to build a blockhouse at Oswego that would act as a "beaver trap" where pelts would accumulate (173–74). Burnet did not offer the Iroquois any choice in the matter and ignored their suggestions that the post be placed on Oneida Lake (which would have preserved geographic middleman status for the Onondagas and Oneidas). Both Haan (1976: 221–31) and Richter (1992: 250–51) take Burnet's heavy-handed conduct as an indication of the lack of Iroquois power at this time.

Trade statistics collected by the Albany Commissioners indicate that Oswego almost instantly transformed the Indian trade. In the spring and summer of 1725, at least 1164 bundles of beaver pelts, deerskins, and other undesignated furs were received at Albany and Schenectady (McIlwain 1915: 159–60); of these, 67 percent were from Oswego, 17 percent from direct trade at Albany, and 15 percent from Canada (mostly via clandestine exchange with St. Lawrence mission Iroquois). Thirty-nine trading parties from Albany involving more than one hundred Europeans went to Oswego during the 1725 trading season; only three used Indian guides (McIlwain 1915: 159–60; Richter 1992: 250). French officials also noted the large volume of Indian canoe traffic on its way to Oswego that year (NYCD 9: 953). By April 1726 the Albany Commissioners reported that "We hear of many [Albany traders] that are gone to Trade to the Westward even to the Number of 50 Canoes. People encourage that Trade now to emulation[,] even those who were at first against it" (McIlwain 1915: 163).

The threat posed by Oswego prompted quick action from the French. In the spring of 1725 a carpenter, blacksmith, and other workers assembled at Fort Frontenac to build two sailboats intended to transport to Niagara materials for a fort (D. Kent 1974: 112). The French assumed a stronger post at Niagara would dissuade at least some western Indians from going to Albany. Faced with Seneca opposition, the French used their usual tactic of searching about until they found a group that would approve their plans, obtaining permission to construct a stone fort at Niagara from the Onondagas (NYCD 9: 953). Notably, the French did not bother to obtain permission until after preparations for the fort had already begun (Haan 1976: 224–25; Richter 1992: 251). Documents suggest that Iroquois leaders (including Senecas) agreed to the French construction in July 1726, but they denied that they had done so in meetings with New York officials that September (D. Kent 1974: 115–28). In September 1727 Joncaire visited both Seneca "Castles" and provided a list of prices for the "great store of goods" held at Niagara (MACIA vol. 1819: 255a–56). By October, 120 Frenchmen had completed a two-story stone citadel at the mouth of the Niagara River, christened Fort Niagara (DHNY 1: 290–91; D. Kent 1974: 111–15; McIlwain 1915: 163–64; P. Scott 1998: 47).

In June 1725 New Yorkers informed the Six Nations that they would build an unfortified trading house instead of a blockhouse at Oswego; the structure was finished by September (McIlwain 1915: 158–61). After the French construction at Niagara, however, a stone fort quickly was erected at Oswego in 1727 (without Iroquois consent) and a permanent military garrison of twenty men assigned there (Bertsch 1914; DHNY 1: 291–92; Haan 1976: 229; McIlwain 1915: 171). In 1728 Governor John Montgomerie asked the Six Nations for land at Oswego so that the garrison could farm and pasture cattle (McIlwain 1915: 173); the Iroquois granted the request with the stipulation that the area be strictly marked out and, once determined, not exceeded.

Although the European powers primarily focused their attention on the major posts at Oswego and Niagara, they continued to contend for subsidiary trade locations. European efforts at Irondequoit probably reflected British nervousness about Niagara, which was "conveniently situated to intercept all the Fur Trade of the Upper Nations & even of our Sennecas who must pass by that place as they come from their Hunting" (McIlwain 1915: 164), and French realization that Niagara alone was not going to capture the western trade from New York. However, Senecas consistently equivocated, stalled, and denied either imperial power the upper hand at Irondequoit. Louis-Thomas Chabert de Joncaire asked Seneca permission for a post there in 1730 (NYCD 5: 911; McIlwain 1915: 180–81), which was denied by

1731 (MACIA vol. 1819: 339). His son Philippe-Thomas Chabert de Joncaire attempted to take three Seneca headmen to Canada in 1736 to arrange for French purchase of Irondequoit, but the New York commissary at Oswego convinced them not to go (MACIA vol. 1820: 85a–86). The elder Joncaire was said to have obtained Seneca permission for a post at Irondequoit and may have constructed one there in 1737 (McIlwain 1915: 199–200). New York Governor George Clarke attempted to have the Iroquois revoke the permission given to Joncaire, but Clarke's own attempt to buy Seneca land at Irondequoit failed, perhaps due to efforts by the Albany Commissioners (E. Fox 1949: 44–45; Parmenter 1999: 71–72).

In 1738 Senecas from the French-leaning village of "Onnaghee" threatened to move from inland (likely near Canandaigua Lake [K. Jordan 2004]) to Irondequoit itself (MACIA vol. 1820: 129–29a). The Albany Commissioners sent an alarmed message to Governor Clarke, stating that "Your Honor will perceive that the Indians are to remove their castle to Ierondequat which if they do will be of dangerous consequence to this Government and give an opportunity to the French to influence all the Indians and entirely cutt off the furr trade at Oswego" (129a). New York agents quickly resumed attempts to purchase Irondequoit from the Senecas, but funding shortages and various intrigues delayed the actual sale to New York until 1741 or 1742 (IIDH, Aug. 16, 1741; McIlwain 1915: 209–11, 213–15, 222–23, 225, 228; NYCD 6: 204). New York's plans for a fort and European settlement went unrealized (E. Fox 1949: 45–46).

At the elder Joncaire's instigation, the French established another trading post in Seneca territory in 1734. Reports from March and April of that year to the Albany Commissioners claimed that a large trading house with two hearths had been built "between the two Sinneke castles named Kannasadagoe and Onnahee on the bank of a large stream or creek" (MACIA vol. 1820: 50), possibly Flint Creek (see chapter 4). Joncaire flew the French flag, kept the post well stocked with French brandy and rum from Oswego, and reportedly had plans to fortify it (MACIA vol. 1820: 50, 52; McIlwain 1915: 189). The post likely also contained smithy facilities.

The New Dynamics of the Great Lakes Fur Trade

Oswego quickly proved itself dangerous to French fur trade interests. The total value of furs the French received at Niagara and Fort Frontenac fell from 40,911 livres in 1723 to 29,297 livres in 1724 and to only 9151 livres in 1725 (White 1991: 121). New France responded to Oswego "by expanding into new areas and by subsidizing the trade in old ones" (White 1991: 122;

Wien 1990). The semi-private Compagnie des Indes, which held the monopoly on the Canadian fur trade, expanded into areas distant from British posts where Indians were willing to obtain fewer goods in order to trade locally. The French crown subsidized prices at Niagara and Fort Frontenac, where private traders were unable to turn a profit, absorbing a financial loss to make these posts competitive with Oswego. Across the Northeast, New France also increased its provision of smiths, diplomatic gifts, and support for the families of Native warriors fighting in French-sponsored conflicts; accepted lower-grade pelts and non-beaver skins even if there was no ready demand for them; and increased brandy sales (White 1991: 122–28). White (1991) views these French policy changes as economic concessions made to maintain diplomatic and military ties to western Indian nations.

To some degree, the strategy appears to have worked, and New France recaptured a portion of the west-east trade. The bar graphs in figure 3.1 illustrate that the Compagnie des Indes routinely received more than 100,000 beaver pelts annually between 1726 and 1757; most of these pelts would have come from sources distant to Oswego. More pertinent to this study, the subsidized trade at Forts Niagara and Frontenac rebounded, although not completely. These posts received furs worth 39,948 livres in 1728 and 52,308 livres in 1730; in 1730 only 30.5 percent of the total fur value was derived from beaver pelts (White 1991: table 3.1). During 1733–1742, the total annual value of furs received at the two posts averaged 24,590 livres, of which value 11.3–25.6 percent was derived from beaver pelts (Standen 1998: table 1). With the exception of high figures in 1730 and 1733, all of these values fall below the 1723 (pre-Oswego) level of 40,911 livres (Standen 1998; White 1991), probably indicating that Oswego captured the bulk of the west-east and local trade during these years.

Indians clearly were more than willing to shift their trade from Oswego to French posts and vice versa based on the current political-economic situation. Oswego essentially was shut down except during the trading season during King George's War (1744–1748), as most New York traders stayed in Albany for protection (Norton 1974; Wien 1990). French figures show that trade at Niagara and Frontenac increased dramatically during 1743–1748, as a consequence of both limited opportunity at Oswego and better management of Niagara and Frontenac by François Chalet (Standen 1998). During 1743, total volume reached 43,238 livres at Niagara and Frontenac, of which 27.8 percent was derived from beaver pelts; in 1744, total trade reached 54,700 livres, 45.7 percent of which was derived from beaver. Beaver values alone reached 50,000 livres in 1747 and more than 60,000 livres

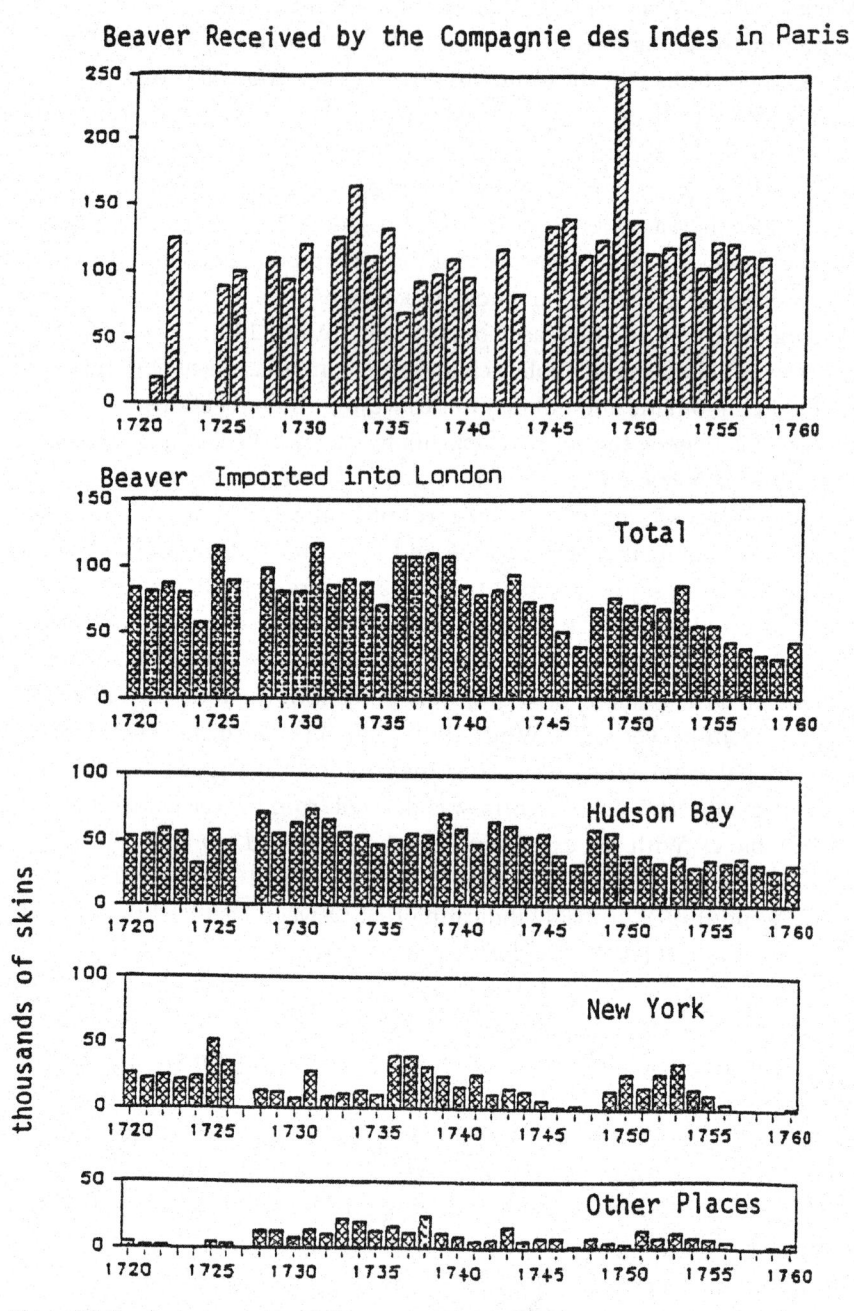

Figure 3.1. Beaver pelts exported from North America to Paris and London, 1720–1760 (from Wien 1990: figure 4). (Image used courtesy of the Canadian Historical Association and Thomas Wien.)

in 1748 (Standen 1998: table 1). However, the two years following the war were easily the best for Oswego since the 1720s and perhaps the best ever: in 1749 Oswego received 193 canoes containing 1385 packs of furs and skins valued at £21,406 (Barnes 1914: 132–33).

Although French reconfiguration and efforts at Niagara, at Irondequoit, and between the Seneca villages carved out a continued role for New France, it is probably accurate to say that Oswego dominated both the west-east beaver trade and the overall fur trade in the lower Great Lakes during 1724–1754. Figure 3.1 shows the volume of beaver sent from New York to London during the 1724–1754 era, including pelts from both the north-south trade terminating at Albany and the west-east trade from Oswego (see also Norton 1974: 149). Despite yearly fluctuations in volume, New York supplied on average 25 percent of the furs received in London during 1720–1755, and even supplied 10 percent of London's furs as late as 1765, when the main focus of the trade was much farther west (101–2). Furthermore, the London beaver figures do not fully measure the overall importance of the New York fur trade. Not all New York beaver pelts were shipped to London; a significant number were sold to hatmakers operating within the North American colonies and some were smuggled to the Netherlands (Norton 1974). British traders also readily accepted other types of furs and skins such as the *menues pelleteries* ("minor pelts": raccoon, fisher, marten, otter, mink, and muskrat), bearskins, and deerskins (see Cutcliffe 1981). Laird's (1995) survey of price data from French and British posts indicates that Oswego routinely offered lower prices for highly valued stroud blankets and rum. Perhaps most significantly, Canadian officials consistently portrayed Oswego as a major threat until its destruction in 1756 during the Seven Years' War (Norton 1974: 172–73).

Local Effects of Oswego

The influence of the post at Oswego on the Senecas turns on whether Senecas still maintained adequate primary access to furs and on how the post affected the Seneca geographic middleman role. In a local political-economic approach, it is of prime importance to assess the post's effects in the short term, at the scale relevant to the Senecas' daily lives.

The Senecas' western geographical position made them an exceptional case within the Confederacy with regard to both primary production and geographic middleman traffic. Senecas had the most direct access of any Iroquois nation to western hunting territories with plentiful supplies of fur-bearing animals. The trading post/fort at Oswego likely changed the *routes* western Indians took to trade with the British, but it did not change the fact that they needed to traverse Seneca territory. Western Indians, even if traveling by the shortest route along the south shore of Lake Ontario to Oswego, still needed to pass through and stop overnight in Seneca territory on the lakeshore. Western groups undoubtedly continued to contact and negotiate with Senecas for passage. The construction at Oswego may have had a greater effect on some of the *central* Iroquois nations, especially the Onondagas and Oneidas, who were bypassed much more completely.

Primary sources suggest that the Senecas found Oswego at least partially working to their advantage. At councils between New York and the Six Nations, the Iroquois frequently were asked if they were convinced of the benefits of Oswego, and although Iroquois headmen protested the trade terms, alcohol sales, and quality of goods they received at Oswego, they did not criticize the existence of the post itself (McIlwain 1915: 173, 187–88). While these statements could reflect Iroquois acquiescence to the inevitable, primary sources also demonstrate that Six Nations people—and Senecas in particular—actively recruited western Indians to trade at Oswego. In 1727 "Two of the Chief Sachims" of "Onah" (the westernmost and supposedly more pro-French Seneca village) reported to the Albany Commissioners that they had been to the west and convinced "4 Nations" of western Indians to come into the British interest (IIDH, Aug. 6, 1727). In 1733 Six Nations representatives told New York Governor William Cosby that the goods at Oswego should be kept low "for the cheaper the goods are there, the more Far Indians will come to trade there" and that Senecas stationed at Niagara Falls would "perswade the Far Indians to trade at Oswego" (NYCD 5: 968). In 1735 when the Iroquois protested that the rum they received at Oswego was half water, they added that this made them "appear as Lyars to the Far Indians who come there upon their Encouragement" (McIlwain 1915: 195). In 1745 and 1746, Senecas informed the "Twightwights" (Miamis) that the trading path to Oswego remained open despite the upheavals of King George's War (MACIA vol. 1820: 358–59).

Oswego and the beaver trade were not the only economic options for the Six Nations. Participation in the north-south trade that primarily tapped hunting grounds north of Lake Ontario (Parmenter 2001b) was an option, and the separate Pennsylvania fur market became increasingly important after 1715, especially as an outlet for deerskins (Cutcliffe 1981; Norton 1974: 93). Senecas undoubtedly used Oswego, Niagara, Irondequoit, and the post between the Seneca villages to reduce their own travel times as compared to previous journeys to Albany and Montreal. Additionally, Senecas likely redirected their trade based on the terms of exchange offered at individual posts and the state of their relations with New France and New York. Some Senecas moved outside of their home region to become service providers to those more directly involved in the fur trade. Senecas continued to act as carriers at the Niagara portage, a prosperous niche over which Norton (1974: 41) claims the Senecas held a monopoly. In 1750 Swedish traveler Peter Kalm viewed about two hundred carriers (mostly Iroquois) working at Niagara; their prime cargo was packs of furs "chiefly of deer and bear," and they were paid in cash at the rate of 20 pence per pack (Kalm 1966 [1751]: 82). Iroquois of both sexes were employed as carriers, and some Iroquois owned horses that they used to move goods (Benson 1937: 696). There is also some indication that the Senecas supplied the French garrison at Niagara with "fresh meat" (NYCD 10: 85).

Additionally, the lower Great Lakes fur trade diversified beyond beaver pelts, incorporating substantial exchange of deerskins, bearskins, and *menues pelleteries* late in the first quarter of the eighteenth century (Cutcliffe 1981; Laird 1995; Standen 1998; White 1991). Increasing European acceptance of skins and pelts other than beaver may have meant that the Iroquois suddenly had a marketable source of furs for primary production right in their homeland. This local alternative to long periods of travel to distant beaver sources may not have been sustainable, since the species that provided the *menues pelleteries* were rare and easily overhunted, and the addition of commercial to subsistence deer hunting may have curtailed local deer populations (as apparently happened in Pennsylvania [McConnell 1992] and the Southeast [White 1983]).

The British presence at Oswego was far from being an unmitigated boon, however. Iroquois trading fortunes there probably mirrored the boom-and-bust pattern seen in the New York export figures. Additionally, as early as 1725—the year after the Oswego post was founded—Onondaga, Cayuga, and Tuscarora representatives came before the Albany Commissioners to protest trade terms, gunpowder quality, and the alcohol trade at Oswego (McIlwain 1915: 160–61; Parmenter 1999: 46). Such complaints were repeated throughout the period; the commissary position created to regulate problems at Oswego in 1726 (Norton 1974: 170) apparently did not much help matters. New York traders frequently watered down their rum; eventually the commissary was instructed to test each keg and "obtain better rum in the event Iroquois are cheated" (McIlwain 1915: 187–88, 195).

While some Iroquois wanted better-quality rum, others desired to have the rum trade eliminated altogether. Initially, Iroquois headmen asked Governor Burnet to completely ban alcohol sales at Oswego, since rum "Debauches their Young Men & renders them incapable of Order & Obedience" and "occasions Bloodshed, Quarrels & Confusion amongst their people" (McIlwain 1915: 160–61). They requested that alcohol sales be limited to Albany, which would make rum more difficult for the young men to obtain and would reduce drunken behavior in the home villages. The New Yorkers replied that it was necessary to have alcohol at Oswego since the Far Indians would not trade without it. In February 1726 Burnet mandated that no alcohol should be sold to the Six Nations (McIlwain 1915: 161–62), a provision that was not enforced and was probably unenforceable. The problem was exacerbated in 1727 when the French decided to supply brandy at Fort Niagara and Fort Frontenac to compete with Oswego (Laird 1995: 24–25; Parmenter 1999: 53); that October, Joncaire offered brandy kept at Niagara to the Senecas (MACIA vol. 1819: 255a–56).

By 1728 Iroquois headmen had abandoned their fruitless opposition to the rum trade at Oswego and instead attempted to prevent traders from bringing alcohol directly into their villages (McIlwain 1915: 173–75). Such direct alcohol sales apparently placed more than the "young men" at risk. In 1731 Iroquois representatives told New York Governor Montgomerie that they

> earnestly desire that no Rum may be sold any where but at Albany & Oswego & not brot into their Castles. they say it is impossible for them to resist it when it is to be sold amongst them, that it destroys Men, Women & Children & unfits them for every kind of Business. that if it was only sold at Oswego & Albany, they could fetch it but in small pcells & not be continually intoxicated with it as they are when its continually to be bot at their Castles. (McIlwain 1915: 183)

Alcohol abuse also was cited as one of the main reasons for Iroquois opposition to the construction of more trading posts in 1731. Headmen related that "the more buildings are made near us, the more liquor is brought unto us, which is the occasion of all mischief. Therefore we do not incline any more should be made" (MACIA vol. 1819: 339–39a).

Descriptions of communal alcohol abuse in mid-century Iroquois villages are frequent (for example, Beauchamp 1916: 70–76 passim; Drake 1855: 218–19; Pilkington 1980: 12). Specific references to Seneca alcohol abuse are documented in 1738 (McIlwain 1915: 207), 1741 (NYCD 9: 1083–84), and 1750 (Beauchamp 1916: 70–76). At least some of these events resulted in serious injuries or deaths. The historical record supports Haan's (1980:

326) and Richter's (1992: 265) claims that alcohol availability and Iroquois alcohol abuse increased dramatically after the opening of Oswego, one of the post's clear negative effects (compare Wallace 1969: 26–27).

Political Relations and Crises

During 1724–1754, the French continued to try to influence Seneca affairs by providing smiths and sending members of the Joncaire family to Seneca villages—Louis-Thomas until his death in 1739, and his sons Philippe-Thomas (1707–ca. 1766) and Daniel-Marie (1714–1771) thereafter (DCB 3: 101–2; 4: 137–38). Philippe-Thomas replaced his father as agent to the Senecas by 1740 (NYCD 9: 1067), and the Joncaire brothers were active in Seneca territory and at Niagara throughout the 1740s and 1750s (D. Kent 1974: 135–83). A French smith and his family frequently were reported among the Senecas during 1726–1744 (IIDH, Apr. 12, 1731; MACIA vol. 1819: 255a–56; McIlwain 1915: 162, 189, 238; NYCD 9: 1067, 1094). One French smith was referred to as "Laforge;" his son eventually took over his duties (NYCD 9: 1090, 1094). Although they are mentioned infrequently in historic documents, independent French traders also traveled to Seneca villages. The Moravian Johann Cammerhoff noted that a French trader had set up at Nuquiage (likely a seasonal Seneca-Cayuga fishing village on the border of Seneca territory), where he traded in rum and other goods in 1750 (Beauchamp 1916: 66).

New York used a similar range of agents and services, keeping delegations in Seneca territory almost year-round during most of the 1724–1746 period (Jordan 2002: 127–28; MACIA vol. 1819: 97, 117, 170a–71a, 278–79, 294–94a, 326–26a; vol. 1820: 24, 35, 52). Some parties contained as many as eleven persons (MACIA vol. 1819: 326), and almost all included smiths. New York's delegations likely were not as effective as those of the French; personnel changed almost every year, and there does not appear to have been the same degree of kinship (or intermarriage) between the Senecas and New York agents as there was between the Senecas, the Joncaires, and the "Laforge" smiths. Agents who resided in Seneca territory and are mentioned by name in primary sources are discussed in chapter 4.

European efforts encouraged chronic factional competition among the Senecas. In 1734 the Albany Commissioners informed Governor Cosby that the French were making significant inroads among the Senecas, possibly as a result of the new trading post between the two villages. Several Senecas (including by some estimates the entire western community) had aligned with the French and most were wavering, so New York sent Colonel

Philip Schuyler to Seneca territory to win them back (MACIA vol. 1820: 52a; McIlwain 1915: 189–91). In 1740 Iroquois (probably Senecas) presented wampum belts to Charles de la Boische de Beauharnois, governor of New France, to rid him of his impression of the "bad cheer in our country" (NYCD 9: 1065). Beauharnois sent Philippe-Thomas Chabert de Joncaire and a blacksmith back with the Seneca delegation but warned the Senecas to take good care of the smith "and not suffer him to be hungry" (NYCD 9: 1067).

The Seneca famine of 1741–1742 is a well-documented instance of severe and tragic food shortage. The problem affected much of the Northeast: the Cayugas, Onondagas, and Oneidas were said to be "in great want of Provisions" in June of 1741 (McIlwain 1915: 221), and the Lorette mission near Quebec also suffered a food shortage in 1742 after failure of the French wheat crop (JR 69: 59–63). However, the situation in Seneca territory was the most dire. It appears that maize crops failed in both 1740 and 1741 and that stored food reserves were inadequate to sustain the Senecas until the next crop ripened in 1742. In August 1741 a Seneca delegate told the Albany Commissioners that his people needed provisions, powder, and lead in order to go hunting (IIDH, Aug. 16, 1741; McIlwain 1915: 222–23); a similar message was delivered to Beauharnois in Montreal the same month (NYCD 9: 1075). In May 1742 Seneca representatives asked the Albany Commissioners for compassion because their people were in great want (IIDH, May 14, 1742) and reported to Beauharnois in July that many lives had been lost (NYCD 9: 1089). Due to the famine, the Senecas did not attend an October 1741 conference in Montreal (IIDH, Oct. 1, 1741) or a July 1742 meeting with Pennsylvania officials (*Minutes of the Provincial Council of Pennsylvania*, ed. Hazard, hereafter PPCM 4: 563–65). At the Pennsylvania meeting, the Onondaga spokesman Canasatego reported that a Seneca "father had been obliged to kill two of his Children to preserve his own and the rest of his family's lives" (564). It is noteworthy that a major outburst of factional competition, the sale of Irondequoit to the British, increased migration to Ohio, and the likely movement of the western Senecas to the Genesee Valley all took place during or immediately after this catastrophic famine.

In the midst of the famine in September 1741, Beauharnois reprimanded the Senecas for attacking Frenchmen, stealing merchandise, and drinking to excess around Niagara; he added that the French blacksmith would not return because he feared starvation, and also because the Senecas took all their work to a New York smith (NYCD 9: 1083–84). Although a July 1742 exchange between the Senecas and Beauharnois evidenced continued friction, the French governor presented the Senecas with symbolic and material gifts, providing a new French flag to replace the worn one the Seneca headman Théruatakonte claimed to have "always borne . . . among the English, in spite of all that could be said to me"; sending Philippe-Thomas and Daniel-Marie Chabert de Joncaire and "Laforge's son" to live with the Senecas; and, most crucially, supplying the Senecas with ammunition for hunting (NYCD 9: 1090–94). Parmenter (1999: 155) contrasts Beauharnois' relatively generous gifts to the spate of criticism the Senecas received from New York Governor Clarke in response to similar requests.

These measures improved the stock of the French: a 1742 New York detachment to Seneca territory found that the French had distributed numerous presents and demolished the house New Yorkers typically resided in; additionally, fifty Seneca warriors had taken French ammunition and gone south to fight the "Flatheads" (McIlwain 1915: 229). In October 1743 the Albany Commissioners related that

> The Sennecas who are the most numerous of the 6 Nations [and] were formerly the most firmly Attached to the British Interest, are of late by the Intrigues & Management of the French become the most wavering, & without proper care be taken on our side for the time to come, they fear the French will get the greatest part of them over to their Interest. The Commissrs propose that a Fort should be built in their Country & garrisoned with an Officer & 20 Men. Also that proper measures be fallen on to remove the French who reside in the Sennecas Country & who are constantly debauching their Affections from us. (McIlwain 1915: 232)

The Senecas were regularly supplied with New York delegations thereafter, but New York authorities never convinced the Senecas to expel the French. Although requests similar to that of 1743 continued to be made (for example, MACIA vol. 1820: 289), chronic funding shortages prevented a New York fort from being built in Seneca territory until 1756, when a stockade was constructed at Kanadesaga (Hamell n.d.; JP 9: 457–58). At the request of the Senecas, this fort was never garrisoned (Pilkington 1980: 11).

Differences between pro-French and pro-British factions among the Senecas appear to have resulted in a major change in the location of Seneca villages in the 1740s. The western Seneca "Castle" near Canandaigua Lake was abandoned, probably in stages, and its residents resettled on the Genesee River. This resulted in a separation of 70 km between the principal Seneca villages, a distance unprecedented in the Seneca sequence and an order of magnitude greater than the 14.5 km separation between the preceding main villages at New Ganechstage and Huntoon (K. Jordan 2004). Western Senecas may have selected Genesee Valley locations to be closer to their French allies at Niagara (Abler and Tooker 1978: 507; Richter 1992: 256). The exact date of the founding of the Genesee villages is uncertain,[5] but Seneca villages on the Genesee were visited by the Moravian Cammerhoff in 1750 (see Beauchamp 1916).

Documents from the 1740s contain repeated British criticisms of the Iroquois' dispersed way of living, exhortations to live more compactly, and encouragements to relocate to areas under greater British control (Parmenter 1999: 84–85). These critiques, often directed specifically at the Senecas, appear to have had little effect. During the famine of 1741 Albany officials recommended that the Six Nations should not scatter but instead gather in their castles (IIDH, Oct. 3, 1741; McIlwain 1915: 223–24). When Claessen and John Lansingh brought that message to the Senecas, Seneca headmen responded that they could not supply an answer since too many of their people were out hunting (MACIA vol. 1820: 218a). In May 1742 the commissioners recommended that the Senecas move their village to a location "on the north side of the old castle" (227); this spot may have been "nearer to Cayougoes [the Cayugas]" (as suggested by NYCD 6: 217). The Senecas agreed and gave a belt of wampum to the New Yorkers to attest to their sincerity (IIDH, May 14, 1742; NYCD 6: 217). At the beginning of King George's War, the commissioners recommended that the Iroquois "live compact together in their Castles wch is absolutely necessary for their own Security in this time of War" and Iroquois headmen again consented (McIlwain 1915: 234–35). In July 1744, Senecas asked that a New York smith and armorer be sent to their territory "very much and speedily especially _____ to mend their hatchets[,] which they will want to build new houses when they remove their castle as they have promised" (MACIA vol. 1820: 290a). Although three New Yorkers, including the smith Myndert Wemp, were sent to Seneca territory expressly to "make their hatchets for them" the next month (295a), a 1754 document noted that the Senecas had not fulfilled any of their promises to move and still lived "very remote from one another" (NYCD 6: 856–57).

In addition to the 1741–1742 famine, the Senecas also suffered from epidemics during the 1724–1754 era. Smallpox swept through the Seneca population in 1732–1733, killing several headmen (MACIA vol. 1820: 24; McIlwain 1915: 187–88; NYCD 5: 966, 9: 1036; Parmenter 1999: 105 note 129). Senecas did not attend October 1745 negotiations in Albany due to a "raging distemper" in their homeland, from which more than sixty people, including eight headmen, died (Parmenter 1999: 211, 286 note 77). Although smallpox has been documented among the Six Nations during 1738–1740 and 1751–1753 (Jennings et al. 1985: 178, 185), I was unable to confirm that the Senecas were affected.

Warfare and War Rumors

Numerous Iroquois war parties that included Senecas journeyed to Virginia and the Carolinas to fight with southern groups, including the Catawbas, Choctaws, Cherokees, and Chickasaws throughout the 1724–1754 period (Aquila 1983: 217–27; Merrell 1987; Perdue 1987). These wars against Indian allies of the southern British colonies solidified Iroquois relations with New France, allowed young warriors to prove themselves, and generated steady supplies of French arms and provisions (Aquila 1983: 227–32). Although many Iroquois warriors were killed or captured in the south, Six Nations war parties were able to strike at the southern nations with little fear of retaliation on their home villages. Aquila (1983: 231) notes that "pro-Iroquois Indian villages on the Susquehanna and Allegheny rivers stood between the homelands of the Iroquois and those of the Flatheads. Iroquois warriors could freely pass down the Susquehanna Trail and along the southern and western warriors' paths to raid the southern Indians, while the Flatheads found it nearly impossible to strike back." Merrell's (1987: 192 note 19) documentation of southern raids to the north is limited to two instances from Pennsylvania sources. Rumors of southern Indian attacks also appear to have been rare. When Mohawks spoke of the threat of a Flathead attack on their villages in 1735, they were chided by Governor Cosby, who told them that such attacks were implausible (Parmenter 1999: 134–35), and in fact the attack never materialized. Southern Indians occasionally visited Seneca territory, either as diplomatic emissaries or, more frequently, as prisoners (for example, Parmenter 1999: 144, 147; Perdue 1987: 139).

To the west, the Foxes proved to be a persistent source of unease due to their continuing agitation against the French and their ties to Senecas dating to the early part of the century. In 1730 Foxes asked permission to resettle among the Senecas and received a lukewarm response; while trying to migrate east, nine hundred Foxes were slaughtered by the French and their Indian allies (Edmunds and Peyser 1993: 135–57; NYCD 5: 911; McIlwain 1915: 180–81). Louis-Thomas Chabert de Joncaire solicited Seneca assistance for a proposed war against the Foxes in 1737 that did not come to fruition (Edmunds and Peyser 1993: 190; McIlwain 1915: 200).

The 1724–1754 era was marked by rumors of local war, especially at the end of the period when events built toward the Seven Years' War. Jennings (1984: 301, 1988: 87; Jennings et al. 1985: 174) asserts that the Six Nations promoted general war against the British in 1726 and French in 1727, but these incitements were likely to have been the work of small groups of disgruntled headmen rather than reflecting a general policy (Richter 1992: 378 note 33). In 1728 a French army of one thousand men was rumored to be readying for an attack on Oswego; the Albany Commissioners advised the Iroquois to keep their warriors at home in case this was true (McIlwain 1915: 172). The Seneca carriers' village at the Niagara portage apparently burned down in 1728 (MACIA vol. 1819: 279–79a); Donald Kent (1974: 127) speculates that this may have been the result of a drunken brawl. In 1739, a French and Indian army commanded by Charles Le Moyne de Longueuil passed through Niagara on its way to battle Chickasaws in Louisiana. While Kent (1974: 139) notes that "the passage of an army of 442 men on its way to punish Indians sixteen hundred miles away gave [Senecas] a strong impression of French power," the size of the force was not unusual by Iroquois standards, and Iroquois forces had on occasion covered similar distances.

In 1744, King George's War, also known as the War of Austrian Succession, ended three decades of French-British peace that had begun in 1713 (Parmenter 1999: 190–239, 2002, 2007a: 57–63). New York and New France both sought alliances with the Iroquois during the four-year war, bringing on what Parmenter (1999: 190) terms a crisis of neutrality. However, all homeland Iroquois except the Mohawks remained neutral throughout the conflict. Seneca delegates to both New York and New France insisted on their neutrality (Parmenter 1999: 196, 198), a claim that appears to be substantiated by the lack of homeland Senecas in documentary accounts of military engagements during the war. Both French and British agents frequented Seneca territory, and Senecas continued to encourage western Indians to travel across their territory to Oswego (MACIA vol. 1820: 295–95a, 309, 311a, 358; vol. 1821: 80). The ingenuity Senecas used to maintain their commitment to neutrality is illustrated by their response to a November 1744 visit by New York agent Jacobus Bleecker in which he demanded that Senecas expel French agents from their territory (MACIA vol. 1820: 309; Parmenter 1999: 197–98). Bleecker was forced to deliver this message to Francophile Seneca headmen because the sachems "that were in the English interest" allegedly were out hunting; unsurprisingly, Bleecker's demand was rejected.

The low level of Iroquois involvement in a full-blown imperial war is remarkable (Parmenter 2007a: 57–63). Confederacy Mohawks offered limited military support to the British, engaging in small raids on the Canadian border until two defeats in 1747 and 1748 ended even these efforts. Mission Mohawks provided greater, but still limited, aid to the French, particularly in the November 1745 attack on Saratoga and raids near Albany in 1746 (Parmenter 1999: 229, 2007a: 58). Ohio Iroquois killed five French traders near Detroit in 1747 (Parmenter 1999: 229) but otherwise did not engage in much partisan military activity. Parmenter (2007a: 62) concludes that "the Iroquois played a key role in determining the scale and intensity of the war by their highly selective and balanced involvement" as allied warriors. The Treaty of Aix-la-Chapelle ended King George's War in 1748. Immediately after the conclusion of the war, eighty Iroquois delegates took the opportunity to formally assert their continued neutrality in a meeting with the governor of New France (Parmenter 2002: 35).

The years following King George's War saw the focus of the fur trade begin to shift away from the Great Lakes to the Ohio Valley in preparation for another "trader's leapfrog" (Aquila 1983; Jennings 1988; McConnell 1992; White 1991). Pennsylvania and Virginia lead the westward expansion of the fur trade; in 1748, Conrad Weiser made the first official Pennsylvania visit to Ohio Indians in an attempt to bring more groups into Pennsylvania's economic orbit (Aquila 1983: 197–99; Jennings 1988: ch. 3; Parmenter 1999: 239–40). These economic maneuvers threatened French-Indian alliances and also the connection between Canada and Louisiana. In the summer of 1749 a two hundred–man French expedition traveled down the Ohio Valley to discourage Indians there from trading with the British. The French incited Mississaugas (Southeastern Ojibwas) to attack the Iroquois in 1750 "in an effort to convince the Confederacy to surrender its claims to the Ohio Country," but the attack was thwarted by last-minute negotiations (Aquila 1983: 150–51; Beauchamp 1916: 45). Forty Confederacy Senecas accompanied Daniel-Marie Chabert de Joncaire to Logstown in May 1751, where Joncaire confronted Pennsylvania official George Croghan (Parmenter 1999: 266).

Confrontations between the French, British, and their Indian allies escalated in 1752 when French-sponsored Indians attacked Pickawillany, a Miami town that had become a center for British traders. In April 1753 a French expedition of more than 1600 men led by Pierre-Paul Marin de la Malgue was dispatched to construct a series of frontier forts in the Ohio Valley, worrying British traders at Oswego on their way (Parmenter 1999:

272–73). Despite recommendations from homeland Senecas and other nations to remain neutral, the Ohio Iroquois headman Tanaghrisson informed Marin in September that further advances and forts would not be tolerated (Jennings 1988: 52–54; Parmenter 1999: 278–79). In April 1754, six hundred French soldiers captured forty-one Virginians building a fort at what is now Pittsburgh, Pennsylvania, and completed the fort themselves, naming it Fort Duquesne. Virginians and Ohio Iroquois commanded by George Washington (then twenty-two years old) attacked a French party in May, and then took refuge from the main French body in the hastily constructed Fort Necessity, where Washington surrendered on July 4, 1754. Another, far more active imperial war had begun; documents indicate that the Townley-Read site was probably in the process of being abandoned in 1754 as well (NYCD 6: 856–57).

Migration and the Turn toward Ohio

Migration, whether within the Seneca homeland or away from it, played an increasingly important role for Senecas as the eighteenth century progressed. Migration occurred in response to economic opportunity or factionalism, and often to a mixture of both. While most scholars (for example, Wonderley 2004: 15) have viewed extra-regional migration as a net loss to the Iroquois Confederacy, Parmenter (1999) views the new communities more as satellites of the Confederacy than migrants. He contends that Iroquois migration

> facilitated the development of a far-ranging network of contacts between the Confederacy and other Native groups throughout northeastern North America. The freedom to migrate . . . kept the Confederacy flexible, unpredictable, and a matter of concern among their European allies. The [St. Lawrence] mission Iroquois and Mingos [Ohio Iroquois], while retaining a considerable degree of local autonomy, maintained contact with their Confederacy kin . . . [supplying] the intelligence necessary for the Six Nations' leadership to continue their precarious balancing act between two competing European empires. Additionally, the migrant communities helped preserve the social flexibility of the Iroquois by providing a viable means of resolving internal factional conflict among Confederacy nations and villages [through physical separation]. (Parmenter 1999: 14, 443)

In this view, Seneca migration proved advantageous to homeland interests.

Economic opportunities outside the Seneca homeland presented themselves during the entire 1677–1754 period. One of the first alternatives to New York and New France as a source of trade goods was the colony of Pennsylvania, established in 1681. Senecas drawn to the Pennsylvania trade reportedly intended to settle on the Susquehanna River by 1690 and definitely had done so by 1697 (B. Kent 1993: 57, 59). There they lived in multinational towns (most notably Conestoga, near present-day Lancaster) with Shawnees, Delawares, Munsees, Piscataways/Conoys from Maryland, and remnants of the Iroquoian Susquehannocks (B. Kent 1993; McConnell 1992). Senecas killed several Delawares in February 1694, allegedly for nonpayment of tribute (Keener 1998: 194–95; NYCD 4: 99). Some Senecas lived in small villages north of Lake Ontario during approximately 1670–1687; some villages may have been reoccupied until about 1704, when attacks by French-allied Indians made them uninhabitable (N. Adams 1986; Konrad 1981, 1987; Poulton 1991; Richter 1992: 219; Schmalz 1991). The French trading post at Niagara offered another prospect for diversified economic activity closer to home (Kalm 1966 [1751]; D. Kent 1974; NYCD 9: 885), as previously noted.

The main economic opportunity outside the homeland was in the Ohio territory, which stretched from the headwaters of the Allegheny River to the Muskingum and Scioto River valleys in present-day Ohio (McConnell 1992). This region, largely depopulated during the wars of the mid-seventeenth century, became the destination for the greatest number of Seneca migrants (McConnell 1992; Parmenter 1999: 154–58). The absence of a year-round human presence in the Ohio territory had allowed animal populations—particularly fur-bearing animals—to rebound, and Ohio was one of the major hunting grounds discussed in the grand peace negotiations of 1700–1701 (Brandão and Starna 1996). Iroquois groups undertook seasonal hunts there starting in about 1680; travel in the region increased by 1718 when the Allegheny and Ohio valleys became the main "warriors' path" to the south, replacing an older route across central Pennsylvania and Virginia that was being settled by Europeans (McConnell 1992: 14, 49).

Some of the first groups to repopulate the Ohio territory were Pennsylvania Indians facing European encroachment and growing shortages of game. McConnell (1992) marks a 1724 migration by Delawares as the first major resettlement of the area; they were soon joined by groups of Shawnees and Iroquois, particularly Senecas. At first, the Seneca presence in the Ohio territory was rather small; in the fall of 1731 traders found only "4 settled families" of Senecas at Aliquippa's Town on the Ohio River near Pittsburgh (now Aliquippa, Pennsylvania). The town appears to have been a seasonal provisioning place for hunters traveling to and from Ohio and warriors coming and going from the south (16, 22). It was named for the Seneca matron Aliquippa; her presence indicates that entire family units had migrated, rather than male hunters or warriors alone.

Iroquois migrations to the Ohio country began in earnest in the 1740s (McConnell 1992: 15, 19, 23; Parmenter 1999: 155–56). The Allegheny Valley was populated first; the Seneca/multinational towns of Conewango (Warren, Pennsylvania), Buckaloons (Irvineton, Pennsylvania), and Kuskuski (New Castle, Pennsylvania) were established there by the mid-1740s. Later migrants traveled along the south shore of Lake Erie to settle at Cuyahoga (near Cleveland, Ohio) and Sandusky (Sandusky, Ohio). Senecas made up a large portion of the Iroquois migrants. French sources estimated that most of the six hundred Iroquois newly settled on the Cuyahoga in 1742 were Senecas and Onondagas (McConnell 1992: 62), and nearly half of the 347 Iroquois living in the upper Ohio Valley in 1748 were said to be Senecas (McConnell 1992: 23). By 1748, Six Nations populations in Ohio may have approached 10–15 percent of the homeland numbers (Parmenter 2001a: 107).

Seneca migrants may have been motivated by the still-abundant game in Ohio or by factionalism at home. The prospect of direct trade in Ohio country, either with itinerant Pennsylvania traders or with French outposts, made it possible for some Senecas to abandon the time-consuming and dangerous travel between homeland villages, extra-regional hunting territories, and trading posts. First-person narratives of captives who lived with Iroquois groups in the Ohio country, such as those of Mary Jemison (Seaver 1990 [1824]) and James Smith (Drake 1855: 178–264), detail lifeways that were fundamentally different from those in the homeland. Year-round home villages were replaced by seasonal camps, and family units tended to stay together except when men departed for hunting or warfare. Group composition and the hunting territories they used were flexible; decisions were based on the presence of fur-bearers, game, and trading opportunities. While by most estimates these self-sufficient Ohio Iroquois groups (who eventually became known as Mingos) operated largely out of the political and economic control of homeland leaders (Hunter 1978; Jennings 1984: 308, 352), Parmenter (1999, 2001a) demonstrates that Ohio migrants continued to provide options, intelligence, and goods to the Confederacy. Many Iroquois appear to have lived in the Ohio country only temporarily, later returning to their homeland villages (Parmenter 1999: 441). The lives of Mary Jemison (Seaver 1990 [1824]) and Joseph Brant (Kelsay 1984: 41–45) provide well-known examples.

The interest the French and the British colonies took in Ohio by the late 1740s and the role the region played in the Seven Years' War indicates that the main part of the fur trade had shifted there along with Delaware, Shawnee, and Iroquois migrants in the 1740s. This occurred at roughly the same time as the new Seneca villages on the Genesee were founded; the combination of migration and homeland settlement movements demonstrates that the 1740s were a period of radical social and economic change for the Senecas.

Discussion

The four historical periods outlined in this chapter can be classified as favorable or unfavorable political-economic times for the Senecas. The Twenty Years' War period (1677–1701) was dominated by conflicts that increasingly went against the Iroquois. Decreasing military strength in comparison to western Indian nations meant that the Senecas had less regular access to contested hunting territories. French hostility prevented trade at posts such as Michilimackinac and Fort Frontenac. The tremendous extra-regional distances covered by Iroquois warriors across areas that lacked friendly trading posts for the disposal of heavy furs meant that the time men devoted to warfare generally was not economically productive. Brandão and Starna (1996) provide an important perspective on the 1700–1701 treaties by outlining the mutual weakness of *all* parties involved in the negotiations, including both the Iroquois and western Indians. There can be no question, however, that the Twenty Years' War should be seen as an unfavorable political-economic period for the Senecas.

In contrast, the middleman period (1713–1724) stands out as the period most likely to have been favorable. The Senecas' geographic position between western Indians and Albany presumably resulted in substantial diplomatic and economic benefits. Access to hunting territories north of Lake Ontario, near the western Great Lakes, and in Pennsylvania and Ohio probably was fairly secure and reasonably profitable. French and British wooing of the Senecas with diplomatic presents and services introduced a fair quantity of European goods into the Seneca homeland. This period is the best candidate for Norton's (1974) time of "peace and prosperity" for the Iroquois, and for the Senecas especially.

The second and fourth periods represent more ambiguous times. The period of uncertainty (1701–1713) witnessed the beginnings of the geographic middleman role as western Indians began to make the trek to Albany, but was threatened by simmering European conflict and European efforts to incite warfare between Far Indians and the Iroquois. The Senecas required time to recover from the demographic, political, and economic stresses of the Twenty Years' War, and Seneca access to prime extra-regional hunting territories was uncertain.

Conditions during the long Oswego Era (1724–1754) were equally ambiguous. Senecas were shaken by epidemics, the devastating famine of 1741–1742, and chronic episodes of factionalism. Open French-British warfare took place during King George's War, and new conflict loomed in the years before the Seven Years' War. Increasing numbers of Senecas migrated to the Ohio country, obtaining direct access to game and new trade outlets but in the process weakening ties with the homeland (perhaps intentionally). Trends in the fur trade signaled that territories to the west had more long-term importance than the Seneca homeland, but the trade also may have diversified from beaver pelts to incorporate considerable numbers of deerskins, bearskins, and *menues pelleteries.* This may have provided a short-term increase in the local availability of saleable skins and pelts to the Senecas. The physical separation between the Genesee and Finger Lakes Senecas isolated pro-French and pro-British factions from each other and made it much less easy to coordinate the efforts of the western and eastern groups. These factors made the Senecas' political-economic position more difficult, but it remains unclear whether any of these problems fundamentally compromised Seneca autonomy. Extreme positions—such as Norton's (1974) time of "peace and prosperity" or Haan's (1976, 1980) and Richter's (1992) implication that Niagara and Oswego signaled the end of the Iroquois fur trade economy—do not seem to be warranted in the Seneca case.

The remainder of this book will explore what archaeology can add to the picture of Seneca local political economy obtained through documents.

4

New Ganechstage in the Library, Museum, and Archive

After the destruction wrought by the 1687 Denonville invasion, the Senecas moved eastward to the area between Seneca and Canandaigua lakes (Conover 1889; K. Jordan 2004; Wray 1983; Wray and Schoff 1953). The two villages initially settled in this area—Snyder-McClure (figure 4.1: Site 1) and White Springs (Site 2)—occupied hilltop locations and were probably nucleated settlements (K. Jordan 2004).[1] This continued the circa 1565–1687 Seneca practice outlined by Wray and Schoff (1953) of building a pair of large, nucleated villages in defensible terrain. Construction of a small homeland satellite village at Kendaia on the eastern shore of Seneca Lake, which likely took place by 1704 (see figure 6.5) resumed another long-standing Seneca practice.

When Snyder-McClure and White Springs were abandoned, major changes in Seneca settlement preferences took place (K. Jordan 2004). The newly established settlement at the north end of Seneca Lake was the first spatially segmented community in the Seneca village sequence. This was noted by nineteenth-century local historian George S. Conover (1885, 1889, n.d.: 83–84), who hypothesized that the White Springs Senecas moved from their nucleated village to resettle in a complex of at least six contemporaneous "neighborhoods" along an 8 km section of Burrell Creek. I have termed this group of sites—which includes the Townley-Read, Brother, Rippey, Rupert, Zindall-Wheadon, and Hazlet sites (figure 4.1: sites 4a–f)—the New Ganechstage Site Complex, following the Moravian missionary Johann Cammerhoff, who called one neighborhood in this area by that name during a 1750 visit (Beauchamp 1916: 67, 82).

The Townley-Read/New Ganechstage Project was initiated in 1996 to locate and excavate domestic deposits within a single Seneca neighborhood in order to obtain data on site structure, residential forms, and household activities in the context of these major changes in settlement preferences. The Townley-Read site appeared to be a promising locale for field research.[2]

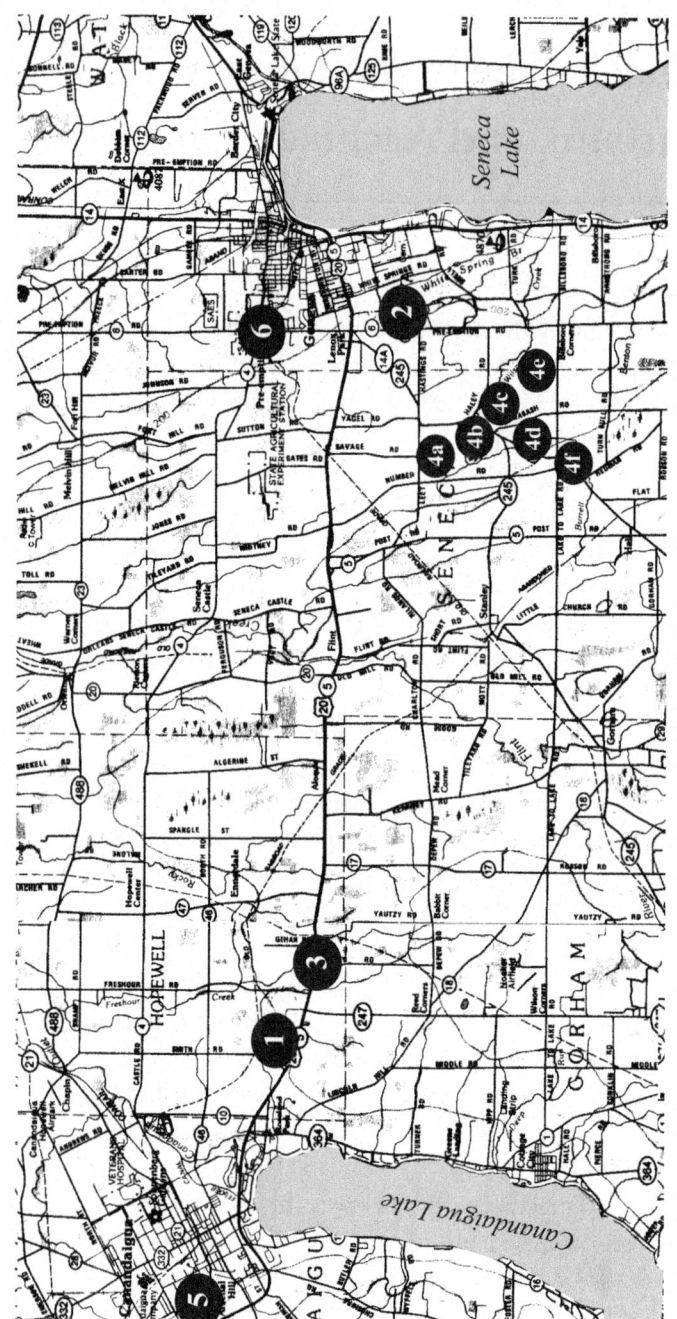

Figure 4.1. Seneca sites between Canandaigua and Seneca lakes, occupied circa 1688–1779. (Base map adapted from *New York State Atlas & Gazetteer*. Freeport, Maine: DeLorme Mapping, 1993).

1. Snyder-McClure, circa 1688 to 1710–1715
2. White Springs, circa 1688–1715
3. Huntoon (likely Onaghee), circa 1710–1715 to 1740–1745
4. New Ganechstage Site Complex (likely Ganundasaga), circa 1715–1754
   a. Brother   b. Townley-Read   c. Rippey   d. Rupert   e. Zindall-Wheadon   f. Hazlet
5. Sackett, circa 1740–1745 to 1770–1779
6. Kanadesaga, circa 1754–1779

First, manuscript writings by Conover (1882, n.d.) and avocational archaeologist Charles F. Wray (n.d.) provided two fairly detailed, although not entirely compatible descriptions of the site's internal structure. Both Conover and Wray suggested that Townley-Read was the principal village within the site complex, and hinted that the site might include orchards and a European-run smithy. Additionally, artifact collections from Townley-Read at the Rochester Museum and Science Center (RMSC) provided a complementary set of data (primarily from mortuary and site-wide surface collection contexts) unavailable for any of the other New Ganechstage sites. Lastly, both Seneca descendants and the landowners were amenable to archaeological investigation of the site.

Townley-Read: Physical and Cultural Setting

The Townley-Read site (figure 4.2) lies about 5 km southwest of the City of Geneva, in the Town of Seneca, Ontario County, New York. Physiographically, the site lies within the Finger Lakes Hills (a subdivision of the Appalachian Hills region), in close proximity to the Lake Ontario Lowland province (Thompson 1966). The site area was deeply scoured by the advance and retreat of Wisconsonian glaciers in the late Pleistocene (Cadwell, Muller, and Fleisher 2003; Ridge 2003); as a result of glacial action, the terrain around Townley-Read is generally quite smooth and surface sediments contain large amounts of glacially deposited material. Climatically, the Geneva area is characterized by cold, snowy winters and warm, dry summers (Thompson 1966: figure 24). Modern measurements find that the area receives an average of 83.49 cm of precipitation per year and has an average growing season of approximately 145 days (Thompson 1966: tables 9, 12). The federal soil survey of Ontario County (Pearson and Cline 1958) categorizes the soils in the immediate vicinity of the Townley-Read site as some of the most productive in the county.

Townley-Read, like many upland archaeological sites in central and western New York state, predominantly has a relatively stable land surface that has been "accessible to artifact deposition from the early Holocene to the present" (Cowan 1999: 598; see also Ritchie 1980: 35–36). There has been little accumulation or removal of sediment except in areas heavily impacted by wind or water, such as floodplains, hilltops, and the bases of hills. Much of central and western New York has been plowed, which frequently results in stratigraphy consisting of an organic plowzone (which may contain the

Figure 4.2. Aerial photograph of the Townley-Read site facing north, July 2007. Note the western Ridgetop (A) and the low-lying East Fields (B). Burrell Creek follows the irregular line of trees, running north from the lower left-hand corner of the image and crossing to the east in the middle of the photo. Figure 5.1 presents a topographic map of the site. (Photo by William S. Hecht.)

mixed remains of cultural deposits made over several thousand years) overlying subsoil, into which features from various cultural periods intrude.

The site is bounded on three sides by Burrell Creek. Despite a sizable floodplain more than 60 m wide in places, Burrell Creek currently does not conduct a particularly large volume of water and even dries up completely at the end of some hot, dry summers. In all probability however Burrell Creek was a year-round water source during the eighteenth century. The presence of a nineteenth-century Euro-American mill a short distance upstream from Townley-Read (Conover 1882: insert map; Lightfoote 1989: 20) demonstrates that water flow definitely was more consistent in the past. Widespread Euro-American forest clearance to create permanent agricultural fields likely decreased groundwater retention and altered the water table around the creek (Cronon 1983: 124–25). Additionally, water levels in Seneca Lake and the Seneca River have been regulated to feed the Cayuga and Seneca Canal, which likely affected the water table in tributary areas (see Heidenreich 1971: 63–66 for a similar example from the Huron homeland). East of the site, the creek (in this section called Wilson Creek on some maps) enters a deep gorge that runs all the way to Clark Point on Seneca Lake. The lake, in turn, drains into the Seneca River, the Oswego

River, Lake Ontario, the St. Lawrence River, and eventually the Atlantic Ocean.

A catchment area with a 2 km radius around the site encompasses the substantial floodplain areas along Burrell Creek and a large marsh to the west (probably part of what Cammerhoff called the "Long Bridge"). A 5 km catchment radius includes extensive marsh areas to the west, north, and south, as well as access to the Flint Creek, Castle Creek, Benton Run, and White Spring Brook drainages. Clark Point on Seneca Lake, which would have provided ample access to the lake's resources, is about 5.7 km from Townley-Read. The pathway from the site to Seneca Lake along the south bank of Burrell/Wilson Creek is fairly direct and crosses few feeder streams.

Townley-Read is about 3.5 km away from the preceding White Springs site and 6 km from the successor village at Kanadesaga (figure 4.1: site 6). Townley-Read also is located 2.5 km west of the Woodley village site, dated to circa 1450–1550 by Niemczycki (1984: tables 6–7). The proximity of a Late Woodland village to Townley-Read indicates that the locality was attractive to at least two separate populations that used a mixture of extensive agriculture, hunting, and gathering. In some ways, therefore, the settlement of Townley-Read can be considered a reoccupation (see Engelbrecht 2003: 105). Isolated surface finds of lithic projectile points, including Archaic points from the Townley-Read site itself and from 2.9 km to the southeast (RMSC site Plp-83), suggest even earlier Indian use of the area.

Euro-American occupation of the Townley-Read site was initiated when land speculators Oliver Phelps and Nathaniel Gorham purchased a large portion of what is now central and western New York from the state of Massachusetts in April 1788. In July of that year, Phelps and Gorham extinguished Seneca claims to about one-third of this land (predominantly east of the Genesee River) in a subsequently contested purchase negotiated at Buffalo Creek (Conover 1893; Wallace 1969: 171, 173–74). A survey laying out 6-mile-square townships within this territory was completed by 1789, after which each township was subdivided into 1-mile-square (259 ha) lots. Most of the Townley-Read site was included in Lot 32 in Range 1, Township 9, of the Phelps and Gorham purchase (Conover n.d.: 75). According to Conover (n.d.: 76), Lot 32 originally was owned by Jonathan Read, who first visited the area in 1791. By 1874 two houses had been constructed on Lot 32, both of which are still standing. At the time of this writing James C. Minns owns most of what was originally Lot 32 (including both houses) and farms the area.

Documentary References

Although the Townley-Read site was occupied during a period when visits from European diplomats, traders, smiths, and missionaries were frequent, most primary-source documents manifest an astounding lack of concern with settlement names, locations, and site structure. The enticing prospect of reading a document that specifically describes Senecas living at Townley-Read—a grail of sorts for archaeologists dealing with Postcolumbian American Indian sites—remains unrealized. Many documents probably do describe visits to Townley-Read, but the depictions of Seneca territory they contain are not precise enough to make a secure link (see K. Jordan 2002: 142–58 for a review of documentary evidence on settlement names and locations).

The linking of documentary references to physical locations is complicated by the frequent Iroquois practice of naming enduring groups of people rather than particular places (Bradley 1987: 116; Engelbrecht 2003: 106–7; Fenton and Tooker 1978: 470; Hamell 1980: 94; Snow 1995: 304). This parallels the Iroquois practice of naming *roles* that were perpetuated from generation to generation, such as the fifty named sachem positions of the Confederacy council; *individuals* added or dropped personal names depending on the role or office they occupied. Besides town names and leadership roles, the Iroquois also used single enduring terms for European leaders—every governor of New York was called "Corlaer," every governor of New France "Onontio"—and even sequential family dogs had the same name (Trigger 1990: 39).

European naming practices do not facilitate the identification of sites either. Colonial-period Europeans referred to Iroquois villages as castles, a label that may have been appropriate for the palisaded villages of the seventeenth century, but which continued to be applied to later nucleated sites that lacked palisades and even to dispersed settlements where houses were more than 50 m apart. In contrast to Iroquois use of the same village name for several separate locations, modern archaeologists' practice of naming sites after Euro-American landowners tends to produce multiple names for a single site as the property changes hands over time. This results in a different sort of identification problem and is the reason why the names of several of the archaeological sites discussed herein are hyphenated.

Throughout the 1709–1742 period there are consistent references to "two" or "both" Seneca villages in both British and French sources (Leder 1956: 210–11; MACIA vol. 1819: 170a, 1820: 50; McIlwain 1915: 189; NYCD

5: 544, 588; 9: 1056, 1091). This information coincides with the picture supplied by archaeology; namely, that there were two main Seneca communities (one eastern and one western) in existence at any given point during this time period, and that Seneca settlement was concentrated in the region between Seneca and Canandaigua lakes (figure 4.1). There are also persistent reports that the Seneca villages differed in size between 1719 and 1742 (MACIA vol. 1819: 111, 329a; vol. 1820: 52a; NYCD 5: 588, 911; 9: 1065, 1090). After 1742, the regional Seneca settlement pattern appears to have diversified considerably (K. Jordan 2004).

The four main Seneca communities of this era (White Springs and the New Ganechstage Site Complex to the east; Snyder-McClure and Huntoon to the west) are described in eighteenth-century documents with what appear to be two sets of names. Due to the idiosyncratic ways Europeans heard and transcribed Iroquois words, there are many variant spellings but they generally are either (1) four- or five-syllable names that begin with a *C*, *K*, or *G* (the Iroquois consonant is voiced somewhere between the sounds of these letters in English); or (2) two- or three-syllable names that begin with an *O*. The *C*, *K*, and *G* names likely refer to the eastern set of villages and the *O* names to the western set.

The *C*, *K*, and *G* names all appear to be variants on Ganundasaga, meaning "a new settlement village" (Gä-nun-dä-sa'-ga, per Morgan 1962 [1851]: 424, 469), "at the new town" (Gă-nă-dă-se'-ge, per Hewitt in Hodge 1907–1910 1: 198), or more simply "new town" (David Maracle, personal communication, 1996). There are documentary references to recognizable variations on Ganundasaga from 1705 to 1750 (Beauchamp 1916: 67, 82; MACIA vol. 1819: 170a, 255a–56, 278a, 287a, 294a; vol. 1820: 50, 52–52a; Waterman 2008). The 1750 Cammerhoff journal explicitly names the abandoned White Springs site "Ganechstage" and the occupied Seneca village "New Ganechstage" (Beauchamp 1916: 67). A later and historically better-known eighteenth-century Seneca village in the Geneva area commonly is known as Kanadesaga (occupied circa 1754–1779; figure 4.1: site 6). The Ganundasaga name therefore appears to have been used for three separate village locations occupied in total for more than ninety years. Conover (1889: 8) found in excess of one hundred variant spellings of Ganundasaga in his documentary research.

The later *O* names appear to be variants on Onaghee, which Conover (1889: 4) relates to the Seneca word *onagheh*, meaning "head." There are documentary references to recognizable variations on Onaghee from 1719 to 1741 (IIDH, Aug. 6, 1727, Aug. 16, 1741; MACIA vol. 1819: 170a, 255a–56,

287, 334a; vol. 1820: 24, 50, 52–52a, 129; McIlwain 1915: 124; NYCD 5: 528, 544, 570–72). Onaghee is specifically identified as the "little" or "small" castle in documents dating to 1725 and 1734 (MACIA vol. 1819: 111, vol. 1820: 52a). All of these accounts probably refer to the later of the two western villages at the Huntoon site. Documents dating to between 1700 and 1710 mention a Seneca town called "Oksaront" (Colden 1935 [1720]: 376), "Sjaunt" (NYCD 4: 691), or "Saront" (Waterman 2008); all likely refer to the earlier western village at the Snyder-McClure site.

Early Eighteenth-Century References to the Eastern Seneca Community

The account book of Albany trader Evert Wendell contains several references to a Seneca village called "Canosedaken" dating from 1705 to 1710 (Waterman 2008). The resemblance between the words *Canosedaken* and *Ganundasaga* suggests that Canosedaken was the eastern principal village, and the dates of these accounts imply that they discuss the White Springs site.

An anomalous documentary reference to the eastern Seneca village derives from the May 1720 New York expedition dispatched to Seneca territory to inquire about French activity at Niagara. Expedition members included Myndert Schuyler, Robert Livingston Jr., and Lawrence Claessen. They arranged a meeting in an initially unnamed Seneca town with its headmen and those from the "neighboring castle" of "Onaghee," and note later in the document that they received the Senecas' response to their message "in Sinnondowaene" (NYCD 5: 542–45). This implies that the New York delegation stayed in the eastern village named Sinnondowaene. Sinnondowaene is unlikely to refer to the White Springs site because by 1720 White Springs would have been occupied for thirty-two years, a very long span for a nucleated Iroquoian village. It is probable that Schuyler and Livingston recorded an alternate name for the New Ganechstage Site Complex, possibly using a variation of "Tsonontouan"—the French term for the Seneca people and territory (see, for example, JR 57: 27)—to refer to the eastern "capital" of the Senecas (MACIA vol. 1819: 255a–56). Thus this is the earliest fairly definite documentary reference to the New Ganechstage Site Complex, and possibly to the Townley-Read site.

Claessen's report from the 1720 diplomatic mission says that on June 7 he went to Irondequoit "where I mett a French Smith sent by the Governor of Canada to work for the Sinnekies gratis he having compassion on them as a father on his children knowing they wanted a smith since they have lay'd out a New Castle" (NYCD 5: 550). Richter (1992: 379 note 5) uses this reference to date the founding of one of the second set of villages, but this cannot be done with confidence. Again, a 1720 founding date would make for a long life span for either the Snyder-McClure or White Springs sites (both settled in 1688 in the aftermath of the Denonville invasion). Additionally, another 1720 document indicates that some Senecas from Onaghee settled in Canada at a location between "Laprerise and Chambly near Montreal" during that year (NYCD 5: 570–72). A "New Castle" definitely was built in Canada during 1720, and it is possible that the smith was journeying to, rather than from, the Montreal region. Alternately, the smith may have been needed for an undetermined small satellite village in the homeland.

In 1726 New York Governor Burnet ordered Captain Evert Bancker "fourthwith to repair to ye Sinnekes country & there to reside till April next, either at Canosedagui or Onahee or go from time to time from ye one castle to the other as you shall think most lending to the publick service" (MACIA vol. 1819: 170a). This is the first mention of a village name that is a recognizable variant of Ganundasaga I was able to locate since the 1710 reference in the Wendell journal.

Factional Politics, Colonial Agents, and Smiths

In October 1727, Lawrence Claessen reported to the Albany Commissioners about his September trip to Seneca territory, where he found

> a French smith in ye Sinneke Castle with his wife children & servant, who sold goods there to ye Indians for skins & peltry. Ye Indians inquired of me if the Smith from here [that is, Albany] should bring goods there to supply their necessity. if he did they would not be displeased about it.... Jean Cour ye french Interpreter had been gone from ye Sinneke Castle called Onnahee for two days before he came to *Canosade ye capitall of ye Sinnekes*. he informed ye Indians yt he has a great store of goods in ye house at Jagara [Niagara] & invited ye In[dians] to trade with him there. He had formerly given strouds at a beaver skin a blanket but ____ he would sell it at three[.] A choice French blanket at ye same price[;] a fine French gune at £7[;] ... ketels of powder their wt in beaver[;] a fine French frise coat or a fine men shirt as appears fine ____ stockings at 1¼ beaver. 4 French potts pure brandy at 1 beaver. he had sent for a cooper to make keggs (MACIA vol. 1819: 255a–56; emphasis added).

Although the reference is ambiguous, it appears likely that Claessen was in "Canosade" when he overheard Louis-Thomas Chabert de Joncaire's announcement, and that the French smith, family, and servant also were living there. "Canosade" appears to be a variant of Ganundasaga.

By 1728, New York officials appear to have consolidated a base of operations in the eastern community. Instructions for New York delegations sent to Seneca territory in 1728, 1729, and 1730 all specified that they should base themselves in "Canosodago" (MACIA vol. 1819: 278–79, 294–94a, 326–26a), a shift in language from Bancker's 1726 instructions to "go from time to time from ye one castle to the other" (MACIA vol. 1819: 170a). New York's prioritization of the eastern community was reinforced in a May 1729 meeting between five principal headmen "of the castle called Onnah" and the Albany Commissioners. When the Onaghee headmen announced that "they desire that they may have a Gunsmith this next winter in their castle" (MACIA vol. 1819: 287), the commissioners replied, "You have desired of us that we should send you a gunsmith this next winter, which according to your device shall be sent to you, a Fitt Person who shall lie in the castle called Canasuedaha, where the smiths tools are kept" (MACIA vol. 1819: 287a). Both "Canosodago" and "Canasuedaha" appear to be additional variations on Ganundasaga.

At the same time, officials from New France (particularly Louis-Thomas Chabert de Joncaire) appear to have preferred to stay in the smaller western village of Onaghee, and apparently were quite welcome there. Joncaire's presence at Onaghee was noted in 1719, 1725, 1727, and 1732 (MACIA vol. 1819: 111, 255a–56; vol. 1820: 24; NYCD 5: 528). The Albany Commissioners received word in 1730 that Joncaire wanted to stay "this ensuing winter in the small castle" of the Senecas (NYCD 5: 911). French documents also note requests for smiths for the "Little Village" in 1740 and 1742 (NYCD 9: 1065, 1090). The residents of Onaghee were said to have "gone over to the French" in 1734 (MACIA vol. 1820: 52a).

There were probably smithy facilities in or near both the eastern and western Seneca communities. French smiths were active in Seneca territory during the first decade of the eighteenth century (McIlwain 1915: 64, 79; NYCD 9: 830), likely in facilities in or near the Snyder-McClure or White Springs sites. French smiths noted between 1715 and 1742 (see, for example, McIlwain 1915: 103–4, 113, 117; NYCD 5: 550, 9: 1065, 1090) probably had their primary facilities in or near the Huntoon site. New York smiths were first dispatched to Seneca territory during 1721–1723 (DHNY 1: 289; Leder 1956: 232–35; NYCD 5: 641–42, 666, 718), but it is unclear whether they operated at Irondequoit or in the Senecas' home villages. New York smiths operating after 1724 probably were based in Ganundasaga, and likely at the

Townley-Read site, based on the local "tradition" cited by Conover (1882: 77) discussed later in this chapter. Smithy facilities also were constructed at the trading posts at Niagara, Irondequoit, and Oswego.

Smiths from New France and New York frequently worked in Seneca territory simultaneously. In an October 1728 meeting with New York Governor Montgomerie, Seneca headmen encouraged the governor to supply them with a smith, since the "French smith who is there now, he can make no worke . . . for he is an old man and can scarcely see" (MACIA vol. 1819: 275a). Although the accuracy and persuasiveness of this depiction of the French smith cannot be judged, two days later Montgomerie nonetheless dispatched a smith and an armorer to Seneca territory for six months (MACIA vol. 1819: 278). In September 1741, New France Governor Beauharnois reprimanded the Senecas for directing all their smithing work to a New Yorker (presumably Hendrick Wemp based on IIDH, Sept. 24, 1740) despite the fact that a French smith also was working in their territory (NYCD 9: 1083–84). Structures and facilities occasionally were endangered when agents departed; in late 1742 New York agent Andries Nack found the "house," which may have contained the smithy, in which "our people used to dwell in there broake down, which the French men had demolished" (MACIA vol. 1820: 238).

It is possible that on occasion smiths from New York and New France sequentially used the same smithy facilities, and perhaps even the same tools. Claessen's October 1727 report shows that the French smith likely was working in the eastern community, and the May 1729 Albany Commissioners statement makes it quite clear that New York smiths based themselves in "Canasuedaha." Several documents demonstrate that smith's "tools & utencills" were left in Seneca territory (MACIA vol. 1819: 278a; see also MACIA vol. 1819: 287a, 294–94a, 326–26a). The Albany Commissioners provided explicit instructions in 1730 as to how their agents were to take possession of the smithy facilities and tools, leaving the language ambiguous enough so as to encompass the possibility that they would find them in the control of Senecas, other Indians, or Frenchmen:

> upon your arrival at the Sinnekes Castle called Canosadago, you and each of you are in the name of His Excy John Montongomerie Esq. Our Governour to demand from the said Sinneke Sachims, or such person or persons as you shall find there residing, all the smiths utencills and tools together wth the shop, from such person or persons who shall or may have such utencills and tools belonging to the pub-

lick in his or their custody... all persons concern'd are hereby strictly charg'd and commanded to deliver the aforesaid utencills tools and shop and every part thereof unto you, as he or they shall answer the contrary at their perill. (MACIA vol. 1819: 326a)

A March 1734 document notes that the French had established a large trading post and smithy "between the two Sinneke castles named Kannasadagoe & Onnahee on the bank of a large stream or creek" (MACIA vol. 1820: 50). In an April document, Jacobus Myndertse noted that this post had "two fires" and flew a French flag; he described the location of the post as "near the castle called Cannosadago[,] on the bank of a brook in the road from Najager [Niagara] and Onahee" (MACIA vol. 1820: 52). Since in 1734 the Senecas are all but certain to have been living at Huntoon and New Ganechstage, the most likely location for the French trading post is on Flint Creek. Although the French reportedly had plans to fortify the post in 1734 (MACIA vol. 1820: 52), I found no additional references to the structure.

The Cammerhoff Journal

In 1750 the Moravian missionaries Johann Cammerhoff and David Zeisberger traversed Seneca territory on their way to the major (and probably recently settled) western Seneca village at Geneseo. Cammerhoff's account (in Beauchamp 1916: 24–112) is the only truly detailed primary-source description of the Seneca villages between Seneca and Canandaigua lakes. Cammerhoff relates that they entered Seneca territory on June 28:

> About four miles from the Lake we came into the neighborhood of the old city of Ganechstage, which is said to have been very large. It was destroyed by Onontio or Governor of Canada, according to what the Indians say, 60 or more years ago. Now we could discover where the farms must have been. It is a very beautiful tract of land, with good springs of fresh water. It lies so high that one could see from here to Gajuka [the main Cayuga village], about 50 miles [80 km] distant. From the road we could see that it must have been a very large city. A few isolated huts are still standing, from which led footpaths.... The Gajuka [Hahotschaunquas, their Cayuga guide] told us that when the French had destroyed the city, they had killed only 7 Indians, but had taken the whole city, which was very large. The surrounding country is very pleasant, like a pleasure garden in the desert, to which I know no comparison in this country. (Beauchamp 1916: 67)

This description of Ganechstage places it conclusively at the White Springs site. Hahotschaunquas supplied the Moravians with the Iroquois conception of the enduring village, which Cammerhoff interpreted literally. When the guide said that Ganechstage was destroyed by the French, he meant that the *predecessor* village (not White Springs itself) had been destroyed by Denonville. The description of the White Springs area as a "pleasure garden" likely indicates that Senecas continued to use their former village site for agricultural purposes.

After being momentarily lost, the Moravian party moved west:

> We saw clearly that we had gone too far south, and out of our course. The Gajuka therefore went to look for the way. He found the huts which constitute new Ganechstage, and asked directions. We started going directly to the right until we came to the footpath, and saw the city, consisting of only 8 or 9 huts. This time we did not enter it, but continued straight on and came into a terrible wilderness. Then we had a worse road than we had on the whole journey . . . we went through swamps and marshes, where the flies troubled us greatly. For miles we were obliged to walk on trees and branches, as on both sides were deep marshes, bushes and thorns, which make an inconvenient bridge, for we sometimes slipped from the trees and branches, and fell into the swamp, and could scarcely get up again with our heavy bundles. We called the road the Long Bridge. It would have been quite impassible with horses, and the Indians say no one can travel this road except on foot. After we had continued in this swamp for about six miles we came to a creek, called Axoquenta or Firestone Creek [now Flint Creek]. From thence the road was a little better. Toward evening we reached an old Indian settlement, where a city by the name of Onnachee is said to have stood, but which is now uninhabited. We were caught in a dreadful thunder and rain storm, and were thoroughly drenched, particularly in going through the tall grass. We went on a little further and encamped along a creek called Otochshiaco [Fall Brook per Beauchamp's footnote]. (Beauchamp 1916: 67–68)

The route that Cammerhoff, Zeisberger, and the Cayuga guide took appears to have been along the north side of Burrell Creek and past one of the components of the New Ganechstage Site Complex, possibly Townley-Read. The "Long Bridge" apparently went through some of the present-day swamps between Number Nine Road and the village of Flint, and it is possible that their guide intentionally took them on a suboptimal route. The vacant Seneca settlement Cammerhoff called "Onnachee" is fairly certainly either Huntoon or Snyder-McClure; the "tall grass" encountered during the thunderstorm is likely to have been growing in abandoned Indian fields. It is most probable that Cammerhoff saw Snyder-McClure, since Huntoon had been abandoned not long before Cammerhoff's visit and houses would still have been standing there. Unless the path they took bypassed the site, why Cammerhoff did not mention Huntoon is somewhat of a mystery.

After this Cammerhoff and Zeisberger visited the Seneca villages of Ganataqueh near Canandaigua Lake (possibly the Sackett site; figure 4.1: site 5), Hachniage on Honeoye Lake, and Zonesschio near what is now Geneseo, New York. The Moravians encountered village-wide drinking episodes in Ganataqueh and Zonesschio, which convinced the Moravians to abandon their idea of a mission among the Senecas. On their return journey, a Seneca in Ganataqueh told them of "a chief living in Ganechsatage by the name of Gajinquechto . . . his house was large and we could put up there" (Beauchamp 1916: 81). After spending a rainy night along Fall Brook, the Moravians again passed between Canandaigua and Seneca lakes on July 6:

> We crossed the fourfold swamp, the long bridge, and many marshes and bogs. Because it was very wet and slippery I often sank deeply into them. The mosquitoes worried us dreadfully, and in spite of all the marshes we found no drinking water. In the afternoon we arrived at Ganechsatage, and repaired to the house of the chief Gajinquechto. He and his wife were not at home, but came after we had been there a short time, received us very kindly, and at once offered us venison. We made inquiries concerning the route we were to take. The sachem's wife went with us and pointed it out, and so we journeyed on, passing old Ganechsatage, and at noon reached a spring. Here we halted because of the heat. We met several Indians who had been hunting with bows and arrows. (Beauchamp 1916: 82)

In sum, Cammerhoff's description of the eastern village is meager—eight or nine huts, with Gajinquechto's "large" house among them—and insufficient to determine exactly which of the six small sites along Burrell Creek he and Zeisberger visited. Conover's (1889) equation of Cammerhoff's New Ganechstage with the Townley-Read site is a possibility but not a definite conclusion.

Later References to the Eastern Seneca Community

The last likely description of occupation of the New Ganechstage Site Complex was penned in 1754 by the Albany Commissioners. They described Seneca territory as follows:

> the Commissrs are of opinion, that his Honr should insist on the Senecas, who at present live very remote from one another, to make a general Castle near the mouth of the Senecas River, where they have already begun to build a new Castle—This point has been several times recommended to them by former Governors, and which they have faithfully promised to do, but have not hitherto effected. (NYCD 6: 856–57)

The location of the new village "near the mouth of the Senecas River" is likely to be that of the large village of Kanadesaga (figure 4.1: site 6), where New York built a small fort in 1756. Kanadesaga was burned by the American Sullivan expedition in 1779, but Senecas reoccupied the site shortly thereafter.

The missionary Samuel Kirkland's description of a June 1788 journey to Buffalo Creek to attend treaty negotiations with the Six Nations about the Phelps and Gorham purchase (Pilkington 1980) provides an additional account of the region. Kirkland stopped at Kanadesaga, where he preached "the 2d sermon ever preached upon this ground" on June 15 (138). A week later he set out for Buffalo Creek, describing the area between Kanadesaga and Canandaigua Lake as follows: "The first four miles [6.4 km] passed thro' the old fields of the ancient Seneka Town called Kanghsadegea. Then entered a swamp, or low lands, thick timber'd about 5 miles [8 km] thro', in the middle of which is good stream called in English Flint Brook. After passing this came to open land where was formerly a seneka settlement called anaye" (139–40). It appears that Kirkland took the same route used by Cammerhoff in 1750. Kirkland's "Kanghsadegea" is likely to have been the New Ganechstage Site Complex, and "anaye" either Snyder-McClure or Huntoon.

Historic Maps

Historic maps provide additional but limited help in locating the villages in question. Beyond the basic problem of European mapmakers simply not having detailed knowledge of the terrain, maps frequently were copied from older sources, replicating outdated or inaccurate information. Old village locations tend to persist on maps long after their abandonment, perhaps because Europeans had difficulty understanding the periodic relocation of Iroquois settlements. For example, Guillaume Delisle's 1718 map "Louisiane et du cours du Mississippi" (IIDH, Dec. 4, 1726 [II]) and the maps that accompanied various editions of Cadwallader Colden's *History of the Five Indian Nations Depending on the Province of New-York in America* (for example, Colden 1958 [1747]; IIDH, Dec. 4, 1726 [III]) include Seneca settlements that had not been inhabited since their burning by the Denonville invasion in 1687.

Unsurprisingly, maps produced by colonial agents and travelers who passed through Seneca territory are the most accurate. New York military engineer Willem Wolfgang Römer's map of 1700 (Römer 1700; see figure 9.4) shows Seneca villages in the approximate locations of the Snyder-McClure and White Springs sites, using images of relatively small, peak-roofed houses to represent them (see Gronim 2001: 378–79 for discussion of this map). This accurate information was not incorporated into the later maps produced by Delisle and Colden.

In 1755 mapmaker Lewis Evans produced "A General Map of the Middle British Colonies in America" (figure 4.3; Evans 1755), which records the approximate locations of Huntoon, New Ganechstage, Kendaia, and three villages on the Genesee River. Although Evans traveled in Iroquoia, he never visited Seneca territory directly (Gipson 1939: 162–63); his information on this region may have been derived from fur trader and Albany County deputy surveyor John Rutger Bleecker (Klinefelter 1971: 42; Mullenneaux 2002), the son of Rutger Janse Bleecker, a prominent member of the Albany Commissioners of Indian Affairs (Parmenter 2007b: table 10.1). While the placement of villages called "Canasadego" and "Onahie" on Evans' map corresponds to the Townley-Read and Huntoon sites, this information was slightly out of date, since by 1755 both Huntoon and the New Ganechstage Site Complex had been largely or completely abandoned (Beauchamp 1916: 67; NYCD 6: 856–57). The various maps later published with Peter Kalm's account of his 1750 travels (Evans 1784; Gibson 1771) either do not show Seneca villages or copy details (including the spelling of village names) from Evans' 1755 map. The lack of original detail in these maps supports the idea that Kalm's observations of Seneca territory on his way to Niagara were limited to the shore of Lake Ontario (see Benson 1937: 695). Thus, I have been unable to find a historic map that shows the location of the New Ganechstage Site Complex during the period in which it was occupied.

Figure 4.3. Detail from Lewis Evans's "A General Map of the Middle British Colonies," 1755. The town marked "Canasadego" is roughly at the location of the New Ganechstage Site Complex. (Library of Congress, Geography and Map Division.)

An anonymous map of New York and Six Nations territory (figure 4.4; "N.W. Parts of New York" 1750–1768) produced between 1758 and 1764, and probably dating to 1761–1764, represents the watercourses at the northwest end of Seneca Lake fairly accurately. It shows the location of "Canossodage" with a triangular mark quite close to the Townley-Read site, and notes that the settlement is abandoned. Another site, labeled "the New Castel," is shown in the approximate location of Kanadesaga.[3]

With the exception of the Römer map, none of these maps contains any of the illustrative embellishments occasionally added by earlier cartographers. I know of no sketches or drawings that represent any of the 1715–1754 Seneca villages.

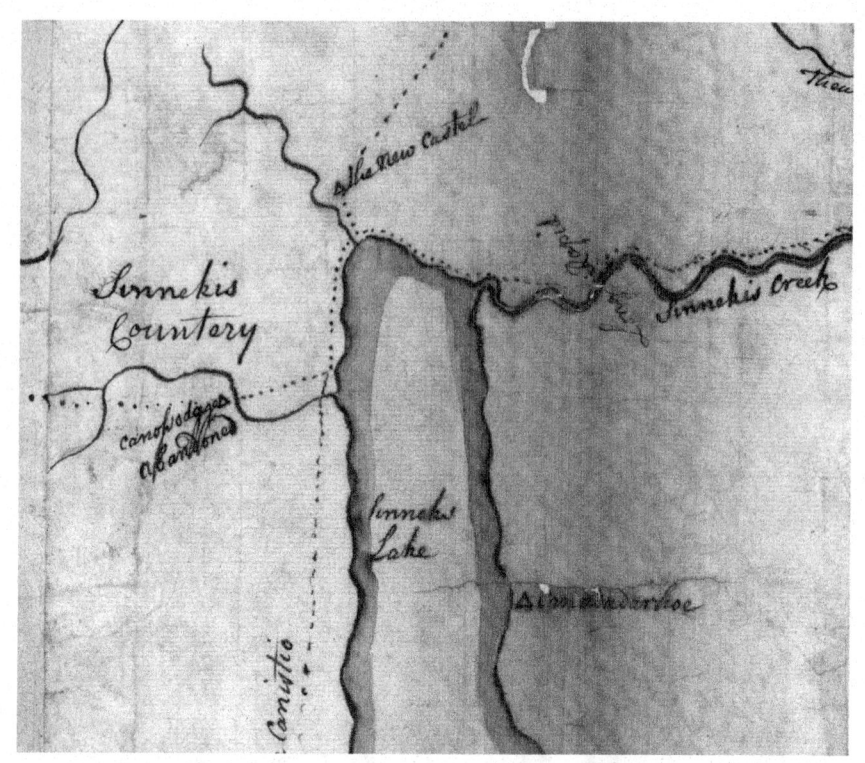

Figure 4.4. Detail from "N.W. Parts of New York, No. 156," circa 1758–1764 (1750–1768). The town marked "Canossodage / Abandoned" is at the location of the Townley-Read Site. (Library of Congress, Geography and Map Division.)

Previous Accounts of Archaeological Resources at Townley-Read

Two main sources of information about the location and structure of archaeological deposits at the Townley-Read site existed at the initiation of the current project: (1) the writings of George S. Conover, a local historian and former president of the Village of Geneva who wrote copiously on the early history of the region (Conover 1882, 1885, 1889, 1893, n.d.); and (2) the field notes of Charles F. Wray (n.d.), an avocational archaeologist who dug at Townley-Read in 1979 and 1982 as part of his extensive investigations of Seneca Iroquois sites.

George S. Conover

Conover gathered a significant amount of material describing the New Ganechstage Site Complex for a June 2, 1882, lecture on Indian history presented at Linden Hall in Geneva. His description of Townley-Read was based on interviews with the owners of the site, examination of their artifact collections, and site visits. Conover's writings and maps must be used with caution. In many cases, multiple versions exist; later versions (for example, Conover n.d.) often show greater insight into the subject matter but also include a significant number of copying errors in sections transferred from earlier works.[4] Conover also frequently misinterpreted archaeological evidence (see K. Jordan 2002: 176–79, 207–11). Despite these shortcomings, Conover's work has much to offer for the study of the site.

Conover (1882) describes several elements within the Townley-Read community, including cemeteries, a European-run blacksmith shop, fruit and nut tree orchards, and the village precinct. Conover first describes the "large Indian burial ground" at the site, which he labeled with an irregular circular mark in his manuscript map (figure 4.5):

> to the west and southwest of the residence of N.A. Read, and distant from 20 to 30 rods [100–151 m] southwesterly from Burrell creek, which at that point runs in a southeasterly direction, is a ridge of ground, portions of which are of a sandy soil, and on this was a large Indian burial ground, and where a very great many skeletons have been uncovered in past times, during the cultivation of the land. Here appears to have been the principal burying ground, but it also extended in a southeasterly direction and across the highway, and into the field on the east side thereof. (Conover 1882: 70–71)

Artifacts recovered from the Seneca burial ground after their exposure by nineteenth-century plowing (1882: 71–75) included kettles, pipes, tomahawks, axes, occasional gun barrels, large quantities of "beads and trinkets" including "blood stone" (red pipestone?) beads, as many as fifty crucifixes, religious medals, and a metal cup that resembled "one of a pair that were sometimes used in Catholic churches in the celebration of mass" (75).

Next, Conover describes what he terms an "Indian Blacksmith Shop" about 150 m northwest of the cemetery area:

> on the edge of the bank on the south side [of the creek] where there is quite a curve or bend, there is evidence of the site of a blacksmith shop which was doubtless there before the settlement of the country by the white people. Such is the tradition, and from its location there seems a probability that the statement is correct. While the situation was accessible and quite convenient for the Indians, it was far otherwise for the white people, being distant from any road that could possibly

have been made or used for any ordinary purpose, and in such an out of the way place, not easily accessible and quite inconvenient. It is well known that the Indians were supplied with blacksmiths by all the governments of the colonies that they were in contact with. (Conover 1882: 77)

Unfortunately, Conover does not discuss what was found at this location that convinced him it was a smithy.

Conover then sets forth what he took to be the Seneca village precinct at Townley-Read:

Some 80 or 100 rods [402–503 m] southwest of the burial ground, and on the bank of high ground east of Burrell creek, on the Read farm in the southwest part of lot 32, was one of the principal sites of the town. At this place there have been abundant indications of the former location of huts or cabins that were occupied by the Indians. In many places the discoloration of the ground, traces and marks of fire on and in the earth and on stones were quite numerous, and every evidence showing that the settlement must have been of good size. Here the bank is high and the ground quite dry; descending the bank, there is quite a flat or low piece of ground before the creek is reached, and here between the water and the site of the huts there were originally evidences of many paths, as likewise was the case between the town and burial ground, and also in other directions. (1882: 78–79)

In figure 4.5, Conover drew C-shaped symbols (likely representing house roofs) on the western Ridgetop that contains the boundary between Lots 31 and 32 to represent the village location.

Conover noted that "a grove of about 3 acres [1.2 ha] of butternut trees" lay between the northern portions of the cemetery area and the "Indian village" (1882: 78), and that "on the west side of the creek on Lot 31 there was another large grove of butternut trees, interspersed with many wild plums. To the north of this there was another Indian burial ground where many burials had been made. Apple trees, both single and in groups, were scattered over the whole neighborhood for a distance of two or three miles" (1882: 79). Early inventories of archaeological sites in central New York compiled by Beauchamp (1900), Follett (n.d.), and Parker (1920) replicate but do not add to the information supplied by Conover.

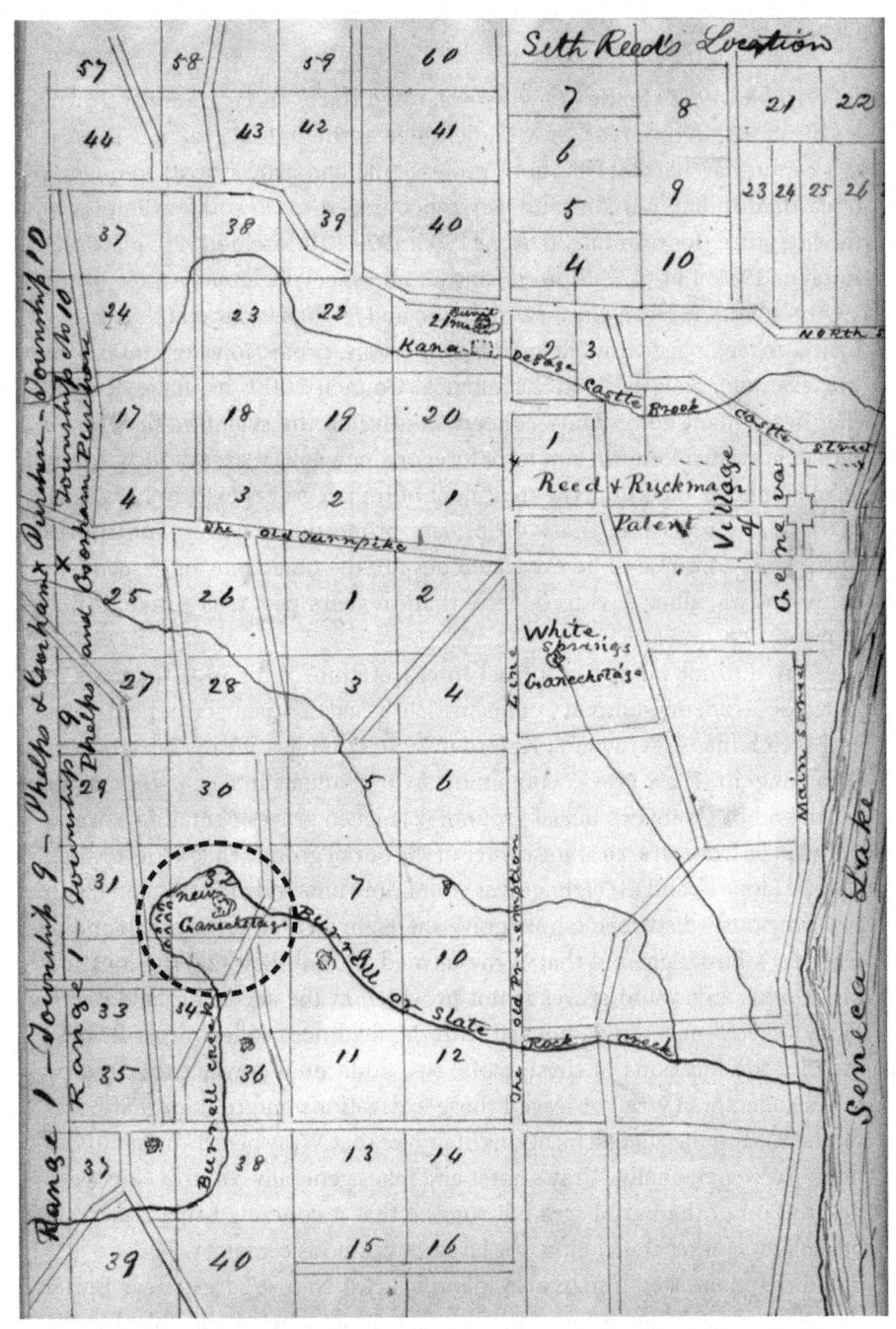

Figure 4.5. George S. Conover's sketch map of Seneca sites in the Geneva, New York, area, with the Townley-Read site circled. Numbers indicate post-1789 Euro-American property lots of one square mile. Original in Conover (n.d.), vol. 3, p. 746. (Courtesy of the Hobart and William Smith Colleges Archives, Geneva, New York.)

Charles F. Wray

In 1979 and 1982 Charles F. Wray excavated thirty-three graves at Townley-Read within the area Conover identified as the "burial ground." Twentieth-century archaeologists (both professional and avocational) frequently unearthed Indian remains and were encouraged to do so by examples in the literature (for example, B. Kent 1993: 197–201; Ritchie 1980: plate 113; Robbins 1981: 134–47). More recently, and especially after passage of the 1990 Native American Graves Protection and Repatriation Act (NAGPRA), many archaeologists (myself included) and some professional organizations (for example, New York Archaeological Council 2000: 16) have decided that descendant community concerns outweigh the scientific benefits of Indian grave exploration and have foregone new burial excavations. Many legal loopholes regarding the treatment of Indian graves exist in New York (particularly regarding those on private property), however, and Indian burial sites continue to be excavated despite the objections of descendant communities, albeit less frequently than in years past (see Amato 2002; Jemison 1997).

Wray did not publish a formal interpretation of his investigations at Townley-Read; my summary of his work is based on manuscript field notes and sketch maps (Wray n.d.; K. Jordan 1996 compiles Wray's burial data). Wray dug up (1) six graves containing six individuals in a cemetery at the north end of Conover's burial ground; (2) eleven graves containing twelve individuals from an area at the center of the burial ground that Wray termed "Burial Plot #1"; and (3) eight graves containing nine individuals, along with two previously disturbed empty grave shafts, in an area at the south end of Conover's burial ground that Wray termed "Burial Plot #2." The location of six other excavated graves is not provided in the surviving field notes. Wray's sketch maps (n.d., housed with the field note collection at RMSC) identify the locations of these plots, two additional graves excavated by other collectors (Wray observed these excavations and took partial notes on them), and the alleged locations of graves that Wray heard about but did not observe personally. Wray's notes and maps generally confirm Conover's description of the burial area but suggest that it contained small, discrete burial plots rather than being one large, continuous cemetery.

Wray's main sketch map also identifies two "refuse" areas near Burial Plot #2 and provides a location for what Wray labeled the "blacksmith shop." None of the materials from the RMSC collections are specifically labeled as being from the refuse areas, and since Wray's surface-collected material contains a significant amount of nineteenth-century Euro-American ceramics, it is uncertain whether these refuse deposits related to the eighteenth-century Seneca or a later Euro-American occupation. Wray's placement of the "blacksmith shop" in the northeast elbow of Burrell Creek bears no relation to Conover's description, and a walkover of the Wray smithy area indicated that it was unlikely to contain cultural deposits.

Information from Other Collectors

I have spoken with several collectors who have dug at the site; because not all collectors authorized publication of their names, I have presented all information obtained from collectors anonymously throughout the book. These collectors provided additional information on the location of Seneca graves and types of material culture recovered at Townley-Read, most of which has not been confirmed or has not yet been examined by the project (see summary in K. Jordan 2002: 183). In all likelihood many other collectors have dug at the site and unidentified—and perhaps sizable—private collections from the site probably exist.

In sum, previous excavations and surface collections have concentrated on burial areas. The information provided by Wray, Conover, and anonymous collectors indicates that there were at least nine burial clusters at Townley-Read (K. Jordan 2002: 183–84); the approximate locations of these cemeteries are shown in figure 5.1. It is possible that some of these represent isolated single graves rather than cemeteries with multiple burials, and some clusters may be segments of larger cemeteries. On present evidence, these cemeteries appear to have contained no more than twenty individuals each, making them relatively small in comparison with earlier Seneca sites (K. Jordan 2004).

Archaeological Collections

Collections of artifacts, faunal materials, and botanical remains from Townley-Read are primarily housed at the Rochester Museum and Science Center and Cornell University.[5] The Townley-Read collections at RMSC are the largest from any Seneca site occupied between 1688 and 1755, and they are accompanied by a significant amount of contextual information. The majority of this material is from mortuary deposits. All of the artifacts Wray recovered during his 1979–1982 grave excavations, as well as additional artifacts surface-collected by Wray, are included in the RMSC's Rock Foundation collection. General locational information for most of the Wray burials is provided by sketch maps; the surface collections from the site are not differentiated by area and therefore are likely to contain a mixture of artifacts from various contexts. Although some of Wray's large artifact collection from Townley-Read has a prominent place in RMSC's "At the Western Door" exhibit on Seneca history, the collection remained essentially unreported at the onset of project fieldwork, with the exception of brief mentions in a handful of comparative studies (Bodner 1999; Karklins 1983; Lorenzini and Karklins 2001; Prisch 1982; Wray 1983).

The Rock Foundation also has acquired additional materials from Townley-Read surface-collected or excavated by at least seven other collectors. Most of this material cannot be provenienced to any particular area within the site, although some of it is labeled as having come from Seneca graves. Some RMSC artifacts are identified as being from the "Townley Farm" site, to which Wray gave a separate site designation; these artifacts are likely to derive from the East Fields "burial ground" area (K. Jordan 2002: 182).

The materials collected by the Townley-Read/New Ganechstage Project during the investigations described in this book are exclusively from domestic contexts. These materials are the property of the Minns family and are currently housed at Cornell University.

Dramatis Personae

Using documentary sources, a good-sized list of individuals known or suspected to have lived at or visited the eighteenth-century Seneca community at New Ganechstage can be reconstructed. As one might expect when relying on texts penned by Europeans, this list is made up primarily of European visitors rather than Seneca residents. In the future, it may become possible to associate archaeological deposits with some of these specific historical figures—if, for example, either Gajinquechto's "large house" or the French trading house between the two Seneca villages were found. Identification of the names of particular individuals associated with New Ganechstage may strengthen the linkage between the site complex and present-day populations, both Seneca and non-Indian. This section represents a trial effort that deserves to be expanded on, particularly through examination of additional manuscript documents and collection of Seneca genealogical information.

As in previous sections, the low level of detail available in primary sources means that historical figures can be linked to the New Ganechstage Site Complex but not specifically to the Townley-Read site. The presence of persons in New Ganechstage can be rated as either definite, highly likely, or possible.

Definite Seneca Residents

The only Seneca who can be linked conclusively to New Ganechstage is Cammerhoff's "Gajinquechto." Conover (1885) equates the Gajinquechto of 1750 with Kaienkwaahton, or Old Smoke, a pro-British headman from the post-1754 village of Kanadesaga, frequent participant in colonial-Iroquois councils, and leader in the American Revolution (see also DCB 4: 404–6). Reverend Samuel Kirkland was adopted by Old Smoke's family during his 1764–1765 stay at Kanadesaga (Pilkington 1980). Kaienkwaahton, a member of the Turtle Clan (moiety 1), died in 1786 (DCB 4: 404). Wallace (1969: 121) describes him as being "a heavily built man over six feet tall, and sixty-some years of age" in 1765; Abler (in DCB 4: 404) translates his name as "disappearing smoke or mist." Kaienkwaahton was likely to have been one of the main leaders, and possibly the primary leader, at New Ganechstage, particularly during the later part of the occupation.

Highly Likely Seneca Residents

Kayenkwarahte (also "Kanakarighton" or "Blewbek") was a Seneca headman described by Colden in 1709 as someone "who had been allways firmly attached to the Interest of ys Governt [that is, to New York]" (Colden 1935 [1720]: 380; see also DCB 2: 111–12). His appearance at diplomatic councils is noted starting in 1699, where he is identified as "the chief sachim of Sinnekis" (NYCD 4: 597), and his diplomatic role continued until at least 1726 (MACIA vol. 1819: 71a; NYCD 5: 545, 801). Kayenkwarahte was removed from his leadership position after intrigue by Louis-Thomas Chabert de Joncaire in 1719 but was apparently restored in 1720 (Colden 1935 [1720]: 434; NYCD 5: 545). The clan mark made by Kanakarighton in 1726 (reproduced in NYCD 5: 801), a bird with long legs and a long neck, is almost certainly a heron (moiety 2) rather than a plover (as asserted by the NYCD editors). Fenton (1998: 339) implies that Blewbek may have held the "Old Smoke" hereditary name before the Revolutionary War leader, which would contradict the apparent differences in recorded versions of their names and the fact that they were from opposite moieties. Given that Blewbek was the main pro-British spokesman among the Senecas, it is likely that he was from the eastern village, was an important figure in New Ganechstage during the latter part of his life, and may have been buried there.

Thanitsaronwee, or Sagonadaragie, of the Beaver clan (moiety 1) was a Seneca leader who accompanied "Kanakarighton" (Kayenkwarahte) to Albany in 1724 and 1726 and drew his clan symbol on the conference record in 1726 (MACIA vol. 1819: 71a; NYCD 5: 801). Given that they traveled together, it is possible that both headmen were from the same village. A 1734 Albany Commissioners document records a conversation between a New York agent and a Seneca headman referred to as "the Doctor" (MACIA vol. 1820: 52–52a). He is described as being a spokesperson commonly inclined to the British interest, and his comments on Seneca factional politics suggest he lived in the eastern village rather than the Francophile western village.

Seneca adults known to have lived at Kanadesaga may have lived a portion of their lives in New Ganechstage, and young adults may have been born there. Persons who fit this criterion include (1) Ah-wey-ne-yohn, mother of the reservation-period leader Red Jacket and a member of the Wolf clan (Densmore 1999); (2) Tekanadie, or Tekanando, Samuel Kirkland's adoptive relative at Kanadesaga in 1764–1765 (Pilkington 1980: 11, 21, 45 note 32); and (3) Onoingwadekha, or "Burnt Milk," a nativist Seneca leader at Kanadesaga who spoke in favor of traditional forms of Iroquois economy and religion and opposed Christianity in 1765 (Pilkington 1980: 21–25, 46 note 48; see also Fenton 1998: 552; McConnell 1992: 223).

Definite European Visitors

One of the most frequent European visitors to New Ganechstage was the ubiquitous Louis-Thomas Chabert de Joncaire (circa 1670–1739), a Frenchman who was captured and adopted by the Senecas in 1689 or 1690, and returned to New France in 1694 (DCB 2: 125–27; Richter 1992: 198; see Severance 1906 for a dated but still useful biography). There are suggestions that Joncaire fathered children with a Seneca woman, but the evidence is equivocal (DCB 2: 127; Severance 1906: 88–89). His presence in New Ganechstage is substantiated by the 1727 document detailing his visit to the village to announce the trade terms available at Niagara (MACIA vol. 1819: 255a–56).

New York agents Myndert Schuyler and Robert Livingston Jr. visited the eastern Seneca village in 1720. At the time, Schuyler (1672–1755) was the mayor of Albany; he also served as a commissioner of Indian affairs for at least thirty-five years between 1706 and 1754, as representative to the New York General Assembly, and in various municipal positions in Albany (Bielinski 2002; Parmenter 2007b: table 10.1). Livingston (1663–1725) was mayor of Albany from 1710 to 1719, commissioner of Indian affairs, and a prominent merchant (Bielinski n.d.).

The 1720 mission also included interpreter Lawrence (or Lourens) Claessen van der Volgen, a frequent visitor to Seneca territory during the 1710–1738 era who brought back the 1727 report detailing Joncaire's efforts to entice Senecas to trade at Niagara (MACIA vol. 1819: 255a–56). In some years, Claessen made more than one trip to Seneca territory. Like Joncaire, Claessen had been captured by the Iroquois at an early age—in his case by Canadian Iroquois who attacked Schenectady in 1690—and learned Iroquoian languages during his captivity (Richter 1992: 220). Claessen apparently spoke no English (220), which may not have been a great hindrance considering that most of the New Yorkers in charge of Indian affairs were of Dutch descent. Born in 1679, Claessen died in January 1742 (McIlwain 1915: 224; Richter 1992: 220).

The presence of the Moravian missionaries Johann Cammerhoff (circa 1719–1751) and David Zeisberger (1721–1808) in New Ganechstage is unquestionable due to the evidence provided in Cammerhoff's journal. Cammerhoff died shortly after the 1750 mission, probably from tuberculosis (Olmstead 1997: 65). Zeisberger was to make several lengthy stays among the Onondagas, and to conduct a mission among the Seneca/multinational communities on the Allegheny in 1767–1770 (Beauchamp 1916; Olmstead 1997).

Highly Likely and Possible European Visitors

New York agent Evert Bancker's 1726 orders to stay for a year in Seneca territory specified that he was to split his time between "Canosedagui" and "Onahee" (MACIA vol. 1819: 170a), making it highly likely that he spent time in the eastern community. Bancker (1665–1734) was mayor of Albany in 1694–1695 and 1707–1709, a prominent fur trader, and part owner of a fraudulent deed to most of Mohawk territory (Bielinski 2003; Richter 1992: 137, 192). Bancker also served as a commissioner of Indian affairs in Albany for at least twenty years between 1696 and 1732 (Parmenter 2007b: table 10.1), making him (along with Schuyler and Livingston) one of the more prominent New York agents dispatched to the Seneca country.

The New York missions to Seneca territory in 1728, 1729, and 1730 each were ordered to proceed to the eastern Seneca community and secure the smithy facilities for themselves (MACIA vol. 1819: 278–79, 294–94a, 326–26a). Personnel who accompanied these missions included Gerardus Bancker, William Fisher, the smith and armorer Barnardus Hartsen, Hendrick Myndertse Roseboom, Abraham Schuyler, Cornelius Ten Broeck, Johannes Hendrichse Ten Eyck, Sybrian (or Sybrant) van Schaick, the armorer Joseph van Size, Johannes van Veghlen Jr., the smith Hendrick Wemp, the smith and interpreter Abraham Wendell, and Evert Harmanuse Wendell.

Primary sources record the names of more than twenty other New York agents who worked in Seneca territory.[6] Their duties probably were similar to those of Evert Bancker and the 1728–1730 missions, so many or all of these people likely spent time in New Ganechstage. Smiths appear to have had the longest tenures in Seneca territory, particularly Abraham Wendell (present 1730–1736),[7] Myndert Wemp (at Irondequoit and probably in Seneca territory in 1721–1722; present in Seneca territory 1744–1746),[8] and Hendrick Wemp (possibly present in 1724 and definitely present in 1728–1729 and 1740–1741).[9]

Philippe-Thomas Chabert de Joncaire (circa 1707–1766), likely the "little son" introduced to the Senecas by Joncaire the elder in 1717, apparently took over his father's duties as French agent to the Senecas in 1735 or 1740 (DCB 3: 101; NYCD 9: 1067). His brother Daniel-Marie Chabert de Joncaire (1714–1771) subsequently assumed the position in 1748 (DCB 4: 137). Both are highly likely to have visited New Ganechstage. The "Laforge" father-and-son duo of smiths probably visited or lived in New Ganechstage (see MACIA vol. 1819: 255a–56). In 1742, Seneca petitioners requested that Laforge's son come to work as a smith in their territory (NYCD 9: 1090), and their language suggests that they were quite familiar with Laforge senior and with the character of his son. A 1744 document noted that the Senecas were expecting the arrival of "two French smiths who where [sic] naturall born Indians" (MACIA vol. 1820: 309), which may indicate that the Laforges were considered Native for reasons of parentage or adoption.

Unfortunately, French documents are not as explicit as New York sources in naming the lesser agents and smiths that represented New France, and independent traders are almost never named. The French official Charles Le Moyne de Longueil (1687–1755), an adopted Onondaga (per Haan 1976: 171) who became the second Baron de Longueil, stopped in Seneca territory on diplomatic missions in 1716, 1721, and 1725, and at Niagara in 1739 (DCB 3: 384–85; D. Kent 1974: 119; McIlwain 1915: 113, 158–59; NYCD 5: 590). He was accompanied in 1721 by Michel Maray de La Chauvignerie (NYCD 5: 590), whom Parmenter (1999: 52) identifies as an Indian agent.

5

Archaeology at the Townley-Read Site, 1996–2000

The Townley-Read/New Ganechstage Project focused on locating and excavating domestic-context archaeological deposits from the eighteenth-century Seneca village at the Townley-Read site (figure 5.1). The 1996–2000 fieldwork at the site described in this book was supported by Columbia University, Hobart and William Smith Colleges, the National Science Foundation, and the Early American Industries Association. The project was advised by Peter Jemison of the Seneca Nation of Indians.

The unpublished records of George S. Conover (1882, n.d.) and Charles F. Wray (n.d.) identified an area of approximately 48 ha that potentially contained eighteenth-century deposits, but offered conflicting opinions about the location of the village. A north-south drainage ditch divides the western part of the site—including the Ridgetop that Conover identified as the village location (Areas A, B, and C)—from the East Fields (Areas D, F, and H), where Wray's notes implied there were domestic deposits as well as cemeteries. Conover's and Wray's accounts suggested different models for Seneca land use at the site.

The Ridgetop where Conover (1882: 78) claimed there were "abundant indications of the former location of huts or cabins that were occupied by the Indians" exhibits many characteristics typical of nucleated Iroquois village sites. It is one of the most defensible settings in the locality: its elevation provides good visibility in all directions around it, and the elbow of Burrell Creek protects the Ridgetop from attack in two directions. The location would have been attractive to Seneca farmers because large amounts of fertile, well-drained floodplain soil were available in the creekbed below. Both the predecessor village to New Ganechstage at White Springs and its successor at Kanadesaga were built on hilltops (K. Jordan 2004). Additionally, Conover's suggestion that the Townley-Read Senecas buried their dead in cemeteries (predominantly in the East Fields) that were spatially isolated from residences implied continuity with earlier Seneca sites such as Snyder-

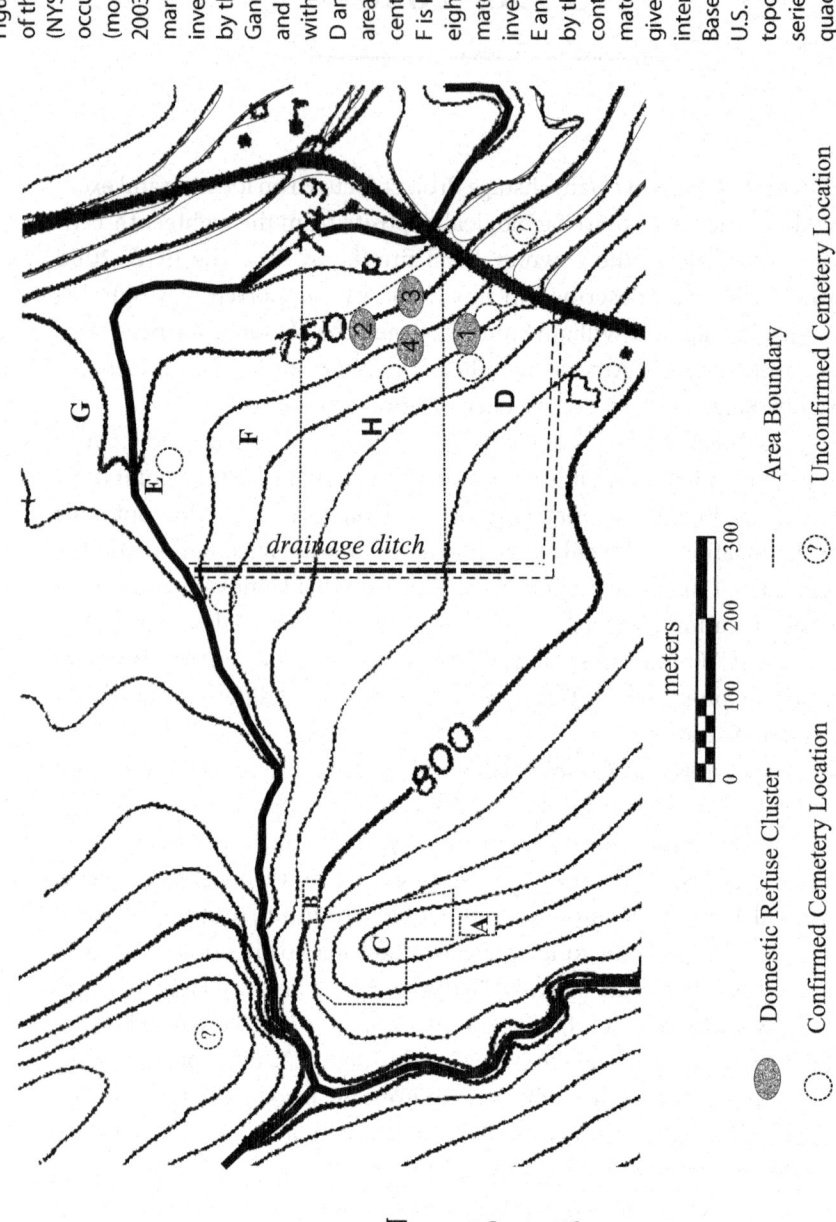

Figure 5.1. Topographic map of the Townley-Read site (NYSM 2440; RMSC PIp-16), occupied circa 1715–1754 (modified from K. Jordan 2003: figure 1). Letters mark areas that have been investigated or considered by the Townley-Read/New Ganechstage Project. A, B, and C are Ridgetop areas with Precolumbian deposits. D and H are low-lying areas with eighteenth-century domestic deposits. F is known to contain eighteenth-century materials but has not been investigated systematically. E and G were examined by the project but did not contain substantial cultural materials. Elevations are given in feet; contour interval is 10 ft (3.0 m). Base map taken from U.S. Geological Survey topographical map, 7.5′ series, Stanley, New York, quadrangle. (Image used courtesy of the New York State Archaeological Association.)

McClure (K. Jordan 2004; Wray n.d.). In short, Conover outlined a model of community structure that was similar to earlier Iroquois villages and has parallels at other eighteenth-century Iroquoian archaeological sites, including the Oneida Primes Hill site (occupied circa 1696–1720; Bennett 1988), the Onondaga Sevier site (circa 1700–1720; T. Tanner 1995), and the multinational Conestoga site near present-day Lancaster, Pennsylvania (circa 1690–1740; B. Kent 1993).

In contrast, Wray's maps suggested that site structure at Townley-Read might differ radically from that of traditional Iroquois villages. Wray's placement of "refuse" areas on either side of a cemetery in the East Fields suggests that the East Fields were not strictly a burial ground. If the refuse deposits were made by Senecas, it could mean that Seneca residences were built in low-lying areas with little defensive value. The possibility that houses and middens might be located quite close to graves also would contrast with earlier Seneca sites. The Wray data could signal a dispersed community structure similar to that documented for the main Onondaga village in 1743 by John Bartram (1966 [1751]: 42) and suggested for eighteenth-century Mohawk settlements at Fort Hunter and Indian Castle (Snow 1995: chs. 13–14). When the Townley-Read/New Ganechstage Project was initiated, dispersed community structure had not been investigated archaeologically at these or other sites.

As a third alternative, it is possible that the Conover and Wray models were not mutually exclusive. Seneca dispersal into many small sites may have been a gradual process: the Ridgetop could have been the original habitation area occupied by Senecas moving from White Springs, and low-lying settlements in the East Fields and other small sites in the New Ganechstage Site Complex could have been settled as "daughter" communities that separated from the Ridgetop village. A composite of the two models therefore might prove to be the most accurate.

Field Methods

Archaeological excavations at the site began in 1996 to evaluate these models of community structure. In determining the field methodology to be used at Townley-Read, my main approach was to rely as much as possible on nonintrusive techniques. This decision represented a convergence between (1) current archaeological ethics that favor site conservation over excavation, and (2) Seneca community opposition to the archaeological disturbance of graves. My incorporation of the Seneca perspective into the

Table 5.1. Summary of Fieldwork Conducted at Townley-Read, 1996–2000

Area	Shovel Test Pits	Test Units	Surface Exam (ha)	Features	Post Molds	Flotation Samples	Other Techniques
A	25	5	—	1	1	6	GPR; magnetometry; conductivity; metal detection
B	17	8	informal	2	—	8	magnetometry; conductivity
C	85	2	informal	1	—	1	magnetometry; conductivity
D	56	34	2.7	15	31	38	GPR; metal detection
E	3	4	—	—	—	—	magnetometry; conductivity (spot)
G[a]	—	—	informal	—	—	—	—
H	66	14	3.8	4	2	22	GPR; magnetometry
Total	252	67	6.5	23	34	75	

Note: a. Area F is known to contain eighteenth-century deposits but has not been systematically examined.

project in part reflected the growing awareness among archaeologists of the impact of their work on descendent communities (see Fine-Dare 2002; Kerber 2006; Mihesuah 2000; Spector 1993; Thomas 2000; Watkins 2000), but also my conviction that new archaeological projects must be vigilant so as to guard against continuing the colonial relationship between archaeologists and indigenous peoples that has too often characterized the archaeology of the past (McNiven and Russell 2005).

Project field methodology was developed in conjunction with Peter Jemison, our liaison to the Seneca Nation of Indians. Jemison is the former chair of the Haudenosaunee Standing Committee on Burial Rules and Regulations, faithkeeper for the bird moiety of the Seneca Nation, author, and editor (for example, Jemison 1995, 1997; Jemison and Schein 2000). His principal concern was that archaeologists must use utmost care to avoid disturbing cemetery areas and grave goods. As a consequence, the project attempted to find ways to distinguish mortuary from domestic areas. This was a continuing process involving a number of trials and experiments, but in the end not one grave was disturbed during the course of the project.

Investigations took place at varying degrees of intensity across various portions of the areas identified by Conover and Wray (table 5.1). In each examined area, project archaeologists first used nonintrusive methods such as field walking, systematic surface examination and collection, and geophysical techniques (including ground-penetrating radar [GPR], proton magnetometer, and soil conductivity surveys) to identify domestic-context deposits. Subsequently, intrusive methods were used to investigate domestic areas, including soil core sampling, systematic metal detector survey, shovel test-pit and test-unit excavation, and stripping of the plowzone (soil previously disturbed by plowing) by earth-moving machinery. All excavated areas were refilled at the conclusion of the project.

Project archaeologists dug shovel test pits (STPs) of approximately 35 cm in diameter and screened the excavated soil with 6 mm mesh hardware cloth. Test units (TUs) primarily were 1 × 1 m in size; excavated soil identified as plowzone or subsoil was screened with 6 mm mesh hardware cloth, while possible feature or post mold soil was screened with 3 mm mesh hardware cloth. Plan views of possible cultural features and post molds were drawn, and these soil stains then were bisected and profiles drawn. With the exception of very small post molds, flotation samples were taken from each soil stain identified in the field as potentially cultural. Kurt Jordan (2002, n.d.) provides feature descriptions, artifact inventories, further details regarding project field and laboratory procedures, evaluation of the field methods used, and additional figures. This chapter draws on unpublished analyses by Adam Watson (2007; faunal materials), Jack Rossen (2006; botanical materials), and Scott Stull (2006; ceramics); the data supplied here supplant those presented in earlier publications and reports.

Chasing Conover: Archaeology on the Ridgetop and the Possible Smithy Area

The project first investigated Conover's (1882, n.d.) claims that the main habitation area at Townley-Read was on the western Ridgetop, and that a European-run smithy was located in the eastern part of the site.

Although the western Ridgetop was similar to the locations of many Iroquoian villages occupied during the fifteenth through seventeenth centuries (Hasenstab 1996; Vandrei 1987), 1996–1999 excavations found no conclusive evidence for an eighteenth-century occupation on the Ridgetop. Not only was Conover's claim that this was "one of the principal sites of the [eighteenth-century Seneca] town" (Conover 1882: 78) in error, but the narrow range and low density of materials found on the Ridgetop appear to preclude a substantial domestic occupation during any time period (K. Jordan 2002: 194–208; n.d.).

Three fire-related features and one possible post mold were located on the Ridgetop. Although diagnostic artifacts were not definitely associated with these deposits, each feature contained botanical remains, suggesting that plant processing occurred there. The entire Ridgetop contained a light scatter of Precolumbian and post-1788 Euro-American artifacts. The greatest concentration of Precolumbian materials was found in Area A. Diagnostic Late Woodland artifacts from Area A included a triangular Madison projectile point made from Onondaga chert and an incised ceramic sherd; non-diagnostic artifacts included an undecorated mica-tempered ceramic pipe stem fragment, four additional chert tools, an exhausted chert core, and one other Native-made ceramic sherd. Two informal lithic tools and two possible Native-made ceramic sherds (both very worn) were recovered in Area B. A calibrated, two-sigma radiocarbon date of 1270–1420 CE (Beta-217626) was obtained for Feature 2 in Area B, the largest of the Ridgetop features, suggesting a Late Owasco or Early Iroquois occupation. The Ridgetop artifacts and features likely are the by-products of short-term, special-purpose indigenous uses of the area as a campsite, hunting station, plant-processing area, agricultural field, or location for initial reduction of lithic cores. Some Precolumbian artifacts from the Ridgetop may be traces of resource-procurement forays or farming by residents of the nearby Woodley village site (occupied circa 1450–1550, based on ceramic data).[1]

Although no unambiguous evidence for an eighteenth-century presence was found, it is virtually certain that Senecas made use of the Ridgetop given the area's close proximity to definite eighteenth-century Seneca residences in the East Fields. The Ridgetop may have functioned as an agricultural field, a location for hunting or gathering, a place to watch for game, or a spot for special-purpose processing such as the boiling of maple sap (Parker 1910: 102–4) or preparation of fuel for use by the on-site blacksmith (Oppenheim n.d.). Eighteenth-century Senecas may have subjected the area to low-temperature ground fires, a practice commonly employed by the Iroquois and many other American Indian groups (O. Stewart 2002: 77–87). These fires facilitated hunting and travel, created conditions favorable for the growth of berries and other gathered foods, destroyed plant diseases and pests, and increased game populations (particularly deer) by selecting for browsable plants (Cronon 1983: 49–51). Many of these activities would leave few artifactual traces.

Conover's account of the "Indian blacksmith shop" seemed to describe its location fairly exactly, although he does not mention how he recognized it as such. Work with measuring tapes and compass narrowed the possible location of Conover's smithy to a 200 m band along the south side of Burrell Creek. This area was surveyed in 1998 using a metal detector, proton magnetometer, and soil conductivity meter. Area E was isolated as the most likely location for Conover's smithy; it contained three low mounds quite close to Burrell Creek. One of the mounds contained distinct magnetic anomalies, and initial shovel tests and metal-detector samples in Area E recovered one hand-wrought nail and possible iron production debris. Further investigation in 1999 recovered artifacts ranging from a single large chert flake to modern brown bottle glass, but no preserved smithy features or other evidence for eighteenth-century occupation was found (K. Jordan 2001).

An eighteenth-century smithy may indeed have been present at Townley-Read, as documentary sources suggest, but Conover's and Wray's writings appear to be poor guides to its location. Blacksmith facilities may have been placed farther from Burrell Creek than Conover's text implies, possibly in an area that is currently plowed. Although wider use of geophysical testing or systematic metal detection would seem to offer the best means of locating the blacksmith facilities, a smithy would have been near a water source, and thus near subsequent Euro-American field borders and trash dumps. New surveys likely would encounter accumulations of iron fence wire and recent metal trash similar to those that hampered the Project, limiting the effectiveness of metal detection and many geophysical techniques.

Conover's detailed and seemingly precise descriptions of the site's structure initially were alluring, but upon further investigation his narrative proved to intermix hard evidence and speculation without differentiating between the two. In the end Conover provided the project with little more than another cautionary tale about using the writings of nineteenth-century local historians. However, our examination of the Ridgetop supplied the first indications that the internal structure of the Townley-Read site was quite different from that of the Iroquois sites that had preceded it.

Surveys in the East Fields

After no eighteenth-century residential deposits were found on the Ridgetop, the project shifted its focus to the low-lying East Fields at Townley-Read, an area with essentially no defensive value. Wray and others had excavated at least thirty-three eighteenth-century burials in the East Fields during 1979–1982 (Wray n.d.). It was possible that some or all of the eighteenth-century materials there were from mortuary deposits, so the project took a very cautious approach to survey and excavation in the East Fields. Peter Jemison and I thought it inappropriate to use invasive survey techniques (such as shovel testing or soil coring) in an area known to contain cemeteries. The project therefore employed noninvasive survey methods, with good results.

The project experimented with ground-penetrating radar and proton magnetometer surveys (Heimmer and De Vore 1995) and systematic metal detection (Connor and Scott 1998) in the East Fields. However, the most successful method proved to be simple surface examination of the plowed portions of the site. We tried a number of different variations, ranging from point-proveniencing each surface artifact in a given area using a total station to counting artifacts within 20 × 20 m squares. Use of 10 × 10 m collection units with diagnostic artifacts point-provenienced within the site grid appears to offer the best compromise between maximizing the level of detail acquired about spatial relations and minimizing the expenditure of time and resources.

I emphasize that the project conducted surface *investigations*, not surface *collections*. Since our intention was to avoid the disturbance of graves and grave goods, artifacts generally were cataloged in the field and then *left in place* unless they were fairly conclusively determined to be from domestic contexts. Artifact collection and subsequent excavation took place only in definite domestic areas. Butler (1979) has identified a number of limitations to a "no-collection strategy" (see also Beck and Jones 1994). While the project's methodology shares some of the limitations identified by Butler ("nice finds" were left on-site, and some information was lost since artifacts left in the field could not be reexamined), it also differs in fundamental respects from the scenario he critiques. First, only the portions of the site that could not be proven to be domestic were left completely uncollected. Second, a substantial artifact assemblage from mortuary deposits at the site already was available for study at RMSC. Lastly, I felt the concessions made to meet the wishes of the Seneca descendant community were a small price to pay in the development of less colonial forms of archaeology.

A total of 6.5 ha were surface mapped within Areas D and H (K. Jordan 2002: 211–20). These surface investigations located four "Domestic Refuse Clusters" (DRCs), in the eastern portion of the survey area (figure 5.2). DRCs were defined primarily by the surface density of small animal bone and tooth fragments, both burned and unburned; the project designated any 20 × 20 m square in which twenty or more pieces of faunal material were found as a DRC. Seneca women's exploitation of bone marrow and bone grease is likely to be responsible for the highly fragmented character of the food bone refuse found at the site (Watson 2000). The DRCs also contained most of the surface finds of eighteenth-century white ball clay

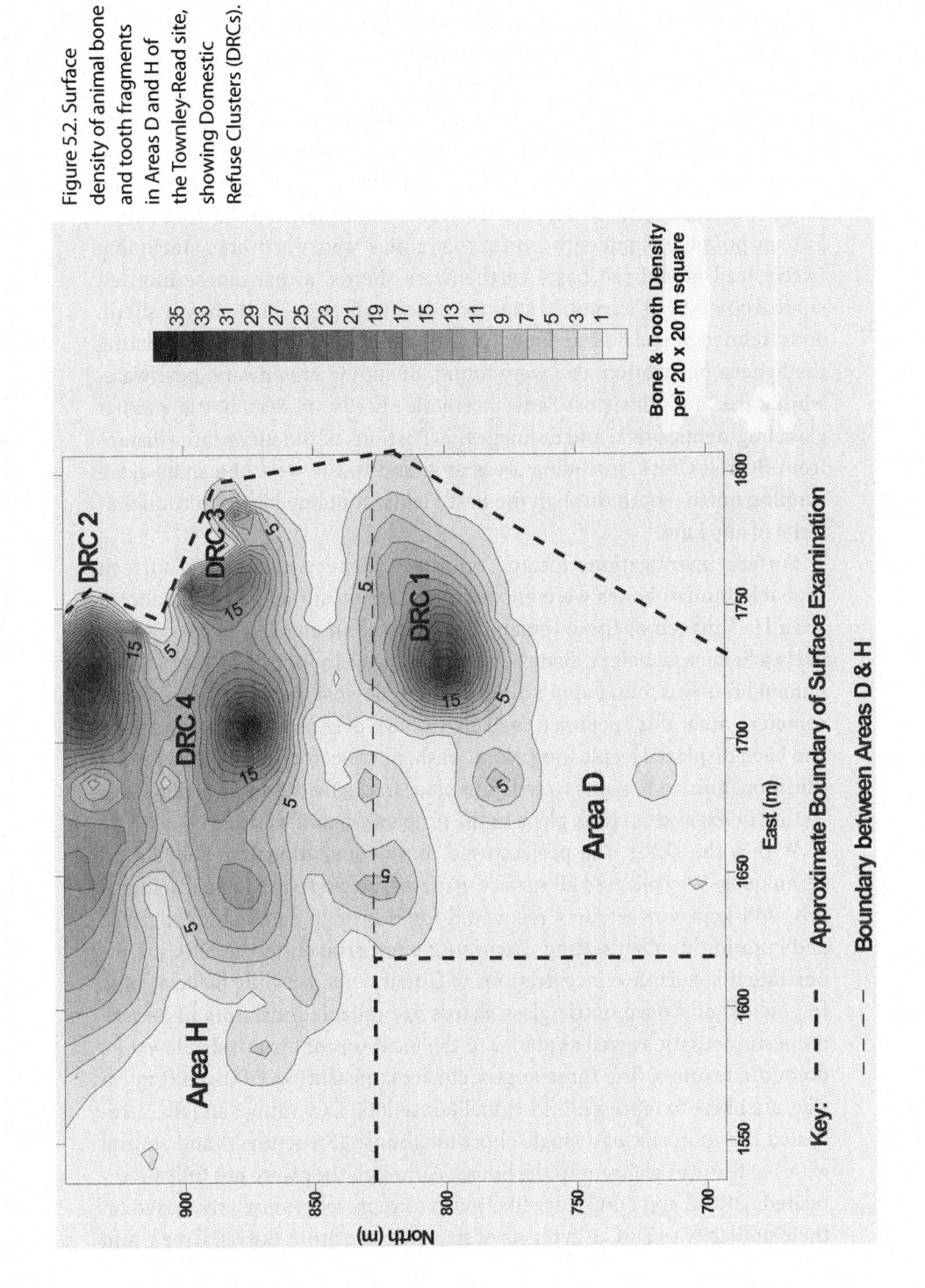

Figure 5.2. Surface density of animal bone and tooth fragments in Areas D and H of the Townley-Read site, showing Domestic Refuse Clusters (DRCs).

smoking pipe and olive bottle glass fragments; these European-made items are almost never found in early eighteenth-century Seneca grave assemblages (K. Jordan 2002: 214).

Other types of cultural material noted during the surface surveys included glass beads; red pipestone and red slate beads and manufacturing debris; lithic debitage and gunflints; Native-made ceramic and stone pipe fragments; iron objects; scrap sheet brass; and marine shell fragments. Fifteen possible eighteenth-century ceramics were recovered, including twelve lead-glazed red paste earthenware sherds, a manganese mottled conical bowl sherd, a combed slip-decorated buff-paste earthenware sherd, and a refined porcelain fragment (Stull 2006). Various materials postdating the Seneca occupation also were found, including creamware, pearlware, whiteware, and other post-Seneca ceramic sherds; modern bottle and flat glass fragments; brick; and drainage tile. Portions of the survey area distant from Burrell Creek, including areas atop and to the west of a small ridge running north–south through the East Fields, contained little cultural material of any kind.

Surface investigations located one likely Seneca cemetery. Fourteen probable human bones were encountered during surface investigation of Area H. Thirteen of these remains were found in an area of 23 × 40 m, likely a Seneca cemetery disturbed by plowing or looting. The one isolated human bone was found approximately 40 m downslope from the probable cemetery area; this specimen is likely to have originated in the cemetery and been displaced by plowing, slope wash, or collector activity. After identification, human remains were left in place in the field, and no artifact collection or excavation took place in the probable cemetery area.

Within the DRCs, the project used more conventional archaeological techniques. We collected all surface artifacts, began to use intrusive methods, and kept any artifacts recovered for thorough cataloging, analysis, and curation in a lab setting. Excavations undertaken in the DRCs demonstrate that surface concentrations of faunal remains, white ball clay pipe fragments, and olive bottle glass shards are reliable indicators of Seneca domestic activity, as well as guides to the locations of intact sub-plowzone domestic features. The three largest clusters, measuring 1100–1700 m^2 in size, are likely to represent individual house lots. Excavations in DRC 1 revealed the footprint of a single short longhouse (Structure 1) and several external features adjacent to the house. Although they were not fully investigated, DRC 2 and DRC 4 are likely also to represent house lots, based on their similarity to DRC 1 in terms of size, distance from Burrell Creek, and placement on the slope leading down to the creek. Excavations in DRC 3 located a midden deposit of at least 15 × 10 m in size, indicating that DRCs cannot automatically be assumed to be houses.

Excavations in Domestic Refuse Cluster 1

The project's most concentrated excavations took place within the 50 × 16 m core of DRC 1 during 1999 (K. Jordan 2002: 224–58). A 10 × 40 m grid of shovel test pits at 5 m intervals, sampling of a set of metal detector "hits" in a separate 10 × 30 m area, and a series of 1 × 1 m test units helped us to locate Post Molds 4 and 5 (later determined to be main support posts for Structure 1) and the large firepit Feature 5. At that point a bulldozer was brought in to strip off the plowzone from an area roughly 14 × 43 m in size (figure 5.3). This enabled us to recover much more information about the broader house lot area than would have been possible using hand excavation alone. Initially, we left an island of plowzone soil around Post Molds 4 and 5 that turned out to enclose just about the entirety of Structure 1; we did not determine the size and alignment of the dwelling until mid-November when this soil was removed by a backhoe. The weather did not permit much more work during the 1999 field season; project archaeologists were able to fully clean and map the structure area (figure 5.4), but the majority of wall posts were not excavated. Although we found several post molds and features likely dating to the eighteenth century outside Structure 1, their positioning was neither dense nor patterned enough to suggest that another structure was present within DRC 1.

Structure 1

The post-mold pattern recovered at the western end of DRC 1 (figure 5.5) is interpreted as the remains of a Seneca "short longhouse" dwelling (see chapter 9 for further analysis of the structure). To date the Townley-Read house is only the fourth full structural plan recovered in the Seneca region from the 1550–1779 period, the others being located at the (1) Factory Hollow (Guthe 1958); (2) Cornish (Hayes 1967); and (3) Ganondagan (Dean 1984) sites.

A total of fifty-three dark, post-mold-sized soil stains were found in the area of the structure. Of these, thirty are interpreted as probable or definite, thirteen as possible, and ten as unlikely eighteenth-century post molds based on their location, color, or the presence of small pieces of bone or charcoal within their fill. Nine probable or definite, four possible, and two

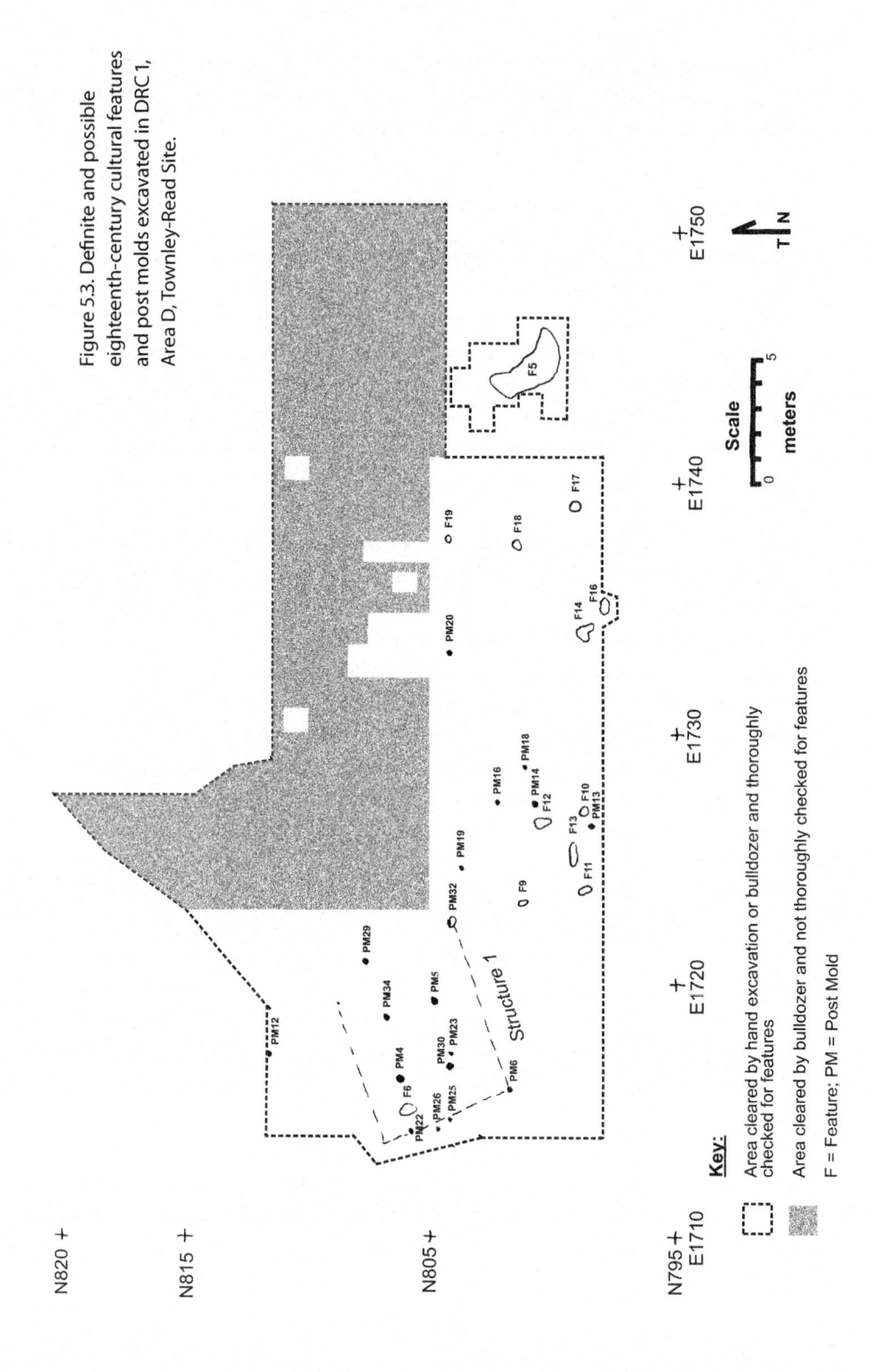

Figure 5.3. Definite and possible eighteenth-century cultural features and post molds excavated in DRC 1, Area D, Townley-Read Site.

Figure 5.4. The author inspects sub-plowzone traces of Structure 1 at the Townley-Read Site, DRC 1 Excavation Trench, Area D, November 1999. Aboveground black markers show locations of large posts; white lines indicate rows of wall posts. (Photo by Pete Vallely.)

unlikely post molds were excavated. Two larger soil stains (Features 6 and 20) were located within the structure area; neither is thought to be cultural. Three smaller unnumbered features not thought to be cultural also were excavated.

As I interpret it (see figure 9.6), Structure 1 at Townley-Read was 5.3 m wide and 7.5 m long. The width measurement is based on the western wall, which contains fourteen definite and two possible posts, five of which were excavated. Post molds were found at close to right angles to the presumed corners of the west wall, making it unlikely that the structure extended beyond the 5.3 m dimension. The length figure has less evidence to support it. The north wall contains six probable posts, none of which was excavated. The south wall is even less substantiated, with only four definite and five possible posts; part of the south wall also was obliterated by a twentieth-century pipe trench (Feature 7). However, the large Post Mold 32 is on the line of the south wall, and its position has been used to mark the eastern end of the structure. Late in the 1999 field season we attempted to chase out the north and south walls and the interior lines established by the two

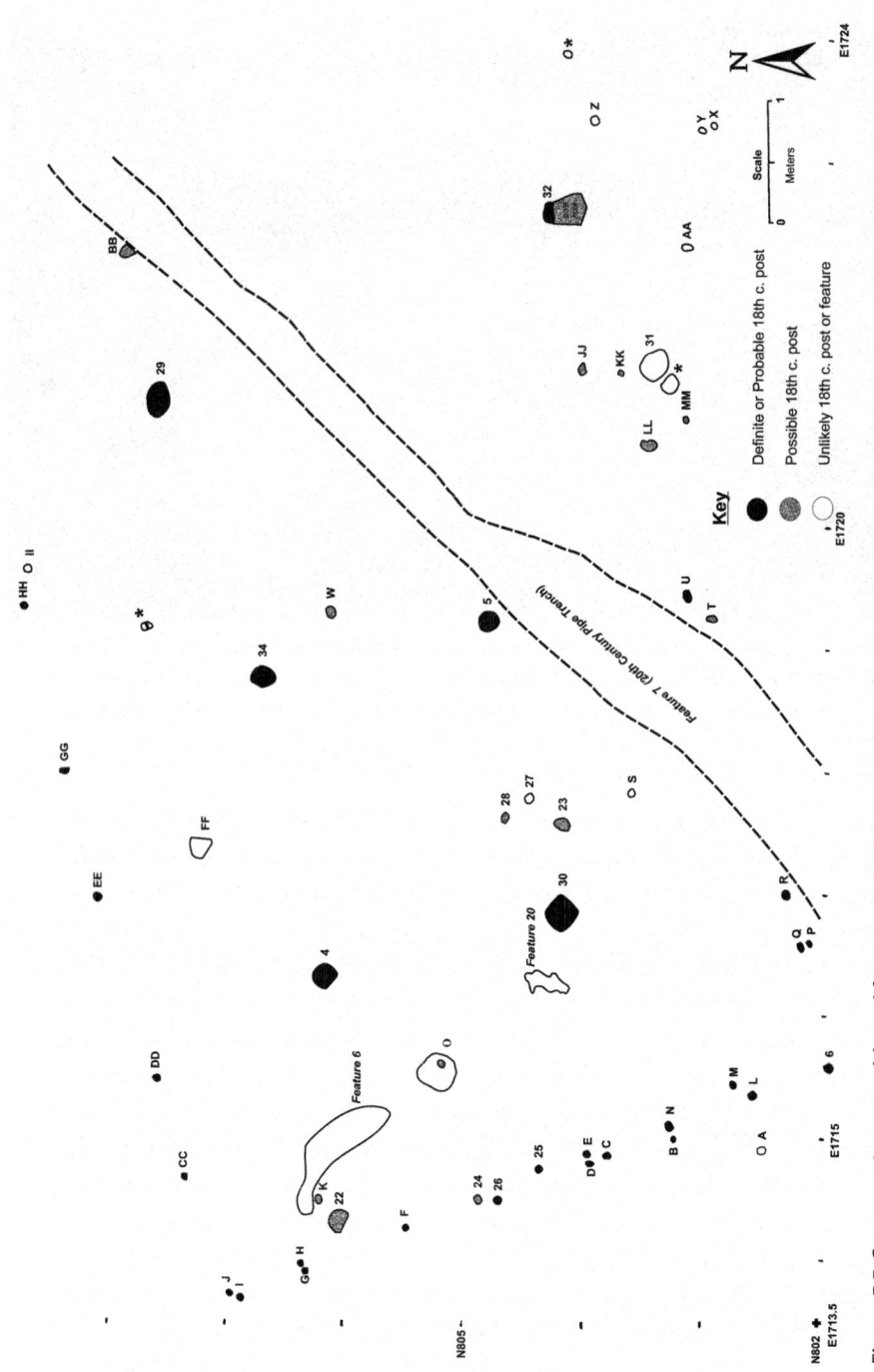

Figure 5.5. Structure 1 post molds and features in DRC 1, Area D, Townley-Read Site (K. Jordan 2003: figure 2). Posts numbered or marked with an asterisk were excavated; posts marked with a letter were not excavated. Portions of Features 6 and 7 were excavated; Feature 20 was not excavated. (Image used courtesy of the New York State Archaeological Association.)

sets of main support posts, but no additional post molds were located. Time constraints did not allow us to clean and map these areas completely, but the lack of any finds of post molds in these areas and the patterning of the post molds recovered makes me reasonably certain that we uncovered the full plan of the house. Based on this interpretation of its size, Townley-Read Structure 1 is defined as a "short longhouse" using Kapches (1984) typology for Iroquoian houses, or less formally, as a "shorthouse." Structure 1 is interpreted as a two-family dwelling based on the presence of four main support posts and a central corridor, which suggest that the house contained two sleeping platforms.

The architecture of the Townley-Read house is in many ways fairly traditional in form. The largest posts are located in the interior of the dwelling, where they provided the main structural support for the house, and presumably framed a central corridor and anchored sleeping platforms. The four main support posts (PMs 4, 5, 30, and 34) ranged from 18 to 23.5 cm in diameter, averaging 19.9 cm, and extended 12–36 cm below subsoil surface; all had rounded bottoms. Three definite small external post molds (PMs 6, 25, and 26) were excavated: these posts extended 11–18 cm below subsoil surface and exhibited both rounded and pointed bottoms. The surface diameters of the thirty-one definite, probable, or possible small wall posts range from 4.0 to 13.0 cm, averaging 6.3 cm.

Post Molds 29 and 32, both of which are located at the eastern extreme of the structure, do not fit either the interior or wall post category particularly well. Both posts are roughly equidistant from the western wall, prompting the interpretation that they formed part of the eastern wall of the house. PM 29, located roughly in line with the northern set of main support posts, was 24.5 cm in diameter but extended only 10 cm below subsoil surface. To date, PM 32 is a unique find at the site: it was a rectangular post 18 cm × 7 cm in size that had been inserted into a dug post hole. Its position in line with the south wall and the fact that we found no similar features makes it almost definite that PM 32 was part of the structure rather than an intrusive feature such as a Euro-American fencepost. Use of these large posts as wall supports represents a departure from the fairly traditional construction methods seen in the rest of the house.

Although we did not recover direct evidence for a central hearth, indirect evidence supports the assumption that one was present. The density of charcoal in the heavy fractions of flotation samples was highest to the east in PMs 32 and 34, intermediate in PMs 5, 6, and 29, and low in western post molds 4 and 30. In contrast, fire-cracked rock was concentrated to the west:

large pieces of fire-cracked rock were present in the matrix of PMs 4 and 30 and smaller pieces were present in PMs 6, 29, and 34. Alternatives to a central hearth (such as a hearthstone fireplace with a chimney or a noncentral firepit) probably would have been located along the doorless western wall, but the low charcoal density in PMs 4, 6, and 30 weighs against this idea.

The contents of post-mold fill recovered by flotation and dry screening with 3 mm mesh hardware cloth provide a solid foundation to the claim that Structure 1 was a domestic dwelling. The post-mold contents have a very "lived in" look, containing many small lost items and artifactual by-products of household activities. Seven of the thirteen excavated possible or probable post molds contained glass seed beads, including all four main support posts and Post Molds 6, 25, 29, and GG. A single tubular, white wampum shell bead was found in the matrix of PM 4. Fish scales were recovered from PMs 4, 6, and 29 and from Feature 6; PM 6 contained a single muskrat tooth; four pieces of sheet brass kettle scrap were found in PM 4; and a single hand-wrought nail was recovered from PM 30.

All four central support posts and PMs 25, 29, and 32 contained maize cupule fragments, and maize kernel fragments were found in PMs 5, 30, and 34. A single bean specimen and gourd rind (*Lagenaria* sp.) fragments were recovered from PM 4; gourd rind also was found in PM 6. Hickory nutshell remains were found in PMs 4, 5, 6, 25, 30, and 32; and butternut remains in PMs 29 and 30. Seeds from wild plants included blackberry or raspberry (*Rubus* sp.), found in PMs 4, 5, and 29; and sumac, recovered from PM 4. Wood charcoal found in the Structure 1 post molds included maple, sycamore, American elm, American chestnut, cedar, and specimens from the red and white oak groups (Rossen 2006).

The western main support posts (PMs 4 and 30) contained significantly more bone remains and artifacts than did the other post molds. Although these posts were larger and were driven deeper into the ground than the other posts within Structure 1, they still showed significant differences in artifact density as well as overall quantity. PM 4 contained 267 faunal specimens (including white-tailed deer bone, fish scales, a muskrat humerus, and the only porcupine specimen recovered by the project) while PM 30 contained 500 pieces of bone (including raccoon maxilla fragments, a deer metacarpal, and fish ribs) and a raccoon tooth (Adam Watson, personal communication, 2007). Heidenreich (1971: 154) and Snow (1995: 100, 124) interpret post molds filled with large pieces of refuse as evidence that these posts were pulled when the structure was abandoned. Following this argument, the high concentrations of bone in PMs 4 and 30 suggest that they were removed while the others rotted in place. PMs 4 and 30 were clearly structural supports (in contrast to Snow's contention that only decorated, nonstructural posts were pulled at abandonment); their removal would imply that the house was at least partially dismantled when it was vacated or at some subsequent point.

Plowzone soil from the Structure 1 area contained a variety of material types (see K. Jordan n.d. for a full inventory). Consumption behavior was indicated by animal bone and tooth remains (including specimens identified as white-tailed deer and black bear), two eighteenth-century olive bottle glass fragments, and Native-made and European white ball clay ceramic pipe fragments. Complete costume items consisted of two drawn round black glass beads and a rolled sheet brass cone bangle. Possible manufacturing debris includes one burned blue-and-white glass pendant fragment that appears to have been discarded during production, a tabular fragment of red slate, one shell fragment, and six pieces of scrap sheet brass.[2] Other artifacts consisted of one sheet brass projectile point; fourteen possible eighteenth-century ceramic sherds (thirteen European-made red or red-buff paste earthenware sherds and one possible Native-made sherd [Stull 2006]); two pieces of clear flat glass that may be mirror fragments; iron nails and objects of indeterminate function; charcoal; ten pieces of lithic debitage; fire-cracked rock; and assorted intrusive nineteenth- and twentieth-century materials.

The density of bone and tooth fragments recovered from the plowzone was significantly higher in test units excavated in the eastern half of the structure than in the western half (K. Jordan 2002: table 5.2). The higher bone density to the east may reflect refuse dumping or bone-related activity (such as the smashing of bones for marrow and grease extraction) immediately outside the eastern door of the structure or in a vestibule area for which no architectural traces were recovered. This pattern provides additional support for the claim that Structure 1 terminated near PMs 29 and 32.

In addition to the hand-wrought nail found within the matrix of PM 30, nine definite hand-wrought nails and four possible hand-wrought nail fragments were recovered from plowzone contexts within Structure 1. These nail finds (particularly the in situ find in the post mold) provide conclusive evidence that nails were used in the construction of Structure 1 (see chapter 8 and table 8.2). The lack of sub-plowzone pits within the structure may mean that most or all of the household's storage was aboveground, possibly in bark "casks" similar to those described by Lafitau (Fenton and Moore 1977: 21) and Morgan (1962 [1851]: 318).

Feature 5

The project recovered the traces of a large outdoor firepit 21.5 m east of Structure 1 (see figure 5.3). There is strong evidence that this firepit, termed Feature 5, was used predominantly for fur and skin processing and bone marrow and grease exploitation, with a secondary focus on the preparation of plant and animal foods (K. Jordan 2002: 236–48; Rossen 2006; Watson 2000, 2007). Feature 5 was 3.5 m in length and 1.7 m across at its widest point, and it extended to a depth of 43 cm below subsoil surface. The firepit contained four main sub-plowzone stratigraphic levels (figure 5.6). The upper two strata (I and II, labeled A–C on the figure) definitely can be linked to the eighteenth-century Seneca occupation and will be the focus of this discussion. Lighter-colored Stratum III (labeled D) contained a very low concentration of artifacts and animal bones, but did incorporate a wide variety of plant remains, including maize cupules, squash seeds, gourd rinds, grass seeds, cherry pits, blackberry/raspberry and sumac seeds, and charcoal from hardwood branches (Rossen 2006). Stratum IV (labeled E) represents an earlier cultural use of the feature that did not involve concentrated processing of animal or plant remains; the botanical sample from Stratum IV contained only wood charcoal and fungus (Rossen 2006). The plowzone soil lying above the feature contained a very high density of faunal remains (K. Jordan 2002: table 5.2), suggesting that Feature 5 was originally larger and deeper and that its upper portions were destroyed by plowing.

The uppermost layer, Stratum I, was about 8 cm thick at its maximum extent. It consisted of several circular concentrations and lenses of ash about 75 cm in diameter and contained substantial amounts of faunal material (2281 specimens were recovered via dry screening and flotation). Stratum II, 19 cm thick in total, consisted of an intentionally created platform of fire-cracked rock intermixed with black soil and charcoal. Dense bone concentration continued in Stratum II, with 1754 faunal specimens recovered. Both levels had fire-related functions, with Stratum II perhaps acting as a platform supporting several small fires in Stratum I. Both levels also served as trash dumps.

The upper two strata were likely to have been created fairly close in time to one another, based on Watson's (2000) determination that an *Ursus americanus* (black bear) maxilla fragment from Stratum I mended with a

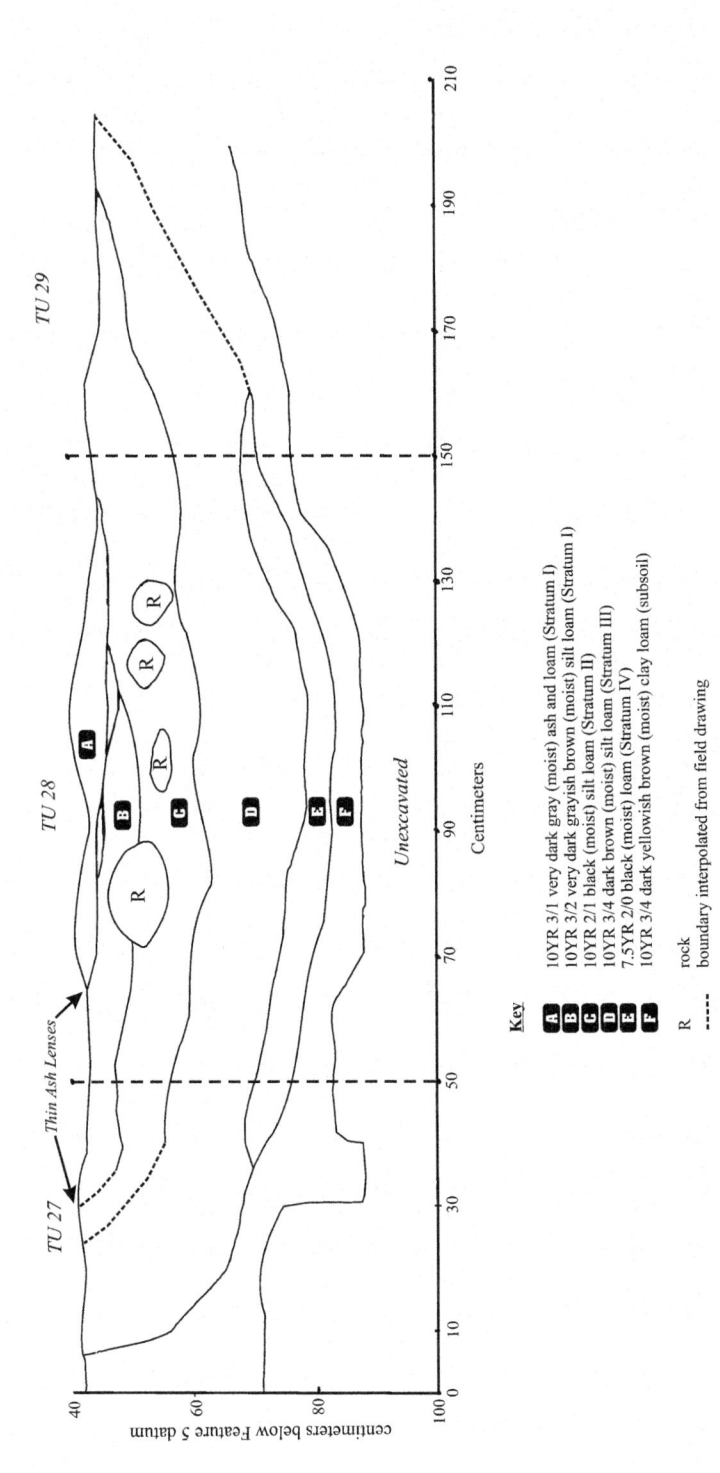

Figure 5.6. Profile of Feature 5, DRC 1, Area D, Townley-Read Site. Profile is shown only for in situ portions of feature below the plow zone.

zygomatic fragment from Stratum II. These layers also contained all of the diagnostic eighteenth-century artifactual material recovered within Feature 5. Stratum I contained sheet brass scrap fragments; three white glass seed beads; two iron fragments; a white ball clay pipe bowl fragment; one small piece of patinated glass; and a complete 4.9 cm tubular shell bead. Stratum II contained a white ball clay pipe bowl fragment; one battered Native-made ceramic sherd; a very large wire-wound (amber?) glass bead fragment; one white glass seed bead; and a second complete tubular shell bead, this example being 10.8 cm long. The complete shell beads in the upper two strata also may tie the levels together in time. That these valued shell artifacts ended up in a feature that otherwise appears to be a trash deposit perhaps can be accounted for by a single episode of loss, possibly the breakage of a necklace while the wearer was working in the area. An account from Oneida territory in the 1660s suggests that Iroquois people expressed grief through "casting off all the adornments" (Brandão 2003: 97), perhaps providing an alternative explanation. Stratum I soil contained a single piece of aqua flat glass, which based on its thickness and overall uniformity is likely to postdate the Seneca occupation. This was the only intrusive artifact found within the feature.

Feature 5 provided a diverse and well-preserved sample of faunal remains. Table 5.2 presents the faunal assemblage from Strata I and II, which have been analytically combined based on the mendable bear cranial fragments and the two complete shell beads. Strata I and II contain representatives of half of the species identified at Townley-Read to date. When species recovered from mixed contexts within the feature (medium-sized mustelid) or from the plowzone soil above and presumably plowed out of Feature 5—pig (*Sus scrofa*) and fisher (*Martes pennanti*)—are factored in, Feature 5 essentially presents Seneca faunal use at the site in microcosm.

Butchering marks and the recovery of limb, vertebra, rib, or pelvis fragments indicate that some of the white-tailed deer, beaver, and raccoon remains found in Strata I and II probably were processed for meat (Watson 2000). Since all these animals were of value in the fur trade, Senecas likely also used these individuals for their hides or pelts (Watson 2000). The bird, fish, and amphibian remains found in Strata I and II probably also represent food remains, while the meadow vole tooth may have been introduced by natural burrowing.

Only 16 percent (11 of 68) of the deer specimens recovered from Strata I and II were axial skeleton elements, and 66 percent (45 of 68) were cranial bones, foot bones, or teeth. This body part distribution suggests that

Table 5.2. Faunal Remains Found In Situ in Strata I and II of Feature 5, Townley-Read Site

Description	Cranial Bone	Vertebra	Rib	Pelvic Bone	Limb Bone[a]	Foot Bone[b]	Tooth	Unknown	Total
White-tailed deer (*Odocoileus virginianus*)	2	3	4	4	12	34	9	0	68
Raccoon (*Procyon lotor*)	0	0	0	2	1	3	0	0	6
Black bear (*Ursus americanus*)	4	0	0	0	0	1	0	0	5
Beaver (*Castor canadensis*)	2	0	0	0	1	0	0	0	3
Passenger pigeon (*Ectopistes migratorius*)	0	0	0	0	3	0	0	0	3
Gray fox (*Urocyon cinereoargenteus*)	1	0	0	0	0	1	0	0	2
Martes sp. (incl. 1 *Martes americanus* spec.)	0	0	0	0	0	2	0	0	2
Cow (*Bos taurus*)	0	0	0	0	0	1	0	0	1
Domestic dog (*Canis familiaris*)	0	0	0	0	0	1	0	0	1
Meadow vole (*Microtus pennsylvanicus*)	0	0	0	0	0	0	1	0	1
Ruffed grouse (*Bonasa umbellus*)	0	0	0	0	1	0	0	0	1
Deer-sized mammal	1	2	1	1	1	1	0	0	7
Hare-sized mammal	0	1	0	0	0	0	0	0	1
Small carnivore	0	0	0	0	1	0	0	0	1
Rodent	4	0	0	0	0	0	0	0	4
Mammal, indeterminate	23	9	33	0	97	0	43	2993	3198
Bird, indeterminate	1	8	0	0	5	1	0	0	15
Fish, indeterminate	1	27	0	0	0	0	0	45	73
Amphibian, indeterminate	0	0	0	0	4	0	0	1	5
Non-mammalian, indeterminate	0	0	0	0	0	0	0	130	130
Indeterminate/unidentified	0	0	0	0	0	0	0	508	508
Total	39	50	38	7	126	45	53	3677	4035

Source: adapted from Watson (2007)

Notes: a. Limb bone category includes long bones and scapula fragments.
b. Foot bone category includes carpals, tarsals, metacarpals, metatarsals, and phalanges.

many of these deer remains were introduced into the area while attached to skins (see Lapham 2005: 90–93; Perkins and Daly 1968: 104). The axial bones of these deer individuals (vertebrae, ribs, and pelvic bones) appear to have been disposed of elsewhere, while cranial and foot remains were removed from the skins during dressing at Feature 5 (Watson 2000, 2007; Nerissa Russell, personal communication, 2001). Rib fragments usually are identifiable even when broken into small pieces; that only thirty-eight rib fragments were found in Strata I and II provides strong evidence that the overall body part distribution was not merely the result of axial bones being highly fragmented and thus unrecognizable.

Black bear, gray fox, cow, domestic dog, and marten/fisher are represented only by cranial or foot bones within Feature 5, which again suggests hide or pelt processing. The large number of cranial fragments in the feature provides another potential link to deer-hide preparation. American Indians used the boiled brains of "any animal" (particularly deer or dog) or "the backbone of the elk" as a tanning solution during the processing of deerskins (Morgan in Tooker 1994: 115–16).[3] Black bear, beaver, white-tailed deer, and gray fox cranial fragments were recovered from Feature 5. The black bear cranial bones (representing two individuals) showed "no sign of burning or roasting, suggesting that the cranium was discarded after the extraction of the brains" (Watson 2000: 43). These bears' brains may have been used for deer-hide processing.

The vast majority of the bone material in the upper layers of Feature 5 was highly fragmented. Average bone weights from the flotation samples ranged from 0.09–0.81 g per piece. Weathering patterns show that the bones were broken up shortly before their burial in the feature, and there is little evidence of gnawing or digestion. As first recognized by Watson (2000), this high degree of predepositional fragmentation of both long and cancellous bone material appears to be most consistent with marrow extraction and bone grease rendering (see Outram 2001, 2003).

Botanical remains recovered from Strata I and II included maize cupules and kernels, squash seeds and peduncles, gourd rinds, hickory and butternut shells, and a possible hazelnut specimen. One flotation sample from Stratum I contained more than 1200 maize cupule specimens. Seeds recovered from these strata included blackberry or raspberry (*Rubus* sp.), grass, hackberry, cherry (*Prunus* sp.), sumac, grape, small-seeded nightshade, morning glory, and hawthorn. Wood charcoal included maple, ash, American chestnut, sycamore, pine, cedar, and red oak group specimens, with maple predominant.

The faunal and artifactual materials recovered from the plowzone above Feature 5 are of the same character as those found in situ within Strata I and II. Faunal remains include specimens of white-tailed deer, beaver, raccoon, fisher, pig, and undetermined fish and bird species. Artifacts consisted of a variety of brass artifacts (including a Jesuit-style heart-shaped ring plaque, two sheet brass projectile points, and a mouth harp fragment), three glass beads, one olive bottle glass fragment, and both European white ball clay and Native-made ceramic smoking pipe fragments.

Of particular interest are eleven iron nail fragments (seven definitely and four possibly hand-wrought) and an aqua crown flat glass fragment (sometimes used in windows) that were found in the plowzone above Feature 5. While these nominally architectural items could indicate that some sort of structure was in the immediate vicinity of the feature, the large dimensions of Feature 5 make it unlikely that it was an indoor firepit, and no sub-plowzone architectural features (such as post molds) were found in the area. A more plausible explanation is that the nails and crown glass fragment were included with the trash materials dumped in Feature 5 or that wood embedded with nails was used for fuel.

In sum, a variety of evidence suggests that Feature 5 Strata I and II were used for the intertwined purposes of hide processing and bone marrow and grease exploitation (see "Animal Use and Men's and Women's Labor at Townley-Read" in chapter 10 for further discussion) as well as for the processing of plant and animal foods. Both layers also served as a trash dump, primarily for the discard of bone- and plant-processing by-products.

General House Lot Area

In what can be considered the house lot area (that is, the area outside Structure 1 and away from Feature 5), twelve feature-sized and eighteen postmold-sized dark soil stains were uncovered and excavated (figure 5.3) and a sizable assemblage of artifacts was recovered from the plowzone. Discussion here concentrates only on those features and posts that are likely to be cultural in origin.[4]

Sub-plowzone finds of diagnostic eighteenth-century material culture were relatively rare in the house lot area. Given that even some very small posts within Structure 1 contained eighteenth-century materials, their absence from most of the exterior features and post molds (even some of significant size) is somewhat puzzling. Although it is possible that the features and posts without diagnostic material are the remnants of Precolumbian activity, it is more likely that they derive from short-term, specialized eighteenth-century usage. Signature eighteenth-century artifacts would be unlikely to collect at the bottoms of limited-use features. The eighteenth-century hypothesis is strengthened by the proximity of the features and posts to Structure 1 and Feature 5 and by the absence of any diagnostic Precolumbian finds in Area D.

Aside from Feature 5, the most substantial features and post molds in DRC 1 clustered to the southeast of the short longhouse; this grouping includes Features 10, 13, and 14 and Post Molds 13, 14, 16, 18, and 19. Feature 10, a shallow bowl-shaped pit 30 cm in diameter and extending 15.5 cm below subsoil surface, contained scrap brass fragments, two glass seed beads, and a ceramic glaze chip from a European-made vessel, as well as faunal material, a single small Native-made ceramic sherd, fire-cracked rock, sycamore charcoal, and two maize cupule fragments. Feature 13 (96 cm across and extending 20 cm into subsoil) and Feature 14 (97 cm across and extending 38 cm into subsoil) were both regularly shaped, fire-related features with three stratigraphic layers interpreted as repeatedly used, special-purpose hearths; they contained small bone fragments (in low quantities), chert debris, fire-cracked rock, coal, burned noncultural chert, and sycamore wood charcoal. Feature 13 contained one black walnut shell fragment, while Feature 14 contained a maize cupule and blackberry or raspberry seed (Rossen 2006).

Post Molds 13, 14, and 16 were tubular soil stains of 19–23 cm in diameter that were heavily disturbed by rodents, but their contents suggest that they were cultural features. PM 14 contained the most material, consisting of bone fragments (including white-tailed deer and eastern cottontail rabbit specimens), a single squash seed, gourd rind, blackberry or raspberry seeds, and wood charcoal derived from American elm, maple, American chestnut, and trees of the red oak group. Flotation samples from PMs 13 and 16 contained low bone and charcoal densities. Charcoal in each of these posts was exclusively from sycamore wood, and PM 13 also contained five fragments of gourd rind (Rossen 2006). Post Mold 18 was 8 cm in diameter at subsoil surface and extended 23 cm into subsoil to a somewhat pointed base; its matrix included a piece of a white ball clay pipe bowl and a white-tailed deer tooth fragment. PM 19 (9 cm in diameter and extending 25.5 cm into subsoil to a pointed base) contained bone, chert debris, one scrap sheet brass fragment, a blackberry or raspberry seed, and maple charcoal.

Farther to the east, the shallow, oval-shaped dark soil stain Feature 16 (60 cm across, extending 6 cm into subsoil) contained bone, small coal fragments, charcoal, seeds, and a single Native-made ceramic sherd. Feature 18 was a bowl-shaped pit 32 cm across that extended 11 cm into B-horizon soil; it contained a fairly high density of bone remains, one tooth fragment, fire-cracked rock, chert debris, and charcoal. Feature 19 was a mottled, tubular soil stain with a very regular negative impression; it measured 21 cm in diameter and extended 16 cm into subsoil. This feature contained bone, chert debris (including a flake fragment), fire-cracked rock, and snail shells. It is possible that this stain represented the traces of a large post that had been pulled out. Post Mold 20 (18 cm in diameter and extending at least 15 cm into subsoil) had been disturbed by rodents but its profile exhibited sufficient cultural characteristics to determine that it was an eighteenth-century feature; its bottom depth and base shape could not be determined due to the rodent activity. PM 20 contained a purple wampum shell bead, substantial bone remains, one fish scale, chert debris, and snail shells. Botanical remains from PM 20 included maize kernels and cupules, a single bean specimen, hickory nutshell, blackberry/raspberry and sumac seeds, and American chestnut and maple charcoal (Rossen 2006).

To the north of the structure, Post Mold 12 was deemed too small to yield a flotation sample, and screened soil did not contain any artifactual material; it is interpreted as a probable to definite post mold based on its very well-preserved shape. This post was 9 cm in diameter and extended 26 cm into subsoil, where it terminated in a pointed base.

Only Feature 10 and Post Mold 20 contain indications of generalized domestic activity similar to those in Structure 1 and Feature 5, reflected by a broad range of artifactual, faunal, and botanical materials. Feature 10 and Post Mold 20 are isolated from Structure 1 and each other. There do not seem to be enough features with domestic signatures nor is the overall distribution of features and post molds outside Structure 1 sufficiently patterned to suggest that another dwelling was present in the DRC 1 trench area.

The most concentrated evidence for extramural Seneca activity was found to the southeast of the house, in the vicinity of Features 13 and 14.[5] The location of these hearths downwind and downslope from Structure 1 may mean that they were cooking fires placed to keep heat and smoke away from the house. The fact that none of the features in the vicinity of Feature 10 exhibited anything close to its range of material types suggests that Feature 10 was used during a different season or even year than the other features. The probable to definite post molds—PMs 12, 13, 14, 16, 18, 19, and 20—are not spatially patterned and do not provide substantial evidence for activity areas; incorporation of the possible large pulled post Feature 19 does not change this picture. Only PM 20 contained archaeological materials reflective of a range of activities, but the food-preparation and burning in evidence around PM 20 appear to have taken place in relative isolation from other features.

Plowzone artifacts recovered in the general house lot area analytically were separated based on their proximity to Structure 1 (K. Jordan n.d.). In the immediate exterior of Structure 1, plowzone finds included animal bone fragments, one white ball clay pipe stem, one glass bead, possibly eighteenth-century red paste earthenware and intrusive ceramic sherds, five possible or definite hand-wrought nail fragments, lithic debitage, one fire-cracked rock, and charcoal. The shovel tests with the densest concentrations of bone in the house lot area were located on the exterior margins of Structure 1, which may indicate that bone processing (potentially the fragmentation of bones for marrow and grease extraction) or refuse dumping took place just outside the house.

Contexts more distant from Structure 1 showed lower food bone density and (less predictably) an increased number of white ball clay smoking pipe remains. Plowzone artifacts from these areas included scrap sheet brass, white ball clay pipe stem and bowl fragments (including two bowls bearing Tippet maker's marks), three possibly eighteenth-century ceramic sherds (one each of red-paste earthenware, porcelain, and 1745–1790 Jackfield [Stull 2006]), six glass beads, olive and emerald green bottle glass, lithic debitage, one red pipestone fragment (possibly manufacturing debris), two shell fragments, and intrusive post-Seneca ceramics, drainage tile, brick, bottle and flat glass, and iron wire. Fifteen possible to definite iron nails were recovered from the general house lot, of which only one (a cut nail) conclusively could be proven to be intrusive. The find of a probable iron pistol-barrel segment crushed at one end (possibly for use as a scraper; see Wray 1973: 22) may indicate that some hide-processing activity took place to the south of Structure 1. Faunal remains from the general house lot area included specimens identified as white-tailed deer and a single pig tooth.

Excavations in Domestic Refuse Cluster 2

Excavations in DRC 2 followed the model established in DRC 1 (for map, see K. Jordan 2002: figure 5.7). A grid of shovel test pits (STPs) at 5 m intervals was dug over the entire 20 × 20 m area, and an additional six shovel tests were dug to investigate anomalies located by magnetometer survey. Cultural material was found in twenty-nine of the thirty-one STPs; animal bone or tooth fragments and chert debitage were the most common materials found. Five test units were dug to investigate high concentrations of cultural material or possible features existing below the plowzone. Three possible cultural features (Features 21–23) and one post-mold-sized stain unlikely to be a cultural feature were located.

Feature 21, an obvious hearth found near the center of the DRC, was an oval-shaped concentration of ash and charcoal 42.5 cm long that extended 6 cm below subsoil surface. Feature soil (all of which was taken for flotation) contained 128 bone and 8 tooth fragments (including one red fox [*Vulpes vulpes*] tooth), 4 fish scales, and other items. Botanical remains from the feature included maize cupules and kernels, a blackberry/raspberry seed, and maple charcoal. No fire-cracked rock was found within Feature 21 or in the plowzone soil above it, indicating that it was probably an informal, short-term hearth. A tubular red pipestone bead reject of 0.8 cm length was found at the interface between the plowzone and subsoil quite near the feature, and a complete 1.4 cm long triangular red pipestone bead and a probable eighteenth-century mirror fragment were recovered from a test unit dug immediately to the northeast.

Features 22 and 23 were small soil stains, neither of which contained definite eighteenth-century materials. Soil from each feature contained bone fragments and chert debris; Feature 22 contained two fish scales, a hickory nutshell, fire-cracked rock, and charcoal from the white oak group. Feature 23 contained two pieces of possible coal cinder.

Plowzone artifacts from DRC 2 consisted of animal bone and tooth fragments (including specimens identified as white-tailed deer, pig, domestic dog, beaver, and raccoon), one piece of sheet scrap brass, both Native- and European-made ceramic pipe fragments, one glass bead, one piece of olive bottle glass, the possible eighteenth-century mirror fragment, three possible or definite hand-wrought nails, one large piece of iron slag, an elongated lead fragment, a possible chert engraving tool, chert debitage, a lithic whetstone, two pieces of red pipestone, and assorted materials postdating the Seneca occupation.

The limited amount of excavation in DRC 2 permits few conclusions to be drawn about eighteenth-century activities there; further investigation (particularly in the central portion of the area) certainly is warranted. Excavations may have caught the edges of two or more areas of domestic activity, such as a house lot (possibly to the west) and a midden (possibly to the east), with the main parts of these deposits lying outside the sampled area. The evidence for red pipestone ornament manufacture in the central portion of the area likely indicates that a domestic structure was in close proximity to, if not directly within, DRC 2.

Excavations in Domestic Refuse Cluster 3

Excavations in DRC 3 (figure 5.7) commenced with a 5 × 5 m grid of shovel tests; ten additional STPs were dug to the east to test the area closer to Burrell Creek for cultural deposits. Thirty-three of the thirty-five shovel test-pits recovered cultural material. While the shovel tests in the western portion of DRC 3 revealed typical plowzone depths of 26–36 cm, most of the shovel tests in the eastern portion found deep organic deposits that appear to have been produced by extensive sediment deposition. Since the eastern part of DRC 3 is both fairly flat and at the base of a slope, it is a likely destination for wind- or water-moved sediments.

Six shovel tests in the northeastern portion of DRC 3 located a very dark grayish brown–to–black, artifact-laden horizon below the modern plowzone, with a bottom depth of 47–55 cm below ground surface. Subsequent excavations determined that this dark layer (designated the Buried Plowed Midden, or BPM, horizon) likely is the remains of an eighteenth-century Seneca midden that was plowed during the early part of the post-1789 Euro-American occupation. All nine test units in DRC 3 were placed to investigate this buried dark horizon. Farther to the east, ten shovel tests revealed deep organic soil ranging from 37 to 59 cm below surface with no visible internal stratigraphy (that is, buried soil was the same as or close to the color of the modern plowzone). Almost certainly all of this stratum had been plowed as well; the portions of it below 35 cm in depth are interpreted as a buried plowzone.

Most of the sediments deposited at the base of the slope likely were displaced as a consequence of Euro-American tree clearance, stump removal, and farming at the site shortly after 1789. It appears that in the early years of Euro-American cultivation, most or all of the Seneca ground surface in DRC 3 was disturbed by plowing. Subsequently, colluvial deposition of sediment at the slope base (slopewash) occurred, to a thickness where modern plowing churns only washed-in sediments and not the sediment that originally made up the eighteenth-century ground surface. Given the level of preservation seen in the lower portion of the organic strata in DRC 3, it is probable that the buried organic horizon soils were capped off only a few years after Euro-Americans began to alter the landscape and therefore were not subject to Euro-American plowing for a great length of time. The variation present in the thickness of organic deposition at the bottom of the slope probably is the result of the filling in of natural declivities.

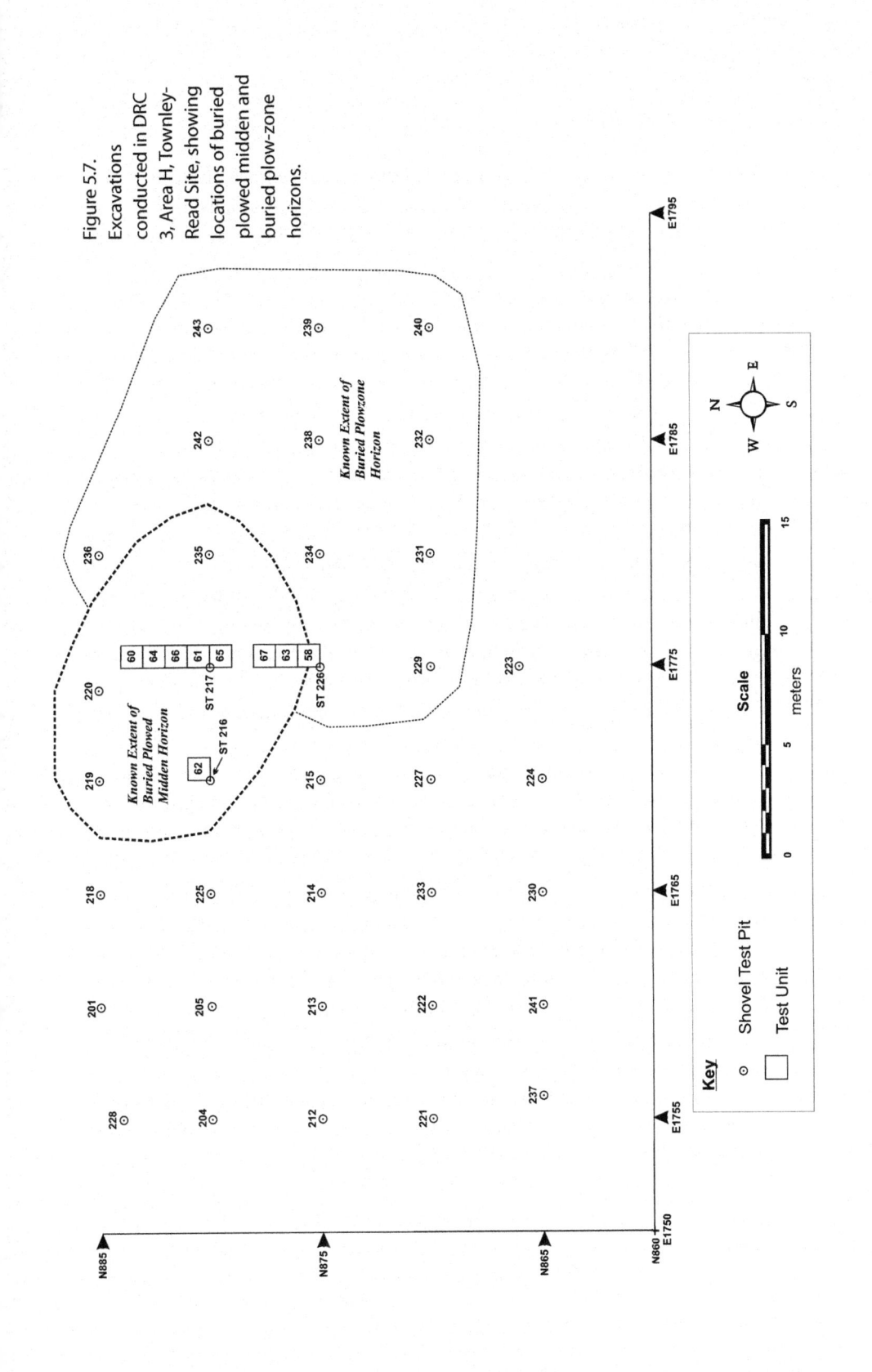

Figure 5.7. Excavations conducted in DRC 3, Area H, Townley-Read Site, showing locations of buried plowed midden and buried plow-zone horizons.

Buried Plowed Midden

Shovel test pits and test units indicated that the BPM horizon measured at least 15 × 10 m in size (figure 5.7). Since the horizon initially appeared to be an intact eighteenth-century deposit, a conservative excavation strategy employing 5 cm thick arbitrary excavation levels, 3 mm mesh hardware cloth for screening, and frequent flotation samples was adopted (figure 5.8). Although the plow scars discovered at the base of the horizon on the penultimate day of excavation proved that the deposit had been plowed, these techniques still provided us with a fine-grained body of data from the BPM. The horizon increased in thickness from 4–5 cm in the southern excavation units to 20–23 cm thickness in the northernmost units. This suggests that the BPM horizon, and perhaps underlying in situ portions of the midden, may extend for some distance to the north of the excavated area.

The types of materials found in the BPM locus included animal bone and tooth fragments, scrap sheet brass and other brass artifacts, European and Native-made ceramic pipe fragments, a limited number of ceramic sherds (most intrusive), glass beads, bottle glass, one possibly Native-made glass pendant fragment, iron hardware, a limited amount of lithic debitage, two lithic core/hammerstones, a single biconcave red pipestone bead, fire-cracked rock, fish scales, charcoal, seeds, nutshell fragments, and small bits of coal. Some evidence for metal production was recovered from flotation samples; namely, two small globular pieces of lead and two pieces of slag.

Faunal and botanical remains recovered from the BPM all appear to relate to the Seneca occupation of the site. Faunal material recovered from above or within the BPM contained specimens identified as white-tailed deer, beaver, pig, bird, cow, domestic dog, gray fox, black bear, mink-sized mustelid, and the only whistling swan (*Cygnus columbianus*) specimen found at the site to date. Botanical remains (Rossen 2006) included maize cupules and kernels, gourd (*Lagenaria* sp.) rinds, blackberry or raspberry (*Rubus* sp.) and elderberry seeds, and hickory and butternut shells. Wood charcoal specimens were identified as sycamore, maple, pine, American elm, and wood from the red oak group.

This deposit is interpreted as a midden, based primarily on the density of faunal remains recovered. Bone and tooth density in the modern plowzone over the BPM (139.7 pieces/m^3) was somewhat less than that found above the Feature 5 work area and trash deposit (193.5 pieces/m^3), and somewhat greater than that found above the work and habitation area in the eastern portion of Structure 1 (111.6 pieces/m^3). Several factors may explain why

Figure 5.8. Hobart and William Smith students at work in the Buried Plowed Midden area, DRC 3, Area H, Townley-Read Site, May 2000. Note the proximity of the area to Burrell Creek, represented by the line of trees in the background. (Photo by the author.)

the BPM density figure is lower than that for Feature 5: (1) the concentrated nutrient extraction and hide processing that took place around Feature 5 may have resulted in a refuse assemblage that contained a higher proportion of faunal remains than the generalized household trash deposited in the BPM; (2) the BPM was disturbed by Euro-American plowing, and materials within it were subject to post-depositional exposure, breakage, and destruction that the in situ remains in Feature 5 did not experience; and (3) the modern plowzone above the BPM consists in part of sediments that washed in from lightly occupied areas to the west. The BPM faunal materials also are on average far smaller than those found in Feature 5. Average bone specimen weights from the BPM flotation samples ranged from 0.01–0.05 g per piece. In contrast, the four flotation samples from the bone-bearing levels of Feature 5 (Strata I and II) had average specimen weights of 0.09–0.81 g per piece. Some of this difference is attributable to the post-depositional breakage and weathering that took place when the BPM deposit was plowed, but it also is likely that Senecas intensively processed the bone that ended up in the BPM, and that some breakage and weathering took place when the DRC 3 trash deposits were open to the air during the Seneca occupation.

In most cases a greater diversity of forms and material subtypes was found in the BPM than in DRCs 1 and 2. For example, bottle glass fragments recovered from the BPM included not only olive glass but also emerald green, aqua green, and light blue-green varieties.[6] Both Native-made and European ceramics were found, including seven small, worn sherds of indigenous pottery and one red paste earthenware sherd; the plowzone above the BPM yielded a small piece of tin-glazed, buff paste earthenware. All eight Native-made pipe fragments recovered appear to derive from separate pipes.

In some material categories, the range of types found in the BPM was narrower than in DRCs 1 and 2. All of the iron recovered consisted of hardware forms (eight possible or definite nail fragments, one spike, and one possible hinge fragment). Twenty-six of the twenty-seven glass beads recovered from the BPM locus were small- or medium-sized circular drawn beads (22 white, 3 clear redwood, and 1 black). One fragment of a very large pale blue wire-wound bead also was recovered. The small- and medium-sized beads are classified as embroidery beads using criteria set out by Silliman (2004: 146). The homogeneity of the BPM bead assemblage and its distinctiveness when compared to beads from other parts of the site suggest that it may be the by-product of beading activities, rather than representing lost or discarded items. Aside from the whistling swan and mustelid specimens, the faunal assemblage contains species found relatively commonly in the rest of the site. The range of materials in a communal deposit consistently should exceed that found in an individual household deposit (B. Smith 2001). That the BPM assemblage is not consistently more diverse than the single-household deposits in DRC 1 may indicate that the BPM also represents refuse from one household.

The finding of plow scars at the base of the BPM proves that the midden deposit was plowed. Additionally, the BPM deposit was relatively homogenous throughout, with no visible internal stratigraphy; the two features found in DRC 3 (Feature 24 and Post Mold 36) both became visible only beneath the BPM horizon. Intrusive, post-Seneca artifacts were found in the modern plowzone above the BPM, but Euro-American plow disturbance does not seem to have introduced a substantial amount of non-Seneca material into the BPM itself. The only artifacts from the BPM identified as definitely post-Seneca were a fragment of aqua flat glass and a single piece of brick or drainage tile. The BPM contains a small amount of potentially Precolumbian material. Six definite Native-made potsherds with mica temper and one possible grit-tempered sherd were recovered by flotation. Each sherd was quite small, suggesting that it had been subject to extended weathering. Much or all of the chipped stone material recovered in and above the BPM (two core/hammerstones, twenty-eight pieces of debitage, and small pieces of possibly cultural chert debris from flotation samples) also may derive from a Precolumbian component. Nonetheless, the overwhelming majority of the material found within the BPM (likely including the Native ceramic sherds and flaked chert) is of eighteenth-century Seneca origin.

The two cultural features found extending below the BPM horizon were more than 6.5 m apart. A large basin-shaped, charcoal-filled stain termed Feature 24 was found in the western half of Test Unit 62; its full spatial extent was not determined. A flotation sample taken from the upper black, charcoal-filled layer within the feature yielded a small white glass bead, bone material, gourd rind fragments, three sumac seeds, and sycamore and maple charcoal (Rossen 2006). Post Mold 36, a round soil stain 32 cm in diameter, was found below the BPM in Test Unit 63. It consisted of a dark central core of black loam 12 cm in diameter surrounded by an oval of dark brown soil, suggesting a post with a dug post hole. All soil from both layers was taken for flotation. The sample from the black core yielded three bone fragments, chert debris, three gourd rind specimens, and sycamore and maple charcoal; the surrounding lighter soil contained bone, chert debris, probable quartz fragments, twenty-six gourd rind fragments, a single sumac seed, sycamore charcoal, and fungus.

Domestic Refuse Cluster 3 General Area

The very deep organic soil to the east of the BPM (figure 5.7) is interpreted as a modern plowzone overlying a buried earlier plowzone. Relatively dense faunal remains and several diagnostic eighteenth-century artifacts, including a fire-flint made of nonlocal "blonde" flint (possibly French chalcedony), a large round white glass bead, and a piece of possible eighteenth-century deep aqua-green bottle glass were recovered from this area. These finds suggest that substantial Seneca activity took place east of the midden area, although the buried plowzone horizon is not likely to have the integrity to allow more than coarse definition of those activities and how they were organized in space.

Artifacts recovered from the remainder of DRC 3 (outside both the BPM and buried plowzone areas) included a small complete red pipestone bead, 0.6 cm square with a circular hole in the center, and a massive tubular shell bead (1.8 cm long, 1.4 cm in diameter) found on the plowzone surface. Bone and tooth fragments (including specimens identified as white-tailed deer and bear), lithic debitage, fire-cracked rock, charcoal, a possibly eighteenth-century porcelain sherd, and post-Seneca ceramic material also were found.

A single human molar (identified by Professor Nerissa Russell of Cornell University) was recovered from plowzone soil in ST 225; this is the only definite human remain disturbed by project excavations to date. I consulted with Seneca advisor Peter Jemison about how this find should affect the project's excavation strategy. We agreed that the presence of an isolated tooth in plowzone soil downhill from known cemetery locations might be explained by slopewash or collector activity rather than the presence of burials in the immediate area. Mr. Jemison advised the project to proceed with caution but not alter the excavation strategy unless additional human remains were disturbed; we found no other human remains during the 2000 field season. The tooth has been repatriated to the Haudenosaunee Standing Committee on Burial Rules and Regulations for reburial.

Dating the Seneca Occupation at Townley-Read

I estimate that Senecas occupied the Townley-Read site from circa 1715 to 1754, a revision of Charles Wray's (1983: 46) generally accepted 1710–1745 dates for the site. My revision is based on a combination of four factors: (1) documentary evidence (including both direct mentions of village moves and document-based reconstructions of the political-economic context); (2) artifactual evidence; (3) topography and community structure at Townley-Read (particularly the lack of attention to defense expressed in the settlement's location); and (4) the length of proposed occupation at the preceding White Springs site, which is likely to have been a nucleated village. The rationale for the new dates will be spelled out after consideration of earlier authors' ideas about occupation spans for Townley-Read.

Previous Occupation Estimates

The earliest detailed consideration of the dates of Seneca occupation at Townley-Read was offered by George S. Conover in a theory repeated in several of his later writings (1889, 1893, n.d.). Conover posits that White Springs had been abandoned as a consequence of a smallpox epidemic in

1732: "most of the remainder [of the White Springs population] fled and settled down in scattered fragments in the neighborhood of Slate Rock [Burrell] creek, some three miles [4.8 km] further southwest" (1889: 5). According to Conover, this move founded the New Ganechstage Site Complex that includes the Townley-Read site. Conover places the abandonment of New Ganechstage in 1756: "In 1756 ... Sir William Johnson erected palisade fortifications in the Indian country, and such was erected for the Senecas on Kanadesaga or Castle brook.... At that time the scattered fragments were gathered from the settlements on Slate Rock creek and located at the new site" (1889: 5). These dates occasionally appear in more recent sources (for example, Emmons 1958; Hodge 1907–1910, 1: 198).

Conover references a 1732 document (NYCD 9: 1036) to date the move from White Springs to the New Ganechstage Site Complex. However, this particular document does not mention a village abandonment; it only notes the presence of smallpox in Seneca territory. Conover tries to bolster his argument by citing an Iroquois "tradition" of uncertain origin that "the Indians being infected with the small-pox and feeling languid and uncomfortable, but not knowing what was the matter concluded to go and bathe in the lake and having done so the result proved very fatal" (n.d.: 65–66). This undocumented "tradition" also neglects to mention a village relocation, and I see no obvious tie between it and the White Springs site. Conover's 1756 date for the abandonment of New Ganechstage is based on primary-source references to fort construction associated with a new Seneca community on Kanadesaga Creek (for example, JP 9: 457–58), but an Albany Commissioners of Indian Affairs document (NYCD 6: 857) illustrates that the village move was already in progress in 1754.

It seems likely that Conover did not understand the impermanent nature of Iroquois settlements resulting from their regime of shifting agriculture. For Conover, Seneca settlements needed a good *external* reason to be abandoned, just as a Euro-American village would. History supplied him with plausible reasons for the abandonment of most of the Seneca settlements: the Denonville destruction in 1687 for Ganondagan, the British construction of the fort at Kanadesaga in 1756 for New Ganechstage, and the American destruction of Kanadesaga in 1779. The only Geneva-area village move that did not have a clear-cut historical cause was the relocation from White Springs to New Ganechstage. To account for the abandonment of White Springs, Conover latched on to the documentary mention of a smallpox epidemic and an Iroquois tradition, neither of which are conclusively linked to a village move in the original sources.

Furthermore, Conover fails to specify why the 1732 epidemic resulted in a village relocation whereas other documented outbreaks of smallpox among the Senecas, such as those in 1696 and 1717 (NYCD 4: 195, 9: 877; McIlwain 1915: 120), did not. Additionally, a 1732 abandonment would make for a forty-five-year occupation for White Springs, significantly longer than most estimates for the maximum lifespan of a large nucleated Iroquoian village (for example, Tooker 1991 [1964]; Trigger 1990). Conover's interpretation of the move from New Ganechstage to Kanadesaga further indicates that he did not fully understand Iroquois village relocation: Conover views the move to Kanadesaga as a *response* to 1756 British fort construction, when the 1754 document clearly states that the Senecas had already started to move *before* the fort was built.

Charles Wray (1973: 8) initially estimated a 1710–1730 occupation for Townley-Read, dates repeated in some later sources (for example, Karklins 1983). This twenty-year occupation appears to have been an extrapolation of the average village duration proposed in Wray and Schoff's (1953) study of the 1550–1687 Seneca sequence. By 1983, Wray had done enough work at Snyder-McClure, White Springs, Huntoon, and Townley-Read (Wray n.d.) to realize that the character of Seneca settlements changed quite dramatically during the early eighteenth century. He hypothesized two sequential Seneca residential patterns: a 1550–1710 "longhouse era," during which villages were occupied for an average of twenty years; and a 1710–1820 "cabin era," in which villages were occupied on average for thirty-five years (Wray 1983: 41; see evaluation in K. Jordan 2004).

Wray seems to have extrapolated from the firm historical dates of the 1687 Denonville expedition and the 1779 Sullivan-Clinton campaign. After placing White Springs in the longhouse era, with an approximate twenty-year occupation from 1687 to 1710, he had seventy years left for Townley-Read and Kanadesaga, which when halved, resulted in the 1710–1745 occupation period for Townley-Read. Wray appears to have been unaware of the 1750 Cammerhoff journal and the 1754 Albany Commissioners' document, both of which indicate that New Ganechstage continued to be occupied into the 1750s.[7] Wray evidently did not attempt to confirm his occupation dates with artifactual evidence, such as by using pipe stem dating (K. Jordan 2002: 277–78). The 1710–1745 span has become the standard set of dates for the site, repeated in many subsequent sources (for example, RMSC's "At the Western Door" exhibit; Grumet 1995; Lorenzini and Karklins 2001; Prisch 1982). The point to be emphasized here is that Wray's occupation span is an estimate, and neither the 1710 nor the 1745 date is backed up by any substantial independent evidence.

Artifactual Evidence

Other evidence dating Townley-Read's occupation can be obtained through the analysis of artifacts of known or narrow manufacturing dates, white ball clay smoking pipe fragments, and glass beads from the site.

Six datable bronze royal medals from the Townley-Read site are contained in the RMSC collections (K. Jordan 2002: 286–87; see B. Kent 1993: 282–83 for manufacturing dates). Five of these are George I medals, which date to 1714–1727; one is a King George II and Queen Caroline medal, which dates to between 1727 (the beginning of George II's reign) and 1737 (the year of Queen Caroline's death). Conover (1882: 91) reports on Mr. Read's 1880 find of a buttplate from a musket with the date 1716 stamped on it in the East Fields at Townley-Read; this artifact is not known to be preserved in any museum collection.

European-made white ball clay pipe fragments from museum, surface collection, and excavated contexts at Townley-Read were examined for temporal clues (K. Jordan 2002: 283–86). The combination of artifacts in the RMSC and project collections provided a sample of 296 measurable pipe bores, of which 89.2 percent measured $5/64$ inch. Harrington (1954) dates pipe assemblages dominated by $5/64$-inch pipe bore fragments to 1710–1750. Binford's (1962) regression formula provides a date of 1742.4 for this assemblage (K. Jordan 2002: table 5.6). Hanson's (1969) date-range regression method, found to be considerably more accurate than Binford's in seventeenth-century contexts (Mallios 2005), provides a date of 1733.6 when the formula for occupations hypothesized to take place during 1710–1800 is used. This is almost exactly at the midpoint of the 1715–1754 date range suggested here.

The project recovered decorated bowl fragments from six separate pipes; each of the five examples with legible inscriptions contains the mark of the English pipe maker Robert Tippet. Unfortunately, Tippet pipes are not precisely diagnostic. Three generations of Robert Tippets made pipes in Bristol, England, from 1660 to 1722, and other pipe makers appear to have continued to use Tippet marks after 1722 (Brewer 1992: 153–56; Walker 1977: 660). McCashion (1979: 69) states that "after c. 1700, varieties of English pipes make their way into New York State Indian sites and by c. 1710 or later, the Bristol products of the Robert Tippetts [sic] are found on both

Indian and domestic sites where they predominate." McCashion appears however to have relied on local experts to date Iroquois sites, including Charles Wray for the Seneca region, so the 1710 date cannot be considered to be independent of the Wray chronology.[8]

Seventy-three glass beads were collected through excavation and surface investigation during the project's 1996–2000 fieldwork at Townley-Read.[9] Table 5.3 presents a bead inventory utilizing the Kidd and Kidd (1983) typology, as modified by Karklins (1982). In terms of manufacturing technique, the collection consists of sixty-two drawn beads (85 percent) and eleven wire-wound beads (15 percent). This breakdown is comparable to other sites roughly contemporaneous with Townley-Read: 17 percent of the 1690–1740 Conestoga bead assemblage (n = 23,336) consisted of wire-wound beads (B. Kent 1993: 215); 32 percent of a sample of 122 beads from the 1696–1720 Oneida Primes Hill site were wire-wound (Bennett 1988: 6). Given this evidence, Wray's frequently quoted claims that wire-wound beads are "dominant" at sites of this era (1973: 19) and that the Townley-Read and Huntoon assemblages are "nearly void of drawn beads except for 'seed' varieties" (1983: 46) appear to be overstatements.

The Townley-Read glass bead assemblage appears to have some utility for dating the site (K. Jordan 2002: table 5.5). Snow's (1995: table 1.15) data on the earliest appearance of bead varieties in the Mohawk Valley provides a *terminus post quem* date for the Townley-Read assemblage of 1693 (based on the finds of IIj2, WIIc11, and WIIc12 variety beads). The Townley-Read assemblage bears a number of similarities to the post-1710 Oneida assemblage defined by Pratt (1961: 19). Brain (1979) provides data on the temporal and geographic range of several bead types and approximate mean dates for some varieties' appearance. While Brain's study draws on few sites in the Northeast, relies uncritically on older site occupation span estimates made by excavators (M. Smith 2002: 57), and after more than twenty-five years is somewhat dated (as is obvious from the discrepancies between Snow's and Brain's dates for specific bead varieties), it still provides a temporal framework for a bead assemblage unavailable from other sources. Utilizing Brain's usage span information, the narrowest date range with which the Townley-Read bead assemblage would be compatible is 1729–1781. Brain provides mean use dates for sixty-six of the Townley-Read beads; their overall mean date is 1744.1, less than two years apart from the Binford pipe stem formula calculated for the site.

Table 5.3. Glass Beads Recovered at the Townley-Read Site, 1996–2000

Kidd & Kidd Variety	Shape	Glass Type	Color	Size VS	S	M	L	VL	VL?	Total
Ia4	tubular	translucent	oyster white	0	0	1	0	0	0	1
IIa6	round	opaque	black	0	0	0	2	0	0	2
IIa7	circular	opaque	black	0	1	0	1	1	0	3
IIa13	round	opaque	white	0	1	0	2	0	0	3
IIa14	circular	opaque	white	1	34	1	0	0	0	36
IIa15	oval	opaque	white	0	0	0	0	0	1	1
IIa27	circular	clear?	emerald green	4	1	0	0	0	0	5
IIa37	circular	opaque	aqua blue?	0	1	0	0	0	0	1
IIa56	circular	clear	bright navy	0	2	0	0	0	0	2
IIa*	circular	clear	redwood	0	3	0	0	0	0	3
IIj2	round	opaque	black w/3 wavy white lines	0	0	0	0	1	0	1
IVa5	round	opaque w/ clear core	redwood w/apple green core	0	0	0	1	0	0	1
IVa6	circular	opaque w/ clear core	redwood w/apple green core	0	0	1	0	0	0	1
IVb10	round	opaque w/ clear core	redwood w/apple green core, 3 white stripes	0	0	0	2	0	0	2
WIb5	round	translucent	pale blue w/golden cast	0	0	0	0	6	1	7
WIb7	round	translucent	amber	0	0	0	0	1	0	1
W1c*	oval	clear	lilac?	0	0	0	0	1	0	1
WIIc11	faceted	clear?	ultramarine?	0	0	0	0	1	0	1
WIIc12	faceted	clear	bright navy	0	0	0	0	1	0	1
Total				5	43	3	8	12	2	73

* Variant on Kidd & Kidd Variety

Evaluating the Evidence

Artifacts from the Townley-Read site provide somewhat conflicting evidence regarding the dates of the site's occupation. The peace medals and dated buttplate predominantly suggest an occupation during the 1716–1727 period, while the Binford formula pipe stem date and the mean glass bead date derived from Brain cluster in the 1742–1744 range; the 1733.6 Hanson pipe stem date essentially splits the difference. The pipe stem and glass bead dates might mark the *midpoint* of the occupation of the site, assuming that these artifact types were regularly available throughout the Seneca occupation. However, there are problems associated with pipe stem formulas, especially for a relatively small assemblage that is dominated by one borehole size, and my use of Brain's data is not a widely recognized dating method. Of themselves, artifact-based dating methods do not provide any firmer settlement and abandonment dates than Wray's estimates, but function best as a means to check an occupation date hypothesis derived from other sources. For example, the peace medals and buttplate weigh against Conover's 1732 founding date for the site, since they suggest substantial activity at the site prior to that time, and the pipe stems and beads suggest a later abandonment date than Wray's 1745.

A more reliable way to estimate the founding and abandonment dates for Townley-Read is to use historical documents in conjunction with evaluation of the site's topographic setting, internal structure, and overall defensibility. The June 15, 1754, Albany Commissioners document provides a relatively firm date for the abandonment of Townley-Read. In it, the commissioners recommended that "the Senecas, who at present live very remote from one another, ... make a general castle near the mouth of the Senecas river, where they have already begun to build a new castle" (NYCD 6: 857). The Senecas in the New Ganechstage Site Complex (including Townley-Read) certainly lived "very remote from one another." While the move from New Ganechstage to Kanadesaga was likely to have been gradual and may have started before and continued after 1754, I have used 1754 for the abandonment of Townley-Read due to this unambiguous documentary reference. There is nothing in the archaeological record to contradict this date, and a move from the fully dispersed New Ganechstage Site Complex to a somewhat more defensible settlement at Kanadesaga (K. Jordan 2004) makes sense given the regional political-economic situation at the beginning of the Seven Years' War.

Establishing a founding date for the settlement is more difficult. That the Townley-Read Senecas ignored the western Ridgetop in favor of a downslope location in the East Fields provides an important clue. The historical record can be assessed to determine when such a non-defensible settlement would have been possible—or even not foolhardy—to construct. Keep in mind that it would have been completely feasible for Senecas to build a dispersed settlement in a defensible location, but they did not do so. The key to the founding date of Townley-Read is to pay careful attention to the political-economic context beyond the locality. One needs to determine when a period of *peace* occurred that Senecas might have perceived as having the potential to be *relatively durable*.

Wray's 1710 founding date does not meet these criteria. The 1709–1712 years were among the most precarious in a "period of uncertainty" (see chapter 3). During this time a series of war scares and actual attacks took place that disrupted the burgeoning trade between western Indian groups and Albany, through which the Senecas received benefits as geographic middlemen. In April 1709 Alexander Montour—who had guided western Indian groups through Iroquois territory to Albany—was killed on French orders. In late 1710 or early 1711 western Indian groups raided Iroquois territory on French instigation. Most significantly, in 1709 and 1711 the British assembled troops and Indian allies (including 182 Senecas in 1711) for assaults on New France; although logistical complications aborted both invasions, the threat of open imperial warfare in the Northeast was very real. New York unsuccessfully solicited Iroquois participation in the western conflict between the Foxes and the French in 1712. It appears that 1710 would have been a terrible time for the Senecas to build a dispersed settlement in a non-defensible location. Furthermore, Senecas are unlikely to have considered a non-defensible setting for a new village at this time either, much less started clearing land and undertaking other preparations necessary for a new settlement adjacent to Burrell Creek.

Within a few years the supra-local diplomatic and military climate had changed considerably. The French and British negotiated the Treaty of Utrecht in 1713, ending the War of Spanish Succession. From 1713 to 1744 "the French and English generally remained at peace" (Aquila 1983: 92), a development aided by the informal alliance between France and Great Britain in opposition to the Holy Roman Empire in 1716. Richter (1992: 234) notes that Iroquois relations with the French, strained by Iroquois participation in the abortive British invasions of New France and the French war with the Foxes, improved by 1714. The passage of western Indians through Iroquoia (including Seneca territory) resumed quickly; White (1991: 120) notes that the value of beaver exports from New York doubled in 1713 and almost doubled again in 1714. In short, the 1713–1724 "middleman period," previously identified as the most favorable decade for the Senecas during the entire 1677–1754 period, exactly meets the criteria of local peace that may have been perceived to be relatively durable.

A final factor to consider is the length of occupation at the White Springs site, which was probably a large nucleated village (K. Jordan 2004). Most scholars specify thirty years as the maximum duration for a large, nucleated Northern Iroquoian settlement (for example, Tooker 1991 [1964]: 42; Trigger 1990: 31); smaller, dispersed villages could be occupied for significantly longer periods (K. Jordan 2004). Since White Springs was settled in 1687 or 1688 immediately following the Denonville expedition, the site presumably would have been abandoned *at the latest* by 1717 or 1718. This is quite consistent with the 1715 founding date for New Ganechstage proposed here. As outlined in chapter 4, Lawrence Claessen's June 1720 report that the Senecas "have lay'd out a New Castle" (NYCD 5: 550) is unlikely to be related to the founding of Townley-Read. This founding date would have required a very long thirty-two-year occupation at White Springs, and Senecas are known to have initiated new settlement near Montreal in 1720.

It would appear that 1713 would be the first year in which the eastern Senecas might realistically have thought about building a village in a nondefensible setting and begun preparing the area for the move. I have chosen 1715 for the founding date of Townley-Read, arbitrarily allocating two years for the Senecas to assess the political-economic situation, find an area for the new village, test soils for their agricultural potential, clear land, and assemble materials for house construction. As with 1754, the 1715 founding date makes sense given the supra-local context, and there is nothing in the archaeological record to contradict this date (particularly since it precedes all of the dated artifacts found at the site, including the 1716 buttplate).

A 1715–1754 occupation span for Townley-Read therefore agrees with the political-economic context derived from historical documents, specific documentary mentions of village moves, ecological constraints on settlement length at the nucleated White Springs site, and dates derived from the Townley-Read artifact assemblage. Although when viewed through the lens of arithmetic the new set of dates does not represent a major change from Wray's 1710–1745 occupation span for the site, it does represent a marked improvement over Wray in terms of the variety of types of evidence that inform the occupation span, and in terms of the new dates' usefulness to researchers. Delineation of more precise and better-supported site occupation spans is crucial to the reconstruction of local political economy and examination of the interplay between local and supra-local factors.

6

Seneca Settlement Pattern and Community Structure, 1677–1779

The main model used to describe Postcolumbian Seneca Iroquois settlement patterns is that of Charles Wray and Harry Schoff (1953), who proposed that from 1550 to 1687 the Senecas consistently built two major villages, each surrounded by one or more smaller local satellite settlements (figure 6.1). Based on historic accounts, Wray and Schoff suggested that Senecas relocated their villages approximately every twenty years, and that the eastern and western villages staggered their moves slightly so that only one community was moving at a given time. Although more comprehensive study of the Seneca evidence by researchers at the RMSC has modified both the sequence of sites and the overall chronology (Sempowski and Saunders 2001; Wray et al. 1987, 1991), Wray and Schoff well approximated a Seneca settlement pattern that endured for almost 150 years. They note that their model described Seneca settlements after 1687 less effectively: "the Seneca moved eastward ten to twenty miles [16–32 km] . . . and subsequently scattered in numerous smaller villages about the Finger Lakes and the middle and upper Genesee Valley" (1953: 53).

Scholars working since 1953 have not described the regional organization and community structure of post-1687 Seneca villages in detail. This chapter summarizes and evaluates archaeological and documentary data on the 1677–1779 Seneca settlement sequence by providing "synchronic snapshots" of Seneca villages during the years 1687, 1700, 1720, 1750, and 1779 (additional details are provided in K. Jordan 2004, from which this chapter is condensed). A final section compares the changes observed in settlement pattern and community structure with the overall political-economic sequence set out in chapter 3.

Following Wray and Schoff (1953; Wray 1983), this chapter examines Seneca settlements in the area often called their "traditional homeland" between the Genesee River and Cayuga Lake in present-day New York State. This boundary is artificial: Senecas resided outside the "homeland" area in

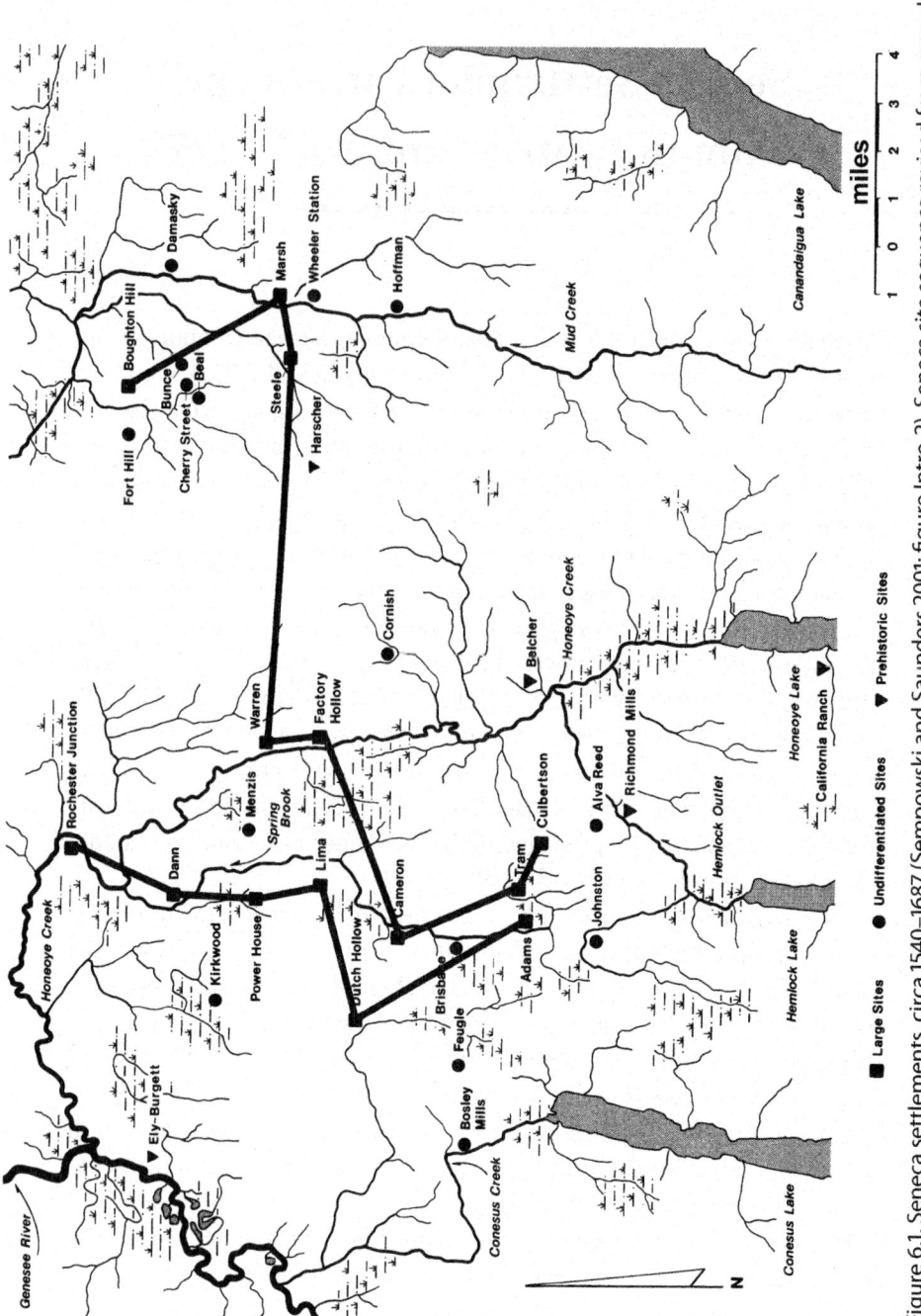

Figure 6.1. Seneca settlements, circa 1540–1687 (Sempowski and Saunders 2001: figure Intro-2). Seneca site sequence revised from map drawn by Charles F. Wray (1973); redrawn by Patricia L. Miller. (Image used courtesy of the Rochester Museum and Science Center.)

each of the periods described in this chapter (see Parmenter [1999, 2001a, 2007a] for a re-evaluation of the relations between homeland and satellite Iroquois populations). There were year-round Seneca settlements on the north shore of Lake Ontario between approximately 1665 and 1704 (Konrad 1981, 1987; Poulton 1991; Richter 1992: 219); in Pennsylvania starting in approximately 1690 (B. Kent 1993); and at Fort Niagara from 1718 through the Seven Years' War, and perhaps earlier (Kalm 1966 [1751]; NYCD 9: 885). Senecas also resided at the multinational mission communities on the St. Lawrence River (JR 59:289; Richter 1992: 120; Tremblay 1981: 59 note 16). Numerous Senecas relocated to the Ohio territory after about 1724 (Hunter 1978; McConnell 1992; Seaver 1990 [1824]), including a large Seneca contingent on the Allegheny River beginning about 1740 (Brodhead in Conover 1887; Deardorff 1946; Hulbert and Schwarze 1912; Hunter 1978). These Seneca settlements deserve greater analytical treatment, but this task is beyond the scope of the present work.

Data for all sites have been derived from historical documents and from publications by, field notes of, and conversations with local historians and avocational archaeologists. Topographic assessments of site locations are based on U.S. Geological Survey topographic maps and site walkovers I conducted at several village locations. Extensive professional excavation targeting habitation areas, which allows much more detail to be provided, has taken place at only three homeland Seneca sites occupied between 1677 and 1779: Ganondagan (Dean 1984, 1986; Hayes, Barber, and Hamell 1978), Townley-Read, and Kanadesaga (Hamell n.d.; Hartgen Archaeological Associates 2002).

Table 6.1 presents founding and abandonment dates for the main Seneca sites occupied during 1670–1779. Occupation dates are based on Wray (1983) with revisions discussed in this volume. A detailed, site-by-site analysis of historical context, topography, and diagnostic artifacts similar to that performed for Townley-Read in chapter 5 is needed to better establish village occupation spans but clearly is outside the scope of this study. Brief examination of artifacts from these sites in the RMSC collections indicates that Wray's temporal assessments are not likely to be far off the mark.

Kurt Jordan (2004) presents a typology for Seneca settlements based on Sanders, Parsons, and Santley's (1979: 52–60) classification scheme for sites in the Basin of Mexico and Kapches' (1984) typology for Northern Iroquoian house forms. In this typology (Table 6.2), Seneca residential sites are classified by three separate elements: (1) a term describing size (large village, small village, hamlet, or farmstead); (2) a modifier (nucleated, semi-

Table 6.1. Occupation Spans for Selected Seneca Sites, 1670–1779

Site	Founding Date	Departure Date
Ganondagan/Boughton Hill	1670–1675	1687
Rochester Junction	1670–1675	1687
Snyder-McClure	1688	1710–1715
White Springs	1688	1715
New Ganechstage Site Complex	1715	1754
Huntoon	1710–1715	1740–1745
Kendaia	1704–1720	1779
Fall Brook	1740–1745	1775
Honeoye	1740–1745	1779
Kanadesaga	1754	1779
Genesee Castle	1775	1779

Source: Wray (1983), with modifications.

dispersed, or fully dispersed) based on the organization of space within that community; and (3) a term indicating the predominant house form (longhouse, short longhouse, Iroquoian-style cabin, European-style house, or mixed if no one type predominates). Although only fully excavated sites can be classified with complete confidence, provisional classification adequate for the task of describing general settlement pattern changes can be undertaken for many sites.

Since few systematic archaeological surveys have been undertaken in the Seneca region, small sites are underrepresented or absent in the maps and discussions that follow. Iroquoian archaeology in general has emphasized village and cemetery excavations over exploring small or seasonally exploited sites. While this has resulted in a biased, village-centered view of Iroquois landscape use, it is likely that virtually all of the year-round sites that housed one hundred or more people have been found through either documentary sources or the work of individuals such as William Beauchamp (1900), Harrison C. Follett (n.d.), Arthur C. Parker (1920), and Charles Wray (1973, 1983, n.d.). This assertion is supported by the fact that no additional village sites have been located in areas of the Seneca region where systematic survey has taken place (for example, Johnson and Berg 1976; Trubowitz 1983).

Period 1: 1687

In 1687 Seneca territory was invaded by the French-led expedition commanded by the Marquis de Denonville, causing the Senecas to either burn or abandon their villages ahead of the French advance. Following the de-

Table 6.2. Seneca Settlement Typology

Each site description involves a size term, an organizational term, and a house form term.

Community Size Terms

1. *Large Village*: a community of more than 500 persons.
2. *Small Village*: a community of 100–500 persons.
3. *Hamlet*: a community of fewer than 100 persons housed in two or more residential structures.
4. *Farmstead*: a site consisting of only one residential structure (population would vary according to household size).

Community Organizational Terms

1. *Nucleated Community*: a community in which the amount of extramural, communal space is limited and highly organized. A lack of household infields or a hilltop location with limited flat space for residences could be indicators of nucleation.
2. *Semi-dispersed Community*: a community in which there is no rigorous organization of extramural, nonresidential space. House lots with specialized external structures or household infields could be indicators of dispersal in an Iroquoian cultural context. Semi-dispersed settlements can be distinguished from fully dispersed communities based on the former's nonlinear arrangement of houses.
3. *Fully Dispersed Community*: a community in which there is no rigorous organization of extramural, nonresidential space. House lots with specialized external structures or household infields could be indicators of dispersal in an Iroquoian cultural context. Fully dispersed settlements can be distinguished from semi-dispersed communities based on the linear arrangement of houses in the former, as for example, along a watercourse.

Residential Terms

1. *Longhouse Community*: a community where the majority of residential structures are longhouses. A longhouse is defined as an Iroquoian-style residential structure with a length-to-width ratio of 2:1 or more (Kapches 1984: 64). This type of structure is sometimes called a "true" longhouse to differentiate it from a "short" longhouse.
2. *Short Longhouse Community*: a community where the majority of residential structures are short longhouses. A short longhouse is defined as an Iroquoian-style residential structure with a length-to-width ratio of 1.26:1 to 1.99:1 (Kapches 1984: 64).
3. *Cabin Community*: a community where the majority of residential structures are cabins. A cabin is defined as an Iroquoian-style residential structure with a length-to-width ratio of 1.25:1 or less (Kapches 1984: 64).
4. *European-style House Community*: a community where the majority of residential structures are built in European architectural styles (see chapter 8).
5. *Mixed Housing Community*: a community where no house type represents 50 percent or more of the total housing inventory.

Source: Modified from K. Jordan 2004: table 2.

struction of 1687, the Senecas abandoned the Honeoye and Mud Creek drainages, ending the orderly sequence of Seneca village relocations and regional ecological transformations that had been progressing for well more than a century (Wray and Schoff 1953; see also Vandrei 1987).

Documented Sites

Scholars generally accept that the sites encountered by the Denonville expedition in 1687 were the same as those documented by New York official Wentworth Greenhalgh in 1677 (Hamell 1980). The 1677 and 1687 accounts both describe two large, nucleated villages and two smaller local satellite villages (figure 6.2). Historians and archaeologists have identified Ganondagan (now Ganondagan State Historic Site; also known as the Boughton Hill or Gannagaro site) and Rochester Junction as the two large sites, and Beal and Kirkwood as the satellite villages (Wray et al. 1991). The Damasky site has been dated to this period archaeologically, but its existence during 1677–1687 was not verified by Greenhalgh or the members of the Denonville expedition.

Greenhalgh's report (Snow, Gehring, and Starna 1996: 191–92) includes house counts for each Seneca village and estimates that the Seneca Nation would be able to field one thousand warriors. He describes two major settlements: Canagaroh (various spellings), an eastern community of 150 houses which is probably the Ganondagan site, and Tiotohattan, a western village of 120 houses which is probably Rochester Junction. Each of these large villages had an associated smaller village about 6.4 km away: the eastern satellite, Canoenada, contained thirty houses and is probably the Beal site; the western satellite, Keint:he, contained twenty-four houses and is probably the Kirkwood site. Greenhalgh relates that Canagaroh was "on top of a great hill" and that Tiotohattan was "on the brincke or edge of a hill" (191). According to Greenhalgh, all of the villages were unpalisaded. He notes that Tiotohattan "contains about 120 houses being the largest of all the houses wee saw, the ordinary being 50 or 60 foott [15–18 m] long, and some 130 or 140 foott [40–43 m] long, with 13 or 14 fires in one house" (191). Greenhalgh's house descriptions will be analyzed in chapter 9.

Because the Senecas abandoned and burned several of their villages before the 1687 Denonville expedition reached them, the French soldiers make few remarks about house forms or settlement organization (see DHNY 1: 237–43; Hamell 1980; NYCD 9: 358–69; Olds 1930: 9–52; Squier 1851: 90–95). The weight of indirect evidence favors the conclusion that the settlements were unpalisaded (K. Jordan 2004), with the possible exception

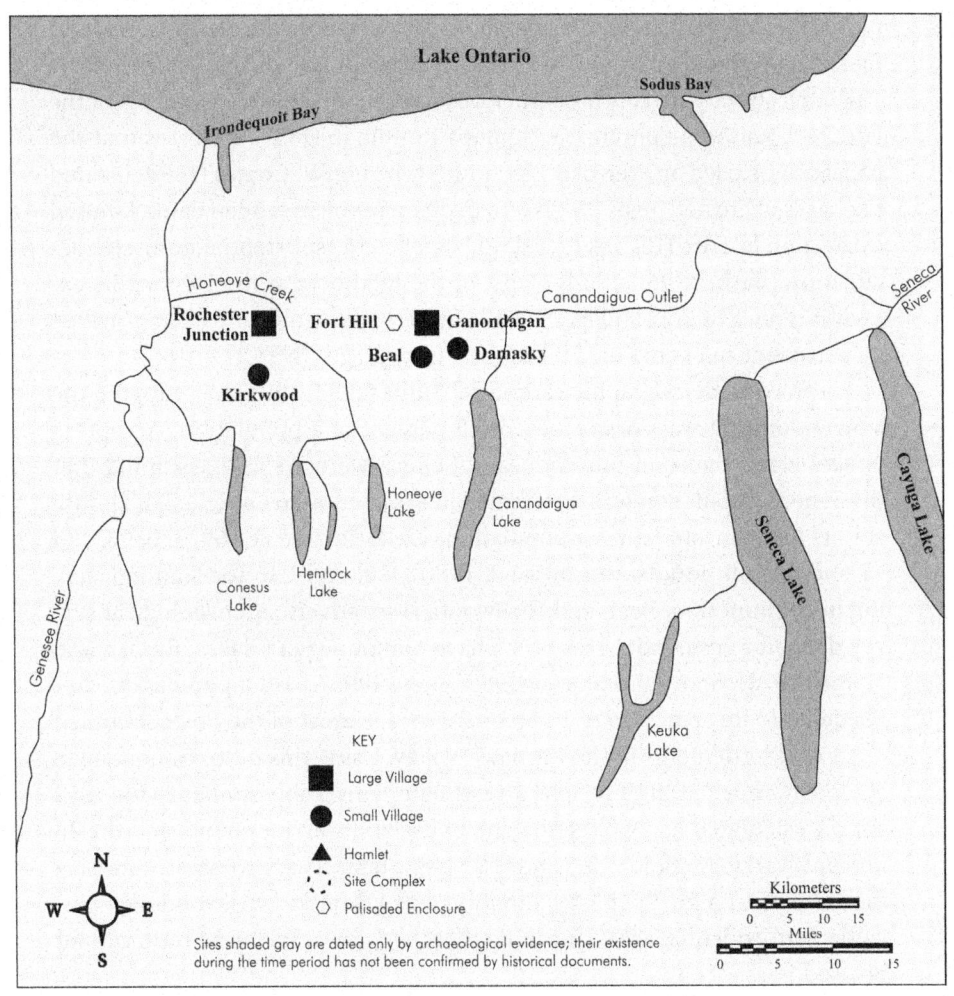

Figure 6.2. Seneca settlements, 1687 (modified from K. Jordan 2004: figure 1). Base map adapted from Wray (1983). (Image used courtesy of *Northeast Anthropology*.)

of the western satellite town, where Denonville relates that he found the coat of arms of the King of England "at the gate of this village" (NYCD 9: 367).

Several members of the Denonville expedition mention an uninhabited fortification at "Fort Hill" on an extremely defensible hilltop 1.7 km west of Ganondagan. At the time of the Denonville expedition, a full palisade had been constructed on this hilltop, with a fortified extension running down one side of the hill to connect to a spring. Documents indicate that the fort may have been built in 1684 in response to rumors of impending French attack (NYCD 9: 254, 261). The members of the Denonville expedition found maize (stored and growing) and possibly pigs but no houses inside the Fort Hill enclosure. Nineteenth-century observers were able to see traces of the Fort Hill palisade. Ephraim G. Squier's 1848 map (1851) indicates that the palisade enclosed an area of 8.1 ha; in 1890 Irving W. Coates (1893) located the bases of burned posts 25–46 cm in diameter in an eroded bank. Limited excavation at Fort Hill has found no evidence for substantial domestic occupation (Barber 1961, 1964). Most of the members of the Denonville expedition refer to Fort Hill as a "fort," but perhaps significantly, Denonville's own account refers to Fort Hill as the "new village" (NYCD 9: 365).

For making demographic estimates, Snow (1994, 1995) has adopted the convention that warriors represent 25 percent of a population. Accepting Greenhalgh's figure of one thousand Seneca warriors and assuming that the Seneca population was distributed in proportion to Greenhalgh's house counts for each site, warrior populations are estimated at 463, 370, 93, and 74 and overall populations at 1852, 1480, 372, and 296 for Ganondagan, Rochester Junction, Beal, and Kirkwood, respectively. Archaeological survey defined a residential area of 3.7 ha at Ganondagan (Hayes, Barber, and Hamell 1978). Snow and Starna (1989; Snow 1995) posit a population-to-residential-site area ratio of 1 person:20 m^2 for most of the Postcolumbian nucleated settlements in the Mohawk Valley. Using this ratio, Ganondagan could have housed 1843 people, an estimate remarkably similar to the 1852 people calculated using Greenhalgh's house and warrior counts and the 25 percent warriors standard. Vandrei's (1987: table 1) approximate site-size figures of 6.1 ha for Rochester Junction and 1.0 ha for Kirkwood likely include nonresidential areas, meaning that the Snow and Starna ratio cannot be used.

The hilltop locations of Canagaroh/Ganondagan and Tiotohattan/Rochester Junction suggest that they were nucleated settlements; excavations at Ganondagan have not revealed any traces of a palisade. There are no published descriptions of the satellite villages, although Kirkwood was built in a highly defensible location (Vandrei 1987: table 2). The eastern satellite village at the Beal site may have been occupied by refugee Hurons (Hamell 1980). Repeated excavation and looting at Ganondagan have revealed at least twelve separate cemeteries located at the margins of the village area; Graham and Wray (1985 [1966]: 5) estimate that the largest cemetery contained about two hundred burials.

Comparison with the fully excavated Mohawk Valley village of Caughnawaga (occupied circa 1679–1693; Snow 1995) in terms of average house lot size and amount of available extramural space reveals that Greenhalgh's estimate of 150 houses for Ganondagan likely was too high (K. Jordan 2004). Modifications of the Ganondagan figures based on the Caughnawaga evidence suggest it is more likely that there were 74–119 Seneca houses at Ganondagan. Coupling these revised estimates with the village population figure of 1843 calculated earlier results in average household sizes of 24.9 and 15.5 persons per house, respectively, both significant increases over the 12.3 persons per house figure for Ganondagan calculated using Greenhalgh's 150-house count.

Overview

The Seneca settlement pattern in both 1677 and 1687 consisted of large, nucleated longhouse villages with local satellite small villages, at least some of which contained a component of short longhouses or storage structures (K. Jordan 2004). The palisaded enclosure at Fort Hill is an anomaly in the Seneca sequence. The very large area enclosed by the palisade—representing a significant amount of wood and labor—would seem to preclude its use solely as a defensive citadel, granary, or animal pen (although the area may have served all of these functions temporarily). During the mid-1680s, the Senecas may have been considering the consolidation of several unpalisaded settlements into one large fortified town, something that Greenhalgh reported the Cayugas were discussing in 1677 (Snow, Gehring, and Starna 1996: 191) and that some assert the Cayugas actually implemented (DeOrio 1998). Barber (1964) was able to identify two springs on Fort Hill, meaning that the area was habitable. Denonville (NYCD 9: 365) may have been entirely correct in identifying Fort Hill as the "new village."

Many scholars (for example, Snow 1995: 471; Taylor 1995: 34; Wray 1983: 41) have claimed that French attacks in the 1680s and 1690s taught the Iroquois a lesson about the futility of palisade construction in the face of European foes. However, there was considerable variability in the defensive posturing of Seneca settlements during the 1565–1687 era (Vandrei 1987; Wray and Schoff 1953), and it appears from the Greenhalgh and Denonville expedition documents that most or all of the 1677–1687 Seneca villages were unpalisaded, meaning that unfortified sites were built prior to Denonville. If the interpretation of Fort Hill as a new village location is correct, the 1687 Seneca towns may represent not the *abandonment* of palisade construction, but merely its *temporary cessation*. A more realistic position is to assume that there was substantial temporal and regional variation in terrain preferences and palisade construction, dependent on local levels of conflict or anticipated conflict.

Period 2: 1700

After spending the winter of 1687–1688 with the Cayugas, the Senecas returned to their homeland and constructed new communities (figure 6.3). Although some scholars (for example, Conover 1889; Fenton 1940; Houghton 1927; Jennings et al. 1985) have claimed that the Senecas settled in the Genesee Valley as early as 1688, current archaeological evidence indicates that the villages built in the immediate aftermath of the Denonville expedition were all to the east of the 1687 sites. Apparently, only two new villages—located at the Snyder-McClure and White Springs sites (Wray 1983)—were built to replace the four sites burned in 1687. Military engineer Willem Wolfgang Römer's 1700 map of Seneca territory (Römer 1700; see figure 9.4) appears to confirm the number and locations of these villages. Although new domestic-context fieldwork commenced at White Springs in 2007 (Aloi 2007), at the time of this writing information on the internal organization of these sites mainly has been derived from accounts of nineteenth- and twentieth-century local historians and avocational archaeologists, site walkovers, and analysis of topographic maps. Published documents from the period mention Seneca villages only in passing and without detailed description (for example, NYCD 4: 597, 691, 750).

Wray (1983: 41) describes the 1688 move as follows: "The Senecas moved about 10 or 15 miles [16–24 km] eastward to an area more remote from Irondequoit Bay and nearer their allies, the Cayugas. Here they built their last compact palisaded villages of longhouses." Wray provides no supporting evidence for the claims made in the last sentence, and there are few data that can address the issues of palisade construction or house form(s). On current evidence, however, Wray's assertion that these settlements were nucleated appears to hold up.

The Western Community at the Snyder-McClure Site

Coates investigated and mapped the Snyder-McClure site in 1891 and published his findings in a series of newspaper articles the following year (1892a–e). He (1892e) documents the looting of burials at the site as early as 1832 and additional disturbance of burials during railroad construction near the site. Coates (1892d) also summarizes local historical accounts of the captivity of William Wyckoff, which describe a short September 1779

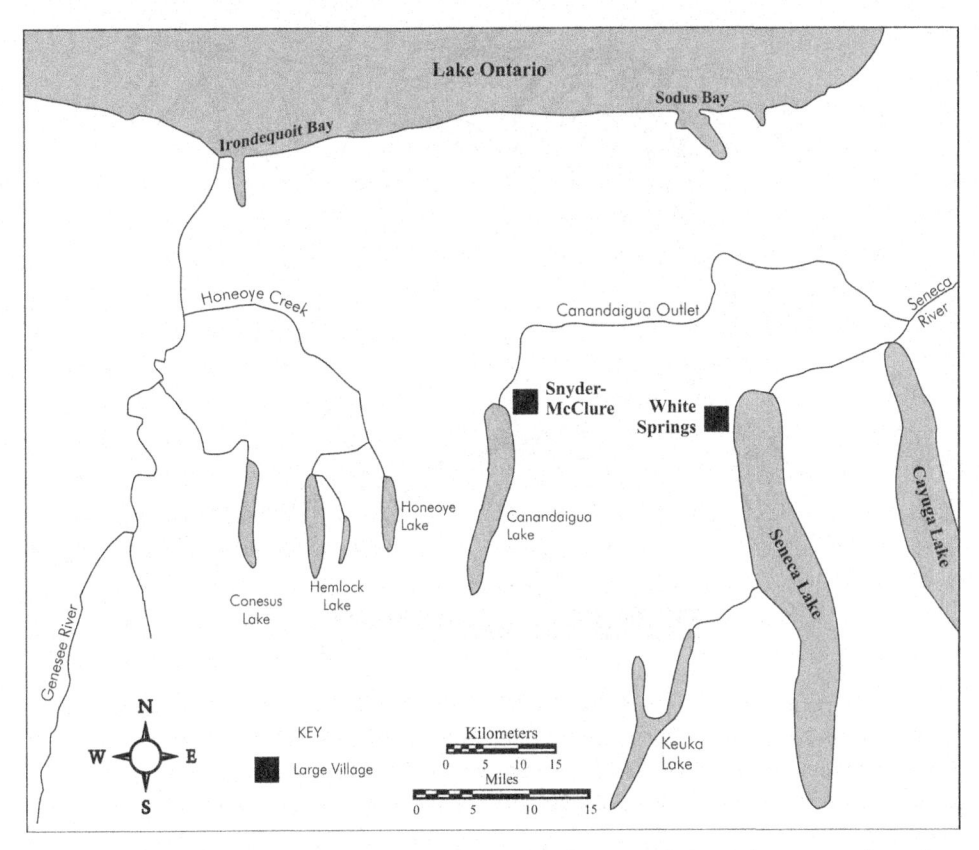

Figure 6.3. Seneca settlements, 1700 (revised from K. Jordan 2004: figure 2). Base map adapted from Wray (1983). (Image used courtesy of *Northeast Anthropology*.)

visit to the site by a group of Iroquois and captives. Wyckoff's captors allegedly showed him around the then-abandoned site, detailing the locations of two springs, twelve giant elm trees which "represented the twelve moons," old agricultural fields and apple orchards, "the medicine man's garden," and the "field of athletic sports," as well as the residential area of the site.

Follett (n.d.: Site 163) relates that Snyder-McClure was "an interesting spot and has a commanding view of the surrounding country . . . the area of the village site is about five acres [2.0 ha] . . . there are a number of spots which show plainly on the surface containing small pieces of animal bones and it is evident these were lodge sites . . . this was probably a village of from five to ten longhouses." Follett also describes a cemetery to the north of Fall Brook. Other avocational archaeologists, including Schoff and Wray, excavated at Snyder-McClure beginning in the 1920s. At least three separate

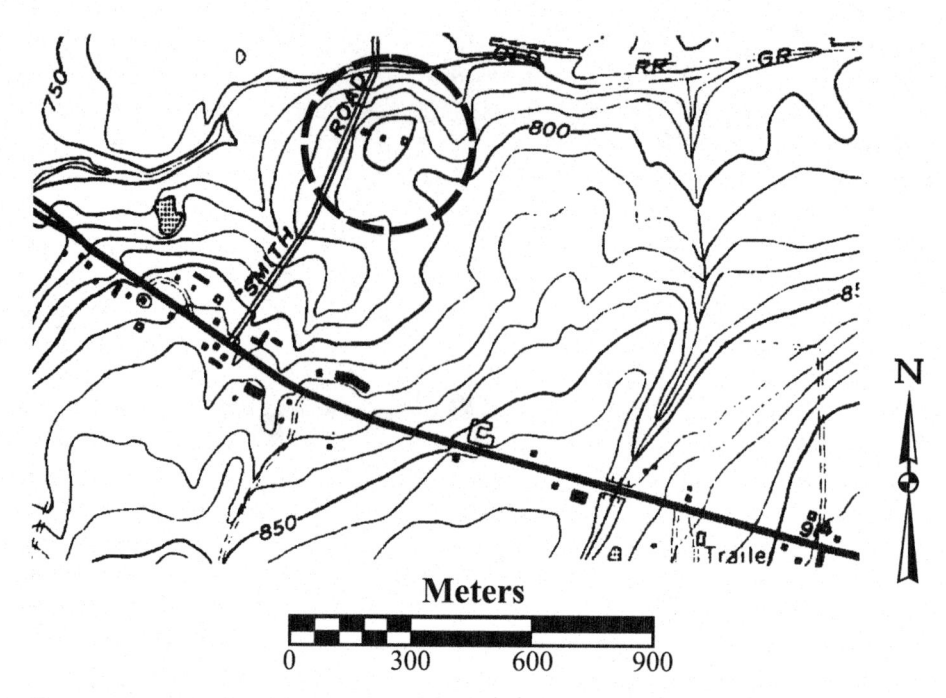

Figure 6.4. Topography of the Snyder-McClure site, occupied 1688 to circa 1710–1715 (modified from K. Jordan 2004: figure 3). Note rising terrain southeast of the site. Elevations are given in feet; contour interval is 10 feet (3.0 m). Base map taken from U.S. Geological Survey topographical map, 7.5' series, Rushville, New York, quadrangle. (Image used courtesy of *Northeast Anthropology*.)

cemetery areas were present at the site: twenty-five and thirty-four burials, respectively, were removed from two knolls, and from surface evidence Wray (n.d.) estimated that a third burial plot north of Fall Brook contained fifty to sixty graves. All of these cemeteries were placed in areas marginal to the hilltop. This is similar to the arrangement of cemeteries and living space at Ganondagan, although the burial plot across Fall Brook at Snyder-McClure is more isolated from the village precinct than were the Ganondagan cemeteries.

There has been little investigation of the presumed habitation area of the site. The hilltop location Coates and Follett described is fairly defensible and provides good visibility in a 300 degree arc, with a rise to the east-southeast (possibly Wyckoff's "field of athletic sports") constituting the one defensive handicap of the site (figure 6.4). The flattest area at the top of the hill is only about 0.8 ha in size, which implies that the village, or at least a part of it, was nucleated. Since no formal excavation has taken place on the hilltop, there is little reason for confidence in Follett's house count and even less for his characterization of the site as a longhouse village. His areal estimate of 2.0 ha is more reliable since it was based on the surface distribution of refuse bone. Assuming that Snyder-McClure was a nucleated settlement, use of Snow and Starna's village population density formula results in an estimate of one thousand residents for a 2.0 ha site.

The Eastern Community at the White Springs Site

Less information is available on the White Springs site, which has been severely impacted by modern residential development. The exact size and boundaries of the village itself are unknown; prior to 2007, only cemeteries had been systematically excavated. In 1750 the Moravian missionaries Johann Cammerhoff and David Zeisberger passed through an abandoned Seneca village that very likely was the White Springs site; Cammerhoff noted that the village was "said to have been very large" (Beauchamp 1916: 67). Conover (n.d.: 63–70) describes 1842 landscaping efforts on the White Springs Manor property which resulted in the grading of two knolls that contained Seneca cemeteries. Witnesses told Conover that at least four wagonloads of human remains were removed, and many local residents had artifacts from the site in their collections during the 1880s. Conover's description of the cemeteries indicates that they could have bounded a sizable village area.

The cemeteries at White Springs all were situated on the margins of a long north-south ridge. The ridge can be characterized as somewhat defensible: while it is only 3 m higher than the land to the west, it occupies a commanding position over lands to the east and has a clear view all the way to Seneca Lake. The southern end of the ridge is well defined, but the northern portion merges gradually into an expanse of flat terrain. In comparison to Snyder-McClure, the more gradual terrain at White Springs does not dictate nucleated village organization. Two pieces of negative evidence, however, indicate that White Springs was indeed a nucleated community. First, an archaeological survey by the State University of New York at Buffalo (Trubowitz 1976: 39–40) failed to find any definite seventeenth- or eighteenth-century artifacts in twenty-six shovel test pits dug along a road adjacent to the site. Wray (n.d.) later determined that this survey had dug in close proximity to a cemetery. Second, the longtime owner of the southern half of the ridge stated that very little artifactual material had been found there despite decades of plowing (Fanny Fribolin, personal communication, 1999), an account confirmed by several field walkovers. The near-total absence of domestic debris in close proximity to the likely village location and to known cemeteries contrasts substantially with the broad scatter of refuse found at the dispersed Townley-Read site. It is not possible to make a population estimate for White Springs due to the lack of data on the size of the village precinct.

Overview

The immediate Seneca response to Denonville was one of *continuity* rather than change. Although the 1687 invasion resulted in a long-distance move away from the Honeoye and Mud Creek drainages and a decrease in the total number of villages, the size of the subsequent main villages and their spatial relation to each other was not altered. The 1700 pattern continued to consist of two large villages which, at 19 km apart, were placed close enough to each other to allow fairly regular interaction. During 1640–1687, the main Seneca villages consistently had been built 15 to 20 km apart (Vandrei 1987; dates from Sempowski and Saunders 2001).

The number and size of the 1700 sites seem to confirm documentary indications that the Seneca population at that time was considerably smaller than the approximately four thousand people seen by Greenhalgh in 1677. Almost certainly, however, both Snyder-McClure and White Springs were large nucleated villages, a claim bolstered by the population estimate of one thousand residents for Snyder-McClure. The size of the cemeteries at both sites indicates that Wray's (1973) transition to "small plots" had not taken place by 1700.

There also may have been palisade construction at the 1700-era sites, the position taken by Wray (1983). Snyder-McClure and White Springs were located in somewhat defensible terrain (although each site has a defensive weakness), and both were likely to have been sufficiently nucleated to allow fortification. Palisaded settlements definitely were built in other parts of Iroquoia well after the 1687–1696 French settlement burnings (for example, the post-1693 Mohawk Milton Smith site [Snow 1995] and possibly the circa 1696–1720 Oneida Primes Hill site [Bennett 1988]). The issue of fortification at Snyder-McClure, White Springs, and other nucleated sites will remain unresolved until sufficient archaeological investigation of village margins takes place.

Period 3: circa 1720

The Seneca settlements occupied around 1720 (figure 6.5) show the first major departures from the Wray and Schoff (1953) model. Changes are evident at the regional level (in the founding of the more distant satellite village at Kendaia), community (construction of the spatially segmented New Ganechstage Site Complex), and site (the dispersed community plan at Townley-Read) levels.

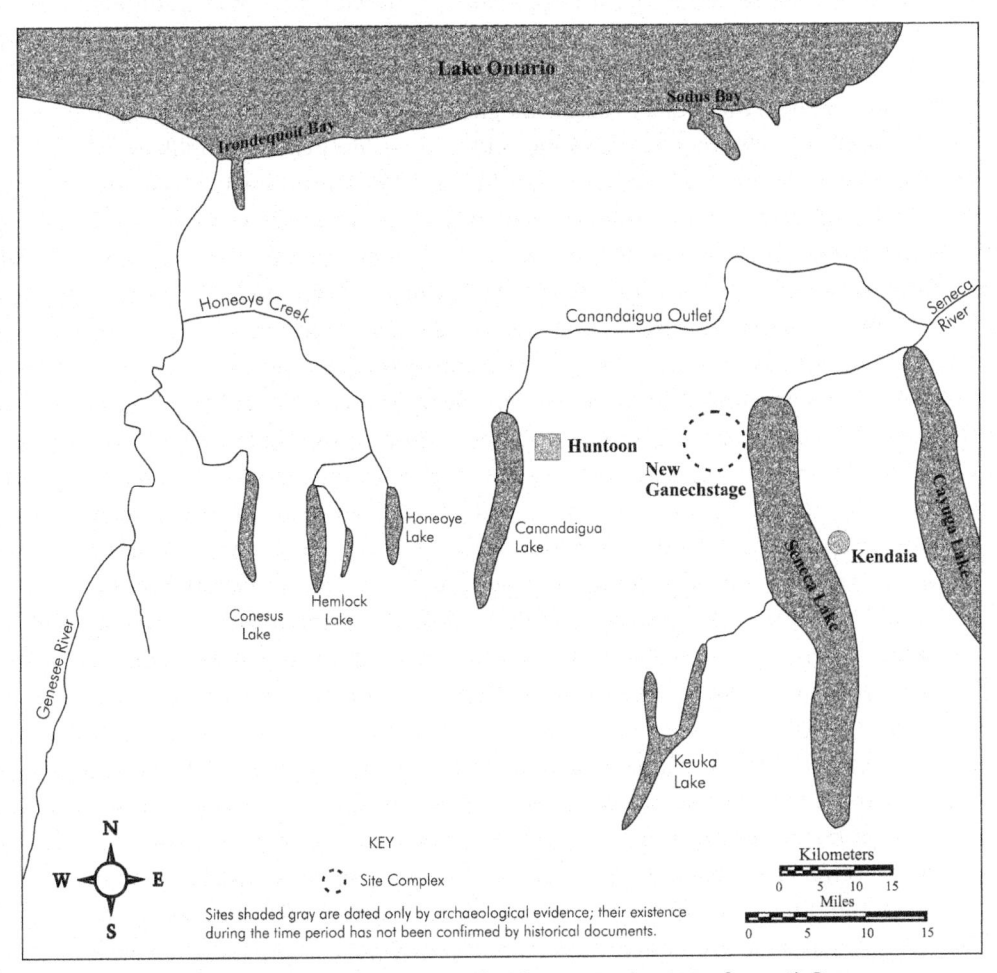

Figure 6.5. Seneca settlements, circa 1720 (modified from K. Jordan 2004: figure 4). Base map adapted from Wray (1983). (Image used courtesy of *Northeast Anthropology*.)

The New Ganechstage Site Complex

The central Seneca community at the New Ganechstage Site Complex (figure 6.6) was organized as a set of at least six spatially distinct "neighborhoods" spread along an 8 km section of Burrell Creek (Conover 1882: 70–88), including the Townley-Read, Brother, Rippey, Rupert, Zindall-Wheadon, and Hazlet sites. Evidence marshaled in the previous chapter indicates that the Townley-Read site, and probably the rest of the New Ganechstage Site Complex, was settled in about 1715. Although previous descriptions of this community (for example, Conover 1882, n.d.; Wray 1983) identify Townley-Read as a large village surrounded by smaller hamlet- or farmstead-sized satellites, the project's archaeological work at Townley-Read has cast doubt on this interpretation. In particular, Townley-Read was unlikely to have housed more than five hundred people, and some of the other sites in the locality (particularly Rupert) may have approached Townley-Read in population. The "site complex" terminology better describes the relationship among the six small sites than does a core-satellite model.

Surface survey and excavations at Townley-Read located and explored four domestic refuse clusters (DRCs) within a total survey area of 6.5 ha. Three clusters of 1100–1700 m² in size likely represent individual house lots; a smaller fourth cluster was centered on a trash midden. The three house lots are arranged in a line 60–80 m apart and about 50–150 m away from Burrell Creek, meaning that Townley-Read should be classified as a fully dispersed community. If the 60–80 m linear spacing between houses holds for the remainder of the site area, a total of fifteen to twenty houses could have been constructed in the Townley-Read neighborhood. If each of these potential house lots contained a two-family short longhouse similar to that built in DRC 1, approximately 150 or 200 people may have resided at Townley-Read.

Conover (1882, n.d.), field notes and collections at RMSC (Wray n.d.), and conversations with local collectors indicate that there were at least nine burial clusters at Townley-Read. Based on excavated evidence, each of these cemeteries contained from two to fourteen individuals, and probably each contained fewer than twenty individuals originally. Burials have been reported at all of the components of the New Ganechstage Site Complex except Brother, meaning that Townley-Read did not serve as a central cemetery for the other sites.

The five sites that make up the remainder of the New Ganechstage Site Complex are poorly known, and much of the information recorded about

Key:

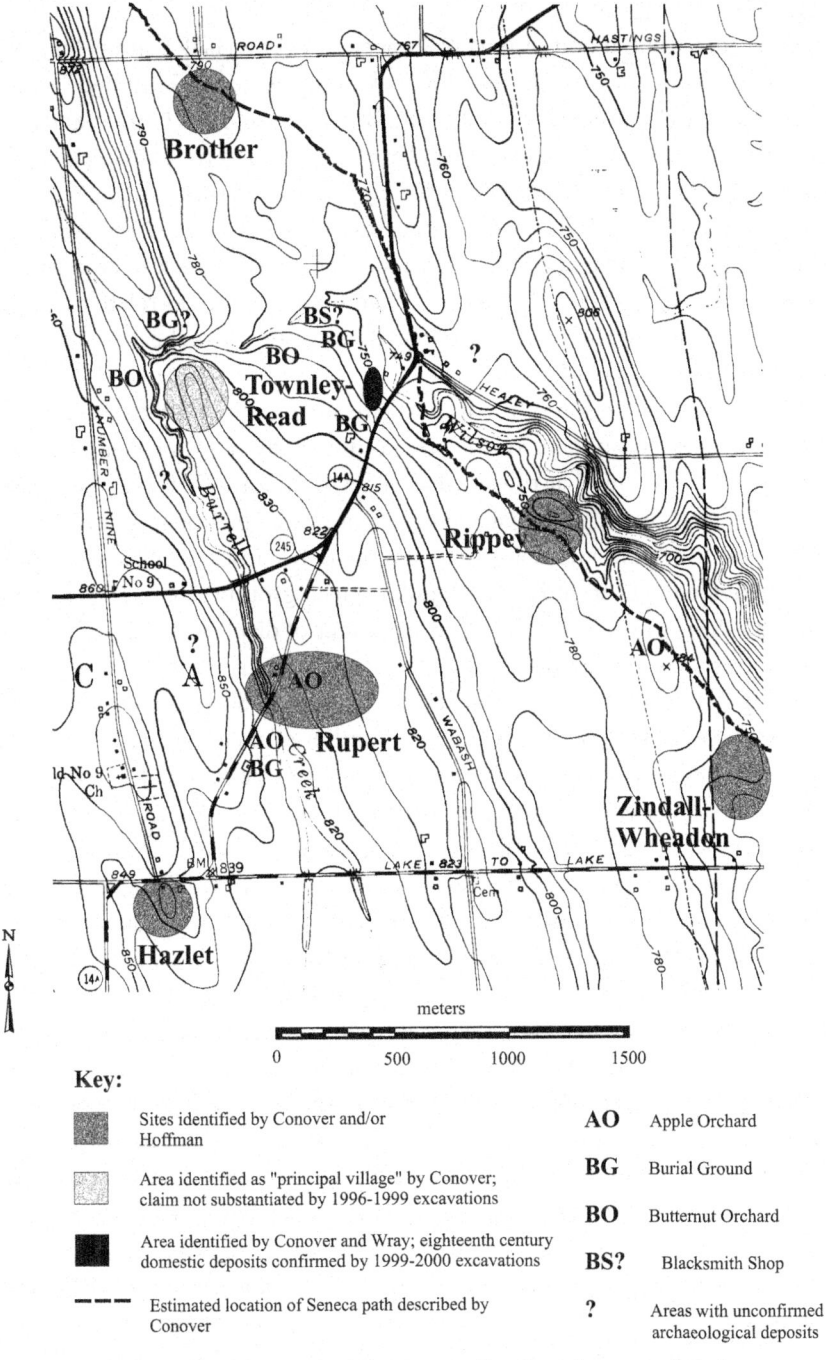

■ Sites identified by Conover and/or Hoffman

▨ Area identified as "principal village" by Conover; claim not substantiated by 1996-1999 excavations

■ Area identified by Conover and Wray; eighteenth century domestic deposits confirmed by 1999-2000 excavations

--- Estimated location of Seneca path described by Conover

AO Apple Orchard
BG Burial Ground
BO Butternut Orchard
BS? Blacksmith Shop
?   Areas with unconfirmed archaeological deposits

Figure 6.6. Topography of the New Ganechstage Site Complex, occupied circa 1715–1754 (modified from K. Jordan 2004: figure 5). Elevations are given in feet; contour interval is 10 feet (3.0 m). Base map taken from U.S. Geological Survey topographical map, 7.5' series, Stanley, New York, quadrangle. (Image used courtesy of *Northeast Anthropology*.)

them is secondhand and of uncertain accuracy. The Hazlet site is located on a slight hill distant from Burrell Creek but reportedly contained "a fine spring of water" (Conover 1882: 87–88). Brass kettles, glass bottles, and red pipestone ornaments have been found at Hazlet (Follett n.d.: Site 393; Hoffman n.d.), conclusively dating it to the eighteenth century. Hoffman (n.d.) states that eight to ten burials had been excavated at Hazlet. The Zindall-Wheadon site is located on the south side of Burrell Creek near another spring (Conover 1882: 87). Follett (n.d.) and Hoffman (n.d.) relate that ten graves had been dug here that contained brass kettles, glass beads, red pipestone ornaments, and iron jackknives.

Conover's description of the Rupert site suggests it was likely to be the second-largest component of the site complex. He describes eighteenth-century artifacts found at the site and remarks that there were "many evidences of fire places" and that a number of graves had been found "scattered over the territory, mainly between the creek and the highway . . . not contiguous enough to indicate a regular burial ground" (n.d.: 83; see also 1882: 85–87). This may indicate that a number of dispersed residences and cemeteries were present at Rupert. The Rippey site contained burials and a spring (Conover 1882: 81–82), which suggests a domestic component. Conover relates that at Rippey "quite a number of skeletons have been exhumed at different times . . . [arranged] lying lengthwise or flat in the grave and alongside of each other," but containing "no relics or trinkets of any kind whatever" (1882: 82). This description is questionable in light of the archaeology of the region. The use of extended burials would seem to date the site to the post-contact era, but an absence of grave goods in an Iroquoian cemetery (especially a Postcolumbian one) would be quite aberrant. Brother is the least known of the New Ganechstage sites; Conover (1882: 81–82) and Townley-Read landowner Jim Minns (personal communication, 1998) could state only that Indian artifacts had been found there.

Based on reported site descriptions and cemetery sizes, on present evidence each of the neighborhoods in the site complex (except for the poorly understood Brother site) likely was occupied by more than one nuclear family.[1] Hazlet and Zindall-Wheadon may have been farmsteads containing individual two-family short longhouses similar to Structure 1 at Townley-Read; Rupert likely contained multiple houses of unknown size; and Rippey contained either a single large household or several smaller households who buried their dead communally. As at Townley-Read, the main consideration in the placement of the other New Ganechstage sites appears to have been access to prime agricultural soil and water rather than defensibility.

The Western Community at the Huntoon Site

The Huntoon site, located 14.5 km west of New Ganechstage, presumably was another major community. As outlined in chapter 4, Huntoon is likely to be the Seneca village of "Onaghee" or "Onnahee" mentioned in 1719–1741 documents, and the "little" or "small" village mentioned in 1719–1742 sources. A 1734 document describes the "small castle called Onnahee consisting of about 160 families" (MACIA vol. 1820: 52a), implying a village population of about eight hundred persons.

At least forty graves have been excavated at Huntoon (Wray n.d.), but no habitation areas have been located. Cemeteries at the site appear similar to the loose clusters of twenty or fewer graves seen at New Ganechstage. My 1995 walkover showed that the terrain in the vicinity of the cemeteries offered little defensive advantage. An area bounded by converging gorges sits about 600 m north of the cemeteries; a former landowner said this area has "a good vantage to the north" (Roger Wolfe, personal communication, 2000). This defensible area (which has not been tested for domestic deposits) is more than 16 ha in size, meaning that community nucleation was not required even if the best defensive terrain at Huntoon was selected for settlement.

Determining more precise dates for the occupation span at Huntoon will require additional archaeological and documentary research. Given political-economic conditions in the Seneca region, if the site proves to be a dispersed community, a 1715 founding date similar to that of New Ganechstage is likely; if it is nucleated, a slightly earlier date between 1710 and 1715 seems feasible. The residents of Onaghee appear somewhat fickle in the documentary record; some persons from Onaghee moved to near Montreal in 1720, and threats were made to move to an unnamed location (possibly on the Genesee River) in 1734 and to Irondequoit in 1738 (MACIA vol. 1820: 52a, 129; NYCD 5: 570–72). Due to the consistency of documentary references, however, Huntoon appears to have been occupied until at least 1741 or 1742,[2] and definitely had been abandoned by 1750 based on the Cammerhoff journal.

The Outlier Village at Kendaia

The newly established Seneca community on the eastern shore of Seneca Lake at Kendaia (on the grounds of present-day Sampson State Park) cannot be considered a satellite of the larger communities in the same way that earlier small communities had been. Kendaia was placed approximately 30 km by land from its closest neighbor, a distance that precluded easy, regular contact. Using the typology for Iroquois uses of space presented in chapter 2, earlier small villages can be defined as *local* satellites in relation to the closest principal village; in contrast, Kendaia is a *regional* satellite village. In 1779 Kendaia was described in terms that suggest a semi-dispersed community plan (Conover 1887: 204; K. Jordan 2004). This type of community structure probably was established in the early years of the settlement; it and the population of Kendaia are discussed in the 1779 section later.

Kendaia was occupied either for an extended period or multiple times. Based on finds of large number of Jesuit artifacts in only one of two excavated cemeteries, Harry Schoff (n.d.) posited a 1700–1730 occupation followed by a 1779-era reoccupation confirmed by historical documents. Although the gap between Schoff's two cemetery dates has led some observers to posit two separate occupations at Kendaia (for example, Grumet 1995; RMSC's "At the Western Door" exhibit), a single, lengthy Seneca occupation at Kendaia seems more feasible. Three avenues of evidence support this claim. First, two occupations of a single site by shifting cultivators during an eighty-year time span appears unlikely; Heidenreich (1971: 188–89) estimates that in the Huron area a fallow period of at least thirty-five years was necessary before reoccupation could be attempted. Second, the site (including additional cemeteries) extends far beyond the area excavated by Schoff (Bob DeOrio, personal communication, 1998); it is quite possible that other, unrecorded cemeteries contain burials from the intervening period. Third, the apple trees at Kendaia were reported to be as much as fifty years old by members of the 1779 Sullivan expedition (Conover 1887: 46), and it is unlikely that the Senecas would have abandoned a large orchard at the peak of its productivity.

Whereas the reported age of the apple trees at Kendaia in 1779 points to a founding date of around 1730, the Jesuit artifacts found at Kendaia by Schoff (n.d.) suggest an earlier founding date. The account book of Albany fur trader Evert Wendell contains references to a Seneca village named "Canadedaerhoo" or close variants dating to 1704 and 1707 (Waterman 2008). These names are quite similar to the "Canadadarhoe" shown in the approximate location of Kendaia on the anonymous "N.W. Parts of New York" map, which likely was produced between 1758 and 1764 (figure 4.4). This may confirm an earlier founding date for Kendaia. If so, Kendaia may represent the resumption of Seneca use of satellite communities after their temporary abandonment during 1688–1704.

Overview

The 1720 settlements exhibit a number of substantial changes in the nature of Seneca settlement preferences. The distance of Kendaia from the main communities at New Ganechstage and Huntoon precluded frequent communication, making Kendaia the first regional satellite small village in the Postcolumbian Seneca sequence. The segmentation of the nucleated community at White Springs into the numerous small neighborhoods of the New Ganechstage Site Complex and the residential dispersal that accompanied it also were unprecedented. The criteria used for selecting settlement location clearly had changed as well; Kendaia, the neighborhoods in the New Ganechstage Site Complex, and possibly Huntoon were situated with little regard for defensive terrain, and the Senecas at Townley-Read selected a low-lying site over a nearby defensible ridgetop. In terms of internal structure, at Townley-Read small graveyards were located fairly close to houses, in contrast to the more isolated, nucleated cemeteries seen on the margins of earlier communities.

These sites were occupied for significantly longer durations than previous nucleated villages. Part of New Ganechstage was still occupied in 1750, as was Kendaia in 1779. The dispersal of houses and the presence of fertile creek-bottom soils may have meant that agricultural resources and firewood were not depleted as quickly as at nucleated settlements. On the limited evidence available from Townley-Read, it is possible that short longhouses may have replaced true longhouses as the predominant residential form (see chapter 9). Finally, it appears that all of the changes in community structure probably occurred *at once* during the move from White Springs. That there was no eighteenth-century occupation on the defensible hilltop at Townley-Read means that the new settlement pattern did not evolve gradually, but was in fact a very rapid, total change from the previous pattern.

The settlement pattern for this time period (at least in the east) appears to consist of site complexes of small villages and hamlets or farmsteads, and of isolated small villages lacking clear spatial association with the larger site complexes. The regional distribution of the 1720 sites maintained some continuity with previous Seneca settlement patterns, in that the major settlements at Huntoon and New Ganechstage were only 14.5 km from each other; only the small community at Kendaia was isolated from the main block of the Seneca population.

Archaeological and documentary evidence indicates that both semi-dispersed and fully dispersed settlements were constructed, and that at least some of the dwellings used were short longhouses. The lack of information about residential arrangements used at Huntoon precludes any more comprehensive statements. Current evidence can account for only approximately 1150 Senecas living in the homeland region in 1720;[3] this figure is admittedly incomplete as it omits those New Ganechstage residents who lived outside the Townley-Read site.

Period 4: 1750

The map of Seneca settlements in 1750 (figure 6.7) is reconstructed from the journal of the Moravian Cammerhoff (Beauchamp 1916: 24–112), which describes his travel to the Seneca towns of New Ganechstage, Ganataqueh, Hachniage, and Zonesschio, as well as his passage through two abandoned Seneca village locations (one fairly definitely White Springs and the other either Huntoon or Snyder-McClure). Although Cammerhoff did not visit every major Seneca site, the journal indicates that new villages had been constructed and that they were more isolated from one another spatially than were the 1720 sites.

Cammerhoff saw "only 8 or 9" houses at what he termed New Ganechstage (Beauchamp 1916: 67), likely meaning he mistook one of the more northerly neighborhoods in the Site Complex (for example, Brother or Townley-Read) for the entire community. Since New Ganechstage's successor village at Kanadesaga was not occupied until around 1754 (NYCD 6: 856–57), additional Senecas almost undoubtedly continued to live in the southern part of the site complex. That the Moravians traveled between New Ganechstage and Canandaigua without encountering any active settlements indicates that Huntoon had been abandoned. Again, archaeological and documentary evidence favors the conclusion that Kendaia was occupied in 1750; other Seneca settlements off Cammerhoff and Zeisberger's route may have been occupied at this time as well.

Newer settlements recorded by Cammerhoff include Ganataqueh, Hachniage, and Zonesschio. Zonesschio in the Genesee Valley is probably Wray's (1983) Fall Brook site; it likely was founded by migrants from Huntoon and possibly other communities during the 1740s. Cammerhoff's Hachniage likely can be equated with the Honeoye site. Ganataqueh was located near Canandaigua Lake; however, by 1779 it apparently had been replaced by a newer village, and it is unclear which of the two settlements

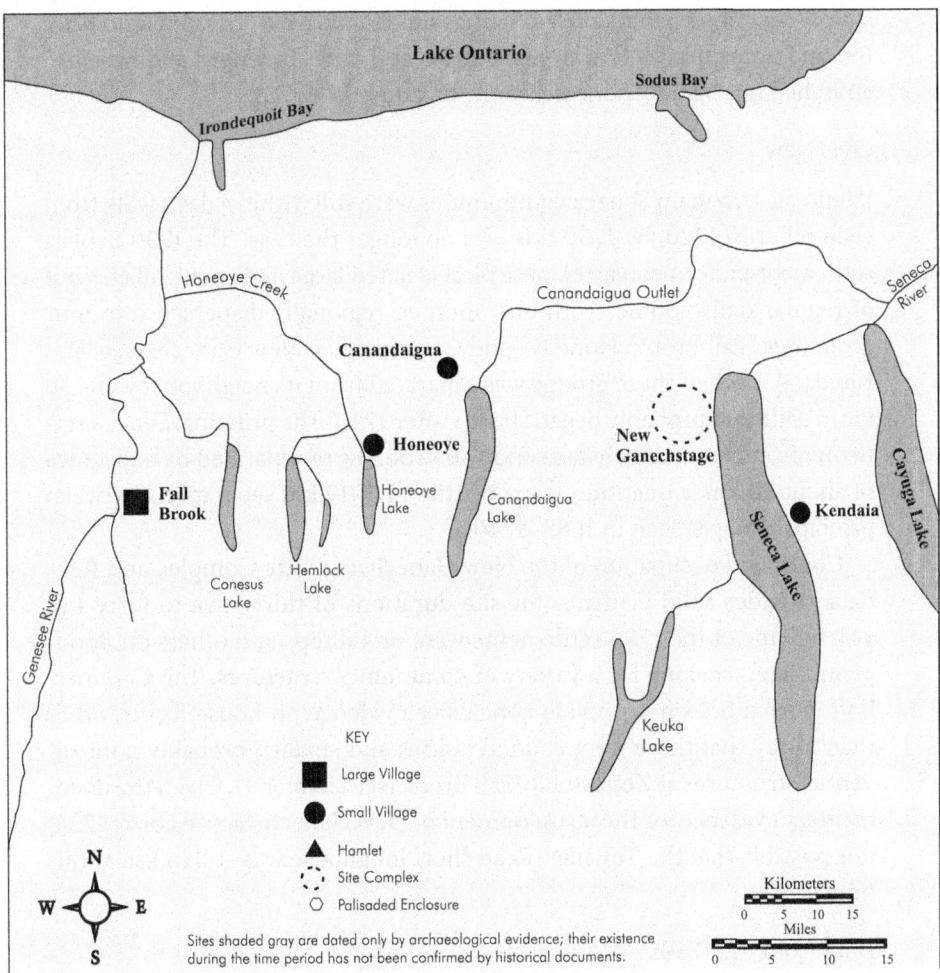

Figure 6.7. Seneca settlements, 1750 (modified from K. Jordan 2004: figure 6). Base map adapted from Wray (1983). (Image used courtesy of *Northeast Anthropology*.)

corresponds to the Postcolumbian component at the Sackett site excavated by William Ritchie in the 1930s (Hayes 1965; Ritchie 1936).

Cammerhoff (Beauchamp 1916: 67, 73) provides house counts only for New Ganechstage (eight or nine "huts") and Zonesschio ("40 or more large huts"). Zonesschio, described as the Seneca capital, probably was the largest of the 1750 settlements. Figure 6.7 classifies Zonesschio/Fall Brook as a large village, although a house count of forty may mean that the site housed fewer than five hundred people. The site complex at New Ganechstage probably was occupied beyond the northern hamlet visited by Cammerhoff, and Ganataqueh and Hachniage appear to have been larger than hamlets. There is little information on community structure in the Cammerhoff journal; he simply describes Ganataqueh as being "situated on a hill" (Beauchamp 1916: 69) and notes that a "fine large plain, several miles in length and breadth" stretched out behind Zonesschio (Beauchamp 1916: 73).

Overview

While the two main Seneca communities were still within a day's walk from each other in 1720, by 1750 this was no longer the case. The 1750 Seneca settlement pattern consisted of several isolated large and small villages out of regular daily contact with one another, regionally dispersed into four groupings (Fall Brook; Honeoye and Canandaigua; New Ganechstage; and Kendaia). Each of these groups was separated from its neighbors by 20–30 km, a shift that probably began shortly after 1740. The principal Seneca settlements at New Ganechstage and Fall Brook were separated by a distance of about 70 km, a quantum leap over the 14.5–19 km separations between principal villages seen in 1688–1740.

Continued occupation of the New Ganechstage Site Complex and Kendaia provides solid evidence for site durations of thirty-five to forty-five years. Some of the 1750 settlements were on hilltops and others on floodplains, likely making for a variety of community structures. The Cammerhoff journal does not provide conclusive evidence on house forms, other than to say that there were council houses and smaller, probably nonresidential structures at Zonesschio/Fall Brook (see chapter 9). Given the documentary evidence for the abandonment of New Ganechstage in about 1754, it is possible that the Townley-Read short longhouse was still in use at this time.

Data from the 1760s

A relatively detailed manuscript map dating to the 1760s ("N.W. Parts of New York" 1750–1768; see discussion in chapter 4) provides a view of Seneca settlements between 1750 and 1779. This map shows settlements in the relative locations of Kendaia (labeled "Canadadarhoe"), Canandaigua (labeled "Canodago," eight houses), Honeoye ("Haneaye"), and Fall Brook ("Chenosious," fifty houses). The map clearly postdates the New Ganechstage Site Complex: "Canossodage," which appears to be on Burrell Creek, is marked abandoned, and a settlement labeled "the New Castel" is shown in the location of Kanadesaga. Other settlements in the Seneca region (which either existed in 1750 but were not noted by Cammerhoff, or were established between 1750 and the map's creation) include "Canawagis" near present-day Avon (six houses), and "Canosseago" located somewhat ambiguously on a watercourse marked "Branch of Ohio" (possibly the Allegheny River). Canosseago also is labeled "30 houses from near Pitsburgh formerly." David Zeisberger's account of a 1768 journey in the Genesee Valley indicates that the large village at "Zoneschio" (likely Fall Brook) was fully dispersed. He states that the "town consists of some twenty houses. Most of the people live outside it, scattered through the forest within a radius of two to three miles [3–5 km]" (Hulbert and Schwarze 1912: 85). Discrepancies in the house counts for Fall Brook—Zeisberger claims there were twenty houses, the "N.W. Parts of New York" map fifty, and Cammerhoff forty in 1750—may be due to the fact that observers viewed and counted different portions of the town. Zeisberger in particular seems to have enumerated only the central part of the community.

Period 5: 1779

In August and September 1779, American soldiers commanded by General John Sullivan destroyed at least seventeen nominally Seneca settlements between Chemung and Genesee Castle (inclusive), and forces under Colonel Daniel Brodhead destroyed approximately eleven settlements on the Allegheny River. Hunter (1956) documents a significant Fox and Munsee presence in the lower Allegheny towns, and also claims that despite its location in the Genesee Valley, the village of Gathtsegwarohare was a Fox, rather than a Seneca, settlement. Records from the American expeditions indicate that there were more Seneca settlements than in previous periods, and that villages continued to be unclustered (figure 6.8; the Chemung and Allegheny settlements are not pictured).

The Sullivan and Brodhead expeditions did not destroy all the Seneca villages, but the number and location of Seneca towns occupied in 1779 that survived the 1779 invasions has not been determined conclusively. Wray (1983) associates the Avon Bridge and Caneadea I sites with this period; Avon Bridge is likely to be the site of Canawaugus known from documentary sources (Abler 1989: 115; "N.W. Parts of New York" 1750–1768; Fenton 1998: 602–3; Jennings et al. 1985: 211). Other unaffected Seneca villages that may have been occupied in 1779, possibly including settlements on the present-day Seneca reservations at Cattaraugus and Tonawanda (Abler 1989: 118; Graymont 1972: 218; Hamell 1992a: 30; Wallace 1969: 143), are not shown in figure 6.8.

Table 6.3 summarizes the village descriptions found in the journals and letters of thirty-two American expedition members published in Conover

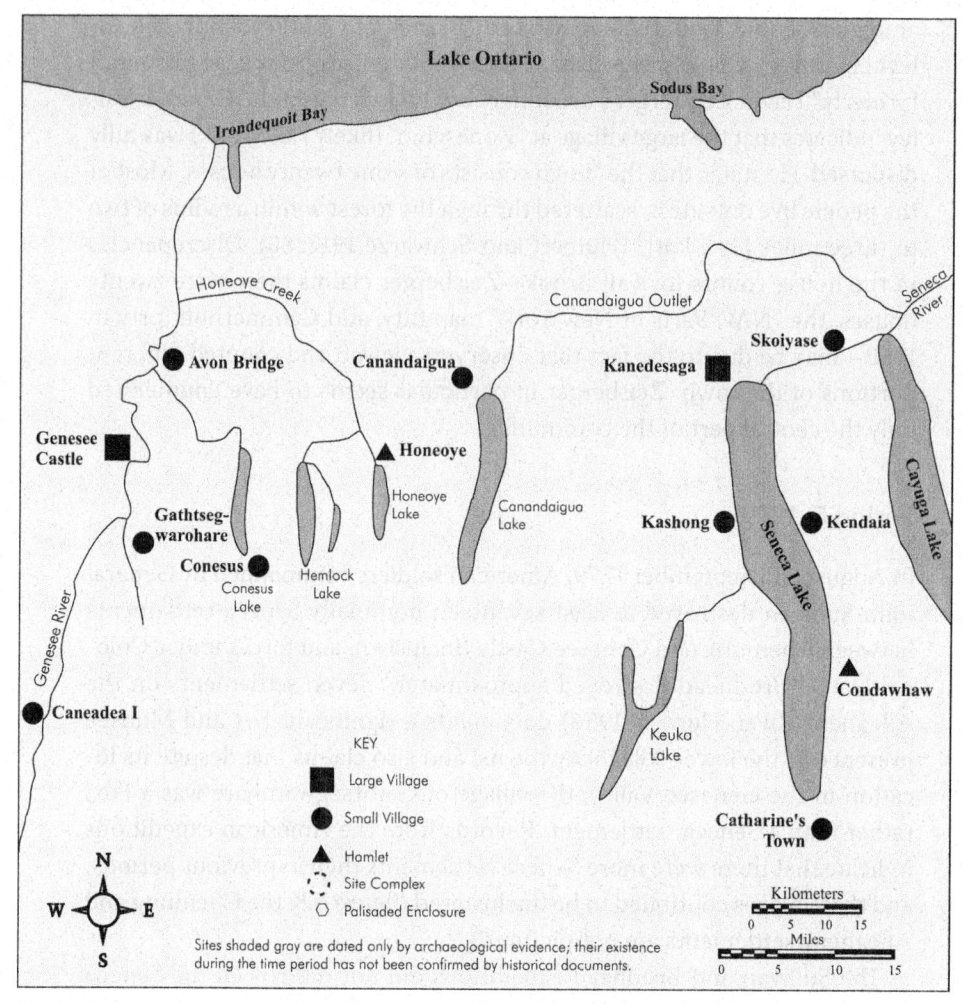

Figure 6.8. Seneca settlements, 1779 (modified from Jordan 2004: Figure 7). Base map adapted from Wray (1983). (Image used courtesy of *Northeast Anthropology*.)

(1887) and Division of Archives and History (1929). It demonstrates that Senecas were using a striking variety of settlement sizes, types of community organization, and house forms in 1779. The median value of all the house counts contained in the journals proved to be the best way to summarize data typically expressed as ranges (for example, "10 to 20 houses") or approximations ("about 20 houses"). Genesee Castle is the only site that definitely can be classified as a large village, as its median house count of 107 would represent a population of more than five hundred even if every house were a nuclear-family residence. Kanadesaga, the second-largest

Table 6.3. Seneca Settlements Destroyed by the American Sullivan Expedition, 1779

Settlement[a]	Number of House Counts	Median House Count	Orchards Mentioned	Community Structure	Comments	Shown in Fig. 6.8
Chemung	12	30	no	scattered	council houses, frame houses	no
Newtown	4	40	no	scattered	new, "Tory houses"	no
Middle Town	1	8	no	n/a	"buildings of English construction"	no
Canaweola	4	20	no	scattered	"Tory Houses"	no
Big Flats	0	n/a	no	n/a	—	no
Catharine's Town	11	30	yes	"middling compact"	council house?	yes
Condawhaw	2	7	no	scattered	—	yes
Kendaia	14	20	yes	compact	old	yes
Kanadesaga	17	50	yes	compact	old, council house	yes
Kashong	5	20	yes	n/a	new, "white" houses	yes
Skoiyase	2	19	no	n/a	fish ponds	yes
Canandaigua	16	28	no	compact	new, "white" houses	yes
Honeoye	13	10	yes	n/a	old	yes
Conesus	11	18	yes	n/a	—	yes
Gathtsegwarohare	8	22	no	n/a	new	yes
Genesee Castle	19	107	no	compact	new, field houses	yes
Painted Post	0	n/a	no	n/a	"white" houses	no

Sources: Conover 1887; Division of Archives and History 1929.
Note: a. Settlements are listed in order of their destruction.

settlement with a median house count of fifty, probably also housed more than five hundred people. Settlements of two to ten houses have been classified as hamlets, as have the small Chemung Valley settlements at Big Flats and Painted Post for which no house counts were given.

Expedition members appear to have accurately described the age of several settlements. By 1779 only two of the 1750 villages, Kendaia and Honeoye, were still occupied; both were described as "old." Kendaia was almost universally labeled the oldest Seneca settlement, and John Burrowes estimated that the apple trees there were fifty years old (Conover 1887: 46). Kanadesaga contained apple trees estimated by Jabez Campfield to be twenty to thirty years old (Conover 1887: 58). Ganataqueh and Fall Brook both had been replaced by new settlements located only a short distance away. Newer settlements did not have well-established fruit tree orchards, and were more likely to contain houses that Sullivan expedition members assumed had been built by Europeans, which they called "Tory houses," among other terms.[4]

There had been no consistent trend toward more dispersed settlement in the Seneca area since 1750. Sullivan expedition members describe various settlements as "scattered," "compact," or "middling compact." Despite the fact that Genesee Castle was at most ten years old (it was on the opposite side of the river from where the Americans expected to find it), it was described by Samuel Shute as "the most compact" of any village he had seen (Conover 1887: 272). This community apparently had consolidated significantly since Zeisberger's observations in 1768, but it is unlikely that Genesee Castle's residents adopted a nucleated community structure like that seen at Ganondagan, since it was in a non-defensible valley setting. Both Kanadesaga and Kendaia, described in more detail later, had semi-dispersed community structures. Communities such as Chemung, Newtown, Canaweola, and Condawhaw, which were built along watercourses, may have been fully dispersed in a manner similar to Townley-Read.

Kanadesaga: Successor Village to Townley-Read

As noted in chapter 5, the Senecas at New Ganechstage began to move to a new location at Kanadesaga no later than 1754 (NYCD 6: 856–57). Kanadesaga was built on a ridgetop, a major change from the settlement locations in the New Ganechstage Site Complex. The defensibility of the Kanadesaga ridgetop was aided by a European-built fort. In 1756 Sir William Johnson ordered the construction of a small (45.7 m^2) fort with two blockhouses in the midst of the new village (JP 9: 457–58). The fort apparently was never garrisoned by European troops. It was being used as a Seneca residence in 1765, when the Reverend Samuel Kirkland spent most of the winter in one of the blockhouses as a guest (Pilkington 1980: 11). Sullivan expedition members describe the fort as being in ruins in 1779; they destroyed the remnants. Lewis Henry Morgan mapped the preserved traces of the stockade in 1845, noting its rectangular shape (measuring 64 × 37 paces), locations of the blockhouses, and two possible European-run smithies within the stockade's walls (Tooker 1994: figures 2, 13).

Even with the presence of the fort, the location of Kanadesaga was not ideal defensively. Although the site is on the eastern end of a ridge, the terrain is relatively flat to the north and slopes upward to the west. To the southeast the site is somewhat protected by Kanadesaga Creek and slight slopes, but in terms of overall defensibility the site cannot compare with earlier locations such as Ganondagan and Fort Hill, or even Snyder-McClure and White Springs. Comparing Morgan's 1845 map to the present-day landscape suggests that the British fort actually may have been built in a low-lying area at the base of a hill, making it all but useless for defensive purposes. Sir William Johnson may have intended the structure to be a fortification, but the location specified by the Seneca hosts may have limited the fort's effective functions to those of smithy and trading post.

Kirkland's account of his 1765 stay at Kanadesaga contains few details about community structure or house forms, beyond that there was a 24.3 m council house at the site and that he slept on "bunks" in two separate houses (Pilkington 1980: 8–11). Sullivan expedition member William McKendry (Conover 1887: 205) described the settlement at Kanadesaga as being "very compact[,] not more than 100 rods [503 m] from outside to outside." A secondary account describing the captivity of Jane Campbell, who was taken to Kanadesaga in 1779, relates that the "village was laid out with some regularity, and in almost circular form, enclosing a large green" (Campbell 1831: 178).[5]

Archaeology conducted at Kanadesaga to date has not located intact eighteenth-century domestic features. Although eighteenth-century artifacts were recovered, RMSC-sponsored excavations in 1975 failed to uncover any definite eighteenth-century features or to confirm the location of the 1756 stockade (Hamell n.d.). In 2002, a large-scale survey of an approximately 29.4 ha area south of Kanadesaga Creek recovered no traces of eighteenth-century Iroquois occupation (Hartgen Archaeological Associates 2002). Based on this evidence, the documentary sources asserting or implying that Kanadesaga had a circular community structure (Campbell 1831: 178; Conover 1887: 205) should not be taken literally. The nonresidential area south of the creek should be removed from site size calculations and the village provisionally considered to be a half-circle in plan, approximately 500 m across in its longest dimension, based on the McKendry journal.

This model of the site area and the median house count of fifty provided by the Sullivan journals for the town can be used to calculate an average house lot size of 1987 m^2 (Jordan 2004: table 4). This estimate is reasonably close to the archaeologically observed size of the larger DRCs at Townley-Read, which may mean that a similar type of house lot organization was used at both sites. Use of the provisional population–to–residential site area relationship of 1 person per 170 m^2 I have posited for Townley-Read results in an estimated population of 584 for Kanadesaga (K. Jordan 2004). Kanadesaga is classified as semi-dispersed based on the combination of the semicircular structure of the site, its hilltop location, and the large average house lot size calculated for the site.

Kendaia

McKendry (Conover 1887: 204–5) estimated that at Kendaia eleven houses had been built on a 302 m × 101 m ridge, producing an average house lot size of 2759 m² (K. Jordan 2004: table 4). Since there is a median count of twenty houses for Kendaia based on fourteen estimates, it appears that McKendry described only a portion of the site. Only burials have been excavated at Kendaia (Schoff n.d.). Although the exact location of the ridge described by McKendry has not been determined, the topography in the area is not particularly well suited for defensive purposes. The implied rectangular or oval structure of the community and the large average house lot size calculated for the site class Kendaia as a semi-dispersed village. Use of the Townley-Read 1 person per 170 m² ratio results in an estimated population of 179 for the portion of Kendaia described by McKendry (K. Jordan 2004).

Overview

In summary, the Seneca settlement pattern in 1779 consisted of two large villages and a number of spatially isolated small villages and hamlets. Continuing the pattern seen in the 1750 sites, the principal Seneca villages at Kanadesaga and Genesee Castle were separated by almost 75 km. Some Seneca towns were placed in locations that were more defensible than the 1720–1750 sites were, but it does not appear that defensibility was the predominant factor in determining village placement. Even communities set on what observers called "hilltops" or "eminences"—such as Kendaia and Kanadesaga—were not placed on steep-sided hills nor did they offer particularly good visibility, and the location of Kanadesaga has a number of defensive flaws for which the British-built fort offered scant compensation.

The Senecas used a wide range of community forms in 1779. The settlements along the Chemung River are described as being the most scattered, and probably were linear, fully dispersed communities; other villages, such as Genesee Castle, are described as more compact. However, even the most compact 1779 settlements in no way approached the level of nucleation present at Ganondagan, and they should be classified as semi-dispersed.

Discussion

The pattern of two large Seneca villages with smaller local satellites (Wray and Schoff 1953) clearly was abandoned during the 1687–1779 period, which concluded with numerous, spatially isolated Seneca villages and hamlets.

It is possible to view the entire period as one in which the overall number of villages and inter-village distances gradually increased, and village size incrementally decreased. However, this linear, normative scenario obscures important exceptions and discontinuities. Changes in Seneca settlement pattern, site defensibility, community structure, cemetery size, and settlement duration instead took place abruptly during two main historical moments: the first during 1710–1720, and the second during 1740–1750.

The sequence of major disjunctions in the Seneca use of space—indications that the daily lives of Senecas changed quite dramatically—provides a counterpoint to a document-based depiction of 1687–1779 Seneca political economy (chapter 3). Spatial data underscore the importance of certain historical moments and downplay others. Two concepts are particularly relevant to this discussion. The first is the distinction between *short-distance* and *long-distance* village relocations. Following Champlain, Snow (2001: 22) suggests that short-distance moves were most often the consequence of "normal" ecological and economic factors, such as local resource exhaustion and demographic pressure, whereas long-distance moves frequently were the result of political factors such as warfare. The second concept is that of *settlement pattern change*, which requires a major shift in settlement preferences with regard to village size, spacing, setting, community organization, or village duration; a village relocation in itself cannot be considered a change in settlement pattern without such major alterations.

The combination of data on the Seneca use of space (derived from archaeology and locally specific readings of documents) and on the political-economic context in which the Senecas lived (mainly derived from documentary sources) offers interesting results. It strongly implies that explanations stressing gradual long-term processes such as demographic decline, increasing colonial domination by Europeans, declining military strength, changes in subsistence practices, and overall cultural disintegration (for example, Fenton 1998; Haan 1976; Jennings 1984; Ramenofsky 1987; Richter 1992; Snow 1994, 1995; Taylor 1995: 34) provide a less satisfactory explanatory framework than does a focus on the specific constraints and opportunities offered by supra-regional political-economic factors during particular time periods.

The first major event in Seneca history during the 1677–1779 period was the destruction wrought by the Denonville expedition. This invasion prompted a long-distance relocation that fits Snow's model perfectly. The settlement pattern at the 1700 villages was not altered however—the Senecas still built large, nucleated, hilltop villages that were close enough for regular communication; cemetery size and placement preferences were unaltered; and village duration was similar to that of pre-Denonville settlements. If palisades were constructed at Snyder-McClure or White Springs, their construction can be seen as the taking up of one of the options within the Seneca settlement repertoire in response to a hostile military climate.

The next major event in Seneca history—the ending of the Twenty Years' War through the peace treaties of 1700–1701—was not accompanied by a village move or major settlement pattern change. The founding of the regional satellite village at Kendaia marked resumption of the pre-1687 settlement pattern with a twist: Senecas again lived in a satellite community, but they constructed it at a greater distance from the principal villages than pre-1687 local satellites had been. It would be reasonable to argue that the peace agreements came so close on the heels of the 1688 relocations that Senecas would have been reluctant to abandon large villages only midway through their life cycles. If the peace had been fully effective, however, the principal settlements could have diversified, perhaps through the construction of local satellite villages or farmsteads. Such a development does not appear to have taken place. The constant fluctuation and uncertain future of military and trade relations with the French, British, and western Indian groups and the continuance of sporadic violence during the 1701–1713 period of uncertainty made it prudent for the bulk of the Seneca population to continue to reside in nucleated, defensible villages. Kendaia may have been built on the border of Cayuga territory, far from any principal villages, in an attempt to evade enemies.

The end of the period of uncertainty in about 1713 appears to have had a major effect on the Senecas' use of space. The changes exhibited by the New Ganechstage Site Complex—eschewal of defensive terrain, segmentation of the community into linear neighborhoods along watercourses, construction of fully dispersed houses, use of relatively small cemeteries, extension of site duration, and possibly a transition to communities with a majority of shorthouses (see chapter 9)—represent a near-complete transformation of the Seneca settlement system.

The length of occupation at White Springs argues that the founding of New Ganechstage (including Townley-Read) occurred soon after the beginning of the geographic middleman period, perhaps by 1715. It is likely that Huntoon was established at close to the same time. The timing of the settlement pattern change appears to be closely linked to transformations in the regional political-economic situation that occurred at the beginning of the middleman period. Political-economic developments included the establishment of relative local peace, Iroquois declarations of neutrality to the French and British, and the transit of increased numbers of pelt-bearing western Indian groups across Iroquoia to trade at Albany. The settlement changes can be seen as a response to broad-scale political transformations, but in this situation it can be argued that the moves were *opportunistic* rather than *reactive* (as they had been in 1687).

The fact that the opening of the British trading post at Oswego in 1724 was not accompanied by Seneca village moves—in particular, there was no move toward Lake Ontario to ensure interception of western Indians traveling to Oswego—runs counter to the assertion made by Haan (1976) and Richter (1992) that the new post was a political-economic disaster for all the Iroquois nations. While inland locations near Seneca and Canandaigua lakes had sufficed during the middleman period, one might expect a village shift toward Lake Ontario after 1724 in response to the increased importance of the lakeside, all-water route to Oswego. But despite sporadic Seneca threats to move north to the lake (such as the proposed move from Huntoon to Irondequoit in 1738 [MACIA vol. 1820: 129]), even the 1750 sites—most of which were settled during the latter part of the Oswego era (chapter 3)—did not relocate in that direction. The regional evidence indicates *long-term stability* in relations between the Senecas and pelt-bearing western Indian groups. This implies that mechanisms for the creation and maintenance of alliances between the Senecas and western Indians used during the middleman period continued to work during the Oswego era.

A long-distance village move took place during 1740–1750 when Senecas directly occupied the Genesee Valley for the first time since the mid-sixteenth century. The main Genesee Valley settlement at Fall Brook was built about 55 km from Lake Ontario. While Fall Brook was not much farther from Lake Ontario than Huntoon (at about 45 km) had been, the settlements on the Genesee River likely were founded in reaction to major changes in the political economy of the fur trade. Documentary sources demonstrate that both French and British traders were focusing more on direct exchange with fur producers in the Ohio territory and Mississippi Valley than on attracting western Indians to their posts on Lake Ontario. The Genesee Valley settlements, probably founded in the early 1740s, were in a locale that was both less connected to Lake Ontario and better positioned for Iroquois hunters to head to the Ohio territory themselves.

There are many documents from the 1740s and 1750s indicating that the Genesee Senecas were more "pro-French" than their eastern counterparts. This would seem to continue the long-standing Francophilia seen at the preceding western village of Huntoon (see chapters 3 and 4). The move to the Genesee Valley placed western Senecas closer to the French fort at Niagara, something that might have seemed sensible as events started to build toward King George's War (1744–1748). Although this war did not actually expand into direct imperial conflict in northeastern North America, the prospect of war may very well have influenced the relocation decision. Some of the eastern villages founded at this time, such as Honeoye and Canandaigua, may have been more nucleated or have occupied more defensible settings than did their predecessors. During the war New York officials encouraged the eastern Seneca towns (perhaps the older ones) to nucleate, but these communities failed to comply.

It is interesting to note that Huntoon was occupied for a substantially shorter time than its eastern contemporaries at New Ganechstage and Kendaia. The overall political-economic climate during the middleman period and the Oswego era favored New York over New France. Since the western village was more Francophile in orientation, its residents may have hedged somewhat by building their village in a position where it could take advantage of western Indian traffic, but at the same time use a more defensible setting and a nucleated (or at least relatively nucleated) village plan. If that proves to be the case, the estimated occupation span of approximately twenty-five years for Huntoon may have had its roots not only in imperial politics and the dynamics of the fur trade, but also in ecological constraints on the duration of nucleated villages.

The next major upheaval in Seneca history was the onset of the Seven Years' War. It is notable that at this point the New Ganechstage Senecas gave up their dispersed settlements along Burrell Creek and moved to a semi-dispersed ridgetop setting at Kanadesaga. The occupation at New Ganechstage therefore coincides almost completely with the period of relative local peace from 1713 to 1754. Although the location of Kanadesaga was not perfect for defense, it represented a substantial improvement over the linear, downslope locations at Townley-Read. Such continued use of large house lots in semi-dispersed settlements represented a compromise between the labor and resource advantages of dispersed villages (see chapter 7) versus the need for increased vigilance and defensibility in a time of heightened imperial hostilities.

After the Seven Years' War, the resultant surrender of New France to Great Britain, and Pontiac's War, the Senecas built smaller villages more isolated from one another. This intra-regional dispersal likely responded to the elimination of the possibility of imperial war between the French and

British, which meant that villages could be situated in response to ecological and economic rather than defensive concerns. This settlement pattern was encountered by the Sullivan and Brodhead expeditions in 1779, themselves products of the new rivalry between Great Britain and the rebellious American colonists. It is interesting to note that the western Seneca "capital" was dispersed in 1768 but rebuilt in "compact" form by 1779, which may further indicate the quickness with which Senecas responded to political-economic changes.

The majority of the Seneca population spent the winter of 1779–1780 as refugees near Fort Niagara in dismal conditions (Calloway 1995: 129–57). Although western portions of Seneca territory were reoccupied or newly settled starting in late 1779 and 1780 (Calloway 1995: 141; Graymont 1972: 220–22; A. Mt. Pleasant 2004), land cessions and reservationization starting with the hotly contested 1784 Treaty of Fort Stanwix began a process in which Euro-American settlers hemmed in the Senecas on smaller and smaller pieces of territory (Graymont 1976; Hauptman 1999; Taylor 2006; Wallace 1969). After 1784, Senecas had much less control over where they could settle.

In short, close comparison of the historical sequence of supra-regional political-economic conditions known from documentary sources with the timing of changes in the Senecas' use of space has much to offer. Such comparison draws attention to the onset of favorable political-economic conditions in 1713 and to the dynamics of the 1740–1750 decade when the Genesee Valley was reoccupied. A focus on particular political-economic conditions (both local and supra-regional) has greater power to explain specific village relocations and changes in settlement pattern than do less-rooted appeals to general processes such as overall "acculturation," cultural decline, linear increases in village dispersal, or continuous decreases in site defensibility. A contextual political-economic approach also highlights the agency of eighteenth-century Senecas: even after one hundred years of direct engagement with Europeans, long-distance village moves and settlement pattern changes were not always reactive; they could also be opportunistic. The 1715 settlement pattern changes responded to just such an opportunity. Some of the reasons why those changes were attractive are discussed in the next chapter.

7

The Logic of Dispersed Settlement

In about 1715, Senecas living at the White Springs site abandoned their nucleated, hilltop village and resettled in several small "neighborhoods" arrayed along Burrell Creek. Although this move, like earlier short-distance relocations to new nucleated settlements, likely was prompted by ecological concerns such as resource depletion and pest infestation, this particular village move involved a complete transformation in the structure of the eastern Seneca community. This chapter provides a detailed look at the uses Townley-Read residents made of space, and offers a new interpretation of the motivations for and consequences of community segmentation and site-level residential dispersal. Although most primary and secondary sources characterize dispersal in negative terms, excavation data collected by the Townley-Read/New Ganechstage Project suggest that Seneca dispersal was a reasoned and rational response to a particular set of political, economic, and ecological conditions.

The task of analyzing Iroquois dispersal is complicated by the fact that Six Nations peoples undertook actions which can be characterized as dispersal at a number of spatial and temporal scales. Eighteenth-century Senecas dispersed extra-regionally, as shown by the establishment of satellite communities in Pennsylvania and Ohio, and at the regional level, as seen in the reoccupation of the Genesee Valley in the 1740s. They also dispersed at the community level, illustrated by the segmented form of the New Ganechstage Site Complex, and at the site level, as seen by the increased distance between houses at the Townley-Read site. Seasonal dispersal (temporary expeditions to procure resources such as passenger pigeons, fish, or deer) also took place. In each of these instances Seneca places of residence shifted and "dispersed," in some cases briefly and in others more or less permanently.

Furthermore, different motivations appear to have caused residential dispersal in the various parts of Iroquoia. Mohawk communities appear to have segmented and Mohawk residences dispersed primarily in order to secure land access in the face of European territorial encroachment, whereas economic opportunism appears to have produced a similar spatial pattern at New Ganechstage (K. Jordan 2009). The analysis presented here is tailored to local political-economic conditions in eastern Seneca territory. Additional targeted research will be necessary to determine whether and why dispersal took place in other parts of the Confederacy, although conditions analogous to the Seneca situation are likely to apply in Cayuga, Onondaga, and Oneida territories (K. Jordan 2002: 325–26).

Negative Interpretations of Iroquois Settlement Dispersal

Most of the descriptions and interpretations of Iroquois residential dispersal found in eighteenth-century documents share several characteristics, regardless of whether the observations were made by Europeans or the Iroquois themselves. First, primary sources are imprecise about the types of dispersal they discuss: documents seldom specify whether they refer to seasonal or relatively permanent dispersal, and whether dispersal took place at the site, community, regional, or extra-regional scale. Second, these accounts consistently express disapproval over Iroquois "spreading out." Although anthropologists and historians looking at eighteenth-century Iroquois society often uncritically repeat these negative comments, it is not altogether clear that the interpretations offered in primary sources should be taken at face value.

Iroquois and European Views from Diplomatic and Missionary Accounts: Loss of Control

Transcribed eighteenth-century Iroquois speeches often describe residential dispersals in mournful tones. Six Nations leaders viewed their current "scattered" state poorly as compared to the past, when their nations were stronger and lived "in a body" (NYCD 6: 217). Native speakers emphasized factionalism, alcohol abuse, and imperial politics as causes for dispersal; most of their comments appear to address extra-regional population movement. In a 1710 conference, Oneida and Onondaga leaders said that unless alcohol sales were ended "it would be impossible to preserve peace in their Castles but that they would be forced to disperse whereby an end would be put to their Nation" (Colden 1935 [1720]: 388; see also McIlwain 1915: 75–76). In 1741 Mohawk sachems complained to the Albany Commissioners that "in former Days the Indians lived near each other in their several Tribes but that now they are become a Scattered People & that great Numbers are removed to Canada & elsewhere & that they fear those who are left will soon be gone" (McIlwain 1915: 223–24; IIDH, Oct. 3, 1741). In 1754 the Mohawk leader Hendrick claimed that dispersal was a product of British neglect (Aquila 1983: 108).

European interpretations also linked Iroquois dispersal to political-economic dissipation. One of the earliest European critiques of Iroquois residential dispersal is found in the record of an April 1700 meeting between New York officials and Onondagas. This document appears to equate community-level dispersal with a loss of political power. The New Yorkers advised the Onondagas to "make your dwellings and habitatiou[n]s compact together, that upon occasion they may be secured and not stragling to and again, as we see they are; which will be a means to preserve your name and keep you from any suddain assault or incursion of an enemy" (NYCD 4: 661). While Richter (1992: 257) has taken this as evidence that the Onondagas built dispersed communities shortly after the 1696 destruction of their villages by Frontenac, there is little archaeological support for this claim, and it is implausible that the Onondagas would have constructed a permanent, indefensible community in the midst of the Twenty Years' War.[1] The remainder of the 1700 document indicates that the New York delegation was impeded and delayed because many Onondagas were living in seasonal fishing camps when they arrived (NYCD 4: 657–60). Perhaps New York officials voiced their frustration with the *seasonal* dispersal of Onondaga men to fish.

Jesuit documents provide other early European interpretations of Iroquois residential dispersal. In 1718 Father Joseph-François Lafitau claimed that some Iroquois had moved to missions on the St. Lawrence River due to alcohol-related disruptions in the homeland villages (JR 67: 39–41). In 1735 Father Luc François Nau echoed these sentiments, writing from the mission at Kahnawake that "the five Iroquois nations, who are with the English, are visibly on the decrease, on account of their incessant quarrels and the use of Intoxicants supplied by the [E]nglish. It is for this reason that the more provident abandon a country where they cannot live peaceably and come to settle among us" (JR 68: 277–79). These explanations overlook other motivations for relocation, such as the opportunities for hunting and trade available to Iroquois living on the St. Lawrence (see Parmenter 2001b).

During the 1740s and 1750s New York officials repeatedly appealed to individual Iroquois nations to end their dispersal and gather themselves together in "a general Castle" (for example, NYCD 6: 857). As noted in chapter 3, Senecas were frequent recipients of such criticism from New York. In response to the Mohawk complaints in October 1741, the commissioners recommended that "100 lb of Pouder" and a proportionate amount of lead "should be lodged at each of their [Iroquois] Castles in order to keep them from settling at a Distance as scarcity of Provisions is partly the reason & also that the French endeavor to draw them toward Cadaraqui Lake [Lake Ontario]"; they also acknowledged that New York did not have the funds necessary to carry out the plan (McIlwain 1915: 224). In June 1742 the lieutenant governor informed the Iroquois that "it is with great concern that he understands most of the 6 Nations have of late years dispersed themselves forgetting their Antient Custom of dwelling together in Castles. [H]e exhorts them to return to their Primitive Way of Living as it will add to their Strength & enlarge their Influence" (McIlwain 1915: 226–27). In 1744 at the beginning of King George's War, New York Governor George Clinton encouraged the Iroquois "to live compact together in their Castles wch is absolutely necessary for their own Security in this time of War" (234). British colonial officials also repeatedly demanded that Iroquois nations recall their kinsmen from Ohio (Parmenter 2001a: 107–8).

Despite frequent Iroquois assertions that they "approved of the Govrs Exhortation to live in their Castles as formerly" (McIlwain 1915: 227), and that they were "buisy in collecting themselves together in order to live in Compact Bodies" (235), Six Nations (and particularly Seneca) compliance with these dictates was markedly incomplete. In 1754 the commissioners were still recommending that "the Six Nations who now live dispersed and confused, should in the most earnest manner be exhorted to unite and dwell together in their respective Castles" (NYCD 6: 856).

Eighteenth-Century European Eyewitness Accounts: Agrocentrism

Whereas diplomatic and missionary sources are written with little discussion of particular villages and virtually no descriptive detail, travelers' accounts written after 1740 provide eyewitness perspectives on locally dispersed Iroquois communities. Travelers' accounts also frequently disparage dispersed villages, but for a very different reason than the more formal records. The disapproval of European visitors is rooted in ethnocentric perceptions about Iroquois agriculture and village life rather than in a desire to perpetuate the political-economic status quo or enhance colonial control.

Eyewitnesses clearly misunderstood the Iroquois regime of semipermanent, extensive hoe agriculture and the types of houses and fields associated with it. These visitors expressed distaste for fields that were filled with many different crops, unplowed, unfenced, and dotted with stumps and rocks. They also objected to communities composed of impermanent houses and lacking well-defined roads. Bartram (1966 [1751]: 42) described the Iroquois capital ("if I may so call it") at Onondaga in 1743 as "scattered." Richard Smith related of the Oneida settlement at Oquaga in 1769 that "the Habitations here are placed straggling without any order on the Banks"; that the houses were "dark and dismal" and "filled too often with squalor and nastiness"; that "each house possesses a paltry garden"; and that their "Fences are miserable and the Land back of the village very indifferent" (Halsey 1906: 65–67). An anonymous 1799 visitor to the Tuscarora reservation near Niagara, which contained houses with paired sleeping platforms and ground-level central hearths, commented on the Tuscaroras' "disgusting way of living" ("Fort Niagara in 1799" 1997 [1799]).

These descriptions of dispersed Iroquois settlements are markedly similar to later documents penned by Euro-Americans from long-settled coastal regions who observed Euro-American frontier communities that subsisted by extensive hoe agriculture. The Euro-American "backwoods" way of life, first developed by Savo-Karelian Finns in the colonial period and later used by much greater numbers of Scots-Irish and other groups (T. Jordan and Kaups 1989), also was characterized by expeditiously constructed, more or less temporary houses and fields. Terry Jordan and Matti Kaups (1989: 4–6) cite post-1790 accounts of Euro-American extensive-farming settlements that describe houses as "insignificant," "of the most inferior quality," and "miserable"; fields as "slovenly" and farmed "with but little care"; and the people themselves as "squatters" who were "ignorant, lazy, and poor." Extensive hoe agriculture is in fact a very labor-efficient crop production system that is highly appropriate where good farmland is abundant (Boserup 1965). European and Euro-American disregard for these practices may be a form of "agrocentrism" that judged harshly any community lacking the trappings of permanent, intensive agriculture.

European visitors also attributed site-level dispersal to problems of alcohol abuse. David Zeisberger noted of the main western Seneca village in 1768 that its dispersed "condition is attributable to the excessive drinking which is all too common in the place. No one, not even those given to drinking, care to live in the town" (Hulbert and Schwarze 1912: 85). In contrast, other primary sources suggest that localized dispersal provided no barrier to alcohol-related unrest. To get Reverend Samuel Kirkland out of harm's way during a contentious 1765 funeral where alcohol was going to be consumed, friendly Senecas took him to an abandoned maple sugaring hut 3.2 km away from Kanadesaga (Pilkington 1980: 12), and even there Kirkland felt he was in danger. For individuals or groups effectively to isolate themselves from alcohol-related violence, a long-distance relocation—such as to the St. Lawrence missions where there was a reduced supply of alcohol—likely was necessary.

Scholarly Interpretations

Anthropologists and historians frequently have echoed the negative interpretations of Iroquois dispersal expressed in historical documents. Even ostensibly neutral scholarly accounts often are laced with negative terms (see the quotations from Morgan 1962 [1851] and Wallace 1969 cited in chapter 1). For example, Abler and Tooker (1978: 507) state that Seneca settlements "drifted" east and west after the Denonville invasion; Snow (1995: 457) claims that dispersed Mohawk houses "were scattered almost randomly." Fenton places settlement dispersal within a list of social ills that beset the Six Nations during the mid-eighteenth century:

> Niagara had passed to the French while Oswego, as a British outpost constantly threatened by the French, survived at the whim of the ambivalent Onondagas, who complained about the cheating traders watering their rum and deplored the violence in drunken routs. Famine stalked the Longhouse [that is, the Six Nations] as crops were not planted or brought to harvest. Men were too weak to hunt. People no longer lived in nucleated, palisaded villages, as settlements spread out in a defenseless pattern. The Senecas and Cayugas were most scattered. (Fenton 1998: 408)

Zeisberger's argument that local dispersal was a way to avoid alcohol-related unrest has been adopted by several scholars (for example, Richter 1992: 266; Tiro 1999: 42) who similarly overestimate the effectiveness of a short hike as a deterrent to drunken people with grudges.

Scholars' portrayal of dispersed settlement locations as haphazardly chosen, hasty responses to social problems contrasts sharply with the typical depiction of nucleated villages as being placed on the basis of carefully considered ecological, economic, and military variables (Heidenreich 1971; Trigger 1987 [1976], 1990). Recently, Jones (2006: 534) has added a new wrinkle to the issue by suggesting that "drastic changes toward more European-style housing and settlement layout occurred during the early eighteenth century" in Onondaga territory. Labeling dispersed Iroquois settlements as a Europeanized form inadvertently bolsters claims for Iroquois decline and does not stand up well against the evidence presented in this chapter.

Discussion

Most Iroquois and European accounts, particularly those dating before the 1740s, appear to refer to *extra-regional* dispersal rather than movement across lesser distances. Viewing these texts as discussions of extra-regional dispersal best accounts for their focus on demographic decline and loss of power. To the European colonial eye, long-distance moves (such as those from the Iroquois homeland to the St. Lawrence missions) were distressing because they often placed Iroquois populations close to imperial or provincial rivals. Parmenter (2001a: 108–9) notes the zero-sum mentality of colonial officials: "both English and French authorities assumed that any dispersion of the Iroquois would weaken the Confederacy, and ultimately result in a defection of these potential allies to the enemy."

The first documents to address local dispersal appear to be the Albany Commissioners' records from the 1740s and 1750s. These documents frequently begin with an assessment of extra-regional dispersal, but then quickly elide to a discussion of "dispersed and confused" settlements at the local level. The critical tone of these texts remains consistent despite the change in scale. New York officials appear to have recognized only two alternatives: Six Nations people either settled in locally compact "castles"—the favored option—or they "dispersed," which represented a loss of control to New York officials no matter whether such dispersal was local or extra-regional. Official dislike for locally dispersed Iroquois villages may have been compounded by agrocentric disapproval of farming done without monocropping, plows, or fences. Eighteenth-century conflation of issues of political control and agrocentrism resulted in a general negativity that recent scholars have readily and uncritically reproduced.

These negative interpretations of local dispersal should not be taken at face value for several reasons. Eighteenth-century documents clearly do not delimit whether their critiques apply to seasonal, site, community, regional, or extra-regional movements. The distress over the loss of military and political power that many of these documents express is most likely a critique of extra-regional movement, and this logic may not apply to more localized residential shifts.

Additionally, one must consider the bias of the speakers, something that scholars have not regularly assessed. Notably, Iroquois negotiators, colonial officials, priests, and their informants all would have been opposed to local dispersal because it made keeping track of individual villagers and factional activities more difficult. European officials, in particular, were greatly annoyed when Iroquois leaders were not where they expected them to be, a frequent occurrence that prevented the smooth operation of diplomacy. Reading between the lines of the documents on dispersal, one finds an Iroquois strategy of stalling and avoidance that allowed Six Nations peoples to follow their own courses of action out of the sight of Europeans. As the 1744 Seneca example detailed in chapter 3 suggests (MACIA vol. 1820: 290a, 295a), Iroquois peoples also may have used promises to relocate as a means to obtain the services of colonial smiths, who were readily dispatched to help with village moves but in the end likely found themselves providing more everyday services.

The thick fog of negativity surrounding eighteenth-century Iroquois communities can only be cut with new evidence and new interpretations. Many Iroquois dispersed settlements were occupied for forty years or more and continued to be occupied despite New York's opposition, suggesting that they were placed on the basis of a durable, positive draw rather than a haphazard response to factionalism, alcohol abuse, or disruption of blood kinship ties.

House Lot and Community Structure at Townley-Read

Archaeological data from the Townley-Read site provide the material foundation for demonstrating the economic and ecological advantages of community segmentation and site-level residential dispersal. The historically unprecedented dispersed house lot was the basic building block of the Townley-Read community. Figure 7.1 provides a schematic model of the five main elements of a dispersed Seneca house lot, derived from domestic-context evidence recovered by the project and mortuary data obtained from Charles Wray's field notes (n.d.) and discussions with collectors. Starting downhill and moving up, they are (1) a floodplain with fertile soil; (2) a trash midden; (3) external work areas; (4) a two-family shorthouse structure; and (5) one or more cemeteries uphill from the house.

Water and fertile soil in the bed of Burrell Creek served as focal points that defined the structure of each house lot and the entire site. In Domestic Refuse Cluster (DRC) 1, the short longhouse dwelling was oriented toward a large basin of floodplain soil only 50 m to the northeast, placing water and naturally renewed soil for farming in close proximity to the house. This basin is just upstream of where Burrell Creek cuts deeply into the local shales and forms a steep-sided gully; even today the basin acts as a silt trap

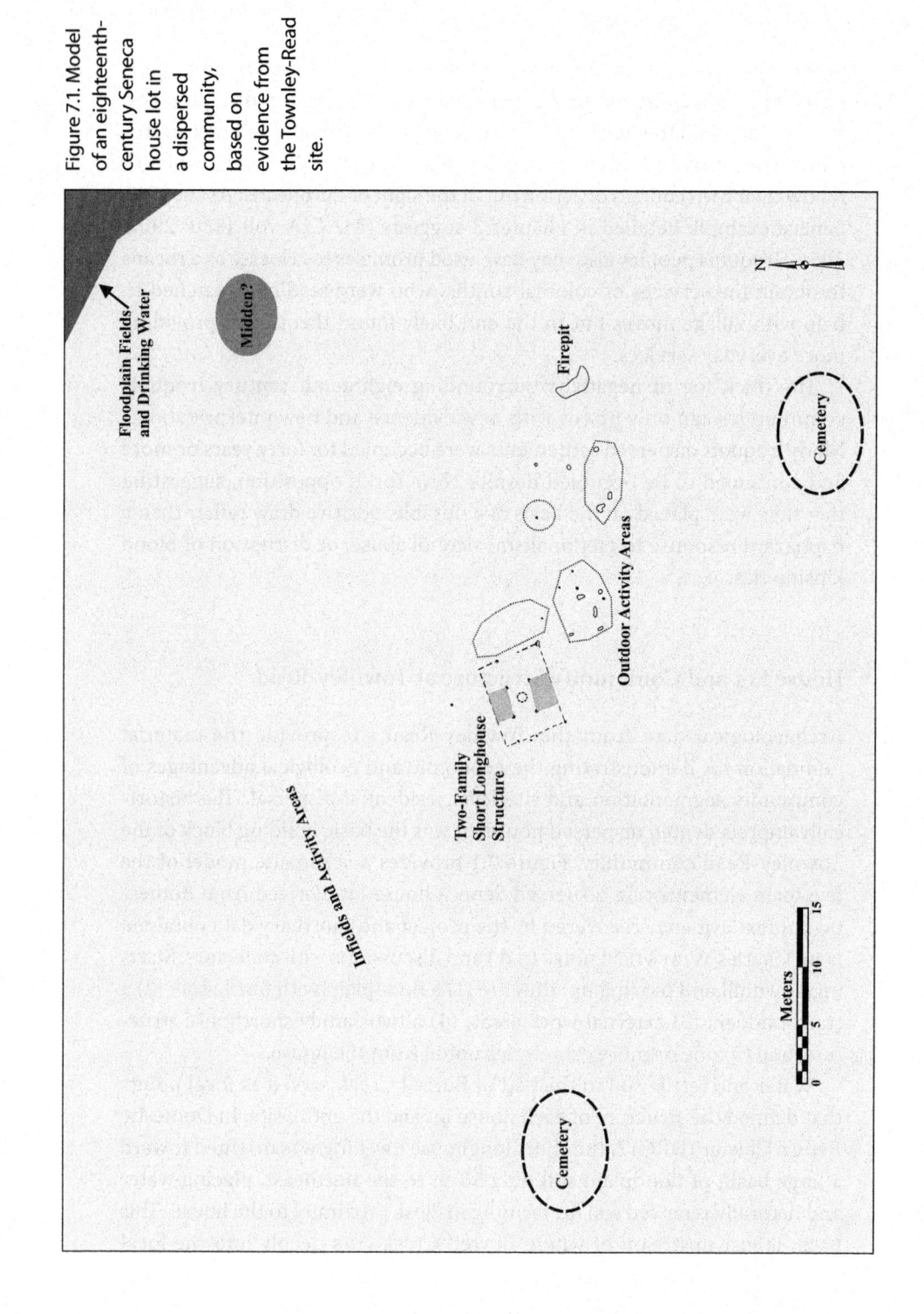

Figure 7.1. Model of an eighteenth-century Seneca house lot in a dispersed community, based on evidence from the Townley-Read site.

where spring floodwaters slow down and dump sediments. The likely house lots in DRC 2 and DRC 4 have a similar relation to the flood basin (figure 5.1). Such fertile floodplain areas were cultivated for "extended periods of time . . . perhaps indefinitely" by American Indians (Doolittle 2004: 187). The linear arrangement of houses along the creek likely resulted in elongated, rectangular house lots (see Stone 1991).

A formal trash midden was found only in DRC 3. The very large Buried Plowed Midden, at least 10 × 15 m in size, appears to have been a household, rather than communal, deposit because it contained a range of trash materials similar to or even narrower than known single-household refuse deposits at the site. The DRC 3 BPM horizon, situated at the very edge of the bank above the Burrell Creek silt trap, may be associated with DRC 4, which is directly uphill and likely to have been the location of a structure. Midden deposits were not found in or near DRC 1 and DRC 2. It is unclear whether these households deposited their trash in middens or pits that have not been located, in a sheet midden that has since been destroyed by plowing, or over the bank of Burrell Creek.

Seneca house lots at Townley-Read incorporated a significant amount of external space. This "yard" area allowed many tasks that would have been undertaken at some distance from residences in nucleated settlements to be done directly beside houses. Outdoor activities are reflected at Townley-Read by large firepits (such as Feature 5), smaller hearths, isolated post molds, and storage pits. In DRC 1, Feature 5 likely was used for the tandem production of pelts and hides for the fur trade and for processing bone grease, foods, and medicines; numerous other pits and post molds were found to the east and south of the short longhouse structure. Concentrations of bone refuse exterior to the east end of Structure 1 suggest that a work area or vestibule was present there as well. Although archaeologists did not recover any direct evidence for infields or orchards at Townley-Read, the spatial organization of the house lots and historic documents suggest that food production also took place in the copious space available between houses.

The architecture of the short longhouse structure found in DRC 1 is discussed in chapter 9. Artifact deposits within Structure 1 demonstrate that a wide variety of activities took place indoors, including the storage, processing, and consumption of both wild and domesticated plant and animal foods; the manufacture of utilitarian and personal adornment items; and smoking.

Cemeteries at Townley-Read were located close to houses instead of outside the village precinct as at earlier sites (see chapter 6). The Townley-Read cemeteries appear to have been much smaller than earlier cemeteries, probably containing fewer than twenty burials each. Wray's field notes (n.d.) and information obtained from collectors indicate that two cemeteries were located near Structure 1, one about 20 m south of Feature 5 that contained at least ten burials and one about 35 m west of Structure 1 that contained at least two burials. Both cemeteries are slightly uphill from the residential portion of the house lot and away from flood-basin agricultural fields. The Townley-Read Senecas buried their dead only a short distance from houses and work areas, where residents did not routinely move through them during the course of daily activities.

Senecas at Townley-Read appear to have built a series of house lots similar to that presented in figure 7.1 in a line along Burrell Creek, with houses located 60–80 m apart. As outlined in chapter 6, the Townley-Read neighborhood of the New Ganechstage Site Complex likely contained fifteen to twenty house lots and a total population of 150–200 people. While this estimate assumes that each house lot contained a two-family short longhouse structure like that in DRC 1, the extent of residential diversity at Townley-Read is uncertain and there may have been larger "true longhouse" structures or smaller nuclear-family houses at the site. Further exploration of residential diversity in the New Ganechstage Site Complex should be a high priority if additional excavations take place.

Although the project was unable to determine its exact location, historic documents and George S. Conover's writings suggest that a European-run smithy was built in or near the site. Conover's description (1882: 77), if accurate, indicates that the smithy was set on the bank of Burrell Creek like the Indian houses, only 150 m from a Seneca graveyard. This would mean that the smithy, and possibly the residence of the European smith, were integrated into the Seneca community rather than being placed at a distance sufficient to maintain the appearance of Seneca neutrality and to prevent the din of the smithy from reaching the site's occupants.

The arrangement of contemporaneous Seneca sites in the vicinity suggests that the house lot and community models presented here may hold for a much larger area than Townley-Read alone. The component sites in the New Ganechstage Site Complex (figure 6.6) all are located along an 8 km stretch of Burrell Creek and its tributary streams. There probably are many other unidentified Seneca house lots or even whole neighborhoods in the spaces between known sites. There were surely at least fifty contemporaneous Seneca house lots in the site complex, and the area easily could have contained one hundred or more house lots. The total population of the site complex presumably was between five hundred and one thousand people.

This model of community and house lot structure at Townley-Read bears a striking resemblance to that at Onondaga as described by John Bartram in 1743. There houses were on average 80–120 m apart: "The town in its present state is about 2 or 3 miles [3.2 or 4.8 kilometers] long, yet the scattered cabins on both sides of the water, are not above 40 in number, many of them hold 2 families, but all stand single, and rarely above 4 or 5 near one another; so that the whole town is a strange mixture of cabins, interspersed with great patches of high grass, bushes and shrubs, some of pease, corn and squashes" (Bartram 1966 [1751]: 42). Two-family dwellings with similar construction details were built at both Townley-Read and Onondaga (see chapter 9). Bartram describes orchards at a satellite community 6.4 km away from the main Onondaga village, relating that "we descended easily for several miles over good land producing sugar-maples, many of which the Indians had tapped to make sugar of the sap, also oaks, hickery, white walnuts [butternuts], plums and some apple trees, full of fruit; the Indians had set long bushes all round the trees at a little distance, I suppose to keep the small children [or animals?] from stealing the fruit before they were ripe" (39–40).

Although it is entirely possible to build a dispersed settlement in a defensible location—which might have been the result had negative factors such as factionalism or alcohol-related unrest caused the move from White Springs—the Senecas at Townley-Read did not do so. They instead ignored settings with defensive advantages, bypassing both the western Ridgetop and a lower ridge running up the middle of the East Fields. The non-defensible character of the site suggests that other, positive factors drew the Senecas to that exact location.

The years from 1713 to 1754, which encompass the occupation of Townley-Read, were a period of relative local peace (see chapter 3). The New Ganechstage Senecas continued to live in their dispersed, non-defensible house lots despite the founding of European posts at Niagara and Oswego, King George's War, and frequent exhortations to nucleate from New York officials. They only abandoned their neighborhoods along Burrell Creek and resettled in a semi-dispersed village on a ridgetop at Kanadesaga in 1754 as events built toward the Seven Years' War. The semi-dispersed structure of Kanadesaga and many later villages suggests that Senecas were reluctant to give up the advantages of dispersed settlement, even when the political-economic situation favored attention to defense and greater nucleation.

Advantages of Dispersed Settlement

Advantages of dispersed over nucleated settlement include decreased competition among households for farmland and firewood, easier access to cropland and water, increased development of edge areas, less frequent village moves, increased wind protection, and lessened danger of village-wide fires. Additionally, settlement dispersal in no way obstructed Seneca access to other resources in the Townley-Read locality, such as the wetlands Cammerhoff called the "Long Bridge" (Beauchamp 1916: 68); fishing spots on Seneca Lake, on the Seneca River, and in local creeks; and abandoned village and field locations (particularly at White Springs).

In a palisaded settlement, all women farmers started their day at the same point: the village gate. In order to reach their fields and firewood sources, some had to walk a considerable distance; this problem would have been exacerbated if the fertility of nearby fields declined and more distant fields were planted. Dispersed settlement alleviated many of these difficulties by starting women off from different points in the landscape, giving them immediate access to different plots of land. While there were certainly differences in the quality of soils adjacent to various house lots, the basic and divisive problem of having some women walk a short distance to their fields while others faced much longer hikes was alleviated.

Linear settlement along Burrell Creek meant every household had ready access to seasonally replenished creekbed soil and water for drinking, cooking, and cleaning. Fields and water sources were close by, decreasing the amount of time women had to spend walking back and forth to their fields, living in field huts, and carrying water. All of these factors no doubt resulted in substantial reallocation of Iroquois women's time as compared to life in nucleated villages, primarily by opening up for other purposes those blocks of time formerly used in transit. When New York officials demanded that Senecas "return to their castles" in 1741, Seneca negotiators said they could not reply until they had consulted with the women, who have "so much to say in that affair" (MACIA vol. 1820: 218a). This exchange may acknowledge the degree of power Iroquois women had over the organization of their communities and their own daily lives. Seneca women may have been particularly concerned with protecting the favorable aspects of dispersed settlement, and Seneca men appear to have been well aware of their opinions.

House lots at Townley-Read were vastly more spacious than those at nucleated sites. At dispersed settlements, many activities that in a nucleated village necessarily had taken place either inside longhouses or outside palisade walls were undertaken in the yard. This provided advantages in terms of proximity to other community members, security, and lighting. It potentially allowed orchards and infields to be added to the repertoire of Iroquoian food production, possibilities that will be discussed in the next section.

Dispersed settlement resulted in the development of a larger amount of "edge areas" than had nucleated settlement. Edge areas between forested land and fields are fertile habitats for deer, turkeys, and gathered crops such as blueberries, raspberries, gooseberries, cherries, hazelnuts, hackberries, and hawthorn (Cronon 1983: 51–52; Wykoff 1991: 16). In a nucleated settlement, edge areas can be envisioned as a ring, the diameter of which gradually expanded as the area under cultivation increased. In contrast, dispersed farmsteads would have generated a complex mosaic of fields, edges, and forests. The total length of edge areas in this mosaic would have been much greater than the perimeter of the ring around a nucleated settlement.

The mosaic created by active fields likely was supplemented by environmental manipulation in areas more distant from the site. Like other American Indian groups, the Iroquois actively transformed local landscapes in order to foster certain resources (Engelbrecht 2003: 99–105; see Hammett 2000 for a detailed southeastern model). Additional edge areas were created through periodic burnings of abandoned fields at old village sites, creating the extensive "meadows" throughout Iroquoia that were mentioned by many European travelers (Engelbrecht 2003: 99–100). These practices undoubtedly increased the numbers of edge-dwelling and -utilizing animal and plant species, particularly the economically crucial white-tailed deer. Analysis of faunal materials indicates that deer supplied the bulk of the meat and a significant portion of the skins exchanged in the fur trade at Townley-Read (chapter 10). Cronon (1983: 52) has termed Native American manipulation of edge areas to increase the deer population "a more distant kind of husbandry." Cammerhoff's description of the area around the abandoned White Springs site as a "pleasure garden in the desert" in 1750 (Beauchamp 1916: 67) demonstrates that New Ganechstage Senecas continued to manipulate the ecosystem in the vicinity of their former village.

In combination, these factors meant that some of the crucial ecological processes forcing the abandonment of Iroquois settlements—particularly exhaustion of nearby firewood sources, pest infestation, waste accumulation, and possibly declining fertility in older, intensively used fields (Engelbrecht 2003: 101–4; Snow 1994: 70–71; Starna, Hamell, and Butts 1984; Trigger 1987 [1976], 1990)—occurred at a slower rate in dispersed than in nucleated settlements. Dispersed settlements could be, and were, occupied for longer periods: Townley-Read was occupied for an estimated thirty-nine years, and Kendaia perhaps for seventy-five years (although some small scale local moves may have taken place during this span). The major inconveniences of resettlement—including soil evaluation, field clearance, materials stockpiling, and house construction (Trigger 1990: 30–32)—were substantially reduced in frequency when settlements could be occupied for more than twice as long as nucleated villages. The longer occupation span of dispersed settlements also made it worthwhile to construct dwellings more durable than bark longhouses. New, creolized house forms applying European tools and hardware to traditional Iroquois architectural forms did in fact appear in the dispersed settlements (chapter 9).

Settlement dispersal had additional advantages. At Townley-Read houses were built on the protected eastern slope of the low rise, out of the prevailing west wind, which can be especially harsh during winter. Furthermore, dwellings were constructed far enough apart so that if one house burned, the fire would not be likely to spread to other houses. House fires were a distinct danger for settlements with wooden dwellings where residents used open fires for heating and cooking. Warrick (1986) outlines extensive evidence for house and village fires in nucleated Iroquoian village sites in Ontario. Champlain (cited in Warrick 1986: 51) noted in 1615 that Huron houses were spaced three to four paces apart to minimize the spread of house fires; the 60–80 m separation at Townley-Read obviously offered considerably greater fire protection.

Many subsistence resources available to the dispersed community at Townley-Read could be accumulated and stored for use during the late winter and early spring, when both domesticated and wild resources were at their nadir. The high level of white-tailed deer use seen at the site consistently included bone grease production, which provided a storable source of fat (K. Jordan and Watson 2005). Nuts from orchards could be stored whole or processed into nut oil, although on present evidence neither of these options seems to have been used frequently (Rossen 2006). Therefore, one of the major effects (and probable goals) of Seneca residential dispersal appears to have been to generate more storable foods that could help Seneca families get through the late winter–early spring "hungry time," the thorniest problem in the Iroquois seasonal cycle of resource availability.

Seneca Plant Use at Townley-Read: Outfields, Infields, Orchards, and Gathering

Documentary sources indicate that by the 1760s some Iroquois communities had adopted a "creolized" agricultural system, in which domesticated plants acquired from European sources were added to cultigens long used by Six Nations peoples. Bartram's description of the dispersed Onondaga village in 1743 indicates that "pease, corn, and squashes" were grown between houses, and that orchards of sugar maple, oak, hickory, butternut, plum, and apple trees were grown at some distance from the village (1966 [1751]: 39–42). Richard Smith noted in 1769 that every house at the dispersed Oneida village at Oquaga "possesses a paltry Garden wherein they plant Corn, Beans, Water Melons, Potatoes, Cucumbers, Muskmelons, Cabbage, French Turneps, some Apple Trees, Sallad, Parsnips, & other Plants" (Halsey 1906: 66–67). Sullivan expedition members named some Six Nations settlements after their fruit orchards, such as Appletown (that is, Kendaia) and the Cayuga Peachtown (Conover 1887; Division of Archives and History 1929). Of the plants mentioned in these accounts, watermelons, potatoes, cucumbers, cabbage, turnips, apples, peaches, and peas (if Bartram was correct in his identification of crops) were introduced to North America by Europeans (T. Jordan and Kaups 1989: 117–18).

Following the local political-economic approach advocated in this volume, we cannot assume that this pattern of plant use existed at Townley-Read, since the site was abandoned fifteen years before Smith's account of Oquaga, and was located at some distance from both Onondaga and Oquaga. While settlement dispersal at New Ganechstage certainly allowed the Seneca plant use system to undergo major alteration, evidence as to whether this indeed took place must be reviewed carefully. Eighteenth-century plant use by Six Nations peoples can be analytically divided into outfield, infield, orchard, gathered plant, and imported plant categories. This section reviews archaeological and documentary evidence for Seneca use of plants in these categories at Townley-Read, relying on Rossen's (2006) analysis of more than 16,000 botanical remains recovered at the site.

Outfields

Iroquoian agriculture was based on semipermanent, extensive hoe cultivation of the "three sisters"—maize, beans, and squash (Engelbrecht 2003: 22–33; Lewandowski 1987; J. Mt. Pleasant 2006; Parker 1910; see Boserup 1965 for a general model of extensive agriculture). Whereas men initially cleared trees and brush from new fields using a process of girding and firing, women were responsible for the remainder of agricultural tasks, including planting, tending, harvesting, processing, and storing of domesticated plant foods. Technologically, Iroquoian agriculture could be undertaken with digging sticks and hoes, and did not require removal of rocks and stumps from fields, plowing, or fencing. Iroquoian farmers especially valued creekbed fields, as spring flooding annually replenished their fertility.

Iroquoian women appear to have expanded their village's cropped area by opening up new fields over time. The conventional view of Iroquoian agriculture posits that the fertility of agricultural soils gradually declined over several years of cultivation and that new fields were needed to maintain production levels. Many models of Iroquois agriculture are based on Huron examples (see Heidenreich 1971; Trigger 1990), but the low organic content of the sandy soils in Huron territory may mean that Huron agriculture does not provide an appropriate model for other locales. Some scholars have questioned whether soil fertility declined as quickly, or at all, in the richer soils of the Iroquois homeland (Engelbrecht 2003: 30–31; Jane Mt. Pleasant, personal communication 2006). Doolittle (2004) suggests that some fields may have been cultivated for a site's entire occupation span and questions whether the field rotation and fallowing necessary in a classic swidden system were used aboriginally in the Northeast. Nonetheless, Iroquois villagers appear to have expanded cultivated land over time, possibly due to short-term fallowing or pest infestations in older fields (Lewandowski 1987; Starna, Hamell, and Butts 1984). Distant fields may have been cultivated to diversify the range of microenvironments in use in order to provide added protection against crop failure (Engelbrecht 2003: 30).

Seneca use of major traditional crops at Townley-Read is confirmed by archaeological evidence (Rossen 2006). Maize remains (including kernels and cupules) and gourd rind (*Lagenaria* sp.) fragments were found in every locus where extensive flotation sampling was employed, including contexts from Structure 1, Feature 5, extramural features in the DRC 1 house lot, and the DRC 3 BPM. The ubiquity of gourd rind fragments likely reflects widespread Seneca use of gourds as containers. Squash (*Cucurbita* sp.) and bean (*Phaseolus vulgaris*) remains were relatively rare. Four squash seeds and one peduncle were found within Feature 5, and a single squash seed was recovered from Post Mold 14 in the DRC 1 house lot. Only two bean specimens were found, one in Post Mold 4 (a central support post within Structure 1), and the other in extramural Post Mold 20. These plants may have been used rarely, or they may be underrepresented because processing methods reduced their chances of being charred and preserved in the archaeological record (Engelbrecht 2003: 26–27). Bodner (1999) reports that 164 uncarbonized sunflower achenes were found within (and preserved by) a brass kettle that was plowed out of a grave at the site. Sunflowers traditionally were intercropped with the "three sisters." No sunflower specimens were recovered during Townley-Read/New Ganechstage Project excavations, which again may reflect rarity of use or a low frequency of charring.

Direct documentary evidence on Seneca plant use while Townley-Read was occupied is contained in the 1750 Cammerhoff journal (in Beauchamp 1916). The fare offered to Johann Cammerhoff and David Zeisberger by Seneca villagers consisted primarily of corn stews: they were served maize and beans in Canandaigua, and stews of venison or trout and maize in Canandaigua and Honeoye (Beauchamp 1916: 69, 71). While traveling in Seneca territory, they ate "Indian bread" made of maize and watered cittamun (Beauchamp 1916: 68, 71). Cittamun, or cornmeal "roasted in the ashes and pounded to flour" (Beauchamp 1916: 61), was typical Northern Iroquoian travelers' fare from the time Europeans began observing them (Trigger 1990: 56–57).

The structure of the Townley-Read site suggests that extensive, hoe-based outfield agriculture was used. Houses at the site clearly were oriented toward the floodplain of Burrell Creek, which would have been quite difficult to access with a plow. The location of several houses next to the silt trap upstream from a steep gully suggests that this feature was the main draw of that particular locale. The soils in the site area are predominantly Ontario Loam "one of the more productive soils of the area" (Pearson and Cline 1958: 66). Palmyra series soils, characterized as "some of the most productive soils in Ontario and Yates Counties" (68), also are found near Burrell Creek (Pearson and Cline 1958: maps 32–33).

Samuel Kirkland described traces of what appears to have been a fairly large field system at the then-abandoned New Ganechstage Site Complex in 1788. Describing his travels from Kanadesaga to Canandaigua Lake, Kirkland noted that the "first four miles [6.4 km] passed thro' the old fields of the ancient Seneka Town called Kanghsadegea" (Pilkington 1980: 139).

In 1779, Sullivan expedition members observed abandoned fields 6–8 km across near where Huntoon had stood (Conover 1887: 90, 160).

Agricultural tools and hardware have been recovered from other Seneca sites of this era. Iron hoes, a technology consistent with Iroquois extensive agriculture, have been found in a grave at the Snyder-McClure site and in unknown contexts at Huntoon. Although iron animal shoes, including specimens identified by the collection catalogue as "ox shoes," have been recovered from the Snyder-McClure and White Springs sites, all of these examples were surface-collected and likely derive from post-1788 Euro-American farming of the land. The archaeological record at Townley-Read contains no evidence—such as fences, outbuildings, harness tackle, or plow fragments—associated with intensive agriculture.

In total, this evidence suggests that the mainstay of Seneca agriculture remained outfields planted in maize, beans, gourds, squash, and sunflowers throughout the occupation of the New Ganechstage Site Complex.

Infields

Large house lots provided space for activities that formerly had been done outside palisades, and also made new types of activities possible. In particular, Seneca households at Townley-Read would have had ample space for infields. Nearby infields had several advantages over outfields of maize, beans, and squash that might have been several kilometers away by the end of a village's life cycle. Infields could be much more closely monitored for plant diseases, pests, and animals, and could be fertilized with household food remains. An expanded repertoire of plants could have been grown, including fragile or labor-intensive plants that would not have survived in an outfield. Historic documents confirm that a wide variety of plant species were grown close to eighteenth-century Iroquois houses, including European domesticates. However, the Townley-Read botanical assemblage of more than 16,000 specimens indicates little deviation from traditional staples. Notably, not a single European-derived plant was recovered.

Contemporaneous documentary sources imply that eighteenth-century Iroquois peoples initially made little use of European infield plants. For example, the 1750 Cammerhoff journal mentions only maize, beans, wild plant foods, and a small amount of European foodstuffs imported whole rather than locally produced. Bartram's (1966 [1751]: 42) description of Onondaga in 1743 mentions only "pease, corn, and squashes" growing between houses. Since he does not mention beans (an Iroquois staple), it appears possible that Bartram mistook aboriginal beans for peas (a crop brought to North America by Europeans). If this is the case, the evidence suggests that Onondaga and Seneca farmers did use infields in the 1740s and 1750s, but had not expanded their repertoire of infield crops beyond traditional staples. Smith's detailed description of diverse infield crops in 1769 thus appears to be a poor fit for the earlier local political economy in the Seneca region.

Orchards

Documentary sources describe widespread Iroquois use of indigenous and imported tree crops during the eighteenth century (for example, Bartram 1966 [1751]; Conover 1887; Division of Archives and History 1929; Halsey 1906). The encouragement of nut trees (probably through planting, tending of natural seedlings, and selective elimination of competing nonproductive trees for firewood) has a long history in the Iroquois region, as witnessed by Champlain's 1615 discovery of groves of nut trees next to abandoned Iroquoian villages near Lake Ontario (cited in Engelbrecht 2003: 28; see also Wykoff 1991). Nuts were processed for oil, a storable fat that could be extracted from cracked nuts by boiling; and were ground into flour, which could then be added to water to make "nut milk" (Wykoff 1991: 11–12). Parker (1910: 100) mentions that hickory and butternut oils were regarded as particularly palatable by Senecas in the early nineteenth century, and that hickory oil was used to feed infants. European-introduced tree fruits, such as apples and peaches, could be used fresh or dried for later use.

Dispersal could have facilitated increased Seneca use of orchards in the eighteenth century. In dispersed settlements, space could be dedicated to crops that were not immediately productive. Longer settlement durations provided time for slow-maturing trees to develop before a site was abandoned. Women could have monitored frail seedlings planted near houses, and tree crops could have been employed more readily since vistas no longer needed to be kept clear in order to watch for attackers.

Moreover, Conover (1882) provides a relatively detailed account of remnant Seneca orchards of apple and butternut trees in and around Townley-Read, although he does not spell out exactly how he knew of their existence. His account suggests that fruit and nut trees had been grown both in high-density orchards and in smaller groups. At Townley-Read itself, Conover (1882: 78–79) mentions a 1.2 ha grove of butternut trees (approximately at the north end of the drainage ditch separating the East from West Fields; figure 5.1), and a second butternut orchard "interspersed with many wild plums" across Burrell Creek to the west of the Ridgetop, distant from known house lot areas. Conover added that apple trees "both single and in groups were scattered over the whole neighborhood for a distance of two or three miles" (79), a pattern that may indicate these trees were associated with individual house lots. Other nucleated apple orchards were found at the Rupert site (including one 0.4 ha in size) and between the Rippey and Zindall-Wheadon sites (85–87). At Rupert, a cache of plum pits was found in a brass kettle recovered from a burial (85).

It is therefore quite surprising that little archaeological evidence for Seneca use of orchard crops was recovered at Townley-Read. A total of only 204 nutshell fragments weighing 2.6 grams was recovered from fifty-nine flotation samples taken in the East Fields. While the nutshell assemblage was diverse, including hickory, butternut, black walnut, and possibly hazelnut specimens, the very low overall density of nutshell remains is virtually unprecedented at American Indian sites in eastern North America (Rossen 2006). It may be notable that no acorn remains were recovered, given that acorns require significant processing before they are edible. Furthermore, no traces of European tree crops such as apple seeds or peach pit fragments were recovered. The lack of apple seeds is particularly puzzling, since Conover described apple orchards in the vicinity of Townley-Read and American soldiers reported seeing fifty-year-old apple trees at Kendaia in 1779 (Conover 1886: 46), meaning that other eastern Senecas were growing apples during the period of Townley-Read's occupation.

Can this discrepancy between textual sources and archaeological data be resolved? Several possibilities present themselves. First, the largest orchards appear to have been spatially isolated from houses at Townley-Read based on Conover's description of the site. Excavations concentrated on house lots and may not have sampled areas where the bulk of orchard crops were processed. Second, the prolific production of bone grease at the site (chapter 10) may have provided sufficient stored fat resources so that other foods (nuts in particular) were de-emphasized. The ubiquity of gourd remnants may reflect their use as bone grease containers.

Third, tree crops planted during the occupation of the Townley-Read site may not have been terribly productive while the site was inhabited. For example, seedling apple trees can take twelve to fifteen years to bear fruit and do not reach peak production until they reach thirty or forty years of age (Ian Merwin, personal communication 2001). Senecas may have planted tree crops during the occupation of Townley-Read, but with the awareness that the main rewards from these labors would come after the site had been abandoned. Fourth, orchards may have been planted primarily in *aban-*

doned areas rather than near inhabited locations. William Wyckoff's 1779 captivity narrative (summarized in Coates 1892d) describes apple orchards at the Snyder-McClure site abandoned sixty-five to seventy years previously, a period in which there are no documentary references to Iroquois use of apples. Therefore, the orchards Conover described may have been planted not by the residents of the Townley-Read site, but by the denizens of its successor village at Kanadesaga, who made use of the fertile, refuse-laden soils at the abandoned Townley-Read site. The final two options presented here suggest that rather than being an immediate-return strategy, planting of fruit and nut orchards may have been an element in the intentional, long-term transformation of the local landscape into a mosaic of resources productive for the human population (see Engelbrecht 2003).

Gathered Plants

The Townley-Read botanical assemblage reflects the astounding variety of wild plants Northern Iroquoian communities used for dietary and medicinal purposes (see Herrick 1995; Parker 1910; Waugh 1973 [1916]). Wild plant seeds recovered at the site included blackberry/raspberry (*Rubus* sp.), sumac, grass, cherry, grape, elderberry, hackberry, nightshade, hawthorn, and morning glory (Rossen 2006). Blackberry/raspberry remains were by far the most frequent, found in 43 percent of East Fields flotation samples and totaling more than four hundred in number. Nine of the listed species (all but elderberry) were recovered from Feature 5, including all of the grass, cherry, grape, hackberry, nightshade, hawthorn, and morning glory specimens. All seven elderberry specimens were recovered from the BPM.

Some significant Iroquois wild foods, including strawberries and blueberries, were not found in the Townley-Read assemblage, but these berries produce very small seeds that are difficult to recover. While in Seneca territory Cammerhoff and Zeisberger gathered what they termed "whortleberries," a name used for European varieties of blueberries which Cammerhoff likely misapplied to indigenous species (Beauchamp 1916: 81). Blueberries, raspberries, cherries, hackberries, and hawthorn are all species that thrive in the edge areas amply generated by dispersed settlement (Cronon 1983: 51–52; Wykoff 1991: 16).

Imported Plants

Although there is no archaeological or documentary evidence for the use of imported foods in the Seneca region during 1715–1754, the Cammerhoff journal indicates that small amounts of European foodstuffs were imported into neighboring Cayuga territory. During the Moravians' initial visit to the main Cayuga village, the "old chief... Onechsagerat" prepared an impromptu tea service for them, which he served in "a very large spoon and a wooden dish" set upon two inverted corn mortars (Beauchamp 1916: 64–65). On their return visit the chief had obtained European "biscuit" from Oswego for them (Beauchamp 1916: 85). The plowzone find of a Jackfield-type ceramic sherd in DRC 1 may provide indirect evidence for the use of tea during the latter part of the occupation at Townley-Read; Jackfield, dating to 1745–1790, was most often used for teapots, tea bowls, and pitchers (Fisher 2003: 29; Stull 2006). French trade records indicate that flour, biscuit, peas, and tobacco were provided at frontier posts (Laird 1995: tables 1.1–1.2).

Ramenofsky (1998: 88–89) notes that increased Indian use of European-made white ball clay pipes in the Southeast accompanied greater importation of tobacco produced under European direction in the mid-Atlantic and elsewhere. Inhabitants of the Townley-Read site may have imported European-controlled tobacco in some quantity beginning in the 1730s or 1740s, based on the quite homogenous white ball clay pipe assemblage recovered at the site (chapter 5).

Discussion

While Seneca settlement dispersal at Townley-Read appears to have provided the opportunity for a new type of subsistence system, continuities in Seneca plant use far outweighed innovations. The main adoptions from Europeans—some domesticated animals and possibly orchard crops and garden plants—were added to previous resources rather than replacing them. The main advantages of dispersal for the Townley-Read Senecas therefore seem to be that they could continue their traditional farming techniques but practice them more easily because women were closer to fields, water sources, and infield plants than they had been in previous nucleated settlements. The range of Seneca and Six Nations plant use appears to have expanded in the second half of the eighteenth century, further realizing some of the potential for diverse plant production inherent in the organization of dispersed communities.

Land Allocation and Agricultural Labor

Anthropologists have identified several ethnographic and archaeological cases where settlement dispersal accompanied agricultural intensification (for example, Drennan 1988; Stone 1996: 42–50). In many instances, intensification (greater levels of output per unit area or, in Stone's [1996: 29] terms, "production concentration") strengthened a household's investment in and connection to particular plots of land, bolstering notions of exclusive land tenure. It is therefore possible that the changes in land-use patterns seen at the Townley-Read site may have disrupted or reduced the importance of traditional Iroquois practices, which relied on clans for both access to land and organization of agricultural labor.

An initial answer is provided by the fact that Townley-Read and the rest of the New Ganechstage Site Complex was abandoned during the 1750s without invasion or other external provocation. Settlement relocation is fundamentally a way to avoid agricultural intensification (Stone 1996: 41). Therefore, even the most intensively used land around Seneca houses at New Ganechstage never became permanent, private property. When the new settlement at Kanadesaga was founded, it is likely that Senecas continued to use time-tested ways of determining which households gained access to which plots of land.

Extensively farmed outfields provided the core of Seneca food production at Townley-Read. Although Seneca households consistently used the fields that were seasonally renewed by the flooding of Burrell Creek, this area was too small to supply the subsistence needs of the entire population. The use and boundaries of more distant fields undoubtedly changed from year to year as household sizes changed, old fields were left fallow, and new fields were brought into production. Year-to-year allocation of land, like the demarcation of plots at a new settlement, was a source of longstanding tension in Iroquois agriculture. It was likely to have been addressed with a usufruct system: use of a plot secured continued access, but unused land could be reallocated to others by clan leaders.

An interesting comparison can be made between Seneca land use at Townley-Read and that of the patrilineal Euro-American groups who settled dispersed farmsteads in the American Midlands (T. Jordan and Kaups 1989). These backwoods pioneers lived in similar ecological settings, practiced an analogous infield-outfield agricultural system, and used domesticated animals in roughly the same proportions as the Townley-Read Senecas. Backwoods settlers primarily organized subsistence production at the household level, which is reflected in inter-residential distances. The dictate that a family should be ready to move "when you can see the smoke of a neighbor's cabin" (77) expressed Midlanders' preferred spacing. Jordan and Kaups (1989: 123) relate that "for the initial stage of pioneer settlement, the term 'isolated' farmstead may be more descriptive [than 'dispersed' habitation], since backwoods settlers tended to scatter, leaving three to eight or ten miles [4.8–16.0 km] between dwellings. The individual cabins later became the focus of loose family or clan clusters, in which the individual houses stood not more than a mile [1.6 km] apart." They estimate that a Midland system required more than 800 ha of land for a typical nuclear family.

The houses at Townley-Read were much closer together than Midland farmsteads, suggesting that Seneca dispersed settlement was not optimized strictly on the basis of ecology. Stone (1991: 352) notes that residential spacing "reflects a balance between the pull of the residence to the plot (by intensification) and the pull to the other farms (by labor mobilization)." There is good reason to suspect that the residential spacing adopted by the Townley-Read Senecas in part reflected the proximity needed for kin-based labor sharing. The Townley-Read neighborhood was likely to have been a "work exchange territory" (349).

Townley-Read Senecas may have used kin-based communal work parties for agriculture, based on documents from other parts of Iroquoia. The "large company of 33 women, who were hoeing corn" that Cammerhoff observed outside the main Onondaga village in 1750 (Beauchamp 1916: 46) likely was a communal work party. Mary Jemison's discussion of later Seneca agriculture describes communal planting and wood collection under the command of a female "driver and overseer" (Seaver 1990 [1824]: 160–61). Parker (1910: 29–31) discusses Seneca customs for organizing work "bees" for preparing soil, hoeing, harvesting, and husking. He translates the Seneca word for the groups formed for these activities as "mutual aid societies" (30). Such groups were led by a "matron of the cornfields," and labor was repaid with a feast (30–31). Neither Jemison's nor Parker's accounts are linked to a particular time period or location, but they support the idea that communal institutions remained important to Seneca agriculture well past the middle of the eighteenth century.

Several authors (for example, Richter 1992: 262) have argued that dispersed houses represent a significant decrease in organized social interaction, but this is not necessarily the case. Stone (1991: 352) has demonstrated ethnographically that "there can be stable, even formalized communal labor pools where households reside in individual farmsteads." Although construction of several free-standing structures at greater distances from one another resulted in decreased daily interaction in comparison to nucleated longhouse settlements (in that fewer people would have used the same doorways, corridors, and pathways), the social functions of Iroquois matrilineal groups (labor sharing and coordination, decision making, and so forth; see Doxtator 1996: 21–23) are unlikely to have been hindered by the 60–80 m spacing between houses seen at New Ganechstage.

Population pressure, market opportunity, and taxation are among the most significant causes of production concentration (Boserup 1965; Stone 1996: 33–34). Although it is tempting to consider some of these options (especially given scattered indications of eighteenth-century Iroquois population increase; see Parmenter 1999), land was not at all scarce in the eighteenth-century Seneca homeland, and market opportunities for agricultural products were few. There are only isolated instances where Senecas are known to have provided food to Europeans—French agent Louis-Thomas Chabert de Joncaire acquired nine hundred bushels of maize for the garrison at Fort Michilimackinac from the Senecas in 1715 (D. Kent 1974: 87), and Senecas reportedly supplied the French at Niagara with "fresh meat" (NYCD 10: 85). The difficulties in transporting large quantities of heavy foods and the very small numbers of Europeans residing near Seneca territory effectively prevented the development of a thriving "frontier exchange economy" (in the sense developed by Usner 1992, 1998) in subsistence products.

Instead, Seneca women grew more food closer to their homes primarily because it was more efficient. When homes were clustered, Seneca women had to walk long distances between houses, fields, and water sources. The establishment of peaceful conditions in Iroquoia removed the need to nucleate for safety; and dispersed housing greatly reduced unproductive transit time. In my view, Seneca "intensification" happened merely through the substitution of economically productive tasks (growing more food) for unproductive ones (walking long distances).

Conclusions

It appears that the Townley-Read Senecas abandoned nucleated settlement, defensive terrain, longhouses, and the isolation of houses from burial grounds when they moved the short distance from White Springs to New Ganechstage. While many ethnohistorians have taken these developments as evidence for political dissipation and the disintegration of traditional values, an alternate, more positive position has greater explanatory power.

The years surrounding the establishment of the dispersed community at Townley-Read were relatively peaceful, and the pelt-bearing western Indian groups who traveled across Iroquoia to trade with the British proved an economic boon to Iroquois nations (such as the Senecas) located along the route. Townley-Read's residents took advantage of these conditions to jettison the landscape of fear that dominated nucleated communities, and to disperse across the landscape in an economically efficient pattern.[2] Peter Kalm overheard comments to this effect made by "someone who had spent three years among them [the Senecas] for purposes of trade" in Albany in 1750: "The Seneca country and the surrounding region is inhabited by Indians only. Formerly because of wars they lived in large villages surrounded by stockades, but now the natives have scattered, one living here, another there" (Benson 1937, 2: 619). This more positive formulation is one of the rare comments on dispersal made by someone not directly interested in managing Seneca political affairs.

The Senecas did not establish these new dispersed neighborhoods haphazardly; instead, they carefully considered the economic and ecological advantages of spreading out across the landscape. The Townley-Read data suggest that settlement dispersal was something the Senecas did from a position of strength in order to lessen the burdens of everyday labor, rather than being the desperate choice of an exhausted population in the throes of social disintegration.

8

Iroquois Housing, 1677–1754

Terminology and Definitions

Were the majority of eighteenth-century Iroquois residences "European-style log cabins," as scholars often claim (for example, Aquila 1983; Graymont 1972; Jones 2006; Richter 1992; Snow 1989, 1995, 2001; Weslager 1969)? Assertions of this sort need to be made carefully and documented thoroughly, since the adoption of European-style house forms has been taken as an index for the overall state of Iroquois culture, and frequently as conclusive evidence for the declining importance of matrilineality to the Six Nations. Despite the significance of housing change to the interpretation of eighteenth-century Iroquois cultures, little sustained empirical study of the issue has taken place, and the few relatively detailed studies (for example, Fenton 1967; Hamell 1992a; Wallace 1969) have not gained much traction in the scholarly literature. The majority of previous interpretations of eighteenth-century housing trends instead (1) rely on narrow definitions of "European" and "traditional" houses; (2) subscribe to overly normative views of the Six Nations' housing stock, both locally and inter-regionally; (3) come to unwarranted conclusions based solely on primary sources' use of words such as "cabin" and "log"; (4) do not make much use of archaeological data; and (5) are not much concerned with the specific material factors that caused changes in house forms.[1] As a result of these shortcomings, many scholarly accounts of eighteenth-century Iroquois architectural change reproduce longstanding acculturationist assumptions that Indians naturally and inevitably adopted European technology and cultural forms.

A second underlying assumption affects "log cabin" studies regardless of who was alleged to be living in them. Log cabins have long been central to American ideas of self-sufficient individualism, and the highly positive connotations surrounding log cabins have resulted in widespread manipulation of their image by political campaigns, localities, and commercial products

(Gunderson 1957; Pessen 1984; Shurtleff 1967 [1939]). These various inventions have given both the public and scholars the impression that log cabins were older and more ubiquitous than they actually were. The architectural historian Harold Shurtleff (1967 [1939]) has gone so far as to call the standard history of log cabin construction in America a "myth." Additionally, Iroquois people *did* construct dwellings that closely resembled popular stereotypes of the log cabin on reservations in New York and Ontario during the nineteenth century, for which there is widespread photographic evidence (for example, Snow 1994: figure 8.1; Tuck 1971: plate 44) and some archaeological data (Kenyon and Ferris 1984; Lantz 1980). But the degree to which eighteenth-century Iroquois houses were built using European models, and when, where, and why particular European forms were adopted largely have been unaddressed by scholars. This chapter provides a set of definitions and classification tools to aid such an inquiry; chapter 9 explores evidence for change in Iroquois house forms from 1677 to 1754.[2]

Traditional Iroquois, European-Style, and Intercultural/Creolized Houses

Scholars typically have tried to place the dwellings used by eighteenth-century Iroquois peoples into two categories: either Iroquois longhouse or European-style house. Previously, I have argued that a third formal category—the intercultural/creolized house—is needed to adequately describe the full range of eighteenth-century Iroquois residential forms (K. Jordan 2002, 2003). To aid in the classification of documentary and archaeological evidence, I outline the most prominent characteristics of each type.

Traditional Iroquois Houses

Many Postcolumbian Iroquoian houses exhibit continuities with Precolumbian dwellings in terms of materials and construction techniques. In the sense that they manifest continuities with Precolumbian forms—but not in the sense that they were timeless and unchanging—it is appropriate to call these house forms traditional. Traditional Iroquois architecture has been well studied (for example, Kapches 1979, 1984, 1990, 1993, 1994; Prezzano 1992: 256–94; Snow 1997; Warrick 1988, 1996; Williams-Shuker 2005; Wright 1995). Traditional houses were fundamentally defined by their temporariness. Iroquoian nucleated villages generally were abandoned every ten to thirty years, and it was not worthwhile to build houses that would outlast the occupation span of the village. Hence the amount of labor invested in the initial production of a traditional house was relatively low, but maintenance costs (such as the frequent need to replace wall posts) were high (see McGuire and Schiffer 1983 for discussion of these parameters).

The main architectural characteristics of traditional Iroquois houses include (1) sets of paired large wooden posts in the house interior that supported the weight of the structure; (2) smaller supports along the walls and on the roof to hold the siding and roofing in place; (3) siding and roofing made of bark; (4) a rounded arbor- or parabola-like shape for the roof; and (5) gable-end doorways. The paired interior support posts framed a central corridor. Hearths were constructed at regular intervals along the corridor, and the main support posts were used to anchor sleeping and storage platforms, so that two sleeping compartments (each housing a nuclear family) faced each other across a hearth. The two-family, one-hearth module—the basic unit of Iroquoian housing—was duplicated end-to-end according to the size of the social unit to be housed. Less formally constructed vestibules or porches often were built at one or both ends of the house; these areas sheltered activities and served as kitchens, wood storage areas, and summer sleeping quarters. Scholars have disagreed about the specifics of roof construction and shape, whether sleeping compartments ran continuously along the sides of the longhouse or were interrupted by storage areas, and the length of longhouse compartments (see Hamell 1992a; Kapches 1993; Snow 1997; Wright 1995), but there is a general consensus about the rest of the architectural form.

The "true longhouse" can be defined as a residential structure with two or more hearths, housing four or more nuclear families. Figure 8.1 illustrates a typical true longhouse, in this case five compartments long. This diagram follows Snow's (1994, 1997) assumptions that living compartments did not run the full length of the house, that areas used purely for storage were present both inside and outside the living area, and that each house segment was 6 m in length.

Recent research has revealed that Iroquoian villages often contained house forms other than true longhouses. Evidence for Iroquoian residential variability is the most copious in Ontario, perhaps because research there has more frequently involved broad-scale village excavation than have studies in New York (see Warrick 2000). However, a growing number of structural forms that are not multiple-hearth true longhouses also have been unearthed in New York (for example, Dean 1984; Hosbach et al. 2006; K. Jordan 2003; Ricklis 1967; Sohrweide 2001). To standardize house descriptions, Kapches has developed (1) the longhouse–short longhouse–cabin ty-

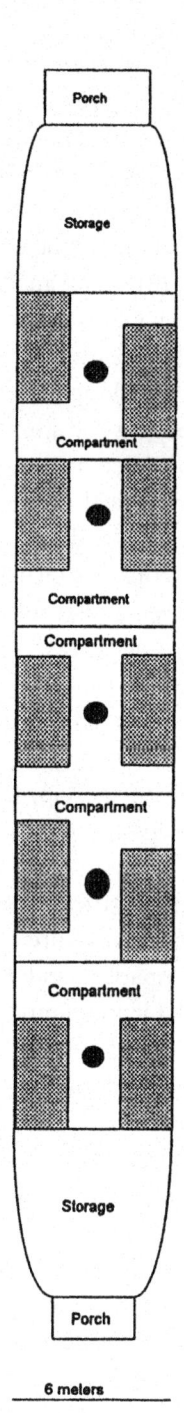

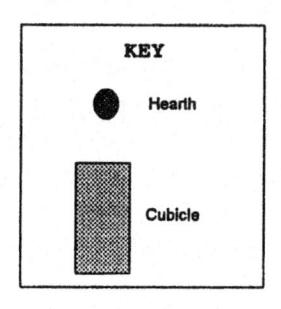

Figure 8.1. Plan view of a traditional Iroquois longhouse (Snow 1994: figure 3.3). (Image used courtesy of Dean R. Snow.)

pology for traditional Iroquoian structures (1984); and (2) a system of "spatial dynamics" (1990) where the proportions of a structure's area devoted to "organized" and "unorganized" space can be used to assess whether or not it functioned as a residence. Used in tandem, Kapches' techniques illustrate that true longhouses and short longhouses (often one hearth, two-family dwellings) were most frequently used as residences, whereas smaller Iroquoian "cabin" forms were often special-purpose nonresidential structures that did not incorporate all of the permanent and semipermanent internal features of dwellings.

European-Style Houses

Europeans constructed houses in a number of forms in colonies adjacent to Iroquoia in the seventeenth and eighteenth centuries, with the form of the house being in part determined by the cultural affiliation of the builder (see McAlester and McAlester 1984 for definitions and illustrations of various architectural elements). European architectural traditions had distinct histories of introduction to and reproduction in North America. Discussion here is limited to those European traditions encountered by Iroquois peoples during the 1677–1754 time frame, and to consideration of wooden house forms, since Iroquois use of masonry and brick for wall construction was a rare and late occurrence.

In European wood architecture, a primary distinction can be made between buildings of framed construction and buildings of log construction. Shurtleff (1967 [1939]: 17) defines a timber-framed house as "consisting of sills, posts, studs, plates, girders, joists, rafters, beams, and braces." One of the main ways to distinguish the various framed forms is to examine how the spaces between external wall studs were filled. In New France, inter-stud spaces in framed houses were filled with (1) stone, mortar, mud, or clay, often coated with a protective sheathing (*colombage*); (2) upright posts or boards that were then chinked or plastered over (*piquet*); or (3) slotted logs fit into grooved upright support posts (*pièces-sur-pièces*) (Moogk 1977; Rempel 1967). Dutch framed wooden houses were covered with boards and, particularly in the early stages of colonization, had thatched roofs (McAlester and McAlester 1984: 112–19; Weslager 1969: 129–31). English immigrants' framed houses were constructed in Post-Medieval and later Georgian forms (Deetz 1977; Glassie 1975; Johnson 1996), and inter-stud spaces typically were filled or covered with brickwork and plaster ("half-timber"), boards, or shingles (McAlester and McAlester 1984: 74–82, 104–11; Rempel 1967). The more affluent immigrants in New Netherland,

New York, and New France often replaced wooden houses with dwellings of stone or brick as soon as they were financially able. The presence of framed construction in Iroquois villages can be considered a definite consequence of interaction with Europeans since traditional Iroquois architecture shares few characteristics with these house forms.

Although some log forms were used by the Dutch, French, and English—particularly in the construction of defensive blockhouses (Shurtleff 1967 [1939])—in main part these cultural groups had little experience with horizontal, notched-log construction. Rempel (1967: 13) notes of the English that even though "log construction was introduced into the future United States as early as the first half of the seventeenth century and although it was speedier and required fewer tools and less skill, the English did not adopt this form until the eighteenth century, and even then it was generally considered only a stop-gap until they could afford a better building of stone, brick, or wooden frame." The geographer Terry Jordan (1985; Jordan and Kaups 1989) identifies three major North American log building traditions that potentially influenced the Six Nations: (1) the Savo-Karelian tradition; (2) the Moravian, or "German-Slavic," tradition; and (3) the Midland or "backwoods" fusion. Jordan (1985) claims that North American log architecture was not influenced significantly by the Schwenkfelders, European neighbors of the Moravians who migrated to Pennsylvania in the 1730s, or by groups from the Alpine-Alemannic region (except in barn construction, largely not of concern here). Importantly, Palatine Germans who settled in the Mohawk Valley after 1711 did not have a tradition of log construction (T. Jordan 1985: 137; Otterness 2004: figure 8).

The earliest log dwellings in North American were built by Europeans who settled in the Delaware Valley (T. Jordan 1985; T. Jordan and Kaups 1989; Rempel 1967). Any search for the European inspirations for Iroquois "log cabins" must look to the history of this region. Savo-Karelian Finns, who migrated to the Delaware Valley shortly after New Sweden's founding in 1638, constructed the first documented examples. Diagnostic aspects of Savo-Karelian log building techniques (T. Jordan 1985: ch. 3) include (1) round-log construction and, less frequently, two-sided planking; (2) logs shaped to fit closely together, requiring minimal or no chinking; (3) saddle-notched, V-notched, or square-notched cornering; (4) logs extending up to the house gable, where they supported a ridgepole; (5) roofs of gentle pitch; (6) one-room-deep layouts in a variety of forms, including the "saddlebag" (two rooms, two front doors), and "dogtrot" (two freestanding rooms separated by a covered, open-air porch) varieties (see figure 8.2).

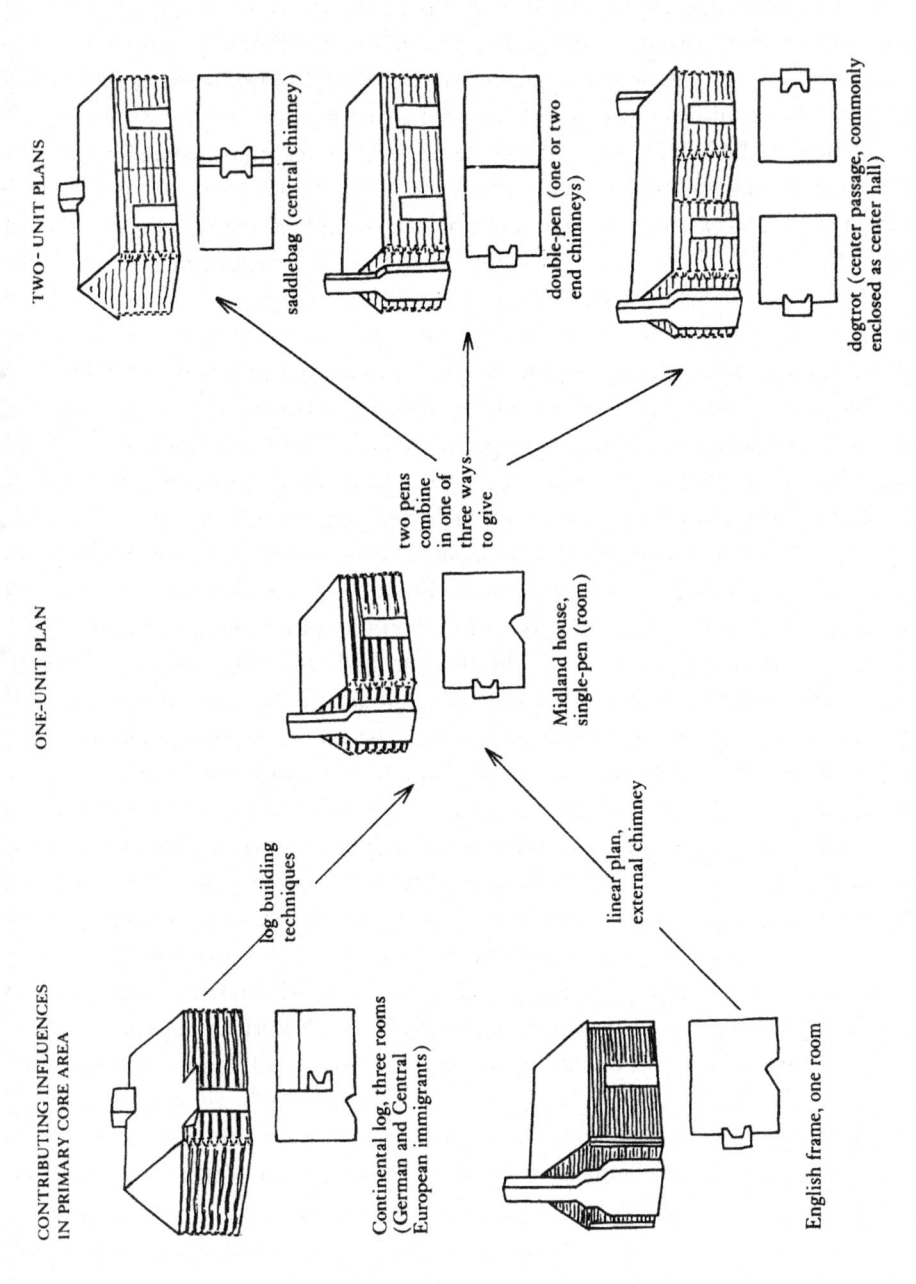

Figure 8.2. Origin and development of the Midland log cabin (McAlester and McAlester 1984: 84). The McAlesters place greater emphasis on German and Central European log constructions than do Jordan and Kaups (1989). (Image used courtesy of Random House/Alfred A. Knopf.)

Moravians from the German-Slavic borderland began to settle in the Delaware Valley in the 1740s, bringing with them another log-building tradition. Although Moravian techniques apparently exerted little influence on nineteenth-century American log architecture (T. Jordan 1985), they are spelled out in detail here due to the important role Moravians played in Indian affairs in the Northeast. German-Slavic building techniques consist of (1) two-sided hewn logs, of greater thickness than those seen in North American Midland examples; (2) chinkless or "false-chinked" gaps between logs; (3) full- and half-dovetailed, and square- and half-notched cornering; and (4) boarded gables (T. Jordan 1985: ch. 5). Moravians appear to have had "almost unanimous allegiance to dovetailing" in America (135).

The largest demographic group that used log architecture was neither Savo-Karelian nor Moravian, but the Scots-Irish practitioners of what Jordan and Kaups (1989) term "backwoods," or "Midland," culture. Midland culture was a hybrid of Savo-Karelian, Native American, and British cultural traditions fused in the "architectural melting pot" (Rempel 1967: 17) of the Pennsylvania colony (figure 8.2). According to Jordan and Kaups (1989), Savo-Karelian log building and subsistence techniques formed the backbone of Midland culture. In their model, Savo-Karelian ideas fused with Native American—especially Delaware—traditions during 1640–1680, forming a "Fenno-Indic" hybrid appropriate to local ecological conditions. Backwoods culture became a major force only after British and Irish populations began migrating to Pennsylvania in about 1680. This immigration intensified after 1717, when large numbers of Scots-Irish left Northern Ireland for Pennsylvania when their English landlords "racked their rents intolerably high" (Jennings 1984: 348). Although these immigrants came to the Delaware Valley with no tradition of log building and little experience in forest colonization, Jordan and Kaups posit that these practices were learned from neighboring "Fenno-Indic" populations. The newly hybridized Midland culture spread after 1700, displacing or replacing Native American populations in Pennsylvania, Ohio, and other locations (T. Jordan and Kaups 1989: figure 1.3).

While Savo-Karelian log building techniques had the most influence on the development of the Midland-style log cabin (T. Jordan 1985; Jordan and Kaups 1989), British architectural practices also had a role:

> An "English plan" single-pen cabin, distinguished by side-facing gables, front and rear doors centered in each eave wall, and square shape, with each wall between 15 and 16 feet [4.6–4.9 m] in length,

became the most common type on the backwoods frontier.... The Scotch-Irish introduced a similar eave-entrance plan for the single-pen cabin which differed from the English type only in being somewhat more elongated, with eave walls five or six feet [1.5–1.8 m] longer than the gabled sides. The doors of the Scotch-Irish cabin were positioned off-center, producing an asymmetry that was absent from the English plan.... Perhaps the most obvious British influence on Midland backwoods cabin plans involved chimney placement.... English chimneys [were] centrally positioned in a gable wall, a concept alien to the northern European tradition. (T. Jordan and Kaups 1989: 209)

Some elements of later log cabins—particularly the centered doors of the "English plan" and symmetrical window placement—evidence a Georgian mindset unlikely to have been expressed by earlier cabin builders. Rempel (1967: 19–21) asserts that the fusion of Georgian principles and log construction was undertaken in Canada by loyalist migrants after the American Revolution.

Intercultural/Creolized Houses

Iroquois peoples adopted some European trappings for their houses at a very early date, as evidenced by the split-plank doors with iron hinges observed by Dutch West India Company official Van den Bogaert in a Mohawk dwelling in 1634 (Gehring and Starna 1988: 4). Similar limited use of European hardware (such as nails and bolts) and wood-shaping tools for making planks, boards, and hewn timbers continued in eighteenth-century structures (Bartram 1966 [1751]: 41; Bennett 1988; Dean 1984; Doblin and Starna 1994: 40; Fenton and Moore 1977: 22). Peaked roofs may have been adopted from Europeans (Hamell 1992a: 50–56; Prezzano 1992: 275), and some archaeologists assert that the large post diameters and flattened ends of Postcolumbian structures were the product of iron tools (for example, Engelbrecht 2003: 163; Prezzano 1992: 259–60, 276; Ritchie 1980: 285). In some senses, therefore, *all* post-contact Iroquois houses were intercultural houses (Engelbrecht 2003: 163–64).

European tools and hardware could be used in two fundamentally distinct ways, however.[3] In the first, European tools were used as substitutes for stone tools to facilitate construction with traditional materials, such as wooden posts and bark. These houses generally incorporated limited amounts of European hardware and materials. In the second, European technology was used to produce recognizably Iroquoian houses, but where most of their features were distinct from traditional bark-covered dwellings. In these "intercultural/creolized" houses, European tools were used to make vital components that had no parallel in traditional construction methods, such as logs, planks, or nails. At the same time, traditional material types such as wooden posts and bark were not entirely abandoned, making the process one of addition rather than replacement. In both instances the ultimate goal was similar—production of a house with a central hearth and sleeping platforms—but distinct sets of methods and materials were used to attain this end.

The two-part *intercultural/creolized* designation is ungainly, but intentionally so. Terminology used to describe various types of cultural hybridization, such as *transculturation*, frequently either connotes or denotes that the social boundaries between groups ceased to exist (see Ortiz 1995 [1940]: 102–3). While this may be an appropriate description for what occurred in colonial settings such as the Caribbean, the Southwest, French Louisiana, or Spanish St. Augustine (Deagan 1983, 1998: 28–29; Loren 2005; Rothschild 2003), such terminology can be misleading when applied in settings where European and indigenous cultures remained relatively distinct or even diverged from one another over time (Roseberry and O'Brien 1991; Sider 1997). For this reason, I have used *intercultural* as opposed to *transcultural* (compare Hamell 1992a).

The term *creolized* indicates that a form of hybridization occurred, something that is not obvious from the use of *intercultural* alone. While some applications of *creolization* blur cultural boundaries in just the sense I seek to avoid (see Singleton 1998: 178), the term does not have a single agreed-upon meaning (Dawdy 2000). I use it here in the sense of Leland Ferguson (1992: xlii), who writes that "processes of creolization produced mixed cultures with divisions within the mixes, a series of interacting subcultures rather than a single creolized blend." Even this statement needs to be modified for application in the Northeast, where creolization took place in the context of interacting *cultures*, rather than a single overarching culture or several subcultures. Parallels to concepts of cultural transfer and *métissage* advanced by Canadian scholars (for example, Turgeon 1996) also exist.

The intercultural/creolized designation should be limited to those houses whose construction would have been impossible without European tools and hardware. Intercultural/creolized houses should be viewed as a specific subtype of Iroquois dwellings, often built alongside more traditional and, by the second half of the eighteenth century, fully European-style forms.

Although solid documentary evidence for intercultural/creolized houses does not exist until 1755, when James Smith noted the use of log siding in a winter dwelling constructed by Kahnawake Mohawks living in Ohio (see next section), archaeological evidence suggests an earlier date for the first appearance of intercultural/creolized houses. Significant variation from traditional Iroquois norms is evident around 1690 in Conestoga House 2 and also by 1715 in Townley-Read Structure 1 (see chapter 9). Intercultural/creolized houses appear to have been built in a variety of sizes, including true longhouses (Halsey 1906: 65–66), short longhouses (Townley-Read Structure 1), and presumably smaller cabin forms as well.

Three Key Descriptions of Specific Iroquois Houses

This section reviews three key documentary descriptions of Iroquois residences that serve to flesh out the typology presented in this chapter. The first account describes a European-style log cabin built in an Iroquois village, and the next two sources describe intercultural/creolized dwellings. Although all three accounts slightly postdate the occupation of the Townley-Read site, each provides a detailed rendering of techniques and circumstances that sheds light on Iroquois architectural practices before 1754. The first and second accounts, dating to 1754 and 1755, respectively, contain the earliest conclusive documentary evidence for log construction at Iroquois villages; in tandem, they illustrate that eighteenth-century Six Nations peoples used logs in both fully European-style log dwellings, and interculturally in Iroquois fashion. The third passage, dating to 1769, describes a traditional house form constructed with hewn timbers and planks, providing another prime example of an intercultural/creolized house.

European-Style Log Construction at Onondaga, 1754–1755

A journal written by the Moravian brother Charles Frederick (Beauchamp 1916) contains the earliest evidence I was able to locate describing the use of European-style log architecture at an Iroquois village. Frederick's journal chronicles his and David Zeisberger's 1754–1755 stay at Onondaga, during which they built several log structures for their hosts. Significantly, all construction work was done by the Moravians themselves.

Frederick and Zeisberger first erected a log house for themselves in November 1754: "Got our house under roof and lodged therein at once, on account of the many drunken Indians. Dimensions: 13 ½ by 12 ½ feet [4.1 × 3.8 m] inside; the walls of hewn logs, roofed with shingles, for we could get no bark at this time of the year. Moreover, it is the smallest but the best house in Onondago" (Beauchamp 1916: 205). A second house then was constructed for "an aged [Onondaga] couple" who intended to use it initially for sugar boiling and then as a residence; the Moravians "made it of wood and rather large. We worked at it about a month" (Beauchamp 1916: 210). Frederick and Zeisberger also built a small sugaring hut and a "little log hut" for a bear cub, and made boards and a door (Beauchamp 1916: 201–9). Of particular interest is the solicitation for the construction of a log building they received from an Onondaga family: "An old woman invited us to her house, to see her son who had just arrived. He asked us to estimate what we would charge to build him a storehouse . . . he inspected our house and declared that he wanted one like this. We made him a bid for building one, at a low price, as he himself admitted" (Beauchamp 1916: 209).

Frederick's journal provides ample indication that the Onondagas were unfamiliar with this type of log construction, and Moravian assistance was solicited even when a standing example was available to copy. However, the acceptance of this type of house seems tentative at best: Onondagas mainly had the Moravians build special-purpose structures, such as maple-sugaring huts and storehouses, and even the house of the "aged couple" was initially to be used as a sugaring hut. Since these log structures were built by Moravians, it is very likely that they employed dovetailed cornering methods (see T. Jordan 1985: 135).

Intercultural Log Construction in the Ohio Country, 1755

The first documentary description of Iroquois people themselves erecting a log dwelling is contained in Colonel James Smith's narrative of his 1755 captivity among a group of French-allied Mohawks from Kahnawake wintering in the Ohio country (Drake 1855). Smith describes Mohawk construction of a small winter house made of logs, split timbers, and bark:

> They cut logs about fifteen feet [4.6 m] long, and laid these logs upon each other, and drove posts in the ground at each end to keep them together; the posts they tied together at the top with bark, and by this means raised a wall fifteen feet [4.6 m] long, and about four feet [1.2 m] high, and in the same manner they raised another wall opposite to this, at about twelve feet [3.7 m] distance; then they drove forks in the ground in the centre of each end, and laid a strong pole from end to end on these forks; and from these walls to the poles, they set up poles

instead of rafters, and on these they tied small poles in place of laths; and a cover was made of lynn bark, which will run even in the winter season.... At the end of these walls they set up split timber, so that they had timber all round, excepting a door at each end. At the top, in place of a chimney, they left an open place, and for bedding they laid down on the aforesaid kind of bark, on which they spread bear-skins. From end to end of this hut along the middle there were fires, which the squaws made of dry split wood, and the holes or open places that appeared the squaws stopped with moss, which they collected from old logs; and at the door they hung a bear-skin; and notwithstanding the winters are hard here, our lodging was much better than what I expected. (Drake 1855: 193–94)

There are many departures from traditional Iroquoian construction in this example, including the lack of internal support posts and sleeping platforms and the use of a ridgepole. However, the structure does not fit European architectural traditions either. The 4.6 m log walls superficially resemble *pièces-sur-pièces* architecture, a distinct possibility given that these Mohawks had associated with French Canadians at the Kahnawake mission. However, the details of the winter house make for a poor match, since neither grooved uprights nor notched horizontal logs were used. Additionally, the winter house's ridgepole was supported by Y-shaped posts, not the topmost log in the gable as in European and Midland log examples (T. Jordan 1985: 22–23, figure 3.24).

The post-in-ground wall supports can be seen as drawing on an Iroquois heritage, but their use differs from traditional practices. It is quite likely that the structure was made possible by European tools and technologies such as axes and saws, particularly for the construction of gable-end boards (a detail also seen in Lafitau's 1724 description of a longhouse at Kahnawake [Fenton and Moore 1977: 22]). The indigenous log form constructed by the Mohawks is therefore a good example of intercultural/creolized architecture.

European Technologies Implementing Iroquoian Architectural Principles at Oquaga, 1769

Richard Smith's 1769 account of the fully dispersed multinational (principally Oneida) settlement at Oquaga provides another description of intercultural/creolized log construction that fits well within the Iroquois architectural tradition:

The Habitations here . . . are composed of clumsy hewn Timbers & hewn Boards or Planks. You first enter an inclosed Shed or Portus which serves as a Wood house or Ketchin and then the Body of the Edifice consisting of an Entry . . . of about 8 Feet [2.4 m] wide[,] on each side whereof is a Row of Stalls or Births resembling those of Horse Stables, raised a Foot [0.3 m] from the Earth, 3 or 4 on either side according to the Size of the House, Floored and inclosed round, except the Front, and covered on the Top. Each Stall contains an entire Family so that 6 or more families sometimes reside together. . . . The fire is made in the Middle of the Entry and a Hole is left in the Roof for the Smoke to escape for there is neither chimney nor window; consequently the place looks dark and dismal. The House is open as a Barn, save the Top of the Stalls which serve to contain their lumber by way of Garret. Beams are fixed lengthways across the house, and on one of these, over the Fire, they hang their wooden Pot Hooks & cook their food. . . .

Furniture they have little; the Beds are dirty Blankets. The stalls are about 8 feet [2.4 m] long & 5 [1.5 m] deep and the whole House perhaps from 30 to 50 feet [9.1–15.2 m] in length by 20 [6.1 m] wide, filled too often with Squalor & Nastiness. Almost every House has a Room at the End opposite to the Ketchin serving as a larder for Provision; there are no cellars. The Roofs are no other than Sheets of Bark fastned crossways and inside to Poles by way of Rafters. Upon the outside are split Logs which keep the Roof on; they are Pitch Roofs and it is about 8 feet [2.4 m] from the Ground to the Eves of the House, and this is said to be the general Form of building their Houses and Towns throughout the 6 Nations. (Halsey 1906: 65–66)

This house provides the best documentary indication that Six Nations peoples applied European technologies in the service of Iroquoian architectural principles. The materials used in the house's construction—especially the hewn timbers, split logs, boards, and planks—evidence concentrated use of European tools. However, the house is also readily recognizable as a traditional Iroquoian house form: it includes interior support posts, sleeping platforms with elevated storage spaces above them, a "shed" at the structure's end, bark roofing, and a central corridor punctuated by open fires. Smith obviously describes a multiple-hearth, multifamily longhouse, and his statement that "6 or more families sometimes reside together" indicates that structures with three or more hearths *sometimes* were built.

Houses of 9.1–15.2 m length could have contained one to three hearths. His claim that "this is said to be the general Form of building their Houses and Towns throughout the 6 Nations" is interesting (especially given the 1769 date of the account) but cannot be assessed given the sparse nature of present evidence.

Identifying Intercultural/Creolized Houses

Several architectural practices recognizable in the documentary and archaeological records can be used to distinguish intercultural/creolized houses from traditional Iroquois and European-style dwellings. These include post size, type, and placement; wall post spacing; iron nail use; and siding type, interior post usage, and cornering methods.[4] The best candidates for the intercultural/creolized designation will depart from traditional Iroquois and European-style norms in more than one of these areas. The archaeological examples mentioned briefly here are discussed in detail in the next chapter.

Post Size, Type, and Placement

Archaeological and documentary data indicate that Iroquois structures in the late seventeenth and the eighteenth centuries employed numerous wall posts. The use of posts is rare in European framed architecture and unnecessary in Savo-Karelian or Moravian log construction.[5] That wall posts were used at all on an Indian site is an important clue that indigenous construction methods may have been used. However, traditional versus intercultural/creolized uses of posts need to be distinguished.

Prezzano's (1992: 259–60) data from thirty-eight Owasco and Iroquois sites containing "traditional" architecture indicate that posts at both Pre- and Postcolumbian sites average 5–10 cm in diameter. Traditional dwellings also tend to exhibit a bimodal distribution of post sizes, with interior weight-bearing support posts being considerably larger than the smaller posts used for wall construction. In some cases (such as the short longhouse at the sixteenth-century Onondaga Atwell site [Ricklis 1967]), three distinct post-size groupings have been recovered.[6]

Iroquoian dwellings constructed with posts that are on average larger than the 10 cm upper boundary suggested by Prezzano, or with posts that lack distinct size groupings may be intercultural/creolized dwellings. Table 8.1 presents post-size information compiled from late seventeenth- and eighteenth-century Iroquoian sites. Data that imply nontraditional post use include the very large rectangular posts, typically 17.8 × 22.8 cm in size,

Table 8.1. Post Mold Diameter Figures for Selected Iroquoian Sites (in Centimeters)

Site	Occupation Dates	Overall Average (all posts)	Smallest Wall Post	Largest Wall Post	Wall Post Average
Rogers Farm: Structure 1	1660–1685	9.4	5.0	15.0	8.6
Bead Hill: Trench 1	1665–1687	5.5	2.0	17.0	n/a
Ganondagan: Trench 4 Structure	1670–1687	10.2[a]	6.1	16.8	9.4
Primes Hill	1696–1720	7.8	5.1	12.7	7.3
Conestoga: House 1	1690–1740	7.0	n/a	n/a	n/a
Conestoga: House 2	1690–1740	12.7	n/a	n/a	n/a
Townley-Read: Structure 1	1715–1754	8.6	4.0[b]	13.0[b]	6.3[b]
Egli	1753–1778	17.8 × 22.8	n/a	n/a	n/a

Sources: Rogers Farm: Williams-Shuker (2005); Bead Hill: Poulton (1991); Ganondagan: Dean (1984); Primes Hill: Monte Bennett, personal communication 2001; Conestoga: Anderson (1995); Egli: Hesse (1975).

Notes: a. includes Features 146 and 162 (possible bench supports)
b. excludes large Wall Posts 29 and 32

found at the Revolutionary War–era Egli site on the Upper Susquehanna River (Hesse 1975) and possibly the 12.7 cm average for posts recovered in Conestoga House 2 (Anderson 1995), although this structure may not have been built by Iroquoian people. Posts at the Seneca Bead Hill site north of Lake Ontario were identified at subsoil surface but not excavated (Poulton 1991: 17). They likely represent a mix of structural and nonstructural posts; I suspect excavations would reveal that many of the alleged post molds with very small dimensions were root holes or other natural disturbances. The 5.5 cm average post size at Bead Hill places it in the "traditional" category.

Squared-off or rectangular posts, such as those at Egli, indicate that European wood-shaping tools were used. The use of dug post holes (traditionally, Iroquois posts were driven into the ground) or atypical post placement (such as the large posts in the eastern wall of Townley-Read Structure 1) also may signal intercultural/creolized construction methods.

Wall Post Spacing

Using slightly different measures, Warrick (1988) and Williams-Shuker (2005) have quantified wall post density for traditional architecture in Five Nations, Huron, and Neutral territories. Warrick (1988: table 8) finds that the average original wall post density (prior to repair and replacement of rotted posts) was 3.3 posts per meter or greater at Huron and Neutral sites for most time periods examined. Williams-Shuker does not distinguish original from replacement posts, measuring wall post density by "dividing the total number of wall posts identified by the total number of exposed linear meters of house circumference that were excavated" (2005: 233). Employing this method, forty Cayuga, Mohawk, and Huron houses built between 1400 and 1600 used an average of 3.7 posts per meter, whereas sixty-nine Cayuga, Mohawk, Onondaga, Seneca, and Huron houses used between 1600 and 1700 used an average of 2.5 posts per meter (2005: table 27). Existing data suggest that intercultural/creolized houses may have employed even fewer wall posts (K. Jordan 2003: 57).

Wall post density figures must be used carefully because they can be dramatically altered by poor post preservation. Density figures are most reliable when one or more sections of a structure's walls have been well preserved. For example, in Townley-Read Structure 1 (figure 9.6), the western wall was set in a clayey deposit, and definite posts as small as 4 cm in diameter were recovered, making the original post density figure for the wall of 2.5 posts per meter quite reliable. Other post density figures are more questionable. For example, the southern wall in the structure recovered at Ganondagan (figure 9.1) has a very low wall post density of 1.5 posts per meter, but it is not clear that post mold preservation conditions were good in this or any other portion of the excavated area.

Iron Nail Use

One of the main European features of intercultural/creolized house forms—the use of iron nails—actually serves to *differentiate* Iroquois houses from European log cabins. Counterintuitively, European log cabins used few if any nails. Expensive nails were not needed to construct a Midland log house; corner-notching served to secure wall logs in position, and the gentle pitch of the Midland cabin roof meant that gravity held roofing elements in place (T. Jordan and Kaups 1989: 168). In intercultural/creolized houses, nails appear to have been used primarily to secure siding (Hesse 1975; K. Jordan 2001).

The extent of iron nail use can be estimated using the ratio between the number of nails recovered and the area excavated at a given site (Table 8.2; K. Jordan 2001 provides additional details on nail use). It is important to assess excavated samples for comparability. For example, the data from Townley-Read, Rogers Farm, Bead Hill, Ganondagan, and Primes Hill make for reasonable comparison because excavations at each site sampled portions of house lots and recovered sub-plowzone features, and disturbance of deposits by plowing occurred to approximately the same depth.[7] To make the data consistent, the Townley-Read statistics include only nails found in shovel test pits or test units.

Table 8.2. Iron Nail Density at Selected Iroquois Sites

Site	Occupation Dates	Excavated Area (m²)	Number of 17th- & 18th-century Nails Recovered [a]	Nails/m² [a]
Rogers Farm	1660–1685	40.0	5	0.13
Bead Hill: Trench 1	1665–1687	46.0	0	0.0
Ganondagan: Trench 4	1670–1687	157.9	22–28	0.14–0.18
Primes Hill	1696–1720	88.3	30	0.34
Townley-Read: Structure 1 area	1715–1754	11.8	10–16	0.85–1.36
Townley-Read: Area D	1715–1754	37.4	25–42	0.67–1.12
Townley-Read: East Fields overall	1715–1754	57.6	31–53	0.53–0.92
Egli (estimated)[b]	1753–1778	455.2	118	1.04–1.30

Sources: Rogers Farm: Williams-Shuker (2005); Bead Hill: Poulton (1991); Ganondagan: Dean (1984), Primes Hill: Bennett (1988), Egli: Hesse (1975)
Notes: a. The lower number in the range is for definitely hand-wrought nails; higher figure includes all possibly hand-wrought nails.
b. See text for estimation procedure.

The raw nail density figure of 0.26 nails/m² for Egli (where 118 hand-wrought rosehead, L-head, T-head, and headless nails were recovered) also requires modification. Most of the topsoil in the examined area at Egli was cleared away by bulldozer; nails were recovered only from the remaining topsoil and from features. Because architectural nails were used primarily aboveground, most nails at Egli would have been deposited in the upper stratigraphic layers at the site and likely were removed by the bulldozer. Consequently, I increased the Egli density figure four- to fivefold to approximate the number of nails present prior to bulldozing. Table 8.2 likely underestimates Iroquois nail use; Six Nations people may well have collected nails for reuse when a site was abandoned, and modern collectors with metal detectors also are likely to have diminished the number of nails in the archaeological record.

Although the figure of 1.04–1.30 nails/m² for Egli must be used with caution, builders at Townley-Read and Egli, the two latest sites, appear to have used nails to a significantly greater extent than did builders at Rogers Farm, Bead Hill, Ganondagan, and Primes Hill. This likely indicates some form of architectural change; the concentrated application of European technology suggests that structures at Townley-Read and Egli are likely to meet the intercultural/creolized definition.

Siding Type, Interior Post Usage, and Cornering Methods

The three documentary descriptions cited earlier in this chapter demonstrate that Iroquois peoples used logs, planks, and other siding materials in both European and non-European ways. Use of these types of siding on a significant part of a structure in itself proves that an Iroquois dwelling was not entirely traditional. Iroquoian log- or plank-sided houses could not have been constructed without European technology; felling and shaping of logs (rounded, split, hewn, or planked) required ownership of iron broadaxes and adzes and considerable technical skill in their application. Although documentary mention of these types of siding alone is inadequate to determine whether a dwelling was constructed in European or intercultural/creolized fashion, information on the presence or absence of sleeping compartments and on cornering details can help distinguish how siding was deployed.

Choices in cornering and interior support methods are related to culturally diagnostic ways of supporting the weight of a structure. European structures bear the weight of the superstructure primarily at the corners and along walls, while traditional Iroquoian structures mainly were supported by large interior posts (Kapches 1993: 145–47). The presence of substantial interior posts—usually described in their role as bench supports—therefore is a clue that indigenous systems of structural support were used in a house. One example is Richard Smith's 1769 description of the intercultural/creolized house at Oquaga (Halsey 1906: 65–66). Although Smith does not state how the Oquaga structure's siding was held up, the overwhelmingly Iroquoian aspects of the rest of the house argue that the interior posts played a major weight-bearing role. The "inclosed round" compartments within the house must have been sturdily constructed, as they supported sleeping platforms and upper storage spaces. If the timbers and boards used in the structure's siding did not bear the majority of its weight, they need not have been as substantial as the logs used in European-style cabins, and they may not have been cornered in the same ways. Siding in this "habitation" may have been nailed to upright posts, or inserted between upright posts in a manner similar to the Kahnawake Mohawks' winter house in Ohio.

In addition to the Oquaga house, many other accounts of eighteenth-century Iroquois log- or plank-sided houses also describe sleeping compartments attached to interior posts (for example, Conover 1887: 60; Division of Archives and History 1929: 176). Some authorities (such as Wonderley 2004: 18) argue that eighteenth-century Iroquois builders added sleeping compartments to European-style log cabins; in this view, the compartment framing was not used structurally but only to preserve the traditional arrangement of interior space and its symbolic associations. Milanese traveler Paolo Andreani suggested otherwise in a 1790 description of Oneida housing (Snow, Gehring, and Starna 1996: 323), noting, "In its construction, this nation has embraced in part the custom of the neighboring European colonies, and instead of building a longhouse with several berths all around as they used to do, they now build a room in which they put various beds." To me, the most likely scenario is that Iroquoian architectural principles and sleeping compartments were put aside at the same time.

In contrast, proper cornering was vital to European-style log structures; a modern estimate suggests that well-executed corner notches support 70–80 percent of the weight of a European-style log building (Langsner 1982: 121). Cornering details are one of the best ways to assess whether a log dwelling was constructed in European style, and also to determine which log-building traditions were drawn upon; Terry Jordan (1985: 130) writes, "Perhaps no other facet of log carpentry is potentially more revealing of antecedents than is the method of joining timbers at the corners of structures." Unfortunately, very few accounts of pre–Revolutionary War Iroquois houses describe cornering details. This may be for reasons other than simple oversight: cornering in houses in which the structure's weight was distributed to interior posts may have been informal or even non-interlocking. This type of construction may have appeared generically "Indian" to European observers.

Since siding types and cornering methods do not preserve archaeologically, inferences about siding and cornering based on excavated data must be made indirectly. Many archaeologically visible departures from traditional norms (including the changes in post size, shape, and placement; increased wall post spacing; and increased iron nail use outlined earlier) may have been rooted in the use of more rigid siding and new means of fastening it to upright wall posts. Smith's description of the Oquaga intercultural/creolized house and other evidence presented in chapter 9 suggest that Six Nations peoples frequently used logs, planks, and other rigid siding materials *as a substitute for bark* in structures that otherwise maintained Iroquoian forms. Intercultural/creolized houses combining siding made using European tools with Iroquoian structural principles may have predominated at many eighteenth-century sites, particularly in the Seneca region (K. Jordan 2004).

Notes on Terminology and Classification

The previous sections demonstrate that scholars should not take documented references to Iroquois use of logs and planks as indications that Six Nations peoples had adopted European-style architectural forms; Iroquois peoples also used these types of siding in their own ways. Uncritical interpretation of other terms commonly used in primary sources also can lead to unwarranted conclusions about Iroquois architectural forms.

The ambiguous term *cabin* is a prime example. A cabin can be defined as

1. a more or less temporary structure;
2. a dwelling of a certain size or proportions, regardless of its method of manufacture. This is the sense of the word used by Kapches (1984), who defines Iroquoian cabins as residential structures with a length-to-width ratio of 1.25:1 or less; or,
3. a dwelling made from notched logs laid parallel to the ground, or in other words, a European-style log cabin.

These three definitions should not be conflated, nor should the use of the word *cabin* (or *cabane* in French) in historical sources be taken to signify more than one of these meanings. Seventeenth- and eighteenth-century Europeans often used the term *cabin* only to convey their perception that a structure was impermanent, without any implications as to the size of the dwelling or the materials from which it was built. This point is clearly illustrated by Champlain's 1616 use of *"cabanne"* to describe bark longhouses with up to twelve hearths (Snow 1997: 62). Contrast this with Tuck's (1971: 182) too-quick assertion that the use of the word *cabane* by late seventeenth-century French observers "is difficult to construe as [a] longhouse or any similar structure" (see also Warrick 1996: 20).

The same caution applies to the English *hut* and the German *Hütte*. For example, the 1750 journal of the Moravian Johann Cammerhoff uses the word translated as "hut" (probably *Hütte*) to describe both an obvious Cayuga longhouse that was "large and roomy, with three or four fireplaces . . . well built and waterproof" (Beauchamp 1916: 43) and a temporary shelter he and his companions built to get themselves out of the rain (29). The multiple referents of the term makes it all but useless for the interpretation of architectural form.

In order to classify small Iroquoian-style structures, their overall size should be assessed and Kapches' (1984) typology applied if length and width measurements are available. The more precise term *short longhouse* should be used in instances where a structure was built in Iroquois style and either (1) its dimensions and internal spatial arrangement meet Kapches' (1984) definition, as with Structure 1 at Townley-Read; or (2) two-family residence can be inferred, as in Bartram's (1966 [1751]: 42) description of

Onondaga houses in 1743. It is essential that anthropologists and historians recognize eighteenth-century short longhouses to be a traditional part of the Iroquoian housing repertoire (Kapches 1984; Ricklis 1967) and not an eighteenth-century aberration or the product of acculturation.

The term *cabin* still has a productive place in ethnohistorical and archaeological parlance, but scholars must be vigilant in its use, since it can refer to structures constructed in either European or traditional Iroquois styles. The term should *always* be preceded by "Iroquoian-style" or "European-style" when used in the context of Iroquoian sites of the seventeenth to nineteenth centuries. Iroquoian-style cabins can be identified by their proportions or their arrangement of interior space (Kapches 1984, 1990).

9

Iroquois Housing, 1677–1754

Archaeological and Documentary Evidence

This chapter assesses archaeological and documentary evidence on house forms used at Iroquois sites occupied between 1677 and 1754 using the classificatory scheme presented in chapter 8. To be comprehensive, I incorporate housing information from extra-regional Iroquois satellite communities outside the homeland, including Bead Hill, Conestoga, Fort Frontenac, and mission communities in the St. Lawrence River valley.

Iroquois Housing, circa 1677–1696

Evidence from across the Confederacy indicates that traditional-style longhouses were the main residential form in use at the end of the seventeenth century. Archaeological data from this period is relatively copious; information on house forms is available from the Seneca, Onondaga, Mohawk, and Cayuga regions, and domestic-context excavation has taken place at a Seneca satellite village north of Lake Ontario.

Homeland Iroquois Settlements

Wentworth Greenhalgh's 1677 journal and excavations conducted at Ganondagan jointly provide a view of homeland Seneca housing during the 1677–1687 period (see figure 6.2 for site locations). These sources indicate that dwellings of at least three different sizes were present in the Seneca region. Greenhalgh describes houses of 15–18 m ("the ordinary") and 40–43 m at Tiotohattan (likely the Rochester Junction site), with the longer having "13 to 14 fires in one house" (Snow, Gehring, and Starna 1996: 191). Both of these house types clearly fall within Kapches' (1984) longhouse category, but the count of "13 to 14 fires" is far too high for a longhouse about 40 m long. Using standard archaeological estimates that longhouse living compartments were 4.5–6.0 m in length (Kapches 1993: table 3; Snow 1997), one would expect 2.5–4.1 hearths in the smaller "ordinary" houses, and 6.6–9.5 hearths in the longer houses. Since many houses likely contained nonresidential storage compartments at one or both ends, the lower figures in each range probably are more accurate. Generally, each hearth supported two nuclear families of about five persons each (Snow 1995), making households of twenty to thirty persons likely for two- to three-hearth "ordinary" longhouses and sixty to eighty residents likely for the longer six- to eight-hearth structures. If one substitutes "families" for Greenhalgh's "fires," the numbers come close to corresponding, since 13–14 families would indicate that approximately 65–70 people lived in the larger houses.

Although structural remains have not been well preserved at Ganondagan (Dean 1986; Huey 1997b), the floor plan of an apparent 11 × 6 m short longhouse structure (figure 9.1) was exposed during 1983–1984 excavations in Trench 4 by Dean and Barbour Associates. Dean's (1984) interpretation of the structure does not conform to the definition of a traditional Iroquois house: (1) he identified no bench support posts (26); (2) a large proportion of the hypothesized floor area was devoted to hearths, with two large hearths each within 30 cm of proposed walls (24); and (3) the arrangement of posts in the alleged northern and southern walls is quite irregular. These discrepancies have caused some to suggest either that excavations did not reveal the structure's full plan or that the structure was nonresidential (Jemison and White 1997; K. Jordan 2002: 306, 395–96).

However, Dean (1984: 21) mentions of the structure that "it is possible to picture a 'bench-like' area along the southern wall depending on where the actual wall line is drawn." It appears plausible to interpret Features 146 and 162 as bench support posts, making a residential function likely. The broad array of cultural materials recovered from features within the structure (24–26) also weighs against a special-purpose function. If it is indeed a dwelling, the Ganondagan structure remains atypical because it apparently contained only a single sleeping platform, and also because its hearths are unusually large (not all of them may have been in use at once). Knight (2002: 34) notes that a significant proportion of the structures at the circa 1590–1620 Huron Ball site have benches on only one side, suggesting that this type of construction may have been introduced to the Seneca region by refugee Hurons if it did not already have a minor presence in the Five Nations housing repertoire.

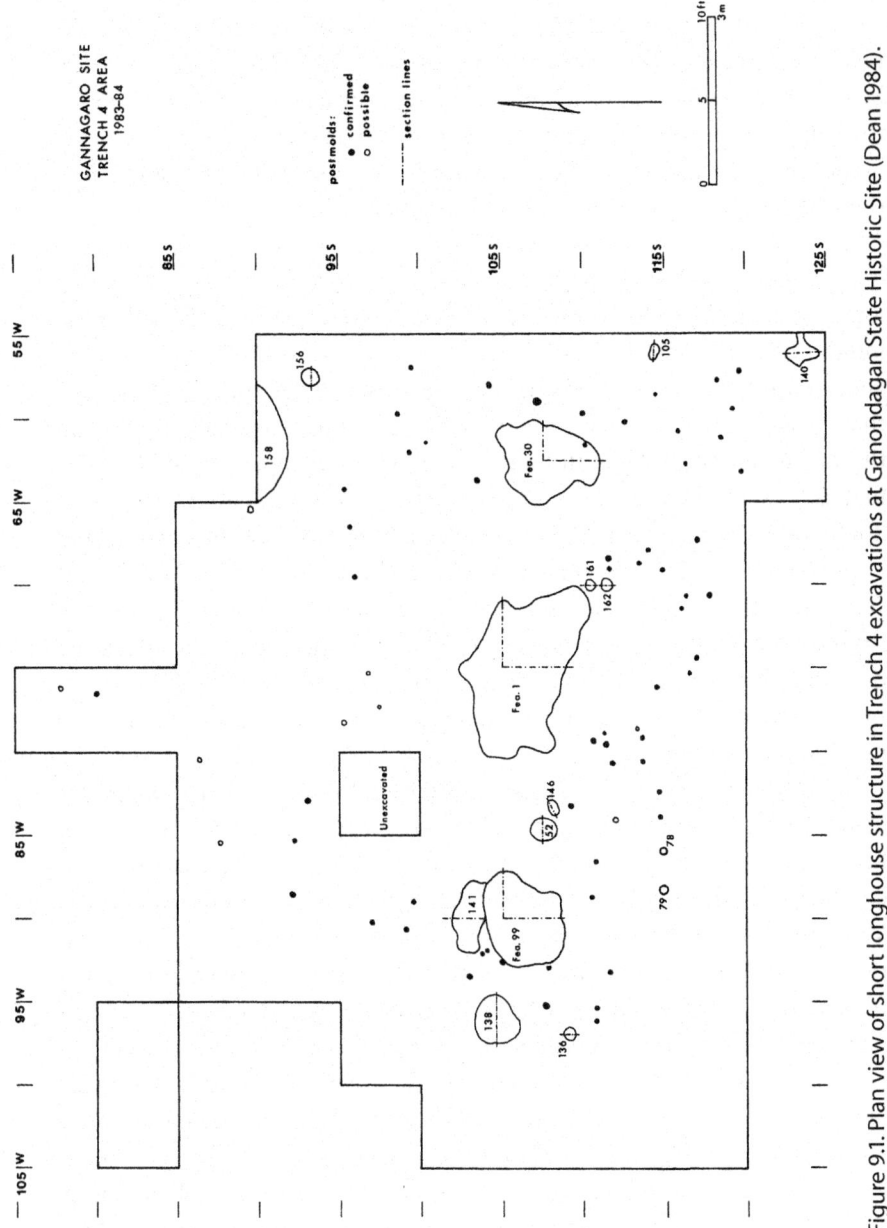

Figure 9.1. Plan view of short longhouse structure in Trench 4 excavations at Ganondagan State Historic Site (Dean 1984). The site was called Gannagaro at the time of excavation. (Image used courtesy of the Bureau of Historic Sites, New York State Office of Parks, Recreation and Historic Preservation.)

Gregory Sohrweide (2001) has argued convincingly that the Onondaga village burned in advance of the 1696 French invasion force led by Louis de Buade de Frontenac was located at the Weston site. Crews under Sohrweide's direction have excavated about 5 percent of the site to subsoil. The residential portion of the site was approximately 3.6 ha in size, of which 2.6 ha was enclosed by a triple-walled palisade. An undated anonymous map of the village likely drawn by a member of the 1696 expedition closely reflects archaeological finds at Weston and provides a reasonably accurate plan of the village at the time of its destruction (figure 9.2).

The 1696 map indicates that Weston contained approximately sixty houses inside and thirteen houses outside the palisade. Using archaeological and cartographic evidence, Sohrweide (2001: 18) estimates that the longest house at site was less than 30 m, most were 15–25 m in length, about 35 percent of the buildings were less than 12 m long, and most of the houses contained two or three hearths (23). The map also suggests that the vast majority (perhaps all) of the dwellings at Weston should be classified as true longhouses rather than short longhouses or cabins (K. Jordan 2002: 395). Excavations at the site recovered traces of both residential and nonresidential structures. Structure 9 was 21.3 m long and 6.1 m wide; it contained storage vestibules at either end, six internal compartments, and three hearths; an external storehouse 19.4 m long ran along one side of the building (Sohrweide 2001: 10, figure 6). Weston Structure 7 (17.5 × 6.1 m in size) was divided into two "storehouses" of equal size and contained no hearths (13–15, figure 8).

The Mohawk site of Caughnawaga (figure 9.3), burned in 1693, is unusual in post-1677 Iroquois archaeology in that the entire community plan has been recovered (Grassman 1969; Snow 1995: 431–43). Excavations conducted in the 1940s and 1950s by Father Thomas Grassman and the Van Epps–Hartley Chapter of the New York State Archaeological Association (NYSAA) revealed twelve structures within a village area of 0.6 ha surrounded by a square, double palisade wall. The twelve structures averaged 25.9 × 6.3 m in size and contained three or four hearths (Snow 1995: 433); each is classified as a true longhouse. Snow (1995: 433) asserts that three of these structures were nonresidential based on the excavation field notes, an interpretation that merits future reevaluation. The relatively uniform longhouse size at Caughnawaga is one of the main pieces of evidence Snow (1989, 1994, 1995) uses to argue that by the late seventeenth century Mohawk kin groups had become so fragmented that families without blood ties were "repackaged" into standardized longhouses, in place of the previous

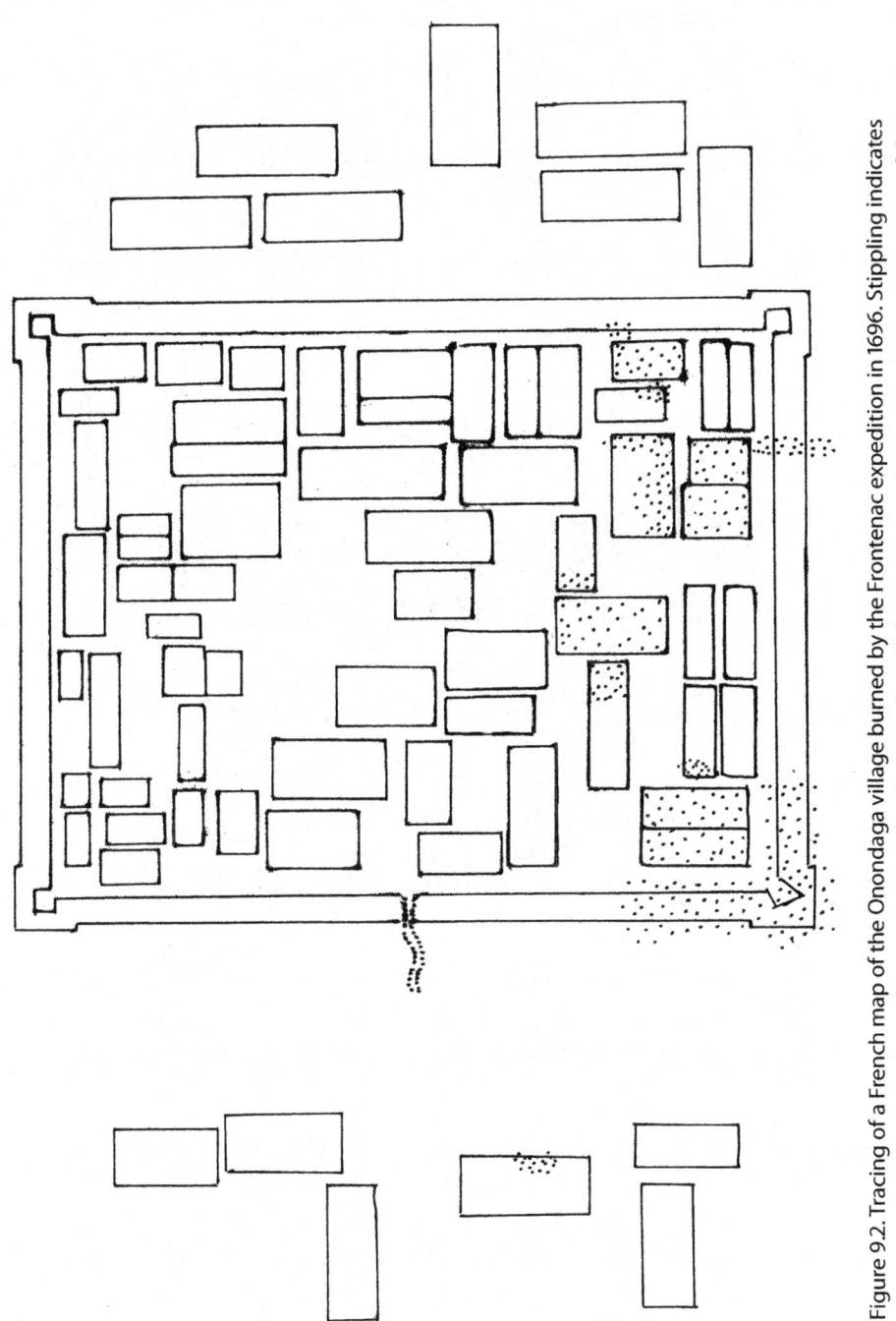

Figure 9.2. Tracing of a French map of the Onondaga village burned by the Frontenac expedition in 1696. Stippling indicates areas of the site excavated by A. Gregory Sohrweide, which confirm that the 1696 map is a reasonable approximation of the plan of the village. (Image used courtesy of A. Gregory Sohrweide.)

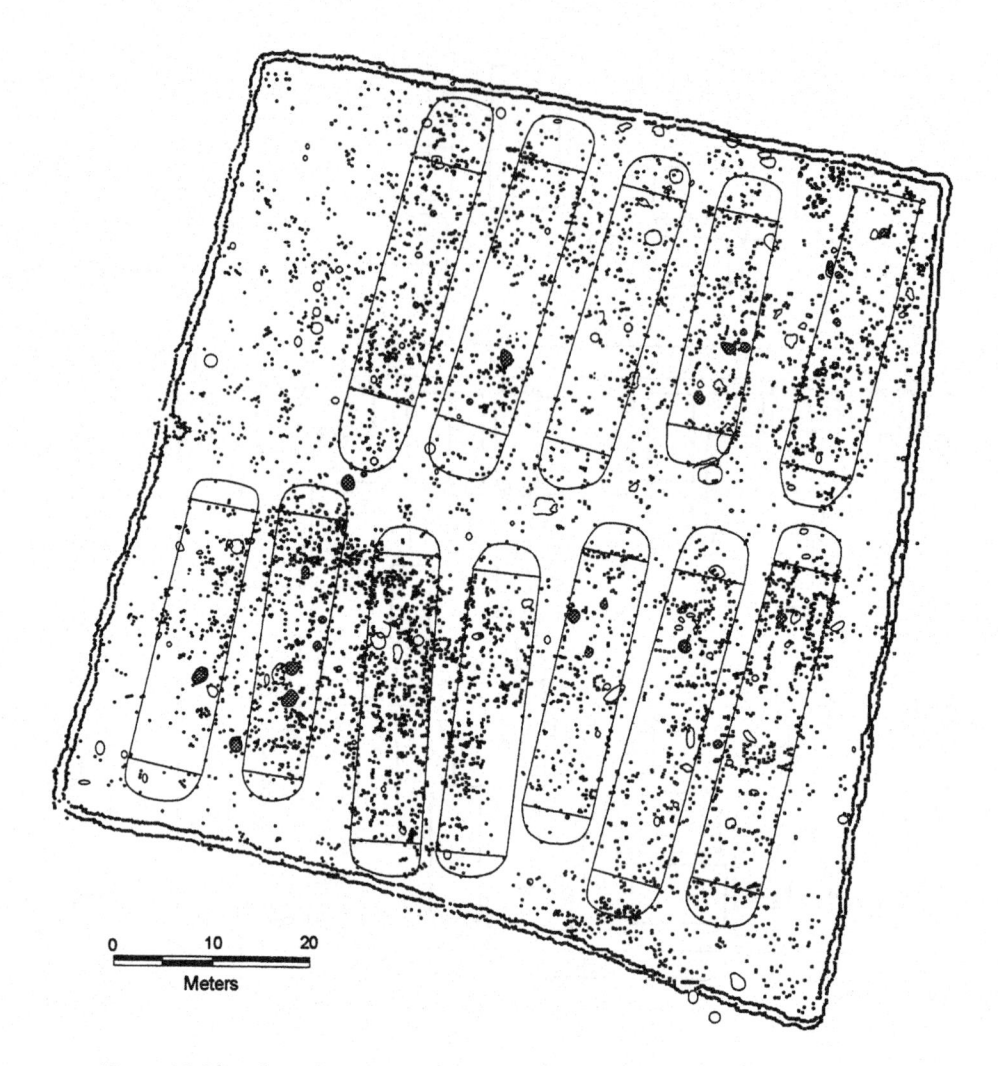

Figure 9.3. Plan view of excavations at the Caughnawaga site, with interpretation of longhouse outlines (Snow 1995: figure 11.3). (Image used courtesy of Dean R. Snow.)

practice of house lengths being dictated by the actual demographic composition of matrilineages. I evaluate this model in chapter 11.

Excavations at the small Cayuga Rogers Farm site (Williams-Shuker 2005) revealed a portion of a dwelling interpreted as a longhouse. Rogers Farm is a 0.4 ha site likely to have been the circa 1660–1685 Cayuga village of Onontaré, which contained the Jesuit chapel called St. René (Mandzy 1990; Williams-Shuker 2005: 15–17). University of Pittsburgh domestic-context excavations in 2000 supervised by Kimberly Williams-Shuker (2005: 142) cleared an area of 40 m². This area contained a portion of a longhouse structure 6.7 m wide; due to topographic limits, the structure was no more than 25 m long (197, 224). Williams-Shuker suggests that a house of this size would have contained three to four hearths and housed six to eight families (224). She also notes that the structure is unusually wide by Five Nations standards, which may signal that its builders were Hurons (239–41).

The data from these four sites allow some comparison of house structure and layout. Thirty-eight measured wall posts from the Ganondagan structure ranged from 6.1 to 16.8 cm and averaged 9.4 cm in diameter (Dean 1984: 22–23). Dean (1984: 21) states that these posts "had either been tapered to blunt points or were of fairly uniform diameters with rounded or blunt tips. All of the posts appear to have been driven into the ground rather than dug." The two probable bench support posts (Features 146 and 162) measured 25.0 cm and 22.9 cm in diameter, respectively. The large Features 1 (3.0 × 1.5 m), 30 (1.8 × 1.5 m), and 99 (1.8 × 1.4 m) at Ganondagan were interpreted as hearths (24). In contrast, hearths at Weston were small and shallow; preserved portions ranged in size from 48 to 91 cm across (Sohrweide 2001: 10, 16, 17). At Caughnawaga, many of the presumably shallow internal hearths appear to have been destroyed by plowing (Snow 1995: 435). At Rogers Farm, forty-five wall posts ranged from 5 to 15 cm and averaged 8.6 cm in diameter. Fourteen interior structural posts, classified as "bench support" or "compartment" posts, ranged from 8 to 15 cm and averaged 11.3 cm in diameter (Williams-Shuker 2005: table 16). Wall post density averaged 2.2 posts per meter for the excavated portion of the structure (210). Feature 31/31B may be a central hearth associated with the structure; it was approximately 1 m in diameter in its preserved dimensions (185, 195). Post mold size data have not been published for Caughnawaga or Weston, although Sohrweide (2001) identifies "large" and "small" posts at Weston.

Bead Hill

Discussion of homeland architectural patterns can be supplemented with excavation data from the Iroquois du Nord Bead Hill site in Scarborough, Ontario (Poulton 1991). Bead Hill is believed to be the circa 1665–1687 Seneca village known as Ganestiquiagon (40); the Seneca component at the site is approximately 2.2 ha in size (5). Excavations by Mayer, Poulton, and Associates in 1991 found the most concentrated evidence for Seneca domestic occupation in Trench 1; 112 post molds and seven features (one hearth and six pits) were identified in a 46 m² area that was cleared but not excavated (13, 17). Although no structure outlines could be determined, the excavators felt that the "nature and density" of post molds and features and the density of plowzone artifact finds "suggests the presence of one or more longhouses" (17). The post molds ranged from 2 to 17 cm and averaged 5.5 cm in diameter (1991: tables 6, 17); as mentioned in the previous chapter, some of the possible post molds are likely to be nonstructural or noncultural. No iron nails were found in Trench 1. A linear feature present at the east end of Trench 1 appears similar to "linear end features" or "slash pits" found at historic Neutral sites (18).

Discussion

There is little evidence to suggest that residences at Ganondagan, Weston, Caughnawaga, Rogers Farm, or Bead Hill were intercultural/creolized structures. Architectural data from these sites have been interpreted within the traditional Iroquoian framework by their excavators, and many structures have the traditional layout of central hearths flanked by paired sleeping benches, interior weight-bearing posts, and smaller posts along exterior walls.

A frequently reproduced illustration depicting the 1687 battle between Senecas and Denonville's forces (for example, Hamell 1980: plate 3; Richter 1992: plate 18) represents Ganondagan with a drawing of three peaked-roof structures, which may imply European influence.[1] However, it is unclear whether the drawing (published in 1703 after an uncertain history of recopying) is accurate, and it is also possible that peaked-roof construction was a feature of traditional indigenous construction (see discussion in Hamell 1992a: 50–56). Iron nails and low wall-post density may suggest that nontraditional construction methods were used in the Ganondagan shorthouse, but nail density in Trench 4 is significantly lower than at later sites where more intercultural/creolized features are in evidence (table 8.2), and the low wall-post density of the structure may be the product of poor preservation.

Sohrweide (2001: 20) notes that of all Iroquois construction practices, fortification systems underwent the greatest change in the seventeenth century. The palisade at Weston was square in shape and had a bastion at each corner (Sohrweide 2001), and Caughnawaga's palisade was square as well (Snow 1995), reflecting the incorporation of European military principles. At Weston, the use of cul-de-sacs and palisade posts driven into the ground represent continued use of traditional Onondaga fortification techniques (Sohrweide 2001: 20–22). Defensive architecture therefore may represent an early example of intercultural/creolized practice that added European principles to existing methods of Iroquois construction. It is noteworthy that Europeans appear to have been involved, at least as consultants or haulers, in the construction of square Iroquoian fortifications at Weston (Sohrweide 2001: 22) and in initial constructions at the Mohawk Lipe site in 1689 (Snow 1995: 444).

Iroquoian Housing, circa 1696–1715

Homeland and Mission Iroquois Settlements

No structural plans dating to this period—spanning the end of the Twenty Years' War and the full period of uncertainty—have been excavated in the Iroquois homeland. One ambiguous clue to Seneca housing of the time is provided by the 1700 map drawn by military engineer Willem Wolfgang Römer (1700; figure 9.4). The ostensible original manuscript for this map is housed in the National Archives of the United Kingdom.[2] It depicts two structures in Seneca territory, placed roughly in the locations of the Snyder-McClure and White Springs sites. They have peaked roofs which descend almost to the ground in a manner reminiscent of an A-frame house. The A-frame was not used by either Iroquoians or Europeans at the time, meaning that these representations are likely to be inaccurate (the banding on the structures' roofs, however, may reflect Iroquoian bark roofing). On the map the gables of the Seneca houses appear to be decorated, perhaps with antlers. An illustration placed south of the Mohawk River on the Römer map (not shown in figure 9.4) depicts one longhouse with a single smoke hole and two smaller arbor-shaped structures, which Dunn (2002: 17) interprets as "sheds, probably for wood storage." Note that some subsequent versions of the Römer map (such as the copy Dunn [2002: figure 21] claims is a faithful rendition of the original) render the roof shapes of the Seneca houses as more arbor-like and convert the apparent gable decorations into two columns of smoke rising from smoke holes. While these details may better match scholars' expectations that the Iroquois housing stock was made up of small traditional longhouses in 1700, the inaccurate copies do not provide direct evidence that this was the case.

In 1695 the Reverend John Miller made a detailed map of the newly established Mohawk refugee village at Schuyler Flats north of Albany, includ-

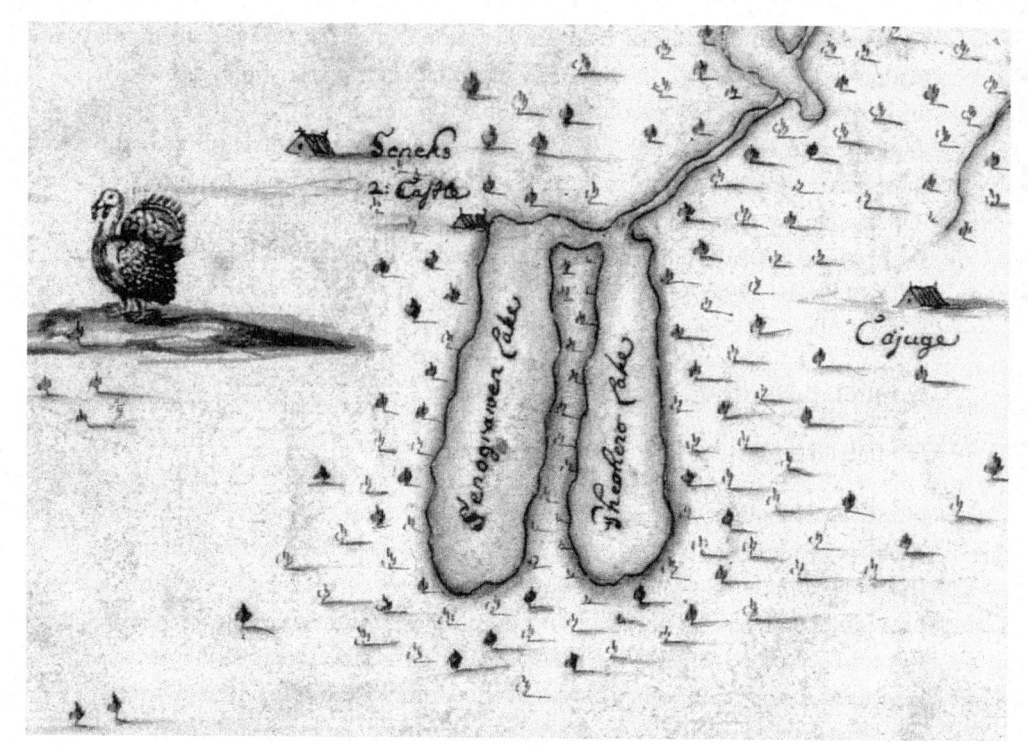

Figure 9.4. Detail from "A Mapp of Coll. Romer His Journey to the 5 Indian Nations..." (Römer 1700). Item C.O. 700/New York 13A. (Image used courtesy of the National Archives of the United Kingdom.)

ing a cutaway view of one longhouse (Dunn 2002: figure 22; Huey 1998: figure 2). Hamell (1992a: 48) indicates that Miller redrew the map after his original and notes were lost at sea, so the depiction may not be completely accurate. The map shows five longhouses, each of which contains three hearths and uniformly rounded ends; in all instances, the houses appear to have two or three *side* entrances. The five dwellings were reported to house a total of only sixty people (Huey 1998: 26), or four persons per hearth. If Miller's information on side entrances and his very low persons-per-hearth figure are correct, they are quite atypical for traditional Iroquois houses. The settlement at Schuyler Flats also included three structures for colonial troops and a square palisade with two bastions; the village has not been located archaeologically (26).

A 1698 deposition in a land fraud case stated that the Mohawk Lower Castle contained "thirty nine houses belonging to the Maquase Nation some of which contain one family, some two, and some four" (NYCD 4: 345). This document demonstrates that the residential uniformity seen at

Caughnawaga did not continue in subsequent Mohawk villages. Use of one-family houses does not seem to be paralleled in other parts of Iroquoia at this time. Society for the Propagation of the Gospel missionary William Andrews noted in 1713 that Mohawk "houses are made of Mats & bark of Trees together with poles about 3 or 4 yards [2.7–3.7 m] high" (quoted in Lydekker 1938: 37), suggesting that Mohawks continued to use traditional construction methods employing bark siding supported by a network of small posts. Andrews may have been describing the Milton Smith archaeological site (Snow 1995: ch. 12).

Joseph-François Lafitau, a Jesuit missionary at the Kahnawake mission on the St. Lawrence, penned a detailed and frequently cited description of a bark-covered true longhouse in his 1724 volume on the customs of the Iroquois (Fenton and Moore 1977: 19–22; see also Snow 1997). Lafitau worked at Kahnawake from 1712 to 1717, and there is enough specific detail in his account to suggest that it was based on firsthand experience (Snow 1997: 68). Beyond providing another indication of the continued construction of traditional longhouses in the first quarter of the eighteenth century, Lafitau also records the use of European-derived features, such as gable-end walls strengthened with planks and hung wooden doors with iron bolts, within the Kahnawake houses (Fenton and Moore 1977: 22). Lafitau (22) suggests these features were protections against theft, but it is also possible that they improved durability or reduced drafts.

The most extensive domestic-context excavation at an Iroquois homeland village occupied during this period has taken place at the circa 1696–1720 Oneida Primes Hill site (Bennett 1988; personal communication, 2001). About 9 percent of the estimated 1.0 ha village area was excavated by the Chenango Chapter of the NYSAA during 1979–1982. Although no structural plans could be determined from the array of post molds uncovered, some tentative conclusions can be drawn based on the fifty-one possible to definite post molds excavated at Primes Hill (Monte Bennett, personal communication, 2001; see table 8.1). Excluding two probable interior support posts of more than 20 cm in diameter, the remaining probable wall posts ranged from 5.1 to 12.7 cm and averaged 7.3 cm in diameter. The bimodal distribution of post sizes and the low overall average of 7.8 cm may indicate that traditional, bark-sided houses were constructed at Primes Hill.

This limited evidence from the homeland and surrounding missions indicates that the Iroquois housing stock predominantly consisted of traditional dwellings during this period. Nucleated community structure also was quite common in 1696–1715, as seen at Primes Hill (Bennett 1988), the Seneca Snyder-McClure and White Springs sites (chapter 6), the Onondaga Jamesville Pen and Sevier sites (Grumet 1995: 392; T. Tanner 1995), and the Mohawk Milton Smith and Allen sites (Lenig 2001; Snow 1995: 389–90, 456). Palisades have been excavated at Jamesville Pen and possibly at Primes Hill (Grumet 1995: 392; Bennett 1988). These continuities with earlier sites in terms of site structure and defensibility support the idea that there was continuity in residential forms as well.

Conestoga

The most substantial archaeological data from this era come from the multinational (in part Seneca) Conestoga site near present-day Lancaster, Pennsylvania (figure 9.5; B. Kent 1993: 379–91). The site, occupied circa 1690–1740, was excavated in 1972 by a Pennsylvania Historical and Museum Commission team led by Barry Kent. Conestoga is estimated to be about 0.8 ha in size; it is located on a small hilltop (383) and can be characterized as semi-dispersed in plan (K. Jordan 2004: 46–48). About 36 percent of the site was cleared of plowzone soil, revealing three separate house plans and a number of burials.

Two complete structures (one 15.2 × 4.5 m and the other 10.7 × 4.5 m) and one incomplete dwelling (6.1 m wide and at least 12.2 m long) were excavated. Feature preservation was poor: no interior hearths were recovered and "only one or two" of the extramural pit features could be conclusively associated with the eighteenth-century occupation. Barry Kent (1993: 382) notes that post molds "in all three houses averaged five inches [12.7 cm] in diameter (somewhat larger than at earlier sites), and usually extended four inches [10.1 cm] into subsoil. The average distance between the post holes was about 20 inches [50.8 cm]. Corners of the houses were at neat right angles." Anderson (1995) provides structure-specific data for the two completely excavated houses.

The three structures differ markedly in layout and construction details. Since a number of ethnic groups (primarily Iroquoian Susquehannocks and Senecas, but also non-Iroquoian peoples) resided at Conestoga, some houses may have been constructed by non-Iroquoian or multinational households. The long duration of the Conestoga site also may mean that the houses represent a *sequence* of architectural forms rather than contemporaneous dwellings, so some or all of these structures therefore might more properly be placed in the 1715–1754 section.

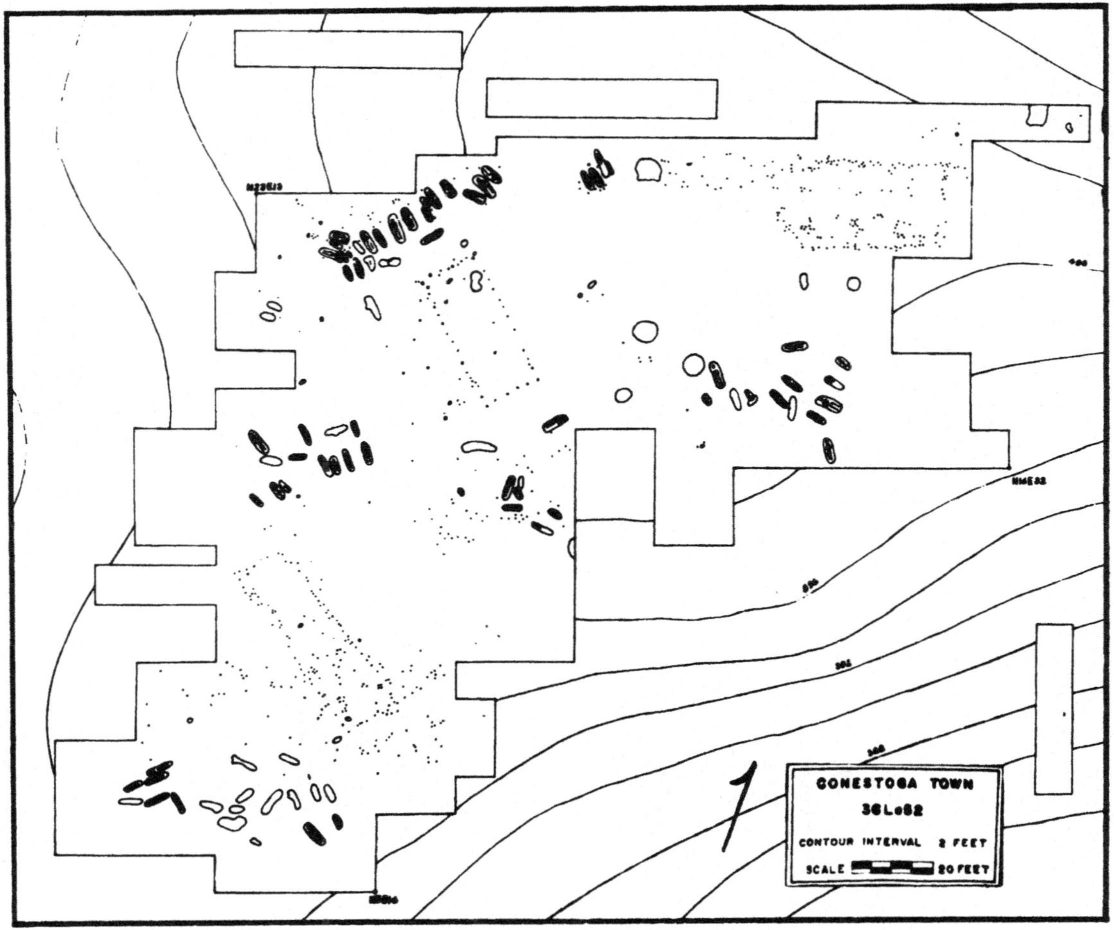

Figure 9.5. Plan view of excavations at the Conestoga site (B. Kent 1993: figure 107). (Image used courtesy of the Pennsylvania Historical and Museum Commission.)

The incompletely excavated dwelling to the northeast is best classified as a traditional-style Iroquoian longhouse. It appears to have (1) a central corridor; (2) a post mold pattern suggestive of internal compartments; (3) an informal storage shed at the west end; and (4) fairly dense wall-post placement. The structure's 6.1 m width also is typical for an Iroquoian longhouse. The other structures do not fit the traditional Iroquois model as easily, particularly in that they appear to be too narrow to allow construction of two sleeping compartments and a central hearth. The longer structure to the southwest (Anderson's [1995] "House 1") has a pattern of paired wall posts suggesting that these posts were used to brace semirigid siding, a fairly traditional construction detail. It also contains a number of internal posts, so this structure differs from a traditional longhouse primarily in terms of its width. The 155 measured posts from House 1 average 7.0 cm in diameter (table 8.1; Anderson 1995: table D-4).

The central house (Anderson's "House 2") exhibits the most nontraditional elements. There is only a single line of wall posts, instead of the double rows seen in the other structures. Wall posts are quite far apart, and interior posts are infrequent. The post mold pattern in the central house also suggests a single side-wall entrance rather than the gable-end doorways typical of Iroquoian structures. The posts utilized in House 2 were much larger than those in House 1; the seventy measured posts in House 2 averaged 12.7 cm in diameter (table 8.1; Anderson 1995: table D-4). At the same time, this structure does not match any of the European architectural forms described in chapter 8 particularly well. It is perhaps a candidate for French *pièces-sur-pièces* architecture, in which slotted logs were fit horizontally into grooved upright support posts (Moogk 1977). There appear to be too many uprights for this type of construction, however: a *pièces-sur-pièces* house could have been built much more efficiently using fewer uprights and longer horizontal logs.

In short, the Conestoga houses differ from traditional Iroquoian houses in a number of ways, but overall they represent more the modification of traditional methods and materials than the adoption of European architectural forms. The larger post sizes and longer distances between posts (especially in the central house) may indicate that something other than bark (perhaps logs or planks) was used for siding. The average size of the posts used in House 2 falls outside the 5–10 cm average post diameter figure for traditional architecture noted by Prezzano (1992: 259–60), also suggesting that House 2 was an intercultural/creolized house. All three structures would be classified as longhouses using Kapches' (1984) Iroquoian house typology, although it may be improper to use this typology at Conestoga since the houses may not be Iroquoian.

Iroquois Housing, circa 1715–1754

For the 1715–1754 period, there are fairly detailed documentary descriptions of houses from many parts of the Six Nations homeland. Excavations at Townley-Read allow detailed interpretation of the layout of Structure 1. Extra-regionally, documentary sources and drawings evidence the persistence of fairly traditional Iroquoian house forms at Fort Frontenac and the St. Lawrence mission communities. Use of traditional architecture in missions is notable because missions may have been sites of persistent, directed culture change efforts.

Homeland Iroquois Settlements

A fairly complete picture of the housing stock at the dispersed village at Onondaga can be re-created from documentary sources. These descriptions probably refer to the Onondaga Castle archaeological site, which may have been first occupied around 1720 (Bradley 1987: 207). In 1737, Conrad Weiser related that the Onondagas "live in huts made of bark, which are very convenient; some of them are 50, 60, to a 100 feet [15.2–30.5 m] long, generally about 12 or 13 feet [3.7–4.0 m] wide. In this length there are generally four or five fires, and as many families, who are looked upon as one" (Weiser 1860 [1737]: 340).

Richter (1992: 381 note 10) rightly questions Weiser's extremely narrow width measurement and his claim that only one family lived at each hearth. Additionally, Weiser's figures for house length and hearth number are not entirely congruent; a four-hearth structure should be about 18–24 m long, given compartment lengths of 4.5–6.0 m (Kapches 1993; Snow 1997). Nevertheless, Weiser's account clearly indicates that some of the Onondaga housing stock in 1737 consisted of traditional bark-sided, multiple-hearth longhouses.

Bartram's description of the same settlement in 1743 provides another perspective. Although Bartram's account (1966 [1751]: 41) centers on a special-purpose council house, he states at the end that "after this model are most of their cabins built." The main difference between the council house and the other "cabins" was in terms of length, since "many" of the dwellings at the site were said to have held two families (42). The council house was about 80 feet [24.4 m] long, and 17 [5.2 m] broad, the common passage 6 feet [1.8 m] wide; and the apartments on each side 5 feet [1.5 m], raised a foot [0.3 m] above the passage by a long sapling hewed square, and fitted with joists that go from it to the back of the house; on these joists they lay large pieces of bark ... the apartments are divided from each other by boards or bark, 6 or 7 foot [1.8–2.1 m] long, from the lower floor to the upper, on which they put their lumber, when they have eaten their homony, as they set in each apartment before the fire, they can put the bowel over head, having not above 5 foot [1.5 m] to reach; they set at the floor sometimes at each end, but mostly at one: they have a shed to put their wood in the winter, or in the summer, to set or converse or play, that has a door to the south; all the sides and roof of the cabin is made of bark, bound fast to poles set in the ground, and bent round on the top, or set aflatt, for the roof as we set our rafters; over each fire they leave a hole to let out the smoake, which in rainy weather they cover with a piece of bark, and this they can easily reach with a pole to push it on one side or quite over the hole, after this model are most of their cabins built. (1966 [1751]: 41)

The two-family version of a dwelling constructed in this manner can be classified fairly definitely as a short longhouse with one hearth and two sleeping compartments. Although there is some indication of nontraditional construction in the use of boards and "a long sapling hewed square," and possibly in the narrower width of the structure and the bark "set aflatt" on the roof, the majority of the elements described are quite traditional in form. Weiser and Bartram's use of the words *hut* and *cabin* should not be taken as precise signifiers for certain house forms; in particular, Bartram's use of *cabin* cannot be taken as evidence that log construction was used at the site.

In tandem the two descriptions potentially describe the entire housing stock at Onondaga: Bartram says that *many* of the houses contained two families, and Weiser says that *some* were 15–30 m long. There is no evidence for Richter's (1992: 261) claim that "others, presumably, were single-family dwellings built in nontraditional styles." Onondaga Castle appears to exhibit continuity with most earlier sites in terms of both construction techniques and intrasite diversity in house forms, since short longhouses, various sizes of true longhouses, and a council house were present.

The Moravian missionary Cammerhoff describes Cayuga, Onondaga, and Seneca housing in 1750. He portrays a Cayuga village as consisting of "about 20 huts altogether, most or [sic] them large and roomy, with three or four fireplaces; they are well built and waterproof. They have small entrance buildings on both sides, and four or five families can lodge in every cabin" (Beauchamp 1916: 43). Although the Moravian's estimate of household size does not exactly match the number of hearths he describes, it is evident that he is describing multifamily true longhouses with storage vestibules on both ends. These structures could be three- to four-hearth structures housing six to eight nuclear families if his hearth number estimates are correct, or two- to three-hearth structures if his household size figures are correct.

Cammerhoff uses the words *house*, *cabin*, and *hut* to describe dwellings at Onondaga (Beauchamp 1916: 46, 60). He mentions "seven large cabins close together" (46), which appear to have been multifamily structures with sleeping platforms and central corridors. One of these dwellings was that of "Ganassateco" (Canasatego), whose house was "very large and roomy, and well built ... an apartment had been prepared for us, we were invited into it, and the one side, which had been covered with beautiful mats, was assigned to us. It was large enough for six [Moravian] Brethren to have lodged there comfortably, and was on the same side of the house as Ganassateco's own apartment. A room opposite us was shown to our Gajuka [Cayuga guide]" (46–47). This house clearly had a fairly traditional floor plan with at least four large sleeping platforms. The dwelling apparently was not the council house; Cammerhoff and Zeisberger had to follow a messenger from Ganassateco's house to a separate building where a council took place (47).

Cammerhoff describes two house types present at the western Seneca site of "Zonesschio" (likely the Fall Brook site; see figure 6.7 for location), neither of which was likely to have been the predominant residential form. The first was the residence of the sachem Garontianechqui, which served as "the meeting place for their Council as well as their fortress" (Beauchamp 1916: 74); this building was described as the largest house in the village. Cammerhoff's reference to this council house and chief's residence acting as a "fortress" is unparalleled in other sources, and I am inclined to discount it given that Cammerhoff was not a military man (Engelbrecht 2003: 164 makes a contrasting interpretation). The large house of the sachem Gajinquechto at New Ganechstage (Beauchamp 1916: 81) also may have served as a council house. The second building at Zonesschio described by Cammerhoff was a small structure "with so little space that 6 or 7 men could scarcely stand within" (74). Cammerhoff and Zeisberger were forced to hide in this building's "loft" or "garret" for two days while two hundred Senecas engaged in a drinking bout. The small structure had a shingled roof and a small window or airhole opening off the loft at the gable end of the building (75); it was likely to have been a special-purpose, nonresidential structure. Richter (1992: 261) appears to have taken aspects of this small structure to be typical of Seneca dwellings, but I find it difficult to support his assertion that "by 1750 most Senecas seem to have been living in single-family cabins built in a European style that often included such features as roughly finished attics" (261) on the basis of this fragmentary evidence.

The 1750 journal of Daniel Claus provides brief accounts of housing in the Mohawk and Oneida regions. Claus depicts what appears for the most part to be a fairly traditional residential stock, but he also provides the first certain description of a European-style Iroquois dwelling. Claus relates that at the Mohawk settlement at Fort Hunter

> most of the inhabitants were Indians [who lived] in houses made of tree bark. We had to take up quarters at one of the Indian chiefs, by the name of Brant, in German, Brand, and we really could not find fault with it; for he lived in a well built, 2 story house, provided with furniture like that of a middle-class family; there was nothing wanting in our food or drink or in our beds. (Doblin and Starna 1994: 35)

The "2 story" house may have been the residence of Brant Canagaraduncka (Kelsay 1984: 51), at that time a Mohawk leader at Fort Hunter and later the stepfather of the better-known Joseph Brant. That the house was two stories tall in itself indicates a substantial departure from Iroquois norms; two-story construction also would have required that the house have a chimney.

Claus gives a detailed description of the house he stayed in at the "Indian Castle Oneida," likely the village of Anajot or "Old Oneida" near present-day Vernon Center (Doblin and Starna 1994: 39 note 138). Claus provides measurements in *schlag*, "an old German measure equal to about one foot [0.3 m]" in length (Doblin and Starna 1994: 37 note 129):

> our place of residence ... was one of the more distinguished [houses] because a gray pole with intermittent red stripes stood in front of it. On the outside they [the houses] were entirely built of bark [and were] about 12 or 13 Schlag [3.7–4.0 m] wide [*sic*] and 18 or 20 [5.5–6.1 m] high [*sic*]. Inside, they were divided on both sides into several rooms, which were rather well fit together with posts and boards, on which

one could sit or lie; on both sides, boards were also nailed below so that one could put something behind. These rooms, of which there were 3 to 6 on each side of the house, appeared to me like box-beds without doors. In the middle of the corridor, which was 5 or 6 Schlag [1.5–1.8 m] wide, a fire was burning in front of each [room] for cooking and on top goods and victuals were laid. The seat was about 2 Schlag [0.6 m] high from the floor. On top, [smoke] holes of about 40 or 50 [12.2–15.2 m] and more Schlag long will be kept open, which did not suffice, however, for all the smoke to escape. (Doblin and Starna 1994: 39–40, except for metric equivalents; insertions in square brackets are by editors Doblin and Starna).

This Oneida structure appears to be a multiple-hearth, bark-sided longhouse. Claus' description indicates that there were three to six compartments on each side of the house, and that in total the house was more than 12.2–15.2 m long, given his description of the length of the smoke holes. Doblin and Starna (1994: 40 note 140) assert that Claus reversed his width and height figures, meaning the structure was 3.7–4.0 m high and 5.5–6.1 m wide.[3] Claus indicates that houses typically had bark siding and roofing, and also that the heights and widths of other houses were similar. Other details he describes may apply only to the structure Claus stayed in, which may have been a council house.

An example of architecture from the Mohawk Valley that is quite difficult to classify is provided by a 1734 map of the Schoharie region (reproduced in Dunn 2002: figure 1). The so-called wigwam drawn on the map near Schoharie is proportioned like a true longhouse, but it contains only a single central smoke hole and two entrances on the eave face of the structure. Some of these details are reminiscent of Miller's 1695 map of the Mohawk settlement at Schuyler Flats.

Townley-Read Structure 1 as an Intercultural/Creolized House

Figure 9.6 shows my interpretation of the layout of the short longhouse at the 1715–1754 Townley-Read site. The 7.5 × 5.3 m structure appears to have been built using a fairly traditional overall plan. The main supports for the house were located in the middle of the structure, with lighter posts around the outside; a central hearth and sleeping platforms also likely were present. Some of the indeterminacy of the eastern portion of the structure may be due to the presence of a poorly defined covered storage compartment or vestibule (Snow 1997: 70), another traditional feature. Given its layout, the

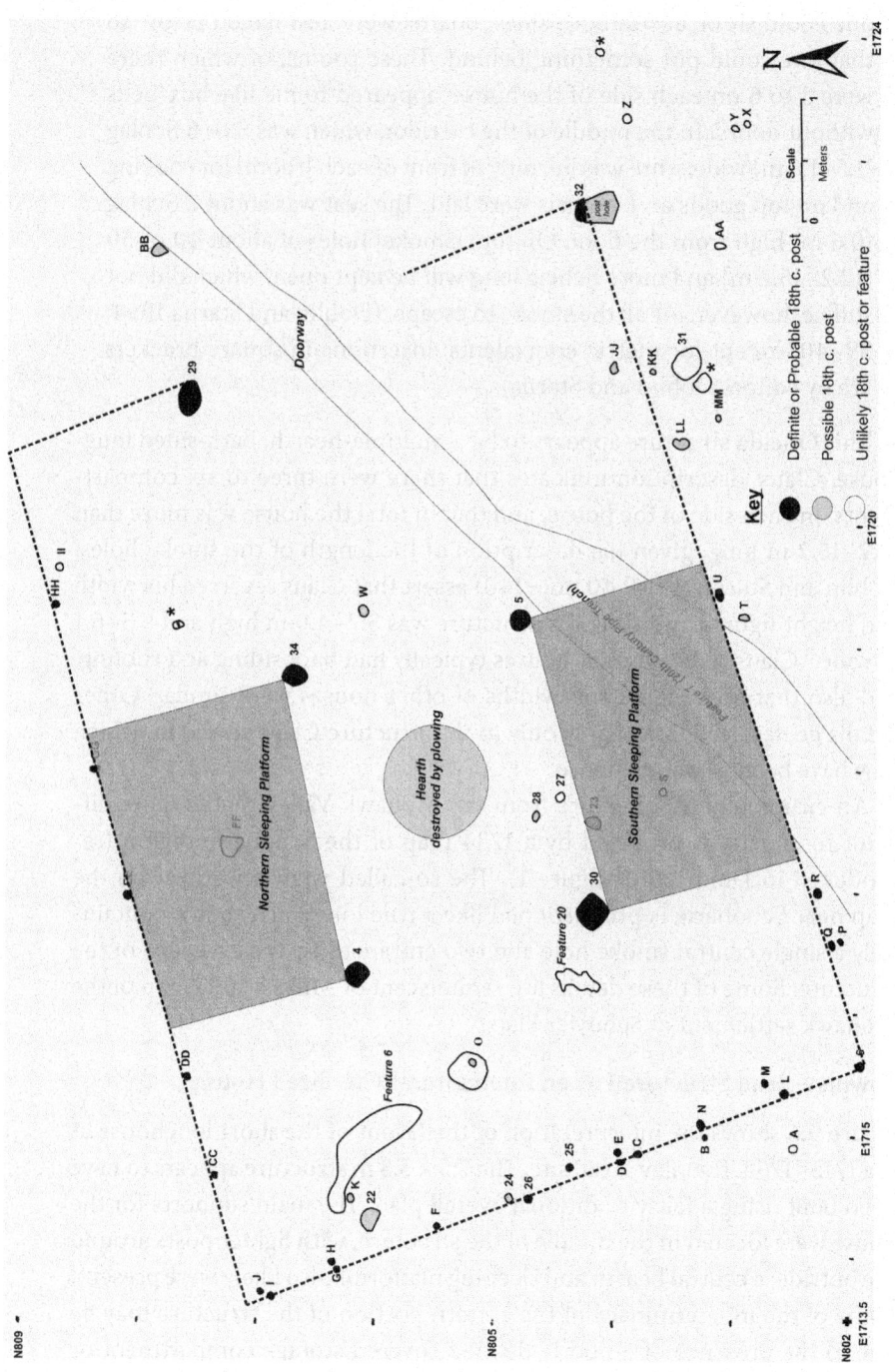

Figure 9.6. Interpretation of size and internal features of Structure 1, DRC 1, Area D, Townley-Read Site (K. Jordan 2003: figure 3). (Image used courtesy of the New York State Archaeological Association.)

shorthouse probably housed two families. It looks very much like one freestanding segment from a longhouse, and in many ways it appears to be a close match for the two-family version of Bartram's "cabin" at Onondaga.

Townley-Read Structure 1 also can be compared to a significantly older short longhouse plan from the sixteenth-century Onondaga Atwell site (figure 9.7; Ricklis 1967).[4] The Atwell structure was constructed before the initiation of direct Iroquois-European engagement when iron tools were rare (Bradley 1987: 75–76); note particularly the rounded ends of the structure, a characteristic of Precolumbian Iroquoian dwellings (Prezzano 1992: 276). Two ornaments made from European brass and one very small piece of iron have been recovered at the site; this assemblage is consistent with an occupation in the second or third quarter of the sixteenth century (Bradley 1980, 1987: 50, 72; compare Tuck 1971: 165, 169–70). The Atwell structure measures 7.9 × 5.5 m and contains clear evidence for bench support posts and central hearths. The ring of small post molds at the western end of the structure has been interpreted as the remains of a storage bin or corncrib (Ricklis 1967: 16–17; Tuck 1971: 167).

The Townley-Read short longhouse manifests a surprising number of continuities with the Atwell structure despite the 140 years or more between their construction dates. The dimensions of the Townley Read house (7.5 × 5.3 m) are extremely close to those of the Atwell structure (7.9 × 5.5 m). Both dwellings have frequent large internal posts, and presumably both had central hearths. Each house has a characteristic double layer of wall posts, signifying that posts were used to brace siding. If the ring of posts at the western end of the Atwell structure is indeed a storage feature, both short longhouses may have had only a single eastern door. Applying Kapches' (1990) spatial dynamics method, it appears that the Townley-Read and Atwell short longhouses also had similar proportions of organized and unorganized space.

At the same time, the Townley-Read structure incorporated a number of innovations that are not present in the Atwell structure or most other earlier houses. This is most apparent in terms of post type and location, wall post frequency, and iron nail use. These departures from traditional practices in sum indicate that Townley-Read Structure 1 should be classified as an intercultural/creolized dwelling.

Excluding the two large probable wall posts used to support the eastern wall (PM 29 and PM 32), the diameter of all twenty-four probable or definite wall posts (as taken at subsoil surface) in the Townley-Read structure range from 4.0 to 8.5 cm and average 5.8 cm. Incorporating seven addi-

ATWELL FORT SITE (CZA 1-1)

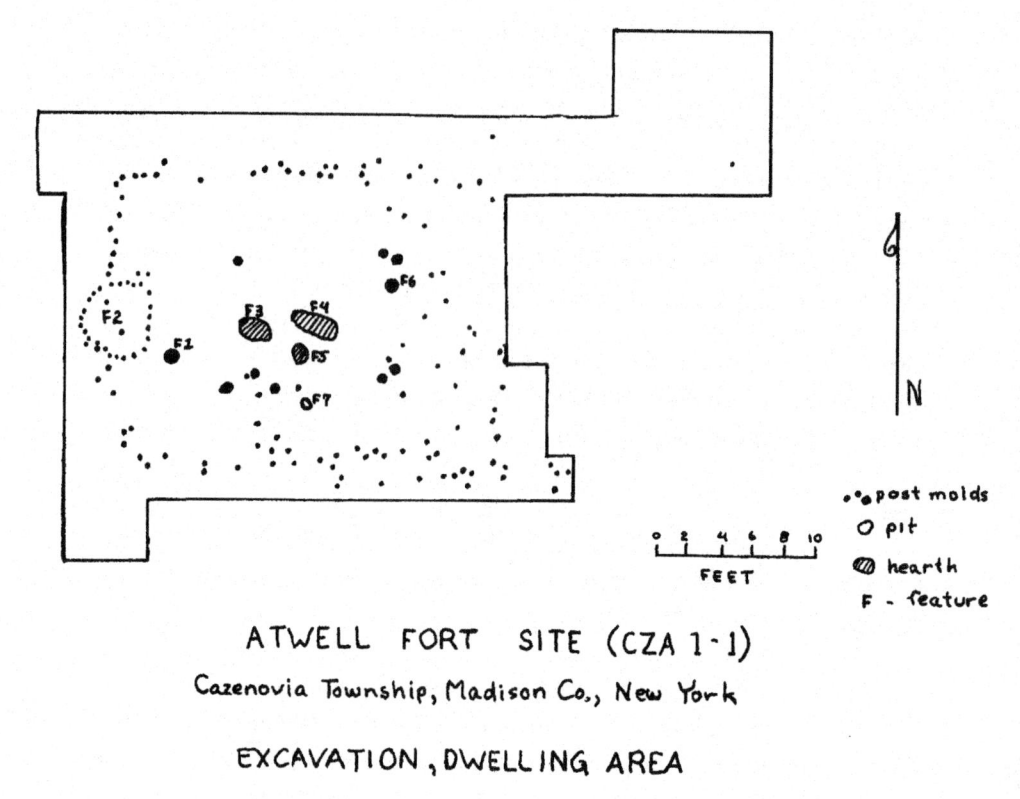

Cazenovia Township, Madison Co., New York

EXCAVATION, DWELLING AREA

Figure 9.7. Plan view of short longhouse structure recovered at the Onondaga Atwell site, circa 1525–1575 (Ricklis 1967: 16). (Image used courtesy of the New York State Archaeological Association.)

tional possible wall posts changes the range to 4.0 to 13.0 cm, and the average to 6.3 cm. When compared to data from other late seventeenth- and eighteenth-century sites (table 8.1), Townley-Read appears most similar to Primes Hill. Additionally, large interior posts range from 18.0 to 23.5 cm in diameter at Townley-Read, while the two probable interior support posts at Primes Hill measure 20.3 cm and 22.9 cm. The wall posts at Townley-Read are somewhat smaller than those used at Rogers Farm and Ganondagan, and much smaller than those used at Egli or Conestoga House 2. The data provided by Ricklis (1967) do not permit direct comparison to the short longhouse structure at Atwell.

Diachronic comparison of post size data thus places the Townley-Read short longhouse with relatively traditional Iroquoian houses. However, the *type* and *location* of some of the posts used in Townley-Read Structure 1 are quite atypical of, and even unparalleled at, any of the earlier sites. The use of the large posts 29 and 32 as part of the eastern wall and the shape of Post Mold 32, an unusual squared-off post with a dug post hole, suggest departure from traditional construction methods at Townley-Read.

Although post preservation certainly is an issue, wall post density at Townley-Read is significantly lower than has been calculated for traditional Iroquoian houses by Warrick (1988: table 8) and Williams-Shuker (2005: table 27). Using Williams-Shuker's method, the Townley-Read structure contains thirty-three wall posts along a total structural perimeter of 25.6 m, for an average of 1.29 posts per meter. This is significantly lower than Williams-Shuker's average overall wall post density of 2.48 posts per meter for Iroquoian houses occupied during 1600–1700 (2005: table 27). Individual walls in the Townley-Read short longhouse exhibit quite varied densities. In the western wall, where preservation and post recovery were quite good, original wall post density is about 2.5 posts per meter; post density in the north wall is approximately 1 post per meter. Even given likely differences in post preservation between Atwell and Townley-Read, the Townley-Read structure assuredly used fewer wall posts than the Atwell short longhouse (contrast figures 9.6 and 9.7).

Iron nail density at Townley-Read (table 8.2) is much higher than those seen at Rogers Farm, Bead Hill, Ganondagan, or Primes Hill, where other archaeological evidence suggests that traditional houses were built. The level of nail use at Townley-Read is much closer to that at Egli, where intercultural/creolized architecture almost certainly was used.

In aggregate, these features suggest that siding materials other than bark were used in the Townley-Read structure, materials which needed markedly less reinforcement. It is possible that the intercultural/creolized architecture used at the Townley-Read site deployed small logs or planks as siding in Iroquoian, but not traditional, fashion. If this interpretation is accurate, the Townley-Read short longhouse differs from the contemporaneous but more traditional bark-sided shorthouse structures Bartram described at Onondaga.

Fort Frontenac and the St. Lawrence Missions

Documents and images from extra-regional satellite Iroquois settlements near Fort Frontenac (present-day Kingston, Ontario) and at the mission communities of Kahnawake (Sault St. Louis) and Kanehsatake (Lake of Two Mountains) on the St. Lawrence (figure 1.1) provide unexpected evidence for the persistence of traditional Iroquois house forms. This is especially noteworthy because these communities were located in close proximity to the French, and directed culture-change efforts may have been particularly intense at mission or trading-post communities.

A frequently used pictorial source is a drawing of a bark-sided true longhouse that details the circa 1720 "Plan du Fort Frontenac ou Cataracouy" (reproduced in Richter 1992: plate 1; Snow 1994: figure 3.4; Snow 1997: figure 6). Snow (1994: 45) interprets the drawing as a representation of a 20 m true longhouse with small exterior posts placed every meter. Hamell (1992a) identifies this structure as probably Oneida. The full map depicts thirteen native dwellings constructed in the fort's vicinity (N. Adams 1986: figure 4). Nick Adams (1986: 16) notes that six of these dwellings, arranged in a group and roughly parallel, are "clearly more Iroquoian than Algonquian"; they range from 8.5 to 22 m in length, and each is about 5 m wide. Using Kapches' (1984) typology, the shortest of these would be defined as a short longhouse, and the remainder as true longhouses. Adams (1986: 16) uses the map data to question the scholarly premise that multiple-hearth longhouses had disappeared from Iroquois sites by the eighteenth century.

Mission communities also provide evidence for continued use of traditional architecture. As mentioned previously, Lafitau was able to describe a traditional, bark-sided true longhouse, probably based on firsthand observations of such structures at the Kahnawake mission during 1712–1717. A mid-eighteenth-century drawing (reproduced in Fenton and Tooker 1978: figure 1) shows true longhouses in the vast majority at Kahnawake. This observation appears to be supported by 1735 comments by Father Luc François Nau, who stated of the Kahnawake Indians that "they would for the most part be as clear-complexioned as the french, were it not for the effects of the Smoke in their cabins, which is so dense I fail to understand how they do not lose Their sight" (JR 68: 265). The smokiness of these dwellings suggests continued use of ground-level hearths without chimneys. A 1743 drawing of the Iroquois mission at Lake of Two Mountains (reproduced in Fenton and Tooker 1978: figure 3) also depicts a number of true longhouses, although here they make up only about half of the community, the other half being what appear to be single-hearth peaked structures, perhaps built on a European model.

Peter Kalm's 1750 description of the Huron mission at Lorette near Quebec differs greatly from these accounts. He described the Indian houses there as built "after the French fashion," with two rooms (a bedroom and a kitchen), a small stone oven topped by an iron plate, and beds near the wall (Benson 1937: 462); the construction methods employed in these houses are not spelled out. Kalm also described the Lorette Indians as engaging in a hybrid form of agriculture, growing maize, wheat, rye, and sunflowers, some of which were planted in rows (463). A 1742 food shortage at Lorette followed the failure of the French wheat crop (JR 69: 59–63), demonstrating a degree of reliance on European crops there.

The extent and effectiveness of directed culture-change efforts at these missions appear to have varied considerably, producing distinctly different local political economies. That the Huron community at Lorette appears to have adopted more elements of French architecture and subsistence practices than the other mission communities perhaps can be explained by the fact that they were refugees from a group that had been displaced far to the west. Hurons at Lorette had fewer ties of kinship and alliance with other groups remaining in the region, ties which the Iroquois residents of Kahnawake and Kanehsatake appear to have cultivated assiduously (Parmenter 1999; Surtees 1985: 69).

Discussion

Researchers have not comprehensively investigated regional sequences of Iroquois adoption of European log and framed architecture, and in many cases scholars' assertions that such adoptions were widespread early in the eighteenth century appear to have more to do with presuppositions than with evidence. The major conclusion of this study of Iroquois housing is that there is almost no evidence for the Iroquois adoption of European log or framed architecture prior to 1754 outside of the Mohawk Valley and St. Lawrence missions.

With the possible exception of peaked-roof dwellings depicted at Ganondagan, known houses of the 1677–1693 period all fall comfortably within the rubric of the traditional, bark-sided Iroquoian house. Longhouses with two to four hearths appear to have made up most of the Iroquois housing stock, and significant residential diversity was present in the Seneca and Onondaga areas. The limited evidence available from the 1693–1715 period indicates that traditional construction techniques continued to predominate, and there are distinct continuities in community structure with earlier sites, which may signal parallel continuities in residential forms. It is not clear whether the departures from traditional architecture seen in the 1695 map of Schuyler Flats and the 1700 Römer map reflect genuine alterations or liberties taken by the mapmakers. Two genuine exceptions were documented: the central house at Conestoga (with nontraditional dimensions and post size) and the one-family houses noted at the Mohawk Lower

Castle in 1698. These alterations do not appear to have been accompanied by significant adoption of European architectural practices. It is important to note that these departures from traditional forms first appear in the Mohawk and Susquehanna valleys, both places where Europeans were present in some numbers nearby.

Iroquois houses of the 1715–1754 period appear surprisingly traditional; bark siding remained quite prevalent, and true, multiple-hearth longhouses were noted in the Onondaga and Cayuga regions. Residential changes in the 1715–1754 period seem to be primarily in house *size* rather than house form (see "Changes in Household Size" later in this chapter): significant numbers of short longhouses were built for the first time, and council houses larger than most or all of the residential stock were common across Iroquoia.

However, a greater degree of change appears to have occurred during this period than in the previous eras. True European-style houses were constructed as Iroquois residences by 1750 in the Mohawk Valley (the two-story Brant house at Fort Hunter) and at the Huron mission of Lorette. Given the lack of evidence for European-style log cabins at contemporaneous Iroquois sites, and the low level of contact between Iroquois populations and European groups that had a tradition of log building at this time, it is quite likely that both the Brant house and French-style structures at Lorette were frame-constructed. Again, these were both locations where Europeans were numerous.

Residential change took place in the more isolated portions of Iroquoia as well, but here (as evidenced by the Townley-Read short longhouse) European technologies and hardware were used in the service of Iroquoian architectural principles, rather than as part of the full-blown adoption of European-style house types. The adoption of intercultural/creolized forms of architecture appears to have been primarily an indigenous development, especially given the high level of continuity seen between the Townley-Read house and earlier short longhouse structures such as the one at Atwell.

Iroquois Adoption of Intercultural/Creolized Dwellings

One of the main reasons that European-style house forms had little impact on Six Nations communities by 1754 was because Iroquois peoples had developed a new type of architecture on their own. Intercultural/creolized dwellings were more durable than their traditional precursors, but they also preserved Iroquoian architectural principles and traditional arrangements of space, which served both functional and symbolic purposes. The apparent prevalence of intercultural/creolized dwellings in the Seneca region through the American Revolution (K. Jordan 2004) indicates that they well served widespread cultural demands.

What factors contributed to the adoption of intercultural/creolized houses? The need for substantial homes that could endure the longer occupation spans of the new dispersed villages appears to have been a key factor (Hamell 1992a: 3; Tiro 1999: 44). In comparison to traditional houses, intercultural/creolized houses may have required greater labor outlays for the durable materials deployed in their construction, but they likely decayed less quickly and needed less maintenance.

I suspect that careful comparison of the seasonal and spatial availability of the components used in traditional and intercultural/creolized houses (such as bark, fibers used for cordage, logs suitable for planking or siding, and posts of various sizes), analytically intermeshed with other labor demands associated with dispersed settlements, would prove fruitful. For example, bark typically needed to be harvested in the spring and flattened and dried before use; work parties were mobilized to produce large quantities (Fenton and Moore 1977: 20). Builders had seasonal difficulty obtaining bark on short notice, particularly in winter (Beauchamp 1916: 205; Drake 1855: 193). The use of log and plank siding may have alleviated some of these logistical difficulties. Archaeological evidence from Townley-Read indicates that the majority of the iron objects likely to have been produced on-site were hardware items (K. Jordan 2001). Iroquois peoples may have requested that the blacksmiths regularly sent to their villages by New York and New France produce large quantities of fasteners, lessening their own inputs to house construction by reducing the amount of cordage and wall posts needed to attach and brace roofing and siding.

Other factors are less certain. Larger logs that previously would have been slated for use in palisades could have been used within houses in unfortified sites. Certain European technologies, such as axes and nails, may have needed to be prevalent for construction of intercultural/creolized houses. The new house forms also might have required the invention or diffusion of novel construction techniques.

Changes in Household Size

While many observers comment on the decrease in household size seen among late seventeenth- and eighteenth-century Iroquois populations, most Iroquois dwellings seem to have been traditional multiple-hearth true longhouses until around 1715. At this point, a transition to a majority of single-hearth short longhouses (constructed in either traditional or intercultural styles) appears to have taken place at Iroquois sites such as Onondaga and possibly Townley-Read. Many scholars have interpreted this decrease in household size in terms of cultural loss or the decline of matrilineal institutions (Fenton 1951: 41; Morgan 1965 [1881]: 128–29; Richter 1992: 256–62; Snow 1989: 298). However, the first communities with a majority of short longhouses were *dispersed* settlements. The change in household size therefore may have been a by-product of economically positive changes in community organization rather than a symptom of matrilineal decline.

Nucleated communities composed of large dwellings, each of which housed several families under one roof, are not the sole way matrilineal, matrilocal societies organize themselves. This can be demonstrated using even a small body of cross-cultural data, such as the 186 societies coded by Murdock and Wilson (1972). These data include information on eighteen matrilineal, matrilocal societies (1972: table 1). Among these groups, normative household composition consisted of large extended families typically "embracing the families of procreation of at least two siblings in each of two adjacent generations" in eight cases; households of small extended families "normally embracing only one family of procreation in the senior generation but at least two in the next generation" in six instances; nuclear families with less than 20 percent polygynous households in three cases; and one example of stem families, "a minimal extended family consisting of only two related families of procreation . . . of adjacent generations" (1972: 260–61).

In terms of community organization, five of the eight societies with large extended families occupied compact villages, and one society each occupied a partially dispersed community, a fully dispersed community, and a community composed of "separated subsettlements" (hamlets), respectively. Of the six groups with small extended families, three occupied compact villages, two dispersed villages, and one a hamlet. All three nuclear family societies occupied hamlets, and the stem family society lived in a compact settlement (1972: table 1). These data demonstrate that matrilineal, matrilocal societies can operate using a variety of community and household forms. The fact that the eighteenth-century Iroquois families changed how they distributed themselves in space may indicate less a decline in the effectiveness of matrilineality than the taking up of another, equally viable option from a repertoire of spatial choices.

All eighteen matrilineal, matrilocal societies in the Murdock and Wilson sample exhibit residential clustering, in that kin-group members either dwell under one roof or build smaller residences in close proximity to one another. Reasonable access to other households is necessary to such systems because clan and lineage members need to come together periodically for decision making, uniting kin who do not live under the same roof. This aggregation is most difficult for the married men of a given clan or lineage, who continue to have important leadership and decision-making roles in their kin groups but are distributed among many different households by matrilocal residence (Schneider 1961). Women do not have as great a problem gathering as men do in a matrilineal-matrilocal system, since mothers and daughters tend to live close together, but it is still necessary for women of the same clan residing in different households to be able to meet regularly without a great deal of travel.

Based on present evidence, there does not seem to have been any significant residential clustering at the *house lot* level at Townley-Read. DRC 1 appears to have contained only one residence, and the similarity of DRCs 2 and 4 to DRC 1 in terms of size and surface signature argue that they also held one structure each. The "neighborhoods" within the site complex may however have served to keep kin groups in relatively close proximity. Neighborhoods similar to New Ganechstage also appear to have been present at the main Onondaga community, where Bartram (1966 [1751]: 42) saw clusters of four to five houses in 1743, and which Cammerhoff described as consisting of "5 small towns, beside the single scattered huts" in 1750 (Beauchamp 1916: 60).

While dispersed short longhouses became the norm at some sites, there is also ample evidence for the continued construction of multiple-hearth true longhouses after 1715 in many eighteenth-century documentary and pictorial sources (for example, Beauchamp 1916: 43; Conover 1887: 308; Halsey 1906: 65–66; Wonderley 1998; see K. Jordan 1997). True longhouses are likely to have been present in varying proportions in many Iroquois settlements throughout the eighteenth century and may have predominated in some locations or even across the entire Confederacy, as Richard Smith claimed in 1769 (Halsey 1906: 66). Documents demonstrate that eighteenth-century true longhouses were constructed in both traditional and intercultural styles.

Conclusions

Starting in 1754, the Iroquois housing stock appears to have diversified far more quickly than during the first half of the eighteenth century. While prior to 1754 there is only limited evidence for the construction of intercultural/creolized dwellings (the houses at the Conestoga and Townley-Read sites) and European-style dwellings (in the Mohawk Valley and at Canadian missions), numbers of both of these types of houses increased significantly in the 1754–1780 period, apparently at the expense of more "traditional" bark-sided structures.

While at first glance this depiction may appear reminiscent of scenarios positing the decline of traditional Iroquoian cultural forms, the proportions of each type adopted, and the timing of their adoption, varied distinctly from region to region within the Iroquois homeland (K. Jordan 2002: 414–67; 2009). As Iroquois local political economies diverged during this period—particularly due to differential encroachment by European settlers (K. Jordan 2009)—so too did Iroquois architecture.

A basic conclusion of my preliminary studies of the 1754–1780 period is that European-style log cabins remained remarkably rare within Iroquois territory even through the time of the American Revolution. Large proportions of Six Nations architecture continued to be made up of intercultural/creolized dwellings, particularly in those areas relatively less influenced by Europeans. Six material factors (in part inspired by Lightfoot 2005) appear to be particularly important to the Iroquois adoption or rejection of European-style architecture: (1) the extent of European local territorial encroachment and European-wrought ecological change; (2) the intensity of European-directed culture-change programs; (3) local European population levels; (4) the level of local development of European infrastructure, including roads, sawmills, grist mills, and smithies; (5) opportunities for social mobility within the Native community; and (6) the duration of intensive local interaction between Europeans and Six Nations peoples. Assessing these factors will highlight differences in Iroquois local political economies and help to explain both why and when certain European practices were adopted.

The categories and concepts developed in chapters 8 and 9 help to focus studies of Iroquois residential change both before and after 1754. Particularly, a typology of structural forms that incorporates intercultural/creolized houses results in a more complete picture of eighteenth-century Iroquois society and culture than the standard bifurcation of "traditional" versus "European" architectural forms allows. Intercultural/creolized houses can be added to the growing list of products that show the *convergence* of Iroquoian and European material practices instead of the envelopment of one culture by another, a list that already includes shell bead wampum, wooden ladles, antler hair combs, brass ornaments and tools, splint basketry, and

Iroquois fortification systems (see Engelbrecht 2003; Sohrweide 2001). This shift in perspective, one that much better fits the available documentary and archaeological evidence than does the traditional/European binary, has important implications. The transformations in eighteenth-century house forms can no longer be taken as automatic and seemingly devastating evidence for the disintegration of Iroquois culture; instead, they must be seen as something much more complex that demonstrates considerable continuity with traditional architecture and culture in the midst of thoroughgoing change.

10

Archaeology and Townley-Read's Economy

Faunal Remains, Red Stone, and Alcohol Bottles

This chapter uses archaeological evidence to examine the Seneca local political economy at Townley-Read in terms of animal use (for both subsistence purposes and the fur trade), involvement as geographic middlemen, and access to alcohol. Although these issues are crucial to the interpretation of eighteenth-century Seneca history, Europeans viewed Seneca local economic practices only infrequently. Even when European observers took pen to paper, they did not document these issues with the level of detail needed for the interpretation of short-term local political economies. Archaeology provides a crucial missing piece in scholarly reconstructions, and the Townley-Read evidence demonstrates that local economic practices, either unseen by or of little interest to Europeans, could be quite different from what contemporary observers and subsequent scholars imagined them to be.

Seneca Animal Use and Participation in the Fur Trade: Archaeology

Seneca participation in the fur trade, dietary stress, and labor allocation can be assessed through an examination of the proportional makeup, the degree of bone fragmentation, and the presence or absence of individual species within the Townley-Read faunal assemblage. Faunal evidence from Townley-Read is consistent with the propositions that (1) the focus of Seneca direct production in the fur trade had shifted from beaver pelts to deerskins; (2) there was little chronic dietary stress, although brief periods of severe stress are likely to have occurred, as indicated by historical documents; and (3) Seneca use of European domesticated animals was minimal and for the

Table 10.1. Mammalian Specimens from the Townley-Read Site Identifiable as to Genus or Species

Species	Common Name	NISP	Pct. NISP	MNI	Pct. MNI
Odocoileus virginianus	white-tailed deer	279	79.7	6	22.2
Castor canadensis	American beaver	11	3.1	1	3.7
Microtus pennsylvanicus[a]	meadow vole	11	3.1	1	3.7
Procyon lotor	raccoon	11	3.1	1	3.7
Ursus americanus	black bear	9	2.6	2	7.4
Sus scrofa	pig	8	2.3	1	3.7
Canis familiaris	domestic dog	4	1.1	2	7.4
Urocyon cinereoargenteus	gray fox	3	0.9	1	3.7
Mustela sp.	weasel species	2	0.6	1	3.7
Ondatra zibethicus	muskrat	2	0.6	1	3.7
Bos taurus	cow	1	0.3	1	3.7
Clethryonimus gapperi[a]	southern red-backed vole	1	0.3	1	3.7
Erethizon dorsatum	porcupine	1	0.3	1	3.7
Martes americana	pine marten	1	0.3	1	3.7
Martes pennanti	fisher	1	0.3	1	3.7
Martes sp.	marten/fisher	1	0.3	1	3.7
Parascalops breweri[a]	hairy-tailed mole	1	0.3	1	3.7
Peromyscus sp.[a]	white-footed deer mouse	1	0.3	1	3.7
Sylvilagus floridanus	eastern cottontail rabbit	1	0.3	1	3.7
Vulpes vulpes	red fox	1	0.3	1	3.7
Total		350	100.1[b]	27	99.9[b]

Source: Watson 2007
Notes: a. Possibly noncultural or nondietary.
b. Total does not equal 100 percent due to rounding.

most part confined to pigs, which presumably were allowed to run feral. When compared to sites in the Mohawk Valley, the Townley-Read evidence also indicates there was substantial regional variation in animal use among contemporaneous Iroquois nations.

The portions of the Townley-Read mammalian assemblage that could be identified as to genus or species are summarized in table 10.1.[1] Only faunal specimens recovered from Areas D and H in the East Fields where definite eighteenth-century Seneca occupations took place are considered in this chapter. Number of individual specimens per taxon (NISP) values are limited to specimens positively identified as to genus or species; those identified by general size class (for example, deer-sized mammal) were excluded. Minimum number of individuals (MNI) figures have been calculated conservatively; multiple specimens found in different areas or loci of the site were considered to be the remains of one individual unless clear repetition of skeletal elements or age or sex differences were found. Most or all of the microfaunal specimens listed in table 10.1 likely represent natural processes rather than dietary use, particularly the eight *Microtus pennsylvanicus* (meadow vole) specimens from the same individual that probably introduced itself into the matrix of Post Mold 5.

Non-mammalian remains recovered at the site that have been identified as to genus or species consist of three passenger pigeon (*Ectopistes migratorius*), one ruffed grouse (*Bonasa umbellus*), and one whistling swan (*Cygnus columbianus*) specimen. Additional bird, fish, and amphibian remains were recovered but have not yet been fully analyzed. Faunal materials recovered from mortuary contexts at the site and housed at RMSC reportedly include a turkey leg bone, turtle shell fragments, and rodent bones (Wray n.d.). These materials have not been examined by a faunal specialist and were not formally incorporated into this analysis.

Faunal remains from Iroquois sites have not been examined or reported consistently, complicating the task of finding comparable data. In many cases, published reports list only the species recovered at a given site without quantification or additional analysis. In the Seneca region, the lack of systematic domestic-context excavation has hindered development of a detailed picture of animal use over time. Excluding Townley-Read, at the time of this writing the only published faunal analyses from Postcolumbian Seneca sites are RMSC studies of sites occupied from 1565 to 1630 (Wray et al. 1987, 1991; Sempowski and Saunders 2001) and a study of the reservation-era Vanatta site, which postdates 1790 (Lantz 1980). Faunal assemblages from some of these sites were derived entirely from mortuary offerings, making their relation to overall subsistence uncertain.

Patterns of faunal usage from the Mohawk Valley are better understood. Kuhn and Funk (2000) compile faunal data from eleven Mohawk Valley sites "with large numbers of identified specimens (NISP) which have been analyzed by professional researchers" (30) and employ cluster analysis to identify long-term trends in animal use within these data. The Townley-Read assemblage (NISP = 355, MNI = 30 for all fauna) is comparable to data from individual Mohawk sites in terms of sample size, number of mammalian species recovered, and mean NISP per species figures (K. Jordan 2002: 471–73). These factors suggest that the field methods used at Townley-Read contributed to the recovery of a wide range of species, and that the proportions and presence/absence of various species within the Townley-Read assemblage are not severely biased by sample size effects in comparison to Kuhn and Funk's Mohawk data.[2]

Patterns of Mammalian Usage

Table 10.2 presents information on the Mohawk Valley "subsistence patterns" identified by Kuhn and Funk (2000: tables 3–4) and parallel statistics from the Townley-Read mammalian assemblage. Although the Townley-Read species distribution bears a superficial resemblance to the Mohawk Valley Climax Prehistoric pattern due to the high percentage of white-tailed deer and low percentages of beaver and bear, the resemblance is misleading because Precolumbian Mohawks did not have access to European cloth as an alternative to deerskins. The Townley-Read assemblage therefore represents a different pattern of faunal usage.

Townley-Read is roughly contemporaneous with the Mohawk Colonial period, but the very small quantity of European domesticated animal remains at Townley-Read clearly differentiates its faunal assemblage from the Mohawk pattern (see "Seneca Use of European Domesticated Animals" later in this chapter). The next point of comparison is the Mohawk Late Fur Trade pattern, which is based solely on evidence from the 1657–1679 Jackson-Everson site (dated by Snow 1995: 403).[3] It could be argued that this pattern might have persisted to a later date in the western parts of Iroquoia, which were less subject to European territorial encroachment. However, the overall Townley-Read assemblage (355 NISP) differs from the larger Jackson-Everson (764 NISP) faunal assemblage in three fundamental ways: (1) there is a lesser percentage of beaver; (2) *menues pelleteries* (minor fur-bearing animals, or smaller luxury furs; Laird 1995: 10) are present; and (3) white-tailed deer remains dominate the assemblage to a greater degree.

The proportion of beaver remains at Townley-Read is less than half of that seen at Jackson-Everson. This comparison is difficult to interpret, and

Table 10.2. Species Frequencies of Mammalian NISP for Kuhn and Funk's Mohawk Subsistence Patterns and the Seneca Townley-Read Site

Subsistence Pattern or Site	Dates	Deer (%)	Beaver (%)	Bear (%)	Other Native (%)	European Domesticates (%)
Climax Prehistoric	ca. 1300–1525	81.2	2.1	2.9	13.8	0.0
Early Fur Trade	ca. 1525–1650	75.1	11.9	5.9	7.1	0.0
Late Fur Trade	ca. 1650–1700	66.8	7.7	7.0	18.2	0.3
Colonial	ca. 1700–1800	30.8	3.2	5.4	7.0	53.6
Townley-Read	ca. 1715–1754	79.7	3.1	2.6	12.1	2.6

Sources: Kuhn and Funk (2000: tables 3–4); Watson (2007).

may not necessarily imply a decreased emphasis on the beaver trade by Townley-Read's residents. As outlined in chapter 2, beaver pelts derived from extra-regional sources may leave few (or no) archaeological traces in homeland villages. It is likely that Townley-Read's residents continued to directly obtain beaver pelts extra-regionally, as is indicated by primary texts that discuss the routes Senecas used to get to hunting territories to the north and west (for example, NYCD 5: 911; McIlwain 1915: 164). Watson (2000: 44–45) claims that a juvenile beaver tibia with filleting cut marks recovered at Townley-Read was a "locally acquired, opportunistic kill" used both for its pelt and for food. Overall, however, the contrast between the 7.7 percent beaver remains at Jackson-Everson and the 3.2 percent figure at Townley-Read is consistent with decreased emphasis on primary beaver production (both local and nonlocal) at Townley-Read.

Five *menues pelleteries* specimens were recovered at Townley-Read (pine marten, fisher, and two specimens from the genus *Mustela* and one from the genus *Martes* that could not be identified as to species). These species are absent from the much larger assemblage recovered using 3 mm mesh hardware cloth at Jackson-Everson. Kuhn and Funk (2000: 51) take this as evidence that Jackson-Everson hunters either had depleted local stocks of *menues pelleteries* or were concentrating on beaver hunting to the point that they bypassed other fur-bearing animals. At Townley-Read, production for the fur trade appears to have been quite diverse; beyond beaver and *menues pelleteries*, other species recovered at Townley-Read that may have provided pelts or skins for trade include deer, raccoon, black bear, pig, domestic dog, gray fox, muskrat, cow, and red fox.

The distribution of mammalian body parts at Townley-Read supports the assertion that many species were used for their skins or pelts, some of them perhaps exclusively so (table 10.3). The recovery of axial bones (including vertebrae, ribs, and pelvic bones) or meaty upper limb bones suggests that a species was used for food. At Townley-Read, axial remains were recovered only from white-tailed deer and raccoon; limb bones of deer, beaver, raccoon, muskrat, and porcupine were recovered. Historical references make it reasonable to assume that most of these species were exploited for their skins or pelts in addition to their archaeologically demonstrated use as food.

When cranial bones, teeth, and foot bones alone are recovered, selective transportation, in which pelts or skins but not meat were brought back to the site, may have been involved. This pattern holds for black bear (9 specimens), pig (8), domestic dog (4), pine marten/fisher (3), gray fox (3),

Table 10.3. Body Part Distribution of Mammalian Remains Found in the East Fields of the Townley-Read Site, Excluding Microfauna

Description	Cranial Bone	Vertebra	Rib	Pelvic Bone	Limb Bone[a]	Foot Bone[b]	Tooth	Total
White-tailed deer (*Odocoileus virginianus*)	21	16	7	20	47	100	68	279
Beaver (*Castor canadensis*)	2	0	0	0	3	1	5	11
Raccoon (*Procyon lotor*)	2	0	0	2	2	4	1	11
Black bear (*Ursus americanus*)	5	0	0	0	0	2	2	9
Pig (*Sus scrofa*)	1	0	0	0	0	1	6	8
Domestic dog (*Canis familiaris*)	0	0	0	0	0	1	3	4
Pine marten and fisher (*Martes* sp.)	0	0	0	0	0	3	0	3
Gray fox (*Urocyon cinereoargenteus*)	1	0	0	0	0	1	1	3
Muskrat (*Ondatra zibethicus*)	0	0	0	0	1	0	1	2
Cow (*Bos taurus*)	0	0	0	0	0	1	0	1
Porcupine (*Erethizon dorsatum*)	0	0	0	0	1	0	0	1
Rabbit (*Sylvilagus floridanus*)	0	0	0	0	0	0	1	1
Red fox (*Vulpes vulpes*)	0	0	0	0	0	0	1	1
Weasel species (*Mustela* sp.)	0	0	0	0	0	1	1	2
Total	32	16	7	22	54	115	90	336

Source: modified from Watson (2007).
Notes: a. Limb bone category includes long bones and scapula fragments.
b. Foot bone category includes carpals, tarsals, metacarpals, metatarsals, and phalanges.

and weasel species (2) remains found at Townley-Read. Single foot bone or tooth specimens were recovered from cow, eastern cottontail rabbit, and red fox; these species provisionally can be assigned to the pelt procurement pattern. Although many of the animals whose remains suggest a pelt procurement strategy undoubtedly served other functions (dogs as companion animals, bears and pigs for food, etc.), on present evidence their role within the fur trade is emphasized.

Third and most important, the high percentage of deer within the Townley-Read assemblage suggests that *deer* were the primary focus of the fur trade at the site. White-tailed deer accounted for 79.7 percent of mammalian NISP at Townley-Read, greater than the percentages at any of the Postcolumbian Mohawk sites in Kuhn and Funk's study, and almost as high as that at late Precolumbian Mohawk sites. That the deer proportion at Townley-Read approaches Precolumbian sites is noteworthy, since a significant amount of Iroquois clothing was made with European trade cloth instead of deer hides by the early eighteenth century. The high level of deer

Table 10.4. Percentage of White-Tailed Deer Specimens within Each Locus of the Townley-Read Site

Locus	Mammalian NISP	White-Tailed Deer NISP	White-Tailed Deer (%)
DRC 1—Structure 1	44	26	59.1
DRC 1—Feature 5	192	163	84.9
DRC 1—General House Lot	28	24	85.7
DRC 2—General	18	11	61.1
DRC 3—BPM	64	52	81.3
DRC 3—General	4	3	75.0
Total	350	279	79.7

in the Townley-Read assemblage suggests that subsistence deer hunting had been supplemented by *commercial* hunting. Table 10.4 demonstrates that deer remains made up from 59 to 86 percent of the mammalian specimens identifiable as to genus or species in every excavated locus at the site, indicating that deer procurement was a consistently important activity for every investigated household, presumably throughout the occupation of the site.

Given the amounts of heavy deer bone present at Townley-Read, it appears that many deer were killed within the locality. Specialized procurement of deer and other fur-bearing animals may have channeled labor away from other types of hunting and may be responsible for the rather puzzling absence of several species from the Townley-Read faunal assemblage (see "Presence/Absence of Individual Species" later in this chapter).

In sum, this interpretation suggests that the Townley-Read faunal assemblage represents a pattern of mammalian acquisition different from those identified by Kuhn and Funk (2000). The Townley-Read pattern, termed the Late Fur Trade/Deerskin Trade pattern, continued to focus on the fur trade but concentrated on deer rather than beaver, supplemented by the taking of a diverse array of other fur-bearing animals. This pattern may fit animal-use practices by other northeastern groups documented to have participated heavily in the eighteenth-century deerskin trade, such as the multinational "Conestogas" of the Susquehanna Valley (see primary-source pelt and skin inventories in B. Kent 1993: 63–65, 383). Since domestic areas at Mohawk sites dating to the first half of the eighteenth century have not been formally excavated, existing faunal data cannot address whether Mohawks ever became substantially involved in the deerskin trade; European territorial encroachment after 1711 may have precluded Mohawk adoption of a deer-focused trade system. The Townley-Read data certainly demon-

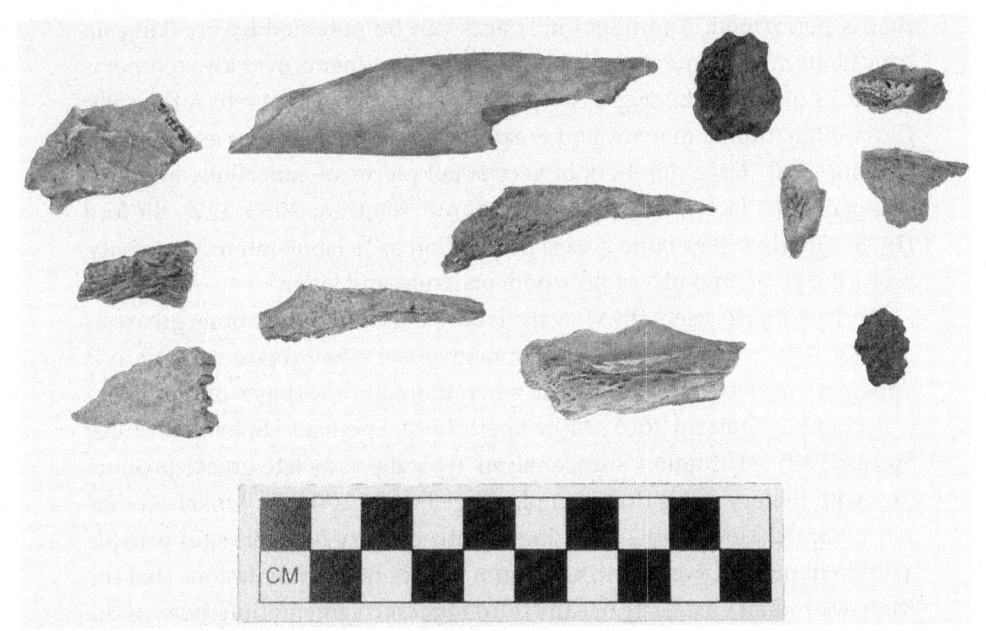

Figure 10.1. Faunal remains recovered during Feature 5 excavation, Townley-Read Site. A sample of larger bone fragments from Stratum I that exhibit characteristics diagnostic of marrow extraction (spiral fractures) and bone grease rendering (fragmented cancellous bone). (Photo by the author.)

strate that the Mohawk Colonial pattern should not be seen as typical of eighteenth-century sites across the Confederacy (K. Jordan 2009).

Bone Fragmentation and Bone Grease Production

Socci (1995) and Watson (2000, 2007) have assessed the degree of bone fragmentation at Iroquois sites using a quantitative method developed by Grayson (1984). Watson (2000) found that Townley-Read has one of the most heavily fragmented assemblages of any Iroquoian site to which the method has been applied; he attributes the fragmentation to production of bone grease (figure 10.1). That heavily fragmented bone has been found in situ in features and post molds at the site, coupled with the lack of significant weathering, trampling, and carnivore gnawing or digestion in intact deposits, strongly suggests that humans were responsible for the fragmentation. Bone grease production and its archaeological correlates have been discussed by many archaeologists (for example, Binford 1978; Brink 1997; Church and Lyman 2003; Leechman 1951; Outram 2001; Sassaman 1995; Vehik 1977). The easiest way to extract lipids from animal bones is to split up long bones to remove marrow; in some settings, this is the only step that is performed. Additional nutrients can be obtained by breaking up cancellous bone elements and simmering the fragments over low-temperature fires to extract bone grease, vitamins, and minerals. Archaeologically, the combination of marrow and grease exploitation produces assemblages composed of "large numbers of very small pieces of cancellous bone accompanied by larger, helical shaft fractures" (Outram 2003: 122). Binford (1978: 158) describes bone grease production as "a labor-intensive activity, requiring great amounts of firewood, patience, and labor."

Archaeologists generally view the labor needed to render bone grease as a major deterrent to its production; many assert that grease extraction is done only in desperate conditions when there are shortages of animal fat (for example, Outram 2001, 2003; Speth 1990; Speth and Spielmann 1983; Spiess 1988). At Iroquois sites, analysts typically associate grease production with dietary stress (for example, Engelbrecht 2003: 11; Junker-Andersen 1983: 152; Socci 1995: 203). Eighteenth-century Iroquois sites provide a different perspective on the motivations for bone fragmentation. That the Mohawk Indian Castle site has the third highest fragmentation index of the sites examined by Socci (1995) illustrates this point. The faunal assemblage from Indian Castle derives from the Brant house lot, residence of one of the wealthiest and most influential Mohawk families (Guldenzopf 1986). Given the affluence of the Brants (as indicated by both the documentary and archaeological records), it is unlikely that they would have suffered from dietary stress.

At Townley-Read, bone grease rendering appears to have been a planned strategy that accumulated storable fat for use in the late winter–early spring "hungry time" (K. Jordan and Watson 2005). Historical and ethnographic accounts indicate that Northern Iroquoian peoples also used bone grease year-round for a variety of culinary, craft, medicinal, and ritual purposes, including as a flavoring for soups and stews, a spread for bread, and oil for frying (Parker 1910; Tooker 1991 [1964]: 66; 1994: 123; Waugh 1973 [1916]: 134). Bone grease rendering therefore may have *prevented* seasonal dietary stress, rather than being an ad-hoc response to shortfall. The claim that there was not consistent dietary stress at Townley-Read is supported by the high overall percentage of deer remains and the lack of significant numbers of Iroquois "famine food" species (see next section). The Townley-Read data fully support Brink's (1997: 272) claim that it "would be inappropriate to assume that archaeological evidence of grease rendering always indicates desperate nutritional conditions or the spring season."

Presence/Absence of Individual Species

Kuhn and Funk (2000: figure 1) inventory the mammalian species recovered at thirteen archaeological sites in the Mohawk Valley. The ecosystems of the Mohawk Valley and the Seneca Lake region were broadly similar, so differences between the overall Mohawk Valley and Townley-Read assemblages are instructive. Since the Mohawk assemblage is derived from thirteen sites from a range of time periods, the comparison is most telling when a species commonly found at Mohawk Valley sites is missing from Townley-Read; absence of species found only rarely in the Mohawk Valley may be a product of sample size (Grayson 1984).

Fourteen of the twenty-seven native mammalian species found on Mohawk sites were recovered at Townley-Read. Of the thirteen species absent from the Townley-Read assemblage, four were found at more than half of the Mohawk Valley sites: in order of frequency, they are woodchuck, American elk, eastern chipmunk, and eastern gray squirrel. Four species were found at 25 to 50 percent of Mohawk Valley sites (bobcat/lynx, snowshoe hare, wolf, and red squirrel), and five species were found at less than 25 percent of Mohawk Valley sites (otter, moose, wolverine [nonlocal], mink, and short-tail shrew). The only Townley-Read species not recovered at Mohawk Valley sites were single specimens of hairy-tailed mole (*Parascalops breweri*) and southern red-backed vole (*Clethryonimus gapperi*). These microfaunal specimens both were found in contexts that suggest they were natural rather than cultural deposits.

Most noteworthy are the absences of woodchuck, American elk, eastern chipmunk, and eastern gray squirrel remains from the Townley-Read assemblage. Senecas definitely traded elk skins while Townley-Read was occupied (for example, Colden 1935 [1720]: 424; McIlwain 1915: 114); their absence can be attributed to rarity of use or a dearth of elks in the region. The absence of woodchucks, chipmunks, gray squirrels, and possibly the rarer red squirrels most likely is attributable to rarity of use, since these mammals surely lived in the environments surrounding Townley-Read. It is notable that mammals commonly found on Mohawk Valley sites but lacking at Townley-Read are predominantly second-tier food species.

In terms of non-mammalian remains, only the bird bone assemblage from Townley-Read has been analyzed at the time of this writing. Like the mammalian record, the bird assemblage from Townley-Read also contains notable gaps. Only the now-extinct passenger pigeon, ruffed grouse, and whistling swan were recovered, while turkey (*Meleagris gallopavo*), goose, and duck bones are missing from the domestic-context assemblage. The passenger pigeon remains are from adult individuals; immature squabs (who generally leave few archaeological traces) were the primary food source for Iroquois peoples, and "countless undetected squabs might have perished for each adult bone found" (Orlandini 1996: 74). A single turkey leg bone was found in the grave of an elderly woman at the site (Wray n.d.). Since bones of both small and large birds were recovered at Townley-Read, the lack of turkey, goose, and duck remains likely reflects rarity of use rather than recovery bias, preservation issues, or destructive Seneca processing.

The apparently low level of turkey use is perhaps the most puzzling aspect of the Townley-Read faunal assemblage. Turkeys were available year-round and frequented the same edge areas preferred by deer (Cronon 1983: 23, 108). Seneca deer hunters must have encountered them frequently; even the Moravian Zeisberger brought down a turkey during his brief stay in Seneca territory (Beauchamp 1916: 72). Waterfowl would have been most abundant in the marshy areas to the west of the site and on the shores of Seneca Lake, particularly during migratory periods in April, May, September, and October (Cronon 1983: 40). Tentative possibilities are that the availability of deer made significant turkey hunting unnecessary, or that seasonal labor obligations took Seneca hunters away from lakes and wetlands during spring and fall. Interestingly, turkey remains were not recovered from the Brant House, Enders House, or Jackson-Everson sites in the Mohawk Valley either (Kuhn and Funk 2000: figure 2), suggesting that turkey hunting had become less important in at least two parts of the Confederacy by the late seventeenth century.

Faunal assemblage composition also provides information about the level of dietary stress within a site's population; in particular, a large proportion of lower-tier food species may provide evidence for chronic shortages. Iroquois famine foods likely to be represented in the faunal record include dogs, freshwater mussels, small birds, eels, muskrats, and mammal bones boiled multiple times (see chapter 2).

The Townley-Read faunal assemblage provides little indication of chronic dietary stress. Second-tier food species such as woodchucks, squirrels, chipmunks, and small birds are entirely absent from the Townley-Read assemblage, and many microfaunal specimens were found in contexts that suggest they died of natural causes. Dog remains are relatively rare (4 specimens making up 1.1 percent of mammalian NISP), in contrast to 6.3 percent of the assemblage at Jackson-Everson (Kuhn and Funk 2000: 53). The Townley-Read shell assemblage is small and highly fragmented, suggesting very minor reliance on shellfish unless consumption or processing took place off-site. Spiess (1988: 418) notes that the predominance of large mammal remains at the eighteenth-century Tunica Trudeau site in Louisiana "suggests a relative affluence, enabling the site's inhabitants to ignore many small species that could have been used for subsistence purposes"; a similar conclusion could be drawn about Townley-Read.

Documents indicate that a major famine occurred in the Seneca region during 1741–1742 (chapter 3). This famine is essentially invisible archaeologically. It is possible that a two-year famine would not have a large impact on the assemblage of a site occupied for almost forty years, especially if famine was atypical. Alternately, preservation biases might weigh against the inclusion of famine foods in the archaeological record, particularly if normal trash-deposition behaviors were suspended in favor of energy-conserving expedient dumping on nearby ground surfaces. Surface materials that could have provided evidence for famine would have faced a greater likelihood of destruction by scavenger consumption, weathering, or trampling. Attempts to get every last bit of nutrition out of bones—such as the repeated boilings of the same set of squirrel bones seen during a 1765 famine at Kanadesaga (Pilkington 1980: 29–30)—also would weaken their structure and make their preservation less likely. Additionally, Townley-Read Senecas may have responded to food shortfalls by increasing their mobility, as is suggested by the Senecas' frequent requests for provisions to go hunting during the 1741–1742 famine (IIDH, Aug. 16, 1741; McIlwain 1915: 222–23; NYCD 9: 1075). In the winter of 1779–1780, Senecas also appear to have responded to the deprivation caused by the Sullivan expedition's destruction of their crops and stored food with increased mobility (Calloway 1995: 137; A. Mt. Pleasant 2004).

In sum, the high proportion of deer, the low numbers of famine foods and second-tier species, and the absence of certain productive food species (especially turkeys) within the Townley-Read assemblage argue for an overall lack of dietary stress during the site's occupation. This does not rule out intermittent bouts of severe stress that may have had devastating effects on Seneca communities, as did the 1741–1742 famine.

Seneca Animal Use and Participation in the Fur Trade: Documentary Evidence

Documents provide ample support for the claim that the eighteenth-century fur trade in the lower Great Lakes diversified and shifted away from its seventeenth-century emphasis on beaver pelts, reinforcing the archaeological evidence that Seneca men and women commercially produced deerskins at Townley-Read. With a few exceptions (for example, Cutcliffe 1981; Laird 1995; Standen 1998), scholars have not recognized that skins and pelts other than beaver were economically important trade items for the Iroquois. For example, Norton's (1974) book on the 1686–1776 New York fur trade discusses deerskins and other pelts only in passing, virtually equating the fur trade with the beaver trade for the entire period. That Senecas and possibly other Iroquois nations apparently found productive alternatives to the beaver trade has important implications regarding the viability of their local political economies.

The full range of New York's fur trade is documented in 1699–1758 statistics from the British Customs Office compiled in Cutcliffe (1981: table 1), which measure exports from New York and Pennsylvania received in London. Cutcliffe (1981: 240) notes that all of these figures are based on "fixed official values" set at the beginning of the eighteenth century; while the statistics do not measure market value, they do provide a standardized expression of trade volume. During the proposed 1715–1754 occupation of the Townley-Read site, furs and skins represented 36.0 percent of New York's total exports to London, with an average annual value of £5917. Of the total value of New York fur and skin exports to London during 1715–1754, beaver skins made up 50.2 percent, deerskins 23.4 percent, and other unspecified skins 26.4 percent. New York exports valued more than £4000 in thirty-two of these forty years, with four of the lowest yearly totals coming during 1745–1748 in the midst of King George's War.

New York's deerskins are likely to have come through the same trade networks as beaver pelts, and due to the weight of deerskins (as compared to beaver pelts and *menues pelleteries*), they are more likely to have come from sources close to trade centers. Seneca participation in the deerskin trade probably increased after the opening of Oswego; Senecas could have transported heavy deerskin cargoes to Oswego on the leg of the trip they made *with the river current* (figure 2.1). During 1715–1754, five of the ten highest yearly New York deer-hide export figures fall immediately after the opening of Oswego during 1724–1728, and two fall within the 1740s. The ten worst years for New York deer-hide exports cluster during three periods: 1715–1716, some of the earliest years that dispersed Iroquois settlements are likely to have been occupied; 1745–1748, when the post at Oswego was largely closed and Indian suppliers may have diverted their trade to French posts (Standen 1998); and 1751–1754, when Pennsylvania consistently exported more than 90 percent of the two colonies' deerskin volume. Notably, two of New York's ten highest and none of the ten lowest yearly beaver export figures come from the 1750–1754 period, illustrating that reports of the death of the New York beaver trade (for example, Richter 1992: 270–71) have been greatly exaggerated.

New France also accepted many varieties of pelts and skins, and French posts likely were the destination for many Iroquois deerskins. Starting no later than 1700, New France preferentially acquired the skins of large animals, including elk, moose, bear, and deer, due to a glut of beaver pelts in Paris (Haan 1976: 116, 203; see also NYCD 4: 799, 804). In 1716 Seneca headmen asked the governor of New France for better terms for elk skins (Colden 1935 [1720]: 424; McIlwain 1915: 114). Standen (1998: table 1) documents fluctuations in the proportion of beaver pelts within the total value of furs received at Forts Niagara and Frontenac between 1730 and 1748. In no year for which complete statistics are available was the percentage of the fur value derived from beaver pelts greater than 45 percent; in 1737 it was only 11.3 percent (see also White 1991: table 3.1). Peter Kalm (1966 [1751]: 82) noted that the packs being carried across the Niagara portage in August 1750 (of uncertain destination) were "chiefly of deer and bear."

The 1750 journal of Johann Cammerhoff provides an eyewitness account of Seneca animal use near the end of Townley-Read's occupation. Cammerhoff traversed Seneca territory during an eight-day period in late June and early July (Beauchamp 1916: 67–82). The animal foods Cammerhoff and fellow Moravian David Zeisberger received from Senecas consisted predominantly of venison and trout; they were offered venison in New Ganechstage, and stews of venison and maize in Canandaigua and boiled trout and maize at Honeoye. The son of the Seneca leader "Tschokagaas" gave the Moravians a 69 cm-long trout as a present; Cammerhoff described it as "the largest and finest David and I had ever seen" (81).

The journal provides frequent indications that midsummer local hunting was of importance to the Seneca local political economy at this time. Just outside the Canandaigua village, the Moravians found an Indian "carrying a deer which he had shot in this neighborhood" (Beauchamp 1916: 69). Cammerhoff and Zeisberger also met an Indian "going on the chase" near Canandaigua, and found upon their arrival at the village that almost all of its male residents had gone hunting (81). Near Old Ganechstage (White Springs), they found "several Indians who had been hunting with bows and arrows" (82), possibly in the fields surrounding the former village.

Zeisberger himself obtained pigeons for at least three meals in Seneca territory, shot a turkey between Honeoye and Hemlock Lakes, and caught "a peculiar kind of fish, unknown to us" in Canandaigua Lake (67, 69, 72, 81, 82). Cammerhoff claims to have seen tracks of "elks" and "buffaloes" (73), but the Moravian may have misidentified the tracks since these species are not found in the Seneca archaeological record. Cammerhoff also saw nearly one hundred domestic dogs at Genesee Castle, a village of "40 or more large huts" (73, 79).

Cammerhoff's descriptions of Cayuga territory provide additional information on the use of lacustrine resources, which Cammerhoff did not observe directly among the Senecas. Cayugas extracted eels (cooked fresh or dried) and turtle eggs from Cayuga Lake and lived in temporary shelters in lakeside caves (Beauchamp 1916: 40, 43, 86; see also Engelbrecht 2003: 16). A French trader living in the nominally Cayuga village of Nuquiage (possibly a seasonal fishing village) at the northeast end of Seneca Lake also presented Cammerhoff and Zeisberger with roasted eels (Beauchamp 1916: 66, 83).

Seneca Use of European Domesticated Animals

Documentary and archaeological evidence indicates there were few European domesticated animals at Seneca sites during 1677–1779, and this pattern apparently extended into the early reservation period. As noted in chapter 7, the small resident populations of Europeans and poorly developed transportation networks in Seneca territory did not permit the growth of a "frontier exchange economy" in domesticated animal products similar to that which arose in the Mississippi Valley (Usner 1992, 1998).

An apparent exception to the pattern of low Seneca use of domesticated animals is the frequently cited mention of pigs at Ganondagan in 1687. According to one account, members of the Denonville expedition found "a vast quantity of hogs which were killed" (DHNY 1: 239). The French officer De Baugy may refer to pigs being within the Fort Hill palisaded enclosure, and also to the possible consequences of eating them: "M. de Tonty was despatched to set fire to this fort [Fort Hill]. Some pigs were found, which did more harm than good, for they started a diarrhoea that has made a large number sick" (Olds 1930: 38).

In contrast to these 1687 accounts, European domesticated animals were not used in great numbers at Townley-Read. European species made up only 2.6 percent of the faunal assemblage (table 10.1), consisting of 2.3 percent pigs and 0.3 percent cows. The eight pig specimens were spread fairly evenly throughout the three investigated Domestic Refuse Clusters: two teeth were recovered from plowzone contexts in DRC 1; two teeth from DRC 2 plowzone contexts; two teeth and a skull fragment from the plowzone above the DRC 3 Buried Plowed Midden; and one metapodial from within the BPM itself. The single cow specimen from the site is a second phalanx from Feature 5 in DRC 1.

At subsequent Seneca sites, use of European animals increased but still remained quite low. Luke Swetland's 1778–1779 captivity narrative mentions that cattle were used for milk, butter, and buttermilk as well as for meat; hogs for meat; and horses for both transportation and meat in the settlements around Seneca Lake (Merrifield 1915: 20, 23, 26, 29, 30, 32, 33, 34, 50); the impression given by the journal is that domesticated animals were infrequent. At the 1779 Seneca villages described by Sullivan expedition members, horses were found at Newtown, Catharine's Town, Condawhaw, Kanadesaga, and Kashong (Conover 1887: 9, 30, 45, 46, 73, 217; Division of Archives and History 1929: 183, 186); cattle at Catharine's Town and Kanadesaga (Conover 1887: 45, 73, 217); hogs at Catharine's Town and Kashong (Conover 1887: 173; Division of Archives and History 1929: 186); and poultry or "fowls" only at Kashong (Conover 1887: 30; Division of Archives and History 1929: 186). Although the Sullivan documents no doubt understate the presence of European animals because Senecas would have hidden their animals from the American army, there is no mention of facilities such as stables, barns, animal pens, or fenced fields that demonstrate significant reliance on such animals. At some early reservation-era sites, European animals continued to be relatively rare. There were few domesticates at Cornplanter's Town in 1798 (Wallace 1969: 191), and they were not plentiful in the faunal assemblage from the post-1790 Vanatta site, where seventeen pig, eight cow, one sheep, and one chicken specimen were found, in comparison to ninety-two deer remains (Lantz 1980).

The pigs at Ganondagan appear to represent an early peak in Seneca use of European animals that was not sustained at later sites. Some notice should be taken that one primary source described "a vast quantity" of pigs, while another mentioned only "some" pigs. It is also not entirely clear from the 1687 French documents that these pigs were penned up on Fort Hill; if true, this situation can best be explained as the expedient use of a palisaded area that had not yet been settled rather than a typical practice. Seneca use of European animals is a perfect illustration that a gradualist model of acculturation does not work: the presence and proportion of European domesticated animals certainly did not build in a steady linear fashion over time.

The small percentage of domesticated animals at Townley-Read and later Seneca sites presents a clear contrast to the situation in the Mohawk Valley. The earliest stratum at the Mohawk Enders House site, occupied prior to the construction of a stone foundation house, dates to approximately 1750–1760 and therefore overlaps with the end of the occupation at Townley-Read. In this layer, a total of 283 mammalian remains identifiable to family level or better were recovered (Rick 1991: table 1). Here 57.2 percent of the identified mammalian NISP was composed of European animal remains, including 108 pig, 38 cow, 10 sheep/goat, 5 horse, and 1 cat specimen; a single chicken bone was also present in this level. A similar proportion of European domesticates is present at later components in the Mohawk Valley, including the post-1760 strata at the Enders House and the post-1762 Brant house lot at Indian Castle; European rats also appear at these later sites (Guldenzopf 1986: Appendix III; Rick 1991: table 2). The contrast between the two regions indicates that European domesticated animals were not adopted by Six Nations peoples as a package, nor did they form a substantial part of the Seneca subsistence regimen even after one hundred years of domesticate use. European animal species instead were adopted individually according to specific ecological and economic factors associated with their management.

Pigs often were the European domesticate adopted earliest by Indians because they could be incorporated relatively easily into existing Native subsistence systems. Pigs adapted to frontier life quickly; taking "advantage of a highly favorable environmental base and an absence of competition in their mast-eating and rooting niche" (T. Jordan and Kaups 1989: 122), they proved advantageous to frontier populations due to their "foraging ability, self-reliance, totality of meat use, and rapid proliferation" (120). Even European New Englanders using intensive agriculture let their pigs run wild in the woods and hunted them in the fall instead of penning them (Cronon 1983: 129). European colonists protected their crops from semi-feral pigs with fences, and maintained some measure of ownership over roaming pigs by branding their ears (129–30).

Faunal data indicate that pigs were the most common European domesticated animal used at Townley-Read, but they made up only 2.3 percent of NISP, 3.7 percent of MNI, and perhaps even less of the diet. Rothschild (2003: 158) suggests that the ratio of deer to pig teeth can indicate the relative importance of these species at a site, but raw counts need to be standardized to account for the different numbers of teeth in each animal's mouth (mature deer have thirty-two teeth, pigs forty-four). Sixty-seven deer teeth and six pig teeth were recovered at Townley-Read, resulting in a corrected ratio of 15.4:1 (produced by multiplying the number of deer teeth by 1.375). I find it implausible that Seneca families "owned" pigs in European fashion, where owners retained exclusive rights to branded animals even when they ran semi-feral. The adoption of pigs by the Senecas (and other western Iroquois) more likely represented the introduction of another source of wild meat into the ecosystem than the taking up of a form of private property.

Horses initially were not adopted in great numbers by Six Nations peoples because existing footpaths were poorly suited to horse-borne travel. The foddering needs of horses also placed demands on stocks of stored grain that often were needed by humans, particularly in the late winter and early spring. Cammerhoff observed several difficulties with the use of horses in the central and western parts of Iroquoia in 1750:

> We have found, here and elsewhere, that traveling on foot is the only way to journey among the Indians, because, with horses, it is frequently impossible to pass over the rough and swampy roads, sometimes covered by fallen trees, making it difficult to lead horses over them, while pedestrians can proceed much more easily; besides, when we reached an Indian settlement, we were harassed day and night by the care of our horses, and were in constant dread of their being shot or injured by drunken Indians. (Beauchamp 1916: 57)

Cammerhoff also recorded an episode where Cayugas shot and killed a loose horse that had "committed depredations in the corn" (Beauchamp 1916: 62). The Moravian party went solely on foot in the Seneca region, and Cammerhoff mentioned that the "Long Bridge" section of trail between New Ganechstage and Canandaigua "would have been quite impassible with horses, and the Indians say that no one can travel this road except on foot" (68). No horse-related remains, either bone material or horse hardware, were recovered by project excavations in the East Fields at Townley-Read.

As soon as paths were cleared and improved to the point where they could be used by horses, the Iroquois adopted them wholeheartedly. Horses also played an important role in hauling, especially firewood (Wonderley 1998: 25) and cargoes at portages (Benson 1937: 696). By Revolutionary War times, horses and horse furniture made up 37 percent of the value of Oneida war claims, exceeding the total value of claims for houses (Wonderley 1998: 25). The increase in Seneca horse usage seen by the time of the Sullivan expedition likely was related to the improvement of trails in the region.

In contrast to pigs, Iroquois horses seem to have been owned individually (Beauchamp 1916: 35; Wonderley 1998: table 3). Six Nations people adopted horses in a way that minimized their impact on agriculture and the seasonal round, apparently allowing them to wander freely in the woods. Cammerhoff notes that his Cayuga guide had to go to "look for his horse, which he had left in the woods" before they could move on, a process that took several days (Beauchamp 1916: 34–35); captive Luke Swetland "caught a horse" in the woods outside Kendaia (Merrifield 1915: 33). Again, Iroquois people appear to have exerted only slightly less control over their animals than did contemporaneous Europeans. Warren Johnson noted in 1760 that European-owned horses in the Mohawk Valley were allowed to "run in the Woods all Winter" (Snow, Gehring, and Starna 1996: 254); their owners then caught them with salt (261). While Europeans cared for their animals *seasonally*, the frontier Iroquois made little provision for their "domesticated" horses, instead catching them whenever they needed the animals for transportation or food. Iroquois communities that coupled extensive agricultural systems with greater numbers of horses (such as the Revolutionary War–era Oneidas) may have tethered or hobbled horses from planting through harvest, the practice of the southeastern Creeks, who kept large numbers of horses but did not use fenced fields or barns (Braund 1993: 76).

Small numbers of cattle appear to have roamed Iroquois field margins and the woods with pigs and horses (Merrifield 1915). This likely was the practice at Townley-Read (where *Bos taurus* bones made up only 0.3 percent of NISP), and at the 1779 Seneca sites destroyed by Sullivan (Conover 1887; Division of Archives and History 1929; Merrifield 1915). Terry Jordan and Matti Kaups (1989: 120) note that a small number of loose cattle could be supported in clearings and abandoned fields without placing active agricultural fields in much danger; Midland pioneers used cattle primarily for their dairy functions rather than for beef or traction. Captive Luke Swetland took over care of two Seneca cows in 1778–1779 because he felt the Senecas were not milking them properly (Merrifield 1915: 29).

The different levels of Mohawk versus Seneca use of domesticated species that required relatively intensive management (such as cattle, and also sheep and goats, the latter of which are absent from pre–Revolutionary War western Iroquois sites) provides another example of the divergent paths local political economies in these regions took after construction of Fort Hunter in 1711. The less encroached-upon Senecas adopted only domesticated species compatible with a system of hoe-based extensive agriculture. The Mohawks' adoption of fencing and large numbers of relatively intensively managed domesticated animals was more a response to the fact that *their previous way of life had become impossible* than the inevitable adoption of useful European animals (K. Jordan 2009).

Animal Use and Men's and Women's Labor at Townley-Read

The Iroquois focus on the acquisition and processing of beaver pelts appears to have continued from the seventeenth century into the 1701–1713 period of uncertainty. Access to beaver-hunting territories was a key part of the 1700–1701 peace treaties with New York, New France, and western Indian nations (Brandão and Starna 1996). Cutcliffe's (1981: table 1) trade figures show that 62.7 percent of the total value of New York fur and skin exports received in London between 1699 and 1713 was derived from beaver pelts, and only 7.5 percent from deerskins. New York's major involvement in the deerskin trade clearly postdated 1713, and this likely is true of Iroquois procurement practices as well. Therefore the eastern Seneca move from White Springs to New Ganechstage in about 1715 also involved a transition from beaver-based to deer-based articulation with the European fur trade. This had major effects on labor patterns for both Seneca men and Seneca women.

Men's Labor at Townley-Read

Seneca men, I assert, did well as a result of the change from beaver to deer hunting that accompanied the move to Townley-Read. Men's beaver hunting tended to take place during the winter, when beavers generally kept to their lodges and their coats were of the best quality (Tooker 1991 [1964]: 67). As beaver populations within Iroquoia and adjoining areas declined in the seventeenth century, Iroquois men hunted at increasingly greater distances from their homeland, resulting in extended periods of dangerous extra-regional travel that lasted for months or even years at a time. Men's hunting journeys alternated or combined with raids on enemy groups that generated captives, plunder, and (at least occasionally) pelts. In addition to the direct threat that they might suffer bodily harm, men's long absences cut down on the amount of labor and sustenance they were able to provide to their households. Their absences also lessened the physical security of homeland villages, a poignant tension for Iroquois families since groups living on the boundaries of then–Five Nations territory generally remained hostile.

Adoption of a deerskin-based role in the fur trade had significant effects on Seneca men's labor allocation. The number of large, heavy deer bones in the Townley-Read assemblage suggests that deer frequently were available *locally*, a supposition strengthened by Cammerhoff's accounts of local hunting in Seneca territory (Beauchamp 1916). Although the impact of nonhuman factors on local deer populations (such as predation levels, the occurrence of persistent deep snow, the availability of mast and browse, and disease rates; Starna and Relethford 1985) must be taken into account, several elements in the relationships among humans, deer, and the environments surrounding Townley-Read suggest that sizable *local and regional* deer populations were likely to have been frequently available. Immediately prior to the occupation of Townley-Read, (1) extra-regional beaver hunting, trade, and warfare consistently had removed Seneca hunters from the localities and regions around homeland villages, allowing deer populations to rebound; (2) the Seneca population had been depleted during the Twenty Years' War, reducing overall levels of deer hunting; (3) fear of bodily harm during the years of war and uncertainty from 1677–1713 probably deterred hunters from certain "no-man's-land" areas (both regional and extra-regional) and allowed deer there to increase; and (4) use of European textiles for clothing deflected some of the hunting pressure that had previously been applied to deer onto beaver. Three additional factors sustained *local* deer populations throughout the occupation of the site. First, dispersed settlement created a complex mosaic of woods, fields, and edge areas conducive to deer; second, dispersed settlement provided individual Seneca hunters with different local hunting territories. Lastly, Seneca pelt-procurement hunting removed deer predators such as bears, wolves, and foxes from the local environment (Adam Dewbury, personal communication, 2007). The other pelt-bearing animals that formed a minor part of the fur trade also were likely to have been available locally or regionally.

Archaeological and documentary evidence also suggests that local white-tailed deer were hunted essentially *year-round*. Observers noted that concentrated Iroquoian deer hunting took place during late fall and early winter (Kuhn and Funk 2000; Trigger 1987 [1976], 1990). Limited season-of-death evidence from the Townley-Read faunal assemblage indicates that local deer hunting took place both in and out of the late fall–early winter season. Using tooth eruption and wear patterns, Adam Watson (2007) determined the season of death for five deer from the Townley-Read site. Watson suspects that all of these kills were local due to the recovery of mandibles or frontal bones. Specimens are present that could have been killed in every month of the year; peaks in hunting intensity appear to have taken place from November through January and May through June.[4] Cammerhoff describes frequent local summer deer hunting and venison availability in the Seneca region in 1750, only about four years prior to the abandonment of Townley-Read. The combination of faunal and textual evidence thus suggests that white-tailed deer were readily available for commercial hunting in the locality or region throughout the occupation of the site, and that local summer hunting may have been a *recurrent* practice at Townley-Read.

Two perspectives view summer hunting as problematic. First, Cammerhoff observed that an acute food shortage impelled Cayuga men to hunt in the summer of 1750, and the nearby Senecas also could have been hunting as the result of a scarcity of vegetable food. However, shortages noted among the Cayugas were not evident in Seneca territory: Cammerhoff and Zeisberger frequently were given stews containing maize, and they easily were able to obtain cornmeal at Genesee Castle for their trip back to Cayuga. Seneca summer hunting therefore does not appear to have been done for emergency reasons. Second, Richard White (1983: 82–87) sees out-of-season hunting as an atypical practice that placed unsustainable pressure on deer populations; he asserts that summer hunting was generated by European traders' extension of credit and increased peddling of addictive alcohol to Indian hunters. In the case of Townley-Read, this scenario is plausible—the Cammerhoff journal contains numerous observations proving that the 1750 Senecas had obtained plenty of alcohol, and they may have increased hunting levels in order to trade for it. However, there would have been a time lapse between the initiation of out-of-season deer hunting and decline in local deer populations. The apparently ready availability of deer among the Senecas in the summer of 1750 suggests that deer decline had not happened by this date, a supposition confirmed by the ubiquity of deer and evidence for summer hunting in the Townley-Read faunal assemblage. There appear to have been thirty-five to forty years of year-round white-tailed deer availability in the Seneca region despite ongoing commercial hunting.

Development of trade in deerskins procured by local and regional hunting allowed Seneca men to stay fairly close to home, in contrast to the beaver-based trade, which had forced them into lengthy and dangerous extra-regional travel and warfare. Men certainly traveled long distances after

1715—some direct Seneca acquisition of extra-local beaver almost definitely took place, and war parties frequently journeyed to the southeast to battle with the so-called Flatheads (Aquila 1983; Merrell 1987; Perdue 1987)—but such travel was likely to have been somewhat more voluntary in character than that in the final years of the beaver-based trade. The increased presence of adult men in the locality and region probably added to the security of the Townley-Read settlement, helped generate a steadier food supply, and facilitated field clearance and construction in the spring and summer, and craft, maintenance, and ritual activities in the winter, among other tasks.

Women's Labor at Townley-Read

The effects of the change in emphasis from beaver to deer on Seneca women at Townley-Read are less clear-cut. Although the direct labor requirements of beaver processing were considerable, the tools and raw materials needed were relatively minimal, consisting of scraping and cutting tools, marrow, and sinew (Jennings 1975: 92). Demands on women's labor for the beaver trade likely concentrated in winter when the majority of beaver hunting occurred, which may have displaced to other parts of the year some tasks women traditionally undertook in winter. In contrast, dressing deerskins was more labor- and material-intensive, partially due to the sheer size of deer hides. Depictions of deerskin processing indicate that each hide had to be subjected to at least six separate processes in order to obtain the most value in exchange.[5] These steps included (1) an optional initial soaking of the skin (apparently in cold water); (2) scraping away of tissue, fat, and hair; (3) softening through pulling, pounding, and stretching; (4) soaking in a solution of water and animal brains previously prepared by boiling; (5) drying by wringing and possibly forcing water out by scraping with a dull hatchet blade or similar tool; (6) a second episode of softening through pulling, pounding, and stretching; and (7) smoking over a shallow firepit or a kettle with burning materials inside. The year-round hunting at Townley-Read meant that these materially involved processes had to be undertaken on a recurring basis. The labor and material requirements of industrial deer-hide processing may have completely eaten up the time saved by residential dispersal (which decreased the amount of time women spent walking to and from fields and carrying water). Involvement in the deerskin-based trade, in short, may have resulted in a net increase in work for Seneca women.

I will evaluate this contention by looking at how Seneca women interdigitated hide working with other tasks. The deer dressing process contains numerous lulls, especially during soaking, heating, and smoking. While some of this time would have been used to prepare for subsequent steps in the process, the procedure inevitably created dead time during which Seneca women could have undertaken other types of work. The organization of space in a dispersed village like Townley-Read presented a variety of opportunities for combining tasks, since water, firewood, infields, nearby outfields, and work areas all were within easy walking distance of one another. If deer-hide processing placed excessive demands on Seneca women, one would expect to see that they used lulls in the process for immediate subsistence tasks. The Townley-Read evidence, in fact, illustrates that the opposite took place: Seneca women filled interstices in the hide-dressing process with an activity that was directed at the future—namely, bone grease rendering.

As outlined in chapter 5, there is strong evidence that Feature 5 at Townley-Read was used primarily for fur and skin processing and bone marrow and grease extraction, with a secondary focus on food preparation. Ethnographic descriptions of bone grease production (for example, Binford 1978: 157–63; Leechman 1951) indicate that many of the raw materials and conditions needed for grease rendering, such as the low-temperature fires required for the slow accumulation of grease, also were used in deer-hide dressing. Tasks associated with grease production included bone smashing, firewood gathering, water carrying, monitoring of low-temperature fires, and skimming off of accumulated grease. The bone grease production process at Townley-Read likely was quite similar to that used ethnographically: bone smashing probably was undertaken with metal tools (perhaps the butt ends of axes or hatchets), using a stone anvil and an outspread hide to catch the bone fragments; boiling undoubtedly was done in brass kettles.

Complementary lulls in the deer-hide dressing and grease rendering processes (particularly when waiting for grease to boil or deerskins to dry, smoke, or soak in a solution of animal brains and water) likely allowed Seneca women to interdigitate the necessary steps and undertake both tasks simultaneously. It is particularly noteworthy that both processes involved heating several kettles over low-temperature fires, meaning that any fires generated could do double duty. Each eighteenth-century excavation locus at Townley-Read showed a high frequency of deer remains and a significant degree of bone fragmentation, suggesting that the deerskin processing–bone grease production pattern identified at Feature 5 extended across the entire site.

Binford observed that Nunamiut grease rendering was undertaken most efficiently when a family had accumulated a large amount of bone, usually in wintertime when freezing would prevent rotting; Leechman notes that in situations where bone storage was impractical, grease needed to be made from bones at most one day old. Women at the Townley-Read site could have done either, depending on the season and the level of men's deer acquisition. Grease rendering appears to have been done throughout most of the year, paralleling hunting and hide dressing. The degree of bone fragmentation is close to uniform across the site; no significant accumulations of unfragmented deer bone have been found, suggesting that grease was rendered in every season.

At Townley-Read, bone grease production was integrated into a subsistence system that made little use of second-tier or starvation food species. Adam Watson and I (K. Jordan and Watson 2005) argue that consistent attention to grease manufacture was a premeditated way to solve the problem of the late winter–early spring hungry time. Indigenous peoples of the eastern woodlands have used a variety of labor-intensive methods to produce storable sources of fat to resolve this seasonal problem. Such solutions included the processing of massive quantities of acorns seen at the Late Archaic Lamoka Lake site (Ritchie 1980: 60) and use of the small-seed crops of the Eastern Agricultural Complex (Gremillion 2004). At the Townley-Read site, Seneca women consistently had time to produce bone grease, which appears to have obviated the need to make frequent use of second-tier species or starvation foods. While grease rendering was labor intensive, it may have proved easier than procuring secondary food sources, and bone grease had many culinary, medicinal, craft, and ritual applications. The opportunity costs of bone grease production were significantly lower due to the facts that hunters were consistently introducing deer bones into Seneca house lots and that many of the tools, raw materials, and conditions needed for grease production already were used in deer-hide processing. The similarities between bone grease rendering and deer-hide processing allowed Seneca women to overlap the two processes and simultaneously engage in both industrial and household production.

The prevalence of bone grease rendering at Townley-Read makes a fundamental point about Seneca women's labor: if deer-hide processing resulted in excessive labor demands at any point during the yearly cycle, women would have devoted their time to tasks more pressing to their subsistence than bone grease production. That they consistently produced a delayed-return resource shows that the yearly cycle associated with dispersed settlement and a deer-hide-based articulation with the fur trade provided sufficient unallocated time for such opportunism.

Red Stone and the Archaeology of the Middleman Role

The controversy over whether the Iroquois acted as middlemen in the fur trade has raged for almost a century (Aquila 1983; Brandão 1997; Haan 1976; Hunt 1940; McIlwain 1915; Trelease 1962). The debate can be clarified by distinguishing between economic and geographic middleman roles, emphasizing the role of gift exchange and alliance in Native American interactions, and specifying the political-economic and temporal contexts in which such activities supposedly took place (see chapters 2 and 3). The debate predominantly has relied on documentary sources, whereas most supposed Iroquois middleman activity would have taken place without Europeans ever seeing it. Archaeology therefore provides another, and perhaps better, way to approach the middleman issue. One way to do this is to monitor changes in what can be termed the "red stone" assemblage on Iroquois sites.

Many eighteenth-century Iroquoian sites contain artifacts made of red-colored stone (Bennett 1982, 1988; Bradley 1987; Fisher 1993; Guldenzopf 1986; Hesse 1975; B. Kent 1993; Kinsey 1981; T. Tanner 1995; Wray 1973, n.d.). Hamell (1983) outlines the value and connotations of the color red in Iroquois cosmology, noting that "redness" connotes the "animate and emotive aspect of Life" and is associated with fire and "blood, certain mineral pigments and stones, native copper, some berries and fruits, 'red willows,' and red cedars" (7). Iroquoian peoples readily collected red-colored objects, including copper-alloy items, red glass beads, and red stone. Red stone was used to make a variety of ornamental forms, including beads, pendants, effigies, maskettes, and pipes.

Eighteenth-century red stone assemblages from Iroquoian sites in New York and Pennsylvania are composed of two main material types. The first is *red pipestone*, a red, siliceous, indurated clay (Rapp and Hill 1998: 124) derived from sources in Minnesota, Wisconsin, Ohio, South Dakota, Kansas, and Arizona (Sigstad 1973). Red pipestone is often referred to as catlinite in the archaeological literature. However, the term *catlinite* is properly confined to a subset of red pipestone quarried from Pipestone National Monument in southwestern Minnesota (Gundersen 1993). The more generic term *red pipestone* should be used for any specimen that has not been sourced conclusively to this area. Red pipestone is characterized by its relative softness, its internal consistency, and the presence of small, light-colored spots within its matrix. I argue in this chapter that fluctuations in Iroquois use of exotic red pipestone provides an index of their interaction with western Indians and of their participation as geographic middlemen.

The second red stone material commonly found on Iroquoian sites in New York and Pennsylvania is *red slate*.[6] Red slate is a relatively coarse material within which cleavage planes are visible to the naked eye. In contrast to red pipestone, red slate could be found within easy quarrying distance from Iroquois territory, with sources near the present-day New York–Vermont border (T. Tanner 1995: 49). Red slate artifacts may derive from the same sources in Washington County, New York, that later produced "New York unfading red" roofing slate for Euro-Americans.[7] Since both red pipestone and red slate are of roughly the same color and both materials were used to make beads and other objects of personal adornment, it is possible that Iroquois peoples used the materials interchangeably, at least to a degree. To gain a comprehensive view of Iroquois red stone use, the volume and relative proportions of red pipestone and red slate on Iroquois sites need to be compared over time.

The presence of red pipestone in eighteenth-century Six Nations sites can be linked fairly conclusively to interaction with western Indian nations, including Ottawas, Foxes, Potawatomis, Miamis, Ojibwas (most frequently referred to as "Mississaugas" in the New York documents), and Huron/Wyandots. Historical documents and archaeological evidence indicate that these groups traversed Iroquois territory on their way to Albany or Oswego during the first half of the eighteenth century, and that they used red pipestone both for personal adornment and in diplomatic negotiations with the Iroquois. These groups' eighteenth-century territories (themselves poorly understood; see various entries in Trigger 1978b) do not appear to coincide with red pipestone source locations in Wisconsin and Minnesota. French reports from the late seventeenth and early eighteenth centuries suggest that the Minnesota pipestone quarries were within Yankton Sioux or Ioway territories (D. Scott et al. 2006: 68–70). Western Indians who traveled to Albany and Oswego were one or two steps removed from these quarries in trade and possibly made direct quarrying expeditions to them.

There is copious evidence for the use of red pipestone at sites on the Straits of Mackinac frequented by Ottawa, Huron/Wyandot, or Ojibwa populations at the turn of the eighteenth century, including Marquette Mission, Lasanen, and Gros Cap (Branstner 1992; Cleland 1971; Nern and

Cleland 1974). Red pipestone was used at the 1680–1730 Bell site in Winnebago County, Wisconsin, probably occupied by Foxes (Quimby 1966: ch. 9), and the 1740–1765 Ottawa or Ojibwa Fletcher site in Bay City, Michigan (Mainfort 1979). The use of red pipestone by Far Indians in negotiations with the Iroquois is illustrated by the presentation of a red pipe by what likely was a group of Mississaugas to Iroquois representatives in Seneca territory in January of 1708. New York official Cadwallader Colden's remark that "a large red stone pipe wch is the greatest present or token used by those Nations in their Treaties" (Colden 1935 [1720]: 364; see also Havard 2001: 81; McIlwain 1915: 52) indicates that this was not a unique occurrence. Archaeological evidence also demonstrates that unmodified red pipestone was brought east and that bead manufacture took place on Iroquois sites.

The red stone sample from the 1996–2000 domestic-context excavations at Townley-Read (figure 10.2) consists of only nine objects: three finished red pipestone beads, one red pipestone bead discarded at a late stage of manufacture (here termed a "bead reject"), one small red pipestone fragment that may be manufacturing debris, three red slate bead rejects, and one probable red slate core. This small sample suggests that both red pipestone and red slate ornaments were manufactured on-site; several samples of small red-colored stone bits that may be in situ manufacturing debris also were recovered via flotation. Although the most extensive excavation took place in Area D, eight of the nine red stone artifacts were found in Area H, possibly suggesting differential household access to red stone.

The sizable collections of red stone artifacts from 1688–1754 Seneca sites curated at RMSC provide a sample large enough to discern temporal trends. The 1688–1754 Seneca red stone assemblage consists of 416 red pipestone and 253 red slate items; 25 artifacts whose raw material could not be specified were excluded from this study. Most of these items were derived from mortuary contexts. For this analysis the assemblage was divided into two temporal groups (see chapter 6 for site details): the first ($n = 191$) contains materials from the White Springs and Snyder-McClure sites, settled in 1688 in the wake of the Denonville expedition and abandoned between 1710 and 1715; the second ($n = 478$) contains materials from sites occupied during 1715–1754, including Townley-Read, Huntoon, Hazlet, Zindall, and Kendaia (analyzed materials from Kendaia derive from what Schoff termed the "Jesuit" cemetery, which dates to the early part of the site's occupation).

Table 10.5 presents data on the RMSC Seneca red stone assemblage, broken down by raw material, time period, and degree of artifact comple-

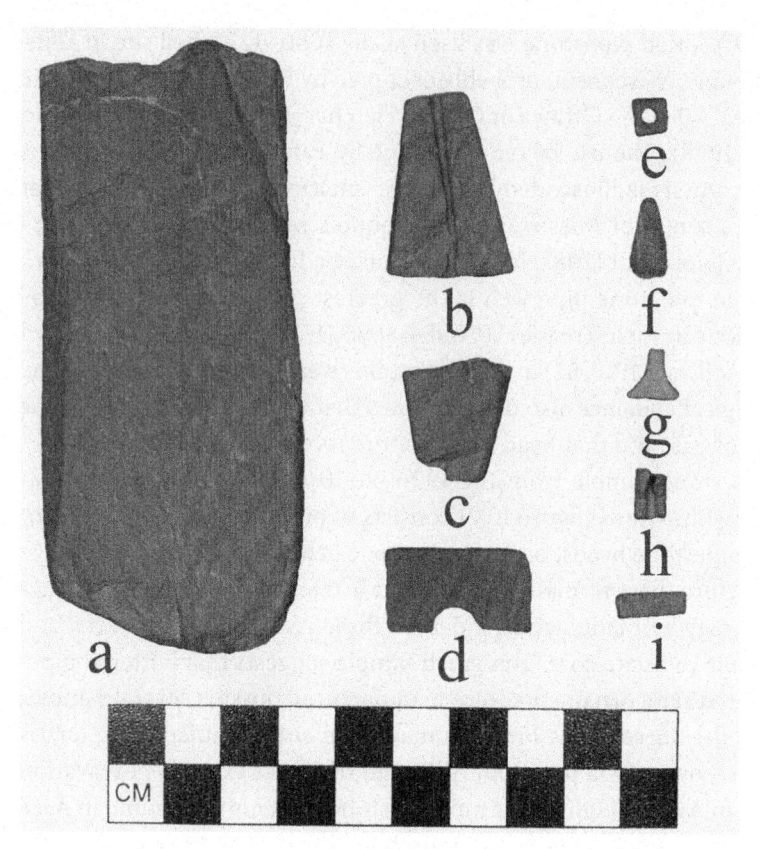

Figure 10.2. Red stone artifacts recovered during Townley-Read fieldwork: *a.* probable red slate core; *b–c.* trapezoidal red slate bead rejects broken during manufacture; *d.* square red slate bead reject broken during manufacture; *e.* complete square red pipestone bead; *f.* complete triangular red pipestone bead; *g.* complete biconcave red pipestone bead; *h.* tubular red pipestone bead reject broken during manufacture; *i.* unperforated rectangular red pipestone fragment. (Photo by the author.)

tion. Seneca raw material use was distinctly different in the two periods: red slate makes up 54 percent of the 1688–1715 red stone assemblage, but only 31 percent in 1715–1754. If only finished artifacts are considered, the proportions change slightly: red slate makes up 42 percent (61 of 146) of finished artifacts in 1688–1715 and 31 percent (145 of 466) of finished artifacts in 1715–1754. Using either measure, the proportion of red pipestone increases dramatically in the later period. There also appears to have been considerably less manufacture of red slate ornaments on Seneca sites in 1715–1754.

Table 10.5. Distribution of Seneca Red Stone Artifacts in the RMSC Collections, by Raw Material, Time Period, and Degree of Completion, 1688–1754

	1688–1715		1715–1754		
	Red Pipestone	Red Slate	Red Pipestone	Red Slate	Total
Unfinished artifacts	3	42	7	5	57
Finished artifacts	85	61	321	145	612
Total	88	103	328	150	669

The analysis can be sharpened by assessing the proportions of red pipestone and red slate in specific contexts. Since the vast majority of the RMSC assemblage was derived from mortuary contexts, this can be done by examining (1) the number of graves containing red stone; and (2) red stone's proportion within total grave offerings during each period. There are eleven well-documented graves from the 1688–1715 sites, and forty-six from the 1715–1754 sites.

At the 1688–1715 sites, only three pieces of red pipestone were found in well-documented graves, divided between two burials. No red slate was found in any of the well-documented assemblages, although poorly contextualized records suggest that red slate was present in graves at Snyder-McClure. In contrast, twenty-three, or fully 50 percent, of 1715–1754 graves contained red stone. Of these, fifteen graves contained solely red pipestone, with an average of 6.2 pieces per grave; one grave contained red slate alone (1 piece); and seven graves contained artifacts of both materials, with an average of 14 pieces of red pipestone, 2.3 pieces of red slate, and 1.1 pieces of undetermined red stone each. Eight graves contained ten or more pieces of red pipestone, and two graves each contained exactly thirty-seven red stone specimens. The maximum amount of red slate included in a 1715–1754 burial is eight pieces.

Clearly, mortuary use of red pipestone increased in the later period; there was a wider distribution of red pipestone during 1715–1754, and some individuals were buried with greater amounts of it. The picture is less clear regarding red slate, but there was only one instance of independent use of red slate in the second period; the material was used intermixed with red pipestone in all other cases.

A second way to assess changes in the consumption of red pipestone is to examine the proportion of red stone in overall grave offerings. This is done by determining the total count of artifacts known to have come from mortuary contexts for each period, regardless of whether exact provenience information is available. This offerings inventory method has the advantage of expanding sample size, which is especially necessary for the 1688–1715 period where well-contextualized data are limited.[8]

Using the total modified artifact count, the percentage of red stone rather counterintuitively *declines* in 1715–1754: red stone artifacts make up 1.4 percent of total offerings in 1688–1715 (45 of 3,244) but only 0.5 percent of the total in 1715–1754 (277 of 53,339). This decline is the product of an enormous increase in glass bead use during 1715–1754: glass beads increase from 74.6 percent of total offerings in 1688–1715 to 96.1 percent in 1715–1754. To eliminate this complicating factor, glass beads were excluded from subsequent calculations. Red stone's part in the total non-glass offering assemblage increases from 5.5 percent in 1688–1715 to 13.5 percent in 1715–1754, which is much more in line with the increased use of red stone in individual graves noted earlier. Most of the change is attributable to greater use of red pipestone, which represents only 1.8 percent of non-glass offerings in 1688–1715 but 10.5 percent of the non-glass assemblage in 1715–1754. Red slate use decreased over the same period, declining from 3.5 percent of non-glass offerings in 1688–1715 to 2.5 percent in 1715–1754. This was accompanied by what appears to be a substantial drop-off in the on-site manufacture of red slate ornaments. The substitution of an exotic material for one available immediately adjacent to Iroquois territory suggests that a ready supply of red pipestone may have been available to Senecas throughout the 1715–1754 period.

These archaeological trends are consistent with increased Seneca interaction with western Indian groups. This interaction most likely took place in a geographic middleman context where western Indians provided gifts to the Senecas during the establishment and renewal of the culturally mandated alliances needed for safe passage across Seneca territory. Western Indians probably began to supply Senecas with red pipestone during the 1701–1713 period of uncertainty, when western groups began to travel to Albany in limited numbers. These initial forays are likely to have introduced the small amounts of red pipestone found at Snyder-McClure and White Springs. Documentary sources indicate that the passage of western Indians to Albany reached a peak during what I have termed the middleman period (1713–1724), the initiation of which roughly corresponds with the founding of the 1715–1754 sites examined here.

Four factors suggest that western Indian transit across Seneca territory continued throughout the 1724–1754 Oswego era. First, Far Indians still needed to cross Seneca territory to reach Oswego, even if they only made brief overnight stays while using the all-water route along the south shore of

Lake Ontario. A 1730 document, written six years after the British founded the post at Oswego, confirms this point. In it New York officials expressed concern about the possibility that French agent Louis-Thomas Chabert de Joncaire would establish a post at Irondequoit, where "foreign Indians especially must pass and repass to and from Oswego, and frequently the Foreign Indians stop there and go by land to the Sinnekes to furnish themselves with provisions, and the Sinnekes very often repass that way from their Beaver hunting" (NYCD 5: 911). Second, documentary sources indicate that the level of trade at Oswego (and therefore middleman traffic) was variable but remained intermittently brisk up to and including the boom years of 1749 and 1750 (see chapter 3 and earlier in this chapter). Third, Senecas remained active in soliciting western Indians to come to Oswego (chapter 3). Lastly, the 1730 document reveals that western Indians went *out of their way* to visit Seneca villages, almost certainly not merely to obtain provisions (the reason attributed to them by Europeans) but also to negotiate alliances. The locations of Seneca settlements did not shift toward Lake Ontario after the founding of Niagara and Oswego, suggesting that the mechanisms that secured the alliance of western Indian travelers during the middleman period continued to work after the construction of the European trading posts/forts. That western Indians in 1730 were willing to make an overland trek totaling 50 km or more indicates that establishing and maintaining alliances with Seneca middlemen was still of vital importance.

The increased presence of red stone can be taken as an indicator that other goods which have left no archaeological traces—most particularly finished beaver pelts, which were still readily available in the West—also were distributed by western Indians to Iroquois middlemen. Middleman traffic continued to provide economic and political support to the Senecas for as long as Oswego continued to be a center of trade. Additionally, the middleman role gave Senecas a further *local* means of involvement in the fur trade, supplementing the new emphasis on deer hunting and deerskin production.

The Archaeology of Seneca Alcohol Consumption

Scholars view alcohol abuse as one of the main social ills of eighteenth-century Iroquois society, and on occasion alcohol has been cited as one of the causes of settlement dispersal and decreased household size. For example, Richter (1992: 266) states that alcohol's "misfortunes were social as well as medical and were probably one reason that many people abandoned compact settlements, communal longhouses, or Iroquoia entirely." This proposition has important implications for the interpretation of Seneca residential dispersal and the decrease in household size that likely accompanied it.

The issue of Iroquois alcohol abuse is complex (Conrad 1999; Mancall 1995; Richter 1992: 85–86) and cannot be discussed in full here. It appears that the Iroquois valued the psychological and sensory distortions induced by alcohol, and may have used alcohol as a "shortcut" to similar states that otherwise required extensive training, self-discipline, and self-deprivation to achieve. Senecas in the 1760s consumed alcohol in association with funerals and mourning (Hulbert and Schwarze 1912: 85; Pilkington 1980: 12). Iroquois leaders also may have used alcohol as a component in feasting behaviors for mobilizing labor, something that frequently has been noted cross-culturally (for example, Dietler 1998). Alcohol was consumed by Six Nations people mainly in group settings, where violence took place with some frequency and deaths sometimes occurred; Iroquois wintertime drinkers also died from exposure.

It is difficult to ascertain temporal trends in Iroquois alcohol consumption using documentary sources because texts describe Iroquois drunkenness with the same highly colored rhetoric regardless of when they were written. Evidence that the situation became more grave over the eighteenth century includes documentary mention of the spread of alcohol abuse to demographic sectors beyond the original drinking population of "young men"; increased reports of drinking within Iroquois villages; and more frequent mention of alcohol-related deaths (see chapter 3). Haan (1976: 234) and Richter (1992: 267) are probably correct in stating that alcohol abuse at least occasionally interfered with Iroquois subsistence by the middle of the eighteenth century, although Haan's supporting evidence (Beauchamp 1916: 199–200) actually refers to Nanticoke refugees living in the Upper Susquehanna Valley, a group in a significantly different political-economic position than homeland Iroquois were.

One should not assume that a linear increase in Iroquois alcohol consumption took place over time. Haan (1976) poses a three-stage model for Iroquois alcohol abuse, claiming there was an early period of severe abuse in the 1670s and 1680s, followed by a lull, then a "reintroduction" after the 1724 construction at Oswego. He states,

> Perhaps more damaging to Iroquois society was the reintroduction of rum to the longhouse [Six Nations territory]. When trade had been conducted at Albany, most drinking occurred before the Iroquois re-

turned home. As the trade at Oswego grew, so did the ease with which Iroquois hunters could bring rum into their villages. By the late 1720s, the towns of the Six Nations began to re-experience the drunken and usually violent brawls that had erupted in the 1670s and 1680s. (Haan 1976: 233)

Haan's model suggests that alcohol consumption was *at a low* during the 1710–1720 era in which Seneca settlement dispersal took place, contradicting Richter's (1992: 266) claim that alcohol abuse was severe during the period in which settlement dispersal took place and was at least partly responsible for it.

Given that documentary sources have been used to come to these diametrically opposed conclusions, it makes sense to examine archaeological evidence for alcohol consumption. Alcohol availability *within* Seneca villages can be assessed by comparing the number of alcohol-related container fragments found at Seneca sites over time. Iroquois peoples acquired alcohol in many types of containers, including kegs of varying sizes and glass and ceramic bottles. Comprehensive study of all varieties of alcohol-related artifacts is needed, but I will limit my discussion here to olive and light blue-green bottle glass. This is a viable, if partial, domain of study for several reasons. First, bottle glass is *representative* of Iroquois alcohol consumption as a whole because smaller glass bottles were cheaper and easier to transport and therefore would have been obtained at least as regularly as larger containers. Second, olive and light blue-green glass bottles were used almost exclusively to store and transport alcohol (Brain 1979, 1988; Noel Hume 1969), making analysis of artifact function much less ambiguous than it is for kegs, which also were used for gunpowder and other substances. Third, bottle glass fragments are durable, and are preserved more consistently than the wood and iron remnants of kegs. Lastly, ceramic bottles are quite rare on late seventeenth- and eighteenth-century Iroquois sites.

If alcohol abuse played a significant role in Seneca community dispersal, as Richter (1992: 266) asserts, one would expect to see substantial accumulations of olive and light blue-green bottle glass at the sites that immediately preceded dispersal. If Haan's model is correct, one would expect lesser amounts of bottle glass at sites occupied between 1690 and 1724. While the 1688–1715 White Springs and Snyder-McClure sites are key to the evaluation of these models in the Seneca region, alcohol bottle use must be contextualized by using longer spans of archaeological data from the eastern Sen-

Table 10.6. Olive and Light Blue-Green Bottle Glass at Seneca Sites, 1688–1754

Site[a]	Dates	Total Surface Items	17th & 18th c. Bottle Glass	Bottle Glass (%)	Thorough Surface Collection?	Bottle Glass in Other Contexts?
Snyder-McClure (RMSC)	1688–1710/5	563	0	0.0	no	yes
White Springs (RMSC)	1688–1715	233	0	0.0	yes	yes
White Springs (Frost)	1688–1715	196	1	0.5	yes	yes
Townley-Read (RMSC)	1715–1754	569	21	3.7	yes	yes
Townley-Read: Area D (TR/NG Nov. 1999)	1715–1754	124[b]	6	4.8	yes	yes
Townley-Read: Area H (TR/NG summer 2000)	1715–1754	142[b]	16	11.3	yes	yes
Huntoon (RMSC)	1710/5–1740	12	0	0.0	no	yes

Notes: a. RMSC: Rochester Museum and Science Center Collections; TR/NG: Townley-Read/New Ganechstage Project; Frost: Eugene Frost Collection (Dewbury and Ryan n.d.)
b. Excludes animal bone and tooth finds.

eca (Ganondagan, White Springs, and Townley-Read) and western Seneca (Rochester Junction, Snyder-McClure, and Huntoon) village sequences (see figures 6.2, 6.3, and 6.5). Due to the lack of well-documented excavations at many of these sites, this analysis also draws on surface-collected materials housed at RMSC and in the private collection of Eugene Frost of Montour Falls, New York (Dewbury and Ryan 2008). Although provenience information for surface collections is often minimal, they presumably sampled the full range of contexts present at a site, including house lots, activity areas, trash middens, and cemeteries. Use of surface collections improves sample sizes and minimizes the biases involved in concentrating on particular contexts; at Townley-Read, for example, bottle glass is rare in mortuary deposits but ubiquitous in domestic contexts.

Data from the 1670–1687 Ganondagan and Rochester Junction sites have not been fully compiled for all types of contexts but they suggest that olive and light blue-green bottle glass were relatively common. Domestic-context excavations at Ganondagan recovered twenty-six seventeenth- or eighteenth-century bottle glass fragments from Trench 4 plowzone contexts in the immediate vicinity of the short longhouse structure; no bottle glass was recovered in situ from Trench 4 features (Dean 1984: 37). Some of the plowzone glass may derive from the early part of the post-1790 Euro-American occupation of the site (see Huey 1994). Olive bottle glass is present in surface collections from the western Rochester Junction site, which are curated at RMSC, but since the overall surface assemblage has not been tabulated the proportion of bottle glass within it is uncertain.

Table 10.6 summarizes information on bottle glass at the four later Seneca sites. Data from Snyder-McClure and Huntoon are derived from surface-collected and mortuary-context materials in the RMSC collections; the White Springs data are from the RMSC and Eugene Frost collections; and the Townley-Read data derive from RMSC and domestic-context investigations by the Townley-Read/New Ganechstage Project (figure 10.3)

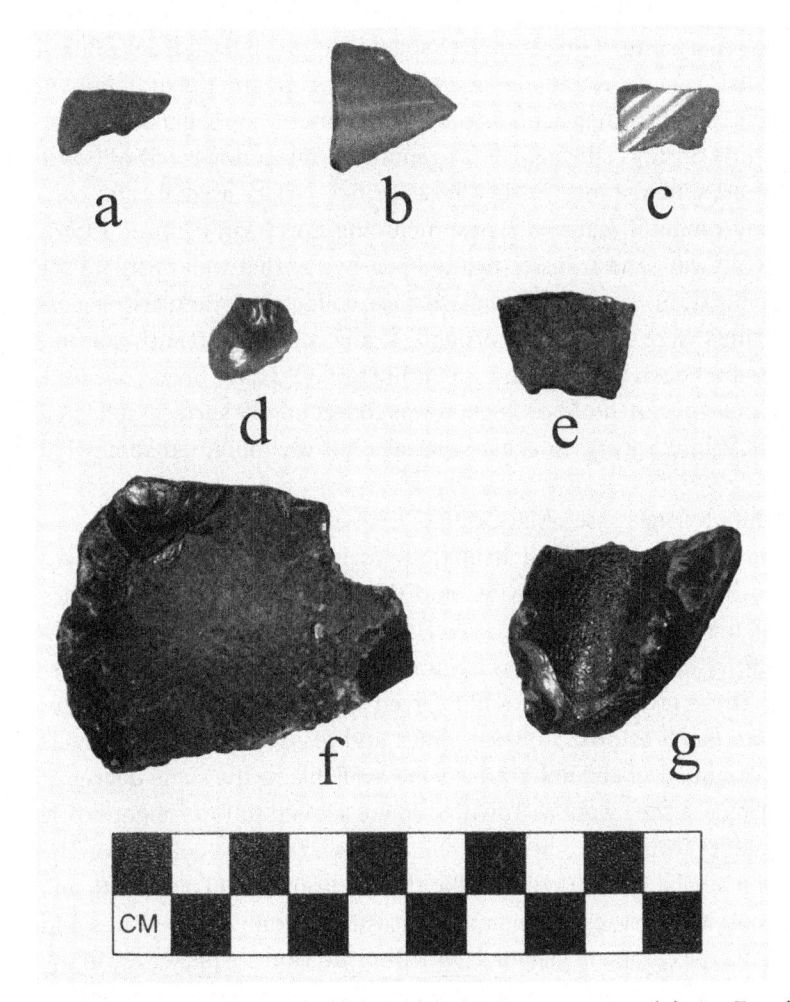

Figure 10.3. Eighteenth-century bottle glass fragments recovered during Townley-Read fieldwork: *a*. emerald green body fragment; *b*. aqua green body fragment; *c*. light blue-green body fragment; *d*. olive glass shard, probably knapped; *e*. dark olive body fragment; *f*. dark olive base fragment with shallow kick-up; *g*. dark olive heel fragment. (Photo by the author.)

Although no bottle glass fragments were found in the sizable surface collection from the western Snyder-McClure site, this information must be interpreted with caution. The surface-collection inventory consists primarily of adornment items made from brass, glass, red stone, and shell, presumably indicating that the collection is biased against relatively prosaic domestic-context items like bottle glass. This point is reinforced by the fact that there is no surface-collected iron from the site. A limited amount of bottle glass from non-surface contexts is present in the Snyder-McClure collections, consisting of one complete small light green flask from a burial and four olive, one clear, and one aqua bottle glass fragments of unknown provenience. On the other hand, the small amount of bottle glass from the eastern White Springs site appears to genuinely reflect low levels of bottle use by the site's inhabitants. Both White Springs surface assemblages contain a broad range of material types, including European ceramic sherds (such as whiteware and transfer-printed pearlware) that well postdate the Seneca occupation, suggesting that surface-collection practices used at White Springs were relatively thorough. If any other eighteenth-century bottle glass had been found at the site, it likely would have been collected. That only one specimen of bottle glass was found in 429 surface-collected artifacts at White Springs suggests that alcohol was obtained somewhat rarely.[9]

The White Springs assemblage differs dramatically from materials surface-collected at Townley-Read. In all three surface collections from Townley-Read—that preserved at RMSC and the Area D and Area H surface collections made by the Townley-Read/New Ganechstage Project—eighteenth-century bottle glass makes up at least 3.7 percent of the overall assemblage. These proportions would be even higher if materials from later components (such as post-1790 ceramics and glass, brick, and drainage tile) were excluded. If alcohol bottles were available to the same degree at White Springs as they were at Townley-Read, sixteen to forty-eight bottle glass fragments would have been recovered in a 429-piece collection. The amount of material surface-collected at the Huntoon site (Townley-Read's western contemporary) is quite small, consisting of only twelve brass and iron items. Three complete glass bottles from Huntoon are preserved in the RMSC collections, two from mortuary deposits and one from an unknown provenience.

Archaeological evidence for the sequence of alcohol bottle availability at eastern Seneca village sites is clear-cut: bottle glass fragments were relatively common at Ganondagan, rare at White Springs, and found readily within every investigated house lot at the Townley-Read site. Although it is based on a subset of alcohol-related material culture, eastern Seneca patterns of bottle glass usage mirror Haan's model of Iroquois alcohol consumption perfectly. Evaluation of the western Seneca sequence remains incomplete; the RMSC collections from Rochester Junction have not been thoroughly examined by the author, and consideration of Snyder-McClure and Huntoon is hampered by collection bias and very small sample sizes.

This information suggests that Iroquois access to alcohol was based on *proximity* and *prosperity*. As Mancall (1995: 7) notes, modern studies have found that proximity to a steady supply of alcohol is a major factor determining the level of its consumption. Fluctuations in Seneca access to Europeans closely correlate with the archaeologically perceived level of Seneca alcohol consumption. Ganondagan was located fairly close to Irondequoit Bay, which made the site quite accessible to Europeans. Additionally, boat-based French traders are known to have exchanged with Iroquois at Niagara (D. Kent 1974: 42, 46; NYCD 3: 442, 9: 287) and likely Irondequoit (NYCD 9: 229) during the 1670s and 1680s. In contrast, the post-Denonville sites of Snyder-McClure and White Springs were more isolated from Lake Ontario, and European visits were irregular, particularly after the expulsion of the Jesuits in 1709. The apparent increase in alcohol availability in the 1720s seen at Townley-Read and in documentary sources can be accounted for by the construction of trading posts/forts near Seneca territory at Niagara and especially the much closer post at Oswego. Several historians (for example, Haan 1976, 1980; McConnell 1992: 18; Richter 1992) have posited that trade at Oswego was the primary reason why alcohol became much more prevalent in Iroquois villages after 1724.

Prosperity is an equally important part of the picture. The 1670s and 1680s were a peak in political-economic prosperity for the Five Nations. Iroquois military power produced ready access to beaver pelts, which could be converted into a steady supply of European goods, including alcohol. The prosperity of this period also is reflected in the plethora of wampum beads and gun parts found at 1650–1687 Seneca sites, including Dann, Marsh, Rochester Junction, and Ganondagan (Ryan and Dewbury 2010; Sempowski 1986; Wray 1985: 106–7). Given the political-economic downturn that began following the Denonville invasion and lasted until the beginning of the middleman era in 1713, it is not surprising that alcohol was less readily available to Senecas during 1687–1713.

The period following 1713 is more problematic, since it is difficult to determine where alcohol obtained out of prosperity ends and alcohol obtained out of addiction, using furs and skins that might better have secured utilitarian items, begins. As noted in chapter 2, the "alcohol brawls" witnessed by Cammerhoff in 1750 in the Seneca villages at Canandaigua and Zonesschio/Fall Brook coincided with a two-year peak in the Oswego fur trade that followed the end of King George's War and were unlikely to have been typical occurrences. However, the repeated instances of alcohol-related distress recorded in primary sources suggest that alcohol likely proved intermittently disruptive to the New Ganechstage Senecas throughout the Oswego era.

In terms of the overall argument regarding the motivations for and consequences of settlement dispersal, the alcohol bottle evidence appears most consistent with the contention that the main increase in Seneca alcohol consumption came *after* settlement dispersal, not before. Richter's claim that alcohol abuse contributed to community dispersal and decreased household size should be reflected by substantial evidence for alcohol consumption at the White Springs site, which was occupied immediately prior to the community segmentation and site-level dispersal seen in the New Ganechstage Site Complex. This does not appear to be the case, reinforcing the conclusion that dispersal took place for *positive* rather than negative reasons.

11

Turning Points in Iroquois History

A Re-Evaluation

Seneca settlement dispersal at New Ganechstage was an opportunistic development, carried out when Senecas took advantage of a period of relative peace to create a localized economy. Seneca women lived closer to fields and water sources, men were able to hunt a resurgent local deer population for subsistence and the fur trade, and the politically and economically advantageous geographic middleman position was developed and maintained. Dispersed settlement sustained core principles of Seneca subsistence and culture, including agriculture centered on maize, beans, and squash; animal use based on wild rather than domesticated animals; and houses constructed using Iroquois architectural principles. Senecas incorporated European technology and domesticated species, but they did so selectively, adopting only those aspects of European culture that fit within their own system of extensive agriculture, hunting, gathering, and communal land access. A close look at regionally specific archaeological and historical evidence reveals a Seneca culture that is much more dynamic and viable than the usual portrayal in the historical and anthropological literature on the Iroquois of the early eighteenth century.

Scholars generally have viewed Iroquois history within a paradigm of gradual decay. Within the confines of this defeatist narrative, any sort of evidence for change is taken as decline. Iroquois populations are portrayed as passive, buffeted by the upheavals of their engagement with Europeans. But what happens to this narrative of decline if significant and reasonably sustainable political, economic, and ecological innovation is acknowledged to have taken place on Iroquoia's "western door" in the early eighteenth century?

Scholars differ on what allegedly initiated the decline of the Iroquois, emphasizing various causal factors and focusing on different time periods.

In general, scholars have identified five main turning points that they claim initiated Iroquois decline. Not all of these accounts align perfectly with one another, and some are mutually contradictory; it is perhaps best to think of each as a model to be tested. Since many of these models cite changes in Iroquois community structure and household form as evidence supporting their case, the data gathered for this volume are particularly pertinent to the evaluation of these five positions.

The first model holds that Iroquois matrilineal institutions were unable to endure the demographic upheavals caused by European-borne epidemic diseases and the warfare and adoption that accompanied them; these upheavals began in the seventeenth and continued into the eighteenth century. A second position maintains that the Iroquois never recovered from their military defeats in the Twenty Years' War, notably the 1687 defeat of the Senecas by the Denonville expedition. Proponents of a third model argue that the Iroquois were defeated and dominated by the unilateral European construction of trading posts/forts at Niagara and Oswego from 1718 to 1724. A fourth interpretation claims that the Iroquois political-economic position was undermined by the shift in European fur trade interests away from Iroquoia to the Ohio and Mississippi valleys in the 1740s and the elimination of the French from Canada in 1760. The final model maintains that Iroquois autonomy was undermined by European territorial encroachment and reservationization after the American Revolution. This chapter summarizes the main points of these models and evaluates each in light of the archaeological and documentary evidence set forth in this study, demonstrating that many of these models fit neither the Seneca region nor the rest of the Confederacy particularly well.

Matrilineal Disintegration

The evidence that European-borne epidemic diseases caused traumatic and massive episodes of mortality among Six Nations populations is irrefutable. There is some scholarly disagreement about the timing of the first "virgin soil" epidemics that spread among Native American populations with no prior exposure to European microbes, but studies by Snow (1992, 1994, 1996) and Warrick (2003) have determined fairly conclusively that the first episodes of massive mortality postdate 1634 in both the Mohawk and Huron regions, based on documentary evidence and major reductions in total settlement area after this date. Snow (1994: 99–100, table 7.1) estimates that the Mohawks lost more than 63 percent of their population within a few months during the 1634 epidemic, and more epidemics followed in later years. In Iroquoian culture, death generated violence against enemies, because it was one of the few culturally effective ways to assuage mourners' grief. "Mourning war" raids were initiated even in the aftermath of deaths from natural or nonviolent causes, and war losses exacerbated the demographic consequences of epidemics (Richter 1992: 32–36, 57–66; Snow 1994: 110–11).

Snow (1989, 1994, 1995, 1996, 1997) asserts that the massive mortality caused by European-borne epidemics, the resulting warfare, and the widespread incorporation of captives to replenish Iroquois populations undermined Iroquois matrilineal institutions to the point where they were no longer viable. Ramenofsky (1987) reaches similar conclusions, linking demographic problems to changes in Iroquois community structure. She writes that in the eighteenth century "when there were too few people to maintain older settlement structures, new structures evolved. These were associated with the hybridization of population" (97). According to Snow, the decay of matrilineal institutions can be seen archaeologically through the decreasing size and increasing homogeneity of Iroquois houses over time.

Snow's initial case study was based on Mohawk data. He states that by the time of the occupation of the Caughnawaga site in 1679

> the Mohawks were living in standardized houses of three to four hearths. This is consistent with the patterns in other longhouse villages in the region. . . . The reason appears to be that these societies were by this time so fragmented that longhouses no longer expanded and contracted to accommodate changing families. Instead, the longhouse became a standardized form and nuclear families were assigned spaces within them in an ad hoc manner. The sets of nuclear families that occupied the longhouses were now apparently only fictive extended families, although some pretense of common clan affiliation was probably maintained by the female residents. (Snow 1995: 443)

During the eighteenth century, Snow asserts that the demographic situation and matrilineal institutions further disintegrated:

> Both the community and the household were evolving rapidly. Mohawk communities were increasingly scattered collections of small individual family houses, and the traditional longhouse was replaced by a house form that looked superficially European. The matrilocal

principles of residence and the matrilineal clan segments that defined earlier longhouses had been under great stress for a century and a half, and the forced relocations of 1693 facilitated the beginning of the final breakup of longhouses into scattered nuclear family residences. The fragmentation meant that compact palisaded villages were no longer socially possible. (1995: 471)

Snow uses similar logic to explain Seneca evidence. He states that by 1677, "Greenhalgh observed the social consequences that absorption of refugees and captives was having for the Senecas. . . . The Senecas maintained their population at around 4,000 throughout the latter part of the seventeenth century, but so much of it was made up of immigrants that even the standardized longhouse had been abandoned for small extended-family cabins. For the Senecas the longhouse was already just a metaphor" (1994: 124). Snow adds that by 1700 traditional means for obtaining leadership positions through matrilineages and matrilocal residence rules also were breaking down among the Senecas: an "able man . . . had little need to subordinate himself to an elderly longhouse matron, and he would have been motivated to live apart in his own cabin, surrounded by his wife, children, and grandchildren" (131–32).

The main evidence for Snow's (1994: 131) claim that the "social stresses of the seventeenth century had already led to individual or two-family Seneca houses" as early as 1677 appears to be his interpretation and modification of Wentworth Greenhalgh's house count and warrior population figures for the Five Nations. Table 11.1 compares Greenhalgh's unmodified numbers (Snow, Gehring, and Starna 1996: 188–92) with Snow's (1995: table 10.3) modifications of them (in the right-hand column). Snow's interpretation can be questioned from several angles. First, he excludes a sixteen-house village (presumably because it was occupied by Huron refugees) and a small outlying ten-house village (for unspecified reasons) from the Mohawk calculations (Snow 1995: 413–14). At the same time, he does not modify the Mohawk warrior count, increasing the mean number of Mohawk warriors per house from 3.1 to 4.3. Snow places question marks in his table for the total number of Seneca houses and warriors/house ratio, presumably because large numbers of Hurons also had settled in the Seneca region (JR 44: 19, 57: 27). However, there is no indication that Greenhalgh excluded Huron refugees or any other captives from his warrior counts. A more conservative procedure is to calculate the number of warriors per house using Greenhalgh's raw numbers. When this is done, the Seneca figure of 3.1 war-

Table 11.1. Iroquois Village Size and Demography in 1677, after Greenhalgh and Snow

Iroquois Nation	Village Size (Nos. of Houses)	Total Houses	Number of Warriors	Warriors per House (raw data)	Warriors per House (Snow 1995)
Mohawk	30, 24, 16, 16, 10	96	300	3.1	4.3
Oneida	100	100	200	2.0	2.0
Onondaga	140, 24	164	350	2.1	2.1
Cayuga	n/a	100	300	3.0	3.0
Seneca	150, 120, 30, 24	324	1000	3.1	?[a]
Total	range: 10–150	784	2150	2.7	n/a

Sources: Snow (1995: table 10.3); Snow, Gehring, and Starna (1996: 188–92)
Note: a. Snow (1995: table 10.3) uses the question mark in his original table, perhaps because of the presence of Huron refugees in Seneca territory.

riors per house does not stand out from the others; the very low figures for the Oneidas and Onondagas (2.0 and 2.1 warriors per house, respectively) appear more problematic.

Additionally, Greenhalgh's house counts at villages with one hundred or more houses are likely to be inflated (K. Jordan 2004: 46). Adjustment of these figures would increase the Oneida, Onondaga, and Seneca warriors-per-house figures, leaving the Mohawks at the middle to low end of the spectrum. Finally, Snow's reliance on Greenhalgh's house and warrior counts neglects Greenhalgh's description of a multifamily true longhouse as the "ordinary" Seneca house. As outlined in chapter 9, it is likely that these true longhouses predominated in Seneca territory, with a minority of one- (cabin) or two-family (short longhouse) dwellings.

While Snow's conclusions about the dramatic decline in Seneca multifamily living are questionable, the Mohawk data that anchor the matrilineal disintegration hypothesis also require re-evaluation. I begin with Snow's claim that late seventeenth-century Iroquois longhouses were standardized in length and form. At first glance, Caughnawaga (figure 9.3) does appear to have quite uniform longhouse lengths, but other evidence weighs against this interpretation. The occupation of Caughnawaga was truncated by its 1693 destruction by the French; the fourteen-year duration of the site was well under the normal lifespan for a nucleated Iroquoian small village. Most alterations to longhouses presumably would have been made toward the end of a village's occupation, when the village's demographic profile would have differed most from the founding population; Caughnawaga was burned and abandoned before significant demographic changes had taken place. Additionally, there is evidence for at least one compartment addition at Caughnawaga; the squared end of House 8 at the northwest corner of the settlement appears to represent a full living compartment built to replace a rounded, informal vestibule of the type seen at the ends of the other longhouses.

Other evidence for standardization cited by Snow (1989: 296; 1995: 443)—1732 drawings of Potawatomi (Clifton 1978: figure 2), Ottawa (Feest and Feest 1978: figure 4), and Huron-Wyandot (Tooker 1978b: figure 2) villages near Detroit and maps and drawings of the Kahnawake mission on the St. Lawrence—offers poor support to the Caughnawaga example. All the 1732 drawings of standardized longhouses near Detroit appear to have been drawn by the same hand; each may have been a stylized rendition that depicted house lengths as more regular than they really were. Even if these drawings are accurate, only the Huron-Wyandot village offers an example of standardized longhouse construction by a matrilineal, matrilocal group. Potawatomi social organization "strongly emphasizes patrilineal descent" (Clifton 1978: 729), and Ottawas traditionally practiced polygyny (Feest and Feest 1978: 777, 783). The dynamics of household formation in these societies therefore were likely to have been quite different than those of the Iroquois. Images of Kahnawake (for example, Fenton and Tooker 1978: figure 1) also may be stylized; directed culture-change efforts by Jesuit missionaries provide a further complicating factor.

Furthermore, data from other Iroquois sites do not evidence standardization. As discussed in chapter 9, the Seneca villages at Ganondagan and Rochester Junction and the Onondaga Weston site—all contemporaries of the "standardized" Caughnawaga site—exhibited notable intrasite diversity in housing, with the Seneca and Onondaga examples each containing true longhouses in at least two sizes plus smaller, perhaps special-purpose, structures. In the Lower Castle village that succeeded Caughnawaga, Mohawks in 1698 were said to live in houses "some of which contain one family, some two, and some four" (NYCD 4: 345). Later sites such as Onondaga Castle in 1737–1743 also contained a variety of house sizes (chapter 9).

Lastly, the evidence for Iroquois adoption of single-family houses during the seventeenth and eighteenth centuries is quite scanty. The best evidence for pre–Revolutionary War Iroquois adoption of single-family houses is from the Mohawk Valley, and these documentary reports have not been confirmed archaeologically. The alleged transformation in Mohawk housing was more likely to have been a product of European territorial encroachment than matrilineal decline, in that Mohawk families likely dispersed to protect their lands from European settlers. The Mohawk example thus provides a poor model for developments in the rest of the Confederacy (K. Jordan 2009).

Given documentary and archaeological evidence for continued Iroquois multiple-family living up to and beyond the American Revolution (chapters 8–9; K. Jordan 2002: 458–65), the positive reasons for early eighteenth-century Iroquois settlement dispersal (chapter 7), and the empirical problems with Snow's matrilineal disintegration hypothesis, it is possible to interpret the history of Iroquois household formation and social organization very differently. I suggest that matrilineal institutions maintained a central place in Iroquois society up to and throughout the eighteenth century. This premise receives support from both cross-cultural parallels and primary-source documentation of Iroquois references to clan affiliation.

Starting with Lewis Henry Morgan, western analysts of kinship have tended to place undue emphasis on genetic, or "blood," ties (Schneider 1984). Although blood ties undoubtedly were of prime importance to Iroquoian peoples, I caution against the quick dismissal of fictive kinship ties, as Snow did in stating that "some pretense of common clan affiliation was probably maintained by the female residents" in the allegedly standardized longhouses of the late 1600s (1995: 443). Fictive kinship ties in fact are essential to matrilineal systems. Matrilineages, whether Pre- or Postcolumbian, are inherently unstable; there is a chronic demographic problem of matrilineages "expiring" due to the lack of female offspring. Mary Douglas (1971: 127) writes "if a woman dies or is barren the group suffers an irreplaceable loss of reproductive powers. Furthermore she cannot multiply her offspring indefinitely by multiplying the number of her husbands." Lineages, if defined in terms of blood ties, quite often die out; as a consequence, "matrilineal descent groups are organized to recruit members by other means additional to direct lineal descent" (127). Recruiting methods such as adoption of captives de-emphasize blood kinship by eventually incorporating outsiders using fictive kinship ties. The Iroquoian emphasis on *role*, where both individuals related by blood and adopted persons took on the personal names of deceased individuals, functioned to incorporate fictive kinship ties while preserving the overall appearance of blood continuity.

Documentary sources further demonstrate the importance of clans to the Iroquois in the eighteenth century. For example, in 1735 the Jesuit Father Nau mentioned the presence of the bear, wolf, and tortoise clans at Kahnawake (JR: 68: 267), a mission that had been in existence since 1676.

The Moravian Cammerhoff noted of the Seneca settlement at "Ganataqueh" (Canandaigua) in 1750 that houses were "ornamented with red paintings of deer, turtles, bears, etc., designating to what clan the inmates belonged" (Beauchamp 1916: 69), and William Morton saw clan symbols depicted on houses and cooking pots among Tonawanda Senecas in 1798 (Hamell 1992a: 31). This information clearly refutes Richter's claim that no eighteenth-century Iroquois houses "featured the elaborate carvings of clan animals or other figures that adorned the entrances to dwellings a century earlier" (1992: 261). Euro-American captives incorporated into Seneca society during 1755–1781 continued to be placed within a network of matrilineal kin; examples include Mary Jemison (Seaver 1990 [1824]: 18–23), Luke Swetland (Merrifield 1915: 21–22), Peter Crouse (Francello 1980: 15–22), and Horatio Jones (Harris 1903: 416–17). Even some of the most Western of documentary records—census data and war claims inventories—emphasize Iroquois clan affiliation. William Johnson's 1758 census of women and children in the highly impacted Mohawk region (cited in Guldenzopf 1986: 66–67) lists the clan affiliation of almost every person, and the Oneidas' post–Revolutionary War claims were organized by the clan membership of the claimants (Wonderley 1998).

Although the demographic disruptions wrought by European-borne epidemics and post-contact warfare were unprecedented in *scale*, they were not unprecedented in *kind*. Precolumbian Iroquoian populations certainly were subject to episodes of mass mortality brought on by famines and indigenously present epidemic diseases (Saunders 1994). The upheavals following engagement with Europeans likely strengthened those preexisting functions of Iroquois clans that incorporated outsiders. Interaction with Europeans may have further bolstered clan ties by emphasizing endeavors that demanded labor mobilization beyond the individual lineage, such as for war parties and trading expeditions. European diplomatic gifts also supplied influence to the clan leaders who mobilized and organized such labor.

The Twenty Years' War and Loss of Military Power

Several authors (for example, Fenton 1998: 330; Jennings 1984) view the Iroquois defeats and French-sponsored village burnings that took place during the Twenty Years' War of 1680–1701 as a turning point in Iroquois history. Jennings (1984: 187, 191) argues that the Iroquois could no longer act unilaterally in conflicts involving the European empires after the defeats of the Twenty Years' War. Homeland Iroquois peoples certainly refrained from military action in French-British conflicts from 1701 until the Seven Years' War in 1754, with the rather lackluster exceptions of the English expeditions against Canada in 1709 and 1711 and Mohawk participation in King George's War in 1744–1748 (Aquila 1983; Parmenter 2007a). Iroquois military power was not completely eliminated, however, as warriors continued to engage nonlocal Native American opponents throughout the first half of the eighteenth century, particularly in the Southeast (Merrell 1987; Perdue 1987).

While the consequences of the Twenty Years' War may have prevented continuation of the old military ways, they did nothing to prevent the Iroquois from developing new, more diplomatically oriented courses of action (Aquila 1983; Parmenter 1999). The success of the Iroquois neutrality policy cannot be written off simply as the consequence of imperial disinterest in northeastern North America. The initiation of relative local peace in the first half of the eighteenth century should be seen as a major diplomatic accomplishment that permitted the Iroquois to maintain their independence between the French and British for several more decades. In the Seneca region, this relative local peace facilitated settlement dispersal, localized deer hunting, and cultivation of the Seneca geographic middleman position.

Scholars (for example, Taylor 1995: 34; Wallace 1969: 22; Wray 1983: 41) also have posited that Iroquois defeats in the Twenty Years' War played a causal role in settlement dispersal. Snow (1995: 471) asserts that "firearms and advanced tactics in warfare had demonstrated the uselessness of traditional stockaded Mohawk villages. The success of French raids in the seventeenth century shows that nucleated villages of longhouses could not be adequately defended, a realization that removed what may have been the last remaining centripetal influence on Mohawk settlement."

The timing of Iroquois adoption of dispersed communities does not support this scenario. As shown in chapters 6 and 9, there was *continuity* in Five Nations settlement forms in the immediate aftermath of the village burnings of the Twenty Years' War. Nucleated and possibly palisaded settlements—such as the Seneca White Springs and Snyder-McClure sites, the Mohawk Milton Smith and Allen sites, and the Oneida Primes Hill site—continued to be built well after the 1687–1696 village burnings. In the Seneca region, there was a lag of almost thirty years between the Denonville burnings and dispersal at the New Ganechstage Site Complex. The length of time between the village burnings in the late seventeenth century and the construction of dispersed Iroquois communities suggests that the two are not directly related. I argue that it is more profitable to look to the positive, peaceful political-economic conditions of the 1710–1720 era as the cause of most of the Iroquois settlement dispersals.

Once more, the Mohawk situation is atypical. Mohawk villages appear to have dispersed following British construction of Fort Hunter in 1711. Mohawks may have perceived the fort as a citadel where they could retreat in the event of attack (Snow 1995: 471). While Mohawks may have allowed the British to provide for their defense (in the process, of course, avoiding the heavy labor and time expenditures of palisade construction and maintenance), this explanation does not apply to other areas of the Confederacy. Dispersed communities in the Seneca, Onondaga, Cayuga, and Oneida regions appear to have abandoned defensibility *entirely*, and in these areas European forts or citadel-type structures were not built until considerably later. Local dispersal occurred because the political-economic situation allowed it, not because self-defense was hopeless.

The Construction of European Trading Posts/Forts at Niagara and Oswego

In his dissertation on 1697–1730 Iroquois diplomacy, Richard Haan (1976) outlines what he interprets as the genesis and dissolution of an Iroquois political-economic scheme that involved maintaining military neutrality between the European powers and encouraging western Indian groups to trade with merchants in Albany. He asserts that this scheme quickly unraveled following construction of the permanent, fortified European outposts at Niagara and Oswego, and that the existence of these posts proves that Iroquois political, economic, and territorial integrity had been fundamentally compromised. This thesis has been adopted and extended by many subsequent researchers, most notably by Richter (1992; see also McConnell 1992). While Haan's interpretation of the 1701–1724 period largely coincides with my own (see chapter 3), I differ with Haan and Richter regarding the consequences of the Niagara and Oswego posts.

For Haan, the French and British trading posts/forts were built in order to undermine the Iroquois geographic middleman position. The British tried to get closer to western pelt sources, while the French reacted to the pro-British slant of Iroquois trade policy, which endangered French alliances with western nations and threatened to cut New France out of the fur trade altogether. Haan (1976: 230) emphasizes Iroquois inability to prevent the founding and subsequent fortification of the European outposts, claiming that Niagara and Oswego "mocked" Iroquois sovereignty and demonstrated that the Six Nations were no longer masters over their own land. Haan concludes that the "completion of Forts Oswego and Niagara in the fall of 1727 signaled defeat for the Six Nations in the diplomatic struggle over the Niagara frontier.... By 1730 the Iroquois' territorial integrity had been questioned, their participation in the western trade constricted, and their society afflicted by problems associated with the shifting of trade from Albany to Oswego" (234–37).

Haan vastly overstates the short-term danger to the Six Nations, and to Senecas in particular. The forts at Niagara and Oswego certainly questioned Iroquois territorial integrity: any Iroquois person could look to the effects of the 1711 construction of Fort Hunter and imagine wagonloads of European settlers in their future. Nonetheless, such settlement in large part did not take place until a much later date and under significantly different political-economic conditions. The numbers of Europeans around Niagara and Oswego remained small and consisted primarily of soldiers and traders. Construction of other European forts outside the Mohawk Valley did not occur until the early years of the Seven Years' War (1754–1763), and the 1756 fort built in Seneca territory was never garrisoned (Pilkington 1980: 11). Up to the American Revolution, few Europeans lived permanently in Iroquois territory outside the Mohawk region, with the largest European concentrations interspersed with multinational Indian settlements on the Upper Susquehanna River rather than around forts. While Niagara and Oswego may have *presaged* the eventual loss of Iroquois territory, to say that Iroquois "defeat" took place in the 1720s or 1730s is to mistake an instance of foreshadowing for the event itself.

The same objection can be raised regarding Haan's position on the western trade. His conclusion that after Oswego the "Iroquois would soon lose all opportunity to profit from Indians passing through Iroquois villages" (1976: 220) overlooks the continued geographic middleman role of some Iroquois groups. Archaeological finds of large quantities of red pipestone (chapter 10), documentary evidence such as the 1730 text describing western Indians trekking overland from Irondequoit to Seneca villages (NYCD 5: 911), and trade figures showing an intermittently high volume of fur and skin exports from New York indicate that western Iroquois nations such as the Senecas and Cayugas, whose territory lay between western Indians and Oswego, continued to profit from middleman traffic. The overall value of the western trade to the Iroquois was diminished (especially for eastern Iroquois nations) but in no way eliminated by the constructions at Niagara and Oswego.

Haan also outlines some negative social consequences of the European outposts, concluding that by the 1730s "the establishments on Lake Ontario, especially Oswego, accelerated the corrosion of Iroquois society" (1976: 231). Haan particularly emphasizes the disruptive effects of alcohol obtained at Oswego, stating that it caused violence, deaths, subsistence problems, and emigration among the Six Nations (234). Haan makes a valuable contribution by demonstrating how major instances of eighteenth-century Iroquois alcohol abuse took place following the founding of Oswego (and therefore, I would add, after Iroquois community dispersal). However, his depiction of the corrosive social effects of alcohol abuse must be tempered because the drinking took place within Iroquois groups that had more economic, cultural, and territorial integrity than Haan allows.

Richter's *The Ordeal of the Longhouse* (1992) goes beyond Haan in its attempt to link broad political-economic trends of the early eighteenth century to community-level changes in Iroquois village location, settlement structure, and house forms. This ambitious effort represents exactly the type of integration of "top-down" diplomatic data with "bottom-up" community-level evidence that historians and archaeologists need to undertake. Richter's model encounters substantial problems, however. First, the timing of settlement changes does not coincide with the most severe periods of Iroquois economic dislocation; second, the evidence for European "economic domination" is not as strong as he claims. Lastly, the "crisis" mode of the interpretation cannot be sustained without support from the community- and household-level portions of the argument.

Richter's reasoning must be examined carefully since his work provides the most detailed model to date for the causes of eighteenth-century transformations in Iroquois settlement and household forms. Richter begins his final chapter, titled "The Iroquois in a Euro-American World," by stating that in the late 1720s and 1730s

> dependence had moved well beyond the simply economic. While each of the Six Nations retained control over much of their day-to-day lives and culture, fundamental political and diplomatic decisions now lay in Euro-American hands. A survey of conditions in Iroquoia reveals that the era of European *colonization* was over; the Six Nations now ranked among the *colonized*. (1992: 256–57; emphasis in original)

He adds that "some of the problems of the late 1720s and 1730s were reflected in transformations in residence patterns" (256), such as emigration from the Iroquois homeland, construction of dispersed hamlets instead of nucleated villages, and abandonment of communal longhouses. Richter immediately runs into timing problems, however. By his own account, settlement dispersal took place in the first two decades of the eighteenth century (257–60), well before the "problems of the late 1720s and 1730s." The evidence presented in this book underscores this point: Senecas founded the dispersed New Ganechstage Site Complex in about 1715, nine years before construction of the New York outpost at Oswego.

Richter's assertions about Iroquois residential transformation are similarly flawed. As outlined in chapter 9, Richter's claims that the Onondaga houses not described by Bartram in 1743 "presumably ... were single-family dwellings built in non-traditional styles" and that by 1750 "most Senecas seem to have been living in single-family cabins built in a European style" (1992: 261) are not supported by documentary or archaeological sources. As noted earlier, his statement that eighteenth-century Iroquois houses no longer were decorated with clan emblems (261) is contradicted by the 1750 Cammerhoff journal and other documents. As I argued in chapters 7 and 9, the unilateral Iroquois adoption of smaller traditional or intercultural houses likely accompanied the settlement dispersals of the 1710–1720 period. Iroquois adoption of European-style house forms occurred only in situations of directed culture change, forced abandonment of the traditional subsistence system, or emerging socioeconomic inequality (K. Jordan 2002: 444–67). These changes in the Iroquois housing mix occurred either before (smaller houses) or after (European-style houses) the "problems of the late 1720s and 1730s." Richter's (1992: 262) conclusion that "the intense communal interaction among members of an ohwachira [matrilineage] characteristic of earlier generations had loosened in fundamental experiential ways" is accurate, but this was hardly fatal to matrilineality. As discussed in chapters 7 and 9, there were many positive aspects to living in smaller houses in a dispersed community, and the short distances between houses seen at Townley-Read in no way precluded the effective operation of a matrilineal society.

Richter considers several other explanations for the changes in Iroquois residence patterns in a paragraph worth quoting at length:

> First, after the treaties of 1701 and the solidification of peace in the region after 1715, there was little reason to rebuild compact, heavily fortified towns. Palisades had not protected the Iroquois from European

enemies, and with no nearby significant native foes, the expenditure of time and resources must have seemed pointless. Moreover, populations decimated by disease, war, and emigration had no need for the large towns of the past, and the land-use patterns of dispersed settlement allowed village relocations to become much less frequent. In addition, the heated political quarrels of the turn-of-the-century years may have led people to feel more comfortable living at some distance from one another even after passions had cooled. One might further speculate that, on some deep social-psychological level, generations of participation in capitalist markets had led to a more individualistic ethos reflected in small one- or two-family dwellings. (1992: 262)

Richter begins the next paragraph by stating "more empirically verifiable sources of the changes in settlement and community patterns lay in the processes of economic domination that the posts at Oswego and Niagara symbolized" (262). Such processes included Iroquois participation in the "capitalist cash economy," alcohol abuse, impoverishment, dependence on trade goods, diminishing role in the fur trade, and loss of territory (262–76).

The long passage quoted here contains the shell of my own argument that settlement dispersal was advantageous—Richter outlines how regional peace facilitated settlement dispersal and how labor previously allocated to palisade construction and village relocation was diverted to other endeavors. However, these positive "possibilities" are intermixed with very negative phrases (palisades were "pointless," there was no longer any need for large towns) and also are framed as "speculations" that cannot be assessed empirically.

Many of these "speculative possibilities" *are* in fact empirically verifiable, and the evidence Richter marshals for "processes of economic domination" is not as strong as he implies. Documentary evidence supports the claim that the regional military position of the Iroquois improved after 1701 and further improved after 1715 (chapter 3). Attention to defense can be measured using the topography of site locations (chapter 6). As noted earlier, the French-sponsored village burnings of the Twenty Years' War did not dissuade the Iroquois from building palisades. Dispersed settlement did mean less frequent village moves, as evidenced by the settlement durations at Townley-Read, Kendaia, and other sites (chapter 6). The organization of Seneca communities, house lots, and residences—avenues of evidence not considered by Richter—provides keys to the benefits of settlement dispersal, rather than serving as signifiers of social decay (chapters 7 and 9).

In order for Richter's argument for "processes of economic domination" to be sustained, his claims must apply to the 1710–1720 period when most of the changes in Iroquois residence patterns occurred. Richter first discusses Iroquois participation in the monetary economy through land sales and wage labor as scouts, porters, guides, and construction laborers (1992: 262). This participation took place mainly among populations near European settlements or forts, including Mohawks near Albany and porters at the Oneida and Niagara portages, however, and did not involve the majority of the Iroquois population. Outside the Mohawk Valley, European settlements in Iroquoia during 1710–1720 were small and of short duration; Six Nations involvement in wage labor and supplying Europeans with food and other goods was mainly an aftereffect of Niagara and Oswego, not a precursor to it. Richter's own statements that "on a day-to-day basis . . . the vast majority of Iroquois continued to operate in a traditional native nexus of reciprocity and redistribution" and that "kin groups rather than individuals apparently still claimed most property" (263) deserve greater emphasis.

Timing problems also plague Richter's point about Iroquois alcohol abuse. Haan's portrayal of the 1690–1720 period as one of low Iroquois alcohol consumption is supported by archaeological evidence from the Seneca region (chapter 10); the main period of increased consumption appears to have occurred *after* settlement dispersal and the construction of smaller houses, and therefore did not cause the changes in residence patterns. Richter's third argument—that residential changes were a consequence of Iroquois poverty—appears to derive not from independent evidence but from his interpretation of the status of the Iroquois role in the fur trade and the extent to which furs were traded for alcohol. Given indications that the 1710–1720 Seneca economy was *expanding* through the geographic middleman role and that alcohol consumption was low, I would argue that Senecas (and likely other Iroquois peoples) were *less* impoverished during the era of settlement dispersal than they were during the Twenty Years' War and period of uncertainty, and that the economic situation in the Oswego era was far less dire than Richter portrays it.

Next, Richter asserts that the fur trade was receding rapidly from Iroquoia, arguing that the primary producers were western Indians, and that the French came to focus on the upper Great Lakes and Mississippi Valley and the British on the Ohio territory. Richter further claims the fur trade became less important to Europe's North American colonies, eclipsed by the exchange of lumber, land, and agricultural products (1992: 270):

> The Iroquois who remained in their traditional homelands were becoming minor players in a game of shrinking economic importance to Euro-Americans. Having never possessed prime hunting territories of their own, they had thrived in the best of times either by raiding for or trading for pelts hunted by their native neighbors. With both alternatives now closed, the Six Nations were slowly sinking into irrelevance in a region more and more dominated by Europeans. (1992: 270–71)

Although comparable diachronic evidence on trade volumes and pelt and skin prices is difficult to secure, drastic conclusions about the "closure" of the Iroquois fur trade cannot be sustained. Six Nations peoples continued to be involved in the fur trade as primary producers, geographic middlemen, and service providers. Trade figures (for example, Cutcliffe 1981; Standen 1998; Wien 1990; see figure 3.1) indicate that beaver exports from New York fluctuated, but intermittently attained high levels, especially in 1734–1741 and the years immediately following King George's War; Compagnie des Indes beaver exports to Paris actually increased after 1745. Deerskins occupied a prominent place in exports to London from New York and Pennsylvania until at least 1754, and European demand for deerskins by some accounts remained brisk until the 1790s, at least in the Southeast (Waselkov 1998). Cutcliffe's (1981) statistics show that for the years 1699–1758 furs and skins made up an average of 32.8 percent of New York's exports to London. Furs and skins made up more than 20 percent of New York exports in all but eleven of the fifty-eight years for which figures are available, and the fur trade was disrupted by war in five of the lowest years. In sum, trade statistics are less indicative of overall decline than that furs and skins made up a smaller, but still significant, piece of an expanding and diversifying colonial economy.

The difference between the long-term consequences and immediate effects of European actions again must be distinguished, and the short-term effects recognized to be less traumatic than Richter takes them to be. This is not to say that fluctuations in the fur trade, changing dynamics of the middleman role, and variation in European demand for different animal species had no effect on Seneca political economy. As with Haan however, Richter's conclusion that the building of trading posts/forts at Niagara and Oswego essentially eliminated the Iroquois role in the fur trade is unfounded.

Richter's final example of "processes of economic domination" is European territorial encroachment, exemplified by post-1711 land grabs in Mohawk territory. Although European encroachment likely prompted Mohawk community dispersal and the adoption of smaller houses (K. Jordan 2009), it cannot be used to explain settlement changes outside the Mohawk Valley. The encroachments at Niagara and Oswego were not of the type seen in the Mohawk Valley because the radius of colonial control exerted by the two posts was not particularly far-reaching. Niagara and Oswego were distant from established Iroquois villages, and the posts did not attract a large European population. The small-scale intensive agriculture and stockraising practiced by the posts' garrisons had little effect on Iroquois subsistence, land-use practices, and ecosystems, and neither post became a center for directed culture-change efforts.

In sum, Richter's attempt to link changes in Iroquois community structure and household organization to Niagara and Oswego is unsuccessful primarily because the trading posts/forts were constructed almost a decade after settlement dispersal and a likely decrease in household size took place. While Richter's attempt to portray European economic domination as an ongoing process potentially remedies this picture, close examination shows that the points he raises to support his argument that the Iroquois were economically dominated turn out to be either *consequences* of Niagara and Oswego or statements that overemphasize negative factors. The more positive reasons for settlement dispersal that Richter presents as speculations have a far more direct relation to the period of Iroquois community and household change than do the negative points he dwells upon.

Diplomatic Retrenchment, Shift of the Fur Trade to Ohio, and Loss of the Play-off System

Several authors have posited that crisis took place in Iroquoia starting in the 1740s due to the declining diplomatic position of the Six Nations and the gradual shift in the focus of the fur trade to the west. Both Aquila (1983) and White (1991) claim that this crisis began during King George's War (1744–1748) and was heightened by the Seven Years' War (1754–1763) and the elimination of the French diplomatic presence in the Northeast in 1763.

Aquila (1983: 237–39) states that what was in his interpretation a very successful Iroquois "restoration policy" started to unravel during King George's War for several reasons: (1) Iroquois conduct during the war angered both the French and British; (2) groups in the Ohio territory had grown more powerful and independent of Iroquois influence; (3) British fur trade interests focused on Ohio, bypassing the Iroquois; (4) the Six Nations lost their tenuous hegemony over Pennsylvania groups, including the Delawares and Shawnees; (5) the Iroquois geographic middleman position had been eliminated; and (6) famine, smallpox, and emigration continued to deplete Iroquois populations. Aquila (1983: 239) concludes that "by the early 1750s, the Iroquois were again in decline."

White (1991: 198–203) provides additional details. During King George's War the flow of French goods to Canada was severely curtailed by a British blockade, and several crown-run posts were turned over to lessees who raised the price of trade goods and cut back on diplomatic gifts. These developments strained French-Native alliances to the breaking point. The problems were exacerbated when persons inexperienced in intercultural diplomacy and opposed to gift giving took over the governorship of Canada in the late 1740s and early 1750s. British officials also reduced the number of diplomatic presents they gave to Great Lakes Indian nations after the conclusion of King George's War in 1748. Imperial and colonial officials increasingly bypassed homeland Iroquois mediators to engage in direct negotiations with Ohio groups. These groups included migrant Iroquois who did not feel compelled to obey homeland elders and Indians from Pennsylvania who had formerly been at least nominally under Iroquois control. Emigration from the Six Nations homeland to the Ohio territory also increased (see chapter 3). French military expeditions to Ohio, starting with Marin in 1753, demonstrated a preference for force over diplomacy. Although French–Native American alliances were reinvigorated as the Seven Years' War approached, the British blockade of oceangoing traffic to Canada again decreased the supply of European goods and weakened the French position (White 1991: 246), and defeat in the Seven Years' War eliminated French influence almost entirely.

After the French surrender of Fort Niagara in 1759 and de facto surrender of the rest of Canada to the British in 1760 (formal transfer of Canada to the British was not completed until 1763), the situation for the Six Nations allegedly became worse because they no longer had the ability to play one European power off the other (Aquila 1983: 240). British commander General Jeffrey Amherst sought to cut costs by replacing the time-tested protocols of alliance with interactions based solely on trade and payment for services rendered. For White (1991: 266–67), this placed tremendous stress on Native leaders whose positions had been solidified by interactions with Europeans. British neglect of the Confederacy leadership diminished imperial influence on outlying groups, such as the western Senecas (who were largely responsible for the Devil's Hole massacre in 1763) and Ohio Mingos (White 1991: 267, 286–89).

Aquila's and White's assertions that Iroquois political and economic decline began during King George's War is not supported by data from the Seneca region. While the war years certainly represented difficult times, this conflict did not result in fundamental changes in the Senecas' political-economic position. As stated earlier, fur continued to be exported from New York at relatively high levels well after 1744; exports included a significant component of furs and skins from Oswego. While the Oswego trade clearly was limited *during* the war (at the same time that trade at Niagara was booming), there is little reason to suspect that Townley-Read's deerskin-based articulation with the fur trade or its middleman traffic were permanently crimped until 1754. Parmenter (1999, 2002, 2007a) takes the very limited Iroquois participation in King George's War as an indicator of the Six Nations' adherence to a policy of "active neutrality." The Senecas faced no significant new encroachments on their territory, and following the war they were still positioned between two empires that could be "played off" each other.

While detailed consideration of the 1754–1779 era is beyond the scope of this book, local political-economic conditions in Seneca territory are likely to have changed dramatically and quickly. Export statistics (Cutcliffe 1981) confirm that the fur trade constricted precipitously starting in 1754. Furthermore, the Seneca middleman role probably was seriously altered by French destruction of the fort at Oswego in 1756 (not rebuilt until 1759) and the British takeover of Fort Niagara in 1759, which largely eliminated the Niagara-Oswego differentials in fur prices and range of trade goods offered that had promoted western Indian traffic across Seneca territory. Senecas also lost their monopoly over the carrying trade at the Niagara portage in 1764 as a consequence of their participation in Pontiac's War (Norton 1974: 212). Merchants began regularly to use sloops to transport furs on the Great Lakes in the 1760s (205), decreasing the cost of obtaining furs from far off sources and in the process removing the need for Indians to haul furs over great distances. Conversely, Parmenter (2001a: 108) asserts that the Iroquois Confederacy cannot be faulted for its intermittent lack of influence over migrant groups, since it never had full control over those groups in the first place. Homeland Iroquois in fact maintained a crucial role in diplomatic negotiations over the Ohio country into the 1790s (117–19).

Systematic examination of 1754–1779 Seneca local political economies clearly is needed. Such a study must address the divergence in the allegiances and actions of the eastern and western ("Chenussio") Senecas during the Seven Years' War and Pontiac's War. Although extra-regional changes suggest that the Senecas' political-economic position after 1754 may have been increasingly difficult, this conclusion needs to be tested with thorough examination of documentary sources, careful domestic-context archaeological investigations, and detailed consideration of existing museum collections. Since this type of local political-economic inquiry has recovered data that seriously question crisis-mode interpretations for the 1713–1754 era, conclusions about Senecas after 1754 should not be made hastily.

I take issue with the "decline" framework Aquila uses to describe the King George's War–Seven Years' War era. It is surprising to see the entire post-1745 period depicted as one of decline in a study that effectively challenges scholarly claims that the whole eighteenth century was a time of ongoing diplomatic, economic, and social crisis. Aquila's account of the years before 1745 is a subtle depiction of political-economic upturns and downturns, good periods and bad. It is a testimony to the strength of tropes of decline in Iroquois studies that even Aquila abandons this subtlety and closes his book with blanket statements more in keeping with the negativism of the majority of scholarly literature.

The American Revolution and Reservationization

The destruction wrought on Iroquois villages during the American Revolution, particularly during 1777–1780, was near total. Wallace (1969: 144) describes it as follows: "before the Revolution, the Six Nations and their dependents had lived largely in some thirty thriving villages scattered from the Mohawk River to Lake Erie and the Ohio country. Of all these towns, by the spring of 1780 only two survived undamaged." Unlike the 1687–1696 French village burnings of the Twenty Years' War, during the American Revolution all Iroquois nations were affected in quick succession. The years in which many Iroquois lived as refugees—outside Fort Niagara for those allied to the British and outside Albany for those allied to the Americans—were trying times. The immediate aftermath of the Revolution included the movement of many loyalist Iroquois to reserves in Canada, particularly on the Grand River. The Senecas—relatively isolated from large European populations—perhaps initially suffered least from dispossession and encroachment, as they were able to resettle much of their territory as soon as late 1779 and 1780, both reoccupying old village sites and establishing new ones (Calloway 1995: 141; Graymont 1972: 220–22; A. Mt. Pleasant 2004).

However, on the heels of British defeat in the Revolution came a series of disastrous and often fraudulent treaties that surrendered land to the Americans, starting with the harsh 1784 Treaty of Fort Stanwix. Even nations that had sided with the American rebels were not exempt from land grabs (Graymont 1976: 451–52). Treaties such as the Canandaigua Treaty of 1794, keystone of modern Iroquois land claims (Jemison and Schein 2000), also have been only selectively honored by the United States, with the federal taking of Seneca land for the Kinzua Dam Project in the 1960s perhaps being the most egregious violation (Bilharz 1998; Hauptman 1986: 105–22).

Destruction and dispossession during and after the American Revolution irrevocably changed Iroquois society, and a series of major changes in subsistence, housing, and culture resulted from it. The post–Revolutionary War period witnessed the expansion of European territorial encroachment from the Mohawk Valley to the rest of the Six Nations. With it came the same effects that Mohawks had experienced beginning in 1711 (K. Jordan 2009): competition for agricultural lands and hunting territories; conversion of wooded areas to permanent agricultural fields; redefinitions of Iroquois land use and forms of property; and expanded opportunities for Euro-Americans to engage in directed culture change. Euro-American territorial encroachment eventually made it impossible for Iroquois peoples to continue a life based on extensive agriculture, hunting, and gathering. Moreover, Iroquois peoples confined to reservations lacked the diplomatic and economic opportunities that Mohawks had drawn upon in their interactions with the British. The old ways were made impossible, and the new setting was one of subjection and poverty.

A close reading of Wallace (1969) supports this view. While the early sections of *The Death and Rebirth of the Seneca* contain mournful passages lamenting the abandonment of longhouses and nucleated villages (see chapter 1), the remainder of the section on pre–Revolutionary War Seneca history supports the case that the Senecas were "an unvanquished Indian nation" (21). Although Wallace has been critiqued for his devotion to modernization theory (see Shoemaker 1991), and he occasionally employs the rhetoric of acculturation (for example, Wallace 1969: 265), these stances do not obscure the causative influence of specific material factors. Wallace's (1969) description of the post-1798 Quaker mission to the Cornplanter Reserve on the Allegheny River provides ample evidence for the continuation of core Iroquois principles of subsistence and housing until they were no longer possible and details the key role directed culture change played in determining the form of the new system that emerged.

On the Allegheny and in many other parts of Iroquoia outside the Mohawk Valley, most of the "acculturative" changes that scholars erroneously claim happened gradually throughout the eighteenth century actually took place in rapid succession during the reservation period. Widespread Iroquois adoption of the fundamental trappings of Euro-American systems of subsistence and property—such as European-style houses, stockraising, and intensive agriculture—did not take place as long as individual nations maintained their autonomy and land base; indeed the evidence indicates that Iroquois groups resisted adoption of these new systems until they could not do otherwise. Iroquois acceptance of Euro-American economic forms reflected neither the gradual realization of the superiority of these forms nor the demise of Iroquois culture. These changes instead took place in local political-economic contexts where Iroquois people confronted the stark facts of reservationization with little power, diminishing amounts of land, and few economic alternatives.

12

Conclusion

Archaeology and the Seneca Restoration

Historians and anthropologists—largely looking at the same documentary sources—have come to diametrically opposite conclusions about the state of Iroquois society during the first half of the eighteenth century. Some, including Richter, Fenton, Haan, and Snow, interpret the era as one of decline; others, such as Aquila and Parmenter, view it as a time of restoration and continued autonomy. Archaeology's value in such a context of scholarly disagreement is that it can test the divergent interpretations. It provides an avenue of evidence that addresses issues different from those written about by European diplomats, missionaries, soldiers, travelers, and captives. Most notably, archaeology provides a record of the conditions of daily life in particular Iroquois villages, which is the material basis upon which local political economies were built.

Incorporation of archaeological data at the regional, community, household, feature, and artifactual levels, coupled with a reassessment of historical documents in light of the picture of daily life provided by archaeology, gives conclusive and solid support for a positive interpretation of the state of Seneca society in the first half of the eighteenth century. The addition of archaeological evidence remedies the gaps in the "restoration" position and in the process considerably strengthens the argument by supplying an account of the *local foundation* that made the restoration in Seneca territory possible. I now summarize major trends during the 1687–1754 period in the Seneca homeland, integrating the documentary information presented in chapter 3 with the archaeological data set out in the remainder of the volume. I emphasize the material conditions of Seneca daily life, political-economic upturns and downturns, and distinctions between Seneca local political economies and those in other parts of Iroquois territory.

Seneca Local Political Economies, 1687–1754

Most scholars emphasize the negative consequences of the Twenty Years' War (circa 1680–1701), which included military defeats and the destruction of Seneca villages and food supplies resulting from the 1687 Denonville expedition. In 1688, Senecas built two new nucleated and perhaps palisaded villages at the White Springs and Snyder-McClure sites. The total area of these villages was considerably smaller than that of the four villages that preceded them, probably reflecting population losses due to violence, disease, and malnutrition during the war years. Primary-source population estimates show a decline of at least two hundred Seneca warriors following Denonville (table 3.1). Despite the ineffectiveness of palisaded villages against French-led expeditions of destruction into Iroquois territory during the 1680s and 1690s, the nucleated and possibly palisaded Seneca villages built in 1688 show continuity with earlier settlement forms. Nucleation and palisade construction may have been intended primarily to protect village inhabitants from small Indian raiding parties rather than large European armies, and nucleated villages may have continued to perform this function effectively during the final years of the Twenty Years' War.

The villages founded in 1688 probably contained a housing mix similar to the sites destroyed the year before, consisting of a majority of true longhouses, a small portion of two-family short longhouses, and perhaps some single-family, Iroquoian-style cabins. Evidence from contemporaneous Iroquoian sites indicates that the structures at White Springs and Snyder-McClure were likely to have been built using Iroquois architectural principles and sided in bark. In comparison to the 1687 settlements, the villages at White Springs and Snyder-McClure were more isolated from Europeans, probably resulting in a decreased supply of alcohol and lesser usage of European domesticated animals. On present evidence, Seneca use of domesticated animals at this time was confined to pigs.

Following the 1700–1701 treaties with the English, French, and western Indian groups that ended the Twenty Years' War, the four elements of Aquila's "Restoration Policy" (neutrality between the English and French empires; alliance with Indians from the upper Great Lakes and Canada; cooperation with the government of Pennsylvania; and warfare against southern Indian groups) began to emerge in fits and starts. Continuation of the peace established in 1700–1701 was never certain during the 1701–1713 period of uncertainty. The Seneca commitment to neutrality was tested by western Indian attacks on their territory (frequently sponsored by the French) and direct participation in the abortive British assault on Canada in 1711. French and British agents were frequent visitors to Seneca country, encouraging factional competition. This period also witnessed the opening of Iroquois territory to western Indian groups who wanted to trade with the British at Albany and the formation of alliances between Senecas and western groups that made transit across Seneca territory possible.

Western Indian passage through Iroquoia initiated what Aquila has called the "geographic middleman" position for the Five Nations. In contrast to some depictions (for example, Norton 1974), western Indians' sojourns in Iroquois territory did not consist solely of exchanges of supplies and services. Amicable relations between Indian groups involved formal declarations and rituals of peace, which included ceremonial hospitality and the transfer of gifts. As noted by Richter (1992), protocols of alliance and the negotiation of safe passage were likely to have provided substantial material benefits to the Iroquois nations that lay along the path to Albany, including the Senecas. Seneca geographic middlemen would have been supplied with furs (primarily beaver pelts, in all likelihood) and ceremonial items (including red pipestone pipes, ornaments, and unprocessed pipestone) during western Indians' passage to Albany, and with European goods during their return. Haan (1976) demonstrates that the Iroquois made serious efforts to encourage western groups to trade at Albany during this period and correctly emphasizes that this policy was at root pro-British, in that it encouraged trade with New York and drew western Indians away from the French alliance.

Although geographic middleman traffic across Seneca territory was occasionally brisk, it frequently was interrupted by rumors of war and instances of actual violence. The danger of war—particularly during 1709–1711—may have prevented Senecas from constructing new settlements. This could have proved problematic for them because the villages built in 1688 probably were at or near the end of their normal life spans due to declining supplies of firewood, growing pest infestation and waste accumulation, and increasing maintenance requirements of aging houses.

On the limited evidence available from other parts of Iroquoia during the first decade of the eighteenth century, settlement and housing patterns appear to have followed the Seneca model. Nucleated and perhaps palisaded settlements were constructed in the Mohawk, Oneida, and Cayuga regions, and primary-source house descriptions all appear to depict traditional, bark-sided dwellings. Although a 1700 document (NYCD 4: 661) implies that Onondagas built a dispersed settlement in the aftermath of the

1696 French invasion, archaeological data suggest that Onondagas continued to use nucleated villages (Grumet 1995: 392; T. Tanner 1995).

British construction of Fort Hunter in the Mohawk Valley in 1711 and subsequent migration of Palatine German refugees into the valley initiated a major divergence in political, economic, and ecological conditions at the eastern and western ends of Confederacy territory (K. Jordan 2009). European encroachment in the Mohawk homeland—protected by the military garrison at Fort Hunter—introduced competition over land; subjected Mohawk fields to depredations by livestock; decreased the supply of wild foods by destroying wooded areas and replacing them with homogenous, monocropped fields; and encouraged Mohawks to define landownership in European terms. The extent and permanence of European fields (primarily due to the huge amounts of land needed to support domesticated animals) radically changed ecology and property in the Mohawk Valley and gradually made the previous Iroquois system of extensive agriculture, hunting, and gathering impossible. At this time these changes were confined to the Mohawk Valley; similar developments did not affect more westerly portions of Iroquoia until the 1760s, or even until after the American Revolution in the Seneca case.

The 1713 formal declaration of peace between Britain and France appears to have caused or coincided with a period of relative local peace in the Northeast. The Iroquois strategy of attracting western Indians to Albany came to fruition as geographic middleman traffic across Iroquoia increased dramatically and continued to build for several more years. This traffic benefited all Iroquois nations on the route to Albany, and Senecas in particular. Even some of the more decline-minded authors see an upturn in Iroquois fortunes during 1713–1724: Richter (1992: 223) relates that the "Iroquois profited both politically and materially" from the exchange and gift giving derived from their middleman position; Haan (1976) views the middleman trade as being successful enough to attract both French and British efforts to undermine it. Increased trade at Albany is well documented in textual sources; the expanded role of Senecas as middlemen is reflected by the dramatic increase in red pipestone usage seen at Townley-Read and Huntoon.

Both documentary sources and archaeological data support the claim that the 1713–1724 middleman period was one of relative local peace, economic upturn, and demographic rebound. During this period, the White Springs Senecas abandoned their defensible, nucleated village and constructed the segmented and dispersed New Ganechstage Site Complex.

This village move, accompanied by a complete transformation in community structure, took place no earlier than 1715, based on the Senecas' need to determine that the post-1713 peace was going to be viable and to have enough time to find a new village location, test soils, clear house lots and fields, and build new houses. The fundamental point here is that settlement dispersal took place during the period in which political-economic conditions were the *most unambiguously positive* of any time during the eighteenth century.

The positive political-economic climate of the times was reflected in the structure of the new dispersed communities. At New Ganechstage, individual houses were located close to floodplain fields and water sources, significantly decreasing the amount of time women spent hauling water and walking to and from their fields. Seneca women likely used some of the time thus freed up to process deer hides (both for home use and trade) and to derive the maximum amount of nutrients from animal bones by extracting storable bone grease. The distance between houses meant that individual households tapped slightly different sources of firewood and cropland, decreasing the rate of resource depletion and allowing the village to be occupied for a considerably longer duration than nucleated settlements were. Dispersal created a complex mosaic of fields and wooded areas that increased the volume of edge habitats conducive to white-tailed deer and wild food plants. Townley-Read faunal data suggest that Seneca hunters focused the majority of their attention on white-tailed deer. Local deer populations had rebounded during the Twenty Years' War and period of uncertainty, and were sustained by the ecological mosaic created by dispersed farmsteads. Continued British and French demand for deerskins (as shown in documentary trade statistics) and local ecology appear to have made the deerskin niche within the fur trade reasonably sustainable, allowing Senecas to hunt locally and maintain access to European goods.

The new Seneca local political economy that accompanied dispersal was (1) highly localized and (2) intercultural. The prior Seneca articulation with the fur trade had been based on beaver pelt procurement; warfare ensured access to productive hunting territories, which became increasingly distant over time. In this local political economy, men were absent for much of the year, and often for years at a time, on extra-regional hunting, trading, and military missions. The new economic system in the dispersed villages focused on locally available animals (deer and *menues pelleteries*), and on beaver pelts and other goods *brought to* the Senecas by western Indians seeking passage to British trading posts. The imperative that men engage in dangerous travel and warfare far from home was lifted in the dispersed settlements, and men may have been able to spend more time in the locality and region than they had in the previous half century. While warfare continued to be practiced and played a significant role in developing Seneca identity, actual combat occurred in the Southeast far from the Iroquois homeland and was not as economically necessary as previous beaver-related conflicts. While Seneca men certainly continued to engage in warfare, they were able to make war more on their own terms. Even slightly longer home stays by adult men would have resulted in increased security and easier subsistence for the homeland settlements.

The new Seneca economic forms were intercultural in that they adopted some of the technologies and subsistence practices of Europeans. These adoptions were not passive and inevitable concessions to the superiority of European customs: Senecas incorporated only those aspects of European technology and subsistence that fit with their own lifeways. For example, Seneca use of European domesticated animals was minor and largely confined to pigs. Pigs were allowed to run feral and represented the introduction of another form of wild meat more than a commitment to protecting, sheltering, and feeding animals. No evidence was recovered for fence construction, harnesses, plows, or barns at Townley-Read. Seneca women living at the site appear to have had little use for European plant species despite their relatively ready availability, although this situation had changed by the occupation of the successor community at Kanadesaga, which was surrounded by orchards of European fruit trees in 1779.

House forms used in the dispersed communities, evidenced by Structure 1 at Townley-Read, also were intercultural in character. The intercultural nature of the structure can be seen in the altered placement and size of its posts and by the increased numbers of European fasteners. These changes in construction details are likely to derive from the replacement of bark siding with more substantial logs or planks made with European axes. But as with subsistence, European construction techniques were incorporated into an overall house design that maintained core Iroquoian features. The new, intercultural houses bore weight on large interior posts, which framed paired sleeping benches around a central hearth. Siding was braced by posts rather than interlocking at the corners or being fastened to a frame, as in European methods of construction. Entrances were placed on the gable ends, and exterior vestibules may have continued to be built. Except in the details of construction, it is likely that the new intercultural/creolized houses would have been quite familiar to the great-grandparents of their builders.

The decrease in household size seen at dispersed communities—from a majority of true longhouses of two or more hearths housing at least four nuclear families to a possible majority of one-hearth, two-family short longhouses—also may have been a response to the improved political-economic situation. Dispersal of people across the landscape had many economic and ecological benefits but in no way inhibited the operation of matrilineal institutions. Dwellings were still close enough to one another to allow regular contact among households and aggregation for decision making by either men or women. Documentary evidence demonstrates the continued importance of the clan system to eighteenth-century Iroquois populations, the functions of which likely included continued allocation of land and organization of men's and women's work groups.

In other parts of Iroquoia, residential dispersal also appears to have taken place during the 1712–1720 era. In the Mohawk Valley, dispersal perhaps was a reaction to the construction of Fort Hunter. Mohawks may have seen the fort as a citadel where they could gather if attacked, or Mohawks may have dispersed as a precautionary measure to protect their lands from European encroachment by settling on them directly (K. Jordan 2009). These motivations do not apply to Iroquois groups outside the Mohawk Valley. The pattern in Onondaga, Oneida (at the Lanz-Hogan site), and Cayuga (at Pattington) territory (Bennett 1982; Bradley 1987: 207; Grumet 1995) appears to match the Seneca model. If this conclusion is sustained by additional targeted research, each Iroquois nation except the Mohawks built dispersed villages during a positive political-economic period, in the absence of substantial European settlement, and without construction of any defensive works whatsoever.

Many of the arguments that take Iroquois settlement dispersal and decreased household size as evidence for Iroquois decline cannot be sustained empirically. Alcohol consumption appears to have been at a distinct low immediately prior to dispersal and increased only subsequent to the founding of Oswego almost a decade later, undermining the claim that alcohol was a primary inducement for households to separate from one another. Palisades had been demonstrated to be ineffective against European armies a generation prior to dispersal, but the Iroquois did not build dispersed communities until the danger of Indian attacks—small-scale raids designed to acquire captives, not destroy villages—had diminished. At the time, Iroquois populations were on the increase rather than in decline. European territorial encroachment was essentially absent outside the Mohawk Valley. The Iroquois role in the fur trade, at least in the Seneca case, had been reconfigured rather than eclipsed; it now emphasized locally acquired deerskins and beaver pelts from the middleman trade rather than primary beaver pelt production.

The positives accumulate: at the regional level, a period of greater local security and increased middleman traffic; at the community level, an arrangement of people in space that placed them in closer proximity to fields and water and sustained local deer populations; at the household level, less walking and water-hauling for women and less hazardous long-distance travel for men. This community- and household-level interpretation supports and solidifies Aquila's (1983) and Parmenter's (1999, 2002, 2007a) Confederacy-level emphasis on the local peace established as a consequence of the restoration or neutrality policies of the Six Nations. In addition to allowing the Iroquois to "trade and farm without having to worry about being attacked" (Aquila 1983: 233–34), local peace gave the Senecas the opportunity to establish a new, highly advantageous system of subsistence and trade.

While the advantages of dispersed settlement were first realized in the positive political-economic setting of the middleman period, benefits continued after the establishment of European trading posts/forts at Niagara and Oswego. The European powers tried to undermine part of the new Iroquois political economy by intercepting western Indians at new trading posts along the route to Albany (Haan 1976). The French sought to provide an alternative to the New York trade by reducing travel distances and offering western Indians prices similar to those in Albany. If successful, French efforts at Niagara or Irondequoit could have all but eliminated the Seneca middleman role by giving western Indians a final destination on the margins of Iroquois territory. This did not occur: the prices and range of goods offered by the British in most years continued to be more attractive than those of the French. The New York trade continued to be the key to the Great Lakes fur trade, and Senecas profited from western Indian transit well after a permanent French post was established at Niagara in 1718.

British efforts to engage in a "trader's leapfrog" by obtaining pelts more directly from western Indians concentrated on creation of a large trading post/fort at Oswego. This process developed quickly, with the New York government clearing the path between Oswego and Albany in 1724 and building a trading house at Oswego in 1725. The actions of the British, who were the primary recipients of the western fur trade, had a greater effect on Iroquois middleman traffic than did those of the French. However, those authors who see the Oswego post as leading to the rapid and total diminution of the Iroquois middleman role overlook the fact that there would have been significant differences in the effects of Oswego on various Iroquois nations. Geographically, it is undeniable that western Indians still needed to cross Seneca and Cayuga territory to reach the post. While Oswego may have reduced the middleman role of the more eastern Iroquois nations, Senecas and Cayugas continued to benefit as long as Oswego remained an important trading center. Textual and archaeological sources support this position. Historical documents indicate that traders at Oswego at least intermittently acquired large amounts of pelts and skins, and Oswego-bound western groups continued to sojourn in Seneca territory well into the 1750s. Archaeological evidence suggests that Senecas received a consistent supply of red pipestone throughout the occupation of the Townley-Read and Huntoon sites. Aquila (1983) does not see an interruption in the geographic middleman position until the 1740s, but even this view of decline may be unwarranted. The total elimination of the Seneca middleman role likely did not occur until the British capture of Fort Niagara from the French in 1759.

The predominance of white-tailed deer bones and red pipestone in deposits across the Townley-Read site argues that the modes of interaction, trade, and subsistence established during the middleman period operated throughout the occupation of the site. That these modes were relatively sustainable suggests that some of the gloomier interpretations of the effects of Oswego and Niagara (for example, Haan 1976; Richter 1992) overemphasize the social and economic downsides of the European trading posts/forts. Haan's position that alcohol availability and consumption increased after Oswego appears to be sustained by the documentary and archaeological records. Greater Seneca alcohol consumption, intermittent famine, and continued epidemic disease were clearly disruptive, but they must be interpreted in the context of a Seneca society that was considerably more viable than Haan and Richter portray it. The New Ganechstage Senecas continued to live in a fully dispersed community through several epidemics, the famine of 1741–1742, King George's War, and the migration of western Senecas to the Genesee Valley, indicating the value of dispersed settlement to eastern Senecas. That they only partially abandoned this community form—by building a semi-dispersed ridgetop community at Kanadesaga as the Seven Years' War approached—suggests that the benefits of dispersal outweighed even the perceived dangers of the war.

My examination of Seneca local political economy thus supports Aquila's (1983) claim for an "Iroquois restoration," in one corner of Iroquoia, but for a slightly different period of time than Aquila suggests. While Aquila views the Iroquois "restoration policy" as operating successfully from 1701 to 1745, I view the Seneca restoration as both starting and ending somewhat later. The 1701–1713 period of uncertainty, clearly an improvement over the Twenty Years' War, was still a troubled time for Senecas. Conditions improved in 1713, or more specifically by 1715 when New Ganechstage was actively being settled. These conditions endured until at least 1750 and perhaps 1754.

In sum, this study demonstrates that archaeological evidence provides an invaluable addition to the standard array of documentary sources. It outlines the local, intercultural basis of the Seneca restoration, in the form of dispersed settlement, infields and outfields, pigs, increased edge areas and local deer hunting for the deerskin trade, two-family intercultural/creolized houses, and cultivation and maintenance of the geographic middleman role. These new forms of community life played an essential part in the Seneca restoration by localizing the economy, decreasing travel, and lessening the burdens of everyday labor for both men and women.

Decline, Tradition, and "Indigenisms"

The conclusions of this study wrest eighteenth-century Seneca settlement dispersal and changed house forms from the clutches of a master narrative of decline. While gradualist acculturative models have been criticized for more than a generation, their influence remains strong, often hidden in the assumptions of older works that are uncritically absorbed by subsequent scholars. Older works steeped in the tonic of "salvage anthropology" viewed the portions of "traditional" cultures that were not already lost as mortally ill. Such scholarship saw Native Americans as buffeted by their interaction with Europeans and Americans, reacting only passively out of a position of supposed weakness. Native Americans found their history defined by scholars such that social change did not operate in the uplifting "ramplike" or "steplike" fashion typically granted to those societies which became "complex" or "civilized" (R. Adams 1966). Any evidence for change was diagnosed as decay. For American Indians, the slope of the ramp was reversed and greased by prevailing models of acculturation: any attempt by Indians to improve their lot only placed them further from "tradition," providing more downward momentum to their slide.

The power of such narrative models is so great as to *capture* the study of certain eras, substituting tropes that lack a firm basis in documentary or archaeological data for detailed research and also discouraging such research. That this process has operated in exemplary fashion in scholarly examination of Iroquois peoples is either surprising, in that part of the history of one of the oldest "case studies" in Americanist anthropology has been misconstrued despite years of scholarship, or is entirely to be expected, given that Iroquois studies is likely to have one of the most entrenched, "foundational" narratives in the discipline (Simpson 2004).

Tropes of gradual decline and gradual assimilation to European technology and lifeways are most obviously refuted by the opportunistic, positive character of Seneca settlement dispersal. The changes made in settlement pattern, community structure, and household organization follow an intercultural but unmistakably Iroquoian logic, rather than an adopted European one. Seneca ability to disperse was based on the major diplomatic accomplishments of establishing and maintaining neutrality between the French and British, while also enticing western Indians—recent enemies— to make the long journey to Albany. These diplomatic endeavors permitted the local changes associated with the Seneca restoration. They evidence an active, opportunistic population rather than one gradually withering away.

The evidence for Iroquois *selectivity* in the adoption of European technology and lifeways presented in this volume further draws attention to Iroquois agency. Agency can be seen in the Seneca adoption of only certain European domesticated animals and plants, and in Seneca use of European tools and fasteners but not European architectural principles in their housing. These resulted in a hybrid Native-European economy and intercultural/creolized houses, with Senecas adopting only those aspects of European culture and technology that fit with their way of life. Bradley (1987: 167) concludes of the 1500–1655 Onondagas that "(1) their response [to Europeans] was active and selective, not passive; (2) continuity marked the process as much as change did; (3) many of the changes were creative, innovative ones." Each of these points equally describes the Seneca local political economy fifty to one hundred years later.

Gradualism also is refuted by the evidence that Iroquois adoption of European technologies and species fluctuated over time rather than increasing in linear fashion. For example, there was an apparent early peak in Seneca alcohol use at Ganondagan, followed by a relative lull at White Springs, then an increase at Townley-Read. Furthermore, documentary sources indicate that pigs were relatively plentiful around Ganondagan in 1687, but they played only a small part in Seneca subsistence at Townley-Read. The linear gradualism that forms the unexamined foundation of tropes of decline obscures local political-economic contexts that much better explain the content and timing of cultural change.

A local political-economic approach demonstrates that it is more accurate to conceive of culture as a *repertoire* of possible solutions than as a static set of norms, as is typical of the "culture patterns" genre of writing. Long-term sequences invariably reveal that Iroquois groups in many times and places departed from the "classic" cultural forms described in normative models. However, this did not mean that they became "less Iroquois" by doing so; in many cases, these groups simply took up other options from their repertoire of cultural practices. For example, the "short longhouse" has a long history as part of the Iroquoian housing stock (Dean 1984; Hosbach et al. 2006; K. Jordan 2003; Kapches 1984; Ricklis 1967); widespread Iroquois use of short longhouses in the eighteenth century signifies nothing about "Europeanization" or the decline of matrilineal institutions. It is even possible to view the dispersed Iroquois settlements of the early 1700s as in some ways a reactivation of the same types of human-ecological relationships that had characterized smaller Iroquois sites of the fifteenth century, such as Getman and Elwood in the Mohawk Valley. These sites are characterized by high proportions of deer bone in faunal assemblages, site durations of approximately fifty years, and modal populations of one hundred to two hundred people (Kuhn and Funk 2000; Snow 1995: 90, 1996, 2001).

Many previous studies of Postcolumbian Iroquois archaeology have (of necessity) relied on material culture to frame their interpretations of Iroquois political, economic, and cultural dynamics (for example, Anselmi 2004; Bradley 1987; Mandzy 1992; Wray and Schoff 1953). Artifact-based studies typically have found that over time (1) the proportions of Precolumbian mainstays such as domestic pottery and stone tools decrease dramatically; (2) European-made goods make up larger percentages of the overall material culture assemblage; and (3) European-made goods increasingly were used without modification by Iroquois peoples. As I argued in the introduction, scholars have been reluctant to address Iroquois sites occupied after 1680 or 1700, perhaps because the amount of "indigenisms" found at these sites is likely to be quite low. To some, this may suggest (perhaps uncomfortably) cultural decline or disarray.

The data presented in this volume demonstrate that archaeologists cannot limit their analyses to material culture; contexts of use also must be studied. Contextual data from the Townley-Read site reveal clear-cut continuities with longstanding Iroquois practices in terms of house construction and (particularly) plant and animal use. These continuities indicate that Senecas maintained control over fundamental social, economic, and ecological processes. This measure of Seneca control over the institutions and conditions governing everyday life demonstrates the autonomy of Senecas living at Townley-Read. But does this perspective simply change the scale of the argument about "indigenisms"? Are maintained systems of house construction, species usage, and agriculture simply "indigenisms writ large"? If so, what criteria will archaeologists working on eras of Indian history more heavily impacted by Euro-Americans (such as the nineteenth century) use to assess indigenous autonomy, since many of these enduring ways of managing territories, social interactions, and resources would have been made impossible by colonialism?

I assert that the contextual continuities at the Townley-Read site are not merely "indigenisms writ large": every domain that showed relative continuity with previous Seneca practices was simultaneously shot through with transformation and innovation. Although the short longhouse form is an enduring part of the Iroquoian housing repertoire, the embodiment of that form at Townley-Read adopted new types of siding and European hardware. The new siding made the house more durable, and the European-provided hardware cut down on the amount of small poles and cordage Seneca builders had to make ready. The plants Seneca women grew and gathered at the site were overwhelmingly traditional resources that had been utilized for centuries, but the dispersed arrangement of the site in space allowed traditional agriculture to be practiced more easily and facilitated the growth of certain wild plants. Seneca hunters concentrated on wild species, as they had in previous years, but emphasized white-tailed deer to a greater extent than their immediate predecessors had and used deerskins to maintain a productive niche in the European fur trade.

The point to be made is that issues of continuity and change are not really of prime importance: what truly needs to be evaluated is autonomy and control. These can best be assessed through the minute changes and rearrangements made in successive local political economies, and how those changes fit together within the overall organization and allocation of labor.

In some cases, indigenisms evidence continued control; in other instances innovations such as local residential dispersal demonstrate autonomy at least as well.

Neither Contact Nor Colonial

The long and tangled debate on how to characterize processes of intercultural engagement indicates that the terms used to describe them provide an all-important shorthand that guides present readers and future scholarship. Take, for example, acculturation. Despite frequent attempts to rescue or rework the concept (for example, Cusick 1998; Henry 2001; B. Little 1994), acculturation remains hopelessly burdened by "implicit assumption[s] of cultural dominance and passiveness" (Cusick 1998: 131). Consumers of acculturation literature are inclined toward gradualism, negativism, and a passive portrayal of American Indian peoples that includes a gloomy view of their future.

Stephen Silliman (2005) has done a great service to anthropologists with his inventory of the shortcomings of the concept of contact. He notes that the term deemphasizes the long-term nature of intercultural encounters, obscures unequal power relations, and veils the potential for creative, creolized cultural products. The *contact period* label fits eighteenth-century Iroquoia particularly poorly: by 1700, European goods had been in circulation in Iroquois territory for at least 175 years and direct engagements between Iroquois peoples and Europeans had taken place since 1609. Much as in, for example, the long-term economic dance between Japan and the United States (only just over sixty years old in its post–World War II incarnation), Europeans, their goods, and their alliances were a fact of life, thoroughly enmeshed in Native existence in the eighteenth-century Northeast. It simply would have been impossible to "break contact." If one seeks a neutral term to describe processes of intercultural encounter, "engagement" provides a better alternative (Torrence and Clarke 2000: 12–16).

With *acculturation* and now *contact* falling into disrepute, there has been in archaeology a widespread and accelerating use of *colonialism* to describe virtually all situations of intercultural engagement (for example, Gosden 2004; Silliman 2005). While it is tempting to describe every Postcolumbian encounter between the materially powerful and well-organized Europeans and indigenous "people(s) without history" as colonial, there is distinct benefit to a more nuanced view of engagement, and a more specific definition of colonialism in particular. Here I draw on Rani Alexander's

(1998) tripartite model for engagement processes, emphasizing her distinction between *colonialism* and *cultural entanglement.*

Alexander (1998: 481) defines colonialism as "an extreme case of core-periphery interaction" that involves political and military control of the peripheral group by the colonizing group from the core, usually through bureaucratic and territorial forms of administration. This definition can be fleshed out with the addition of an *ecological* component, wherein the options of the colonized group are fundamentally constrained because the colonizers intentionally or inadvertently changed local ecological conditions (see Cronon 1983).

Cultural entanglement can be defined as

> a process whereby interaction with an expanding territorial state gradually results in change of indigenous patterns of production, exchange, and social relations. Development of the interaction network may lead to increasingly unbalanced political and economic relations, but these asymmetries are not characteristic of the original encounter.... The larger and more organized polity may initiate contact in seeking specific resources, but direct political and economic control of the hinterland by the state is not evident. Although differences in power and demographic potential between interacting parties may generate unbalanced trade, the flow of resources from the hinterland to the center may not at first be particularly voluminous or unidirectional. Territorial states may establish enclaves in distant areas to facilitate the flow of desired resources, but contact does not entail the subordination of indigenous groups. The power to allocate labor is left in native hands.... Entanglement is a long-term, gradual, and non-directed process of interaction, often spanning centuries or even millennia. (Alexander 1998: 485)

Use of *cultural entanglement* and *colonialism* as analytical alternatives better characterizes the range of political and economic interactions that accompanied the post-1415 European expansion. *Cultural entanglement* in particular grants agency to indigenous peoples and makes the history of intercultural engagement an open, as opposed to predetermined, process (Dietler 1998: 298).

The concepts of cultural entanglement and colonialism well capture the variation observed over time and across space in European-Iroquois relations. European and Iroquois cultures became entangled no later than 1525, when Native groups began to transport European objects inland from the

Atlantic coast. For the Iroquois, this entanglement generated a new economic focus on furs, changed trade routes and warfare patterns, introduced new goods of spiritual significance, altered the basic technology used in daily life, and resulted in drastic population losses due to European-borne epidemics and warfare. Throughout all these changes, however, fundamental decisions about production, diplomacy, and warfare were still made by Iroquois social actors. These decisions necessarily incorporated Europeans as sources of goods and power, and as military forces that could be alienated only at high cost. But Europeans did not directly dictate Iroquois choices, and ecological and demographic factors largely did not constrain Iroquois options.

The Seneca situation described in this volume supplies a textbook case of long-term cultural entanglement. Data from the Seneca region 175 years after the first entanglements with Europeans still indicate substantial Seneca *control* over key economic, political, and ecological decisions. The various positive causes and consequences of settlement dispersal even demonstrate that the Senecas were operating from a position of *strength* during the 1713–1754 period. Cultural entanglement, in fact, characterized Iroquois-European relations in all parts of Iroquoia into the first decade of the eighteenth century, and this mode of interaction continued in every part of Iroquoia outside the Mohawk Valley until the 1760s.

A brief period of stability and decreased everyday labor occurred in the Seneca region at the precise time that substantial social and ecological dislocation and growing economic inequalities were taking place in the Mohawk Valley following the construction of Fort Hunter and encroachment by thousands of European settlers (K. Jordan 2009). As the Mohawk system of shifting agriculture, impermanent settlement, and hunting and gathering became impossible (at the same time preventing emergence of the type of hybrid economy seen at Townley-Read), Mohawks adopted more substantial trappings of European subsistence, housing, and property systems, a process sped by the actions of colonial agents and missionaries who engaged in directed culture change. European actions markedly constrained Mohawk alternatives, eventually creating a situation that clearly must be labeled as *colonialism*.

The contrast between the Seneca and Mohawk cases illustrates two points. First, there was significant regional variation in local political-economic conditions across Iroquoia. While there had been muted regional variation in Iroquoia throughout the Postcolumbian period, as some groups had better access to trade routes and European trading posts, the post-

1711 European population influx made Mohawks diverge in fundamental ways from the rest of the Confederacy. The second point is that the major instances of Iroquois adoption of European lifeways during the eighteenth century are linked to territorial encroachment, directed culture change, and obliteration of the possibility of a functioning Native subsistence system. In short, Iroquois adoption of European lifeways was not the inevitable and gradual consequence of acculturation, it instead was caused by encroachment and colonialism. The parallel changes in housing, agriculture, and animal use in post-1711 Mohawk country, Oneida territory after 1760, and post–Revolutionary War reservation settings in the rest of the Confederacy suggest that similar processes of colonialism were taking place, separated by half a century or more in time.

The picture of Seneca local political economy at Townley-Read suggests that scholars need to reassess their depictions of eighteenth-century Iroquois society. Scholars' discussion of colonialism in eighteenth-century Iroquoia must be done carefully and with geographic and temporal limits. My differences with Richter's (1992: 256) assertion that all Iroquois "ranked among the colonized" by the 1720s and 1730s at this point should be obvious. Guldenzopf's (1986) "Late Colonial Mode of Production" and Kuhn and Funk's (2000) "Colonial Period of Economic Transformation" (somewhat arbitrarily dated to 1700–1800) must be explicitly tied to the post-1711 Mohawk local political economy in order to preclude inaccurate application in the rest of the Confederacy. Furthermore, this study casts doubt on claims that "the disintegration of traditional Iroquois culture" occurred in the second half of the seventeenth century (Kuhn et al. 1986: 30) and that Iroquois political actions in the eighteenth century resulted in "the chaotic uncertainty of neutrality" (Snow 1994: 134).

In short, a framework of cultural entanglement makes no a priori decisions about the direction or pace of culture change. The very ambiguity of the term *invites* a concentration on specific political-economic contexts in the same way that acculturative tropes of gradual decline discourage it. The concentration on political-economic factors operating in particular regions and localities has the potential to generate a more nuanced and solidly based depiction of Indian history. Local political economy works particularly well when document-based views can be supplemented and challenged by archaeological data on the material underpinnings of daily community life. Multi-scalar investigations of specific contexts—both top-down from diplomatic sources and bottom-up from archaeology—have the potential to uncover unexpected results. From the midst of an eighteenth-century Iroquois history that some scholars have dismissed as a time of social turmoil and gradual decline can emerge a picture of an active Seneca people building a reasonably sustainable localized economy in the face of tremendous pressure from European empires and Native rivals. Dispersal can no longer be seen as the passive response of a people buffeted by the upheavals of engagement with Europeans, but instead must be regarded as an instance of active opportunism where Iroquois peoples took advantage of a hard-won neutrality to improve their daily lives.

Notes

Chapter 1. Introduction: Colonialism and Decline in Eighteenth-Century Iroquois Studies

1. In this volume I follow the lead of other archaeologists (e.g., Rothschild 2003; Thomas 2000; Warrick 2000) who have responded to indigenous observations that the chronological terms *prehistoric* and *historic* are derogatory, as they imply that prior to European documentation no "history" was taking place, and that indigenous forms of historical documentation (including in the North American context oral tradition, wampum belts, "winter counts," and rock art) are of little value. I have tried to employ more neutral terminology, including *Precolumbian* and *Postcolumbian*, even though the results (e.g., "The Period of Indirect European Influence") sometimes are ungainly.

2. My use of the terms *English* and *British* requires clarification. When referring to governmental actions, I use English to describe actions before the 1707 formation of the United Kingdom of Great Britain (which united Scotland, England, and Wales), and British for actions in and after 1707. When referring to cultural traditions, I use the labels English, Scotch, and Irish to designate particular cultural groups; these distinctions are important to the discussion of housing traditions in chapters 8 and 9. In cultural terms, *British* refers to more than one of the English, Scotch, and Welsh traditions. Some of the direct quotations in the text are inconsistent with these definitions because other scholars do not use the terms in the same way.

3. Rubertone (2002: 96) notes the "unfortunate title" of *Societies in Eclipse*.

4. Fenton's (1971) assessment of the indigeneity of wampum provides an excellent example. Fenton opposed the repatriation of wampum belts in the collections of the New York State Museum to the Onondaga Nation because (1) wampum is a post-contact phenomenon, "as American as apple pie, the log cabin, and the splint basket" (1971: 437); (2) because contemporary Six Nations peoples cannot "read" the belts or use them in the same way that their seventeenth- and eighteenth-century ancestors did; and (3) because the League of the Iroquois no longer exists in the same form that it once did. Excellent arguments can be marshaled against the first two points, and the third exhibits a clear double standard. One doubts, for example, that the New York State Museum exists in the same form it always has.

5. This Seneca "restoration" is distinct from the Seneca "renaissance" described by Hauptman (1981: 136–63), which refers to the federally funded Seneca Arts Project organized by Arthur C. Parker at the Rochester Municipal Museum. Parker's 1935–1941 project sponsored about one hundred Seneca artists to create works of art and handicrafts for the museum's collections, including the famed paintings by Ernest Smith.

Chapter 2. Local Political Economy

1. Lightfoot's (2005) synthetic treatment of Spanish missions in the same volume is not a work of local political economy because it does not emphasize conditions in

particular localities. As a consequence, this section of Lightfoot's book in my view is not as strong as the part on Colony Ross.

2. *Reservationized* is derived from *reservationization*, defined here as the process of being confined to a reservation. Reservationization is a social process that has some regularities cross-culturally. The word is not a neologism, having been used previously by Rayna Green (1988: 37) and Michaelsen and Shershow (2002).

3. This study relies exclusively on the 1722–1748 manuscript commissioners' minutes maintained by the National Archives of Canada. These records are available on microfilm in their totality (see MACIA 1722–1748) and in part in the fifty-reel microfilm compendium of primary sources titled *Iroquois Indians: A Documentary History* (Jennings et al. 1984, hereafter IIDH). The 1753–1755 commissioners' minutes at the University of Michigan were not consulted.

Chapter 3. Toward a History of the Seneca Homeland, 1677–1754

1. My sortie into the documentary record has relied exclusively on English-language sources and primarily on published materials. Expanded use of manuscript originals and French-language sources has the potential to expand and evaluate the conclusions of this study, and I hope that this book will encourage exploration of less-accessible sources.

2. The issue of price comparisons between French and British posts remains a sticky one. Laird (1995) uses documentary data to claim that British and French goods were priced similarly, with the possible exception of lower British prices for stroud blankets and rum, during the 1720–1760 period. However, Laird was able to generate a detailed price comparison for only two years (1735 and 1754), and extension of his conclusions to other years (particularly earlier ones) remains problematic.

3. Ideas for strengthening the west-east trade had been circulated by both New Yorkers and Iroquois since the 1670s. This policy appears to have originated in Iroquois actions taking place as early as 1673 (Haan 1980: 318; see also Brandão 1997: 124, 342–43 notes 48–49; Havard 2001: 81; Laird 1995: 68–69; Norton 1974: 152–54). Aquila (1984: 54) asserts that New York officials came up with this policy but provides evidence in lesser quantity and with later dates.

4. The Jesuit François Vaillant de Gueslis had left Seneca territory for Montreal in 1706 (DCB, 2: 643).

5. Determining a founding date for the Genesee villages is made particularly difficult due to threats made by residents of the western village of Onaghee to move to an unnamed location (possibly on the Genesee River) in 1734 and to Irondequoit in 1738 (MACIA 1820: 52a, 129). Given evidence for persistence in the Seneca settlement pattern (including village names and size descriptions in primary sources) until 1742, I view a move to the Genesee Valley prior to this date as unlikely.

Chapter 4. New Ganechstage in the Library, Museum, and Archive

1. Cornell University excavations under my direction began at the White Springs site in June 2007 (see Aloi 2007).

2. The Townley-Read site is identified as New York State Museum (NYSM) site

number 2440, Rochester Museum and Science Center site Plp-16, and Wray site number 160. The Townley-Read name for the site was coined in the 1970s by Charles Wray, who combined the names of the owner of the site at that time (Leon Townley) and the original Euro-American owners (the Reads). Other sources (e.g., Conover n.d.; NYSM site records; Wray 1973) refer to it simply as the "Read" or "Reed" site.

3. Despite the 1750–1768 date range given by the Library of Congress, this map almost certainly was produced between 1758 and 1764. It shows Fort Stanwix (built 1758) and mentions Pittsburgh (given that name by John Forbes in 1758) as well as "Sir William Johnsons" at the location of Johnson Hall (completed 1763) and the location of the multinational Indian village at Canisteo, burned in 1764. Moreover, the map is most likely to have been produced between 1761 (when plans for Johnson Hall were well underway [Feister 1995: 16]) and 1764. I am surprised that an abandoned "Canossodage" was still important enough to represent and that Kanadesaga was still considered "new" on a map of this late date. I am grateful to Jim Folts at the New York State Archives for directing me to this and other historic maps.

4. My dissertation relied on the description of Townley-Read contained in Conover's three-volume manuscript "Kanadesaga and Geneva" (Conover n.d., completed circa 1889), currently housed at the Hobart and William Smith Colleges Archives in Geneva, New York. This document contains a considerable number of errors, imprecise statements, and misinterpretations of archaeological evidence. I have since located Conover's 1882 manuscript lecture notes at the Ontario County Historical Society in Canandaigua, New York (Conover 1882). This document includes a physical description of Townley-Read almost identical to the circa 1889 version, but with fewer factual errors, which appear to have been introduced when Conover recopied the 1882 manuscript. The 1882 document cannot completely supplant the later work, since by 1889 Conover had a significantly better understanding of the occupation sequence for the Geneva-area Seneca sites.

5. A single glass "man-in-the-moon" bead (Kidd and Kidd [1983] Type WIIIc1) likely to derive from Townley-Read (Conover 1889: 6–7) is now in the collections of the National Museum of the American Indian in Suitland, Maryland (Mary Jane Lenz, personal communication, 2003). There are no artifacts in the NYSM collections that definitely derive from Townley-Read (Penelope Drooker and Beth Wellman, personal communications, 2001).

6. A complete list of New York agents, dates of their tenure in Seneca territory, and primary-source references that provide this information is available from the author.

7. Primary-source references to Wendell's service in Seneca territory include IIDH, Apr. 12, 1731, July 29, 1735; MACIA vol. 1819: 326, 334a, 346a; vol. 1820: 24, 35, 63, 76a, 80; and NYCD 5: 911.

8. Primary-source references to Myndert Wemp's service in Seneca territory include MACIA vol. 1820: 295, 333a, 383; vol. 1821: 80; and NYCD 5: 718. Myndert Wemp also worked at Kanadesaga, the successor village to the New Ganechstage Site Complex, in 1755–1756 (JP 1: 765).

9. Primary-source references to Hendrick Wemp's service in Seneca territory include IIDH, Sept. 24, 1740; MACIA vol. 1819: 93, 277a, 294; and NYCD 5: 719.

Chapter 5. Archaeology at the Townley-Read Site, 1996–2000

1. Woodley is RMSC site number Plp-078. MacNeish (1952) and Niemczycki (1984) provide contrasting interpretations of Woodley's place in the Seneca and Cayuga sequences.

2. M. Smith (1981) identifies triangular blue-and-white glass pendants from the Seneca Honeoye site (occupied circa 1740–1745 to 1779) as Native-made. These pendants likely were manufactured from crushed trade beads, which were then formed into a paste, shaped, and heated on a copper plate until fusion took place. The blue-and-white pendants recovered in DRC 1 and DRC 3 by the project at Townley-Read (both possibly rejects discarded during the production process) appear to provide evidence for Seneca manufacture. If so, glass pendants may have been produced by multiple households, since pendant rejects were found in two separate DRCs. The RMSC collections contain blue-and-white, monochrome blue, and monochrome green pendants from the Snyder-McClure, Huntoon, and Townley-Read sites, and the private collection of Eugene Frost of Montour Falls, New York, includes a monochrome blue pendant from the White Springs site (Dewbury and Ryan n.d.). In conjunction, these artifacts suggest that both eastern and western Senecas manufactured glass pendants dating back at least to 1688; I have not examined collections from earlier Seneca sites. Alternately, some or all of these pendants may have been European-made (Mike Galban, personal communication 2008).

3. Morgan's published mention that "the back bone of the eel" was sometimes used in deer-hide processing (in Tooker 1994: 180) appears to be the result of a typesetting error; Tooker's (1994: 116) transcription of Morgan's original field notes instead describes the use of the "backbone of the elk."

4. Based on shape, color, and bone and charcoal concentration, Features 10, 13, 14, 16, 18, and 19 were determined to be cultural features, while Features 9, 11, 12, and 17 are not certain to be cultural in origin. Feature 8, a very shallow soil stain, and Feature 15, interpreted as a rodent burrow, were determined to be noncultural during excavation; Feature 7 proved to be a twentieth-century pipe trench. Post Molds 18, 19, and 20 had a postlike shape in part or all of their profile, and each contained eighteenth-century material; the very small PM 12 contained no artifactual material but easily could be recognized as cultural based on its shape. The soil stains labeled PM 13, 14, and 16 were all highly impacted by rodents, but their contents suggest that they are cultural in origin. The soil color, contents, and shape of PMs 7, 8, 9, 10, 11, 15, 17, 21, and 33 make them unlikely to be cultural. Possible post molds NN and PP were not excavated, but they appeared to lack the characteristics diagnostic of culturally formed post stains. See Kurt Jordan (n.d.) for additional details about these features and post molds.

5. Project excavations did not extensively sample the areas to the north and west of Structure 1.

6. Brain (1988: 404) has termed light blue-green bottle glass a "characteristically French artifact."

7. Wray (1983) does not mention Kanadesaga, an apparent oversight.

8. Two pipe bowl fragments in the RMSC collections appear to postdate the primary Seneca occupation of the site, including a ribbed bowl fragment dating to circa 1760–1820 and a pipe fragment with a stem-bowl back angle characteristic of 1780–1840 (K.

Jordan 2002: 286). These two artifacts—a very small proportion of the total white ball clay pipe assemblage—may have been deposited at Townley-Read by later Seneca visitors or by the post-1789 Euro-American occupants of the site.

9. The RMSC collections contain more than thirty thousand glass beads from Townley-Read, primarily derived from mortuary contexts, that were not examined for this volume. This assemblage contains fifteen "man-in-the-moon" beads (Kidd and Kidd [1983] type WIIIc1), which date to 1700–1750 according to Lorenzini and Karklins (2001: 42, table 1). Jessica Herlich's 2008 Cornell University senior honors thesis (on file with the Department of Anthropology) catalogs and analyzes almost 23,000 glass beads from the RMSC assemblage, providing a substantial resource on eighteenth-century Iroquois glass bead use.

Chapter 6. Seneca Settlement Pattern and Community Structure, 1677–1779

1. It may be possible to estimate the populations of the New Ganechstage sites based on the sizes of their cemeteries. If we assume that all New Ganechstage burials were made adjacent to where the deceased person had been living, and also posit an orderly replacement of generations every twenty years, the life cycle of a nuclear family household over a forty-year occupation would result in approximately four burials; a two-family household would generate approximately eight burials over the same period. The frequency of epidemics during the occupation of the site complex suggests the New Ganechstage burial rate would have been somewhat higher.

2. In a 1741 document, New France Governor Beauharnois reprimanded the Senecas for directing all of their smithing work to a New York smith, despite the fact that a French smith was available (NYCD 9: 1083–84). This suggests that the main Seneca towns were close enough together that the western Senecas easily could travel to the eastern community where the New York smith was located. This would have been the case if Huntoon was still occupied, but not if the western Senecas had moved to the Genesee Valley. A 1742 French document requests a smith for the "Little Village" of the Senecas using the same language that had been employed in prior years (NYCD 9: 1090), again suggesting that Huntoon was still occupied.

3. The 1734 Albany Commissioners document indicates a population of about 160 families (or 800 total residents) at Huntoon (MACIA vol. 1820: 52a). Approximately 150–200 people may have lived at Townley-Read if the observed 60–80 m distance between houses extends across the entire site and if each house lot was occupied by a two-family structure. Kurt Jordan (2004) tentatively estimates a population of 179 for a part of Kendaia in 1779, a figure which may have held during the early years of the site as well.

4. I am grateful to Jim Folts and George Hamell (personal communications, 2004) for information on the presence of Europeans in Seneca territory in 1779, which caused me to rethink my previous position that Senecas lived in most of the "Tory houses" in their territory (K. Jordan 2002: 425–26; 2004: 42–43). It remains possible, however, that some of the alleged "Tory houses" were Seneca residences.

5. The historian Milton W. Hamilton (1976: 326) declares the alleged 1765 description of Kanadesaga by colonial official Ezra Buell, which was published in 1903 by Augustus C. Buell, to be "a concoction" of Augustus Buell's. Hamilton (1953, 1956, 1976)

documents errors and forgeries in a number of works by Augustus Buell, and I have been unable to trace the original 1765 manuscript, so the information from it must be used with extreme caution. The narrative states that in 1765 Kanadesaga contained 72 dwellings, 6 log storehouses, and 427 residents (quoted in Buell 1903: 238). Buell notes that a "broad street, I would say a hundred and fifty feet [45.7 m] wide" radiated out from each side of the stockade, and that houses were "at distances of one or two hundred feet [30.5–61.0 m] from each other" (237). Although this description of the site's structure resonates with those provided by McKendry and Campbell, Buell's account of house construction details is inconsistent with other sources and general principles of Iroquois architecture. These empirical problems and the prior record of Augustus Buell documented by Hamilton suggest that the 1765 narrative probably is indeed a fabrication.

Chapter 7. The Logic of Dispersed Settlement

1. The best candidates for the locations of Onondaga villages in 1700 are the Jamesville Pen (Gregory Sohrweide, personal communication, 2001) and Sevier (T. Tanner 1995) sites. The Jamesville Pen site was nucleated and palisaded (Grumet 1995: 392), and the Sevier site occupied a defensible hilltop 2.4–2.8 ha in size (T. Tanner 1995: 41); Grumet's (1995: 393) characterization of Sevier as a "sprawling settlement" does not seem to be warranted. It is possible that New York officials may have wanted the Onondagas to tightly nucleate specifically to facilitate construction of a proposed European fortification around their village, a fortification which in the end never was built (NYCD 4: 660, 750, 783, 873).

2. The phrase *landscape of fear* is from Tuan (1979); see K. Jordan (1998) for application in an Iroquois context.

Chapter 8. Iroquois Housing, 1677–1754: Terminology and Definitions

1. My writing on Iroquois housing owes a considerable debt to the work of George Hamell (especially Hamell 1992a, an important but unpublished conference paper). Hamell has traced Seneca use of traditional, bark-sided Iroquois house forms well into the reservation period. While chapters 8 and 9 are inspired by Hamell's work and cover some of the same ground, my treatment differs from Hamell's in that I examine more formally the large proportion of Iroquois housing during the eighteenth century that falls into neither the "traditional" nor the "European-style" categories; stress the importance of considering the short longhouse to be a continued form of *multiple family* residence; and provide more extensive coverage of truly European-style Iroquois dwellings and the reasons for their construction.

2. Preliminary studies of Iroquois residential architecture after 1754 are provided in Jordan (2002: 414–67, 2004, 2009). I intend to return to this research in subsequent publications.

3. This distinction roughly parallels Rogers' (1990: 106–7) delineation of "replacement" and "addition" as artifact processes.

4. My earlier studies (K. Jordan 2002, 2003) suggested that the smaller proportion of organized space that characterized the Townley-Read short longhouse might distinguish it from traditional dwellings. Using Kapches' (1990) definitions, the area of

the Townley-Read shorthouse contains 22.7 percent organized space (composed of the sleeping bench area and the estimated area of a plowed-away central hearth). This is significantly lower than Kapches' (1990) organized space figures for most "prehistoric" and "early historic" true longhouses in Ontario. However, preliminary study of Post-columbian short longhouse plans (Dean 1984; Hosbach et al. 2006; K. Jordan 2003; Ricklis 1967) suggests that short longhouses consistently had less organized area than did true longhouses, regardless of when they were built, something Kapches (1990) also found true of Iroquoian "cabins." Thus, the small organized area at Townley-Read appears to be a product of the dwelling's short longhouse form, not a consequence of its intercultural/creolized construction.

5. Post-in-ground construction is an integral part of the "earthfast" architectural forms commonly used in the British Middle Atlantic colonies (Deetz 1993) and *pieux en terre* structures used by French colonists (Gums 2002). The archaeological traces of these houses appear to be readily distinguishable from those of Indian dwellings. Earthfast houses employ very large dug post holes and use posts only around the perimeter of the house, while *pieux en terre* structures use wall trenches and fill inter-post spaces with a mixture of clay and organic material (*bousillage*).

6. Posts at Atwell ranged from 6.4 to 30.5 cm in size. Two unusually large probable roof supports measured 30.5 cm and 22.9 cm, other likely interior support posts ranged from 12.7 to 17.8 cm, and wall posts formed the grouping of smallest posts (Ricklis 1967: 15–16).

7. Iron "hardware" was recovered at Conestoga but not quantified (B. Kent 1993: 389), thus eliminating the site from this discussion.

Chapter 9. Iroquois Housing, 1677–1754: Archaeological and Documentary Evidence

1. This drawing and (somewhat anachronistically) a structural plan from the early seventeenth-century Seneca Cornish site (Hayes 1967) provided models for the reconstructed peaked-roof longhouse at Ganondagan State Historic Site.

2. This map is the same map formerly held by the Public Records Office (PRO); an administrative reorganization has placed the PRO within the National Archives.

3. I am puzzled by Doblin and Starna's idea that Bartram "described what may have been the same house at Onondaga" (1994: 40 note 140), because the text clearly indicates Claus was describing an Oneida, not Onondaga, house.

4. The summary presented by Tuck (1971: 165–70) differs fundamentally from Ricklis' (1967) original account. Most significantly, Ricklis states that the structure is 7.9 × 5.5 m in size, while Tuck inexplicably substitutes dimensions of 9.1 × 5.5 m without providing a reason for the change.

Chapter 10. Archaeology and Townley-Read's Economy: Faunal Remains, Red Stone, and Alcohol Bottles

1. Watson (2000) initially analyzed the dry-screened faunal assemblage from Areas A through D, and West (2001) examined the dry-screened faunal assemblage from Area H and the flotation faunal material from the entire site. Watson (2007) re-examines and reports on the entire assemblage. Stephen Cox Thomas of Bioarchaeological Research

is in the process of analyzing the microfaunal and non-mammalian specimens from the site; his study was incomplete at the time of this writing. While the faunal analysis presented here is therefore preliminary, Thomas' study of a relatively small component of the assemblage is unlikely to alter the main points presented here.

2. Townley-Read was occupied during an important seventy-year gap in Kuhn and Funk's data between the 1657–1679 Jackson- Everson site (as dated by Snow 1995: 403) and the Fort Hunter site (where deposits at the Enders House postdate 1750; Fisher 1993; Rick 1991) and Indian Castle site (where deposits from the Brant House postdate 1762; Guldenzopf 1986]).

3. The 1683–1693 date for Jackson-Everson cited by Kuhn and Funk (2000: table 1) appears to be an error.

4. The two deer specimens potentially killed during February–April when whitetails are at their leanest (Madrigal and Holt 2002: 752) were both subadults aged twenty to twenty-four months. These individuals likely were killed by opportunistic local hunting during the spring hungry time; one is female and the sex of the other is indeterminate (Watson 2007). Stored bone grease buffered Seneca subsistence in the late winter and early spring, and there is ample evidence for the use of prime late-spring resources, such as passenger pigeons and fish, at the site. The taking of subadults in February–April therefore does not necessarily represent subsistence stress.

5. Morgan's description of Seneca hide processing on the Tonawanda Reservation in the late 1840s (in Tooker 1994: 115–16, 179–80) is closest temporally and culturally to Townley-Read. Braund (1993: 68), Jennings (1975: 92), Spector (1993: 106), and Waselkov (1998) provide additional details.

6. Identification of the Townley-Read materials as red slate was confirmed by Hobart and William Smith Colleges geologist Brooks McKinney (personal communication, 2000).

7. I am currently in the early stages of a project with Darren Dale of the Cornell High Energy Synchrotron Source (CHESS) that is attempting to source red pipestone and red slate artifacts using x-ray fluorescence. The project compares the elemental compositions of artifacts from Iroquois sites to raw material samples quarried from known locations. Mike Galban (personal communication, 2007) made the interesting suggestion that Iroquois peoples might have acquired red slate from Euro-Americans in Albany who used it as roofing slate. However, red slate has a long history of circulation in the Northeast (Bradley 1987: 102; B. Kent 1993: 167), and it was used commonly on Iroquois sites dating to the 1650s and 1660s (Bradley 1987: 206; Ryan and Dewbury 2010) which appears to predate Albany residents' use of red slate for roofing. I am grateful to Mike Galban and Paul Huey for their input on this issue.

8. K. Jordan (2002: 524–25) details procedures used to generate the overall count figures presented here.

9. Domestic-context excavations conducted at White Springs in 2007 under my direction recovered only a small amount of alcohol bottle glass, reinforcing the overall impression of its rarity based on surface-collection data.

Bibliography

Abler, Thomas S.
1989 *Chainbreaker: The Revolutionary War Memoirs of Governor Blacksnake.* Edited by Thomas S. Abler. Lincoln: University of Nebraska Press.
1992 Beavers and Muskets: Iroquois Military Fortunes in the Face of European Colonization. In R. Brian Ferguson and Neil L. Whitehead, eds., *War in the Tribal Zone*, 151–74. Santa Fe, N.Mex.: School of American Research Press.
2000 Iroquois Policy and Iroquois Culture: Two Histories and an Anthropological Ethnohistory. *Ethnohistory* 47(2): 483–91.

Abler, Thomas S., and Elisabeth Tooker
1978 Seneca. In Bruce G. Trigger, ed., *Handbook of North American Indians.* Vol. 15, *Northeast*, 505–17. Washington, D.C.: Smithsonian Institution Press.

Adams, Nick
1986 Iroquois Settlement at Fort Frontenac in the Seventeenth and Early Eighteenth Centuries. *Ontario Archaeologist* 46: 5–20.

Adams, Robert McC.
1966 *The Evolution of Urban Society.* Chicago: Aldine.

Alexander, Rani T.
1998 Afterword: Toward an Archaeological Theory of Culture Contact. In James G. Cusick, ed., *Studies in Culture Contact*, 476–95. Center for Archaeological Investigations Occasional Paper No. 25. Carbondale: Southern Illinois University.
2004 *Yaxcabá and the Caste War of Yucatán: An Archaeological Perspective.* Albuquerque: University of New Mexico Press.

Alfred, Taiaiake
1999 *Peace, Power, Righteousness: An Indigenous Manifesto.* Oxford: Oxford University Press.

Aloi, Daniel
2007 Students Dig into Iroquois Culture. *Cornell Chronicle Online*, June 22. Available online at <www.news.cornell.edu/stories/June07/fieldArch.da.html> (accessed January 11, 2008).

Amato, Christopher A.
2002 Digging Sacred Ground: Burial Site Disturbances and the Loss of New York's Native American Heritage. *Columbia Journal of Environmental Law* 27(1): 1–44.

Anderson, David A.
1995 Susquehannock Longhouses and Culture Change during the Contact Period in Pennsylvania. Master's thesis, Department of Anthropology, University of Pittsburgh, Pittsburgh, Pa.

Anselmi, Lisa Marie
2004 *New Materials, Old Ideas: Native Use of European-Introduced Metals in the*

Northeast. Ph.D. diss., University of Toronto. Ann Arbor, Mich.: University Microfilms.

Aquila, Richard

1983 *The Iroquois Restoration.* Detroit: Wayne State University Press.

1984 The Iroquois as "Geographic" Middlemen: A Research Note. *Indiana Magazine of History* 80: 51–60.

Barber, Daniel M.

1961 Fort Hill Site. *The Bulletin: New York State Archeological Association* 23: 12–13.

1964 Fort Hill at Victor, New York. *Museum Service: Bulletin of the Rochester Museum of Arts and Sciences* 37(4): 58–61.

Barnes, Frederick W.

1914 The Fur Traders of Early Oswego. *New York Historical Association Proceedings* 13: 128–37.

Bartram, John

1966 [1751] *Observations on the Inhabitants, Climate, Soil, Rivers, Productions, Animals, and Other Matters Worthy of Notice Made by Mr. John Bartram in His Travels from Pensilvania to Onondago, Oswego, and the Lake Ontario, in Canada.* March of America No. 41. Ann Arbor, Mich.: University Microfilms.

Baugher, Sherene, and Kathleen M. Quinn

1996 *Phase Two Archaeological Investigation of Inlet Valley, Town of Ithaca, New York.* Vol. 1, *Text.* Ithaca, N.Y.: Cornell University and the Town of Ithaca Planning Department.

Beauchamp, William M.

1900 *Aboriginal Occupation of New York.* Bulletin of the New York State Museum No. 32. Albany: New York State Museum.

1916 *Moravian Journals Relating to Central New York, 1745–66.* Edited by William M. Beauchamp. Syracuse, N.Y.: Dehler Press.

Beck, Charlotte, and George T. Jones

1994 On-Site Artifact Analysis as an Alternative to Collection. *American Antiquity* 59(2): 304–15.

Bennett, Monte R.

1982 A Salvage Burial Excavation on the Lanz-Hogan Site, OND 2-4. *Bulletin of the Chenango Chapter of the New York State Archaeological Association* 19(4).

1988 The Primes Hill Site, MSV 5-2: An Eighteenth-Century Oneida Station. *Bulletin of the Chenango Chapter of the New York State Archaeological Association* 22(4): 1–21.

Benson, Adolph B., ed.

1937 *Peter Kalm's Travels in North America.* 2 vols. New York: Wilson-Erickson.

Bernbeck, Reinhard

1995 Lasting Alliances and Emerging Competition: Economic Developments in Early Mesopotamia. *Journal of Anthropological Archaeology* 14(1): 1–25.

Bertsch, W. H.

1914 The Defenses of Oswego. *New York Historical Association Proceedings* 13: 108–27.

Bieder, Robert E.
1986   *Science Encounters the Indian, 1820–1880*. Norman: University of Oklahoma Press.

Bielinski, Stefan
2002   Myndert Schuyler. Biography by Colonial Albany Social History Project. Available online at <www.nysm.nysed.gov/albany/bios/s/mynschuyler101.html> (accessed January 11, 2008).
2003   Evert Bancker. Biography by Colonial Albany Social History Project. Available online at <www.nysm.nysed.gov/albany/bios/b/ebancker6454.html> (accessed January 11, 2008).
n.d.   Robert Livingston, Jr. Biography by Colonial Albany Social History Project. Available online at <www.nysm.nysed.gov/albany/bios/l/rlivingstonjr.html> (accessed January 11, 2008).

Bilharz, Joy A.
1998   *The Allegany Senecas and Kinzua Dam*. Lincoln: University of Nebraska Press.

Binford, Lewis R.
1962   A New Method of Calculating Dates from Kaolin Pipe Stem Samples. *Southeastern Archaeological Conference Newsletter* 9(1): 19–21.
1978   *Nunamiut Ethnoarchaeology*. New York: Academic Press.
1980   Willow Smoke and Dogs' Tails: Hunter-Gatherer Settlement Systems and Archaeological Site Formation. *American Antiquity* 45: 4–20.

Bodner, Connie Cox
1999   Sunflower in the Seneca Iroquois Region of Western New York. In John P. Hart, ed., *Current Northeast Paleobotany*, 27–45. New York State Museum Bulletin No. 494. Albany: New York State Museum.

Boserup, Ester
1965   *The Conditions of Agricultural Growth*. New York: Aldine.

Bradley, James W.
1980   Ironwork in Onondaga, 1550–1650. In Nancy Bonvillain, ed., *Studies on Iroquoian Culture*, 109–17. Occasional Publications in Northeastern Anthropology No. 6. Rindge, N.H.: Dept. of Anthropology, Franklin Pierce College.
1987   *Evolution of the Onondaga Iroquois: Accommodating Change, 1500–1655*. Syracuse, N.Y.: Syracuse University Press.

Brain, Jeffrey P.
1979   *Tunica Treasure*. Papers of the Peabody Museum of Archaeology and Ethnology Vol. 71. Cambridge, Mass.: Peabody Museum, Harvard University.
1988   *Tunica Archaeology*. Cambridge, Mass.: Harvard University Press.

Brandão, José António
1997   *Your Fyre Shall Burn No More: Iroquois Policy Toward New France and Its Native Allies to 1701*. Lincoln: University of Nebraska Press.
2003   *Nation Iroquoise: A Seventeenth-Century Ethnography of the Iroquois*. Edited by José António Brandão. Translated by José António Brandão and K. Janet Ritch. Lincoln: University of Nebraska Press.

Brandão, José António, and William A. Starna
1996   The Treaties of 1701: A Triumph of Iroquois Diplomacy. *Ethnohistory* 43: 209–44.

Branstner, Susan M.
1992 Tionontate Huron Occupation at the Marquette Mission. In John A. Walthall and Thomas E. Emerson, eds., *Calumet and Fleur-de-Lys: Archaeology of Indian and French Contact in the Midcontinent*, 177–201. Washington, D.C.: Smithsonian Institution Press.

Braund, Kathryn E. Holland
1993 *Deerskins & Duffels: The Creek Indian Trade with Anglo-America, 1685–1815*. Lincoln: University of Nebraska Press.

Brewer, Floyd I.
1992 Albert Brandt, Tobacco Planter, and the Smoking-Pipe Story in Early Bethlehem, New York. In Charles F. Hayes III, ed., *Proceedings of the 1989 Smoking Pipe Conference*, 151–61. Rochester Museum and Science Center Research Records No. 22. Rochester, N.Y.: Rochester Museum and Science Center.

Brink, John W.
1997 Fat Content in Leg Bones of *Bison bison*, and Applications to Archaeology. *Journal of Archaeological Science* 24(3): 259–74.

Brose, David S., C. Wesley Cowan, and Robert C. Mainfort Jr., eds.
2001 *Societies in Eclipse: Archaeology of the Eastern Woodlands Indians, A.D. 1400–1700*. Washington, D.C.: Smithsonian Institution Press.

Brown, George W. et al., eds.
1966–2005 *Dictionary of Canadian Biography*. 15 vols. Toronto: University of Toronto Press.

Bruseth, James E., and Toni S. Turner
2005 *From a Watery Grave: The Discovery and Excavation of La Salle's Shipwreck, La Belle*. College Station: Texas A&M University Press.

Buell, Augustus C.
1903 *Sir William Johnson*. New York: D. Appleton and Co.

Butler, William B.
1979 The No-Collection Strategy in Archaeology. *American Antiquity* 44(4): 795–99.

Cadwell, Donald H., Ernest H. Muller, and P. Jay Fleisher
2003 Geomorphic History of New York State. In David L. Cremeens and John P. Hart, eds., *Geoarchaeology of Landscapes in the Glaciated Northeast*, 7–14. New York State Museum Bulletin 497. Albany: New York State Museum.

Calloway, Colin G.
1995 *The American Revolution in Indian Country*. Cambridge: Cambridge University Press.

Campbell, William W.
1831 *Annals of Tryon County; or, The Border Warfare of New-York During the Revolution*. New York: J. & J. Harper.

Ceci, Lynn
1989 Tracing Wampum's Origins. In Charles F. Hayes III, ed., *Proceedings of the 1986 Shell Bead Conference*, 63–80. Rochester Museum and Science Center Research Records No. 20. Rochester, N.Y.: Rochester Museum and Science Center.

Church, Robert R., and R. Lee Lyman
2003   Small Fragments Make Small Differences in Efficiency when Rendering Grease from Fractured Artiodactyl Bones by Boiling. *Journal of Archaeological Sciences* 30: 1077–84.
Cleland, Charles E., ed.
1971   *The Lasanen Site*. Publications of the Museum, Michigan State University, Anthropological Series Vol. 1, No. 1. East Lansing: Michigan State University.
Clifton, James A.
1978   Potawatomi. In Bruce G. Trigger, ed., *Handbook of North American Indians*. Vol. 15, *Northeast*, 725–42. Washington, D.C.: Smithsonian Institution Press.
Coates, Irving W.
1892a   The Castle of "Onnaghee." *Ontario County Times*, July 6.
1892b   The Castle of "Onnaghee." *Ontario County Times*, July 13.
1892c   The Castle of "Onnaghee." *Ontario County Times*, July 20.
1892d   The Castle of "Onnaghee." *Ontario County Times*, July 27.
1892e   The Castle of "Onnaghee." *Ontario County Times*, August 3.
1893   *In the Footprints of Denonville*. Canandaigua, N.Y.: Ontario County Times Printing House.
Cobb, Charles R.
1993   Archaeological Approaches to the Political Economy of Nonstratified Societies. *Archaeological Method and Theory* 5: 43–100.
Colden, Cadwallader
1935 [1720]   Continuation of Colden's History of the Five Indian Nations, for the Years 1707 through 1720. *New York Historical Society Collections* 68: 357–434.
1958 [1747]   *The History of the Five Indian Nations Depending on the Province of New-York in America*. Ithaca, N.Y.: Cornell University Press.
Connor, Melissa, and Douglas D. Scott
1998   Metal Detector Use in Archaeology: An Introduction. *Historical Archaeology* 32(4): 76–85.
Conover, George S.
1882   Indian History. Paper presented at Linden Hall, Geneva, N.Y. Lecture notes in bound manuscript, Ontario County Historical Society, Canandaigua, N.Y.
1885   *Sayenqueraghta, King of the Senecas*. Waterloo, N.Y.: Observer Steam Job Printing House.
1887   *Journals of the Military Expeditions of Major General John Sullivan against the Six Nations of Indians in 1779*. Edited by George S. Conover. Auburn, N.Y.: Knapp, Peck, and Thompson.
1889   *Seneca Villages*. Geneva, N.Y.: n.p.
1893   *History of Ontario County, New York*. Syracuse, N.Y.: D. Mason and Co.
n.d.   Kanadesaga and Geneva. 4 vols. Unpublished manuscript available in Archives, Warren Hunting Smith Library, Hobart and William Smith Colleges, Geneva, N.Y.
Conrad, Maia
1999   Disorderly Drinking: Reconsidering Seventeenth-Century Iroquois Alcohol Abuse. *American Indian Quarterly* 23: 1–11.

Cowan, Frank L.
1999 Making Sense of Flake Scatters. *American Antiquity* 64: 593–607.
Cronon, William
1983 *Changes in the Land: Indians, Colonists, and the Ecology of New England*. New York: Hill and Wang.
Cusick, James G.
1998 Historiography of Acculturation: An Evaluation of Concepts and Their Application in Archaeology. In James G. Cusick, ed., *Studies in Culture Contact*, 126–45. Southern Illinois University at Carbondale Center for Archaeological Investigations Occasional Paper No. 25. Carbondale: Southern Illinois University.
Cutcliffe, Stephen H.
1981 Colonial Indian Policy as a Measure of Rising Imperialism: New York and Pennsylvania, 1700–1755. *Western Pennsylvania Historical Magazine* 64(3): 237–68.
Darnell, Regna
1998 *And Along Came Boas: Continuity and Revolution in Americanist Anthropology*. Philadelphia: John Benjamins.
Dawdy, Shannon Lee
2000 Preface to Special Issue of Historical Archaeology on Creolization. *Historical Archaeology* 34(3): 1–4.
DCB. *See* Brown, George W. et al., eds.
Deagan, Kathleen
1983 *Spanish St. Augustine: The Archaeology of a Creole Community*. New York: Academic Press.
1998 Transculturation and Spanish American Ethnogenesis: The Archaeological Legacy of the Quincentenary. In James G. Cusick, ed., *Studies in Culture Contact*, 23–43. Southern Illinois University at Carbondale Center for Archaeological Investigations Occasional Paper No. 25. Carbondale: Southern Illinois University.
Dean, Robert L.
1984 Archaeological Investigations at Gannagaro State Historic Site, Victor, Ontario County, New York, 1983–1984. Edited by Robert L. Dean. Unpublished report on file at the New York State Bureau of Historic Sites, Waterford, N.Y.
1986 Archaeology at Ganondagan State Historic Site. In Ben Kroup, ed., *Art from Ganondagan*, 11–15. Waterford, NY: New York State Office of Parks, Recreation, and Historic Preservation.
Deardorff, Merle H.
1946 Zeisberger's Allegheny River Indian Towns: 1767–1770. *Pennsylvania Archaeologist* 16(1): 2–19.
Deetz, James
1977 *In Small Things Forgotten*. Garden City, N.Y.: Anchor Press/Doubleday.
1993 *Flowerdew Hundred*. Charlottesville: University of Virginia Press.
Deloria, Philip J.
1998 *Playing Indian*. New Haven: Yale University Press.

Deloria, Vine Jr.
1991 Sacred Lands and Religious Freedom. *NARF Legal Review* 16(2): 1–6.

Densmore, Christopher
1999 *Red Jacket: Iroquois Diplomat and Orator.* Syracuse, N.Y.: Syracuse University Press.

DeOrio, Robert N.
1998 Cayuga Update. Paper presented at the Northeast Archaeological Symposium, October 23, 1998, Cayuga Museum, Auburn, N.Y.

Dewbury, Adam G., and Beth Ryan
n.d. The Eugene Frost Collection: Artifacts from the Seneca Iroquois White Springs Site, circa 1688–1715. Unpublished report submitted to author.

DHNY. *See* O'Callaghan, E. B., ed. 1849–1851.

Dietler, Michael
1998 Consumption, Agency, and Cultural Entanglement: Theoretical Implications of a Mediterranean Colonial Encounter. In James G. Cusick, ed., *Studies in Culture Contact*, 288–315. Southern Illinois University at Carbondale Center for Archaeological Investigations Occasional Paper No. 25. Carbondale: Southern Illinois University.

Division of Archives and History
1929 *The Sullivan-Clinton Campaign in 1779.* Albany: University of the State of New York.

Doblin, Helga, and William A. Starna, eds.
1994 The Journals of Christian Daniel Claus and Conrad Weiser: A Journey to Onondaga, 1750. *Transactions of the American Philosophical Society* 84(2).

Doolittle, William E.
2004 Permanent vs. Shifting Cultivation in the Eastern Woodlands of North America Prior to European Contact. *Agriculture and Human Values* 21: 181–89.

Douglas, Mary
1971 Is Matriliny Doomed in Africa? In Mary Douglas and Phyllis M. Kaberry, eds., *Man in Africa*, 123–37. Garden City, N.Y.: Anchor-Doubleday.

Doxtator, Deborah
1996 What Happened to the Iroquois Clans?: A Study of Clans in Three Nineteenth-Century Rotinonhsyonni Communities. Ph.D. diss., University of Western Ontario.

Drake, Samuel G., ed.
1855 *Indian Captivities, or Life in the Wigwam.* New York: Miller, Orton, and Mulligan.

Drennan, Robert D.
1988 Household Location and Compact Versus Dispersed Settlement in Prehispanic Mesoamerica. In Richard R. Wilk and Wendy Ashmore, eds., *Household and Community in the Mesoamerican Past*, 273–93. Albuquerque: University of New Mexico Press.

Dunn, Shirley W.
2002 The Longhouses of Seventeenth-Century Maps: Real or Imagined? *The Bulletin: Journal of the New York State Archaeological Association* 118: 2–18.

Edmunds, R. David, and Joseph L. Peyser
1993   *The Fox Wars*. Norman: University of Oklahoma Press.

Elliott, Dolores
1977   Otsiningo, an Example of an Eighteenth-Century Settlement Pattern. In Robert E. Funk and Charles F. Hayes III, eds., *Current Perspectives in Northeastern Archaeology: Essays in Honor of William A. Ritchie*, 93–105. Researches and Transactions of the New York State Archeological Association 17, No. 1. Rochester, N.Y.: New York State Archeological Association.
1996   Otsiningo: From Prehistory to the Present. *Journal of Middle Atlantic Archaeology* 12: 179–87.

Emmons, E. Thayles
1958   Senecas Abandoned Ganechstage after Smallpox Epidemic. *Geneva Times*, October 28.

Engelbrecht, William
2003   *Iroquoia: The Development of a Native World*. Syracuse, N.Y.: Syracuse University Press.

Evans, Lewis
1755   A General Map of the Middle British Colonies in America. Engraved by Jas. Turner. Map held by the Library of Congress Geography and Map Division, Washington D.C. Available online through the American Memory Project at <http://hdl.loc.gov/loc.gmd/g3710.ar070900> (accessed January 11, 2008).
1784   Pensilvaniæ, Novæ-Cæsareæ, Novi-Eboraci, Aquanishuonigæ et Canadæ, Brevis Delineatio, Juxta Itinera P. Kalm a Ludovico Evans, 1750. Map held by the Library of Congress Geography and Map Division, Washington D.C. Available online through the American Memory Project at <http://hdl.loc.gov/loc.gmd/g3710.ar070500> (accessed January 11, 2008).

Feest, Johanna E., and Christian F. Feest
1978   Ottawa. In Bruce G. Trigger, ed., *Handbook of North American Indians*. Vol. 15, *Northeast*, 772–86. Washington, D.C.: Smithsonian Institution Press.

Feister, Lois M.
1995   *Johnson Hall Outbuildings, Landscape History, and Forgotten Features: Documentary and Archeological Research*. Waterford, N.Y.: Bureau of Historic Sites, New York State Office of Parks, Recreation, and Historic Preservation.

Fenton, William N.
1940   Problems Arising from the Historic Northeastern Position of the Iroquois. In *Essays in Historical Anthropology of North America*, 159–252. Smithsonian Miscellaneous Collections No. 100. Washington, D.C.: Smithsonian Institution.
1951   Locality as a Basic Factor in the Development of Iroquois Social Structure. *Bureau of American Ethnology Bulletin* 149: 35–54.
1967   From Longhouse to Ranch-type House: The Second Housing Revolution of the Seneca Nation. In Elisabeth Tooker, ed., *Iroquois Culture, History, and Prehistory: Proceedings of the 1965 Conference on Iroquois Research*, 7–22. Albany: New York State Museum and Science Service.
1971   The New York State Wampum Collection: The Case for the Integrity of Cultural Treasures. *Proceedings of the American Philosophical Society* 115(6): 437–61.

1978 Northern Iroquoian Culture Patterns. In Bruce G. Trigger, ed., *Handbook of North American Indians*. Vol. 15, *Northeast*, 296–321. Washington, D.C.: Smithsonian Institution Press.
1998 *The Great Law and the Longhouse: A Political History of the Iroquois Confederacy*. Norman: University of Oklahoma Press.

Fenton, William N., and Merle H. Deardorff
1943 The Last Passenger Pigeon Hunts of the Cornplanter Senecas. *Journal of the Washington Academy of Sciences* 33(10): 289–315.

Fenton, William N., and Elizabeth L. Moore, eds.
1974 *Customs of the American Indians Compared with the Customs of Primitive Times*, by Joseph-Francois Lafitau. Vol. 1. Publications of the Champlain Society 48. Toronto: Champlain Society.
1977 *Customs of the American Indians Compared with the Customs of Primitive Times*, by Joseph-Francois Lafitau. Vol. 2. Publications of the Champlain Society 49. Toronto: Champlain Society.

Fenton, William N., and Elisabeth Tooker
1978 Mohawk. In Bruce G. Trigger, ed., *Handbook of North American Indians*. Vol. 15, *Northeast*, 466–80. Washington, D.C.: Smithsonian Institution Press.

Ferguson, Leland
1992 *Uncommon Ground: Archaeology and Early African America, 1650–1800*. Washington, D.C.: Smithsonian Institution Press.

Fine-Dare, Kathleen S.
2002 *Grave Injustice: The American Indian Repatriation Movement and NAGPRA*. Lincoln: University of Nebraska Press.

Fisher, Charles L.
1993 Catlinite and Red Slate Ornaments from the Enders House Site, Schoharie Crossing State Historic Site, Montgomery County, New York. *The Bulletin: Journal of the New York State Archaeological Association* 106: 17–23.
2003 *An Archeological Report on the 18th-Century Mohawk Iroquois Occupation of the Enders House Site at Schoharie Crossing State Historic Site, Montgomery County, New York*. Waterford, N.Y.: Bureau of Historic Sites, New York State Office of Parks, Recreation, and Historic Preservation.

Flannery, Kent V.
1968 Archaeological Systems Theory and Early Mesoamerica. In Betty J. Meggers, ed., *Anthropological Archeology in the Americas*, pp. 67–87. Washington, D.C.: Anthropological Society of Washington.

Follett, Harrison C.
n.d. Archeology of the Counties of Monroe, Ontario, Livingston, and Genesee, New York. Unpublished manuscript on file at Rochester Museum and Science Center Research Division, Rochester, N.Y.

Fort Niagara in 1799.
1997 [1799] *OFN Now & Then: The Newsletter of the Old Fort Niagara Association* 47(11): 1–2. (The author is listed as "An American Gentleman lately from Niagara.")

Fox, Edith M.
1949 *Land Speculation in the Mohawk Country*. Ithaca, N.Y.: Cornell University Press.

Fox, Richard Allan Jr.
1993 *Archaeology, History, and Custer's Last Battle*. Norman: University of Oklahoma Press.

Francello, Joseph A.
1980 *The Seneca World of Ga-No-Say-Yeh*. Lanham, Md.: University Press of America.

Galloway, Patricia
1991 The Archaeology of Ethnohistorical Narrative. In David Hurst Thomas, ed., *Columbian Consequences*. Vol. 3, *The Spanish Borderlands in Pan-American Perspective*, 453–69. Washington, D.C.: Smithsonian Institution Press.
1995 *Choctaw Genesis, 1500–1700*. Lincoln: University of Nebraska Press.

Gehring, Charles T., and William A. Starna, eds.
1988 *A Journey into Mohawk and Oneida Country, 1634–1635: The Journal of Harmen Meyndertsz van den Bogaert*. Syracuse, N.Y.: Syracuse University Press.

Gibson, John
1771 A New and Accurate Map of Part of North-America, Comprehending the Provinces of New England, New York, Pensilvania, New Jersey, Connecticut, Rhode Island & Part of Virginia, Canada and Hallifax, for the Illustration of Mr. Peter Kalm's Travels. J. Gibson, sculp. Manuscript map held by the Library of Congress Geography and Map Division, Washington D.C. Available online through the American Memory Project at <http://hdl.loc.gov/loc.gmd/g3710.ar072600> (accessed January 11, 2008).

Gipson, Lawrence Henry
1939 *Lewis Evans*. Philadelphia: Historical Society of Pennsylvania.

Glassie, Henry
1975 *Folk Housing in Middle Virginia*. Knoxville: University of Tennessee Press.

Gosden, Chris
2004 *Archaeology and Colonialism*. Cambridge: Cambridge University Press.

Graham, Robert J., and Charles F. Wray
1985 [1966] The Boughton Hill Site, Victor, New York. *The Iroquoian: Newsletter of the Lewis Henry Morgan Chapter of the New York State Archaeological Association* 10. (Reprint of a 1966 conference paper).

Grassman, Thomas
1969 *The Mohawks and Their Valley*. Schenectady, N.Y.: J. S. Lischynsky.

Graymont, Barbara
1972 *The Iroquois in the American Revolution*. Syracuse, N.Y.: Syracuse University Press.
1976 New York State Indian Policy after the Revolution. *New York History* 57: 438–74.

Grayson, Donald K.
1984 *Quantitative Zooarchaeology*. Orlando, Fla.: Academic Press.

Green, Rayna
1988 The Tribe Called Wannabee: Playing Indian in America and Europe. *Folklore* 99(1): 30–55.

Gremillion, Kristen J.
2004 Seed Processing and the Origins of Food Production in Eastern North America. *American Antiquity* 69(2): 215–33.

Gronim, Sara Stidstone
2001 Geography and Persuasion: Maps in British Colonial New York. *William and Mary Quarterly*, 3rd. ser., 58(2): 373–402.

Grumet, Robert S.
1995 *Historic Contact*. Norman: University of Oklahoma Press.

Guldenzopf, David
1986 *The Colonial Transformation of Mohawk Iroquois Society*. Ph.D. diss., State University of New York–Albany. Ann Arbor, Mich.: University Microfilms.

Gums, Bonnie L.
2002 Earthfast (*Pieux en Terre*) Structures at Old Mobile. *Historical Archaeology* 36(1): 13–25.

Gundersen, James Novotny
1993 "Catlinite" and the Spread of the Calumet Ceremony. *American Antiquity* 58(3): 560–62.

Gunderson, Robert Gray
1957 *The Log-Cabin Campaign*. Lexington: University of Kentucky Press.

Guthe, Alfred K.
1958 A Possible Seneca House Site, A.D. 1600. *Pennsylvania Archaeologist* 28(1): 33–38.

Haan, Richard
1976 *The Covenant Chain: Iroquois Diplomacy on the Niagara Frontier, 1697–1730*. Ph.D. diss., University of California, Santa Barbara. Ann Arbor, Mich.: University Microfilms.
1980 The Problem of Iroquois Neutrality: Suggestions for Revision. *Ethnohistory* 27: 317–30.

Hagerty, Gilbert W.
1985 *Wampum, War and Trade Goods West of the Hudson*. Interlaken, N.Y.: Heart of the Lakes Publishing.

Halsey, Francis W., ed.
1906 *A Tour of the Hudson, the Mohawk, the Susquehanna, and the Delaware in 1769*. New York: Charles Scribner's Sons.

Hamell, George R.
1980 Gannagaro State Historic Site: A Current Perspective. In Nancy Bonvillain, ed., *Studies on Iroquoian Culture*, 91–108. Occasional Publications in Northeastern Anthropology No. 6. Rindge, N.H.: Dept. of Anthropology, Franklin Pierce College.
1983 Trading in Metaphors: The Magic of Beads. In Charles F. Hayes III, ed., *Proceedings of the 1982 Glass Trade Bead Conference*, 5–28. Rochester Museum and

Science Center Research Records No. 16. Rochester, N.Y.: Rochester Museum and Science Center.

1992a From Longhouse to Loghouse: At Home among the Senecas, 1790–1828. Paper presented at the United States Capitol Historical Society's Native Americans in the Early Republic Symposium, March 5, 1993. Washington, D.C.

1992b The Iroquois and the World's Rim: Speculations on Color, Culture, and Contact. *American Indian Quarterly* 16(4): 451–69.

n.d. Field notes on the Kanadesaga site, on file at Rochester Museum and Science Center Research Division, Rochester, N.Y.

Hamilton, Milton W.
1953 Myths and Legends of Sir William Johnson. *New York History* 38: 18–28.
1956 Augustus C. Buell: Fraudulent Historian. *Pennsylvania Magazine of History and Biography* 80: 478–92.
1976 *Sir William Johnson: Colonial American, 1715–1763.* Port Washington, N.Y.: Kennikat Press.

Hammett, Julia E.
2000 Ethnohistory of Aboriginal Landscapes in the Southeastern United States. In Paul E. Minnis and Wayne J. Elisens, eds., *Biodiversity and Native America*, 248–99. Norman: University of Oklahoma Press.

Hanson, Lee
1969 Kaolin Pipestems: Boring in on a Fallacy. *The Conference on Historic Site Archaeology Papers* 4: 2–15.

Harrington, J. C.
1954 Dating Stem Fragments of Seventeenth- and Eighteenth-Century Clay Tobacco Pipes. *Quarterly Bulletin of the Archaeological Society of Virginia* 9(1): 10–14.

Harris, George H.
1903 The Life of Horatio Jones. *Publications of the Buffalo Historical Society* 6(9): 383–526.

Hartgen Archaeological Associates, Inc.
2002 Phase IA Literature Review & Phase IB Archeological Field Investigation: Cornell Agriculture and Food Technology Park. Unpublished report prepared for Saratoga Associates, Saratoga Springs, N.Y.

Hasenstab, Robert J.
1996 Aboriginal Settlement Patterns in Late Woodland Upper New York State. *Journal of Middle Atlantic Archaeology* 12: 17–26.

Hauptman, Lawrence M.
1980 Refugee Havens: The Iroquois Villages of the Eighteenth Century. In Christopher Vecsey and Robert W. Venables, eds., *American Indian Environments*, 128–39. Syracuse, N.Y.: Syracuse University Press.
1981 *The Iroquois and the New Deal.* Syracuse, N.Y.: Syracuse University Press.
1986 *The Iroquois Struggle for Survival: World War II to Red Power.* Syracuse, N.Y.: Syracuse University Press.
1999 *Conspiracy of Interests: Iroquois Dispossession and the Rise of New York State.* Syracuse, N.Y.: Syracuse University Press.

Havard, Gilles
2001 *The Great Peace of Montreal of 1701*. Translated by Phyllis Aronoff and Howard Scott. Montreal: McGill-Queen's University Press.

Hawley, Charles
1884 *Early Chapters of Seneca History*. Cayuga County Historical Society Collections 3. Auburn, N.Y.: Cayuga County Historical Society.

Hayes, Charles F. III
1965 *The Orringh Stone Tavern and Three Seneca Sites of the Late Historic Period*. Research Records of the Rochester Museum of Arts and Sciences No. 12. Rochester, N.Y.: Rochester Museum of Arts and Sciences.
1967 The Longhouse at the Cornish Site. In Elisabeth Tooker, ed., *Iroquois Culture, History, and Prehistory: Proceedings of the 1965 Conference on Iroquois Research*, 91–97. Albany: New York State Museum and Science Service.

Hayes, Charles F. III, Daniel M. Barber, and George R. Hamell
1978 An Archaeological Survey of Gannagaro State Historic Site, Ontario County, N.Y. Unpublished report on file at the Research Division, Rochester Museum and Science Center, Rochester, N.Y.

Hazard, Samuel, ed.
1838–1853 *Minutes of the Provincial Council of Pennsylvania*. 15 vols. Harrisburg: n.p.

Hefner, Robert W.
1993 Introduction: World Building and the Rationality of Conversion. In Robert W. Hefner, ed., *Conversion to Christianity*, 3–44. Berkeley: University of California Press.

Heidenreich, Conrad E.
1971 *Huronia: A History and Geography of the Huron Indians, 1600–1650*. Toronto: McClelland and Stewart.

Heimmer, Don H., and Steven L. De Vore
1995 *Near-Surface, High Resolution Geophysical Methods for Cultural Resource Management and Archaeological Investigations*. Rev. ed. Denver, Colo.: Interagency Archaeological Services, National Park Service.

Hendon, Julia A.
1996 Archaeological Approaches to the Organization of Domestic Labor: Household Practice and Domestic Relations. *Annual Review of Anthropology* 25: 45–61.

Henry, Dixie Lynn
2001 *Cultural Change and Adaptation among the Oneida Iroquois, A.D. 1000–1700*. Ph.D. diss., Cornell University. Ann Arbor, Mich.: University Microfilms.

Herrick, James W.
1995 *Iroquois Medical Botany*. Edited and with a foreword by Dean R. Snow. Syracuse, N.Y.: Syracuse University Press.

Hesse, Franklin J.
1975 The Egli and Lord Sites: The Historic Component—"Unadilla" 1753–1778. *The Bulletin: New York State Archaeological Association* 63: 14–31.

Hester, Thomas R., Harry J. Shafer, and Kenneth L. Feder
1997 *Field Methods in Archaeology*. 7th ed. Mountain View, Calif.: Mayfield Publishing Co.

Hinsley, Curtis M. Jr.
1981 *Savages and Scientists: The Smithsonian Institution and the Development of American Anthropology, 1846–1910.* Washington, D.C.: Smithsonian Institution Press.

Hodge, Frederick Webb, ed.
1907–1910 *Handbook of American Indians North of Mexico.* 2 vols. Washington, D.C.: Bureau of American Ethnology.

Hoffman, Albert
n.d. Field notes, on file at Rochester Museum and Science Center Research Division, Rochester, N.Y.

Hosbach, Richard E., Alexander B. Neill, Francis J. Hailey, Gerald L. Hayes, and Daryl E. Wonderly
2006 The Dungey Site (MSV-6): An Historic Oneida Village—A Short Longhouse. *Bulletin of the Chenango Chapter of the New York State Archaeological Association* 29(1): 37–71.

Houghton, Frederick
1927 The Migrations of the Seneca Nation. *American Anthropologist* 29(2): 241–50.

Howson, Jean E.
1990 Social Relations and Material Culture: A Critique of the Archaeology of Plantation Slavery. *Historical Archaeology* 24(4): 78–91.

Huey, Paul R.
1994 Archaeological Testing for an Electrical Line at Ganondagan State Historic Site, July 12, 1994. *The Bulletin: Journal of the New York State Archaeological Association* 108: 11–17.

1997a The Origins and Development of Historical Archaeology in New York State. *The Bulletin: Journal of the New York State Archaeological Association* 113: 60–96.

1997b Annotated Bibliography of Reports, Published Articles, and Books Relating to the Archeology at Ganondagan State Historic Site through August 1997. Report on file at the New York State Bureau of Historic Sites, Waterford, N.Y. Available online at <www.nysl.nysed.gov/edocs/parks/ganonbib.htm> (accessed January 11, 2008).

1998 Schuyler Flatts Archaeological District National Historic Landmark. *The Bulletin: Journal of the New York State Archaeological Association* 114: 24–31.

Hulbert, Archer B., and William N. Schwarze, eds.
1912 The Moravian Records II. *Ohio Archaeological and Historical Quarterly* 21: 1–125.

Hunt, George T.
1940 *The Wars of the Iroquois.* Madison: University of Wisconsin Press.

Hunter, William A.
1956 Refugee Fox Settlements among the Senecas. *Ethnohistory* 3(1): 11–20.

1978 History of the Ohio Valley. In Bruce G. Trigger, ed., *Handbook of North American Indians.* Vol. 15, *Northeast,* 588–93. Washington, D.C.: Smithsonian Institution Press.

IIDH. *See* Jennings, Francis, William N. Fenton, Mary A. Druke, and David R. Miller, eds. 1984

Jaimes, M. Annette
1992 Federal Indian Identification Policy: A Usurpation of Indigenous Sovereignty in North America. In M. Annette Jaimes, ed., *The State of Native America*, 123–38. Boston, Mass.: South End Press.
Jemison, G. Peter
1995 Repatriation. *Akwesasne Notes* 1(September 30): 30.
1997 Who Owns the Past? In Nina Swidler, Kurt Dongoske, Roger Anyon, and Alan Downer, eds., *Native Americans and Archaeologists: Stepping Stones to Common Ground*, 57–63. Walnut Creek, Calif.: Altamira Press.
Jemison, G. Peter, and Anna M. Schein, eds.
2000 *Treaty of Canandaigua 1794: 200 Years of Treaty Relations between the Iroquois Confederacy and the United States*. Santa Fe, N.M.: Clear Light Publishers.
Jemison, G. Peter, and John White
1997 Ganondagan's Longhouse: Connecting the Past with the Future. Paper presented at the Conference on the Iroquois Longhouse, Rochester Museum and Science Center, November 15, 1997. Rochester, N.Y.
Jennings, Francis
1975 *The Invasion of America*. New York: Norton.
1984 *The Ambiguous Iroquois Empire*. New York: Norton.
1988 *Empire of Fortune*. New York: Norton.
Jennings, Francis, William N. Fenton, Mary A. Druke, and David R. Miller, eds.
1984 *Iroquois Indians: A Documentary History*. Set of 50 microfilms. Woodbridge, Conn.: Research Publications.
1985 *The History and Culture of Iroquois Diplomacy*. Syracuse, N.Y.: Syracuse University Press.
Johnson, Matthew
1996 *An Archaeology of Capitalism*. Cambridge, Mass.: Blackwell Publishers.
Johnson, William, and Gary Berg
1976 Archeological Impact Evaluation: Stage One Archeological Survey, Canandaigua Lake County Sewer District Project. Unpublished report prepared for Hershey, Malone & Associates, Rochester, N.Y.
Jones, Eric E.
2006 Using Viewshed Analysis to Explore Settlement Choice: A Case Study of the Onondaga Iroquois. *American Antiquity* 71(3): 523–38.
Jordan, Kurt A.
1996 Burial Summaries for Seneca Sites, ca. 1688–1754. Data summary on file with the Research Division, Rochester Museum and Science Center, Rochester, N.Y.
1997 Pan-Iroquoian Trend or Mohawk Exceptionalism: A Reconsideration of the Longhouse to Loghouse Transition, 1687–1779. Paper presented at the Rochester Museum and Science Center Conference on the Iroquois Longhouse, November 15, 1997. Rochester, N.Y.
1998 Cultivating a Landscape of Fear: Warfare and Contact Period Northern Iroquoian Landscapes. Paper presented at the Society for Historical Archaeology Annual Meeting, January 8, 1998. Atlanta, Ga.
2001 Smiths and Senecas: Iron Tool Production and Use at the Townley-Read Site,

ca. A.D. 1715–1754. Unpublished report submitted to the Early American Industries Association in fulfillment of 1999 John S. Watson Grant.
2002 *The Archaeology of the Iroquois Restoration: Settlement, Housing, and Economy at a Dispersed Seneca Community, ca. A.D. 1715–1754*. Ph.D. diss., Columbia University. Ann Arbor, Mich.: University Microfilms.
2003 An Eighteenth-Century Seneca Iroquois Short Longhouse from the Townley-Read Site, c. A.D. 1715–1754. *The Bulletin: Journal of the New York State Archaeological Association* 119: 49–63.
2004 Seneca Iroquois Settlement Pattern, Community Structure, and Housing, 1677–1779. *Northeast Anthropology* 67: 23–60.
2009 Regional Diversity and Colonialism in Eighteenth-Century Iroquoia. In Laurie E. Miroff and Timothy D. Knapp, eds., *Iroquoian Archaeology and Analytic Scale*, 215–30. Knoxville: University of Tennessee Press.
n.d. The Townley-Read/New Ganechstage Project: Investigations of Eighteenth-Century and Precolumbian Components at the Townley-Read Site, 1996–2000. Site report draft in the author's possession.

Jordan, Kurt A., and Adam S. Watson
2005 Rethinking Northern Iroquoian Use of Bone Grease. Paper presented at the New York State Archaeological Association Annual Meeting, May 7, 2005. Watertown, N.Y.

Jordan, Terry G.
1985 *American Log Buildings: An Old World Heritage*. Chapel Hill: University of North Carolina Press.

Jordan, Terry G., and Matti Kaups
1989 *The American Backwoods Frontier*. Baltimore: Johns Hopkins University Press.

Joyce, Rosemary A.
2004 Embodied Subjectivity: Gender, Femininity, Masculinity, Sexuality. In Lynn Meskell and Robert W. Preucel, eds., *A Companion to Social Archaeology*, 82–95. Malden, Mass.: Blackwell.

JP. *See* Sullivan, James, Alexander C. Flick, and Milton W. Hamilton, eds.

JR. *See* Thwaites, Reuben Gold, ed.

Junker-Andersen, Christian
1986 Faunal Remains from the Jackson-Everson (NYSM 1213) Site. In Robert D. Kuhn and Dean R. Snow, eds., *The Mohawk Valley Project: 1983 Jackson-Everson Excavations*, 93–160. Albany: Institute for Northeast Anthropology, State University of New York.

Kalm, Peter
1966 [1751] A Curious Account of the Cataracts at Niagara. In John Bartram, *Observations on the Inhabitants, Climate, Soil, Rivers, Productions, Animals, and Other Matters Worthy of Notice Made by Mr. John Bartram in His Travels from Pensilvania to Onondago, Oswego, and the Lake Ontario, in Canada*, 79–94. March of America Series No. 41. Ann Arbor, Mich.: University Microfilms.

Kapches, Mima
1979 Intra-Longhouse Spatial Analysis. *Pennsylvania Archaeologist* 49: 24–29.
1984 Cabins on Ontario Iroquois Sites. *North American Archaeologist* 5:63–71.

1990 The Spatial Dynamics of Ontario Iroquoian Longhouses. *American Antiquity* 55: 49–67.
1993 The Identification of an Iroquoian Unit of Measurement. *Archaeology of Eastern North America* 21: 137–62.
1994 The Iroquoian Longhouse: Architectural and Cultural Identity. In Martin Locock, ed., *Meaningful Architecture*, 253–70. Worldwide Archaeology Series 9. Brookfield, Vt.: Ashgate Publishing.

Karklins, Karlis
1982 Guide to the Description and Classification of Glass Beads. *History and Archaeology* [Ottawa: Parks Canada] 59: 83–117.
1983 Dutch Trade Beads in North America. In Charles F. Hayes III, ed., *Proceedings of the 1982 Glass Trade Bead Conference*, 111–26. Rochester Museum and Science Center Research Records No. 16. Rochester, N.Y.: Rochester Museum and Science Center.

Keener, Craig S.
1998 *An Ethnohistoric Perspective on Iroquois Warfare during the Second Half of the Seventeenth Century (A.D. 1649–1701)*. Ph.D. diss., Ohio State University. Ann Arbor, Mich.: University Microfilms.

Kelsay, Isabel Thompson
1984 *Joseph Brant, 1743–1807*. Syracuse, N.Y.: Syracuse University Press.

Kent, Barry C.
1993 *Susquehanna's Indians*. Anthropological Series No. 6. Harrisburg: Pennsylvania Historical and Museum Commission. (Reprint of 1984 edition with new preface).

Kent, Donald H.
1974 Historical Report on the Niagara River and the Niagara River Strip to 1759. In David Agee Horr, ed., *Iroquois Indians II*, 11–201. New York: Garland Publishing.

Kenyon, Ian T., and Neal Ferris
1984 Investigations at Mohawk Village, 1983. *Arch Notes* 84(1): 19–49.

Kerber, Jordan E., ed.
2006 *Cross-Cultural Collaboration: Native Peoples and Archaeology in the Northeastern United States*. Lincoln: University of Nebraska Press.

Kidd, Kenneth E., and Martha A. Kidd
1983 A Classification System for Glass Beads for the Use of Field Archaeologists. In Charles F. Hayes III, ed., *Proceedings of the 1982 Glass Trade Bead Conference*, 219–57. Rochester Museum and Science Center Research Records No. 16. Rochester, N.Y.: Rochester Museum and Science Center. (Reprint of 1970 article originally published by Parks Canada.)

Kinsey, W. Fred III
1981 Catlinite and Red Pipestone: A Preliminary Report. Paper presented at the Annual Meeting of the Eastern States Archaeological Federation, November 6–9, 1981. Harrisburg, Pa.

Klinefelter, Walter
1971 Lewis Evans and His Maps. *Transactions of the American Philosophical Society*, n.s., 61(7): 3–65.

Knight, Dean H.
2002 The Function of Longhouses: An Example from the Ball Site. *The Bulletin: Journal of the New York State Archaeological Association* 118: 27–40.

Konrad, Victor
1981 An Iroquois Frontier: The North Shore of Lake Ontario during the Late Seventeenth Century. *Journal of Historical Geography* 7: 129–44.
1987 The Iroquois Return to Their Homeland. In Thomas E. Ross and Tyrel G. Moore, eds., *A Cultural Geography of North American Indians*, 191–211. Boulder, Colo.: Westview Press.

Kuhn, Robert D., and Robert E. Funk
2000 Boning Up on the Mohawk: An Overview of Mohawk Faunal Assemblages and Subsistence Patterns. *Archaeology of Eastern North America* 28: 29–62.

Kuhn, Robert D., David B. Guldenzopf, Pamela E. Sugihara, and Mary Schwarz
1986 The Jackson-Everson Site (NYSM 1213). In Robert D. Kuhn and Dean R. Snow, eds., *The Mohawk Valley Project: 1983 Jackson-Everson Excavations*, 7–33. Albany: Institute for Northeast Anthropology, State University of New York.

Kuhn, Robert D., and Martha L. Sempowski
2001 A New Approach to Dating the League of the Iroquois. *American Antiquity* 66: 301–14.

Laird, Matthew R.
1995 *The Price of Empire: Anglo-French Rivalry for the Great Lakes Fur Trade, 1700–1760.* Ph.D. diss., The College of William and Mary. Ann Arbor, Mich.: University Microfilms.

Landsman, Gail
1997 Informant as Critic: Conducting Research on a Dispute between Iroquoianist Scholars and Traditional Iroquois. In Thomas Biolsi and Larry J. Zimmerman, eds., *Indians and Anthropologists: Vine Deloria, Jr., and the Critique of Anthropology*, 160–76. Tucson: University of Arizona Press.

Langsner, Drew
1982 *A Logbuilder's Handbook.* Emmaus, Pa.: Rodale Press.

Lantz, Stanley W.
1980 Seneca Cabin Site: Historic Component of the Vanatta Site (30CA46). *Pennsylvania Archaeologist* 50(1–2): 9–41.

Lapham, Heather A.
2005 *Hunting for Hides: Deerskins, Status, and Cultural Change in the Protohistoric Appalachians.* Tuscaloosa: University of Alabama Press.

Leder, Lawrence H., ed.
1956 *The Livingston Indian Records, 1666–1723.* Gettysburg: Pennsylvania Historical Association.

Leechman, Douglas
1951 Bone Grease. *American Antiquity* 16(4): 355–56.

Lenig, Wayne
2001 Where Was Canajoharie?: The Mohawk Western or Upper Castle, 1700–1777. Paper presented at the Regional Archaeology Symposium, Cayuga Museum, October 20, 2001. Auburn, N.Y.

Lewandowski, Stephen
1987 Diohe'ko, the Three Sisters in Seneca Life. *Agriculture and Human Values* 4(2–3): 76–93.
Lightfoot, Kent G.
2005 *Indians, Missionaries, and Merchants: The Legacy of Colonial Encounters on the California Frontiers.* Berkeley: University of California Press.
Lightfoote, Rodney S.
1989 *A History of the Town of Seneca.* Interlaken, N.Y.: I-T Publishing.
Little, Barbara J.
1994 People with History: An Update on Historical Archaeology in the United States. *Journal of Archaeological Method and Theory* 1: 5–40.
Little, Elizabeth A.
1987 Inland Waterways in the Northeast. *Midcontinental Journal of Archaeology* 12(1): 55–76.
Loren, Diana DiPaolo
2005 Creolization in the French and Spanish Colonies. In Timothy R. Pauketat and Diana D. Loren, eds., *North American Archaeology*, 297–318. Malden, Mass.: Blackwell.
Lorenzini, Michele, and Karlis Karklins
2001 Man-in-the-Moon Beads. *Beads: Journal of the Society of Bead Researchers* 12–13: 39–47.
Lydekker, John Wolfe
1938 *The Faithful Mohawks.* New York: Macmillan.
Lynch, James
1985 The Iroquois Confederacy and the Adoption and Administration of Non-Iroquoian Individuals and Groups Prior to 1756. *Man in the Northeast* 30: 83–99.
MACIA. *See* Minutes of the Albany Commissioners for Indian Affairs
MacNeish, Richard S.
1952 *Iroquois Pottery Types.* Bulletin 124. Ottawa: National Museum of Canada.
Madrigal, T. Cregg
1999 *Zooarchaeology and Taphonomy of Late Archaic Hunter-Gatherer Complexity in Central New York.* Ph.D. diss., Rutgers University. Ann Arbor, Mich.: University Microfilms.
Madrigal, T. Cregg, and Julie Zimmerman Holt
2002 White-Tailed Deer Meat and Marrow Return Rates and Their Application to Eastern Woodlands Archaeology. *American Antiquity* 67(4): 745–59.
Mainfort, Robert C.
1979 *Indian Social Dynamics in the Period of European Contact.* Publications of the Museum, Anthropological Series Vol. 1, No. 4. East Lansing: Michigan State University.
Mallios, Seth
2005 Back to the Bowl: Using English Tobacco Pipebowls to Calculate Mean Site-Occupation Dates. *Historical Archaeology* 39(2): 89–104.
Mancall, Peter C.
1995 *Deadly Medicine: Indians and Alcohol in Early America.* Ithaca, N.Y.: Cornell University Press.

Mandzy, Adrian Oleh
1990 The Rogers Farm Site: A Seventeenth-Century Cayuga Site. *The Bulletin: Journal of the New York State Archaeological Association* 100: 18–25.
1992 History of Cayuga Acculturation: An Examination of the 17th-Century Cayuga Iroquois Archaeological Data. Master's thesis, Department of Anthropology, Michigan State University, East Lansing.

Marquardt, William H.
1992 Dialectical Archaeology. *Archaeological Method and Theory* 4: 101–40.

Marshall, Orsamus H., ed.
1848 *Narrative of the Expedition of the Marquis de Nonville, against the Senecas, in 1687*. Translated by O. H. Marshall. New York: Bartlett and Welford.

McAlester, Virginia, and Lee McAlester
1984 *A Field Guide to American Houses*. New York: Alfred A. Knopf.

McCashion, John H.
1979 A Preliminary Chronology and Discussion of Seventeenth and Early Eighteenth-Century Clay Tobacco Pipes from New York State Sites. In Peter Davey, ed., *The Archaeology of the Clay Tobacco Pipe*. Part II, *The United States of America*. BAR International Series 60: 63–149. Oxford: BAR.

McConnell, Michael N.
1992 *A Country Between: The Upper Ohio Valley and Its Peoples, 1724–1774*. Lincoln: University of Nebraska Press.

McGuire, Randall H.
2002 *A Marxist Archaeology*. Clinton Corners, N.Y.: Percheron Press. (Reprint of 1992 edition with new prologue).

McGuire, Randall H., and Michael B. Schiffer
1983 A Theory of Architectural Design. *Journal of Anthropological Archaeology* 2: 277–303.

McIlwain, Charles Howard, ed.
1915 *An Abridgement of the Indian Affairs Contained in Four Folio Volumes, Transacted in the Colony of New York, from the Year 1678 to the Year 1751*. By Peter Wraxall. Cambridge, Mass.: Harvard University Press.

McKelvey, Blake
1951 The Seneca "Time of Troubles." *Rochester History* 13: 1–24.

McNiven, Ian J., and Lynette Russell
2005 *Appropriated Pasts: Indigenous Peoples and the Colonial Culture of Archaeology*. Lanham, Md.: Altamira Press.

Merrell, James H.
1987 "Their Very Bones Shall Fight": The Catawba-Iroquois Wars. In Daniel K. Richter and James H. Merrell, eds., *Beyond the Covenant Chain: The Iroquois and Their Neighbors in Indian North America, 1600–1800*, 115–33. Syracuse, N.Y.: Syracuse University Press.
1989 *The Indians' New World: Catawbas and Their Neighbors from European Contact through the Era of Removal*. New York: Norton.

Merrifield, Edward
1915 *The Story of the Captivity and Rescue from the Indians of Luke Swetland*. Scranton, Pa.: n.p.

Michaelsen, Scott, and Scott Cutler Shershow
2002 Practical Politics at the Limits of Community: The Cases of Affirmative Action and Welfare. *Postmodern Culture* 12(2). Available online at <http://muse.jhu.edu/journals/pmc/index.html> (accessed January 11, 2008).

Michelson, Gunther
1977 Iroquois Population Statistics. *Man in the Northeast* 14: 3–17.

Mihesuah, Devon A., ed.
2000 *The Repatriation Reader. Who Owns American Indian Remains?*. Lincoln: University of Nebraska Press.

Minutes of the Albany Commissioners for Indian Affairs (MACIA)
1722–1748 Minutes of the Albany Commissioners for Indian Affairs. Record Group 10, vols. 1819–1821, microfilm reels C-1220 and C-1221. Ottawa: National Archives of Canada.

Mohawk, John
1986 *War against the Seneca: The French Expedition of 1687*. Victor, N.Y.: Ganondagan State Historic Site, New York State Office of Parks, Recreation, and Historic Preservation.

Moogk, Peter N.
1977 *Building a House in New France*. Toronto: McClelland and Stewart.

Morgan, Lewis Henry
1962 [1851] *League of the Ho-de-no-sau-nee, or Iroquois*. New York: Citadel Press.
1965 [1881] *Houses and House-Life of the American Aborigines*. Chicago: University of Chicago Press.
1985 [1877] *Ancient Society*. Tucson: University of Arizona Press.
1997 [1871] *Systems of Consanguinity and Affinity of the Human Family*. Lincoln: University of Nebraska Press.

Mt. Pleasant, Alyssa
2004 Exploring Buffalo Creek: Perspectives on a 19th-Century Haudenosaunee Community. Paper presented as part of the Revisiting Native America series, Buffalo State College, April 29, 2004. Buffalo, N.Y.

Mt. Pleasant, Jane
2006 The Science behind the Three Sisters Mound System. In John E. Staller, Robert H. Tykot, and Bruce F. Benz, eds., *Histories of Maize*, 529–37. Boston, Mass.: Elsevier Academic Press.

Mullenneaux, Nan
2002 John R. Bleecker. Biography by Colonial Albany Social History Project. Available online at <www.nysm.nysed.gov/albany/bios/b/jorbleecker201.html> (accessed January 11, 2008).

Murdock, George P., and Suzanne F. Wilson
1972 Settlement Patterns and Community Organization: Cross-Cultural Codes 3. *Ethnology* 11: 254–95.

Nern, Craig F., and Charles E. Cleland
1974 The Gros Cap Cemetery Site, St. Ignace, Michigan. *Michigan Archaeologist* 20(1): 1–58.

New York Archaeological Council
2000 *Cultural Resource Standards Handbook*. Available online at <http://bingweb.binghamton.edu/~ccobb/nystand.pdf> (accessed January 11, 2008).

Niemczycki, Mary Ann Palmer
1984 *The Origin and Development of the Seneca and Cayuga Tribes of New York State*. Rochester Museum and Science Center Research Records No. 17. Rochester, N.Y.: Rochester Museum and Science Center.

Noble, William C.
2004 The Protohistoric Period Revisited. In James V. Wright and Jean-Luc Pilon, eds., *A Passion for the Past: Papers in Honour of James F. Pendergast*, 179–91. Canadian Museum of Civilization Mercury Series, Archaeology Paper 164. Ottawa: Canadian Museum of Civilization.

Noel Hume, Ivor
1969 *A Guide to Artifacts of Colonial America*. New York: Vintage Books.

Norton, Thomas Elliott
1974 *The Fur Trade in Colonial New York, 1686–1776*. Madison: University of Wisconsin Press.

N.W. Parts of New York, No. 156.
1750–1768 Manuscript map held by the Library of Congress Geography and Map Division, Washington D.C. Available online through the American Memory Project at <http://hdl.loc.gov/loc.gmd/g3800.ar108100> (accessed January 11, 2008).

NYCD. *See* O'Callaghan, E. B., ed. 1969 [1853–1887].

O'Callaghan, E. B., ed.
1849–1851 *Documentary History of the State of New York*. 4 vols. Albany: Weed, Parsons, and Co.
1969 [1853–1887] *Documents Relative to the Colonial History of the State of New York*. 15 vols. New York: A.M.S. Press.

Olds, Nathaniel S., ed.
1930 Journal of the Expedition of the Marquis de Denonville against the Iroquois, 1687, by Chevalier de Baugy. *Rochester Historical Society Publication Fund* 9: 3–56.

Olmstead, Earl P.
1997 *David Zeisberger: A Life among the Indians*. Kent, Ohio: Kent State University Press.

Oppenheim, Samuel D.
n.d. Eighteenth-Century Blacksmiths on the Iroquois Frontier. Unpublished paper prepared as part of the 1998 Columbia University Archaeological Field School; manuscript in the author's possession.

Orlandini, John B.
1996 The Passenger Pigeon: A Seasonal Native American Food Source. *Pennsylvania Archaeologist* 66(2): 71–77.

Ortiz, Fernando
1995 [1940] *Cuban Counterpoint: Tobacco and Sugar*. Translated by Harriet de Onis. Durham, N.C.: Duke University Press.

Otterness, Philip
2004 *Becoming German: The 1709 Palatine Migration to New York*. Ithaca, N.Y.: Cornell University Press.

Outram, Alan K.
2001 A New Approach to Identifying Bone Marrow and Grease Exploitation. *Journal of Archaeological Science* 28(4): 401–10.
2003 Comparing Levels of Subsistence Stress amongst Norse Settlers in Iceland and Greenland using Levels of Bone Fat Exploitation as an Indicator. *Environmental Archaeology* 8: 119–28.

Parker, Arthur C.
1910 Iroquois Uses of Maize and Other Food Plants. *New York State Museum Bulletin* 144: 5–113.
1920 *The Archeological History of New York*. Bulletin of the New York State Museum Nos. 235–39. Albany: New York State Museum.

Parmenter, Jon William
1999 *At the Wood's Edge: Iroquois Foreign Relations, 1727–1768*. Ph.D. diss., University of Michigan. Ann Arbor, Mich.: University Microfilms.
2001a The Iroquois and the Native American Struggle for the Ohio Valley, 1745–1794. In David C. Skaggs and Larry L. Nelson, eds., *The Sixty Years' War for the Great Lakes, 1754–1814*, 105–124. East Lansing: Michigan State University Press.
2001b The Significance of the "Illegal Fur Trade" to the Eighteenth-Century Iroquois. In Louise Johnston, ed., *Aboriginal People and the Fur Trade: Proceedings of the Eighth North American Fur Trade Conference, Akwesasne*, 40–47. Cornwall, Ont.: Akwesasne Notes Publishing.
2002 Neutralité active des Iroquois durant la guerre de la succession d'Autriche, 1744–1748. *Recherches Amérindiennes au Québec* 32(1): 29–37.
2007a After the Mourning Wars: The Iroquois as Allies in Colonial North American Campaigns, 1676–1760. *William and Mary Quarterly*, 3rd. ser., 64(1): 39–82.
2007b "Onenwahatirighsi Sa Gentho Skaghnughtudigh": Reassessing Haudenosaunee Relations with the Albany Commissioners of Indian Affairs, 1723–1755. In Nancy Rhoden, ed., *English Atlantics Revisited: Essays Honouring Professor Ian K. Steele*, 235–83. Montreal: McGill-Queens University Press.

Pearson, C. S., and M. G. Cline
1958 *Soil Survey of Ontario and Yates Counties, New York*. Washington, D.C.: U.S. Government Printing Office.

Perdue, Theda
1987 Cherokee Relations with the Iroquois in the Eighteenth Century. In Daniel K. Richter and James H. Merrell, eds., *Beyond the Covenant Chain: The Iroquois and Their Neighbors in Indian North America, 1600–1800*, 135–49. Syracuse, N.Y.: Syracuse University Press.

Perkins, Dexter Jr., and Patricia Daly
1968 A Hunters' Village in Neolithic Turkey. *Scientific American* 219(5): 97–106.

Pessen, Edward
1984 *The Log Cabin Myth: The Social Backgrounds of the Presidents*. New Haven: Yale University Press.

Piker, Joshua A.
2003 "White & Clean" & Contested: Creek Towns and Trading Paths in the Aftermath of the Seven Years' War. *Ethnohistory* 50(2): 315–47.

Pilkington, Walter, ed.
1980 *The Journals of Samuel Kirkland*. Clinton, N.Y.: Hamilton College.

Porter, Robert B.
2002 The Onodowaga (Seneca) in New York State. In Tom Greaves, ed., *Endangered Peoples of North America: Struggles to Survive and Thrive*, 117–35. Westport, Conn.: Greenwood Press.

Poulton, Dana R.
1991 Report on the 1991 Archaeological Investigations of the Bead Hill Site, City of Scarborough, Ontario. Unpublished report on file with Ontario Service Center, Parks Canada, Cornwall, Ontario.

PPCM. *See* Hazard, Samuel, ed.

Pratt, Peter P.
1961 *Oneida Iroquois Glass Trade Bead Sequence, 1585–1745*. Rome, N.Y.: Fort Stanwix Museum.

Prezzano, Susan Carol
1992 *Longhouse, Village, and Palisade: Community Patterns at the Iroquois Southern Door*. Ph.D. diss., State University of New York at Binghamton. Ann Arbor, Mich.: University Microfilms.

Prisch, Betty Coit
1982 *Aspects of Change in Seneca Iroquois Ladles, A.D. 1600–1900*. Rochester Museum and Science Center Research Records No. 15. Rochester, N.Y.: Rochester Museum and Science Center.

Quimby, George Irving
1966 *Indian Culture and European Trade Goods*. Madison: University of Wisconsin Press.

Quimby, George Irving, and Alexander Spoehr
1951 Acculturation and Material Culture. *Fieldiana: Anthropology* 36(6): 107–47.

Ramenofsky, Ann F.
1987 *Vectors of Death: The Archaeology of European Contact*. Albuquerque: University of New Mexico Press.
1998 Evolutionary Theory and the Native American Record of Artifact Replacement. In James G. Cusick, ed., *Studies in Culture Contact*, 77–101. Southern Illinois University at Carbondale Center for Archaeological Investigations Occasional Paper No. 25. Carbondale: Southern Illinois University.

Rapp, George Jr., and Christopher L. Hill
1998 *Geoarchaeology*. New Haven, Conn.: Yale University Press.

Recht, Michael
1995 The Role of Fishing in the Iroquois Economy, 1600–1792. *New York History* 76(1): 4–30.

Rempel, John I.
1967 *Building with Wood and Other Aspects of Nineteenth-Century Building in Ontario*. Toronto: University of Toronto Press.

Richter, Daniel K.
1983 War and Culture: The Iroquois Experience. *William and Mary Quarterly*, 3rd. ser., 40: 528–59.
1992 *The Ordeal of the Longhouse*. Chapel Hill: University of North Carolina Press.
Richter, Daniel K., and James H. Merrell, eds.
1987 *Beyond the Covenant Chain: The Iroquois and Their Neighbors in Indian North America, 1600–1800*. Syracuse, N.Y.: Syracuse University Press.
Rick, Anne M.
1991 Faunal Remains from the Enders House: An Historic Mohawk Dwelling. Unpublished report prepared for the Zoological Identification Centre, Canadian Museum of Nature, Ottawa.
Ricklis, Robert
1967 Excavation of a Probable Late Prehistoric Onondaga House Site. *The Bulletin: New York State Archeological Association* 39: 15–17.
Ridge, John C.
2003 The Last Deglaciation of the Northeastern United States. In David L. Cremeens and John P. Hart, eds., *Geoarchaeology of Landscapes in the Glaciated Northeast*, 15–45. New York State Museum Bulletin 497. Albany: New York State Museum.
Ritchie, William A.
1936 *A Prehistoric Fortified Village Site at Canandaigua, Ontario County, New York*. Research Records of the Rochester Museum of Arts and Sciences No. 3. Rochester, N.Y.: Rochester Museum of Arts and Sciences.
1980 *The Archaeology of New York State*. Rev. ed. Fleischmanns, N.Y.: Purple Mountain Press.
Robbins, Maurice
1981 *The Amateur Archaeologist's Handbook*. 3rd ed. Cambridge, Mass.: Harper and Row.
Rogers, J. Daniel
1990 *Objects of Change: The Archaeology and History of Arikara Contact with Europeans*. Washington, D.C.: Smithsonian Institution Press.
Römer, Willem Wolfgang
1700 A Mapp of Coll. Romer His Journey to the 5 Indian Nations. Manuscript map held by the National Archives of the United Kingdom. Item number C.O. 700/ New York 13A.
Roseberry, William
1988 Political Economy. *Annual Review of Anthropology* 17: 161–85.
1989 *Anthropologies and Histories*. New Brunswick, N.J.: Rutgers University Press.
Roseberry, William, and Jay O'Brien
1991 Introduction to Jay O'Brien and William Roseberry, eds., *Golden Ages, Dark Ages: Imagining the Past in Anthropology and History*, 1–18. Berkeley: University of California Press.
Rossen, Jack
2006 Archaeobotanical Remains from the Townley-Read Site. Unpublished report submitted to author.

Rothschild, Nan A.
2003 *Colonial Encounters in a Native American Landscape: The Spanish and Dutch in North America*. Washington, D.C.: Smithsonian Institution Press.

Rubertone, Patricia E.
2000 The Historical Archaeology of Native Americans. *Annual Review of Anthropology* 29: 425–46.
2002 Review of *Societies in Eclipse: Archaeology of the Eastern Woodland Indians, A.D. 1400–1700*, edited by David S. Brose, C. Wesley Cowan, and Robert C. Mainfort, Jr. *Northeast Anthropology* 64: 95–96.

Ryan, Beth, and Adam G. Dewbury
2010 The Eugene Frost Collection: Artifacts from the Seneca Iroquois Dann Site, circa 1655–1675. Report on file with Division of Rare and Manuscript Collections, Cornell University Library, Ithaca, N.Y.

Sanders, William T., Jeffrey R. Parsons, and Robert S. Santley
1979 *The Basin of Mexico*. New York: Academic Press.

Sassaman, Kenneth E.
1995 The Social Contradictions of Traditional and Innovative Cooking Technologies in the Prehistoric American Southeast. In William K. Barnett and John W. Hoopes, eds., *The Emergence of Pottery*, 223–40. Washington, D.C.: Smithsonian Institution Press.

Saunders, Lorraine P.
1994 A Consideration of Local Origins for Epidemic Disease in Certain Native American Populations. In Charles F. Hayes III, ed., *Proceedings of the 1992 People to People Conference*, 105–14. Rochester Museum and Science Center Research Records No. 23. Rochester, N.Y.: Rochester Museum and Science Center.

Schiffer, Michael B.
1987 *Formation Processes of the Archaeological Record*. Albuquerque: University of New Mexico Press.

Schmalz, Peter S.
1991 *The Ojibwa of Southern Ontario*. Toronto: University of Toronto Press.

Schneider, David M.
1961 Introduction: The Distinctive Features of Matrilineal Descent Groups. In David M. Schneider and Kathleen Gough, eds., *Matrilineal Kinship*, 1–29. Berkeley: University of California Press.
1984 *A Critique of the Study of Kinship*. Ann Arbor: University of Michigan Press.

Schoff, Harry L.
1949 "Black Robes" among the Seneca and Cayuga. *Pennsylvania Archaeologist* 19: 18–26.
n.d. Field notes, on file at Rochester Museum and Science Center Research Division, Rochester, N.Y.

Scott, Douglas D., Thomas D. Thiessen, Jeffrey J. Richner, and Scott Stadler
2006 *An Archaeological Inventory and Overview of Pipestone National Monument, Minnesota*. Midwest Archaeological Center Occasional Studies in Anthropology 34. Lincoln, Neb.: National Park Service, Midwest Archaeological Center.

Scott, Patricia Kay
1998 Historic Contact Archaeological Deposits within the Old Fort Niagara National

Historic Landmark. *The Bulletin: Journal of the New York State Archaeological Association* 114: 45–57.

Scott, Stuart D., and Patricia Kay Scott

1998 Lower Landing Archaeological District National Historic Landmark. *The Bulletin: Journal of the New York State Archaeological Association* 114: 58–72.

Seaver, James E., ed.

1990 [1824] *A Narrative of the Life of Mrs. Mary Jemison.* Syracuse, N.Y.: Syracuse University Press.

Sempowski, Martha L.

1986 Differential Mortuary Treatment of Seneca Women: Some Social Inferences. *Archaeology of Eastern North America* 14: 35–44.

Sempowski, Martha L., and Lorraine P. Saunders

2001 *Dutch Hollow and Factory Hollow.* Rochester Museum and Science Center Research Records No. 24. Rochester, N.Y.: Rochester Museum and Science Center.

Severance, Frank H.

1906 The Story of Joncaire. *Publications of the Buffalo Historical Society* 9(3): 85–217.

Shimony, Annemarie Anrod

1994 [1961] *Conservatism among the Iroquois at the Six Nations Reserve.* Syracuse, N.Y.: Syracuse University Press.

Shoemaker, Nancy

1991 From Longhouse to Loghouse: Household Structure among the Senecas in 1900. *American Indian Quarterly* 15: 329–38.

Shurtleff, Harold R.

1967 [1939] *The Log Cabin Myth.* Gloucester, Mass.: Peter Smith.

Sider, Gerald M.

1997 The Making of Peculiar Local Cultures: Producing and Surviving History in Peasant and Tribal Societies. In Alf Lüdtke, ed., *Was Bleibt von Marxistschen Perspektiven in der Gechichtsforschung?*, 99–148. Göttingen: Wallstein.

2003a *Between History and Tomorrow: Making and Breaking Everyday Life in Rural Newfoundland.* Peterborough, Ont.: Broadview Press.

2003b *Living Indian Histories: Lumbee and Tuscarora People in North Carolina.* Chapel Hill: University of North Carolina Press.

Sider, Gerald M., and Gavin A. Smith

1997 Introduction to Gerald M. Sider and Gavin A. Smith, eds., *Between History and Histories: The Making of Silences and Commemorations*, 3–28. Toronto: University of Toronto Press.

Sigstad, John S.

1973 The Age and Distribution of Catlinite and Red Pipestone. Ph.D. diss., University of Missouri. Ann Arbor, Mich.: University Microfilms.

Silliman, Stephen W.

2004 *Lost Laborers in Colonial California: Native Americans and the Archaeology of Rancho Petaluma.* Tucson: University of Arizona Press.

2005 Culture Contact or Colonialism? Challenges in the Archaeology of Native North America. *American Antiquity* 70(1): 55–74.

Simpson, Audra
2004 *To the Reserve and Back Again: Kahnawake Mohawk Narratives of Self, Home and Nation.* Ph.D. diss, McGill University. Ann Arbor, Mich.: University Microfilms.

Singleton, Theresa A.
1998 Cultural Interaction and African American Identity in Plantation Archaeology. In James G. Cusick, ed., *Studies in Culture Contact*, 172–88. Center for Archaeological Investigations Occasional Paper No. 25. Carbondale: Southern Illinois University.

Smith, Beverley
2001 Spatial Organization of Economic Activity at an Upper Great Lakes Contact-Period Site. Paper presented at the Annual Meeting of the Society for American Archaeology, April 20, 2001. New Orleans, La.

Smith, Marvin T.
1981 European and Aboriginal Glass Pendants in North America. *Ornament: A Quarterly of Jewelry and Personal Adornment* 5(2): 21–23.
2002 Eighteenth-Century Glass Beads in the French Colonial Trade. *Historical Archaeology* 36(1): 55–61.

Snow, Dean R.
1989 The Evolution of Mohawk Households, A.D. 1400–1800. In Scott MacEachern, David J. W. Archer, and Richard D. Garvin, eds., *Households and Communities: Proceedings of the 21st Annual Chacmool Conference*, 293–300. Calgary: Archaeological Association of the University of Calgary.
1992 Disease and Population Decline in the Northeast. In John W. Verano and Douglas H. Ubelaker, eds., *Disease and Demography in the Americas*, 177–86. Washington, D.C.: Smithsonian Institution Press.
1994 *The Iroquois.* Cambridge, Mass.: Blackwell.
1995 *Mohawk Valley Archaeology: The Sites.* Albany: Institute for Archaeological Studies, State University of New York at Albany.
1996 Mohawk Demography and the Effects of Exogenous Epidemics on American Indian Populations. *Journal of Anthropological Archaeology* 15: 160–82.
1997 The Architecture of Iroquois Longhouses. *Northeast Anthropology* 53: 61–84.
2001 Evolution of the Mohawk Iroquois. In David S. Brose, C. Wesley Cowan, and Robert C. Mainfort Jr., eds., *Societies in Eclipse: Archaeology of the Eastern Woodlands Indians, A.D. 1400–1700*, 19–25. Washington, D.C.: Smithsonian Institution Press.

Snow, Dean R., Charles T. Gehring, and William A. Starna, eds.
1996 *In Mohawk Country: Early Narratives about a Native People.* Syracuse, N.Y.: Syracuse University Press.

Snow, Dean R., and William A. Starna
1989 Sixteenth-Century Depopulation: A View from the Mohawk Valley. *American Anthropologist* 91: 142–49.

Socci, Mary Catherine
1995 The Zooarchaeology of the Mohawk Valley. Ph.D. diss., Yale University. Ann Arbor, Mich.: University Microfilms.

Sohrweide, A. Gregory
2001 Onondaga Longhouses in the Late Seventeenth Century on the Weston Site. *The Bulletin: Journal of the New York State Archaeological Association* 117: 1–24.

Speck, Frank G.
1995 [1940] *Midwinter Rites of the Cayuga Long House.* Lincoln: University of Nebraska Press.

Spector, Janet D.
1991 What This Awl Means: Toward a Feminist Archaeology. In Joan M. Gero and Margaret W. Conkey, eds., *Engendering Archaeology*, 388–406. Cambridge, Mass.: Blackwell.

1993 *What This Awl Means: Feminist Archaeology at a Wahpeton Dakota Village.* St. Paul: Minnesota Historical Society Press.

Speth, John D.
1990 Seasonality, Resource Stress, and Food Sharing in So-Called "Egalitarian" Societies. *Journal of Anthropological Archaeology* 9: 148–88.

Speth, John D., and Katherine A. Spielmann
1983 Energy Source, Protein Metabolism, and Hunter-Gatherer Subsistence Strategies. *Journal of Anthropological Archaeology* 2: 1–31.

Spiess, Arthur
1988 Appendix H: Archaeozoology of a Trudeau Trash Pit. In Jeffrey P. Brain, *Tunica Archaeology*, 418–22. Cambridge, Mass.: Harvard University Press.

Squier, Ephraim G.
1851 *Antiquities of the State of New York.* Buffalo, N.Y.: George H. Derry.

Stahl, Ann B.
2000 What Is the Use of Archaeology in Historical Anthropology? In M. Boyd, J. C. Erwin, and M. Hendrickson, eds., *The Entangled Past: Integrating History and Archaeology*, 4–11. Calgary: Archaeological Association of the University of Calgary.

Standen, S. Dale
1998 François Chalet and the French Trade at the Posts of Niagara and Frontenac, 1742–1747. In David Buissert, ed., *France in the New World*, 225–40. East Lansing: Michigan State University Press.

Starna, William A., and José António Brandão
2004 From the Mohawk-Mahican War to the Beaver Wars: Questioning the Pattern. *Ethnohistory* 51(4): 725–50.

Starna, William A., George R. Hamell, and William L. Butts
1984 Northern Iroquoian Horticulture and Insect Infestation: A Cause for Village Removal. *Ethnohistory* 31(3): 197–207.

Starna, William A., and John H. Relethford
1985 Deer Densities and Population Dynamics: A Cautionary Note. *American Antiquity* 50(4): 825–32.

Steele, Ian K.
1994   *Warpaths: Invasions of North America*. New York: Oxford University Press.
Stewart, Alexander M.
1970   *French Pioneers in the Eastern Great Lakes Area, 1609–1791*. Occasional Papers of the New York State Archaeological Association No. 3. Rochester, N.Y.: New York State Archaeological Association.
Stewart, Omer C.
2002   *Forgotten Fires: Native Americans and the Transient Wilderness*. Norman: University of Oklahoma Press.
Stone, Glenn Davis
1991   Agricultural Territories in a Dispersed Settlement System. *Current Anthropology* 32: 343–53.
1993   Agricultural Abandonment: A Comparative Study in Historical Ecology. In Catherine M. Cameron and Steve A. Tomka, eds., *The Abandonment of Settlements and Regions*, 74–81. Cambridge: Cambridge University Press.
1996   *Settlement Ecology: The Social and Spatial Organization of Kofyar Agriculture*. Tucson: University of Arizona Press.
Stone, Glenn Davis, Robert McC. Netting, and M. Priscilla Stone
1990   Seasonality, Labor Scheduling, and Agricultural Intensification in the Nigerian Savanna. *American Anthropologist* 92: 7–23.
Stull, Scott D.
2006   Ceramics at the Townley-Read Site. Unpublished report submitted to author.
Sturm, Circe
2002   *Blood Politics: Race, Culture, and Identity in the Cherokee Nation of Oklahoma*. Berkeley: University of California Press.
Sullivan, James, Alexander C. Flick, and Milton W. Hamilton, eds.
1921–1965   *The Papers of Sir William Johnson*. 14 vols. Albany: State University of New York.
Surtees, Robert J.
1985   The Iroquois in Canada. In Francis Jennings, William N. Fenton, Mary A. Druke, and David R. Miller, eds., *The History and Culture of Iroquois Diplomacy*, 67–83. Syracuse, N.Y.: Syracuse University Press.
Tanner, Helen Norbeck, ed.
1987   *Atlas of Great Lakes Indian History*. Norman: University of Oklahoma Press.
Tanner, Tyree
1995   The Sevier Site. *William A. Beauchamp Chapter, NYSAA* 7(1): 40–66.
Taylor, Alan
1995   *William Cooper's Town*. New York: Alfred A. Knopf.
2006   *The Divided Ground: Indians, Settlers, and the Northern Borderland of the American Revolution*. New York: Alfred A. Knopf.
Thomas, David Hurst
2000   *Skull Wars: Kennewick Man, Archaeology, and the Battle for Native American Identity*. New York: Basic Books.
Thompson, John H., ed.
1966   *Geography of New York State*. Syracuse, N.Y.: Syracuse University Press.

Thwaites, Reuben Gold, ed.
1959 [1896–1901]   *The Jesuit Relations and Allied Documents.* 73 vols. New York: Pageant Book Co.

Tiro, Karim Michel
1999   *The People of the Standing Stone: The Oneida Indian Nation from Revolution through Removal, 1765–1840.* Ph.D. diss., University of Pennsylvania. Ann Arbor, Mich.: University Microfilms.
2000   A 'Civil' War? Rethinking Iroquois Participation in the American Revolution. *Explorations in Early American Culture* 4: 148–65.

Tooker, Elisabeth
1970   *The Iroquois Ceremonial of Midwinter.* Syracuse, N.Y.: Syracuse University Press.
1978a   The League of the Iroquois. In Bruce G. Trigger, ed., *Handbook of North American Indians.* Vol. 15, *Northeast,* 418–41. Washington, D.C.: Smithsonian Institution Press.
1978b   Wyandot. In Bruce G. Trigger, ed., *Handbook of North American Indians.* Vol. 15, *Northeast,* 398–406. Washington, D.C.: Smithsonian Institution Press.
1984   The Demise of the Susquehannocks: A 17th-Century Mystery. *Pennsylvania Archaeologist* 54(3–4): 1–10.
1991 [1964]   *An Ethnography of the Huron Indians, 1615–1649.* Syracuse, N.Y.: Syracuse University Press.
1994   *Lewis H. Morgan on Iroquois Material Culture.* Edited by Elisabeth Tooker. Tucson: University of Arizona Press.

Torrence, Robin, and Anne Clarke
2000   Negotiating Difference: Practice Makes Theory for Contemporary Archaeology in Oceania. In Robin Torrence and Anne Clarke, eds., *The Archaeology of Difference: Negotiating Cross-Cultural Engagements in Oceania,* 1–31. New York: Routledge.

Trelease, Allen W.
1962   The Iroquois and the Western Fur Trade: A Problem in Interpretation. *Mississippi Valley Historical Review* 49: 32–51.

Tremblay, Louise
1981   La politique missionaire des Sulpiciens au XVIIe et debut du XVIIIe siècle, 1668–1735. Master's thesis, Department of History, Université de Montréal, Montreal, Quebec.

Trigger, Bruce G.
1978a   Early Iroquoian Contacts with Europeans. In Bruce G. Trigger, ed., *Handbook of North American Indians.* Vol. 15, *Northeast,* 344–56. Washington, D.C.: Smithsonian Institution Press.
1978b   *Handbook of North American Indians.* Vol. 15, *Northeast.* Edited by Bruce G. Trigger. Washington, D.C.: Smithsonian Institution Press
1985   *Natives and Newcomers: Canada's "Heroic Age" Reconsidered.* Montreal: McGill-Queen's University Press.
1987 [1976]   *The Children of Aataentsic.* Kingston, Ont.: McGill-Queen's University Press.

1990 *The Huron: Farmers of the North.* 2nd ed. Fort Worth, Tex.: Harcourt Brace Jovanovich College Publishers.

Trigger, Bruce G., and William R. Swagerty

1996 Entertaining Strangers: North America in the Sixteenth Century. In Bruce G. Trigger and Wilcomb E. Washburn, eds., *The Cambridge History of the Native Peoples of the Americas*, vol. 1, part 1, 325–98. Cambridge: Cambridge University Press.

Trubowitz, Neal L.

1976 SUNY Buffalo Archaeological Survey: 1976 Highway Program Annual Status Report. Unpublished report on file at the New York State Historic Preservation Office, Waterford, N.Y.

1983 *Highway Archeology and Settlement Study in the Genesee Valley.* Occasional Publications in Northeastern Anthropology, No. 8. Rindge, N.H.: Franklin Pierce College.

Tuan, Yi-fu

1979 *Landscapes of Fear.* New York: Pantheon Books.

Tuck, James A.

1971 *Onondaga Iroquois Prehistory.* Syracuse, N.Y.: Syracuse University Press.

Turgeon, Laurier

1996 From Acculturation to Cultural Transfer. In Laurier Turgeon, Denys Delâge, and Réal Ouellet, eds., *Tranferts culturels et métissages Amérique/Europe XVIe–XXe siècle*, 33–54. Paris: L'Harmattan.

1998 French Fishers, Fur Traders, and Amerindians during the Sixteenth Century: History and Archaeology. *William and Mary Quarterly* 55(4): 585–610.

Usner, Daniel H. Jr.

1992 *Indians, Settlers, & Slaves in a Frontier Exchange Economy: The Lower Mississippi Valley before 1783.* Chapel Hill: University of North Carolina Press.

1998 *American Indians in the Lower Mississippi Valley.* Lincoln: University of Nebraska Press.

Vandrei, Charles E.

1987 Observations on Seneca Settlement in the Early Historic Period. *The Bulletin: Journal of the New York State Archaeological Association* 95: 8–17.

Vehik, Susan C.

1977 Bone Fragments and Bone Grease Manufacturing. *Plains Anthropologist* 22: 169–82.

Versaggi, Nina M.

1987 *Hunter-Gatherer Settlement Models and the Archaeological Record: A Test Case from the Upper Susquehanna Valley of New York.* Ph.D. diss., State University of New York at Binghamton. Ann Arbor, Mich.: University Microfilms.

Walker, Ian

1977 Clay Tobacco Pipes, with Particular Reference to the Bristol Industry. *History and Archaeology* [Ottawa: Parks Canada] 11.

Wallace, Anthony F. C.

1957 Origins of Iroquois Neutrality: The Grand Settlement of 1701. *Pennsylvania History* 34: 223–35.

1969   *The Death and Rebirth of the Seneca.* New York: Vintage Books.
1978   Origins of the Longhouse Religion. In Bruce G. Trigger, ed., *Handbook of North American Indians.* Vol. 15, *Northeast,* 442–48. Washington, D.C.: Smithsonian Institution Press.

Warrick, Gary A.
1986   In Case of Fire: Burned Longhouses in a Neutral Village. In William A. Fox, ed., *Studies in Southwestern Ontario Archaeology,* 49–53. Occasional Publications of the London Chapter of the Ontario Archaeological Association No. 1. London, Ont.: London Chapter of the Ontario Archaeological Association.
1988   Estimating Ontario Iroquoian Village Duration. *Man in the Northeast* 36: 21–60.
1996   Evolution of the Iroquoian Longhouse. In Gary Coupland and E. B. Banning, eds., *People Who Lived in Big Houses,* 11–16. Monographs in World Archaeology No. 27. Madison, Wis.: Prehistory Press.
2000   The Precontact Iroquoian Occupation of Southern Ontario. *Journal of World Prehistory* 14(4): 415–66.
2003   European Infectious Disease and Depopulation of the Wendat-Tionontate (Huron-Petun). *World Archaeology* 35(2): 258–75.

Waselkov, Gregory A.
1998   The Eighteenth-Century Anglo-Indian Trade in Southeastern North America. In Jo-Anne Fiske and Susan Sleeper-Smith, eds., *New Faces of the Fur Trade,* 193–222. East Lansing: Michigan State University Press.

Waterman, Kees-Jan
2008   *"To Do Justice to Him and Myself": Evert Wendell's Account Book for the Fur Trade with Indians in Albany, N.Y., 1695–1726.* Edited and translated by Kees-Jan Waterman. Philadelphia: American Philosophical Society.

Watkins, Joe
2000   *Indigenous Archaeology: American Indian Values and Scientific Practice.* Walnut Creek, Calif.: Altamira Press.

Watson, Adam S.
2000   Subsistence and Change at Townley-Read. Unpublished senior honors thesis on file with the Department of Anthropology, Cornell University, Ithaca, N.Y.
2007   Economy and Subsistence at Townley-Read: A Faunal Analysis of an Eighteenth-Century Seneca Iroquois Community. Unpublished report submitted to author.

Waugh, Frederick W.
1973 [1916]   *Iroquois Foods and Food Preparation.* Ottawa: National Museum of Man.

Weiser, Conrad
1860 [1737]   Narrative of a Journey from Tulpehocken, Pennsylvania, to Onondaga, in 1737. In Henry R. Schoolcraft, ed., *Information Respecting the History, Conditions, and Prospects of the Indian Tribes of the United States,* vol. 4, 324–41. Philadelphia: J. B. Lippincott.

Weslager, Clinton A.
1969   *The Log Cabin in America.* New Brunswick, N.J.: Rutgers University Press.

West, Michael C.
2001   Early 18th-Century Environment and Trade at Townley-Read: A Seneca Iroquois Site Faunal Analysis. Unpublished senior thesis on file with the Archaeology Program, Cornell University, Ithaca, N.Y.

White, Richard
1983   *The Roots of Dependency*. Lincoln: University of Nebraska Press.
1991   *The Middle Ground*. Cambridge: Cambridge University Press.

Wien, Thomas
1990   Selling Beaver Skins in North America and Europe, 1720–1760. *Journal of the Canadian Historical Association*, n.s., 1: 293–317.

Williams-Shuker, Kimberly Louise
2005   *Cayuga Iroquois Households and Gender Relations during the Contact Period: An Investigation of the Rogers Farm Site, 1660s-1680s*. Ph.D. diss., University of Pittsburgh. Ann Arbor, Mich.: University Microfilms.

Wolf, Eric R.
1982   *Europe and the People without History*. Berkeley: University of California Press.
2001   *Pathways of Power*. Berkeley: University of California Press.

Wonderley, Anthony
1998   An Oneida Community in 1780: Study of an Inventory of Iroquois Property Losses during the Revolutionary War. *Northeast Anthropology* 56: 19–41.
2004   *Oneida Iroquois Folklore, Myth, and History*. Syracuse, N.Y.: Syracuse University Press.

Wray, Charles F.
1973   *A Manual for Seneca Iroquois Archeology*. Honeoye Falls, N.Y.: Cultures Primitive.
1983   Seneca Glass Trade Beads c. A.D. 1550–1820. In Charles F. Hayes III, ed., *Proceedings of the 1982 Glass Trade Bead Conference*, 41–49. Rochester Museum and Science Center Research Records No. 16. Rochester, N.Y.: Rochester Museum and Science Center.
1985   Firearms among the Seneca—The Archaeological Evidence. Abstract published in Charles F. Hayes III, ed., *Proceedings of the 1984 Trade Gun Conference*. Part II: *Selected Papers*, 106–7. Rochester Museum and Science Center Research Records No. 18. Rochester, N.Y.: Rochester Museum and Science Center.
n.d.   Field notes, on file at Rochester Museum and Science Center Research Division, Rochester, N.Y.

Wray, Charles F., and Harry L. Schoff
1953   A Preliminary Report on the Seneca Sequence in Western New York, 1550–1687. *Pennsylvania Archaeologist* 23: 53–63.

Wray, Charles F., Martha L. Sempowski, Lorraine P. Saunders, and Gian Carlo Cervone
1987   *The Adams and Culbertson Sites*. Rochester Museum and Science Center Research Records No. 19. Rochester, N.Y.: Rochester Museum and Science Center.

1991   *Tram and Cameron: Two Early Contact-Era Seneca Sites.* Rochester Museum and Science Center Research Records No. 21 Rochester, N.Y.: Rochester Museum and Science Center.

Wright, James V.
1995   Three-Dimensional Reconstructions of Iroquoian Longhouses: A Comment. *Archaeology of Eastern North America* 23: 9–21.

Wykoff, M. William
1991   Black Walnut on Iroquoian Landscapes. *Northeast Indian Quarterly* 8(2): 4–17.

Index

Page numbers in italics refer to figures, maps, and tables

Abler, Thomas S., 2, 3, 26, 27, 28, 47, 52, 57, 84, 117, 187, 203
acculturation: autonomy, and relationship to, 338, 354; encroachment/colonialism, and relationship with, 337–38, 352, 355; gradualist model, and relationship to, 8, 18, 294–95; house forms, and relationship to, 225, 246, 350; implicit assumptions of model for, 352; opportunistic responses vs., 23, 197, 349; proportions of types of artifacts, and model for, 10
Adams, Nick, 52, 89, 270
Adams, Robert McC., 348
adornment artifacts, 140, 314. *See also* beads, glass; beads, shell; red stone artifacts
Africanisms, 10–11
agriculture, Iroquoian: creolized agricultural system and, 213, 216, 221, 222, 344; dispersed settlements and, 183, 221–23, 317, 343; documentary sources for, 215–16; land allocation and, 221, 222, 271; models for, 214; tools/hardware artifacts and, 216
agrocentrism, 201–4
Albany, 58. *See also* New York
Albany Commissioners of Indian Affairs, 36, 74, 79, 83, 86, 102. *See also* Minutes of the Albany Commissioners for Indian Affairs
alcohol consumption: addiction and, 7, 299, 316; archaeological data about, 278, 311–15, *312, 313,* 331, 340, 350; dispersed settlements, and role of, 34, 199, 200, 202–3, 205, 209, 309–10, 311, 316, 328, 345; disruptions caused by, 78, 79–81, 199, 200, 202–3, 310–11, 316, 328, 331, 345, 347; documentary sources about, 278; fur trade, and role in, 299, 331; Iroquois and, 79–80, 310, 328; missionaries, and protests against, 36; political-economic prosperity, and role in, 34, 315; proximity to alcohol supply, and effects on, 315; scholarship on, 309–10
Alexander, Rani T., 31, 36, 352–53
Alfred, Taiaiake, 16

Allegany Reservation, 34, 337–38
Allegheny Valley: acculturation model, and settlements in, 17–18, 34, 337–38; extra-regional trips to, 42; house forms in, 20; Senecas in, 37, 90, 119, 165, 187; warrior path through, 85, 89
Aloi, Daniel, 172, 358n1
Amato, Christopher A., 114
American Indians. *See* Native Americans
American Midland farmsteads, 221–22, 230, *231,* 232–33, 237, 241, 296
American Revolution era: Europeans living in homelands during, 327; house forms used during, 273, 276; Iroquois, and effects of, 7, 8, 22–23, 117, 323, 336–37, 342; reservationization during, 318, 336
American Sullivan-Clinton expeditions, 37, 187–90, *189,* 197
Anajot village, 264
Anderson, David A., 240, *240,* 258, 260
Andrews, William, 257
Anselmi, Lisa Marie, 12, 350
anthropology, salvage, 8, 13, 348
Aquila, Richard, 2, 7, 22, 23, 26, 49, 50, 52, 53, 57, 62, 64, 65, 66, 72, 85, 87, 161, 200, 225, 300, 325, 333, 334, 335, 336, 339, 341, 346, 347, 348, 358n3
archaeological data: artifact-origin conclusions from, 10–11; in documentary sources, 111, 127, 359n4; domestic-context artifacts preservation/recognizability and, 20–21, 23, 207, 339, 348, 351; event-based archaeology and, 26; hybrid/nontraditional products and, 12, 14, 129–30, 154, 220, 314; long-term sequences, and analysis of, 26, 350; microscale studies, and use of, 26–27; plowzone, and preservation of, 19, 20, 95–96, 111; Postcolumbian period gaps in, 29–30; scholarly interpretation of, 1, 10, 11, 350; supra-regional context and, 31, 32; top-down sources linked with bottom-up, 328, 355

architectural artifacts, 20, 137, 143, 241–42, 242, 254, 269, 363n7. *See also* house forms; post molds (PMs)
Areas A, B, and C in Townley-Read site, 121, *122*, 125–26, 363–64n1
Area D in Townley-Read site, *122*, 124–47, *129*, 279, *312*, 363–64n1
Area E in Townley-Read site, *122*, 126–27
Area F in Townley-Read site, 121, *122*
Area H in Townley-Read site, *122*, 128, *129*, 146–54, 279, *312*, 363–64n1
autonomy: demographic statistics, and relationship to, 7; domestic-context artifact data as demonstration of, 92, 351–52; fur trade, and relationship to, 7; of Iroquois, 7–8, 92, 318, 351–52; military power and, 7, 205, 341; reservationization era and, 8, 14, 17–18, 197, 318, 336–38; territorial encroachment of Europeans, and effects on, 318, 327, 345, 354. *See also* restoration experience
Atwell site, 239, 267–68, *268*, 269, 272, 363n4
Avon Bridge site, 187, *188*
Avon area (New York), 186

Ball site, 248
Bancker, Evert, 101, 102, 119
Barber, Daniel M., 165, 170, 171
Barnes, Frederick W., 34, 77
de la Barre, Joseph-Antoine Le Febvre, 51
Bartram, John, 38, 123, 202, 209, 216–17, 233, 245, 261–62, 267, 269, 275, 329, 363n3
Baugher, Sherene, 19
Bead Hill site, 240, *240*, 241, *242*, 253–54
beads, glass: labor-based interpretation of, 31; "man-in-the-moon," 359n5, 361n9; native, 12, 21, 31, 136, 360n2, 361n9
beads, shell, 21, 136, 140, 145, 154, 276, 314
Beal site, 11, 168, 170
bearskin trade: faunal material and, 44, 140, *141*, 142, *279*, *281*, 282, *283*; during Oswego era, 77, 79, 92
Beauchamp, William M., 31, 33, 36, 45, 80, 81, 84, 87, 93, 99, 104, 105, 106, 108, 112, 119, 166, 175, 184, 185, 186, 210, 215, 219, 220, 222, 235, 236, 245
beaver trade: dates for, 7, 297, 343; documentary sources for, 290; exports to Europe and, 3, *76*, 77, 290, 291, 297; faunal material and, 44, 46, *141*, *281*, *283*, 342; fur-bearing animal populations and, 54, 56, 58, 72, 334; local political economy, and effects of, 46, 297–98, 342, 343; pelt acquisition for, 297, 300; space/time evaluation of, 343–44; trading posts/forts, and role in, 291; transition from, 297
Beck, Charlotte, 30, 128
Bell site, 305
Bennett, Monte R., 18, 19, 123, 158, 176, 233, 240, *242*, 257, 258, 303, 345
Benson, Adolph B., 38, 108, 224, 279, 295
Berg, Gary, 166
Bernbeck, Reinhard, 30
Bertsch, W. H., 73
Bieder, Robert E., 8
Bielinski, Stefan, 68, 118, 119
Big Flats site, 189, *189*
Bilharz, Joy A., 3, 337
Binford, Lewis R., 39, 40, 157, 285, 286, 301–2
Bleecker, Jacobus, 86
Bleecker, John Rutger, 108
Blewbek (Kayenkwarahte), 70, 117
Bodner, Connie Cox, 116, 215
bone marrow/grease exploitation, 138, 142, 143, *285*, 285–86, 301–3, 364n4
Boserup, Ester, 214, 223
botanical remains, 115, 125, 136, 138, 142, 150, 212–15, 219
bottle glass fragments: alcohol consumption and, *312*, 313, 314, 316, 340, 350, 364n9; aqua green, 140, 143, 152, 153, *313*, 314; emerald green, 146, 152, *313*; light blue-green bottle glass, 152, 311, 312, *312*, *313*, 360n6; olive bottle glass, 129–30, 137, 143, 146, 147, 152, 311, 312, *312*, *313*
Boughton Hill site. *See* Ganondagan/Boughton Hill site
BPM. *See* Buried Plowed Midden
Bradley, James W., 3, 10, 11–12, 20, 26, 98, 261, 267, 303, 345, 349, 350, 364n7
Brain, Jeffrey P., 158, 311, 360n6
Brandão, José António, 2, 26, 41, 42, 47, 49, 50, 51, 52, 53, 54, *55*, *55*, 56, 58, 64, 65, 89, 91, 140, 297, 303, 358n3
Branstner, Susan M., 304
Brant, Joseph, 21, 91, 264
Brant Canagaraduncka, 264

Brant House site: classification of, 264, 272; faunal material from, 286, 288, 294, 364n2; lot structure, 19, 20, 21, 272, 286, 294, 364n2. *See also* Indian Castle site
Braund, Kathryn E. Holland, 296, 364n4
Brewer, Floyd I., 157
Brink, John W., 285, 286
British, use of term, 357n2. *See also* English; New York
British Customs Office, 290
British-Iroquoian forces, and invasion of Canada, 61, 62, 341
Brodhead, Daniel, 187, 197
Brose, David S., 9
Brother site, 93, *94*, *179*, 180
Brown, George W., 38, 60, 61, 117, 118, 120, 358n4
Bruseth, James E., 26
Buell, Augustus C., 38, 361–62n5
Buell, Ezra, 38, 361–62n5
Buried Plowed Midden area, 31, 150–53, *151*, 293
Burrell Creek, 93, 96, 97, 105, 106, *151*, 161
Butler, William B., 128
Butts, William L., 212, 214

cabin, Iroquoian-style: archaeological data and, 112; cabin, use of term, 225, 262, 263; connotations surrounding log cabins and, 225–26; described, 17; dispersed settlements and, 209; documentary sources for, 68, 121; European inspiration for, 230, *231*; house form classification using, *167*, 362–63n4; log, use of term, 225; nuclear-family houses and, 2, 17, 20, 156, 208, 274, 320, 361n1; reservationization era and, 226; site classification using, 166; typology of house forms and, 227, 229. *See also* European-style log cabins
Cadwell, Donald H., 95
Calloway, Colin G., 197, 289, 337
Cammerhoff, Johann, 34, 36–37, 45, 81, 93, 97, 99, 104–6, 107, 117, 119, 156, 175, 181, 184–87, 210, 211, 215, 216, 219, 245, 263–64, 275, 291, 292, 295, 296, 298, 299, 316, 324
Campbell, William W., 191, 361–62n5
Canada: British-Iroquoian forces, and invasions of, 61, 62, 341; France's surrender of, 334; fur-bearing animals in, 72; Iroquois, and relations with Indians in, 22, 57; Senecas, and relocation of members to, 71, 181. *See also* New France
Canadadarhoe site. *See* Kendaia site
Canagaraduncka, Brant, 262
Canagaroh village. *See* Ganondagan/Boughton Hill site
Canandaigua Lake: fish resources in, 292; Moravian missionaries, and travels near, 106, 107; settlements between Seneca Lake and, 74, 83, 93, *94*, 99, 104, 106–7, 184, 186
Canandaigua site: alcoholic consumption at, 316; clan symbols at, 324; deer hunting and, 291; described, *189*; food resources and, 215, 291; location of, *185*, 186, *188*; Long Bridge trail near, 295. *See also* Ganataqueh village
Canandaigua Treaty, 337
Canasadego village, 109, *110*. *See also* New Ganechstage Site Complex
Canasatego, 263
Canasuedaha village, 102. *See also* Ganundasaga village
Canawagis/Canawaugus village, 186, 187
Canaweola village, *189*, 190
Caneadea I site, 187
Canodago village, 186. *See also* Canandaigua site
Canoenada village, 168. *See also* Beal site
Canosedaken village, 100
Canosodago village, 102. *See also* Ganundasaga village
Canosseago village, 186–87
Canossodage village, 109, 110, 186–87, 359n3. *See also* New Ganechstage Site Complex; Kanadesaga site
captivity narratives, 35, 36, 38, 172–73
Carolinas, 49, 57, 66, 85
castle, use of term, 98
Catharine's Town village, *188*, *189*, 293
catlinite, 303. *See also* red stone artifacts
cats, 294
Cattaraugus Reservation, 38, 187
cattle, 73, *141*, 241, *279*, *283*, 293, 296
Caughnawaga site: house forms at, 250–53, *252*, 254, 321–22; occupation span for, 170, 321; palisade construction at, 254; post mold size data and, 253

Cayuga nation: deer hunting and, 299; demographic statistics for, *321*; European presence in territory of, 7; Five Nations and, 3; food resources and, 45, 52, 171, 292; fortified settlements and, 171; hearths, and use by, 263; horses adopted for use by, 295, 296; house forms and, 241, 262–63, 272, 341; location of, 3, *5*; orchards of, 213; palisade construction and, 341; settlement patterns of, 199, 341; Twenty Years' War and, 53

Ceci, Lynn, 46

cemetery sites; bottle glass fragments at, 314; changes in size of, 193; decline narratives, and decrease in size of, 2; excavations at, 95, 114, 123–24, 130; faunal material from, 280; glass beads found at, 361n9; indigenisms, and artifacts from, 9; NAGPRA and, 114; New York excavation policies at, 114; red stone artifacts from, 307–8, 364n8; small plots vs. large, 114, 115, 176, 178, 208

ceramic sherds: European, 154, 220, 314; Native, 126, 130, 137, 140, 144, 146, 150, 152, 153

Champlain, Samuel de, 4, 193, 212, 217, 245

Chemung Valley settlements, 42, 187, 189, *189*, 190, 192

Chenosious village, 186. *See also* Fall Brook site

Christianity, 24

Church, Robert R., 285

Claessen, Lawrence, 67–70, 84, 100–101, 103, 119, 162

clan system, 221, 323–24, 329, 345

Clarke, Anne, 352

Claus, Daniel, 264–65, 363n3

Cleland, Charles E., 304, 305

Clifton, James A., 322

Cline, M. G., 95, 215

cloth, European, 281, 283, 298

Coates, Irving W., 31, 52, 170, 172, 174, 219

Cobb, Charles R., 27

Colden, Cadwallader, 35, 36, 60, 61, 62, 67, 70, 100, 108, 117, 199, 287, 291, 305

colonialism: cultural entanglement vs., 30, 352–55; field methods as reflection of, 124, 128; "Indianness" during frontier, 24; Iroquoianist scholarship, and theories about, 6–9, 21–22, 349; use of term, 353

comfort site, 19

community structure: changes in, 2, 23, 83, 192–97, 319; dispersed settlements, and effects on, 211; house forms, and definition of communities, *167*; household size and, 273–75, 345; outfields and, 215–16; typologies and, 165–66, *167*. *See also* settlement patterns

Compagnie des Indes, 75, *76*, 332

Condawhaw village, *188*, *189*, 190, 293

Conestoga site: community structure at, 123; deerskin trade and, 284; described, 258, *259*; house forms and, 260, 271; iron hardware and, 363n7; multinational site, 89, 258; occupation span for, 258; post mold diameter figures for, *240*; semi-dispersed settlements at, 258

Conesus village, *188*, *189*

Confederacy. *See* Iroquois Confederacy of Five Nations

Connor, Melissa, 128

Conover, George S., 31, 33, 37, 93, 95, 96, 97, 99, 103, 106, 110–13, *113*, 117, 121, 123, 124, 125–27, 154–56, 157, 160, 165, 172, 175, 178, 180, 182, 187, 189, *189*, 190, 191, 192, 208, 213, 216, 217–19, 243, 275, 293, 296, 358–59n2, 359nn4–5

Conoy/Piscataway group, 89

Conrad, Maia, 87, 261, 310

contact period, use of term, 352

Cornish site, 363n1

Cornplanter Reserve. *See* Allegany Reservation

Cornplanter's Town village, 17, 34, 293, 337–38

Covenant Chain alliance, 51

Cowan, C. Wesley, 9

Cowan, Frank L., 9, 95

cows, 73, *141*, 241, *279*, *283*, 293, 294, 296

Creeks, southeastern, 296

creolized agricultural system, 213, 216, 221, 222, 344

creolized houses. *See* intercultural/creolized houses

Cronon, William, 96, 126, 211, 219, 288, 294, 353

Cuillerier, René, 41

cultural entanglement, 30, 353–55

Cusick, James G., 352

Customs of the American Indians (Fenton and Moore), 36

Cutcliffe, Stephen H., 48, 77, 78, 290, 297, 332, 335

Dale, Darren, 364n7
Daly, Patricia, 141
Damasky site, 168
Darnell, Regna, 8
Dawdy, Shannon Lee, 234
DCB (*Dictionary of Canadian Biography*, Brown), 38, 60, 61, 117, 118, 120, 358n4
Deagan, Kathleen, 234
Dean, Robert L., 131, 165, 227, 233, *240*, *242*, 248, 253, 312, 350, 362–63n4
Dean and Barbour Associates, 248
Deardorff, Merle H., 33, 37, 41, 42, 44, 45, 165
The Death and Rebirth of the Seneca (Wallace), 9, 16–18, 34, 337
deer, as food resource, 44, 79, 299
deerskin trade: acquisition of skins for, 298–99, 343, 364n4; documentary sources for, 290; exports to Europe and, 290–91, 297, 343; faunal material and, *141*, *281*, *283*, 283–85, *284*, 298–99, 364n4; hide processing for, 300–303, 343, 364n5; Senecas and, *141*, *281*, 284, 298–300, 325, 335, 343, 351; transition to, 297; western Indian trade activities and, 48, 79, 92, 290
Deetz, James, 229, 363n5
Delawares, 89, 91, 232, 334
Delaware Valley, 38, 230, 232
Delisle, Guillaume, 108
Deloria, Philip J., 8
Deloria, Vine, Jr., 9
demographic statistics: archaeological data, and estimates for, 22, 29, 54–55; Twenty Years' War, and effects on population and, 54–56; warrior data in documentary sources and, 50, 54–56, *55*, 170, 320–22, *321*
Denonville expedition: described, 38, 51–52; effects of, 4, 7, 57, 105, 166, 193–94; textual sources from, 37, 168–70
Densmore, Christopher, 118
DeOrio, Robert N., 171, 182
De Vore, Steven L., 128
Dewbury, Adam G., 312, *312*, 315, 360, 3664n7
DHNY (*Documentary History of the State of New York*, O'Callaghan), 36, 37, 69, 73, 102, 168, 292
Dictionary of Canadian Biography (Brown), 38, 60, 61, 117, 118, 120, 358n4
diet. *See* food resources
Dietler, Michael, 310, 353

diplomatic sources, 2, 35–36, 37, 50, 98, 100
diseases: effects of European-borne, 4, 47, 55, 66, 71, 84–85, 318, 319, 324, 347; epidemics of 1634, 7, 318; epidemics of 1724–1754 era, 84–85, 92, 154–55, 156
dispersed settlements: advantages of, 1, 198–99, 210–13, 224, 330–31, 343–46, 347–48, 349; agrocentrism, and interpretation of, 201–2; alcohol consumption, and role in formation of, 34, 199, 200, 202–3, 205, 209, 309–10, 311, 316, 328, 345; archaeological data for, 19, 21, 184; Cayuga nation, and interpretations of, 199; change to, 2, 165–66, 177, 183, 192–97, 198–99, 223–24, 343; community structure model for, 205–10, *206*; cultural factors and, 39; dates for, 19, 186; described, 186; ecological forces, and effects on, 39; ecological manipulation and, 211; Europeans, and interpretation of, 108, 155, 201–3, 204–5; famine food storage in, 212–13; fire protection in, 212; frequency of village moves, and effects of, 330; fully, *167*, 184, 190; house lot structure for, 205–10, *206*, 211, 275, 351; house size reduction, and effects of, 274, 345; infields, and logic of, 213, 216–17; intercultural/creolized houses, and use in, 212; Iroquoian agriculture and, 183, 221–23, 317, 343; local political economy and, 326, 330, 343; matrilineal institutions, and effects of, 222–23, 225, 274–75, 319–24, 320, 329; men, and labor allocation in, 317, 345; middleman period and, 71, 343; Midlands farmsteads as, 221–24; missionaries, and interpretation of, 200, 203, 204, 247; model for, 19; nucleated settlements, and change to, 2, 165–66, 177, 183, 192–97, 198–99, 223–24, 343; occupation span for, 212, 343; orchards, and logic of, 213, 217–19; outfields, and logic of, 213, 214–16; plant use, and logic of, 213–20, 343, 351; production concentration and, 223; scholarship, and interpretation of, 199, 203, 349; semi-dispersed, 93, *167*, 182, 183, 184, 190, 192, 209–10, 258, 348; social life/relations, and effects of, 222–23; storage in, 212–13; summary of logic of, 223–24; women, and labor allocation in, 210, 214, 220, 222, 223, 317, 343, 345. *See also* settlement patterns; *specific sites*

Division of Archives and History, 37, 188, *189*, 217, 293, 296

Doblin, Helga, 233, 264–65, 363n3

Documentary History of New York (O'Callaghan), 36, 37, 69, 73, 102, 168, 292

documentary sources: archaeological data in, 111, 127, 359n4; linking bottom-up data with top-down, 328, 355; Postcolumbian period gaps in, 29–30; scholarly interpretation of, 1, 23, 339; sites, and links to, 98

Documents Relative to the Colonial History of New York (O'Callaghan), 35, 36, 37, 44, 46, 51, 52, 54, 55, 59, 60–66, 68–74, 78–85, 88, 89, 98–103, 107, 108, 117, 118, 120, 155, 156, 160, 162, 165, 168–72, 181, 199–201, 223, 256, 282, 289, 291, 309, 315, 322, 327, 341, 359nn7–9, 361n2, 362n1

dogs: as companions, 283; documentary sources about, 292; as famine food, 45; faunal material of, *141*, 142, 147, 150, *279*, 282, *283*, 288; Iroquois names for, 98; tanning process, and brains of, 142

domesticated animals: cats, 294; cows/cattle, 73, *141*, 241, *279*, *283*, 293, 296; faunal material and, *141*, 278–79, *281*, 292–97, 340; gradualism, and use of, 293–94; horses, 293, 294, 295–96; pigs, 279, 282, 283, *283*, 293, 294–95, 296, 340, 344; reservationization era and, 292

domesticated plant resources, 44–45, 214–15, 216–17, 291, 295, 316. *See also* agriculture, Iroquoian

domestic-context artifacts/archaeology: artifact preservation/recognizability and, 20–21, 23, 207, 339, 348, 351; autonomy theory and, 92, 351–52; identification techniques for, 20; indigenisms, and collection of, 9–10; plowzone refuse used in, 19, 20, 95–96; scholarship on, 18–21; social life/relations, and analysis of, 12–13

Domestic Refuse Cluster 1: artifacts from, 136, 137, 140, 142, 360n2; botanical remains from, 136, 138, 142; cultural features at, 131, *132*, *266*; deer distribution at, 283–85, *284*; faunal material from, 136–37, 138, 140–42, *141*, 283–85, *284*, 293, 360n3; Feature 5 in, 131, 138–43, *139*, 215, 219, *284*, *285*, 293, 301; field methods for excavations at, 131; firepit and, 138, *139*; fur and skin processing evidence at, 138, 140–42, 143,

360n3; glass beads at, 360n2; house lot structure at, 143–46, 205, 207, 360n4; iron nail fragments, 137, 143, 269; map of, *122*, 128, *129*; plow disturbances and, 140; post molds at, 131, *132*; storage aboveground at, 138. *See also* Structure 1 at DRC 1

Domestic Refuse Cluster 2: deer distribution at, 283–85, *284*; excavations in, 146–47; faunal material from, 283–85, *284*, 293; house lot structure at, 130–31, 207; map of, *122*, 128, *129*

Domestic Refuse Cluster 3: artifacts from, 150, 152, 153–54; botanical material from, 150; bottle glass fragments in, 152, 360n6; BPM area, 31, 150–53, *151*, 293; cultural features at, 153; deer distribution at, 283–85, *284*; excavations in, 148–54, *149*; faunal material from, 150–52, 283–85, *284*, 293; general area of, 153–54; glass beads at, 31, 152, 360n2; house lot structure at, 207; human tooth from, 154; iron fragments at, 152; map of, *122*, 128, *129*, *149*; midden deposit, and excavations in, 131; plow disturbances at, 148, 152

Domestic Refuse Cluster 4, 130–31, 207

Domestic Refuse Clusters: Area H and, *122*, 128, *129*, 279, *312*, 363–64n1; bottle glass fragments in, 312; European-made artifact fragments in, 129–30; faunal material in, 128, *129*; field methods for excavations at, 130, 131; map of, *122*, 128, *129*

domesticated plant resources, 44–45, 214–15, 216–17, 291, 295, 316. *See also* agriculture, Iroquoian

Doolittle, William E., 207, 214

Douglas, Mary, 323

Dowaganhaes. *See* Ottawa nation

Doxtator, Deborah, 8, 16, 28, 223

Drake, Samuel G., 38, 42, 80, 90, 236, 237, 273

DRCs. *See* Domestic Refuse Clusters

Drennan, Robert D., 221

Drooker, Penelope, 395n5

Dunn, Shirley W., 255, 256, 265

Dutch Hollow site, 11

Early American Industries Association, 121

earthfast architectural forms, 363n5

East Fields area of Townley-Read site: cemeteries in, 121, 130; cultural material in surface surveys in, 130; European-made artifact fragments in, 129–30; faunal material in, 128, *129*, 282–83, *283*; glass beads at, 130; iron nails, and use in houses at, *242*; MNI figures for, 279; NISP values for, 279; plow disturbances and, 128; surveys in, 127–31

ecology, regional: colonialism, and effects on, 353; labor processes, and effects of, 39, 44; relocation due to exhaustion of, 212; seasonal availability of resources and, 42; settlement patterns, and effects on, 42, 52, 193, 196–97, 198, 211, 220–22; wild foods and, 44–45, 213, 219, 351

Edmunds, R. David, 62, 66, 85

eels, 45, 288, 292

Egli site, *240*, *242*, *242*, 269

Elliott, Dolores, 19

Elwood site, 350

Emmons, E. Thayles, 155

Enders House site, 19, 288, 294

Engelbrecht, William, 3, 29, 40, 42, 45, 97, 98, 211, 214, 215, 217, 219, 233, 263, 277, 286, 292

English: conflict among Seneca nation, and encouragement from, 341; factional conflicts, and role of, 101–4; missions, and rivalry between French and, 88; native proxy battles, and role of, 51, 53, 61–63, 66, 161; Senecas, and relations with, 61, 119–20, 341; smithies, 103, 119; southern Indians, and alliances with, 85; trading post/fort developed by, 71–72, 73; use of term, 357n2; western Indians, and alliances/trade with, 59–60

"Era of Colonial wars," 2, 37

Erie nation, 3, 47

ethnogenesis, 24

ethnography, salvage, 13–15

Euro-Americans: convergence of Iroquoian material practices with ways of, 8–9, 276–77, 337, 338; dispersed settlements, and ways of, 221–24; territorial encroachment by, 6, 337

Europeans: architectural tools/technologies of, 225, 233–34, 237–39, 344, 362n3; colonialism vs. cultural engagement with, 352–53; creolized agricultural system, and plants introduced by, 213, 344; degrees of engagement with, 4, 6; diseases from, 4, 47, 55, 66, 71, 84–85, 318, 319, 324, 347; dispersed settlements, and interpretation by, 108, 155, 201–3, 204–5; early engagement between Indians and, 3–4, 6, 327, 353–54, 355; factional competition encouraged by, 81–82, 341, 346; factional conflicts, and role of, 101–4; fishing industry and, 3; fur trade with, 3, *76*, 77, 290–91, 297, 343; historic maps made by, 107–9; house forms, and influence of, 272; hybrid/nontraditional products made of goods from, 12, 14, 129–30, 154, 220, 314; influences of, 237, 272, 354; location of settlements of, *5*; maps drawn by, 107–8; naming practices of Iroquois for, 98; palisade construction period, and protection against armies of, 345; political-economic approach of Iroquois for engagement with, 197, 223, 317, 326–27, 356; selective adoption of technology/lifeways of, 349–50; tensions/conflicts during Indian engagement with, 29; territorial encroachment of, 6, 7, 23, 198, 284, 318, 322, 327, 331–33, 337, 342, 345, 354–55; textiles from, 281, 283, 298; trading posts/forts development by, 67–74, 327; visitors to Indian villages by, 118–20; western Indian/Iroquois conflicts, and role of, 53, 59, 61, 62, 87, 92. *See also* English; France; missionaries; New France; New York

European-style houses: American Midland farmsteads and, 230, *231*, 241; archaeological data for, 226, 239, 363n5; cabin, use of term, 225, 248; classification of house forms and, 226; described, 229–33, *231*, 235–36; documentary sources for, 235–36, 271; earliest use of, 230; iron nails, and use in, 241; Iroquois' use of, 203, 272, 362n1 (chap.8); log, use of term, 225; Midland cabin style, 222; pieux en terre house forms and, 239, 363n5. *See also* Brant house

Evans, Lewis, 108, *109*

Evolution of the Onondaga Iroquois (Bradley), 12

Factory Hollow site, 11, 131

Fall Brook site: demographic estimate for, 185; dispersed settlement at, 187; house count for, 187; house forms at, 186, 263–64; location of, *185*; occupation span for, *166*. *See also* Zonesschio village

famines: disruptive effect of, 347; foods/food storage for, 45, 212–13, 286, 289, 302, 347; mortality episodes due to, 63, 84, 324; survival during, 37, 82, 84, 92, 289
Far Indians. *See* western Indians
faunal material: animal use variation, and analysis of, 279; dietary stress, and analysis of, 278, 286, 288–89, 299, 364n4; distribution of, 282–83, *283*; documentary sources for, 289–92; domesticated animal use and, *141*, 278–79, *281*, 292–97, 340; in DRC 1, 136–37, 138, 140–42, *141*, 360n3; food resources and, 44, 79, 282, 299; fur trade economy, and analysis of, 278, 281–82; labor allocation, and analysis of, 278, 286; menues pelleteries and, 77, 79, 92, 281, 282; presence/absence of species and, 287–89; surface density of animal bone and tooth fragments, *129*. See also *specific animals*
Feature 5, DRC 1, 131, 138–43, *139*, 215, 219, *284*, *285*, 293, 301
Feder, Kenneth L., 30
Feest, Christian F., 322
Feest, Johanna E., 322
Feister, Lois M., 359n3
Fenton, William N., 2, 3, 4, 7, 13, 15–16, 26–27, 28, 33, 34, 37, 39–42, 44, 45, 49, 57, 117, 118, 138, 172, 187, 193, 203, 225, 233, 237, 257, 273, 274, 324, 339, 357n4; and Tooker, Elisabeth, 98, 270, 322
Ferguson, Leland, 10–11, 234
Ferris, Neal, 21, 226
field methods, 123–25, *124*, 127–28, 130, 131
Fine-Dare, Kathleen S., 9, 124
firepits: bone marrow/grease exploitation and, 138, 142, 143, 301; food preparation at, 138, 140, 142; fur/skin processing at, 138, 140–42, 143, 360n3
Fisher, Charles L., 19, 220, 303, 364
fisher/marten species, 77, 142, *279*, 282, 283
fishing industry, 3, 292
Flannery, Kent V., 39
Flatheads, 62, 83, 85, 300. *See also* southern Indians
Fleisher, P. Jay, 95
Fletcher site, 305
Flick, Alexander C., 83, 155, 190, 359n8
Follett, Harrison C., 31, 112, 173–75
Folts, Jim, 359n3, 361n4
food resources: dietary stress analysis, 278,
286, 288–89, 299, 364n4; domesticated plants, 44–45, 214–15, 216–17, 291, 295, 316; famine foods, 45, 212–13, 286, 289, 347; faunal material, as indication of, 44, 79, 282, 299; fishing industry and, 3, 292; fruit trees, 111, 189, 209, 213, 217–19, 344; gathered plants, 213, 219, 343, 351; imported plants, 213, 219–20; nut trees, 112, 136, 142, 144, 145, 147, 150, 217, 218; Twenty Years' War, and effects on, 52, 56–57; wild foods, 44–45, 213, 219, 351. *See also* agriculture, Iroquoian; *specific animals*
Fort Frontenac, 52, 59, 75, 261, 270, 291
Fort Hill site, 169–70, 171, 293
Fort Hunter site: dates for, 19; domestic-context artifacts from, 19, 23; faunal material from, 364n2; house forms at, 264, 272; territorial encroachment of Europeans and, 23, 327, 342, 345, 354
Fort Michilimackinac, 67, 91, 223
Fort Niagara. *See* Niagara trading post/fort
"Fort Niagara" (anon.), 38
Fort Saint-Louis, 51
Fort St. Joseph, 53
forts/trading posts. *See* trading posts/forts
fowl, 44, 211, 280, 287–89, 292, 293
fox, *141*, 142, *279*, 282, 283, *283*, 298
Fox, Edith M., 74
Fox, Richard Allan, Jr., 26
Fox nation, 50, 62–63, 66, 85, 161, 187, 304, 305
France: British rivalry with, 59–60, 83, 86, 101–3, 161, 196; chronic threat of war between England and, 54, 59, 61–62, 63; influence of, 59, 333, 334; Iroquoian neutrality in rivalry between England and, 22, 208, 335, 340–41; military forces from, 4, 51, 52; Native proxy battles, and role of, 51, 53, 61–63, 66, 161, 325; smithies from, 60–61, 81, 83, 102, 103, 104; trading posts/forts developed by, 72–74. *See also* Canada; Denonville expedition; Europeans; French agents; New France
Francello, Joseph A., 324
French agents: diplomatic activities of, 61, 66, 70, 75, 83, 91, 120, 161, 334; Indian nations, and conflicts encouraged by, 53, 59, 61, 62, 87, 92; Indian nations, and warfare against, 4, 51; Seneca nation, and relationship with, 53, 59–62, 67, 70–71, 85, 87, 92, 117, 119,

223; west-east trade activities, and role of, 53, 59, 75, 346. *See also* France
Frontenac, Louis de Buade de, 250
Frontenac expedition, 250, *251*
frontier exchange economy, 223, 292
fruit trees, 111, 189, 209, 213, 217–19, 344
Funk, Robert E., 7, 26, 29, 46, 280–84, *281*, 287, 288, 298, 350, 355, 364n3
fur trade: alcohol consumption, and role in, 299, 331; archaeological data for, 47; autonomy, and relationship to, 7; commercial hunting and, 45–46; diversification of, 79, 92; documentary sources for, 289–92; with Europeans, 3, *76*, 77, 290–91, 297, 343; extra-regional trips, 46–47; faunal material analysis and, 278, 281–82; Great Lakes hunting territories, and source of animals for, 58, 74–77; Indian nations, and competition for, 58; Iroquoian fur-based articulation and, 45–46, 297, 303, 335, 343; King George's War, and effects on, 34, 75, 78, 290, 333–36; labor allocation and, 297–300; military power, and effects on, 46, 47; with missions, 22, 72; New France and, 70, 74–75, 291, 332; north-south, 47, 72, 77, 78; with New York, 22, 46, 47, 63, 64, 346; population levels of animals, and effects on, 46; relations with neighboring groups, and effects on, 46; relocation of, 87, 195, 318, 333–36; Seven Years' War, and effects on, 333; skins exported in, *76*, 77, 290; space/time evaluation of, 45–48, 331–32, 335, 343–44; trading posts/forts and, 71–72, 75, 77, 291, 309, 327, 331–32, 346; Twenty Years' War, and effects on, 27–28, 56; viability of, 1, 92. *See also* beaver trade; deerskin trade; west-east trade activities

Gajinquechto, 106, 116, 117, 263
Galban, Mike, 364n7
Galloway, Patricia, 24, 32
Ganassateco, 263
Ganataqueh village, 106, 184–85, 186, 189, 324. *See also* Canandaigua site
Ganestiquiagon village, 253. *See also* Bead Hill site
Ganondagan/Boughton Hill site: bottle glass fragments, and alcohol consumption at, 312, 314, 350; cemeteries at, 170; cultural decline at, 11; defensibility of, 190; demographic estimates for, 170, 171; described, 168, 170; domesticated animals at, 293; hearths at, 253; house count for, 171; house forms at, 248, *249*, 254, 322, 363n1; interpretive displays and, 38, 363n1; iron nails, and use in houses at, 241, *242*, 254; nucleated community structure at, 168, 170; occupation span for, *166*, 168; post molds and, *240*, 241, 253
Ganondagan State Historical site. *See* Ganondagan/Boughton Hill site
Ganundasaga village, 94, 99, 101–2. *See also* New Ganechstage Site Complex
Gathtsegwarohare village, 187, *188, 189*
Gehring, Charles T., 42, 233
gendered labor, 44–45, 79, 297–303. *See also* men; women
gendered social actors, 39–40, 42, 44, 90, 343–44
"A General Map of Middle British Colonies" (Evans), 108, *109*
Genesee Castle village, 42, *166*, 187–89, *188, 189*, 190, 192, 292, 299
Genesee Valley settlements: Moravian missions to, 37; occupation span for, 42, 84, 172, 187, 195, 358n5; regional trips to, 42 Seneca communities in, 82, 84, 163, 172, 195–98, 358n5
Geneva area (New York), 1, 37, 95, 99, 110, *113*, 359n4
Getman site, 350
Gibson, John, 108
gift exchange: Europeans and, 56, 75, 324; western Indians and, 60, 65, 92, 303, 308, 341, 342
Gipson, Lawrence Henry, 108
glass fragments, bottle. *See* bottle glass fragments
Glassie, Henry, 229
goats/sheep, 294
Gonnor, Nicholas de, 36
Gorham, Nathaniel, 97
Gosden, Chris, 252
GPR (ground-penetrating radar), 124, *124*
gradualist model, 8, 18, 293–95, 348–50, 352
Graham, Robert J., 170
Grassman, Thomas, 250
Graymont, Barbara, 2, 26, 52, 187, 197, 337
Grayson, Donald K., 285, 287

grease/bone marrow exploitation, 138, 142, 143, *285*, 285–86, 301–3, 364n4
Great Lakes area: alliances with Indians from upper, 22, 57, 334, 340; artifact data within, 10; French influence in, 331; fur trade, and pelts from, 47, 58, 59, 64, 74–77, 79, 91, 289–90, 346; Iroquoian homeland adjacent to, 3; warfare in area of, 59, 62
The Great Law and the Longhouse (Fenton), 15–16
Green, Rayna, 358n2
Greenhalgh, Wentworth, 37, 50, 150, 168, 170, 171, 176, 247–48, 320–21, *321*
Gremillion, Kristen J., 302
Gronim, Sara Stidstone, 108
ground-penetrating radar (GPR), 124, *124*
Grumet, Robert S., 2, 19, 20–21, 156, 182, 258, 342, 362n1
Guldenzopf, David, 19, 29, 286, 294, 303, 324, 355, 364n2
Gums, Bonnie L., 363
Gundersen, James Novotny, 303
Gunderson, Robert Gray, 226
Guthe, Alfred K., 10, 131

Haan, Richard, 2, 7, 26, 49, 59, 60, 62–64, 66, 68, 69–73, 80, 92, 120, 193, 195, 291, 303, 310, 311, 315, 326–28, 331, 332, 339, 341, 342, 346, 347, 358n3
Hachnaige village, 106, 184, 185. *See also* Honeoye site
Hagerty, Gilbert W., 19
Halsey, Francis W., 38, 202, 213, 217, 235, 238, 243, 275
Hamell, George R., 2, 11, 12, 19, 37, 52, 83, 98, 165, 168, 170, 187, 191, 212, 214, 225, 227, 233, 234, 254, 256, 270, 273, 303, 324, 361n4, 362n1
Hamilton, Milton W., 38, 83, 155, 190, 359n8, 361–62n5
Hammett, Julia E., 211
Handbook of American Indians of North of Mexico (Hodge), 33
Haneaye village, 186. *See also* Honeoye site
Hanson, Lee, 157, 160
Harrington, J. C., 157
Harris, George H., 324
Hartgen Archaeological Associates, 19
Hasenstab, Robert J., 125
Haudenosaunees, 1, 13. *See also* Iroquois Confederacy of Five Nations; Iroquois Confederacy of Six Nations; *specific nations*
Haudenosaunee Standing Committee on Burial Rules and Regulations, 124, 154
Hauptman, Lawrence M., 8, 24, 197, 337, 357n5
Havard, Gilles, 2, 53, 54, 59, 62, 305, 358n3
Hawley, Charles, 36
Hayes, Charles F., III, 10, 18, 21, 131, 165, 170, 185, 363n1
Hazard, Samuel, 82
Hazlet site, 93, *94*, 178, *179*, 180
hearths: central, 135–36, 202, 234; longhouses and, 227, 238, 245, 248, 250, 253, 345; short longhouses and, 229, 345; short-term, 147; smoke holes and, 255, 265; special-purpose, 144
Hefner, Robert W., 24
Heidenreich, Conrad E., 2, 96, 136, 182, 203, 214
Heimmer, Don H., 128
Hendon, Julia A., 40
Hendrick (Theyanoguin; Mohawk leader), 66, 200
Henry, Dixie Lynn, 19, 352
Herlich, Jessica, 361n9
Herrick, James W., 219
Hesse, Franklin J., 19, *240*, 241, 242, 303
Hester, Thomas R., 30
Hill, Christopher L., 303
Hinsley, Curtis M., Jr., 8, 13
historic, use of term, 357n1
historical sources: domestic-content excavations, and use of, 31; drawings, 38; evaluating/contextualizing, 30, 31–34; maps, 30, 31–34, 38, 193, 355; space and time evaluation of, 32–33
History of the Five Indian Nations (Colden), 35
Hobart and William Smith Colleges, 113, 121, 359n4
Hodge, Frederick Webb, 33, 99, 155
Hoffman, Albert, 31, 180
hogs, 293
Holt, Julie Zimmerman, 364n4
Honeoye site: crops and, 215; described, *189*; food resources and, 215; glass beads at, 360n2; location of, *185*, *188*; occupation span for, *166*, 168, 189. *See also* Hachnaige village
horses, 293, 294, 295–96

Hosbach, Richard E., 227, 363n4
Houghton, Frederick, 172
house forms: about, 225–26; acculturation, and relationship to, 225, 350; archaeological and documentary evidence for (1677–1784), 247, 275–76; architectural artifacts and, 20; central hearths and, 135–36, 202; clan symbols marked on different, 324, 329; classification of, 1, 226, 245–46; cornering methods and, 242–44; documentary sources for, 235, 261; European influence on, 272; hearths and, 147; homeland settlements c.1677–1696 and, *169*, 247–53, *249, 251, 252*, 254–55, 271, 363n1; homeland settlements c.1696–1715 and, 255–58, *256*; homeland settlements c.1715–1754, 258, 261–69, *266, 268*, 272, 363nn3–4; homeland settlements c.1754–1780 and, 276; household size and, 272, 273–75, 309, 316, 345; interior post usage and, 242–44; iron nails, and use in, 20, 143, 241–42, *242*, 254, 269, 363n7; matrilineal institutions, and relationship to, 222–23, 274–75, 319; at Midland farmsteads, 230, *231*, 232–33, 237, 241; at mission settlements, 261, 269–71, 272, 322; reservationization era and, 226, 362n1; satellite settlements c.1677–1696 and, 253–54, 271–72; satellite settlements c.1696–1715 and, 258–61, *259*; scholarship on changes in, 225–26; short-term hearths and, 147; siding type and, 242–44; site classification using, 166; special-purpose hearths and, 144; terminology and classification of, 244–46; Tory houses, 189, *189*, 361n4; typology for, 135, 166, *167*, 276. See also *specific types of house forms*
house lot structure: dispersed settlement model and, 205–10, *206*, 211, 275, 351; Structure 1 at DRC 1 and, 143–44, 205–8, *206*
Houses and House-Life of the American Aborigines (Morgan), 13–14
house size: scholarship on changes in, 319–23, *321*; single-family houses, 264, 322, 329, 340. See also matrilineal institutions
Howson, Jean E., 11
Huey, Paul R., 9, 248, 256, 312, 364n7
Hunt, George T., 47, 64, 303
Hunter, William A., 90, 165, 187

Huntoon site: agricultural fields, and preservation of, 19; bottle glass fragments, and alcohol consumption at, *312*, 313, 314, 315; cemeteries at, 181; defensibility at, 181, 183; demographic estimate for, 181, 361n3; described, 181; documentary sources for, 106; glass beads in, 360n2; house forms and, 184; local travel areas and, 42; location of, 93, *94*, 108, *109*, 177; names for, 99, 100; occupation span for, 106, *166*, 181, 196, 361n2; red stone artifacts from, 347; relocation of village from, 195
Huron nation: agricultural models and, 214; diseases epidemics, and effects on, 318; homeland of, 3; house forms and, 253; political economy at missions and, 271; red pipestone artifacts and, 304; as refugees, 50, 53, 170, 248, 271, 320; Senecas, and warfare against, 51, 52; wall post spacing for houses built by, 240, 241

IIDH (*Iroquois Indians: A Documentary History,* Jennings et al.), 74, 78, 81, 82, 84, 99, 103, 108, 200, 289, 358n3, 359n7, 359n9
Indian Castle site, 19, 123, 264, 286, 294, 364n2. *See also* Brant House site
indigenisms, 9–12, 18, 350–52
intercultural/creolized houses: architectural tools/technologies and, 225, 233–34, 237–39, 344, 362n3; central hearths and, 234; classification of house forms and, 226, 362n1; convergence of material practices and, 272, 273, 276–77; cornering methods used in, 243, 244; dates for, 235; described, 233, 235, 236–37, 344–45; dispersed settlements, and use of, 212, 229, 349; documentary sources for, 235, 236–37; identification of, 239–44; iron nails, and use in, 241–44, *242*, 269; multiple-hearths/multi-family, 238; palisade construction and, 254–55; post molds and, 239–41, *240*, 240–41, 243, 268–69; settlements c.1696–1715 and, 260–61; settlements c.1715–1754 and, 272–73, 275–76; siding materials for, 242–43, 244, 269; sleeping compartments in, 243–44; Structure 1, 265–69, *266*, 344–45; use of term, 234
Irish cultural traditions, 202, 232, 233, 357n2
Irondequoit bay, 42, 52, 65, 66, 181, 195, 358n5

Irondequoit trading post/fort: British post at, 67–68, 69, 71, 74, 82; Denonville expedition and, 52; French post at, 67–68, 69, 70, 74, 77, 309; Senecas and, 73–74, 78, 181, 315; smithy at, 69, 102–3, 120; west-east trade activities and, 327, 346

iron nails, and use in house forms, 20, 137, 143, 241–42, *242*, 254, 269, 363n7

Iroquoia. *See* Iroquois nations

Iroquois Confederacy of Five Nations: diplomatic missions from, 53, 54; France, and relations with, 53; house forms and, 253; Illinois country, and warfare in, 50; Indian groups, and warfare with, 4, 50–51; location of, *5*; nations of, 3; New France, and peace with, 54; New York, and relations with, 50, 51, 53, 54, 58, 61–62; political-economic position of, 4; traditional homeland of, 3; wall post spacing for houses built by, 240, 241; western Indian alliances, and travel through territory of, 53, 54, 57, 58–59, 60, 62, 64–65, 67, 304–5, 308–9, 341. *See also* Northern Iroquoian cultures; *specific nations*

Iroquois Confederacy of Six Nations: archaeological data and, 18–21; captives taken by, 4, 7, 47, 319, 320; ceded territory to U.S., 7; colonization of, 6, 7; dispersed settlements, and interpretations of, 199–200; domesticated animals adopted for use by, 294; factional conflicts and, 86, 92; gradualist model and, 9; horses adopted for use by, 295–96; map of, 109, *110*, 359n3; mourning war complex and, 4, 47; nations of, 3; political economy of, 4, 6, 7–8; refugees adopted by, 7, 320; satellite villages of, 196. *See also* Northern Iroquoian cultures; *specific nations*

Iroquois Indians: A Documentary History (Jennings et al.), 74, 78, 81, 82, 84, 99, 103, 108, 200, 289, 358n3, 359n7, 359n9

Iroquois nations: acculturation theory and, 337, 338, 352; agricultural models and, 214, 317; American Revolution, and effects on, 7, 8, 22–23, 117, 323, 336–37, 342; autonomy of, 7–8, 318, 351–52; bead manufacture and, 130, 305, 360n2; colonialism, 352–53; control, and effects on, 351–52; convergence of European material practices with practices of, 276–77; decline narratives for, 2, 7, 9, 13–18, 349, 357n4; diplomatic activities based on local political economy of, 23, 333–35; diplomatic activities between Europeans and, 50, 53, 61–62, 71, 91, 161, 334–35; dispersed settlements model for, 19; encroachment of Europeans into territory of, 3–4, 8, 276, 281, 318, 324, 326, 327, 328, 337–38, 355; European-borne diseases, and effects on, 4, 318; European presence in, 6, 355; food resources and, 214; fur-based articulation with Europeans and, 45–46, 70, 297, 303, 335, 343; fur trade relocation, and effects on, 87, 195, 318, 333–36; geographical factors, and effects on, 4, 6; historiography of, 26–27; hybrid/nontraditional products made of goods and, 12, 14, 129–30, 154, 220, 314; messengers from, 40; monetary economy and, 331; naming practices among, 98; neutrality policies of, 22, 66, 85, 86, 87, 208, 325, 335, 346, 349; New France, and relations with, 85; New York, and relationship with, 83, 86; north-south trade activities and, 47, 72, 77, 78; Ohio country, and diplomatic activities of, 335; Ohio country, and negotiations with, 335; Ohio country, and relocation of, 89–90; Ottawa, and negotiations with, 63; paths used by, 65, 85, 89, 97; peaceful conditions, and prosperity for, 92, 223, 224; political economy at missions and, 271; redness, and cosmology of, 303; as refugees in Canada, 7; regional political economy and, 354–55; reservationization, and effects on, 197, 336–38; restoration experience of, 22, 57–58, 333–34, 339, 340–41, 346, 348; scholarship on, 1–2, 6–9, 21–22, 349; selective adoption of European technology/lifeways by, 349–50; Seven Years' War, and effects on, 333, 336; southern Indians, and raids by, 22, 49, 51, 52, 53, 55, 57, 62, 66, 85, 300, 325, 344; trading post/fort construction and, 94, 318, 326–33; traditional homeland of, 3; treaties, and surrendered land of, 337; Twenty Years' War, and effects on, 50–57, 318, 324–26; western Indians, and relations with, 51, 53–54, 57–58, 61, 62, 64–65, 91, 304, 305. *See also* Northern Iroquoian culture; *specific nations*

Jackson, Halliday, 34
Jackson-Everson site, 46, 281, 288, 364nn2–3
Jaimes, M. Annette, 9
Jamesville Penn site, 258, 362n1
Jemison, G. Peter, 114, 121, 124, 127, 154, 248, 337
Jemison, Mary, 38, 90, 91, 222, 324
Jennings, Francis, 2, 4, 7, 26, 74, 78, 81, 82, 84, 99, 103, 108, 200, 289, 358n3, 359n7, 359n9
Jesuit missionaries: artifacts from, 142; cemeteries and, 305; chapels built by, 252–53; expulsion of, 315; influences of, 24, 322; Iroquoian relationships with France, and role of, 21, 60, 61, 358n4; as sources, 36, 200, 257, 323. See also *specific missionaries*
Jesuit Relations (Thwaites), 36, 37, 42, 46, 50, 82, 100, 165, 200, 270, 271, 320
Johnson, Matthew, 229
Johnson, Warren, 296
Johnson, William, 155, 166, 190, 191, 324, 359n3
Joncaire, Daniel-Marie Chabert de, 81, 83, 87, 120
Joncaire, Louis-Thomas Chabert de: alcoholic beverage trade and, 80; biography of, 61, 118; as French agent, 102; Senecas, and relationship with, 59, 60–61, 67, 70–71, 85, 117, 119, 223; trading post/fort established by, 67, 68, 69, 73–74, 309
Joncaire, Philippe-Thomas Chabert de, 67, 74, 81, 82, 120
Jones, Eric E., 2, 12, 203, 225
Jones, George T., 30, 128
Jordan, Kurt A., 2, 6, 7, 13, 18, 19, 125, *167, 169, 173, 174, 177, 179, 185, 188*, 212
Jordan, Terry G., 202, 213, 221, 230, *231*, 232–33, 236, 237, 241, 294, 296
Joyce, Rosemary A., 40
JP (*The Papers of Sir William Johnson*, Sullivan et al.), 83, 155, 190, 359n8
JR (*Jesuit Relations*, Thwaites), 36, 37, 42, 46, 50, 82, 100, 165, 200, 270, 271, 320
Junker-Andersen, Christian, 29, 45

Kahnawake mission: agricultural labor at, 271; dates for 323; dispersed settlements, and interpretations of, 200; documentary sources from, 36, 257, 270; European influences on Mohawks and, 237; house forms and, 237, 257, 269, 270, 322; Senecas, and fights with Iroquois at, 53
Kahnawake Mohawks, 38, 235, 236, 270, 322, 323. See also Kanehsatake mission
Kalm, Peter, 38, 79, 89, 108, 165, 224, 270, 291
"Kanadesaga and Geneva" (Conover), 359n4
Kanadesaga site: archaeological data from, 191; community structure at, 191, 361–62n5; defensibility of, 160, 190–91; demographic estimate for, 191, 361–62n5; described, 188–89, *189*, 190–91; domesticated animals and, 293; famine foods, 289; house count from, 191, 361–62n5; house forms at, 191, 361–62n5; land allocation/agricultural labor in, 221; location/topography of, 93, *94*, 109, *110*, 121, *188*, 190, 191, 192, 359n3; occupation span for, 83, 97, 155, 156, *166*; orchards at, 344; semi-dispersed settlement at, 190, 192, 209–10, 348; smithy at, 190, 191; trading post/fort at, 74, 104, 190–91. See also Canossodage village
Kanakarighton (Kayenkwarahte), 70, 117
Kanehsatake mission. See Kahnawake mission
Kanghsadegea village, 107, 215. See also New Ganechstage Site Complex
Kannasadagoe village, 74. See also New Ganechstage Site Complex
Kapches, Mima, 135, 165, 167, 226, 227, 229, 243, 245–46, 247–48, 260, 261, 267, 270, 350, 362–63n4
Karklins, Karlis, 116, 156, 158, 361n9
Kashong site, *188, 189*, 293
Kaups, Matti, 202, 213, 221, 230, *231*, 232–33, 241, 294, 296
Kayenkwarahte, 70, 117
Keener, Craig S., 47, 51, 53, 89
Kelsay, Isabel Thompson, 27, 91, 264
Kendaia site: burials at, 182, 192; community structure at, 192; defensibility of, 192; demographic estimate for, 192, 361n3; described, 181–82, *189*, 192; house count at, 192; local travel areas and, 42; location/topography of, *177*, 185, *185, 188*, 192, 194; occupation span for, *166*, 177, 182, 183, 184, 189, 194, 212; orchards, and age of, 182, 189; semi-dispersed settlement at, 93, 182, 183, 190, 192
Kent, Barry C., 3, 19, 47, 89, 114, 123, 157, 158, 165, 258, 284, 303, 363n7, 364n7

Kent, Donald H., 60, 67, 68, 69, 71, 73, 81, 89, 120, 223, 315
Kerber, Jordan E., 124
Kidd, Kenneth E., 31, 158, 359n5, 361n9
Kidd, Martha A., 31, 158, 359n5, 361n9
King George's War: British-French rivalry, and effects of, 84, 86, 92; French-Indian relations, and effects of, 196, 334; fur trade, and effects of, 34, 75, 78, 290, 333–36; Iroquois, and effects of, 84, 196, 201, 209; Mohawk participation in, 86, 87, 325; Native proxy battles for French and British and, 325; Senecas and, 85–87, 333–36; Treaty of Aix-la-Chapelle (1748), and end of, 87
King of England, arms of the, 52, 169
Kinsey, W. Fred, III, 303
kinship ties, 81, 205, 271, 323–24
Kinzua Dam Project, 337
Kirkland, Samuel, 37, 65, 107, 117, 190, 191, 202, 215
Kirkwood site, 11, 168, 170
Klinefelter, Walter, 108
Knight, Dean H., 248
Konrad, Victor, 89, 165
Kuhn, Robert D., 6, 7, 24, 26, 29, 46, 280–84, *281*, 287, 288, 298, 350, 355, 364n3

lacustrine resources, 45, 288, 292
Lafitau, Joseph-François, 36, 138, 200, 237, 257, 270
LaForge smiths, 81, 83, 120
Laird, Matthew R., 36, 45, 47, 70, 72, 77, 79, 80, 220, 281, 358nn2–3
Landsman, Gail, 16
Langsner, Drew, 244
Lantz, Stanley W., 20, 21, 226, 280, 293
Lapham, Heather A., 141
League of the Ho-de-no-sau-nee, or Iroquois (Morgan), 1, 14
Leder, Lawrence H., 35, 61, 62, 69, 98, 102
Leechman, Douglas, 285, 301, 302
Lenig, Wayne, 258
Lenz, Mary Jane, 395n5
Lewandowski, Stephen, 214
Lightfoot, Kent G., 8, 27, 276, 357–58n1
Lightfoote, Rodney S., 96
Lipe site, 255
lithic debitage, 97, 126, 130, 137, 146, 147, 150, 154
Little, Barbara J., 30, 352

Little, Elizabeth A., 10, 41
Livingston, Robert, Jr., 35, 68, 70, 100, 118, 119
local political economy: analytical view of, 29, 197; archaeological data, and reconstruction of, 26, 29, 30–31; cultural patterns genre vs. studies of, 33–34; dispersed settlements and, 326, 330, 343; inter-community differences in, 28; labor-based distinctions and, 31; local, use of term, 28; methodological approaches to study of, 30; political economy, use of term, 27–28; primary textual sources for reconstruction of, 31–34; space/time evaluation of, 39, 355–56; structure of, 38–40; tensions/contradictions and, 29; trading posts/forts, and effects on, 327–28, 331–32; Twenty Years' War, and effects on, 91; types of primary textual sources for reconstruction of, 34–38. See also *specific trade economies*
longhouses, bark: classification of house forms and, *167*, 226, 362n1, 362–63n4; described, 226–29, *228*; era of, 156, 223, *228*, 236; hearths and, 227, 245, 248, 250, 253, 345; homeland settlements c.1715–1754, 261–62, 270, 272; longhouse, use of term, 203; multiple-family, 2, 3, 6, 13, 15, 17, 320–23; occupation span of, 212; plan view of, *228*; settlements c.1677–1696 and, 247–53, *249, 252*, 271; settlements c.1696–1715 and, 255–58, *256*, 260, 271; short longhouse, and replacement of, 183; Townley-Read site and, 208; typology of house forms and, 227
Longueil, Charles Le Moyne de, 120
Loren, Diana DiPaolo, 234
Lorenzini, Michele, 116, 156, 361n9
Lorette Indians, 270–71
Lorette mission, 36, 272
Lower Castle village, 256–57, 271–72, 286, 322
Lydekker, John Wolfe, 257
Lyman, R. Lee, 285
Lynch, James, 7, 2

MACIA. See *Minutes of the Albany Commissioners for Indian Affairs*
MacNeish, Richard S., 360
Madrigal, T. Cregg, 44, 364n4
Mainfort, Robert C., 305
Mallios, Seth, 157
mammalian remains. See faunal material

Mancall, Peter C., 310, 315
Mandzy, Adrian Oleh, 12, 252, 350
maps, as sources, 38, 107–9, *110*, 255, *256*, 359n3, 363n2
marine resources, 3, 130, 145, 146, 280, 288–89
Marquardt, William H., 28, 29
Marshall, Orsamus H., 37, 38, 52
marten species, 77, 142, *279*, 282, 283
master narrative of cultural decline, 18, 348
matrilineal institutions: dispersed settlements, and effects on, 222–23, 225, 274–75, 319–24, 320, 329; house forms, and relationship to, 222–23, 274–75, 319, 350; kinship ties and, 81, 205, 250, 323–24
Mayer, Poulton and Associates, 253
McAlester, Lee, 229, *231*
McAlester, Virginia, 229, *231*
McCashion, John H., 157–58
McConnell, Michael N., 79, 87, 89, 90, 118, 165, 315, 326
McGuire, Randall H., 28, 227
McIlwain, Charles Howard, 35, 46, 59–62, 64, 66–69, 71–74, 78–86, 98, 100, 102, 119, 120, 156, 199–201, 282, 287, 289, 291, 303, 305
McKelvey, Blake, 36
McKendry, William, 191, 192, 361–62n5
McNiven, Ian J., 124
men: animal use, and labor of, 297–300; dispersed settlements, and labor allocation of, 317, 345; fur trade, and labor allocation of, 297–300; hunting, and warfare by, 90, 343–44; as social actors in landscape of, 42, 44; travel patterns of, 42, 44
menues pelleteries, 77, 79, 92, 282, 343
Merrell, James H., 24, 49, 85, 300, 325
Merrifield, Edward, 38, 45, 293, 296, 324
Miami nation, 50, 54, 59, 87, 304
Michaelsen, Scott, 358n2
Michelson, Gunther, 55, *55*
microscale studies, 26–27
middleman period: British-French rivalry during, 326, 341, 347; dispersed settlements during, 71, 325, 343; geographic vs. economic middleman role of Iroquois during, 46, 54, 303; red stone artifact assemblages, and role of Iroquois during, 303–9, *306*, *307*, 327–28, 342, 347, 364n6. *See also* west-east trade activities

Middle Town village, *189*
Midland farmsteads, American, 221–22, 230, *231*, 232–33, 237, 241, 296
Mihesuah, Devon A., 9, 124
military power: autonomy and, 7, 205, 341; fur trade, and effects of, 46, 47; power relations and, 39, 205, 341; Twenty Years' War, and effects on Iroquoian, 7, 22, 50–57, 91, 318, 324–26, 340; warrior data, and demographic statistics for Senecas, 50, 54–56, *55*, 170, 320–22, *321*
military sources, 2, 35, 37, 168–70, 172
Miller, John, 255–56, 265
Milton Smith site, 176, 257, 258, 325
Mingos group, 88, 90, 335
minimum number of individuals (MNI) figures, 279
Minns, James C., 97
Minutes of the Albany Commissioners for Indian Affairs, 35, 36, 65, 73–74, 80–86, 98–104, 117–20, 181, 195, 205, 210, 358n3 (chap.2), 358n5 (chap.5), 359nn7–9, 361n3
Minutes of the Provincial Council of Pennsylvania, 82
missionaries/missions: British-French rivalry and, 88; dispersed settlements, and interpretations of, 200, 203, 204, 247; fur trade and, 22, 72; house forms at, 261, 269–71, 272, 322; political economy at settlements, 271; Postcolumbian period, and effects of, 24; refugee villages and, 237, 255; as sources, 35, 36–37. *See also specific missionaries; specific missions*
Mississauga group, 87, 304, 305. *See also* Ojibwa nation
Mississippi Valley, 195, 292, 318, 331
MNI (minimum number of individuals) figures, 279
modernization theory, 8, 337
Mohawk, John, 52
Mohawk nation: colonialism and, 354; community structure and, 198, 333; deerskin trade and, 284; diseases epidemics, and effects on, 318–19; dispersed settlements and, 198, 199–200, 250, 319–20, 321–22, 326, 345; domesticated animal use and, 294, 296–97; European influences on, 237, 354; extra-regional trips of, 46; faunal material and usage in, 280, 281, *281*; Five Nations and, 3; fur trade, and effects of

Mohawk nation—*continued*
decline in beaver population on, 46, 342; homeland of, 3; house forms and, 236–37, 250, 252, 257, 264, 265, 272, 322, 333, 341; King George's War, location of, 5; matrilineal institutions in, 250, 319–20, 321–22; New France, and attacks on, 53; nucleated settlements and, 341; palisade construction and, 341; and participation of, 86, 87, 325; political-economic changes in homeland of, 297, 342; presence/absence of species in homeland of, 287–89; refugee village at missions for, 237, 255; Seneca studies, compared with studies of, 6, 354–55; territorial encroachment of Europeans into homeland of, 6, 7, 23, 198, 284, 322, 327, 333, 337, 342, 345, 354; wall post spacing for houses built by, 241; warrior data, and demographic statistics for, 320–21, *321. See also* Kahnawake Mohawks

Mohawk Valley. *See* Mohawk nation

Montour, Alexander, 60, 61, 161

Moogk, Peter N., 229, 260

Moore, Elizabeth L., 26, 138, 233, 237, 257, 273

Moravian missionaries, 34, 37, 230, 232, 239. See also *specific missionaries*

Morgan, Lewis Henry, 1–2, 3, 13–17, 40–42, 65, 99, 138, 142, 190, 203, 274, 323, 360n3, 364n5

mortality episodes, 63, 84, 324. *See also* diseases; famines

mortuary sites. *See* cemetery sites

Mt. Pleasant, Alyssa, 197, 337

Mt. Pleasant, Jane, 214

mourning practices: alcohol consumption and, 310; discarding adornments and, 140; raids and, 4, 47, 52, 59, 66, 319

Mud Creek sites, 168, 176

Mullenneaux, Nan, 108

Muller, Ernest H., 95

multinational communities, 37, 89, 119, 165, 187. *See also* Conestoga site

multiple-family houses. See *specific house forms*

Munsees, 89

Murdock, George P., 274

museum collections, 1, 23, 24. *See also* Rochester Museum and Science Center

muskrat, 27, 45, 136, *279,* 282, *283,* 288

NAGPRA (Native American Graves Protection and Repatriation Act), 114

Nanticoke refugees, 271

Native American Graves Protection and Repatriation Act (NAGPRA), 114

Native Americans: demographic estimates for, 54; gradualist model and, 8–9, 18, 293–94, 294–95, 348–50, 352; passive portrayals of, 11, 14, 17, 18, 317, 348, 352. *See also* southern Indians; western Indians; *specific nations*

Nau, Luc François, 36, 200, 270, 323

negativism, 14, 204–5, 336, 352

Nern, Craig F., 304

Netting, Robert McC., 39

Neutral nation, 3, 47, 240

New Castle, 186. *See also* Kanadesaga site

New France: beaver trade and, 291; British-French rivalry, and relations between Iroquois and, 86, 101–3, 196, 341; British-Iroquoian attacks on, 53, 61, 62, 341; diplomatic sources from, 36; fur trade and, 70, 74–75, 291, 332; Iroquois names for officials in, 98; Ohio country, and interests of, 90. *See also* Canada

New Ganechstage Site Complex: archaeological resources for, 110–13, *113*; bottle glass fragments, and alcohol consumption at sites in, 316; British-French rivalry, and factional politics at, 101–3; cemeteries at, 178, *179,* 194, 361n1; community structure and, 177, 178, 194, 208, 342–43; crops and, 216; demographic estimate for, 184, 361n1, 361n3; dispersed settlement, and changes at, 183, 194, 199; documentary references for, 95; ecology manipulation at, 211; European visitors to, 118–20; house count for, 185; house forms and, 194, 263; house lot structure at, 275; King George's War period, and dispersed settlements of, 347; land allocation/agricultural labor in, 222; leaders linked with, 117–18; location/topography of, 93, *94, 109, 177, 179,* 185; long bridge section of trail in, 97, 105–6, 210, 295; map of, 108, *109*; Moravian missionaries, and contact with members at, 93, 104–6; names for, 93, 99–100; non-defensibility of settlement and, 180, 181, 183, 194, 209; occupation span for, 155, *166,* 183; outfields and, 215–16; planned/opportunistic relocation and, 317; restoration experience at, 348; short longhouses and, 178, 184; sites included in, 93; smithy at, *179*; transition from beaver to deerskin trade and, 297; visitors/inhabitants and, 116–20; west-east trade and, 194, 317

Newtown village, *189*, 190, 293

New York: aid to Iroquois from, 65, 67; Albany as center for trade in, British-French rivalry, and relations between Iroquois and, 59–60, 83, 86, 101–3, 161, 196; deerskins exported to London from, 297; diplomatic activities of, 61, 71, 91, 161, 334–35; diplomatic sources from, 35, 50, 100; dispersed settlements, and interpretations of, 200–201, 204, 362n1; excavation policies at cemetery sites in, 114; fur trade and, 22, 46, 47, 63, 64, 346; Geneva area in, 1, 37, 95, 99, 110, *113*, 359n4; Iroquois homeland in western, 3, 163; Iroquois names for officials in, 98; map of, 109, *110*, 359n3; negotiations with, 54, 58, 61, 67–68, 69–70; New France, and relations with, 66; north-south trade activities and, 47, 72, 77, 78; peaceful relations with, 57; pelts exported to London from, *76*, 77, 290, 291, 297; red pipestone artifacts from, 303–4; red slate roofing in, 304, 364n7; requests to nucleate from, 84, 196, 201; smithies from, 119–20; trading centers in, 58, 68–69, 71–72; west-east trade activities and, 59, 60, 62, 64, 66, 71–72, 341, 358n3

Niagara trading post/fort: beaver trade and, 291; British-French rivalry during era of, 346; extra-regional trips to, 42; French post at, 68–71, 73, 334: French surrender of, 334, 347; fur trade and, 75; Iroquois, and effects of, 326–33; location of, *5*, 68; occupation span for, 6, 52, 73; political economy, and effects of, 7–8; Seneca siege of, 52; territorial encroachment of Europeans and, 333; west-east trade activities and, 346

Niemczycki, Mary Ann Palmer, 24, 97, 360n1

NISP (number of individual species) values, 279

Noble, William C., 3

Noel Hume, Ivor, 311

Northern Iroquoian cultures, 3, 39. See also Iroquois Confederacy of Five Nations; Iroquois Confederacy of Six Nations; *specific nations*

north-south trade activities, 47, 72, 77, 78

Norton, Thomas Elliott, 2

nucleated settlements: archaeological evidence for, 19, 21, 50, 121, 342, 361n2; change from, 2, 165–66, 177, 183, 192–97, 198–99, 223–24, 343; described, 274; documentary sources for, 341–42; Indian raiding parties, and protection in, 340; landscape of fear and, 224; New York's requests to nucleate and, 84, 196, 201; nucleated, use of term, *167*; regional ecology, and effects of, 212

number of individual specimens per taxon (NISP) values, 279

Nunamiuts, and grease rendering, 301–2

nut trees, 112, 136, 142, 144, 145, 147, 150, 217, 218

"N.W. Parts of New York, No. 156" (map), 65, 109, *110*, 182, 186–87, 359n3

NYCD. See *Documents Relative to the Colonial History of New York* (O'Callaghan)

NYSAA (New York State Archaeological Association), *122*, 250, 257, *268*

NYSM (New York State Museum), 358–59n2, 395n5

Objects of Change (Rogers), 11

O'Brien, Jay, 28, 234

O'Callaghan, E. B., 35, 36, 37, 69, 73, 102, 168, 292

Ohio country: British influences in, 87, 331; extra-regional trips to, 42, 91; French influences in, 87–88; fur trade shift to, 87, 195, 318, 333–36; group composition in, 90; intercultural/creolized houses in, 235, 236–37; intercultural log houses in, 235, 236–37; Iroquois and, 88, 335; satellite villages of Six Nations in, 196; Senecas in, 90; Seven Years' War, and role of, 91

Ojibwa nation, 50, 304, 305

Old Ganechstage, 291. See also White Springs site

Old Oneida village, 264

Olds, Nathaniel S., 37, 168

Old Smoke (Seneca headman), 117

olive bottle glass, 129–30

Olmstead, Earl P., 37, 119

Onaghee, use of term, 99–100

Onaghee village, *94*, 99–102, 181, 358n5
Oneida nation: alcohol abuse issues, 199; clan membership in, 324; creolized agricultural system used by, 213; European presence in territory of, 7, 355; Five Nations and, 3; France, and attacks on, 53; homeland of, 3; horses adopted for use by, 295, 296; house forms and, 264–65, 270, 341, 363n3; location of, 5; middleman role in fur trade of, 72, 78; palisade construction and, 341; settlement patterns and, 199, 341, 345; warrior data, and demographic statistics for, 321, *321*
Onnahee village, 71, 74, 101, 104, 119, 181
Onondaga Castle site, 100–101, 102, 261–62, 322
Onondaga nation: alcohol abuse issues, 199; borrowing grain during scarcity of resources from, 45; dispersed settlements, and interpretations of, 199; European presence in territory of, 7, 53, 250; Five Nations and, 3; homeland of, 3; house forms and, 241, 246, 271, 272, 274, 329; location of, 5; middleman role in fur trade of, 72, 78; Ohio country, and relocation of, 90; palisade construction at settlements of, 254; scholarship, and effects on Seneca scholarship, 6; selective adoption of European technology/lifeways by, 349; settlement patterns and, 199, 200, 341–42, 362n1; warrior data, and demographic statistics for, 321, *321*
Onondaga sites: community organization at, 209; creolized agricultural system at, 213; European objects used by settlers at, 12; European-style log cabins at, 203, 235–36; house forms and, 262–63; house lot structure at, 209, 275; infields and, 217; preservation/recognizability of, 20; village plan and, 250, *251*
Onontaré village, 252. *See also* Rogers Farm site
Oppenheim, Samuel D., 126
Oquaga village, 213, 235, 237–39, 244
orchards: archaeological evidence for, 95, 112, 218–19; dating sites using age of, 182, 189; dispersed settlements, and logic of harvesting, 213, 217–19; fruit trees, 111, 189, 209, 213, 217–19, 344; imported trees for, 217, 218, 220; nut trees, 111, 112, 136, 142, 144, 145, 147, 150, 209, 213, 217, 218, 219; sites with, *179*, 182, 189, 213, 344
The Ordeal of the Longhouse (Richter), 328
Orlandini, John B., 288
Ortiz, Fernando, 234
Oswego trading post/fort era: alcohol trade, and disruptions during, 78, 79–81, 316, 345, 347; British-French rivalry during, 346; European encouragement of factional competition during, 81–82, 346; French influence over Senecas during, 81, 82–83; fur trade during, 74–78, *76*, 290, 316, 332, 335; Iroquois, and effects of, 92, 326–33, 347; Iroquois warfare against Indians during, 85; King George's War, and effects on trade during, 34, 75, 78, 290, 334–36; land given by Senecas for post, 73; local effects on Senecas during, 7–8, 77–81, 92, 195, 334–36, 346–48; occupation span for, 6, 73, 77, 335; political relations/crises during, 81–85; regional trips to post during, 42; territorial encroachment of Europeans during, 333; war rumors during, 85–88, 196, 341; west-east trade activities and, 71–72, 75, 77, 309, 331–32
Ottawa nation, 50, 53, 54, 59, 63, 304, 305, 322
Otterness, Philip, 230
Outram, Alan K., 142, 285, 286

Painted Post village, 189, *189*
Palatine German immigrants, 230, 341, 342. *See also* Moravian missionaries
palisade construction period: Cayuga nation, 341; cessation of, 2, 326, 330; described, 3, 171–72, 254; European armies, and protection during, 171, 345; Indian raiding parties, and protection during, 340; intercultural/creolized houses during, 254–55; Iroquois and, 254, 258, 330, 341; settlement patterns and, 98, 155, 169, 171–72, 176, 194, 254, 326, 330, 340, 342
Parker, Arthur C., 2, 31, 45, 112, 126, 166, 214, 217, 219, 222, 286, 357n5
Parmenter, Jon William, 2, 22–23, 26, 35, 36, 42, 47, 51, 56, 57, 62, 63, 74, 78–80, 83–91, 108, 118–20, 200, 201, 204, 223, 271, 325, 335, 339, 346
Parsons, Jeffrey R., 165
Pattington site, 19, 345

Pearson, C. S., 95, 215
Pennsylvania: deer resources and deerskin trade from, 79, 290; documentary sources from, 82, 85; encroachment of Europeans into Indian territory in, 89; French influences in, 88; fur market in, 78, 87; homeland and, 3; Iroquois and, 22, 57; red stone artifacts from, 303–4; satellite villages in, 196; westward expansion of fur trade led by, 87
Pennsylvania Historic and Museum Commission, 258, *259*
People of the Great Hill, 3. *See also* Seneca nation
Perdue, Theda, 85, 300, 325
period of uncertainty, 57–63, 92, 161, 194, 325
Perkins, Dexter, Jr., 141
Pessen, Edward, 226
Petun nation, 3, 47
Peyser, Joseph L., 62, 66, 85
Phelps, Oliver, 97
pieux en terre house form, 239, 363n5
pigs, 279, 282, 283, *283*, 293, 294–95, 296, 340, 344
Piker, Joshua A., 26
Pilkington, Walter, 37, 42, 45, 65, 80, 83, 107, 117, 118, 190, 191, 202, 215, 289, 310, 327
pine marten/fisher, 282
Piscataway/Conoy group, 89
plants: botanical remains of, 115, 125, 136, 138, 142, 150; creolized agricultural system, and introduction of, 213, 344; dispersed settlements, and use of, 213–20, 343, 351; domesticated plant resources, 44–45, 214–15, 216–17, 291, 295, 316; gathered, 213, 219, 343, 351; imported, 213, 219–20; processing sites for, 125; wild, 44–45, 213, 219, 351. *See also* agriculture, Iroquoian
plowzone refuse, domestic-context archaeology using, 19, 20, 95–96
political economy, use of term, 27–28. *See also* local political economy
Pontiac's War, 196, 335, 336
population statistics. *See* demographic statistics
Porter, Robert B., 3
Postcolumbian period, 9–10, 11–12, 23–27, 357n1
post molds (PMs): diameter figures for, 239–40, *240*; DRC 1, and evidence of, 131–36, *132, 133, 134*, 144–45; for identification of intercultural/creolized houses, 239–41, *240*, 344
Potawatomi nation, 50, 54, 304, 322
Poulton, Dana R., 89, 165, 240, *240*, 242, 253
poultry, 44, 211, 280, 287–89, 292, 293, 294
power relations, 39, 205, 341. *See also* military power
PPCM (*Minutes of the Provincial Council of Pennsylvania*), 82
Pratt, Peter P., 158
Precolumbian period, 24, 357n1
prehistoric, use of term, 357n1
Prezzano, Susan Carol, 19, 226, 233, 239, 260, 267
Primes Hill site, 19, 123, 176, *240*, 241, *242*, 257, 258
Prisch, Betty Coit, 116, 156
Protestant missionaries, 36–37

Quaker missionaries, 17, 34, 337
Queen Anne's War, 36, 57, 61, 63, 64, 69, 161
Quimby, George Irving, 10, 11, 305
Quinn, Kathleen M., 19

rabbits, 44, *279*, 283, *283*
raccoons, 136, 140, *141*, 142, 147, *279*, 282, *283*
Ramenofsky, Ann F., 7, 193, 220, 319
Rapp, George, Jr., 303
rats, 294
Read, Jonathan, 97, 358–59n2
Recht, Michael, 41, 44
red stone artifacts: red pipestone, and middleman role of Iroquois, 303–8, *306, 307*, 327–28, 341–42, 347, 364n7; red slate artifacts, and middleman role of Iroquois, 130, 137, 304, 305–8, *306, 307*, 364nn6–7; sources of materials for, 303, 364nn6–7; treaties, and use of red stone pipes, 305
Relethford, John H., 298
Rempel, John I., 229–30, 232, 233
reservationization: Allegany Reservation, 17, 34, 293, 337–338; during American Revolution era, 318, 336; autonomy, and effects of, 8, 14, 17–18, 197, 318, 336–38; Cattaraugus Reservation, 38, 187; domesticated animals and, 292, 355; house forms and, 20, 226, 355, 362n1; Iroquois, and effects of, 34, 197, 336–38; Tonawanda Reservation, 38, 187, 324, 364n5; use of term, 358n2

restoration experience: of Iroquois, 22, 57–58, 333–34, 339, 340–41, 346, 348; of Senecas, 21–24, 339, 340–41, 348, 349, 357n5

Richter, Daniel K., 2, 4, 6, 7, 26, 27, 34, 45–47, 49, 51, 53–55, 58, 59, 61, 63–65, 72, 73, 81, 84, 86, 89, 92, 100, 118, 119, 161, 165, 193, 195, 200, 203, 222, 225, 254, 261, 262, 264, 270, 274, 291, 309–11, 315, 316, 319, 324, 326, 328–33, 339, 341, 342, 347, 355

Rick, Anne M., 19, 294, 364n2

Ricklis, Robert, 227, 239, 246, 267, 268, 350, 362–63n4, 363n6, 363n4(chap.9)

Ridge, John C., 95, 111, 130, 175, 192, 209

Ridgetop area: community structure from excavations at, 121, 126, 127; defensibility of, 121, 160, 183, 209; described, 121; excavations at, 125–27; map of, 96, 112, 113, 122; occupation site at, 123, 125; plant processing/botanical remains on, 125; Senecas, and use of, 126

Rippey site, 93, 94, 178, 179, 180

Ritchie, William A., 19, 95, 114, 185, 233, 302

RMSC. See Rochester Museum and Science Center

Robbins, Maurice, 114

Robert C. Mainfort, Jr., 9

Rochester Junction site, 11, 166, 168, 170, 247–48, 312, 315, 322

Rochester Museum and Science Center: artifact collections at, 4, 31, 95, 115, 128; bottle glass fragments at, 312, 312, 313, 314, 315; field notes at, 4, 31; glass bead collections at, 360n2, 361n9; red stone artifact collections at, 305–6, 307; Seneca scholarship at, 4; site-wide surface collection at, 95

Rogers, J. Daniel, 11, 30, 362n3

Rogers Farm site, 240, 241, 242, 252–54, 253, 254, 269

Römer, Willem Wolfgang, 108, 109, 172, 255, 256, 271

Roseberry, William, 27, 28, 234

Rossen, Jack, 125, 136, 138, 144, 145, 150, 153, 212–14, 219

Rothschild, Nan A., 24, 30, 46, 294, 357n1

Rubertone, Patricia E., 8, 26, 357n3

rum trade, 74, 78, 79–81, 203, 311

Rupert site, 93, 94, 178, 179, 180

Russell, Lynette, 124

Ryan, Beth, 312, 312, 315, 360, 364n7

Sackett site, 93, 94, 185

St. Lawrence missions: British-French rivalry and, 88; dispersed settlements, and role of, 200, 203, 204, 247; documentary sources from, 36, 257, 261; fur trade with, 22, 72; house forms at, 261, 269–71, 322; multinational sites and, 165

salvage anthropology, 8, 13, 348

Sanders, William T., 165

Santley, Robert S., 165

Sassaman, Kenneth E., 285

Saunders, Lorraine P., 4, 11, 163, 176, 280, 324

Savo-Karelian log construction, 202, 230, 232, 239

Schein, Anna M., 124, 337

Schenectady, 64, 65, 72, 119

Schiffer, Michael B., 30, 227

Schmalz, Peter S., 53, 56, 89

Schneider, David M., 275, 323

Schoff, Harry L., 4, 11, 12, 26, 46, 93, 127, 156, 163, 168, 171, 173, 177, 182, 192, 305, 350

Schoharie region, 265

Schuyler, Myndert, 68, 100, 118

Schuyler Flats site, 255–56, 271

Scots-Irish cultural traditions, 202, 232, 233, 357n2

Scott, Douglas D., 128, 304

Scott, Patricia Kay, 52, 68, 73

Scott, Stuart D., 68

Seaver, James E., 38, 42, 90, 91, 165, 222, 324

Sempowski, Martha L., 4, 11, 24, 46, 163, 176, 280

Seneca Arts Project, 357n5

Seneca Lake: access to resources of, 97, 210; footpaths near, 65, 97; map of, 109, 109; Moravian missionaries, and travels near, 104–6; regulation of water levels in, 97; sites near, 38, 93, 94, 99, 104, 293

Seneca nation: in Allegheny Valley, 37, 90, 119, 165, 187; American Revolution, and effects on, 336–37; archaeological excavations, and effects on, 95, 124; artifact collections, and conclusions about, 11; autonomy and, 92; colonization of, 21; decline narratives for, 349; deerskin-based articulation with fur trade and, 141, 281, 284, 298–300, 325, 335, 343, 351; demographic statistics for, 54–56, 55, 320–21, 321; diplomatic activities of, 51, 117, 349; documentary sources for, 104–6, 107; domesticated animal use and, 292–96, 296–97, 317; domestic-context artifact analysis to determine social life/relations in, 23–24, 207, 339; encroachment of Europeans into territory of, 6–7, 21, 41, 335, 337; English, and relations with, 61, 119–20, 341; epidemics and, 84–85, 92; European-borne diseases, and effects on, 55, 66, 71, 84–85, 347; European technology/lifeways, and selective adoption by, 349; factional conflicts in, 70–71, 81–84, 90, 92, 101–4, 205, 209, 341; famines, and survival of, 37, 52, 82, 84, 92, 171, 289; food resources and, 291–92; France, and relations with, 51–52, 53, 54, 62–63, 65, 81, 82–83; French agents, and relationship with, 53, 59–62, 67, 70–71, 85, 87, 92, 117, 119, 223; fur trade and, 56–58, 64–71, 77–78, 91–92, 334, 335–36; in Genesee Valley, 82, 84, 163, 172, 195, 197, 198, 358n5; glass pendant manufacture and, 360n2; historic maps, and overview of, 107–9, *109*, *110*; house forms and, 241, 260, 262–63, 271, 272–73, 321, 329, 363n1; Indian groups, and warfare with, 51–53, 85, 344; isolation of, 6; King George's War and, 85–87, 333–36; land for trading posts/forts and, 73–74; local political economy of, 6, 49, 317, 333–36, 340–48; location of, 3, *5*, 20, 184, 187, 195; names for, 3; names/locations of villages of, 33; New York, and relations with, 61–63, 69–70, 102, 341; Niagara portage monopoly of, 68, 79, 335; in Ohio country, 90; Oswego trading post/fort era, and local effects on, 7–8, 77–81, 92, 195, 334–36, 346–48; period of uncertainty, and political-economic conditions of, 57–63, 92, 161, 194, 325; refugees adopted by, 320; as refugees near Ft. Niagara, 197, 336; relocation due to warfare, 52, 57, 92, 101, 162, 166, 168, 196; relocation of, 71, 82–84, 88–91, 101, 162, 168, 177, 181, 205, 209; reservationization, and effects on, 34, 197; restoration experience of, 21–24, 339, 340–41, 348, 349, 357n5; scholarship on, 4, 6, 354–55; Seneca castles and, 67, 69, 74, 84, 98; social life/relations using artifacts and, 207, 339; supra-regional context and, 49, 193, 197; trading posts/forts and, 70–71, 73–74, 78, 181, 315; traditional homeland of, 163–65, 163–66, *164*; Twenty Years' War, and effects on, 50–57, *55*, 91, 194, 340; west-east trade, and role of, 194, 278, 331–32, 341–46, 347, 351; western Indians, and relations with, 49, 50–51, 53–54, 62–63, 195, 341. *See also* settlement patterns; Townley-Read site; *specific sites*

settlement patterns: agricultural resources, and effects of, 183; archaeological surveys and, 166; community structure and, 177, 325–26; data sources for, 165; defensibility of site and, 29, 93, 171, 192, 193, 197; definition of changes in, 193; diversification of, 99, 123; duration of settlements and, 193; family units, 90; local level changes, and effects on, 197, 346; long distance relocation and, 176, 193, 195, 197, 203, 204; model of core and satellite villages, 40, 90, 93, 98, 121, 123, 162, 163, *164*, 194, 341; occupation span of settlements and, 29, 165, *166*, 205; palisade construction period and, 2, 98, 155, 169, 171–72, 176, 194, 254, 326, 330, 340, 342; Period 1 (1687), 166, 168–72, *169*; Period 2 (1700), 172–76, *173*; Period 3 (1720), *177*, 177–84; Period 4 (1750), 184–87, *185*; Period 5 (1779), 187–92, *188*, *189*; planned/opportunistic relocation and, 1, 29, 193, 195, 197, 317; political-economic changes, and effects on, 197; regional ecology, and effects of, 52, 193, 196–97, 198; regional level changes, and effects on, 177, 193–97, 346; seasonal camps of Senecas in, 90; Seven Years' War, and effects on, 196; short-distance relocation and, 193, 198; sites, and studies of, 2, 163, 164; synchronic snapshots of, 163; transformations in system of, 2, 192–97; Twenty Years' War, and effects on, 194, 340; typology for, 165–66, *167*; war rumors, and effects on, 341. *See also* dispersed settlements; *specific sites*

Seven Years' War: French-Indian alliances, and effects of, 334; fur trade, and effects of, 333; Iroquois, and effects of, 333, 336; Ohio country, and role in, 91; regional political-economic situation preceding, 86, 92, 160, 209; settlement patterns, and effects of, 196; trading posts/forts during, 77, 327

Severance, Frank H., 60, 118

422 Index

Sevier site, 123, 258, 362n1
Shafer, Harry J., 30
Shawnees, 89–90, 91, 334
sheep/goats, 294
shellfish remains, 130, 145, 146, 288–89
sherds. *See* ceramic sherds
Shershow, Scott Cutler, 358n2
Shimony, Annemarie Anrod, 2, 15
Shoemaker, Nancy, 337
short longhouses: Atwell site, 239, 267–68, *268*, 269, 272, 363n4; classification of house forms and, *167*, 245–46, 362–63n4; hearths and, 229, 345; house lot structure and, 143–44, 205–8, *206*; iron nails, and use in, 254; multiple family residences and, 229, 345, 362n1; settlements c.1677–1696 and, 248; settlements c.1715–1754 and, 261–62; use of, 229, 246, 350. *See also* Structure 1 at DRC 1
shovel test pits (STPs), 125, 131, 146
Shurtleff, Harold R., 226, 229, 230
Sider, Gerald M., 9, 24, 28, 29, 39, 45, 234
Sigstad, John S., 303
Silliman, Stephen W., 11, 27, 30, 31, 352
Simpson, Audra, 8, 15, 16, 349
Singleton, Theresa A., 11, 234
Skoiyase village, *188, 189*
Smith, Beverley, 152
Smith, Ernest, 357n5
Smith, Gavin A., 28, 29
Smith, James, 38, 90, 235, 236
Smith, Marvin T., 158, 360n2
Smith, Richard, 38, 213, 217, 237–38, 243, 244, 275
smithies: English, 103, 119; factional politics and, 101–4; French, 60–61, 81, 83, 102, 103, 104, 120; at Kanadesaga site, 190, 191; LaForge smiths, 120; from New York, 119–20; relocation promises, in exchange for, 205; at Townley-Read site, 95, 111–12, 114–15, 125–27, *179*, 208; at trading posts/forts, 69, 74, 102–3, 120, 190, 191
Snow, Dean R., 2, 3, 4, 6, 7, 19, 26, *228*
Snyder-McClure site: agricultural tools/hardware at, 216; bottle glass fragments, and alcohol consumption at, *312*, 313, 314, 315, 340; cemeteries at, 121, 123, 172, 173–74; community structure at, 258, 340; defensibility of, 174, 176; demographic estimate for, *55*, 175, 176, 340; domesticated animals and, 340; glass beads in, 360n2; house count for, 175; house forms and, 255, 340; location/topography of, 93, *94*, 108, *173, 174, 256*; Moravian missionaries, and documentary source for, 106; names for, 99, 100; nucleated community structure at, 176; occupation span for, 52, 63, 93, 101, *166*, 172; palisade construction and, 176, 194, 340; red stone artifacts from, 307, 308
Socci, Mary Catherine, 29, 285, 286
social life/relations: dispersed settlements, and effects on, 222–23; domestic-context artifact analysis and, 12–13, 21, 23–24; gendered social actors and, 39–40, 42, 44, 90, 343–44; inter-community differences and, 28; kinship ties and, 81, 205, 271, 323–24. *See also* matrilineal institutions
Societies in Eclipse (Brose, Cowan, and Mainfort), 9, 357n3
Society for the Propagation of the Gospel missionaries, 37, 257
Sohrweide, A. Gregory, 19, 227, 250, *251*, 253–55, 277, 362n1
southern Indians: English, and alliances with, 85; Iroquois raids against, 22, 49, 52, 53, 57, 62, 66, 85, 300, 325, 344; white ball clay smoking pipes and, 220, 344. See also *specific groups*
Speck, Frank G., 2
Spector, Janet D., 27, 39, 124, 364
Speth, John D., 45, 286
Spielmann, Katherine A., 45
Spiess, Arthur, 286, 289
Spoehr, Alexander, 10, 11
Squier, Ephraim G., 37, 168, 170
squirrel, 44, 287–89
Stahl, Ann B., 30
Standen, S. Dale, 48, 75, 77, 79, 290, 291, 332
Starna, William A., 26, 37, 42, 47, 49, 50, 54, 56, 58, 89, 91, 168, 171, 212, 214, 233, 243, 247, 264–65, 296, 297, 298, 303, 320, *321*, 358n3, 363n3
Steele, Ian K., 52
Stewart, Alexander M., 36, 61
Stewart, Omer C., 126
Stone, Glenn Davis, 29, 39, 207, 221
Stone, M. Priscilla, 39
STPs (shovel test pits), 125, 131, 146
Straits of Mackinac sites, 304–5
Structure 1 at DRC 1: excavations of, 131–38,

133, 134; house lot structure and, 143–44, 205–8, *206*; intercultural/creolized houses and, 265–69, *266*, 344–45; occupation span for, 186; post mold diameter figures and, *240*; short longhouse form and, 130, 265–69, 362–63n4
Stull, Scott D., 125, 130, 137, 146, 220
Sturm, Circe, 9
Sullivan, James, 83, 155, 187, 190, 359n8. *See also* American Sullivan-Clinton expeditions
Surtees, Robert J., 271
Susquehannock nation, 3, 47, 50, 89, 258
Swagerty, William R., 3
Swetland, Luke, 38, 293, 296, 324

Tanner, Helen Norbeck, 33
Tanner, Tyree, 19, 123, 258, 303, 304, 342, 362n1
Taylor, Alan, 2, 8, 171, 193, 197, 325
tea, and evidence of use, 220
test units (TUs), 125, 131, 146, 150, 241
textiles, European, 281, 283, 298
Thanitsaronwee (Sagonadaragie), 117–18
Theyanoguin (Hendrick), 66, 200
Thomas, David Hurst, 8, 124, 357n1
Thompson, John H., 95
Thwaites, Reuben Gold, 36
Tiotohattan village, 168, 170, 247. *See also* Rochester Junction/Tiotohattan site
Tiro, Karim Michel, 2, 7, 22, 23, 273
tobacco, 220
Tonawanda Reservation, 38, 187, 324, 364n5
de Tonty, Henry, 51, 292
Tooker, Elisabeth, 2, 3, 15, 28, 41, 47, 55–56, 84, 98, 142, 156, 162, 190, 203, 270, 286, 297, 322, 360n3, 364n5
Torrence, Robin, 352
Townley-Read/New Ganechstage Project, 93, 121, *122*, *312*, 313. *See also* New Ganechstage Site Complex
Townley-Read site: agricultural activities at, 213, 216, 221, 222; agricultural fields, and preservation of, 19; animal use at, 278, 297–300, 351; archaeological resources for, 95, 110–16, 115, 359n5; Area D in, *122*, 128, *129*, 131–46, 279, *312*, 363–64n1; Area E in, *122*, 126–27; Area F in, 121, *122*; Area H in, *122*, 128, *129*, 146–54, 279, *312*, 363–64n1; area identified in sources for, 121–23; Areas A, B, and C in, 121, *122*, 125–26,

363–64n1; bone marrow/grease exploitation and, 138, 142, 143, *285*, 285–86, 301–3, 364n4; botanical remains from, 115; bottle glass fragments, and alcohol consumption at, 278, 312, *312*, 313, *313*, 314, 315; brass, 130; cemeteries at, 95, 111, 112, 114, 115, 121, *122*, 130, 178, *206*, 208; central hearths and, 135–36; ceramic pipe fragments, 130; ceramics, 130; community structure at, 198, 205, 222; crops and, 214–15, 216–17; cultural features and post molds excavated in DRC 1, Area D of, *132*; dating occupation span for, 151, 154–62; deerskin-based articulation with fur trade and, *141*, *281*, 298–300, 335, 343, 351; demographic estimate for, 361n3; demographic statistics, and artifact data at, 157–62, *159*; dispersed settlements and, 123, 177, 178, 183, 190, 198–99, *206*; diversification of settlement patterns at, 123; documentary evidence for occupation span for, 154–57, 160; documentary references for, 95, 98–109, 358–59n2; domesticated animal use and, 279, 283, 292–93; domestic-content excavations at, 31; DRC 4 at, 130–31, 207; earlier archaeological resources for, *113*; ecological manipulation at, 211; economy at, 161–62, *281*, 351; Euro-American occupation of, 97; faunal material from, 115, *129*, *141*, 279–85, *279*, *281*, 291, 364n2; field methods at, 123–25, *124*, 127–28, 130, 131; fire protection in, 212; glass beads at, 130, 158, 360n2, 361n9; gunflints at, 130; hearths and, 147; house forms at, 208, 351; house lot structures at, 205–10, *206*, 275, 351; house size and, 274; iron artifacts at, 130, 143, 241–42, *242*, 269; Iroquoian-style cabins used at, 235; land allocation and, 221, 222; lithic debitage at, 130; location/topography of, *5*, 93, *94*, 95–97, *96*, 108, *109*, 121, *179*; manufacturing debris at, 130, 360n2; maps of, 109, *110*, 111, *113*, 359n3; marine shell at, 130; models for land use at, 121, 123; naming of, 358–59n2; non-defensibility of, 123, 127, 161, 162, 183, 209; occupation span for, 88, 154–62, *159*, 178, 212, 360–61n8; orchards and, 95, 112, 218–19; permission for excavations at, 95; pigs at, 294–95, 344; plant use at, 213, 220, 351; plow disturbances and, 127; post mold

Townley-Read site—*continued*
diameter figures for, *133*, 241; presence/absence of species and, 287–89; red stone artifacts at, 111, 130, 137, 146, 147, 150, 154, 305–8, *306*, 364n6; reoccupation evidence at, 97; restoration experience at, 23–24, 339; scholarly interpretation of Iroquoian culture at, 1; short longhouses and, 186; short-term hearths and, 147; smithy at, 95, 111–12, 114–15, 125–27, *179*, 208; special-purpose hearths and, 144; stone pipe fragments at, 130; surface density of animal bone and tooth fragment in Areas D and H of, *129*; topographic map of, *122*; village precinct at, 112, *113*, 121; west-east trade and, 194, 278, 347, 351; wind protection in, 212. *See also* Domestic Refuse Cluster 1; Domestic Refuse Cluster 2; Domestic Refuse Cluster 3; Domestic Refuse Clusters (DRCs); Seneca nation; Structure 1 at DRC 1

trading posts/forts: British-French price comparisons at, 58–59, 335, 346, 358n2; European development of, 67–74, 327; fur trade and, 71–72, 75, 77, 291, 309, 327, 331–32, 346; Iroquois and, 70–71, 94, 318, 326–33; locations of, *5*; smithies at, 69, 74, 102–3, 120, 190, 191; territorial encroachment of Europeans during era of, 23, 327, 331, 332–33, 342, 345, 354; wester Indians, and shift in trade between different, 71–72, 75, 77–78, 309, 327–28, 331–32, 346. *See also specific trading posts/forts*

traditional Iroquoian houses. *See* longhouses, bark

trans-Appalachian region, 20–21

travelers' accounts sources, 35, 36, 37–38

travel patterns, 40–42, *42*, 44–45, 46, 65

Treaty of Fort Stanwix, 337

Treaty of Ryswick, 53

Treaty of Utrecht, 36, 57, 61, 63, 64, 69, 161

Trelease, Allen W., 58, 64, 65, 303

Tremblay, Louise, 165

Trigger, Bruce G., 2, 3, 7, 33, 40, 44–47, 52, 98, 156, 212, 214, 215, 298, 304

Trubowitz, Neal L., 2, 20, 166, 175

Tuan, Yi-fu, 362n2

Tuck, James A., 2, 19, 26, 226, 245, 267, 363n4

Turgeon, Laurier, 3, 234

turkeys, 44, 211, 280, 287–89, 292

Turner, Toni S., 26

turtle shells, 280

Tuscarora nation, 3, 38, 79, 202

TUs (test units), 125, 131, 146, 150, 241

Twenty Years' War: demographic consequences of, 54–56, *55*; food supplies, and effects of, 52, 56–57; fur trade, and effects of, 27–28, 56; military power, and effects of, 7, 22, 91, 318, 324–26, 340; Senecas, and effects of, 50–57, *55*, 91, 194; settlement patterns after, 194, 340

upstreaming method, and decline narratives, 15–16, 357n4

Usner, Daniel H., Jr., 223, 292

Vanatta site, 20, 280, 293

Vandrei, Charles E., 125, 168, 170, 171, 176

Vehik, Susan C., 285

Vernon Center area (New York), 264

Versaggi, Nina M., 44

Virginia, 49, 51, 57, 66, 85, 87, 89

Vita-Taft site, 11

Wagenhaws. *See* Ottawa nation

Walker, Ian, 157

Wallace, Anthony F. C., 2, 3, 8, 9, 13, 16–18, 33–34, 54, 81, 97, 117, 187, 197, 203, 225, 293, 325, 336, 337

wampum belts, 71, 82, 84, 136, 145, 276, 315, 357n1, 357n4

War of Austrian Succession. *See* King George's War

War of Spanish Succession, 36, 57, 61, 63, 64, 69, 161

Warrick, Gary A., 4, 29, 47, 212, 226, 227, 240, 245, 269, 318, 357n1

Waselkov, Gregory A., 332

Waterman, Kees-Jan, 64, 99, 100, 182

Watkins, Joe, 124

Watson, Adam S., 21, 125, 128, 136, 138, *141*, 212, *279*, *281*, 282, 283, 285, 286, 292, 298–99, 302, 363–64n1, 364n4

Waugh, Frederick W., 219, 286

weasel species, 283, *283*

Weiser, Conrad, 87, 261–62

Wellman, Beth, 395n5

Wemp, Hendrick, 103, 120

Wemp, Myndert, 69, 84, 120, 359n8

Wendell, Abraham, 119, 120
Wendell, Evert, 100, 182
Wendell, Evert Harmanuse, 120
Wenros nation, 3, 47
Weslager, Clinton A., 225, 229
west-east trade activities: French agents, and role in, 53, 59; New York, and role in, 59, 60, 62, 64, 66, 341, 358n3; trading posts/forts and, 71–72, 75, 77, 309, 327, 331–32, 346; water-borne trade routes and, 65. *See also* fur trade; middleman period
western Indians: European nations, and conflicts between Iroquois and, 53, 59, 61, 62, 87, 92; footpaths, and trade routes of, 65; fur-bearing animals in territories of, 54, 56, 58, 334; red stone artifacts, and links between Iroquois and, 303–9, *306, 307,* 327–28, 341–42, 347, 364nn6–7; Senecas, and relations with, 49, 50–51, 53–54, 62–63, 195, 341; trading post/fort construction, and effects on trade between Iroquois and, 71–72, 75, 77–78, 309, 327–28, 331–32, 346
Weston site, 250, *251,* 253, 254, 322
White, John, 114, 248
White, Richard, 64–75, 79, 87, 291, 334, 335
white ball clay smoking pipes, 128, 130, 137, 140, 143, 144, 146, 157, 220, 361
White Springs site: agricultural tools/hardware at, 216; bottle glass fragments, and alcohol consumption at, *312,* 313, 314, 316, 340, 350, 364n9; cemeteries at, 175; community structure at, 258, 340, 342–43; defensibility of, 176, 342; demographic estimate for, 55, 176, 340; described, 175, 176; documentary sources for, 100–101, 104–5; domesticated animals used at, 340; excavations at, 358n1; faunal usage patterns at, 291; glass beads at, 360n2; house forms at, 255, 340; location/topography of, 93, *94,* 108, 121, *173, 256*; names for, 99, 100; nucleated community structure at, 93, 154,

162, 175, 176; occupation span for, 52, 63, 93, 97, 100–101, 154–56, 162, *166,* 172; palisade construction and, 176, 194, 340, 342; red stone artifacts at, 308
Wien, Thomas, 34, 75, 76, 332
wild plants, 44–45, 213, 219, 351
William (king of England), 53
Williams-Shuker, Kimberly Louise, 226, 240, *240,* 242, 252–53, 269
Wilson, Suzanne F., 274
Wolf, Eric R., 28, 33, 118
women: bone marrow/bone grease exploitation, and labor allocation of, 128, 301–3, 343; decision-making, and labor allocation of, 210–11, 345; deerskin processing, and labor allocation of, 300–303, 343; dispersed settlements, and labor allocation of, 210, 214, 220, 222, 223, 317, 343, 345; gathered plants and, 213, 219, 343, 351; outfields, and labor allocation of, 214, 351; seasons, and labor allocation of, 44, 300; social actors, and role of, 42, 44; travel patterns of, 41, 42
Wonderley, Anthony, 88, 243, 275, 295, 296, 324
Woodley site, 97, 126, 360n1
Wray, Charles F., 2, 4, 11, 12, 18, 26, 45, 46, 93, 110, 114–15, 116, 127, 146, 156, 163, *164, 166,* 168, 170, 171, 173, 177, *177,* 178, *185, 188,* 280, 303, 315, 325, 350, 358–59n2, 360n7
Wright, James V., 226, 227
Wyandots (Huron refugees), 50, 53, 170, 248, 271, 320, 322
Wykoff, M. William, 211, 217, 219

Zeisberger, David, 34, 37, 104, 105–6, 119, 175, 184, 187, 202, 203, 215, 219, 235–36, 263–64, 288, 291–92, 299
Zindall-Wheadon site, 93, *94,* 178, *179,* 180
Zonesschio village, 106, 184, 185, 186, 263–64, 316. *See also* Fall Brook site

CPSIA information can be obtained
at www.ICGtesting.com
Printed in the USA
LVOW13s2233070218
565706LV00007B/30/P